THE
EXPERIENCE
OF
LITERATURE

PRENTICE-HALL INTERNATIONAL, INC., *London*
PRENTICE-HALL OF AUSTRALIA, PTY. LTD., *Sydney*
PRENTICE-HALL OF CANADA, LTD., *Toronto*
PRENTICE-HALL OF INDIA PRIVATE LIMITED, *New Delhi*
PRENTICE-HALL OF JAPAN, INC., *Tokyo*

THE
EXPERIENCE
OF
LITERATURE
SECOND EDITION

Edited by

GENE MONTAGUE
Department of English
The University of Detroit

MARJORIE HENSHAW
Department of English
University of the Americas

NICHOLAS A. SALERNO
Department of English
Arizona State University

PRENTICE-HALL, INC., ENGLEWOOD CLIFFS, N.J.

Library of Congress Catalog Card No.: 70-116548

Printed in the United States of America

13-294728-5

Current Printing (Last Digit):

10   9   8

Contents

v

POETRY, 301

AN INTRODUCTION, 301

THE LYRIC VOICE, 459

WAR AND PEACE, AS SEEN IN THE LYRIC AND OTHER FORMS, 460

THE
EXPERIENCE
OF
LITERATURE

General
Introduction

People read poems, novels, short stories, plays for many different reasons. Some read for pleasure, some for profit, some—and these are the lucky ones—for both. Some seek an escape, a temporary respite in another character, another place, another time; others want to experience the feelings of a character, to exist vicariously in another place or time. Most people read for a combination of these reasons.

The kind of enjoyment that people find in literature varies considerably. Those who read to escape, to kill time, to relax all enjoy what they're doing, but theirs is obviously a limited enjoyment. The reader who adds to these motives a desire to understand thoroughly what he is reading must work harder, but he adds another kind of enjoyment: the satisfaction of encountering and assimilating a new intellectual or emotional experience. This reader does not escape, but rather he expands his personality: He gains something from the experience.

Whatever their motives, all readers have one thing in common: They read to *experience*.

Because literature is one of the arts, it is not, like a science, a body of knowledge; it is a method of handling and presenting knowledge. Literature draws on other bodies of knowledge but retains its own nature. It is not philosophy, although philosophy is inherent in its nature; it is not history, sociology, or economics, although it embodies something of all these. Like any art, literature is basically a manipulation of experience. It recreates an experience—emotional, intellectual, physical—but *manipulates* that experience so that it always emerges distinct from reality through the author's selection of particular aspects of that experience or his isolation of that experience.

Part of the value of all art forms is that they afford experiences that we as readers can get in no other way. There are many reasons

1

for the reader's inability to experience in reality what he experiences in literature. Perhaps the reader is physically incapable of grasping an experience in the real world because of the limitations of time and space. Literature brings it to him. Perhaps he is incapable of distinguishing the important parts of the experience from the trivial. Literature selects the consequential parts and condenses the experience. Perhaps he is incapable of seeing the significance of an often-recurring experience because its monotony obscures its significance. Literature organizes experience so that it can be examined closely and carefully. What the reader has seen only once, and then too quickly to absorb, or what he has seen repeatedly, but never bothered to observe carefully, takes on meaning. Because human beings are often disorganized creatures, they tend to respect and admire order. The difference between a real experience and that same experience in literature is that what may have been chaotic becomes ordered, organized by the author's selection.

If art is the manipulation of experience, that experience will be meaningless to anyone who does not try to participate in it as re-created by the writer; a writer cannot reach an unreceptive reader. The first thing, then, that a reader owes a writer is a fair hearing. Only a very thoughtless person could say that he does not like poetry. Maybe he does not like the poems he has read so far; but they do not represent all poetry, and his taste may mature and change. And since each poem is a recreation of an experience, one cannot say he does not like poetry without being logically absurd. If a reader condemns all poems on the basis of a few, it becomes virtually impossible for him to enjoy a poem since he has destroyed his receptivity at the beginning. A reader should not go to a new experience, in this case, a poem, with unfair prejudices; rather he should give the writer a fair hearing. Then if he does not like the poem for concrete and specific reasons, he can voice his opinion. Opinions formed without reading the material are meaningless.

Further understanding between reader and writer is also necessary. Like all the arts, literature has certain *conventions*, some of them centuries old, by which it organizes experience. A convention can be defined as a customary artificiality, a device used to organize artistic material. Conventions are a kind of shorthand, convenient ways of condensing and emphasizing and underlining, which make the work of reader and writer easier. The reader must be willing to spend the time necessary to understand the various conventions, or techniques, by which the writer manipulates his material. Otherwise, his concentration will be disturbed by conventions that hamper, even destroy, the recreation of experience. For example, rhymed verse in a play will annoy the reader who thinks that "real people" do not talk in rhyme. One can argue that people in a highly emotional state speak a language that differs more from common speech than do most rhymed lines in plays. It is unnecessary to be this ingenious to convince the reader of his mistake. Rhyme is a convention—consciously and subconsciously we are pleased to hear the chime of the recurring sound; rhyme is a guide to the reader and actors—cue lines and scene and act endings are often signaled by strong rhyme; rhyme is a means of emphasis—strongly rhymed lines call attention to themselves and tell the reader that they are important. What one reads in a play or sees on a stage is not real life; it is life manipulated and organized. To say that a play or a novel or a short story was not good because it wasn't real is meaningless criticism. Plays, novels, and short stories never achieve more than an illusion of reality, and many of them do not attempt even that. Literature cannot be real because it never was real; its origin is the imagination, often inspired by experiences that were real.

Nor is it true that short stories and novels achieve something closer to reality than do poems or plays; they are simply easier to read in most cases because they either use fewer conventions or are less condensed and compressed than poems or plays. Finally, such a thing as a poetic experience as distinguished from a prose experience does not exist. Poems, short stories, novels, and plays do not so much render different kinds of experiences, as they use different conventions to recreate and manipulate similar experiences. A work becomes more highly organized as it uses more conventions because, as noted, conventions are a means of ordering, condensing, and unifying raw experience. Poetry is more highly organized than prose; it has at its command more conventions than does prose. Dramatic poetry (that is, a play in verse) is the most highly organized form of literature because it adds to the conventions of verse the conventions of drama. Nondramatic verse is generally more highly organized than prose drama, if only because of its condensation and precision. Certainly the least complicated form is the prose narrative, which in its formally organized shape becomes the novel or short story.

The Short
Story

Defining the short story is like trying to define democracy; the definition is usually too narrow ("a form roughly 2500 words in length, which presents a full-fledged plot aiming at a single effect") or too broad ("a short prose narrative").

Logically, a short story can be defined on the basis of its conventions. Thus, the short story can be defined as

> a fictional prose narrative (distinguishing it from verse and narrative nonfiction);
>
> usually containing a theme (distinguishing it from an incident and giving it an idea around which it is built);
>
> usually embodied in a plot (distinguishing it from a series of random incidents or tales and giving it formal organization)
>
> which is arranged to allow the greatest economy of character and setting (distinguishing it from the novel, which has fewer time and space limitations).

We do not say that only the short story has these separate characteristics; but we do say that only the short story has this combination of these characteristics.

Defining the short story pinpoints the areas of convention that the reader must know in this form: conventions of plot, character, setting, and so forth. The following story illustrates some of the means by which the writer manipulates experience.

Bernard Malamud

The Bill

Though the street was somewhere near a river, it was land-locked and narrow, a crooked row of aged brick tenement buildings. A child throwing a ball straight up saw a bit of pale sky. On the corner, opposite the blackened tenement where Willy Schlegel worked as janitor, stood another like it except that this included the only store on the street—going down five stone steps into the basement, a small, dark delicatessen owned by Mr. and Mrs. F. Panessa, really a hole in the wall.

They had just bought it with the last of their money, Mrs. Panessa told the janitor's wife, so as not to have to depend on either of their daughters, both of whom, Mrs. Schlegel understood, were married to selfish men who had badly affected their characters. To be completely independent of them, Panessa, a retired factory worker, withdrew his three thousands of savings and bought this little delicatessen store. When Mrs. Schlegel, looking around—though she knew the delicatessen quite well for the many years she and Willy had been janitors across the way—when she asked, "Why did you buy this one?" Mrs. Panessa cheerfully replied because it was a small place and they would not have to overwork; Panessa was sixty-three. They were not here to coin money but to support themselves without working too hard. After talking it over many nights and days, they had decided that the store would at least give them a living. She gazed into Etta Schlegel's gaunt eyes and Etta said she hoped so.

She told Willy about the new people across the street who had bought out the Jew, and said to buy there if there was a chance; she meant by that they would continue to shop at the self-service, but when there was some odd or end to pick up, or something they had forgotten to buy, they could go to Panessa's. Willy did as he was told.

He was tall and broad-backed, with a heavy face seamed dark from the coal and ashes he shoveled around all winter, and his hair often looked gray from the dust the wind whirled up at him out of the ash cans when he was lining them up for the sanitation truck. Always in overalls—he complained he never stopped working—he would drift across the street and down the steps when something was needed, and lighting his pipe, would stand around talking to Mrs. Panessa as her husband, a small bent man with a fitful smile, stood behind the counter waiting for the janitor after a long interval of talk to ask, upon reflection, for a dime's worth of this or that, the whole business never amounting to more than half a dollar. Then one day Willy got to talking about how the tenants goaded him all the time and what the cruel and stingy landlord could think up for him to do in that smelly five-floor dungeon. He was absorbed by what he was saying and before he knew it had run up a three-dollar order, though all he had on him was fifty cents. Willy looked like a dog that had just had a licking, but Mr. Panessa, after clearing his throat, chirped up it didn't matter, he could pay the rest whenever he wanted. He said that everything was run on credit, business and everything else, because after all what was credit but the fact that people were human beings, and if you were really a human being you gave credit to somebody else and he gave credit to you. That surprised Willy because he had never heard a storekeeper say it before. After a couple of days he paid the two fifty, but when Panessa said he could trust whenever he felt like it, Willy sucked a flame into his pipe, then began to order all sorts of things.

When he brought home two large bagfuls of stuff, Etta shouted he must be crazy. Willy answered he had charged everything and paid no cash.

"But we have to pay sometime, don't we?" Etta shouted. "And we have to pay higher prices than in the self-service." She said then what she always said, "We're poor people, Willy. We can't afford too much."

Though Willy saw the justice of her remarks despite her scolding he still went across the street and trusted. Once he had a crumpled ten-dollar bill in his pants pocket and the amount came to less than four, but he didn't offer to pay, and let Panessa write it in the book. Etta knew he had the money so she screamed when he admitted he had bought on credit.

"Why are you doing it for? Why don't you pay if you have the money."

He didn't answer but after a time he said there were other things he had to buy once in a while. He went into the furnace room and came out with a wrapped package which he opened, and it contained a beaded black dress.

Etta cried over the dress and said she would never wear it because the only time he ever brought her anything was when he had done something wrong. Thereafter she let him do all the grocery shopping and she did not speak when he bought on trust.

Willy continued to buy at Panessa's. It seemed they were always waiting for him to come in. They lived in three tiny rooms on the floor above the store, and when Mrs. Panessa saw him out of her window, she ran down to the store. Willy came up from his basement, crossed the street and went down the steps into the delicatessen, looming large as he opened the door. Every time he bought, it was never less than two-dollars' worth and sometimes it would go as high as five. Mrs. Panessa would pack everything into a deep double bag, after Panessa had called off each item and written the price with a smeary black pencil into his looseleaf notebook. Whenever Willy walked in, Panessa would open the book, wet his finger tip and flip through a number of blank pages till he found Willy's account in the center of the book. After the order was packed and tied up, Panessa added the amount, touching each figure with his pencil, hissing to himself as he added, and Mrs. Panessa's bird eyes would follow the figuring until Panessa wrote down a sum, and the new total sum (after Panessa had glanced up at Willy and saw that Willy was looking) was twice underscored and then Panessa shut the book. Willy, with his loose unlit pipe in his mouth, did not move until the book was put away under the counter; then he roused himself and embracing the bundle—with which they offered to help him across the street though he always refused—plunged out of the store.

One day when the sum total came to eighty-three dollars and some cents, Panessa, lifting his head and smiling, asked Willy when he could pay something on account. The very next day Willy stopped buying at Panessa's and after that Etta, with her cord market bag, began to shop again at the self-service, and neither of them went across the street for as much as a pound of prunes or box of salt they had meant to buy but had forgotten.

Etta, when she returned from shopping at the self-service, scraped the wall on her side of the street to get as far away as possible from Panessa's.

Later she asked Willy if he had paid them anything.

He said no.

"When will you?"

He said he didn't know.

A month went by, then Etta met Mrs. Panessa around the corner, and though Mrs. Panessa, looking unhappy, said nothing about the bill, Etta came home and reminded Willy.

"Leave me alone," he said. "I got enough trouble of my own."

"What kind of trouble have you got, Willy?"

"The goddam tenants and the goddam landlord," he shouted and slammed the door.

When he returned he said, "What have I got that I can pay? Ain't I been a poor man every day of my life?"

She was sitting at the table and lowered her arms and put her head down on them and wept.

"With what?" he shouted, his face lit up dark and webbed. "With the meat off of my bones?

"With the ashes in my eyes. With the piss I mop up on the floors. With the cold in my lungs when I sleep."

He felt for Panessa and his wife a grating hatred and vowed never to pay because he hated them so much, especially the humpback behind the counter. If he ever smiled at him again with those goddam eyes he would lift him off the floor and crack his bent bones.

That night he went out and got drunk and lay till morning in the gutter. When he returned, with filthy clothes and bloodied eyes, Etta held up to him the picture of their four-year-old son who had died from diphtheria, and Willy weeping splashy tears swore he would never touch another drop.

Each morning he went out to line up the ash cans, he never looked the full way across the street.

"Give credit," he mimicked, "give credit."

Hard times set in. The landlord ordered cut down on heat, cut down on hot water. He cut down on Willy's expense money and wages. The tenants were angered. All day they pestered Willy like clusters of flies and he told them what the landlord had ordered. Then they cursed Willy and Willy cursed them. They telephoned the Board of Health but when the inspectors arrived they said the temperature was within the legal minimum though the house was drafty. However the tenants still complained they were cold and goaded Willy about it all day but he said he was cold too. He said he was freezing but no one believed him.

One day he looked up from lining up four ash cans for the truck to remove and saw Mr. and Mrs. Panessa staring at him from the store. They were staring up through the glass front door and when he looked at them at first his eyes blurred and they appeared to be two scrawny, loose-feathered birds.

He went down the block to get a wrench from another janitor, and when he got back they then reminded him of two skinny leafless bushes sprouting up through the wooden floor. He could see through the bushes to the empty shelves.

In the spring, when the grass shoots were sticking up from the cracks in the sidewalk, he told Etta, "I'm only waiting till I can pay it all."

"How, Willy?"

"We can save up."

"How?"

"How much do we save a month?"

"Nothing."

"How much have you got hid away?"

"Nothing any more."

"I'll pay them bit by bit. I will, by Jesus."

The trouble was there was no place they could get the money. Sometimes when he was trying to think of the different ways there were to get money his thoughts ran ahead and he saw what it would be like when he paid. He would wrap the wad of bills with a thick rubber band and then go up the stairs and cross the street and go down the five steps into the store. He would say to Panessa, "Here it is, little old man, and I bet you didn't think I would do it, and I don't suppose nobody else did and sometimes me myself, but here it is in bucks all held together by a fat rubber band." After hefting the wad a little, he placed it, like making a move on a checkerboard, squarely in the center of the counter, and the diminutive man and his wife both unpeeled it, squeaking and squealing over each blackened buck, and marveling that so many ones had been tied to- gether into such a small pack.

Such was the dream Willy dreamed but he could never make it come true.

He worked hard to. He got up early and scrubbed the stairs from cellar to roof with soap and a hard brush then went over that with a wet mop. He cleaned the woodwork too and oiled the bannister till it shone the whole zigzag way down and rubbed the mailboxes in the vestibule with metal polish and a soft rag until you could see your face in them. He saw his own heavy face with a surprising yellow mustache he had recently grown and the tan felt cap he wore that a tenant had left behind in a closetful of junk when he had moved. Etta helped him and they cleaned the whole cellar and the dark courtyard under the crisscrossed clotheslines, and they were quick to respond to any kind of request, even from tenants they didn't like, for sink or toilet repairs. Both worked themselves to exhaustion every day, but as they knew from the beginning, no extra money came in.

One morning when Willy was shining up the mailboxes, he found in his own a letter for him. Removing his cap, he opened the envelope and held the paper to the light as he read the trembling writing. It was from Mrs. Panessa who wrote her husband was sick across the street, and she had no money in the house so could he pay her just ten dollars and the rest could wait for later.

He tore the letter into bits and hid all day in the cellar. That night, Etta, who had been searching for him in the streets, found him behind the furnace amid the pipes, and she asked him what he was doing there.

He explained about the letter.

"Hiding won't do you any good at all," she said hopelessly.

"What should I do then?"

"Go to sleep, I guess."

He went to sleep but the next morning burst out of his covers, pulled on his overalls and ran out of the house with an overcoat flung over his shoulders. Around the corner he found a pawnshop, where he got ten dollars for the coat and was gleeful.

But when he ran back, there was a hearse or something across the street, and two men in black were carrying this small and narrow pine box out of the house.

"Who's dead, a child?" he asked one of the tenants.

"No, a man named Mr. Panessa."

Willy couldn't speak. His throat had turned to bone.

After the pine box was squeezed through the vestibule doors, Mrs. Panessa, grieved all over, tottered out alone. Willy turned his head away although he thought she wouldn't recognize him because of his new mustache and tan cap.

"What'd he die of?" he whispered to the tenant.

"I really couldn't say."

But Mrs. Panessa, walking behind the box, had heard.

"Old age," she shrilly called back.

figurative language

He tried to say some sweet thing but his tongue hung in his mouth like dead fruit on a tree, and his heart was a black-painted window.

Mrs. Panessa moved away to live first with one stonefaced daughter, then with the other. And the bill was never paid.

A theme is a central idea around which a piece of literature is developed. It is not the plot or subject matter but the idea that they embody. It is not necessarily a moral because not all experiences teach moral lessons—they simply have effects or consequences. The theme of "The Bill" is that trust is easy enough for humans to accept but difficult to fulfill and destructive when betrayed.

Theme is the simultaneous effect of character, plot, and setting. Theme is therefore largely dependent on conventions of plot, character, and setting.

PLOT

Point of View

Point of view refers to the person who tells the story and determines the grammatical structure of the narrative. *Who* tells the story is very important in determining *what* is in the story: Different narrators will see different things. Some contemporary critics distinguish as many as a dozen different points of view. For our purposes, three are sufficient:

(1) Narrator acting: The narrator is himself an actor in the story, often the main character, and he tells the story in the first person.

("I went to the window. . . ." "I saw her . . .") Writing from this point of view, the narrator can see only what a normal person would see, hear only what a normal person would hear. He therefore can record only what other people say and do within earshot and eyesight; he cannot read others minds and he cannot leap great distances

(2) Narrator observing: The narrator is not directly involved in the story; he tells it from the sidelines. This means that he can see and hear and report the same details that the "narrator acting" does, but he speaks in the third person. ("He went to the window. . . ." "He saw her. . . .")He has the same physical and mental limitations as in the first point of view, but the narrator here is not necessarily emotionally involved in the situations he describes. Therefore, he achieves a degree of objectivity not possible in the first person point of view. At its most objective stage of development, this point of view is often called "reportage"; the story is told by an objective, unemotional observer, totally without personality himself.

(3) Narrator omniscient: The narrator is obviously the author, above and beyond the story. He tells it in the third person ("He went to the window. . . ." "He saw her. . . ."),but he is not restricted by normal human limitations. He can report what people anywhere do, say, and think. He knows all, tells all—or all that he wants to tell.

More than any other age the twentieth century has been concerned with the convention of point of view, which is considered crucial to establishing the illusion of reality necessary in the realistic or naturalistic story. The more rigid (that is, consistent) and restricted the point of view, the more highly organized the experience will be and the easier it will be for the reader to recreate it: The harder it is for the writer, the easier it is for the reader. The easiest point of view for the writer is the omniscient, but it can be the least profitable one if the author meddles too obviously with the story. The reader often finds it hard to share an experience that is being so artificially manipulated by an ever-present author who combines the omnipresence of Superman with the omniscience of a god.

Authors adopt and adapt these points of view as they see fit, choosing the point of view that allows the best manipulation of material to develop the theme. For example, the most successful point of view in the popular short story today is a blend of narrator acting and narrator observing; a distinguished writing teacher, K.P. Kempton of Harvard University, calls it "stream of experience." The author tells the story through one main character, but he tells it in the third person. The author, then, is omniscient only about that character and can only observe the others.

The special advantage of this point of view is that the reader will identify himself with the main character as in the acting point of view, and yet the author can avail himself of the objectivity possible in the observing point of view. In other words, the author appropriates some of the psychological advantages of the first two points of view. The stream of experience point of view is a compromise; the author's job is made easier without sacrificing plausibility. This partly accomplishes what seems to be the goal of many twentieth-century authors: the elimination of the author as narrator.

Authors generally are consistent in their point of view. One lapse may destroy the pattern because the reader usually notices the break, and the illusion consequently is shattered. However, interrupting the point of view, like disturbing any pattern, can be a means of emphasis. In his novel *Darkness at Noon,* a story involving Communist brainwashing to produce fraudulent confessions, Arthur Koestler breaks his stream of experience point of view only twice. In each instance the short passage that breaks it summarizes how far the prisoner's breakdown has progressed and predicts what new methods will follow. It may be argued that what Koestler sacrifices in consistency by these breaks is more than offset by the emphasis they receive, largely because of their inconsistency.

Authors often do not so much select a point of view as the story itself imposes its own point of view. Thus "The Bill" could not be told from another point of view without serious loss or without becoming an entirely different story. The author must show us truthfully and dispassionately the resolution of an emotionally charged situation. He cannot allow one of the characters to tell the story since each has such a strong emotional stake in the situation that his feelings of guilt or injury would warp the story. Yet those feelings of guilt and injury have to be communicated to the reader, or the theme of the story will be buried. In addition, the story covers a long period of time. There is, then, only one point of view feasible: the omniscient, disciplined to avoid sentimentality. You will notice that whenever he can, Malamud makes the authority for a statement rest with a character, not with the author, thus making the story as self-contained and self-sustaining as possible.

Narrative Structure

The basis of any situation, incident, or action in life itself is conflict. When one person or force says "yes" and another says "no," conflict results, and action grows out of it. To be actual this yes-no condition need not be violent or even external. Wanting to buy a meal (yes) but lacking money (no); hating to get up in the morning (no) but finding it necessary to do so (yes); needing a job (yes) but despising work (no); wanting to do the "right thing" (yes) but thinking that doing it is a financial, social, or physical risk (no); desiring to advance yourself (yes) but realizing that the means to that end are not ethical (no)—all these are conflicts. Moreover, in real life, as in literature, conflict resolves itself into a series of steps or divisions of action. In literature they are more easily distinguishable than in life because the author has usually eliminated superfluous material that might clog the action. Nevertheless, the steps are the same. Traditionally, the convention of narrative structure involves seven divisions.

(1) Exposition: the background information necessary to make the story understandable to the reader.

(2) Inciting force: the spark that begins the story itself. Before this point the story has not been moving because only the yes or no force was represented; no active conflict has been established.

(3) Rising action: the complication or impetus for the plot, a series of incidents that make the plot "thicken."

(4) Crisis: the turning point of the story, the point past which the story can go only in one direction, although that fact may be obvious to the reader only after he has finished the story.

(5) Climax: the high point, emotionally or intellectually, of the story. Sometimes crisis and climax are combined. If, for instance, the major problem in a story is a character's making up his mind, the moment he does that will probably be both the crisis and climax.

(6) Falling action: the unraveling of the plot, sometimes referred to as "counteraction" as opposed to the "action" of rising action. To avoid anticlimax falling action is generally much shorter than rising action.

(7) Conclusion: the outcome. In tragedy, the conclusion is called "catastrophe," in comedy, often "solution."[1]

Let us see briefly how this works out in our story. "The Bill" contains several conflicts: Willy vs. the Panessas, Willy vs. Etta, Willy vs. himself, and so on. The central conflict is this last. Willy has accepted a trust without really considering what it involves. He is happy to accept the trust that Mr. Panessa places in him; but he disregards the second half of Mr. Panessa's definition: "If you were really a human being you gave credit to somebody else and he gave credit to you." Willy forgets that trust involves mutual obligation. He takes without giving because the taking perhaps makes him feel important and dignified and human. But when the time comes for Willy to validate the dignity and humanity, he will not. He must pay (yes) but he will not (no)—and later he cannot.

"The Bill" has a very simple plot structure because the author has eliminated everything that might distract the reader and has kept all details in strict chronological order.

The story begins with exposition. The reader is told immediately where the action happens, to whom it happens, and how these people happen to be related. Furthermore, in the first two-and-a-half paragraphs, the author suggests that we are to sympathize with the Panessas (who are introduced as timid and alone, with overtones of being born victims) and with Etta Schlegel (whose outward no-nonsense manner is made attractive by her quiet, good-hearted concern for the Panessas), although about Willy, the main character, the author is as yet noncommittal.

So far, however, there is no action because there is no conflict. Mr. Panessa's offer of credit and Willy's acceptance introduces the conflict and incites the action. Willy has assumed an obligation that he does not fully understand and that, we suspect, he will not be able to live up to.

The rising action follows. Mr. Panessa fulfills his side of the bar-

---

[1]One type of story—the "slice-of-life"—does not manifest these divisions. The "slice-of-life" attempts to get as close to reality as possible by presenting a situation with little or no exposition to establish the circumstances or to establish motive, little or no setting, and little or no emphasis to direct the reader's attention to a crisis or climax. In real life we have to think about these things to establish them clearly in our minds; the "slice-of-life" presents the material without "thought" in this sense; it presents it as if we had stumbled on the situation by accident and were dispassionate observers.

gain; he trusts Willy. Minor conflicts emerge. Etta, for example, knows Willy is involved beyond his depth. She remonstrates, explaining in her own way what mutual trust involves. He will not listen.

The crisis arrives when Mr. Panessa must ask Willy to pay. Willy makes his choice: He will not pay, and he abandons the Panessas. At this point, Willy's decision is not a matter of money so much as a matter of principle. We know he could have paid something earlier, but he would not. Later we learn that even at his poorest he had means of raising some money—not $83, but enough to keep trust alive. However, when Willy decides he will not pay, he has destroyed all possibility of trust by betraying another human being. Willy tries irrationally to shift his guilt by blaming his woes on the tenants, on the landlord, even on the Panessas.

The climax comes when Willy rationalizes a "solution"—that is, a myth that he thinks he can live with. He will pay them in full, he says; he is saving to do it. But the reader knows, and Etta confirms it, that Willy has no way of raising the total amount. Any hope the reader had for Willy evaporates here. He has not decided to pay; he has simply made up another way of not paying.

And when Willy dreams of paying, the reader sees that he is still wrongly motivated. He dreams of tossing the total amount in front of the Panessas, not to discharge his obligation, but to vindicate himself. He still clings to the false pride that brought about his ruin. The climax, then, has grown logically from the inciting force and the crisis.

The falling action shows Willy compensating for his guilt. He becomes the model janitor; working endlessly for the tenants, he does for them what he will not do for the Panessas. But he cannot escape his guilt. The letter from Mrs. Panessa finally shatters Willy's illusions. He runs to get money, but he is too late. Mr. Panessa is dead.

The conclusion is consistent. Mrs. Panessa's ironic cry that Mr. Panessa died of "old age" pierces Willy; he cannot make even the smallest human gesture—he cannot say "some sweet thing" to her. As the author's metaphor ("his heart was a black-painted window") suggests, no light can penetrate or shine out of Willy's heart now. The illusions are gone, and Willy supposedly knows what he is. "And the bill," it is said, "was never paid." In one sense, the bill could not have been paid after the crisis; Willy had betrayed what the bill represented.

Although the story is not pat or mechanical, the action is quite balanced. In the rising action Mr. Panessa discharges his side of the trust: He gives and Willy takes. In the falling action Willy responds to trust: He refuses to pay, and the consequences of his action ensue. This narrative structure is natural in one sense but highly artificial in another: Real life is simply not that precise. Furthermore, an enormous amount of material has been left out of the story. The progressive concentration on Willy's consciousness has allowed the author to eliminate many details, and his use of the omniscient point of view has allowed him to cover long periods of time economically and, at the end, to jump far into the future without furnishing connecting links.

But he has used omniscience judiciously. The reader depends on the author only for the *facts* of the story. Nowhere does the author overtly draw an inference for the reader or intrude a value judgment: Thus, he does not destroy plausibility or lessen the impact of compressed experience. The conventions of point of view and narrative structure make the experience vivid, compact, and meaningful.

A novelist can shed light on a major plot by constructing a minor plot that contains a character similar to the protagonist, caught in circumstances similar to that of the protagonist, or a character unlike the protagonist but caught in similar circumstances, or a character similar to the protagonist but caught in unlike circumstances. By observing the two plots, the reader can form an opinion on the relative merit, intelligence, and so on, of the protagonist. But a short story writer has no time or space for this method. He must often imply comparisons, largely through the use of symbol, metaphor, allusion, and supporting characters.

CHARACTER

Readers and writers talk about major and minor (or supporting) characters, round and flat characters, and dynamic and static characters. These three systems of classifying characters represent three additional conventions that authors use to manipulate experience.

Major and Minor Characters

In real life it is often hard to distinguish between important and unimportant people in a situation. When a person is involved in a situation, he regards himself as the most important "character," even if he is not the main actor in the incident. A writer cannot permit himself this luxury; he must distinguish clearly between the leading character or characters and the supporting characters, or the experience loses all focus and meaning. The way he does this is quite simple. First, he observes the convention that a supporting character justifies his existence in a story only by having a significant relationship to a major character; that is, a supporting character is mainly there to *do something* rather than to *be somebody*. When a supporting character opposes a major character or reacts to him or tells the reader something about him or parallels his action or helps him in some way, he is functioning significantly in the story. The relationship, then, between a major and a minor character is the same as that between a major and a minor conflict. Remove the minor character (or conflict) and we do not destroy the major character (or conflict) although we may remove one aspect of it; but remove the major character (or conflict) and the minor character (or conflict) ceases to be meaningful or important.

The two main characters in "The Bill" are Willy and Mr. Panessa. They are the partners to the trust. Mrs. Panessa and Etta are minor characters. Mrs. Panessa exists, so to speak, to get us into the story and out of it. Consider what she does: She tells us who she and her husband are, how they got into the neighborhood, what they hope for. She is the convenient means of communicating Mr. Panessa's plight to Willy. She states, ironically, the point of the story in her two-word explanation of her husband's death, and she illustrates the continuing repercussions of the unpaid bill in the fate she suffers at the very end. All these things illuminate the two main characters and the theme.

Etta exists first, like Mrs. Panessa, as a means of exposition; second, as a kind of commentator; and third, as Willy's conscience. She exists, in other words, for what she can show us about Willy, by statement and contrast.

Round and Flat Characters

A round character is one who, because the author has given him sufficient time and detail, projects an illusion of reality, of being a real personality rather than just one aspect of a personality. He is believable and whole. Obviously this kind of treatment is necessary when an author creates a major character.

A flat character is one who is not fully drawn. The author portrays him only enough to qualify him for whatever role he plays in the story. Flat characters are not whole although they are sometimes believable. When a flat character is used as a symbol there is no particular reason why he ought to be believable. Most supporting characters are flat for a number of reasons. First, economy dictates flatness. Second, if all characters were round, the focus of the story would be endangered, because the reader, at the worst, might not able to distinguish major from minor characters and, at best, would divide his attention among the round characters.

Dynamic and Static Characters

A dynamic character is one who "develops," that is, he grows and changes, takes on added dimensions as the story or play or poem progresses. He is not the same character at the end of the plot as he was at the beginning. Willy in "The Bill" is dynamic. The young schizoid boy in Conrad Aiken's "Silent Snow, Secret Snow" is strikingly dynamic, since the story concentrates on tracing the distintegration of his sense of reality.

A static character does not develop, does not change. Often he springs full-blown upon the stage, although that is not necessary. He maintains his characteristics unchanged throughout the reader's acquaintance with him. Etta in "The Bill" is static. The title character of Thurber's "The Secret Life of Walter Mitty" is static. He has evolved a method of self-dramatization that helps him escape reality, and he practices it continually in the story. At one point, when he flashes out at his domineering wife, he has, it seems, a chance to change, but he slides back into his fantasies of heroism. The theme of the story depends on his being static.

A writer may choose to tell the story of a character who changes, or he may choose to tell the story of one who maintains his character with good or bad results. There is nothing inherently better in one plot or the other; they are simply different.

Nor is a round character better than a flat one. These terms are all descriptive; they do not imply value judgments.

SETTING

We remarked before that the success of a story depends on a close interrelationship between plot, character, setting, and theme. These things can, with some difficulty, be separated for discussion, but they function simultaneously in the story. Nowhere is it more difficult to separate conventions than in dealing with setting, since it is a matter of place and time. Both of these are closely bound up with plot. Moreover, setting can function as a character, and it also is sometimes the strongest determinant of theme.

A story at its simplest level is about something (plot) that happened to someone (character), somewhere, sometime (setting). Setting can, therefore, be only another word for the background of the story. Frequently, however, it functions in other ways.

(1) It can take the place of a character. In Conrad's "An Outpost of Progress," the setting functions as a kind of antagonist.

(2) It can be a determinant of theme when it functions as more than background but less than character. The short stories and novels of William Faulkner are perhaps the best example. In them the South is an all-pervading force. The cast of mind of Faulkner's Southerners seems often only an outgrowth of the tone of the geographical area.

 (3) It can function symbolically. In Poe's "The Fall of the House of Usher," the house is equated with the character of Usher; the dream setting can be interpreted in terms of Usher's basic fears.

The absence of setting is often significant. In "The Bill" Malamud has reduced setting to a bare minimum. By eliminating details that tie the situation to a specific place and time, Malamud is able to give his theme a wider application, to suggest that the point he is making is applicable at many times in many places.

SYMBOL

A symbol is something that has a real existence in a story, poem, or play but has a significance above and beyond itself. It stands for something more than what it is. The bill itself in "The Bill" is symbolic; it represents much more than a sum of money owed one man by another. It is a gesture of faith and trust that one makes toward another with the understanding that the other will reciprocate. One might even call symbolic a recurring image in "The Bill"—the image of caged birds. One recalls that Malamud says, when Mr. Panessa offers credit and defines trust, that the old man "chirped up"; when the bill is being added up, "Mrs. Panessa's bird eyes would follow the figuring"; and after Willy refuses to pay, "They were staring up through the glass front door and when he looked at them at first his eyes blurred and they appeared to be two scrawny, loose-feathered birds." The association of birds with the Panessas suggests their pitiful, dependent, caged existence. But to call the bird image symbolic is perhaps to use the term so loosely as to make it shed its primary meaning. The term is better preserved for things that are clearly and indisputably emblematic.

In "Silent Snow, Secret Snow," for example, the imaginary snow represents something in the boy's mind. He is unconscious of its symbolic significance, but the reader sees that the boy is hallucinating a creeping death in his desire for what is cold, stifling, secret, and silent. The fly in Mansfield's "The Fly" symbolizes something to the central character; he is not just pestering an insect but recreating part of his past experience.

What symbols are conspicuous in the Hawthorne story that follows?

Nathaniel Hawthorne

My Kinsman,
Major Molineux

After the kings of Great Britain had assumed the right of appointing the colonial governors, the measures of the latter seldom met with the ready and generous approbation which had been paid to those of their predecessors, under the original charters. The people looked with most jealous scrutiny to the exercise of power which did not emanate from themselves, and they usually rewarded their rulers with slender gratitude for the compliances by which, in softening their instructions from beyond the sea, they had incurred the reprehension of those who gave them. The annals of Massachusetts Bay will inform us, that of six governors in the space of about forty years from the surrender of the old charter, under James II, two were imprisoned by a popular insurrection; a third, as Hutchinson inclines to believe, was driven from the province by the whizzing of a musketball; a fourth, in the opinion of the same historian, was hastened to his grave by continual bickerings with the House of Representatives; and the remaining two, as well as their successors, till the revolution, were favored with few and brief intervals of peaceful sway. The inferior members of the court party, in times of high political excitement, led scarcely a more desirable life. These remarks may serve as a preface to the following adventures, which chanced upon a summer night, not far from a hundred years ago. The reader, in order to avoid a long and dry detail of colonial affairs, is requested to dispense with an account of the train of circumstances that had caused much temporary inflammation of the popular mind.

It was near nine o'clock of a moonlight evening, when a boat crossed the ferry with a single passenger, who had obtained his conveyance at that unusual hour by the promise of an extra fare. While he stood on the landing-place, searching in either pocket for the means of fulfilling his agreement, the ferryman lifted a lantern, by the aid of which, and the newly risen moon, he took a very accurate survey of the stranger's figure. He was a youth of barely eighteen years, evidently country bred, and now, as it should seem, upon his first visit to town. He was clad in a coarse gray coat, well worn, but in excellent repair; his under garments were durably constructed of leather, and fitted tight to a pair of serviceable and well-shaped limbs; his stockings of blue yarn were the incontrovertible work of a mother or a sister; and on his head was a three-cornered hat, which in its better days had perhaps sheltered the graver brow of the lad's father. Under his left arm was a heavy cudgel formed of an oak sapling, and retaining a part of the hardened root; and his equipment was completed by a wallet, not so abundantly stocked as to incommode the vigorous shoulders on which it hung. Brown, curly hair, well-shaped features, and bright, cheerful eyes were nature's gifts, and worth all that art could have done for his adornment.

The youth, one of whose names was Robin, finally drew from his pocket the half of a little province bill of five shillings, which, in the depreciation in that sort of currency, did but satisfy the ferryman's demand, with the surplus of a sexangular piece of parchment, valued at three pence. He then walked forward into the town, with as light a step as if his day's journey had not already exceeded thirty miles, and with as eager an eye as if he were entering London city, instead of the little metropolis of a New England colony. Before Robin had proceeded far, however, it occurred to him that he knew not whither to direct his steps; so he paused, and looked up and down the narrow street, scrutinizing the small and mean wooden buildings that were scattered on either side.

"This low hovel cannot be my kinsman's dwelling," thought he, "nor yonder old house, where the moonlight enters at the broken casement; and truly I see none hereabouts that might be worthy of him. It would have been wise to inquire my way of the ferryman, and doubtless he would have gone with me, and earned a shilling from the Major for his pains. But the next man I meet will do as well."

He resumed his walk and was glad to perceive that the street now became wider, and the houses more respectable in their appearance. He soon discerned a figure moving on moderately in advance and hastened his steps to overtake it. As Robin drew nigh, he saw that the passenger was a man in years, with a full periwig of gray hair, a wide-skirted coat of dark cloth, and silk stockings rolled above his knees. He carried a long and polished cane, which he struck down perpendicularly before him at every step; and at regular intervals he uttered two successive hems, of a peculiarly solemn and sepulchral intonation. Having made these observations, Robin laid hold of the skirt of the old man's coat, just when the light from the open door and windows of a barber's shop fell upon both their figures.

"Good evening to you, honored sir," said he, making a low bow, and still retaining his hold of the skirt. "I pray you tell me whereabouts is the dwelling of my kinsman, Major Molineux."

The youth's question was uttered very loudly; and one of the barbers, whose razor was descending on a well-soaped chin, and another who was dressing a Ramillies wig, left their occupations, and came to the door. The citizen, in the mean time, turned a long-favored countenance upon Robin, and answered him in a tone of excessive anger and annoyance. His two sepulchral hems, however, broke into the very center of his rebuke, with most singular effect, like a thought of the cold grave obtruding among wrathful passions.

"Let go my garment, fellow! I tell you, I know not the man you speak of. What! I have authority, I have—hem, hem—authority; and if this be the respect you show for your betters, your feet shall be brought acquainted with the stocks by daylight, tomorrow morning!"

Robin released the old man's skirt and hastened away, pursued by an ill-mannered roar of laughter from the barber's shop. He was at first considerably surprised by the result of his question, but, being a shrewd youth, soon thought himself able to account for the mystery.

"This is some country representative," was his conclusion, "who has never seen the inside of my kinsman's door and lacks the breeding to answer a stranger civilly. The man is old, or verily—I might be tempted to turn back and smite him on the nose. Ah, Robin, Robin! even the barber's boys laugh at you for choosing such a guide! You will be wiser in time, friend Robin."

He now became entangled in a succession of crooked and narrow streets, which crossed each other and meandered at no great distance from the waterside. The smell of tar was obvious to his nostrils, the masts of vessels pierced the moonlight above the tops of the buildings, and the numerous signs, which Robin paused to read, informed him that he was near the centre of business. But the streets were empty, the shops were closed, and lights were visible only in the second stories of a few dwelling houses. At length, on the corner of a narrow lane, through which he was passing, he beheld the broad countenance of a British hero swinging before the door of an inn, whence proceeded the voices of many guests. The casement of one of the lower windows was thrown back, and a very thin curtain permitted Robin to distinguish a party at supper, round a well-furnished table. The fragrance of the good cheer steamed forth into the outer air, and the youth could not fail to recollect that the last remnant of his travelling stock of provision had yielded to his morning appetite, and that noon had found and left him dinnerless.

"Oh, that a parchment three-penny might give me a right to sit down at yonder table!" said Robin, with a sigh. "But the Major will make me welcome to the best of his victuals; so I will even step boldly in and inquire my way to his dwelling."

He entered the tavern and was guided by the murmur of voices and the fumes of tobacco to the public room. It was a long and low apartment, with oaken walls, grown dark in the continual smoke, and a floor which was thickly sanded, but of no immaculate purity. A number of persons—the larger part of whom appeared to be mariners, or in some way connected with the sea—occupied the wooden benches, or leather-bottomed chairs, conversing on various matters, and occasionally lending their attention to some topic of general interest. Three or four little groups were draining as many bowls of punch, which the West India trade had long since made a familiar drink in the colony. Others, who had the appearance of men who lived by regular and laborious handicraft, preferred the insulated bliss of an unshared potation and became more taciturn under its influence. Nearly all, in short, evinced a predilection for the Good Creature in some of its various shapes, for this is a vice to which, as Fast Day sermons of a hundred years ago will testify, we have a long hereditary claim. The only guests to whom Robin's sympathies inclined him were two or three sheepish countrymen, who were using the inn somewhat after the fashion of a Turkish caravansary they had gotten themselves into the darkest corner of the room, and heedless of the Nicotian atmosphere, were supping on the bread of their own ovens, and the bacon cured in their own chimney smoke. But though Robin felt a sort of brotherhood with these strangers, his eyes were attracted from them to a person who stood near the door, holding whispered conversation with a group of ill-dressed associates. His features were separately striking almost to grotesqueness, and the whole face left a deep impression on the memory. The forehead bulged out into a double prominence, with a vale between; the nose came boldly forth in an irregular curve, and its bridge was of more than a finger's breadth; the eyebrows were deep and shaggy, and the eyes glowed beneath them like fire in a cave.

While Robin deliberated of whom to inquire respecting his kinsman's dwelling, he was accosted by the innkeeper, a little man in a stained white apron, who had come to pay his professional welcome to the stranger. Being in a second generation from a French Protestant, he seemed to have inherited the courtesy of his parent nation; but no variety of circumstances was ever known to change his voice from the one shrill note in which he now addressed Robin.

"From the country, I presume, sir?" said he, with a profound bow. "Beg leave to congratulate you on your arrival and trust you intend a long stay with us. Fine town here, sir, beautiful buildings, and much that may interest a stranger. May I hope for the honor of your commands in respect to supper?"

"The man sees a family likeness! the rogue has guessed that I am related to the Major!" thought Robin, who had hitherto experienced little superfluous civility.

All eyes were now turned on the country lad, standing at the door, in his worn three-cornered hat, gray coat, leather breeches, and blue yarn stockings, leaning on an oaken cudgel, and bearing a wallet on his back.

Robin replied to the courteous innkeeper, with such an assumption of confidence as befitted the Major's relative. "My honest friend," he said, "I shall make it a point to patronize your house on some occasion, when"—here he could not help lowering his voice—"when, I may have more than a parchment three-pence in my pocket. My present business," continued he, speaking with lofty confidence, "is merely to inquire my way to the dwelling of my kinsman, Major Molineux."

There was a sudden and general movement in the room, which Robin interpreted as expressing the eagerness of each individual to become his guide. But the innkeeper turned his eyes to a written paper on the wall, which he read, or seemed to read, with occasional recurrences to the young man's figure.

"What have we here?" said he, breaking his speech into little dry fragments. 'Left the house of the subscriber, bounden servant, Hezekiah Mudge—had on, when he went away, —gray coat, leather breeches, master's third-best hat. One pound currency reward to whosoever shall lodge him in any jail of the providence.' Better trudge, boy; better trudge!"

Robin had begun to draw his hand towards the lighter end of the oak cudgel, but a strange hostility in every countenance induced him to relinquish his purpose of breaking the courteous innkeeper's head. As he turned to leave the room, he encountered a sneering glance from the bold-featured personage whom he had before noticed; and no sooner was he beyond the door, than he heard a general laugh, in which the innkeeper's voice might be distinguished, like the dropping of small stones into a kettle.

"Now, is it not strange," thought Robin, with his usual shrewdness, "is it not strange that the confession of an empty pocket should outweigh the name of my kinsman, Major Molineux? Oh, if I had one of those grinning rascals in the woods, where I and my oak sapling grew up together, I would teach him that my arm is heavy though my purse be light!"

On turning the corner of the narrow lane, Robin found himself in a spacious street, with an unbroken line of lofty houses on each side, and a steepled building at the upper end, whence the ringing of a bell announced the hour of nine. The light of the moon, and the lamps from the numerous shop-windows, discovered people promenading on the pavement, and amongst them Robin had hoped to recognize his hitherto inscrutable relative. The result of his former inquiries made him unwilling to hazard another, in a scene of such publicity, and he determined to walk slowly and silently up the street, thrusting his face close to that of every elderly gentleman, in search of the Major's lineaments. In his progress, Robin encountered many gay and gallant figures. Embroidered garments of showy colors, enormous periwigs, gold-laced hats, and silver-hilted swords glided past him and dazzled his optics. Travelled youths, imitators of the European fine gentlemen of the period, trod jauntily along, half dancing to the fashionable tunes which they hummed and making poor Robin ashamed of his quiet and natural gait. At length, after many pauses to examine the gorgeous display of goods in the shop-windows and after suffering some rebukes for the impertinence of his scrutiny into people's faces, the Major's kinsman found himself near the steepled building, still unsuccessful in his search. As yet, however, he had seen only one side of the thronged street; so Robin crossed and continued the same sort of inquisition down the opposite pavement, with stronger hopes than the philosopher seeking an honest man but with no better fortune. He had arrived about midway towards the lower end, from which his course began, when he overheard the approach of some one who struck down a cane on the flagstones at every step, uttering at regular intervals, two sepulchral hems.

"Mercy on us!" quoth Robin, recognizing the sound.

Turning a corner, which chanced to be close at his right hand, he hastened to pursue his researches in some other part of the town. His patience now was wearing low, and he seemed to feel more fatigue from his rambles since he crossed the ferry, than from his journey of several days on the other side. Hunger also pleaded loudly within him, and Robin began to balance the propriety of demanding, violently, and with lifted cudgel, the necessary guidance from the first solitary passenger whom he should meet. While a resolution to this effect was gaining strength, he entered a street of mean appearance, on either side of which a row of ill-built houses was straggling towards the harbor. The moonlight fell upon no passenger along the whole extent, but in the third domicile which Robin passed there was a half-opened door, and his keen glance detected a woman's garment within.

"My luck may be better here," said he to himself.

Accordingly, he approached the door and beheld it shut closer as he did so; yet an open space remained, sufficing for the fair occupant to observe the stranger, without a corresponding display on her part. All that Robin could discern was a strip of scarlet petticoat, and the occasional sparkle of an eye, as if the moonbeams were trembling on some bright thing.

"Pretty mistress," for I may call her so with a good conscience, thought the shrewd youth, since I know nothing to the contrary, "my sweet pretty mistress, will you be kind enough to tell me whereabouts I must seek the dwelling of my kinsman, Major Molineux?"

Robin's voice was plaintive and winning, and the female, seeing nothing to be shunned in the handsome country youth, thrust open the door and came forth into the moonlight. She was a dainty little figure, with a white neck, round arms, and a slender waist, at the exremity of which her scarlet petticoat jutted out over a hoop, as if she were standing in a balloon. Moreover, her face was oval and pretty, her hair dark beneath the little cap, and her bright eyes possessed a sly freedom, which triumphed over those of Robin.

"Major Molineux dwells here," said this fair woman.

Now, her voice was the sweetest Robin had heard that night, yet he could not help doubting whether that sweet voice spoke Gospel truth. He looked up and down the mean street, and then surveyed the house before which they stood. It was a small, dark edifice of two stories, the second of which projected over the lower floor, and the front apartment had the aspect of a shop for petty commodities.

"Now, truly, I am in luck," replied Robin, cunningly, "and so indeed is my kinsman, the Major, in having so pretty a housekeeper. But I prithee trouble him to step to the door; I will deliver him a message from his friends in the country, and then go back to my lodgings at the inn."

"Nay, the Major has been abed this hour or more," said the lady of the scarlet petticoat, "and it would be to little purpose to disturb him tonight, seeing his evening draught was of the strongest. But he is a kind-hearted man, and it would be as much as my life's worth to let a kinsman of his turn away from the door. You are the good old gentleman's very picture, and I could swear that was his rainy-weather hat. Also he has garments very much resembling those leather small-clothes. But come in, I pray, for I bid you hearty welcome in his name."

So saying, the fair and hospitable dame took our hero by the hand; and the touch was light, and the force was gentleness, and though Robin read in her eyes what he did not hear in her words, yet the slender-waisted woman in the scarlet petticoat proved stronger than the athletic country youth. She had drawn his half-willing footsteps nearly to the threshold, when the opening of a door in the neighborhood startled the Major's housekeeper, and leaving the Major's kinsman, she vanished speedily into her own domicile. A heavy yawn preceded the appearance of a man, who, like the Moonshine of Pyramus and Thisbe, carried a lantern, needlessly aiding his sister luminary in the heavens. As he walked sleepily up the street, he turned his broad, dull face on Robin, and displayed a long staff, spiked at the end.

"Home, vagabond, home!" said the watchman, in accents that seemed to fall asleep as soon as they were uttered. "Home, or we'll set you in the stocks by peep of day!"

"This is the second hint of this kind," thought Robin. "I wish they would end my difficulties, by setting me there tonight."

Nevertheless, the youth felt an instinctive antipathy towards the guardian of midnight order, which at first prevented him from asking his usual question. But just when the man was about to vanish behind the corner, Robin resolved not to lose the opportunity, and shouted lustily after him,—

"I say, friend! will you guide me to the house of my kinsman, Major Molineux?"

The watchman made no reply but turned the corner and was gone; yet Robin seemed to hear the sound of drowsy laughter stealing along the solitary street. At that moment, also, a pleasant titter saluted him from the open window above his head; he looked up, and caught the sparkle of a saucy eye; a round arm beckoned to him, and next he heard light footsteps descending the staircase within.

But Robin, being of the household of a New England clergyman, was a good youth, as well as a shrewd one; so he resisted temptation, and fled away.

He now roamed desperately, and at random, through the town, almost ready to believe that a spell was on him, like that by which a wizard of his country had once kept three pursuers wandering, a whole winter night, within twenty paces of the cottage which they sought. The streets lay before him, strange and desolate, and the lights were extinguished in almost every house. Twice, however, little parties of men, among whom Robin distinguished individuals in outlandish attire, came hurrying along; but, though on both occasions, they paused to address him, such intercourse did not at all enlighten his perplexity. They did but utter a few words in some language of which Robin knew nothing, and perceiving his inability to answer, bestowed a curse upon him in plain English and hastened away. Finally, the lad determined to knock at the door of every mansion that might appear worthy to be occupied by his kinsman, trusting that perseverance would overcome the fatality that had hitherto thwarted him. Firm in this resolve, he was passing beneath the walls of a church, which formed the corner of two streets, when, as he turned into a shade of its steeple, he encountered a bulky stranger, muffled in a cloak. The man was proceeding with the speed of earnest business, but Robin planted himself full before him, holding the oak cudgel with both hands across his body as a bar to further passage.

"Halt, honest man, and answer me a question," said he, very resolutely. "Tell me, this instant, whereabouts is the dwelling of my kinsman, Major Molineux!"

"Keep your tongue between your teeth, fool, and let me pass!" said a deep, gruff voice, which Robin partly remembered. "Let me pass, or I'll strike you to the earth!"

"No, no, neighbor!" cried Robin, flourishing his cudgel, and then thrusting its larger end close to the man's muffled face. "No, no, I'm not the fool you take me for, nor do you pass till I have an answer to my question. Whereabouts is the dwelling of my kinsman, Major Molineux?"

The stranger, instead of attempting to force his passage, stepped back into the moonlight, unmuffled his face, and stared full into that of Robin.

"Watch here an hour, and Major Molineux will pass by," said he.

Robin gazed with dismay and astonishment on the unprecedented physiognomy of the speaker. The forehead with its double prominence, the broad hooked nose, the shaggy eyebrows, and fiery eyes were those which he had noticed at the inn, but the man's complexion had undergone a singular, or, more properly, a twofold change. One side of the face blazed an intense red, while the other was black as midnight, the division line being in the broad bridge of the nose; and a mouth which seemed to extend from ear to ear was black or red, in contrast to the color of the cheek. The effect was as if two individual devils, a fiend of fire and a fiend of darkness, had united themselves to form this infernal visage. The stranger grinned in Robin's face, muffled his party-colored features, and was out of sight in a moment.

"Strange things we travellers see!" ejaculated Robin.

He seated himself, however, upon the steps of the church-door, resolving to wait the appointed time for his kinsman. A few moments were consumed in philosophical speculations upon the species of man who had just left him; but having settled this point shrewdly, rationally, and satisfactorily, he was compelled to look elsewhere for his amusement. And first he threw his eyes along the street. It was of more respectable appearance than most of those into which he had wandered; and the moon, creating, like the imaginative power, a beautiful strangeness in familiar objects, gave something of romance to a scene that might not have possessed it in the light of day. The irregular and often quaint architecture of the houses, some of whose roofs were broken into numerous little peaks, while others ascended, steep and narrow, into a single point, and others again were square; the pure snow-white of some of their complexions, the aged darkness of others, and the thousand sparklings, reflected from bright substances in the walls of many; these matters engaged Robin's attention for a while, and then began to grow wearisome. Next he endeavored to define the forms of distant objects, starting away, with almost ghostly indistinctness, just as his eye appeared to grasp them; and finally he took a minute survey of an edifice which stood on the opposite side of the street, directly in front of the church door, where he was stationed. It was a large, square mansion, distinguished from its neighbors by a balcony, which rested on tall pillars, and by an elaborate Gothic window, communicating therewith.

"Perhaps this is the very house I have been seeking," thought Robin.

Then he strove to speed away the time, by listening to a murmur which swept continually along the street, yet was scarcely audible, except to an unaccustomed ear like his; it was a low, dull, dreamy sound, compounded of many noises, each of which was at too great a distance to be separately heard. Robin marvelled at this snore of a sleeping town and marvelled more whenever its continuity was broken by now and then a distant shout, apparently loud where it originated. But altogether it was a sleep-inspiring sound, and, to shake off its drowsy influence, Robin arose and climbed a window frame, that he might view the interior of the church. There the moonbeams came trembling in, and fell down upon the deserted pews, and extended along the quiet aisles. A fainter yet more awful radiance was hovering around the pulpit, and one solitary ray had dared to rest upon the open page of the great Bible. Had nature, in that deep hour, become a worshipper in the house which man had builded? Or was that heavenly light the visible sanctity of the place, visible because no earthly and impure feet were within the walls? The scene made Robin's heart shiver with a sensation of loneliness stronger than he had ever felt in the remotest depths of his native woods; so he turned away and sat down again before the door. There were graves around the church, and now an uneasy thought obtruded into Robin's breast. What if the object of his search, which had been so often and so strangely thwarted, were all the time mouldering in his shroud? What if his kinsman should glide through yonder gate, and nod and smile to him in dimly passing by?

"Oh that any breathing thing were here with me!" said Robin.

Recalling his thoughts from the uncomfortable track, he sent them over forest, hill, and stream and attempted to imagine how that evening of ambiguity and weariness had been spent by his father's household. He pictured them assembled at the door, beneath the tree, the great old tree, which had been spared for its huge twisted trunk and venerable shade, when a thousand leafy brethren fell. There, at the going down of the summer sun, it was his father's custom to perform domestic worship, that the neighbors might come and join with him like brothers of the family, and that the wayfaring man might pause to drink at the fountain and keep his heart pure by freshening the memory of home. Robin distinguished the seat of every individual of the little audience; he saw the good man in the midst, holding the Scriptures in the golden light that fell from the western clouds; he beheld him close the book and all rise up to pray. He heard the old thanksgivings for daily mercies, the old supplications for their continuance, to which he had so often listened in weariness but which were now among his dear remembrances. He perceived the slight inequality of his father's voice when he came to speak of the absent one; he noted how his mother turned her face to the broad and knotted trunk; how his elder brother scorned, because the beard was rough upon his upper lip, to permit his features to be moved; how the younger sister drew down a low hanging branch before her eyes; and how the little one of all, whose sports had hitherto broken the decorum of the scene, understood the prayer for her playmate and burst into clamorous grief. Then he saw them go in at the door; and when Robin would have entered also, the latch tinkled into its place, and he was excluded from his home.

"Am I here, or there?" cried Robin, starting; for all at once, when his thoughts had become visible and audible in a dream, the long, wide, solitary street shone out before him.

He aroused himself and endeavored to fix his attention steadily upon the large edifice which he had surveyed before. But still his mind kept vibrating between fancy and reality; by turns, the pillars of the balcony lengthened into the tall, bare stems of pines, dwindled down to human figures, settled again into their true shape and size, and then commenced a new succession of changes. For a single moment, when he deemed himself awake, he could have sworn that a visage—one which he seemed to remember, yet could not absolutely name as his kinsman's—was looking towards him from the Gothic window. A deeper sleep wrestled with and nearly overcame him but fled at the sound of footsteps along the opposite pavement. Robin rubbed his eyes, discerned a man passing at the foot of the balcony, and addressed him in a loud, peevish, and lamentable cry.

"Hallo, friend! must I wait here all night for my kinsman, Major Molineux?"

The sleeping echoes awoke and answered the voice; and the passenger, barely able to discern a figure sitting in the oblique shade of the steeple, traversed the street to obtain a nearer view. He was himself a gentleman in the prime, of open, intelligent, cheerful, and altogether prepossessing countenance. Perceiving a country youth, apparently homeless and without friends, he accosted him in a tone of real kindness, which had become strange to Robin's ears.

"Well, my good lad, why are you sitting here?" inquired he. "Can I be of service to you in any way?"

"I am afraid not, sir," replied Robin, despondingly; "yet I shall take it kindly, if you'll answer me a single question. I've been searching, half the night, for one Major Molineux; now, sir, is there really such a person in these parts, or am I dreaming?"

"Major Molineux! The name is not altogether strange to me," said the gentleman, smiling. "Have you any objection to telling me the nature of your business with him?"

Then Robin briefly related that his father was a clergyman, settled on a small salary, at a long distance back in the country, and that he and Major Molineux were brothers' children. The Major, having inherited riches, and acquired civil and military rank, had visited his cousin, in great pomp, a year or two before, had manifested much interest in Robin and an elder brother, and, being childless himself, had thrown out hints respecting the future establishment of one of them in life. The elder brother was destined to succeed to the farm which his father cultivated in the interval of sacred duties; it was therefore determined that Robin should profit by his kinsman's generous intentions, especially as he seemed to be rather the favorite and was thought to possess other necessary endowments.

"For I have the name of being a shrewd youth," observed Robin, in this part of his story.

"I doubt not you deserve it," replied his new friend, good-naturedly, "but pray proceed.

"Well, sir, being nearly eighteen years old, and well grown, as you see," continued Robin, drawing himself up to his full height, "I thought it high time to begin in the world. So my mother and sister put me in handsome trim, and my father gave me half the remnant of his last year's salary, and five days ago I started for this place, to pay the Major a visit. But, would you believe it, sir! I crossed the ferry a little after dark and have yet found nobody that would show me the way to his dwelling; only, an hour or two since, I was told to wait here, and Major Molineux would pass by."

"Can you describe the man who told you this?" inquired the gentleman.

"Oh, he was a very ill-favored fellow, sir," replied Robin, "with two great bumps on his forehead, a hook nose, fiery eyes; and, what struck me as the strangest, his face was of two different colors. Do you happen to know such a man, sir?"

"Not intimately," answered the stranger, "but I chanced to meet him a little time previous to your stopping me. I believe you may trust his word, and that the Major will very shortly pass through this street. In the mean time, as I have a singular curiosity to witness your meeting, I will sit down here upon the steps and bear you company."

He seated himself accordingly and soon engaged his companion in animated discourse. It was but of brief continuance, however, for a noise of shouting, which had long been remotely audible, drew so much nearer that Robin inquired its cause.

"What may be the meaning of this uproar?" asked he. "Truly, if your town be always as noisy, I shall find little sleep while I am an inhabitant."

"Why, indeed, friend Robin, there do appear to be three or four riotous fellows abroad tonight," replied the gentleman. "You must not expect all the stillness of your native woods here in our streets. But the watch will shortly be at the heels of these lads and"—

"Ay, and set them in the stocks by peep of day," interrupted Robin, recollecting his own encounter with the drowsy lanternbearer. "But, dear sir, if I may trust my ears, an army of watchmen would never make head against such a multitude of rioters. There were at least a thousand voices went up to make that one shout."

"May not a man have several voices, Robin, as well as two complexions?" said his friend.

"Perhaps a man may, but Heaven forbid that a woman should!" responded the shrewd youth, thinking of the seductive tones of the Major's housekeeper.

The sounds of a trumpet in some neighboring street now became so evident and continual that Robin's curiosity was strongly excited. In addition to the shouts, he heard frequent bursts from many instruments of discord, and a wild and confused laughter filled up the intervals. Robin rose from the steps, and looked wistfully towards a point whither people seemed to be hastening.

"Surely some prodigious merry-making is going on," exclaimed he. "I have laughed very little since I left home, sir, and should be sorry to lose an opportunity. Shall we step round the corner by that darkish house and take our share of the fun?"

"Sit down again, sit down, good Robin," replied the gentleman, laying his hand on the skirt of the gray coat. "You forget that we must wait here for your kinsman; and there is reason to believe that he will pass by, in the course of a very few moments."

The near approach of the uproar had now disturbed the neighborhood; windows flew open on all sides; and many heads, in the attire of the pillow, and confused by sleep suddenly broken, were protruded to the gaze of whoever had leisure to observe them. Eager voices hailed each other from house to house, all demanding the explanation, which not a soul could give. Half-dressed men hurried towards the unknown commotion, stumbling as they went over the stone steps that thrust themselves into the narrow footwalk. The shouts, the laughter, and the tuneless bray, the antipodes of music, came onwards with increasing din, till scattered individuals, and then denser bodies, began to appear round a corner at the distance of a hundred yards.

"Will you recognize your kinsman, if he passes in this crowd?" inquired the gentleman.

"Indeed, I can't warrant it, sir; but I'll take my stand here and keep a bright lookout," answered Robin, descending to the outer edge of the pavement.

A mighty stream of people now emptied into the street and came rolling slowly towards the church. A single horseman wheeled the corner in the midst of them, and close behind him came a band of fearful wind-instruments, sending forth a fresher discord now that no intervening buildings kept it from the ear. Then a redder light disturbed the moonbeams, and a dense multitude of torches shone along the street, concealing, by their glare, whatever object they illuminated. The single horseman, clad in a military dress, and bearing a drawn sword, rode onward as the leader, and, by his fierce and variegated countenance, appeared like war personified; the red of one cheek was an emblem of fire and sword; the blackness of the other betokened the mourning that attends them. In his train were wild figures in the Indian dress, and many fantastic shapes without a model, giving the whole march a visionary air, as if a dream had broken forth from some feverish brain, and were sweeping visibly through the midnight streets. A mass of people, inactive, except as applauding spectators, hemmed the procession in; and several women ran along the sidewalk, piercing the confusion of heavier sounds with their shrill voices of mirth or terror.

"The double-faced fellow has his eye upon me," muttered Robin, with an indefinite but an uncomfortable idea that he was himself to bear a part in the pageantry.

The leader turned himself in the saddle and fixed his glance full

upon the country youth, as the steed went slowly by. When Robin
had freed his eyes from those fiery ones, the musicians were passing
before him, and the torches were close at hand; but the unsteady
brightness of the latter formed a veil which he could not penetrate.
The rattling of wheels over the stones sometimes found its way to
his ear, and confused traces of a human form appeared at intervals
and then melted into the vivid light. A moment more, and the leader
thundered a command to halt: the trumpets vomited a horrid breath
and then held their peace; the shouts and laughter of the people died
away, and there remained only a universal hum, allied to silence.
Right before Robin's eyes was an uncovered cart. There the torches
blazed the brightest, there the moon shone out like day, and there,
in tar-and-feathery dignity, sat his kinsman, Major Molineux!

He was an elderly man, of large and majestic person, and strong,
square features, betokening a steady soul; but steady as it was his
enemies had found means to shake it. His face was pale as death,
and far more ghastly; the broad forehead was contracted in his agony,
so that his eyebrows formed one grizzled line; his eyes were red and
wild, and the foam hung white upon his quivering lip. His whole
frame was agitated by a quick and continual tremor, which his pride
strove to quell, even in those circumstances of overwhelming humiliation. But perhaps the bitterest pang of all was when his eyes
met those of Robin; for he evidently knew him on the instant, as the
youth stood witnessing the foul disgrace of a head grown gray in
honor. They stared at each other in silence, and Robin's knees shook,
and his hair bristled, with a mixture of pity and terror. Soon, however, a bewildering excitement began to seize upon his mind; the
preceding adventures of the night, the unexpected appearance of
the crowd, the torches, the confused din and the hush that followed,
the spectre of his kinsman reviled by that great multitude—all this,
and, more than all, a perception of tremendous ridicule in the whole
scene, affected him with a sort of mental inebriety. At that moment
a voice of sluggish merriment saluted Robin's ears, he turned instinctively, and just behind the corner of the church stood the lanternbearer, rubbing his eyes, and drowsily enjoying the lad's amazement. Then he heard a peal of laughter like the ringing of silvery
bells; a woman twitched his arm, a saucy eye met his, and he saw
the lady of the scarlet petticoat. A sharp, dry cachinnation appealed

to his memory, and standing on tiptoe in the crowd, with his white apron over his head, he beheld the courteous little innkeeper. And lastly, there sailed over the heads of the multitude a great, broad laugh, broken in the midst by two sepulchral hems; thus, "Haw, haw, haw—hem, hem—haw, haw, haw, haw!"

The sound proceeded from the balcony of the opposite edifice, and thither Robin turned his eyes. In front of the Gothic window stood the old citizen, wrapped in a wide gown, his gray periwig exchanged for a nightcap, which was thrust back from his forehead, and his silk stockings hanging about his legs. He supported himself on his polished cane in a fit of convulsive merriment, which manifested itself on his solemn old features like a funny inscription on a tombstone. Then Robin seemed to hear the voices of the barbers, of the guests of the inn, and of all who had made sport of him that night. The contagion was spreading among the multitude, when all at once, it seized upon Robin, and he sent forth a shout of laughter that echoed through the street—every man shook his sides, every man emptied his lungs, but Robin's shout was the loudest there. The cloud-spirits peeped from their silvery islands, as the congregated mirth went roaring up the sky! The Man in the Moon heard the far bellow. "Oho," quoth he, "the old earth is frolicsome tonight!"

When there was a momentary calm in that tempestuous sea of sound, the leader gave the sign, the procession resumed its march. On they went, like fiends that throng in mockery around some dead potentate, mighty no more, but majestic still in his agony. On they went, in counterfeited pomp, in senseless uproar, in frenzied merriment, trampling all on an old man's heart. On swept the tumult and left a silent street behind.

. . .

"Well, Robin, are you dreaming?" inquired the gentleman, laying his hand on the youth's shoulder.

Robin started and withdrew his arm from the stone post to which he had instinctively clung, as the living stream rolled by him. His cheek was somewhat pale, and his eye not quite as lively as in the earlier part of the evening.

"Will you be kind enough to show me the way to the ferry?" said he, after a moment's pause.

"You have, then, adopted a new subject of inquiry?" observed his companion, with a smile.

"Why, yes, sir," replied Robin, rather dryly. "Thanks to you, and to my other friends, I have at last met my kinsman, and he will scarce desire to see my face again. I begin to grow weary of a town life, sir. Will you show me the way to the ferry?"

"No, my good friend Robin, not tonight, at least," said the gentleman. "Some few days hence, if you wish it, I will speed you on your journey. Or, if you prefer to remain with us, perhaps, as you are a shrewd youth, you may rise in the world without the help of your kinsman, Major Molineux."

My Kinsman, Major Molineux

For Analysis

1. Throughout the story Robin is described as a "shrewd" youth. Trace the various meanings that coalesce about this word as the story progresses, and note who applies the word to Robin. Does the last application imply a different meaning from those suggested before?

2. A basic contrast between the country and the city is built into "My Kinsman, Major Molineux." What symbolic values accrue to the rural and urban, respectively, in the progress of the story?

3. Hawthorne partially creates the setting for his tale by describing the type of light that falls on various scenes. Does the illumination vary from scene to scene? If it does, is there a symbolic significance in this variation?

4. A realistic level of incident and setting are carefully maintained throughout the story. Does this realism hinder or facilitate the generation of symbolic values?

Edgar Allan Poe

The Fall of the
House of Usher

Son coeur est un luth suspendu;
Sitôt qu'on le touche il résonne.
—DE BERANGER

During the whole of a dull, dark, and soundless day in the autumn of the year, when the clouds hung oppressively low in the heavens, I had been passing alone, on horseback, through a singularly dreary tract of country, and at length found myself, as the shades of the evening drew on, within view of the melancholy House of Usher. I know not how it was—but, with the first glimpse of the building, a sense of insufferable gloom prevaded my spirit. I say insufferable; for the feeling was unrelieved by any of that half-pleasurable, because poetic, sentiment with which the mind usually receives even the sternest natural images of the desolate or terrible. I looked upon the scene before me—upon the mere house, and the simple land-scape features of the domain—upon the bleak walls—upon the va-cant eye-like windows—upon a few rank sedges—and upon a few white trunks of decayed trees—with an utter depression of soul which I can compare to no earthly sensation more properly than to the after-dream of the reveller upon opium—the bitter lapse into every-day life—the hideous dropping off of the veil. There was an iciness, a sinking, a sickening of the heart—an unredeemed dreari-ness of thought which no goading of the imagination could torture into aught of the sublime. What was it—I paused to think—what was it that so unnerved me in the contemplation of the House of Usher? It was a mystery all insoluble; nor could I grapple with the shadowy fancies that crowded upon me as I pondered. I was forced

41

to fall back upon the unsatisfactory conclusion, that while, beyond doubt, there *are* combinations of very simple natural objects which have the power of thus affecting us, still the analysis of this power lies among considerations beyond our depth. It was possible, I reflected, that a mere different arrangement of the particulars of the scene, of the details of the picture, would be sufficient to modify, or perhaps to annihilate its capacity for sorrowful impression; and, acting upon this idea, I reined my horse to the precipitous brink of a black and lurid tarn that lay in unruffled luster by the dwelling, and gazed down—but with a shudder even more thrilling than before—upon the remodeled and inverted images of the gray sedge, and the ghastly tree-stems, and the vacant and eye-like windows.

Nevertheless, in this mansion of gloom I now proposed to myself a sojourn of some weeks. Its proprietor, Roderick Usher, had been one of my boon companions in boyhood; but many years had elapsed since our last meeting. A letter, however, had lately reached me in a distant part of the country—a letter from him—which, in its wildly importunate nature, had admitted of no other than a personal reply. The MS. gave evidence of nervous agitation. The writer spoke of acute bodily illness—of a mental disorder which oppressed him—and of an earnest desire to see me, as his best and indeed his only personal friend, with a view of attempting, by the cheerfulness of my society, some alleviation of his malady. It was the manner in which all this, and much more, was said—it was the apparent *heart* that went with his request—which allowed me no room for hesitation; and I accordingly obeyed forthwith what I still considered a very singular summons.

Although, as boys, we had been even intimate associates, yet I really knew little of my friend. His reserve had been always excessive and habitual. I was aware, however, that his very ancient family had been noted, time out of mind, for a peculiar sensibility of temperament, displaying itself, through long ages, in many works of exalted art, and manifested, of late, in repeated deeds of munificent yet unobstrusive charity, as well as in a passionate devotion to the intricacies, perhaps even more than to the orthodox and easily recognizable beauties, of musical science. I had learned, too, the very remarkable fact, that the stem of the Usher race, all time-honored as it was, had put forth, at no period, any enduring branch; in other words, that the entire family lay in the direct line of descent, and had always, with very trifling and very temporary variation, so lain. It was this deficiency, I considered, while running over in thought the perfect keeping of the character of the premises with the accredited character of the people, and while speculating upon the possible influence which the one, in the long lapse of centuries, might have exercised upon the other—it was this deficiency, perhaps, of collateral issue, and the consequent undeviating transmission, from sire to son, of the patrimony with the name, which had, at length, so identified the two as to merge the original title of the estate in the quaint and equivocal appellation of the "House of Usher"—an appellation which seemed to include, in the minds of the peasantry who used it, both the family and the family mansion.

I have said that the sole effect of my somewhat childish experiment—that of looking down within the tarn—had been to deepen the first singular impression. There can be no doubt that the consciousness of the rapid increase of my superstition—for why should I not so term it?—served mainly to accelerate the increase itself. Such, I have long known, is the paradoxical law of all sentiments having terror as a basis. And it might have been for this reason only, that, when I again uplifted my eyes to the house itself, from its image in the pool, there grew in my mind a strange fancy—a fancy so ridiculous, indeed, that I but mention it to show the vivid force of the sensations which oppressed me. I had so worked upon my imagination as really to believe that about the whole mansion and domain there hung an atmosphere peculiar to themselves and their immediate vicinity—an atmosphere which had no affinity with the air of heaven, but which had reeked up from the decayed trees, and the gray wall, and the silent tarn—a pestilent and mystic vapor, dull, sluggish, faintly discernible, and leaden-hued.

Shaking off from my spirit what *must* have been a dream, I scanned more narrowly the real aspect of the building. Its principal feature seemed to be that of an excessive antiquity. The discoloration of ages had been great. Minute fungi overspread the whole exterior, hanging in a fine tangled web-work from the eaves. Yet all this was apart from any extraordinary dilapidation. No portion of the masonry had fallen; and there appeared to be a wild inconsistency between its still perfect adaptation of parts and the crumbling condition of the individual stones. In this there was much that reminded me of the specious totality of old wood-work which has rotted for long years in some neglected vault, with no disturbance from the breath of the external air. Beyond this indication of extensive decay, however, the fabric gave little token of instability. Perhaps the eye of a scrutinizing observer might have discovered a barely perceptible fissure, which, extending from the roof of the building in front, made its way down the wall in a zigzag direction, until it became lost in the sullen waters of the tarn.

Noticing these things, I rode over a short causeway to the house. A servant in waiting took my horse, and I entered the Gothic archway of the hall. A valet, of stealthy step, thence conducted me, in silence, through many dark and intricate passages in my progress to the *studio* of his master. Much that I encountered on the way contributed, I know not how, to heighten the vague sentiments of which I have already spoken. While the objects around me—while the carvings of the ceilings, the sombre tapestries of the walls, the ebon blackness of the floors, and the phantasmagoric armorial trophies which rattled as I strode, were but matters to which, or to such as which, I had been accustomed from my infancy—while I hesitated not to acknowledge how familiar was all this—I still wondered to find how unfamiliar were the fancies which ordinary images were stirring up. On one of the staircases, I met the physician of the family. His countenance, I thought, wore a mingled expression of low cunning and perplexity. He accosted me with trepidation and passed on. The valet now threw open a door and ushered me into the presence of his master.

The room in which I found myself was very large and lofty. The windows were long, narrow, and pointed, and at so vast a distance from the black oaken floor as to be altogether inaccessible from within. Feeble gleams of encrimsoned light made their way through the trellised panes, and served to render sufficiently distinct the more prominent objects around; the eye, however, struggled in vain to reach the remoter angles of the chamber, or the recesses of the vaulted and fretted ceiling. Dark draperies hung upon the walls. The general furniture was profuse, comfortless, antique, and tattered. Many books and musical instruments lay scattered about but failed to give any vitality to the scene. I felt that I breathed an atmosphere of sorrow. An air of stern, deep, and irredeemable gloom hung over and pervaded all.

Upon my entrance, Usher arose from a sofa on which he had been lying at full length and greeted me with a vivacious warmth which had much in it, I at first thought, of an overdone cordiality—of the constrained effort of the *ennuyé* man of the world. A glance, however, at his countenance convinced me of his perfect sincerity. We sat down; and for some moments, while he spoke not, I gazed upon him with a feeling half of pity, half of awe. Surely, man had never before so terribly altered, in so brief a period, as had Roderick Usher! It was with difficulty that I could bring myself to admit the identity of the wan being before me with the companion of my early boyhood. Yet the character of his face had been at all times remarkable. A cadaverousness of complexion; an eye large, liquid, and luminous beyond comparison; lips somewhat thin and very pallid, but of a surpassingly beautiful curve; a nose of a delicate Hebrew model, but with a breadth of nostril unusual in similar formations; a finely moulded chin, speaking, in its want of prominence, of a want of moral energy; hair of a more than web-like softness and tenuity— these features, with an inordinate expansion above the regions of the temple, made up altogether a countenance not easily to be forgotten. And now in the mere exaggeration of the prevailing character of these features, and of the expression they were wont to convey, lay so much of change that I doubted to whom I spoke. The now ghastly pallor of the skin, and the now miraculous lustre of the eye, above all things startled and even awed me. The silken hair, too, had been suffered to grow all unheeded, and as, in its wild gossamer texture, it floated rather than fell about the face, I could not, even with effort, connect its Arabesque expression with any idea of simple humanity.

In the manner of my friend I was at once struck with an incoherence—an inconsistency; and I soon found this to arise from a series of feeble and futile struggles to overcome an habitual trepidancy— an excessive nervous agitation. For something of this nature I had indeed been prepared, no less by his letter, than by reminiscences of certain boyish traits, and by conclusions deduced from his peculiar physical conformation and temperament. His action was alternately vivacious and sullen. His voice varied rapidly from a tremulous indecision (when the animal spirits seemed utterly in abeyance) to that species of energetic concision—that abrupt, weighty, unhurried, and hollow-sounding enunciation—that leaden, self-balanced, and perfectly modulated guttural utterance, which may be observed in the lost drunkard, or the irreclaimable eater of opium, during the periods of his most intense excitement.

It was thus that he spoke of the object of my visit, of his earnest desire to see me, and of the solace he expected me to afford him. He entered, at some length, into what he conceived to be the nature of his malady. It was, he said, a constitutional and a family evil, and one for which he despaired to find a remedy—a mere nervous affection, he immediately added, which would undoubtedly soon pass off. It displayed itself in a host of unnatural sensations. Some of these as he detailed them, interested and bewildered me; although, perhaps, the terms and the general manner of their narration had their weight. He suffered much from a morbid acuteness of the senses; the most insipid food was alone endurable; he could wear only garments of certain texture; the odors of all flowers were oppressive; his eyes were tortured by even a faint light; and there were but peculiar sounds, and these from stringed instruments, which did not inspire him with horror.

To an anomalous species of terror I found him a bounded slave. "I shall perish," said he, "I *must* perish in this deplorable folly. Thus, thus, and not otherwise, shall I be lost. I dread the events of the future, not in themselves, but in their results. I shudder at the thought of any, even the most trivial, incident, which may operate upon this intolerable agitation of soul. I have, indeed, no abhorrence of danger, except in its absolute effect—in terror. In this unnerved, in this pitiable, condition I feel that the period will sooner or later arrive when I must abandon life and reason together, in some struggle with the grim phantasm, FEAR."

I learned, moreover, at intervals, and through broken and equivocal hints, another singular feature of his mental condition. He was enchained by certain superstitious impressions in regard to the dwelling which he tenanted, and whence, for many years, he had never ventured forth—in regard to an influence whose supposititious force was conveyed in terms too shadowy here to be restated—an influence which some peculiarities in the mere form and substance of his family mansion had, by dint of long sufferance, he said, obtained over his spirit—an effect which the *physique* of the gray walls and turrets, and of the dim tarn into which they all looked down, had, at length, brought about upon the *morale* of his existence.

He admitted, however, although with hesitation, that much of the peculiar gloom which thus afflicted him could be traced to a more natural and far more palpable origin—to the severe and long-continued illness—indeed to the evidently approaching dissolution

—of a tenderly beloved sister, his sole companion for long years, his last and only relative on earth. "Her decease," he said, with a bitterness which I can never forget, "would leave him (him, the hopeless and the frail) the last of the ancient race of the Ushers." While he spoke, the lady Madeline (for so was she called) passed through a remote portion of the apartment, and, without having noticed my presence, disappeared. I regarded her with an utter astonishment not unmingled with dread; and yet I found it impossible to account for such feelings. A sensation of stupor oppressed me as my eyes followed her retreating steps. When a door, at length, closed upon her, my glance sought instinctively and eagerly the countenance of the brother; but he had buried his face in his hands, and I could only perceive that a far more than ordinary wanness had overspread the emaciated fingers through which trickled many passionate tears.

The disease of the lady Madeline had long baffled the skill of her physicians. A settled apathy, a gradual wasting away of the person, and frequent although transient affections of a partially cataleptical character were the unusual diagnosis. Hitherto she had steadily borne up against the pressure of her malady, and had not betaken herself finally to bed; but on the closing in of the evening of my arrival at the house, she succumbed (as her brother told me at night with inexpressible agitation) to the prostrating power of the destroyer; and I learned that the glimpse I had obtained of her person would thus probably be the last I should obtain—that the lady, at least while living, would be seen by me no more.

For several days ensuing, her name was unmentioned by either Usher or myself; and during this period I was busied in earnest endeavors to alleviate the melancholy of my friend. We painted and read together, or I listened, as if in a dream, to the wild improvisations of his speaking guitar. And thus, as a closer and still closer intimacy admitted me more unreservedly into the recesses of his spirit, the more bitterly did I perceive the futility of all attempt at cheering a mind from which darkness, as if an inherent positive quality, poured forth upon all objects of the moral and physical universe in one unceasing radiation of gloom.

I shall ever bear about me a memory of the many solemn hours I thus spent alone with the master of the House of Usher. Yet I should fail in any attempt to convey an idea of the exact character of the studies, or of the occupations, in which he involved me, or led me the way. An excited and highly distempered ideality threw a sulphureous luster over all. His long improvised dirges will ring forever in my ears. Among other things, I hold painfully in mind a certain singular perversion and amplification of the wild air of the last waltz of Von Weber. From the paintings over which his elaborate fancy brooded, and which grew, touch by touch, into vaguenesses at which I shuddered the more thrillingly, because I shuddered knowing not why—from these paintings (vivid as their images now are before me) I would in vain endeavor to educe more than a small portion which should lie within the compass of merely written words. By the utter simplicity, by the nakedness of his designs, he arrested and overawed attention. If ever mortal painted an idea, that mortal was Roderick Usher. For me at least, in the circumstances then surrounding me, there arose out of the pure abstractions which the hypochondriac contrived to throw upon his canvas, an intensity of intolerable awe, no shadow of which felt I ever yet in the contemplation of the certainly glowing yet too concrete reveries of Fuseli.

One of the phantasmagoric conceptions of my friend, partaking not so rigidly of the spirit of abstraction, may be shadowed forth, although feebly, in words. A small picture presented the interior of an immensely long and rectangular vault or tunnel, with low walls, smooth, white, and without interruption or device. Certain accessory points of the design served well to convey the idea that this excavation lay at an exceeding depth below the surface of the earth. No outlet was observed in any portion of its vast extent, and no torch or other artificial source of light was discernible; yet a flood of intense rays rolled throughout, and bathed the whole in a ghastly and inappropriate splendor.

I have just spoken of that morbid condition of the auditory nerve which rendered all music intolerable to the sufferer, with the exception of certain effects of stringed instruments. It was, perhaps, the narrow limits to which he thus confined himself upon the guitar which gave birth, in great measure, to the fantastic character of his performances. But the fervid *facility* of his *impromptus* could not be so accounted for. They must have been, and were, in the notes, as well as in the words of his wild fantasias (for he not unfrequently accompanied himself with rhymed verbal improvisations), the result of that intense mental collectedness and concentration to which I have previously alluded as observable only in particular moments

of the highest artificial excitement. The words of one of these rhap-
sodies I have easily remembered. I was, perhaps, the more forcibly
impressed with it as he gave it, because, in the under or mystic current of its meaning, I fancied that I perceived, and for the first time,
a full consciousness on the part of Usher of the tottering of his lofty
reason upon her throne. The verses, which were entitled "The Haunted
Palace," ran very nearly, if not accurately, thus:

I

In the greenest of our valleys,
    By good angels tenanted,
Once a fair and stately palace—
    Radiant palace—reared its head.
In the monarch Thought's dominion—
    It stood there!
Never seraph spread a pinion
    Over fabric half so fair.

II

Banners yellow, glorious, golden,
    On its roof did float and flow
(This—all this—was in the olden
    Time long ago);
And every gentle air that dallied,
    In that sweet day,
Along the ramparts plumed and pallid,
    A winged odor went away.

III

Wanderers in that happy valley
    Through two luminous windows saw
Spirits moving musically
    To a lute's well-tuned law;
Round about a throne, where sitting
    (Porphyrogene!)
In state his glory well befitting,
    The ruler of the realm was seen.

IV

And all with pearl and ruby glowing
    Was the fair palace door,
Through which came flowing, flowing, flowing
    And sparkling evermore,
A troop of Echoes whose sweet duty
    Was but to sing,

In voices of surpassing beauty,
The wit and wisdom of their king.

V

But evil things, in robes of sorrow,
Assailed the monarch's high estate;
(Ah, let us mourn, for never morrow
Shall dawn upon him, desolate!)
And, round about his home, the glory
That blushed and bloomed
Is but a dim-remembered story
Of the old time entombed.

VI

And travellers now within that valley,
Through the red-litten windows see
Vast forms that move fantastically
To a discordant melody;
While, like a rapid ghastly river,
Through the pale door;
A hideous throng rush out forever,
And laugh—but smile no more.

I well remember that suggestions arising from this ballad led us into a train of thought wherein there became manifest an opinion of Usher's which I mention not so much on account of its novelty (for other men have thought thus), as on account of the pertinacity with which he maintained it. This opinion, in its general form, was that of the sentience of all vegetable things. But, in his disordered fancy, the idea had assumed a more daring character, and trespassed, under certain conditions, upon the kingdom of inorganization. I lack words to express the full extent, or the earnest *abandon* of his persuasion. The belief, however, was connected (as I have previously hinted) with the gray stones of the home of his forefathers. The conditions of the sentience had been here, he imagined, fulfilled in the method of collocation of these stones—in the order of their arrangement, as well as in that of the many *fungi* which overspread them, and of the decayed trees which stood around—above all, in the long undisturbed endurance of this arrangement, and in its reduplication in the still waters of the tarn. Its evidence—the evidence of the sentience—was to be seen, he said (and I here started as he spoke), in the gradual yet certain condensation of an atmosphere of their own about the waters and the walls. The result was discoverable, he added, in that silent yet importunate and terrible influence which for centuries had moulded the destinies of his family, and which made *him* what I now saw him—what he was. Such opinions need no comment, and I will make none.

Our books—the books which, for years, had formed no small portion of the mental existence of the invalid—were, as might be supposed, in strict keeping with this character of phantasm. We pored together over such works as the Ververt et Chartreuse of Gresset; the Belphegor of Machiavelli; the Heaven and Hell of Swedenborg; the Subterranean Voyage of Nicholas Klimm of Holberg; the Chiromancy of Robert Flud, of Jean D'Indaginé, and of De la Chambre; the Journey into the Blue Distance of Tieck; and the City of the Sun of Campanella. One favorite volume was a small octavo edition of the *Directorium Inquisitorium*, by the Dominican Eymeric de Gironne; and there were passages in Pomponius Mela, about the old African Satyrs and Ægipans, over which Usher would sit dreaming for hours. His chief delight, however, was found in the perusal of an exceedingly rare and curious book in quarto Gothic—the manual of a forgotten church—the *Vigliæ Mortuorum secundum Chorum Ecclesioe Maguntinæ.*

I could not help thinking of the wild ritual of this work, and of its probable influence upon the hypochondriac, when, one evening, having informed me abruptly that the lady Madeline was no more, he stated his intention of preserving her corpse for a fortnight (previously to its final interment), in one of the numerous vaults within the main walls of the building. The worldly reason, however, assigned for this singular proceeding, was one which I did not feel at liberty to dispute. The brother had been led to his resolution (so he told me) by consideration of the unusual character of the malady of the deceased, of certain obtrusive and eager inquiries on the part of her medical men, and of the remote and exposed situation of the burial-ground of the family. I will not deny that when I called to mind the sinister countenance of the person whom I met upon the staircase, on the day of my arrival at the house, I had no desire to oppose what I regarded as at best but a harmless, and by no means an unnatural, precaution.

At the request of Usher, I personally aided him in the arrangements for the temporary entombment. The body having been encoffined, we two alone bore it to its rest. The vault in which we placed it (and which had been so long unopened that our torches, half smothered in its oppressive atmosphere, gave us little opportunity for investigation) was small, damp, and entirely without means of admission for light; lying, at great depth, immediately beneath that portion of the building in which was my own sleeping apartment. It had been used, apparently, in remote feudal times, for the worst purposes of a donjon-keep, and, in later days, as a place of deposit for powder, or some other highly combustible substance, as a portion of its floor, and the whole interior of a long archway through which we reached it, were carefully sheathed with copper. The door, of massive iron, had been, also, similarly protected. Its immense weight caused an unusually sharp, grating sound, as it moved upon its hinges.

Having deposited our mournful burden upon tressels within this region of horror, we partially turned aside the yet unscrewed lid of the coffin, and looked upon the face of the tenant. A striking similitude between the brother and sister now first arrested my attention; and Usher, divining, perhaps, my thoughts, murmured out some few words from which I learned that the deceased and himself had been twins, and that sympathies of a scarcely intelligible nature had always existed between them. Our glances, however, rested not long upon the dead—for we could not regard her unawed. The disease which had thus entombed the lady in the maturity of youth, had left, as usual in all maladies of a strictly cataleptical character, the mockery of a faint blush upon the bosom and the face, and that suspiciously lingering smile upon the lip which is so terrible in death. We replaced and screwed down the lid, and, having secured the door of iron, made our way, with toil, into the scarcely less gloomy apartments of the upper portion of the house.

And now, some days of bitter grief having elapsed, an observable change came over the features of the mental disorder of my friend. His ordinary manner had vanished. His ordinary occupations were neglected or forgotten. He roamed from chamber to chamber with hurried, unequal, and objectless step. The pallor of his countenance had assumed, if possible, a more ghastly hue—but the luminousness of his eye had utterly gone out. The once occasional huskiness of his tone was heard no more; and a tremulous quaver, as if of extreme terror, habitually characterized his utterance. There were times, indeed, when I thought his unceasingly agitated mind was laboring with some oppressive secret, to divulge which he struggled for the necessary courage. At times, again, I was obliged to resolve all into the mere inexplicable vagaries of madness, for I beheld him gazing upon vacancy for long hours, in an attitude of the profoundest attention, as if listening to some imaginary sound. It was no wonder that his condition terrified—that it infected me. I felt creeping upon me, by slow yet certain degrees, the wild influences of his own fantastic yet impressive superstitions.

It was, especially, upon retiring to bed late in the night of the seventh or eighth day after the placing of the lady Madeline within the donjon, that I experienced the full power of such feelings. Sleep came not near my couch—while the hours waned and waned away. I struggled to reason off the nervousness which had dominion over me. I endeavored to believe that much, if not all of what I felt, was due to the bewildering influence of the gloomy furniture of the room —of the dark and tattered draperies, which, tortured into motion by the breath of a rising tempest, swayed fitfully to and fro upon the walls, and rustled uneasily about the decorations of the bed. But my efforts were fruitless. An irrepressible tremor gradually pervaded my frame; and, at length, there sat upon my very heart an incubus of utterly causeless alarm. Shaking this off with a gasp and a struggle, I uplifted myself upon the pillows and, peering earnestly within the intense darkness of the chamber, hearkened—I know not why, except that an instinctive spirit prompted me—to certain low and indefinite sounds which came, through the pauses of the storm, at long intervals, I knew not whence. Overpowered by an intense sentiment of horror, unaccountable yet unendurable, I threw on my clothes with haste (for I felt that I should sleep no more during the night) and endeavored to arouse myself from the pitiable condition into which I had fallen, by pacing rapidly to and fro through the apartment.

I had taken but few turns in this manner, when a light step on an adjoining staircase arrested my attention. I presently recognized it as that of Usher. In an instant afterward he rapped, with a gentle touch, at my door, and entered, bearing a lamp. His countenance was, as usual, cadaverously wan—but, moreover, there was a species of mad hilarity in his eyes—an evidently restrained *hysteria* in his whole demeanor. His air appalled me—but any thing was preferable to the solitude which I had so long endured, and I even welcomed his presence as a relief.

"And you have not seen it?" he said abruptly, after having stared about him for some moments in silence—"you have not then seen it? —but, stay! you shall." Thus speaking, and having carefully shaded his lamp, he hurried to one of the casements and threw it freely open to the storm.

The impetuous fury of the entering gust nearly lifted us from our feet. It was, indeed, a tempestuous yet sternly beautiful night, and one wildly singular in its terror and its beauty. A whirlwind had apparently collected its force in our vicinity; for there were frequent and violent alterations in the direction of the wind; and the exceeding density of the clouds (which hung so low as to press upon the turrets of the house) did not prevent our perceiving the life-like velocity with which they flew careering from all points against each other, without passing away into the distance. I say that even their exceeding density did not prevent our perceiving this—yet we had no glimpse of the moon or stars, nor was there any flashing forth of the lightning. But the under surfaces of the huge masses of agitated vapor, as well as all terrestrial objects immediately around us, were glowing in the unnatural light of a faintly luminous and distinctly visible gaseous exhalation which hung about and enshrouded the mansion.

"You must not—you shall not behold this!" said I, shuddering, to Usher, as I led him, with a gentle violence, from the window to a seat. "These appearances, which bewilder you, are merely electrical phenomena not uncommon—or it may be that they have their ghastly origin in the rank miasma of the tarn. Let us close this casement; the air is chilling and dangerous to your frame. Here is one of your favorite romances. I will read, and you shall listen—and so we will pass away this terrible night together."

The antique volume which I had taken up was the "Mad Trist" of Sir Launcelot Canning; but I had called it a favorite of Usher's more in sad jest than in earnest; for, in truth, there is little in its uncouth and unimaginative prolixity which could have had interest for the lofty and spiritual ideality of my friend. It was, however, the only book immediately at hand; and I indulged a vague hope that the excitement which now agitated the hypochondriac, might find relief (for the history of mental disorder is full of similar anomalies) even in the extremeness of the folly which I should read. Could I have judged, indeed, by the wild overstrained air of vivacity with which he hearkened, or apparently hearkened, to the words of the tale, I might well have congratulated myself upon the success of my design.

I had arrived at that well-known portion of the story where Ethelred, the hero of the Trist, having sought in vain for peaceable admission into the dwelling of the hermit, proceeds to make good an entrance by force. Here, it will be remembered, the words of the narrative run thus:

"And Ethelred, who was by nature of a doughty heart, and who was now mighty withal, on account of the powerfulness of the wine which he had drunken, waited no longer to hold parley with the hermit, who, in sooth, was of an obstinate and maliceful turn, but, feeling the rain upon his shoulders, and fearing the rising of the tempest, uplifted his mace outright, and, with blows, made quickly room in the plankings of the door for his gauntleted hand; and now pulling therewith sturdily, he so cracked, and ripped, and tore all asunder, that the noise of the dry and hollow-sounding wood alarumed and reverberated throughout the forest."

At the termination of this sentence I started and, for a moment, paused; for it appeared to me (although I at once concluded that my excited fancy had deceived me)—it appeared to me that, from some very remote portion of the mansion, there came, indistinctly to my ears, what might have been, in its exact similarity of character, the echo (but a stifled and dull one certainly) of the very cracking and ripping sound which Sir Launcelot had so particularly described. It was, beyond doubt, the coincidence alone which had arrested my attention; for, amid the rattling of the sashes of the casements, and the ordinary commingled noises of the still increasing storm, the sound, in itself, had nothing, surely, which should have interested or disturbed me. I continued the story:

"But the good champion Ethelred, now entering within the door, was sore enraged and amazed to perceive no signal of the maliceful hermit; but, in the stead thereof, a dragon of a scaly and prodigious demeanor, and of a fiery tongue, which sate in guard before a palace of gold, with a floor of silver; and upon the wall there hung a shield of shining brass with this legend enwritten—

> Who entereth herein, a conqueror hath bin;
> Who slayeth the dragon, the shield he shall win.

And Ethelred uplifted his mace, and struck upon the head of the dragon, which fell before him, and gave up his pesty breath, with a shriek so horrid and harsh, and withal so piercing, that Ethelred had fain to close his ears with his hands against the dreadful noise of it, the like whereof was never before heard."

Here again I paused abruptly, and now with a feeling of wild amazement—for there could be no doubt whatever that, in this instance, I did actually hear (although from what direction it proceeded I found it impossible to say) a low and apparently distant, but harsh, protracted, and most unusual screaming or grating sound—the exact counterpart of what my fancy had already conjured up for the dragon's unnatural shriek as described by the romancer.

Oppressed, as I certainly was, upon the occurrence of this second and most extraordinary coincidence, by a thousand conflicting sensations, in which wonder and extreme terror were predominant, I still retained sufficient presence of mind to avoid exciting, by any observation, the sensitive nervousness of my companion. I was by no means certain that he had noticed the sounds in question; although, assuredly, a strange alteration had, during the last few minutes, taken place in his demeanor. From a position fronting my own, he had gradually brought round his chair, so as to sit with his face to the door of the chamber; and thus I could but partially perceive his features, although I saw that his lips trembled as if he were murmuring inaudibly. His head had dropped upon his breast—yet I knew that he was not asleep, from the wide and rigid opening of the eye as I caught a glance of it in profile. The motion of his body, too, was at variance with this idea—for he rocked from side to side with a gentle yet constant and uniform sway. Having rapidly taken notice of all this, I resumed the narrative of Sir Launcelot, which thus proceeded:

"And now, the champion, having escaped from the terrible fury of the dragon, bethinking himself of the brazen shield, and of the breaking up of the enchantment which was upon it, removed the carcass from out of the way before him, and approached valorously over the silver pavement of the castle to where the shield was upon the wall; which in sooth tarried not for his full coming, but fell down at his feet upon the silver floor, with a mighty great and terrible ringing sound."

No sooner had these syllables passed my lips, than—as if a shield of brass had indeed, at the moment, fallen heavily upon a floor of silver—I became aware of a distinct, hollow, metallic, and clangorous, yet apparently muffled, reverberation. Completely unnerved, I leaped to my feet; but the measured rocking movement of Usher was undisturbed. I rushed to the chair in which he sat. His eyes were bent fixedly before him, and throughout his whole countenance there reigned a stony rigidity. But, as I placed my hand upon his shoulder, there came a strong shudder over his whole person; a sickly smile quivered about his lips; and I saw that he spoke in a low, hurried, and gibbering murmur, as if unconscious of my presence. Bending closely over him, I at length drank in the hideous import of his words.

"Now hear it?—yes, I hear it, and *have* heard it. Long—long—long—many minutes, many hours, many days, have I heard it—yet I dared not—oh, pity me, miserable wretch that I am!— I dared not —I *dared* not speak! *We have put her living in the tomb!* Said I not that my senses were acute? I *now* tell you that I heard her feeble first movements in the hollow coffin. I heard them—many, many days ago—yet I dared not—*I dared not speak!* and now—tonight—Ethelred—ha! ha!—the breaking of the hermit's door, and the death-cry of the dragon, and the clangor of the shield—say, rather, the rending of her coffin, and the grating of the iron hinges of her prison, and her struggles within the coppered archway of the vault! Oh! whither shall I fly? Will she not be here anon? Is she not hurrying to upbraid me for my haste? Have I not heard her footstep on the stair? Do I not distinguish that heavy and horrible beating of her heart? Madman!"—here he sprang furiously to his feet, and shrieked out his syllables, as if in the effort he were giving up his soul—"MADMAN! I TELL YOU THAT SHE NOW STANDS WITHOUT THE DOOR."

As if in the superhuman energy of his utterance there had been found the potency of a spell, the huge antique panels to which the speaker pointed threw slowly back, upon the instant, their ponderous and ebony jaws. It was the work of the rushing gust—but then without those doors there *did* stand the lofty and enshrouded figure of the lady Madeline of Usher. There was blood upon her white robes, and the evidence of some bitter struggle upon every portion of her emaciated frame. For a moment she remained trembling and reeling to and fro upon the threshold—then, with a low moaning cry, fell heavily inward upon the person of her brother, and in her violent and now final death-agonies, bore him to the floor a corpse, and a victim to the terrors he had anticipated.

From that chamber, and from that mansion, I fled aghast. The storm was still abroad in all its wrath as I found myself crossing the old causeway. Suddenly there shot along the path a wild light, and I turned to see whence a gleam so unusual could have issued; for the vast house and its shadows were alone behind me. The radiance was that of the full, setting, and blood-red moon, which now shone vividly through that once barely discernible fissure, of which I have before spoken as extending from the roof of the building, in a zigzag direction, to the base. While I gazed this fissure rapidly widened—there came a fierce breath of the whirlwind—the entire orb of the satellite burst at once upon my sight—my brain reeled as I saw the mighty walls rushing asunder—there was a long tumultuous shouting sound like the voice of a thousand waters—and the deep and dank tarn at my feet closed sullenly and silently over the fragments of the HOUSE OF USHER.

The Fall of the House of Usher

For Analysis

1. How does Roderick Usher account for the troubles of his family? What are the theories of the narrator on this subject? What do you think is the true explanation?
2. How does the opening scene of the tale, in which the narrator is seated on horseback before the house, help define the narrator's character?
3. Is there a relationship between the physician's supposed desire to perform an unauthorized autopsy on Madeline and the narrator's incessant theorizing?
4. What is the significance of Usher's painting of the white underground vault?
5. What is the source of the fear that Usher has for his life, before and after Madeline's entombment; what are the sources of the sensations of terror that the narrator feels? What does such a comparative analysis tell one about their respective characters?

Joseph Conrad

An Outpost
of Progress

There were two white men in charge of the trading station. Kayerts, the chief, was short and fat; Carlier, the assistant, was tall, with a large head and a very broad trunk perched upon a long pair of thin legs. The third man on the staff was a Sierra Leone nigger, who maintained that his name was Henry Price. However, for some reason or other, the natives down the river had given him the name of Makola, and it stuck to him through all his wanderings about the country. He spoke English and French with a warbling accent, wrote a beautiful hand, understood bookkeeping, and cherished in his innermost heart the worship of evil spirits. His wife was a negress from Loanda, very large and very noisy. Three children rolled about in sunshine before the door of his low, shedlike dwelling. Makola, taciturn and impenetrable, despised the two white men. He had charge of a small clay storehouse with a dried-grass roof, and pretended to keep a correct account of beads, cotton cloth, red kerchiefs, brass wire, and other trade goods it contained.

Besides the storehouse and Makola's hut, there was only one large building in the cleared ground of the station. It was built neatly of reeds, with a veranda on all the four sides. There were three rooms in it. The one in the middle was the living room and had two rough tables and a few stools in it. The other two were the bedrooms for the white men. Each had a bedstead and a mosquito net for all furniture. The plank floor was littered with the belongings of the white men; open half-empty boxes, torn wearing apparel, old boots; all

AN OUTPOST OF PROGRESS: From TALES OF UNREST by Joseph Conrad. Reprinted by permission of J. M. Dent & Sons Ltd. and the Trustees of the Joseph Conrad Estate.

the things dirty, and all the things broken, that accumulate mysteriously round untidy men.

There was also another dwelling place some distance away from the buildings. In it, under a tall cross much out of the perpendicular, slept the man who had seen the beginning of all this, who had planned and had watched the construction of this outpost of progress. He had been, at home, an unsuccessful painter who, weary of pursuing fame on an empty stomach, had gone out there through high protections. He had been the first chief of that station. Makola had watched the energetic artist die of fever in the just finished house with his usual kind of "I told you so" indifference. Then, for a time, he dwelt alone with his family, his account books, and the Evil Spirit that rules the lands under the equator. He got on very well with his god. Perhaps he had propitiated him by a promise of more white men to play with, by and by. At any rate the director of the Great Trading Company, coming up in a steamer that resembled an enormous sardine box with a flat-roofed shed erected on it, found the station in good order and Makola as usual quietly diligent. The director had the cross put up over the first agent's grave and appointed Kayerts to the post. Carlier was told off as second in charge. The director was a man ruthless and efficient, who at times, but very imperceptibly, indulged in grim humor. He made a speech to Kayerts and Carlier, pointing out to them the promising aspect of their station. The nearest trading post was about three hundred miles away. It was an exceptional opportunity for them to distinguish themselves and to earn percentages on the trade. This appointment was a favor done to beginners. Kayerts was moved almost to tears by his director's kindness. He would, he said, by doing his best, try to justify the flattering confidence, etc., etc. Kayerts had been in the Administration of the Telegraphs, and knew how to express himself correctly. Carlier, an ex-noncommissioned officer of cavalry in an army guaranteed from harm by several European powers, was less impressed. If there were commissions to get, so much the better; and, trailing a sulky glance over the river, the forests, the impenetrable bush that seemed to cut off the station from the rest of the world, he muttered between his teeth, "We shall see, very soon."

Next day, some bales of cotton goods and a few cases of provisions having been thrown on shore, the sardine-box steamer went off, not to return for another six months. On the deck the director touched his cap to the two agents, who stood on the bank waving their hats, and turning to an old servant of the Company on his passage to headquarters, said, "Look at those two imbeciles. They must be mad at home to send me such specimens. I told those fellows to plant a vegetable garden, build new storehouses and fences, and construct a landing stage. I bet nothing will be done! They won't know how to begin. I always thought the station on this river useless, and they just fit the station!"

"They will form themselves there," said the old stager with a quiet smile.

"At any rate, I am rid of them for six months," retorted the director.

The two men watched the steamer round the bend, then, ascending arm in arm the slope of the bank, returned to the station. They had been in this vast and dark country only a very short time, and as yet always in the midst of other white men, under the eye and guidance of their superiors. And now, dull as they were to the subtle influences of surroundings, they felt themselves very much alone, when suddenly left unassisted to face the wilderness; a wilderness rendered more strange, more incomprehensible by the mysterious glimpses of the vigorous life it contained. They were two perfectly insignificant and incapable individuals, whose existence is only rendered possible through the high organization of civilized crowds. Few men realize that their life, the very essence of their character, their capabilities and their audacities, are only the expression of their belief in the safety of their surroundings. The courage, the composure, the confidence; the emotions and principles; every great and every insignificant thought belongs not to the individual but to the crowd: to the crowd that believes blindly in the irresistible force of its institutions and of its morals, in the power of its police and of its opinion. But the contact with pure unmitigated savagery, with primitive nature and primitive man, brings sudden and profound trouble into the heart. To the sentiment of being alone of one's kind, to the clear perception of the loneliness of one's thoughts, of one's sensations—to the negation of the habitual, which is safe, there is added the affirmation of the unusual, which is dangerous; a suggestion of things vague, uncontrollable, and repulsive, whose discomposing intrusion excites the imagination and tries the civilized nerves of the foolish and the wise alike.

Kayerts and Carlier walked arm in arm, drawing close to one another as children do in the dark, and they had the same, not altogether unpleasant, sense of danger which one half suspects to be imaginary. They chatted persistently in familiar tones. "Our station is prettily situated," said one. The other assented with enthusiasm, enlarging volubly on the beauties of the situation. Then they passed near the grave. "Poor devil!" said Kayerts. "He died of fever, didn't he?" muttered Carlier, stopping short. "Why," retorted Kayerts, with indignation, "I've been told that the fellow exposed himself recklessly to the sun. The climate here, everybody says, is not at all worse than at home, as long as you keep out of the sun. Do you hear that, Carlier? I am chief here, and my orders are that you should not expose yourself to the sun!" He assumed his superiority jocularly, but his meaning was serious. The idea that he would, perhaps, have to bury Carlier and remain alone, gave him an inward shiver. He felt suddenly that this Carlier was more precious to him here, in the center of Africa, than a brother could be anywhere else. Carlier, entering into the spirit of the thing, made a military salute and answered in a brisk tone, "Your orders shall be attended to, chief!" Then he burst out laughing, slapped Kayerts on the back and shouted, "We shall let life run easily here! Just sit still and gather in the ivory those savages will bring. This country has its good points, after all!" They both laughed loudly while Carlier thought: "That poor Kayerts; he is so fat and unhealthy. It would be awful if I had to bury him here. He is a man I respect." . . . Before they reached the veranda of their house they called one another "my dear fellow."

The first day they were very active, pottering about with hammers and nails and red calico, to put up curtains, make their house habitable and pretty; resolved to settle down comfortably to their new life. For them an impossible task. To grapple effectually with even purely material problems requires more serenity of mind and more lofty courage than people generally imagine. No two beings could have been more unfitted for such a struggle. Society, not from any tenderness, but because of its strange needs, had taken care of those two men, forbidding them all independent thought, all initiative, all departure from routine; and forbidding it under pain of death. They could only live on condition of being machines. And now, released from the fostering care of men with pens behind the ears, or of men with gold lace on the sleeves, they were like those life-long prisoners who, liberated after many years, do not know what use to make of their freedom. They did not know what use to make of their faculties, being both, through want of practice, incapable of independent thought.

At the end of two months Kayerts often would say, "If it was not for my Melie, you wouldn't catch me here." Melie was his daughter. He had thrown up his post in the Administration of the Telegraphs, though he had been for seventeen years perfectly happy there, to earn a dowry for his girl. His wife was dead, and the child was being brought up by his sisters. He regretted the streets, the pavements, the cafés, his friends of many years; all the things he used to see, day after day; all the thoughts suggested by familiar things—the thoughts effortless, monotonous, and soothing of a Government clerk; he regretted all the gossip, the small enmities, the mild venom, and the little jokes of Government offices. "If I had had a decent brother-in-law," Carlier would remark, "a fellow with a heart, I would not be here." He had left the army and had made himself so obnoxious to his family by his laziness and impudence, that an exasperated brother-in-law had made superhuman efforts to procure him an appointment in the Company as a second-class agent. Having not a penny in the world he was compelled to accept this means of livelihood as soon as it became quite clear to him that there was nothing more to squeeze out of his relations. He, like Kayerts, regretted his old life. He regretted the clink of saber and spurs on a fine afternoon, the barrack-room witticisms, the girls of garrison towns; but besides, he had also a sense of grievance. He was evidently a much ill-used man. This made him moody, at times. But the two men got on well together in the fellowship of their stupidity and laziness. Together they did nothing, absolutely nothing, and enjoyed the sense of the idleness for which they were paid. And in time they came to feel something resembling affection for one another.

They lived like blind men in a large room, aware only of what came in contact with them (and of that only imperfectly) but unable to see the general aspect of things. The river, the forest, all the great land throbbing with life, were like a great emptiness. Even the brilliant sunshine disclosed nothing intelligible. Things appeared and disappeared before their eyes in an unconnected and aimless kind of way. The river seemed to come from nowhere and flow nowhither. It flowed through a void. Out of that void at times came canoes, and men with spears in their hands would suddenly crowd the yard of the station. They were naked, glossy black, ornamented with snowy shells and glistening brass wire, perfect of limb. They made an uncouth babbling noise when they spoke, moved in a stately manner, and sent quick, wild glances out of their startled, never-resting eyes. Those warriors would squat in long rows, four or more deep, before the veranda, while their chiefs bargained for hours with Makola over an elephant tusk. Kayerts sat on his chair and looked down on the proceedings, understanding nothing. He stared at them with his round blue eyes, called out to Carlier, "Here, look! look at that fellow there—and that other one, to the left. Did you ever see such a face? Oh, the funny brute!"

Carlier, smoking native tobacco in a short wooden pipe, would swagger up twirling his mustaches, and surveying the warriors with haughty indulgence, would say:

"Fine animals. Brought any bone? Yes? It's not any too soon. Look at the muscles of that fellow—third from the end. I wouldn't care to get a punch on the nose from him. Fine arms, but legs no good below the knee. Couldn't make cavalry men of them." And after glancing down complacently at his own shanks, he always concluded, "Pah! Don't they stink! You, Makola! Take that herd over to the fetish" (the storehouse was in every station called the fetish, perhaps because of the spirit of civilization it contained) "and give them up some of the rubbish you keep there. I'd rather see it full of bone than full of rags."

Kayerts approved.

"Yes, yes! Go and finish that palaver over there, Mr. Makola. I will come round when you are ready, to weigh the tusk. We must be careful." Then turning to his companion: "This is the tribe that lives down the river; they are rather aromatic. I remember, they had been once before here. D'ye hear that row? What a fellow has got to put up with in this dog of a country! My head is split."

Such profitable visits were rare. For days the two pioneers of trade and progress would look on their empty courtyard in the vibrating brilliance of vertical sunshine. Below the high bank, the silent river flowed on glittering and steady. On the sands in the middle of the stream, hippos and alligators sunned themselves side by side. And stretching away in all directions, surrounding the insignificant cleared spot of the trading post, immense forests, hiding fateful complications of fantastic life, lay in the eloquent silence of mute greatness. The two men understood nothing, cared for nothing but for the passage of days that separated them from the steamer's return. Their predecessor had left some torn books. They took up these wrecks of novels, and, as they had never read anything of the kind before, they were surprised and amused. Then during long days there were interminable and silly discussions about plots and personages. In the center of Africa they made acquaintance of Richelieu and of d'Artagnan, of Hawk's Eye and of Father Goriot, and of many other people. All these imaginary personages became subjects for gossip as if they had been living friends. They discounted their virtues, suspected their motives, decried their successes; were scandalized at their duplicity or were doubtful about their courage. The accounts of crimes filled them with indignation, while tender or pathetic passages moved them deeply. Carlier cleared his throat and said in a soldierly voice, "What nonsense!" Kayerts, his round eyes suffused with tears, his fat cheeks quivering, rubbed his bald head and declared, "This is a splendid book. I had no idea there were such clever fellows in the world." They also found some old copies of a home paper. That print discussed what it was pleased to call "Our Colonial Expansion" in high-flown language. It spoke much of the rights and duties of civilization, of the sacredness of the civilizing work, and extolled the merits of those who went about bringing light, and faith and commerce to the dark places of the earth. Carlier and Kayerts read, wondered, and began to think better of themselves. Carlier said one evening, waving his hand about, "In a hundred years, there will be perhaps a town here. Quays, and warehouses, and barracks, and—and —billiard rooms. Civilization, my boy, and virtue—and all. And then, chaps will read that two good fellows, Kayerts and Carlier, were the first civilized men to live in this very spot!" Kayerts nodded, "Yes, it is a consolation to think of that." They seemed to forget their dead predecessor; but, early one day, Carlier went out and replanted the cross firmly. "It used to make me squint whenever I walked that way," he explained to Kayerts over the morning coffee. "It made me squint, leaning over so much. So I just planted it upright. And solid, I promise you! I suspended myself with both hands to the cross-piece. Not a move. Oh, I did that properly."

At times Gobila came to see them. Gobila was the chief of the neighboring villages. He was a gray-headed savage, thin and black, with a white cloth round his loins and a mangy panther skin hanging over his back. He came up with long strides of his skeleton legs, swinging a staff as tall as himself, and, entering the common room of the station, would squat on his heels to the left of the door. There he sat, watching Kayerts, and now and then making a speech which the other did not understand. Kayerts, without interrupting his occupation, would from time to time say in a friendly manner: "How goes it, you old image?" and they would smile at one another. The two whites had a liking for that old and incomprehensible creature, and called him Father Gobila. Gobila's manner was paternal, and he seemed really to love all white men. They all appeared to him very young, indistinguishably alike (except for stature), and he knew that they were all brothers, and also immortal. The death of the artist, who was the first white man whom he knew intimately, did not disturb this belief, because he was firmly convinced that the white stranger had pretended to die and got himself buried for some mysterious purpose of his own, into which it was useless to inquire. Perhaps it was his way of going home to his own country? At any rate, these were his brothers, and he transferred his absurd affection to them. They returned it in a way. Carlier slapped him on the back and recklessly struck off matches for his amusement. Kayerts was always ready to let him have a sniff at the ammonia bottle. In short, they behaved just like that other white creature that had hidden itself in a hole in the ground. Gobila considered them attentively. Perhaps they were the same being with the other—or one of them was. He couldn't decide—clear up that mystery; but he remained always very friendly. In consequence of that friendship the women of Gobila's village walked in single file through the reedy grass, bringing every morning to the station, fowls, and sweet potatoes, and palm wine, and sometimes a goat. The Company never provisions the stations fully, and the agents required those local supplies to live. They had them through the good will of Gobila and lived well. Now and then one of them had a bout of fever, and the other nursed him with gentle devotion. They did not think much of it. It left them weaker, and their appearance changed for the worse. Carlier was hollow-eyed and irritable. Kayerts showed a drawn, flabby face above the rotundity of his stomach, which gave him a weird aspect. But being constantly together, they did not notice the change that took place gradually in their appearance, and also in their dispositions.

Five months passed in that way.

Then, one morning, as Kayerts and Carlier, lounging in their chairs under the veranda, talked about the approaching visit of the steamer, a knot of armed men came out of the forest and advanced towards the station. They were strangers to that part of the country. They were tall, slight, draped classically from neck to heel in blue fringed cloths, and carried percussion muskets over their bare right shoulders. Makola showed signs of excitement, and ran out of the storehouse (where he spent all his days) to meet these visitors. They came into the courtyard and looked about them with steady, scornful glances. Their leader, a powerful and determined-looking Negro with bloodshot eyes, stood in front of the veranda and made a long speech. He gesticulated much and ceased very suddenly.

There was something in his intonation, in the sounds of the long sentences he used, that startled the two whites. It was like a reminiscence of something not exactly familiar, and yet resembling the speech of civilized men. It sounded like one of those impossible languages which sometimes we hear in our dreams.

"What lingo is that?" said the amazed Carlier. "In the first moment I fancied the fellow was going to speak French. Anyway, it is a different kind of gibberish to what we ever heard."

"Yes," replied Kayerts. "Hey, Makola, what does he say? Where do they come from? Who are they?"

But Makola, who seemed to be standing on hot bricks, answered hurriedly, "I don't know. They come from very far. Perhaps Mrs. Price will understand. They are perhaps bad men."

The leader, after waiting for a while, said something sharply to Makola, who shook his head. Then the man, after looking round, noticed Makola's hut and walked over there. The next moment Mrs. Makola was heard speaking with great volubility. The other strangers—they were six in all—strolled about with an air of ease, put their heads through the door of the storeroom, congregated round the grave, pointed understandingly at the cross, and generally made themselves at home.

"I don't like those chaps—and, I say, Kayerts, they must be from the coast; they've got firearms," observed the sagacious Carlier.

Kayerts also did not like those chaps. They both, for the first time, became aware that they lived in conditions where the unusual may be dangerous and that there was no power on earth outside of themselves to stand between them and the unusual. They became uneasy, went in and loaded their revolvers. Kayerts said. "We must order Makola to tell them to go away before dark."

The strangers left in the afternoon, after eating a meal prepared for them by Mrs. Makola. The immense woman was excited and talked much with the visitors. She rattled away shrilly, pointing here and there at the forests and at the river. Makola sat apart and watched. At times he got up and whispered to his wife. He accompanied the strangers across the ravine at the back of the station-ground and returned slowly looking very thoughtful. When questioned by the white men he was very strange, seemed not to understand, seemed to have forgotten French—seemed to have forgotten how to speak altogether. Kayerts and Carlier agreed that the nigger had had too much palm wine.

There was some talk about keeping a watch in turn, but in the evening everything seemed so quiet and peaceful that they retired as usual. All night they were disturbed by a lot of drumming in the villages. A deep, rapid roll near by would be followed by another far off—then all ceased. Soon short appeals would rattle out here and there, then all mingle together, increase, become vigorous and sustained, would spread out over the forest, roll through the night, unbroken and ceaseless, near and far, as if the whole land had been one immense drum booming out steadily an appeal to heaven. And through the deep and tremendous noise sudden yells that resembled snatches of songs from a madhouse darted shrill and high in discordant jets of sound which seemed to rush far above the earth and drive all peace from under the stars.

Carlier and Kayerts slept badly. They both thought they had heard shots fired during the night—but they could not agree as to the direction. In the morning Makola was gone somewhere. He returned about noon, with one of yesterday's strangers and eluded all Kayerts' attempts to close with him: had become deaf apparently. Kayerts wondered. Carlier, who had been fishing off the bank, came back and remarked while he showed his catch, "The niggers seem to be in a deuce of a stir; I wonder what's up. I saw about fifteen canoes cross the river during the two hours I was there fishing." Kayerts, worried, said, "Isn't this Makola very queer today" Carlier advised, "Keep all our men together in case of some trouble."

II

There were ten station men who had been left by the Director. Those fellows, having engaged themselves to the Company for six months (without having any idea of a month in particular and only a very faint notion of time in general), had been serving the cause of progress for upwards of two years. Belonging to a tribe from a very distant part of the land of darkness and sorrow, they did not run away, naturally supposing that as wandering strangers they would be killed by the inhabitants of the country; in which they were right. They lived in straw huts on the slope of a ravine overgrown with reedy grass, just behind the station buildings. They were not happy, regretting the festive incantations, the sorceries, the human sacrifices of their own land; where they also had parents, brothers, sisters, admired chiefs, respected magicians, loved friends, and other ties supposed generally to be human. Besides, the rice rations served out by the Company did not agree with them, being a food unknown to their land, and to which they could not get used. Consequently they were unhealthy and miserable. Had they been of any other tribe they would have made up their minds to die—for nothing is easier to certain savages than suicide—and so have escaped from the puzzling difficulties of existence. But belonging, as they did, to a warlike tribe with filed teeth, they had more grit, and went on stupidly living through disease and sorrow. They did very little work, and had lost their splendid physique. Carlier and Kayerts doctored them assiduously without being able to bring them back into condition again. They were mustered every morning and told off to different tasks—grass-cutting, fence-building, tree-felling, etc., etc., which no power on earth could induce them to execute efficiently. The two whites had practically very little control over them.

In the afternoon Makola came over to the big house and found Kayerts watching three heavy columns of smoke rising above the forests. "What is that?" asked Kayerts. "Some villages burn," answered Makola, who seemed to have regained his wits. Then he said abruptly: "We have got very little ivory; bad six months' trading. Do you like get a little more ivory?"

"Yes," said Kayerts, eagerly. He thought of percentages which were low.

"Those men who came yesterday are traders from Loanda who have got more ivory than they can carry home. Shall I buy? I know their camp."

"Certainly," said Kayerts. "What are those traders?"

"Bad fellows," said Makola, indifferently. "They fight with people and catch women and children. They are bad men and got guns. There is a great disturbance in the country. Do you want ivory?"

"Yes," said Kayerts. Makola said nothing for a while. Then: "Those workmen of ours are no good at all," he muttered, looking round. "Station in very bad order, sir. Director will growl. Better get a fine lot of ivory, then he say nothing."

"I can't help it; the men won't work," said Kayerts. "When will you get that ivory?"

"Very soon," said Makola. "Perhaps tonight. You leave it to me, and keep indoors, sir. I think you had better give some palm wine to our men to make a dance this evening. Enjoy themselves. Work better tomorrow. There's plenty palm wine—gone a little sour."

Kayerts said "yes," and Makola, with his own hands carried big calabashes to the door of his hut. They stood there till the evening, and Mrs. Makola looked into every one. The men got them at sunset. When Kayerts and Carlier retired, a big bonfire was flaring before the men's huts. They could hear their shouts and drumming. Some men from Gobila's village had joined the station hands, and the entertainment was a great success.

In the middle of the night, Carlier waking suddenly, heard a man shout loudly; then a shot was fired. Only one. Carlier ran out and met Kayerts on the veranda. They were both startled. As they went across the yard to call Makola, they saw shadows moving in the night. One of them cried, "Don't shoot! It's me, Price." Then Makola appeared close to them. "Go back, go back, please," he urged, "you spoil all." "There are strange men about," said Carlier. "Never mind; I know," said Makola. Then he whispered, "All right. Bring ivory. Say nothing! I know my business." The two white men reluctantly went back to the house but did not sleep. They heard footsteps, whispers, some groans. It seemed as if a lot of men came in, dumped heavy things on the ground, squabbled a long time, then went away. They lay on their hard beds and thought: "This Makola is invaluable." In the morning Carlier came out, very sleepy, and pulled at the cord of the big bell. The station hands mustered every morning to the sound of the bell. That morning nobody came. Kayerts turned out also, yawning. Across the yard they saw Makola come out of his hut, a tin basin of soapy water in his hand. Makola, a civilized nigger, was very neat in his person. He threw the soapsuds skillfully over a wretched little yellow cur he had, then turning his face to the agent's house, he shouted from the distance, "All the men gone last night!"

They heard him plainly, but in their surprise they both yelled out together: "What!" Then they stared at one another. "We are in a proper fix now," growled Carlier. "It's incredible!" muttered Kayerts. "I will go to the huts and see," said Carlier, striding off. Makola coming up found Kayerts standing alone.

"I can hardly believe it," said Kayerts tearfully. "We took care of them as if they had been our children."

"They went with the coast people," said Makola after a moment of hesitation.

"What do I care with whom they went—the ungrateful brutes!" exclaimed the other. Then with sudden suspicion, and looking hard at Makola, he added: "What do you know about it?"

Makola moved his shoulders, looking down on the ground. "What do I know? I think only. Will you come and look at the ivory I've got there? It is a fine lot. You never saw such."

He moved towards the store. Kayerts followed him mechanically, thinking about the incredible desertion of the men. On the ground before the door of the fetish lay six splendid tusks.

"What did you give for it?" asked Kayerts, after surveying the lot with satisfaction.

"No regular trade," said Makola. "They brought the ivory and gave it to me. I told them to take what they most wanted in the station. It is a beautiful lot. No station can show such tusks. Those traders wanted carriers badly, and our men were no good here. No trade, no entry in books; all correct."

Kayerts nearly burst with indignation. "Why!" he shouted, "I believe you have sold our men for these tusks!" Makola stood impassive and silent. "I—I—will—I," stuttered Kayerts. "You fiend!" he yelled out.

"I did the best for you and the Company," said Makola, imperturbably. "Why you shout so much? Look at this tusk."

"I dismiss you! I will report you—I won't look at the tusk. I forbid you to touch them. I order you to throw them into the river. You —you!"

"You very red, Mr. Kayerts. If you are so irritable in the sun, you will get fever and die—like the first chief!" pronounced Makola impressively.

They stood still, contemplating one another with intense eyes, as if they had been looking with effort across immense distances. Kayerts shivered. Makola had meant no more than he said, but his words seemed to Kayerts full of ominous menace! He turned sharply and went away to the house. Makola retired into the bosom of his family; and the tusks, left lying before the store, looked very large and valuable in the sunshine.

Carlier came back on the veranda. "They're all gone, hey?" asked Kayerts from the far end of the common room in a muffled voice. "You did not find anybody?"

"Oh, yes," said Carlier, "I found one of Gobila's people lying dead before the huts—shot through the body. We heard that shot last night."

Kayerts came out quickly. He found his companion staring grimly over the yard at the tusks, away by the store. They both sat in silence for a while. Then Kayerts related his conversation with Makola. Carlier said nothing. At the midday meal they ate very little. They hardly exchanged a word that day. A great silence seemed to lie heavily over the station and press on their lips. Makola did not open the store; he spent the day playing with his children. He lay full-length on a mat outside his door, and the youngsters sat on his chest and clambered all over him. It was a touching picture. Mrs. Makola was busy cooking all day as usual. The white men made a somewhat better meal in the evening. Afterwards, Carlier smoking his pipe strolled over to the store; he stood for a long time over the tusks, touched one or two with his foot, even tried to lift the largest one by its small end. He came back to his chief, who had not stirred from the veranda, threw himself in the chair and said:

"I can see it! They were pounced upon while they slept heavily after drinking all that palm wine you've allowed Makola to give them. A put-up job! See? The worst is, some of Gobila's people were there, and got carried off too, no doubt. The least drunk woke up, and got shot for his sobriety. This is a funny country. What will you do now?"

"We can't touch it, of course," said Kayerts.

"Of course not," assented Carlier.

"Slavery is an awful thing," stammered out Kayerts in an unsteady voice.

"Frightful—the sufferings," grunted Carlier with conviction.

They believed their words. Everybody shows a respectful deference to certain sounds that he and his fellows can make. But about feelings people really know nothing. We talk with indignation or enthusiasm; we talk about oppression, cruelty, crime, devotion, self-sacrifice, virtue, and we know nothing real beyond the words. Nobody knows what suffering or sacrifice mean—except, perhaps the victims of the mysterious purpose of these illusions.

Next morning they saw Makola very busy setting up in the yard the big scales used for weighing ivory. By and by Carlier said: "What's that filthy scoundrel up to?" and lounged out into the yard. Kayerts followed. They stood watching. Makola took no notice. When the balance was swung true, he tried to lift a tusk into the scale. It was too heavy. He looked up helplessly without a word, and for a minute they stood round that balance as mute and still as three statues. Suddenly Carlier said: "Catch hold of the other end, Makola —you beast!" and together they swung the tusk up. Kayerts trembled in every limb. He muttered, "I say! O! I say!" and putting his hand in his pocket found there a dirty bit of paper and the stump of a pencil. He turned his back on the others, as if about to do something tricky, and noted stealthily the weights which Carlier shouted out to him with unnecessary loudness. When all was over Makola whispered to himself: "The sun's very strong here for the tusks." Carlier said to Kayerts in a careless tone: "I say, chief, I might just as well give him a lift with this lot into the store."

As they were going back to the house Kayerts observed with a sigh: "It had to be done." And Carlier said: "It's deplorable, but, the men being Company's men the ivory is Company's ivory. We must look after it." "I will report to the Director, of course," said Kayerts. "Of course; let him decide," approved Carlier.

At midday they made a hearty meal. Kayerts sighed from time to time. Whenever they mentioned Makola's name they always added to it an opprobrious epithet. It eased their conscience. Makola gave himself a half-holiday, and bathed his children in the river. No one from Gobila's villages came near the station that day. No one came the next day, and the next, nor for a whole week. Gobila's people might have been dead and buried for any sign of life they gave. But they were only mourning for those they had lost by the witchcraft of white men, who had brought wicked people into their country. The wicked people were gone but fear remained. Fear always remains. A man may destroy everything within himself, love and hate and belief, and even doubt; but as long as he clings to life he cannot destory fear: the fear, subtle, indestructible, and terrible, that pervades his being; that tinges his thoughts; that lurks in his heart; that watches on his lips the struggle of his last breath. In his fear, the mild old Gobila offered extra human sacrifices to all the Evil Spirits that had taken possession of his white friends. His heart was heavy. Some warriors spoke about burning and killing, but the cautious old savage dissuaded them. Who could foresee the woe those mysterious creatures, if irritated, might bring? They should be left alone. Perhaps in time they would disappear into the earth as the first one had disappeared. His people must keep away from them and hope for the best.

Kayerts and Carlier did not disappear but remained above on this earth, that, somehow, they fancied had become bigger and very empty. It was not the absolute and dumb solitude of the post that impressed them so much as an inarticulate feeling that something from within them was gone, something that worked for their safety, and had kept the wilderness from interfering with their hearts. The images of home; the memory of people like them, of men that thought and felt as they used to think and feel, receded into distances made indistinct by the glare of unclouded sunshine. And out of the great silence of the surrounding wilderness, its very hopelessness and savagery seemed to approach them nearer, to draw them gently, to look upon them, to envelop them with a solicitude irresistible, familiar, and disgusting.

Days lengthened into weeks, then into months. Gobila's people drummed and yelled to every new moon, as of yore, but kept away from the station. Makola and Carlier tried once in a canoe to open communications but were received with a shower of arrows and had to fly back to the station for dear life. That attempt set the country up and down the river into an uproar that could be very distinctly heard for days. The steamer was late. At first they spoke of delay jauntily, then anxiously, then gloomily. The matter was becoming serious. Stores were running short. Carlier cast his lines off the bank, but the river was low, and the fish kept out in the stream. They dared not stroll far away from the station to shoot. Moreover, there was no game in the impenetrable forest. Once Carlier shot a hippo in the river. They had no boat to secure it, and it sank. When it floated up it drifted away, and Gobila's people secured the carcass. It was the occasion for a national holiday, but Carlier had a fit of rage over it and talked about the necessity of exterminating all the niggers before the country could be made habitable. Kayerts mooned about silently, spent hours looking at the portrait of his Melie. It represented a little girl with long bleached tresses and a rather sour face. His legs were much swollen, and he could hardly walk. Carlier, undermined by fever, could not swagger any more, but kept tottering about, still with a devil-may-care air, as became a man who remembered his crack regiment. He had become hoarse, sarcastic, and inclined to say unpleasant things. He called it "being frank with you." They had long ago reckoned their percentages on trade, including in them that last deal of "this infamous Makola." They had also concluded not to say anything about it. Kayerts hesitated at first—was afraid of the Director.

"He has seen worse things done on the quiet," maintained Carlier, with a hoarse laugh. "Trust him! He won't thank you if you blab. He is no better than you or me. Who will talk if we hold our tongues? There is nobody here."

That was the root of the trouble! There was nobody there; and being left there alone with their weakness, they became daily more like a pair of accomplices than like a couple of devoted friends. They had heard nothing from home for eight months. Every evening they said, "Tomorrow we shall see the steamer." But one of the Company's steamers had been wrecked, and the Director was busy with the other, relieving very distant and important stations on the main river. He thought that the useless station, and the useless men, could wait. Meantime Kayerts and Carlier lived on rice boiled without salt and cursed the Company, all Africa, and the day they were born. One must have lived on such diet to discover what ghastly trouble the necessity of swallowing one's food may become. There was literally nothing else in the station but rice and coffee; they drank the coffee without sugar. The last fifteen lumps Kayerts had solmnly locked away in his box, together with a half-bottle of cognac, "in case of sickness," he explained. Carlier approved. "When one is sick," he said, "any little extra like that is cheering."

They waited. Rank grass began to sprout over the courtyard. The bell never rang now. Days passed, silent, exasperating, and slow. When the two men spoke, they snarled; and their silences were bitter, as if tinged by the bitterness of their thoughts.

One day after a lunch of boiled rice, Carlier put down his cup untasted, and said: "Hang it all! Let's have a decent cup of coffee for once. Bring out that sugar, Kayerts!"

"For the sick," muttered Kayerts, without looking up.

"For the sick," mocked Carlier. "Bosh! . . . Well! I am sick."

"You are no more sick than I am, and I go without," said Kayerts in a peaceful tone.

"Come! Out with that sugar, you stingy old slave dealer."

Kayerts looked up quickly. Carlier was smiling with marked insolence. And suddenly it seemed to Kayerts that he had never seen that man before. Who was he? He knew nothing about him. What was he capable of? There was a surprising flash of violent emotion within him, as if in the presence of something undreamt-of, dangerous, and final. But he managed to pronounce with composure:

"That joke is in very bad taste. Don't repeat it."

"Joke!" said Carlier, hitching himself forward on his seat. "I am hungry—I am sick—I don't joke! I hate hypocrites. You are a hypocrite. You are a slave dealer. I am a slave dealer. There's nothing but slave dealers in this cursed country. I mean to have sugar in my coffee today, anyhow!"

"I forbid you to speak to me in that way," said Kayerts with a fair show of resolution.

"You!—What?" shouted Carlier, jumping up.

Kayerts stood up also. "I am your chief," he began, trying to master the shakiness of his voice.

"What?" yelled the other. "Who's chief? There's no chief here. There's nothing here: there's nothing but you and I. Fetch the sugar —you pot-bellied ass."

"Hold your tongue. Go out of this room," screamed Kayerts. "I dismiss you—you scoundrel!"

Carlier swung a stool. All at once he looked dangerously in earnest. "You flabby, good-for-nothing civilian—take that!" he howled.

Kayerts dropped under the table, and the stool struck the grass inner wall of the room. Then, as Carlier was trying to upset the table, Kayerts in desperation made a blind rush, head low, like a cornered pig would do, and overturning his friend, bolted along the veranda, and into his room. He locked the door, snatched his revolver, and stood panting. In less than a minute Carlier was kicking at the door furiously, howling, "If you don't bring out that sugar, I will shoot you at sight, like a dog. Now then—one—two—three. You won't? I will show you who's the master."

Kayerts thought the door would fall in and scrambled through the square hole that served for a window in his room. There was then the whole breadth of the house between them. But the other was apparently not strong enough to break in the door, and Kayerts heard him running round. Then he also began to run laboriously on his swollen legs. He ran as quickly as he could, grasping the revolver, and unable yet to understand what was happening to him. He saw in succession Makola's house, the store, the river, the ravine, and the low bushes; and he saw all those things again as he ran for the second time round the house. Then again they flashed past him. That morning he could not have walked a yard without a groan.

And now he ran. He ran fast enough to keep out of sight of the other man.

Then as, weak and desperate, he thought, "Before I finish the next round I shall die," he heard the other man stumble heavily, then stop. He stopped also. He had the back and Carlier the front of the house, as before. He heard him drop into a chair cursing, and suddenly his own legs gave way, and he slid down into a sitting posture with his back to the wall. His mouth was as dry as a cinder, and his face was wet with perspiration—and tears. What was it all about? He thought it must be a horrible illusion; he thought he was dreaming; he thought he was going mad! After a while he collected his senses. What did they quarrel about? That sugar! How absurd! He would give it to him—didn't want it himself. And he began scrambling to his feet with a sudden feeling of security. But before he had fairly stood upright, a common-sense reflection occurred to him and drove him back into despair. He thought: "If I give way now to that brute of a soldier, he will begin this horror again tomorrow—and the day after—every day—raise other pretensions, trample on me, torture me, make me his slave—and I will be lost! Lost! The steamer may not come for days—may never come." He shook so that he had to sit down on the floor again. He shivered forlornly. He felt he could not, would not move any more. He was completely distracted by the sudden perception that the position was without issue—that death and life had in a moment become equally difficult and terrible.

All at once he heard the other push his chair back; and he leaped to his feet with extreme facility. He listened and got confused. Must run again! Right or left? He heard footsteps. He darted to the left, grasping his revolver, and at the very same instant, as it seemed to him, they came into violent collision. Both shouted with surprise. A loud explosion took place between them; a roar of red fire, thick smoke; and Kayerts, deafened and blinded, rushed back thinking: "I am hit—it's all over." He expected the other to come round—to gloat over his agony. He caught hold of an upright of the roof—"All over!" Then he heard a crashing fall on the other side of the house, as if somebody had tumbled headlong over a chair—then silence. Nothing more happened. He did not die. Only his shoulder felt as if it had been badly wrenched, and he had lost his revolver. He was disarmed and helpless! He waited for his fate. The other man made no sound. It was a stratagem. He was stalking him now! Along what side? Perhaps he was taking aim this very minute!

After a few moments of an agony frightful and absurd, he decided to go and meet his doom. He was prepared for every surrender. He turned the corner, steadying himself with one hand on the wall; made a few paces, and nearly swooned. He had seen on the floor, protruding past the other corner, a pair of turned-up feet. A pair of white naked feet in red slippers. He felt deadly sick, and stood for a time in profound darkness. Then Makola appeared before him, saying quietly: "Come along, Mr. Kayerts. He is dead." He burst into tears of gratitude; a long, sobbing fit of crying. After a time he found himself sitting in a chair and looking at Carlier, who lay stretched on his back. Makola was kneeling over the body.

"Is this your revolver?" asked Makola, getting up.

"Yes," said Kayerts; then he added very quickly, "He ran after me to shoot me—you saw!"

"Yes, I saw," said Makola. "There is only one revolver; where's his?"

"Don't know," whispered Kayerts in a voice that had become suddenly very faint.

"I will go and look for it," said the other, gently. He made the round along the veranda, while Kayerts sat still and looked at the corpse. Makola came back empty-handed, stood in deep thought, then stepped quietly into the dead man's room and came out directly with a revolver, which he held up before Kayerts. Kayerts shut his eyes. Everything was going round. He found life more terrible and difficult than death. He had shot an unarmed man.

After meditating for a while, Makola said softly, pointing at the dead man who lay there with his right eye blown out:

"He died of fever." Kayerts looked at him with a stoney stare. "Yes," repeated Makola, thoughtfully, stepping over the corpse, "I think he died of fever. Bury him tomorrow."

And he went away slowly to his expectant wife, leaving the two white men alone on the veranda.

Night came, and Kayerts sat unmoving on his chair. He sat quiet as if he had taken a dose of opium. The violence of the emotions he had passed through produced a feeling of exhausted serenity. He had plumbed in one short afternoon the depths of horror and despair and now found repose in the conviction that life had no more secrets for him: neither had death! He sat by the corpse thinking; thinking very actively, thinking very new thoughts. He seemed to have broken loose from himself altogether. His old thoughts, convictions, likes and dislikes, things he respected and things he abhorred, appeared in their true light at last! Appeared contemptible and childish, false and ridiculous. He reveled in his new wisdom while he sat by the man he had killed. He argued with himself about all things under heaven with that kind of wrong-headed lucidity which may be observed in some lunatics. Incidentally he reflected that the fellow dead there had been a noxious beast anyway; that men died every day in thousands; perhaps in hundreds of thousands—who could tell?—and that in the number, that one death could not possibly make any difference; couldn't have any importance, at least to a thinking creature. He, Kayerts, was a thinking creature. He had been all his life, till that moment, a believer in a lot of nonsense like the rest of mankind—who are fools; but now he thought! He knew! He was at peace; he was familiar with the highest wisdom! Then he tried to imagine himself dead, and Carlier sitting in his chair watching him; and his attempt met with such unexpected success, that in a very few moments he became not at all sure who was dead and who was alive. This extraordinary achievement of his fancy startled him, however, and by a clever and timely effort of mind he saved himself just in time from becoming Carlier. His heart thumped, and he felt hot all over at the thought of that danger. Carlier! What a beastly thing! To compose his now disturbed nerves—and no wonder!—he tried to whistle a little. Then, suddenly, he fell asleep, or thought he had slept; but at any rate there was a fog, and somebody had whistled in the fog.

He stood up. The day had come, and a heavy mist had descended upon the land: the mist penetrating, enveloping, and silent; the morning mist of tropical lands; the mist that clings and kills; the mist white and deadly, immaculate and poisonous. He stood up, saw the body, and threw his arms above his head with a cry like that of a man who, waking from a trance, finds himself immured forever in a tomb. *"Help! . . . My God!"*

A shriek inhuman, vibrating and sudden, pierced like a sharp dart the white shroud of that land of sorrow. Three short, impatient screeches followed, and then, for a time, the fog-wreaths rolled on, undisturbed, through a formidable silence. Then many more shrieks, rapid and piercing, like the yells of some exasperated and ruthless creature, rent the air. Progress was calling to Kayerts from the river. Progress and civilization and all the virtues. Society was calling to its accomplished child to come, to be taken care of, to be instructed, to be judged, to be condemned; it called him to return to that rubbish heap from which he had wandered away, so that justice could be done.

Kayerts heard and understood. He stumbled out of the veranda, leaving the other man quite alone for the first time since they had been thrown there together. He groped his way through the fog, calling in his ignorance upon the invisible heaven to undo its work. Makola flitted by in the mist, shouting as he ran:

"Steamer! Steamer! They can't see. They whistle for the station. I go ring the bell. Go down the landing, sir. I ring."

He disappeared, Kayerts stood still. He looked upwards; the fog rolled low over his head. He looked round like a man who has lost his way; and he saw a dark smudge, a cross-shaped stain, upon the shifting purity of the mist. As he began to stumble towards it, the station bell rang in a tumultuous peal its answer to the impatient clamor of the steamer.

The Managing Director of the Great Civilizing Company (since we know that civilization follows trade) landed first, and incontinently lost sight of the steamer. The fog down by the river was exceedingly dense; above, at the station, the bell rang unceasing and brazen.

The Director shouted loudly to the steamer:

"There is nobody down to meet us; there may be something wrong, though they are ringing. You had better come, too!"

And he began to toil up the steep bank. The captain and the en-

gine-driver of the boat followed behind. As they scrambled up
the fog thinned, and they could see their Director a good way ahead.
Suddenly they saw him start forward, calling to them over his
shoulder: "Run! Run to the house! I've found one of them. Run,
look for the other!"

He had found one of them! And even he, the man of varied and
startling experience, was somewhat discomposed by the manner of
this finding. He stood and fumbled in his pockets (for a knife) while
he faced Kayerts, who was hanging by a leather strap from the cross.
He had evidently climbed the grave, which was high and narrow, and
after tying the end of the strap to the arm, had swung himself off.
His toes were only a couple of inches above the ground; his arms
hung stiffly down; he seemed to be standing rigidly at attention, but
with one purple cheek playfully posed on the shoulder. And, irrev-
erently, he was putting out a swollen tongue at his Managing Director.

An Outpost of Progress

For Analysis

1. Conrad several times makes use of the parenthetical remark when
    speaking in the omniscient voice. What is the effect achieved by his
    use of this device? Is the effect in any way aesthetically inappropriate?
2. The Director is spoken of as "ruthless and efficient." What act in the
    story, for which he is directly responsible, casts doubt on his effi-
    ciency, if not on his ruthlessness?
3. Conrad describes the wilderness frequently during the narrative. What
    do these descriptions contribute to the meaning of the story?
4. What meanings does Conrad seem to attach to the words "savage"
    and "primitive," to the words "progress" and "civilization"?
5. Who are the Christ-figures in "An Outpost of Progress"? How do
    they function within the total context of the story?

James Joyce

The Boarding
House

Mrs. Mooney was a butcher's daughter. She was a woman who
was quite able to keep things to herself: a determined woman. She
had married her father's foreman and opened a butcher's shop near
Spring Gardens. But as soon as his father-in-law was dead Mr.
Mooney began to go to the devil. He drank, plundered the till, ran
headlong into debt. It was no use making him take the pledge: He
was sure to break out again a few days after. By fighting his wife in
the presence of customers and by buying bad meat he ruined his
business. One night he went for his wife with the cleaver and she had
to sleep in a neighbor's house.

After that they lived apart. She went to the priest and got a separation from him with care of the children. She would give him neither
money nor food nor house-room; and so he was obliged to enlist himself as a sheriff's man. He was a shabby stooped little drunkard with
a white face and a white moustache and white eyebrows, pencilled
above his little eyes, which were pink-veined and raw; and all day
long he sat in the bailiff's room, waiting to be put on a job. Mrs.
Mooney, who had taken what remained of her money out of the
butcher business and set up a boarding house in Hardwicke Street,
was a big imposing woman. Her house had a floating population
made up of tourists from Liverpool and the Isle of Man and, occasionally, *artistes* from the music halls. Its resident population was
made up of clerks from the city. She governed the house cunningly
and firmly, knew when to give credit, when to be stern and when to

let things pass. All the resident young men spoke of her as *The
Madam*.

Mrs. Mooney's young men paid fifteen shillings a week for board
and lodgings (beer or stout at dinner excluded). They shared in
common tastes and occupations and for this reason they were very
chummy with one another. They discussed with one another the
chances of favorites and outsiders. Jack Mooney, the Madam's son,
who was clerk to a commission agent in Fleet Street, had the reputation of being a hard case. He was fond of using soldiers' obscenities:
Usually he came home in the small hours. When he met his friends
he had always a good one to tell them and he was always sure to be
on to a good thing—that is to say, a likely horse or a likely *artiste*.
He was also handy with the mitts and sang comic songs. On Sunday
nights there would often be a reunion in Mrs. Mooney's front draw-
ing-room. The music-hall *artistes* would oblige; and Sheridan played
waltzes and polkas and vamped accompaniments. Polly Mooney, the
Madam's daughter, would also sing. She sang:

> *I'm a . . . naughty girl.*
> *You needn't sham:*
> *You know I am.*

Polly was a slim girl of nineteen; she had light soft hair and a
small full mouth. Her eyes, which were grey with a shade of green
through them, had a habit of glancing upwards when she spoke with
anyone, which made her look like a little perverse madonna. Mrs.
Mooney had first sent her daughter to be a typist in a corn factor's
office but, as a disreputable sheriff's man used to come every other
day to the office, asking to be allowed to say a word to his daughter,
she had taken her daughter home again and set her to do house-
work. As Polly was very lively the intention was to give her the run
of the young men. Besides, young men like to feel that there is a young
woman not very far away. Polly, of course, flirted with the young
men but Mrs. Mooney, who was a shrewd judge, knew that the young
men were only passing the time away: None of them meant business. Things went on so for a long time and Mrs. Mooney began to
think of sending Polly back to typewriting when she noticed that
something was going on between Polly and one of the young men.
She watched the pair and kept her own counsel.

Polly knew that she was being watched, but still her mother's persistent silence could not be misunderstood. There had been no open complicity between mother and daughter, no open understanding but, though people in the house began to talk of the affair, still Mrs. Mooney did not intervene. Polly began to grow a little strange in her manner and the young man was evidently perturbed. At last, when she judged it to be the right moment, Mrs. Mooney intervened. She dealt with moral problems as a cleaver deals with meat: And in this case she had made up her mind.

It was a bright Sunday morning of early summer, promising heat, but with a fresh breeze blowing. All the windows of the boarding house were open and the lace curtains ballooned gently towards the street beneath the raised sashes. The belfry of George's Church sent out constant peals and worshippers, singly or in groups, traversed the little circus before the church, revealing their purpose by their self-contained demeanor no less than by the little volumes in their gloved hands. Breakfast was over in the boarding house and the table of the breakfast-room was covered with plates on which lay yellow streaks of eggs with morsels of bacon-fat and bacon-rind. Mrs. Mooney sat in the straw arm-chair and watched the servant Mary remove the breakfast things. She made Mary collect the crusts and pieces of broken bread to help to make Tuesday's bread-pudding. When the table was cleared, the broken bread collected, the sugar and butter safe under lock and key, she began to reconstruct the interview which she had had the night before with Polly. Things were as she had suspected: She had been frank in her questions and Polly had been frank in her answers. Both had been somewhat awkward, of course. She had been made awkward by her not wishing to receive the news in too cavalier a fashion or to seem to have connived and Polly had been made awkward not merely because allusions of that kind always made her awkward but also because she did not wish it to be thought that in her wise innocence she had divined the intention behind her mother's tolerance.

Mrs. Mooney glanced instinctively at the little gilt clock on the mantelpiece as soon as she had become aware through her revery that the bells of George's Church had stopped ringing. It was seventeen minutes past eleven: She would have lots of time to have the matter out with Mr. Doran and then catch short twelve at Marlborough Street. She was sure she would win. To begin with she had all the

weight of social opinion on her side: She was an outraged mother.
She had allowed him to live beneath her roof, assuming that he was
a man of honor, and he had simply abused her hospitality. He was
thirty-four or thirty-five years of age, so that youth could not be
pleaded as his excuse; nor could ignorance be his excuse since he
was a man who had seen something of the world. He had simply taken
advantage of Polly's youth and inexperience: That was evident.
The question was: What reparation would he make?

There must be reparation made in such case. It is all very well
for the man: He can go his ways as if nothing had happened, having
had his moment of pleasure, but the girl has to bear the brunt. Some
mothers would be content to patch up such an affair for a sum of
money; she had known cases of it. But she would not do so. For her
only one reparation could make up for the loss of her daughter's
honour: marriage.

She counted all her cards again before sending Mary up to Mr.
Doran's room to say that she wished to speak with him. She felt sure
she would win. He was a serious young man, not rakish or loud-voiced
like the others. If it had been Mr. Sheridan or Mr. Meade or Bantam
Lyons her task would have been much harder. She did not think he
would face publicity. All the lodgers in the house knew something of
the affair; details had been invented by some. Besides, he had been
employed for thirteen years in a great Catholic wine-merchant's
office and publicity would mean for him, perhaps, the loss of his
job. Whereas if he agreed all might be well. She knew he had a good
screw for one thing and she suspected he had a bit of stuff put by.

Nearly the half-hour! She stood up and surveyed herself in the pier-
glass. The decisive expression of her great florid face satisfied her
and she thought of some mothers she knew who could not get their
daughters off their hands.

Mr. Doran was very anxious indeed this Sunday morning. He
had made two attempts to shave but his hand had been so unsteady
that he had been obliged to desist. Three days' reddish beard fringed
his jaws and every two or three minutes a mist gathered on his glasses
so that he had to take them off and polish them with his pocket-
handkerchief. The recollection of his confession of the night before
was a cause of acute pain to him; the priest had drawn out every
ridiculous detail of the affair and in the end had so magnified his sin
that he was almost thankful at being afforded a loophole of repara-

tion. The harm was done. What could he do now but marry her or run away? He could not brazen it out. The affair would be sure to be talked of and his employer would be certain to hear of it. Dublin is such a small city: Everyone knows everyone else's business. He felt his heart leap warmly in his throat as he heard in his excited imagination old Mr. Leonard calling out in his rasping voice: "Send Mr. Doran here, please."

All his long years of service gone for nothing! All his industry and diligence thrown away! As a young man he had sown his wild oats, of course; he had boasted of his free-thinking and denied the existence of God to his companions in public-houses. But that was all passed and done with . . . nearly. He still bought a copy of *Reynold's Newspaper* every week but he attended to his religious duties and for nine-tenths of the year lived a regular life. He had money enough to settle down on; it was not that. But the family would look down on her. First of all there was her disreputable father and then her mother's boarding house was beginning to get a certain fame. He had a notion that he was being had. He could imagine his friends talking of the affair and laughing. She *was* a little vulgar; some times she said "I seen" and "If I had've known." But what would grammar matter if he really loved her? He could not make up his mind whether to like her or despise her for what she had done. Of course he had done it too. His instinct urged him to remain free, not to marry. Once you are married you are done for, it said.

While he was sitting helplessly on the side of the bed in shirt and trousers she tapped lightly at his door and entered. She told him all, that she had made a clean breast of it to her mother and that her mother would speak with him that morning. She cried and threw her arms round his neck, saying:

"O Bob! Bob! What am I to do? What am I to do at all?"

She would put an end to herself, she said.

He comforted her feebly, telling her not to cry, that it would be all right, never fear. He felt against his shirt the agitation of her bosom.

It was not altogether his fault that it had happened. He remembered well with the curious patient memory of the celibate, the first casual caresses her dress, her breath, her fingers had given him. Then late one night as he was undressing for bed she had tapped at his door, timidly. She wanted to relight her candle at his for hers had been blown out by a gust. It was her bath night. She wore a loose open combing-jacket of printed flannel. Her white instep shone in the opening of her furry slippers and the blood glowed warmly behind her perfumed skin. From her hands and wrists too as she lit and steadied her candle a faint perfume arose.

On nights when he came in very late it was she who warmed up his dinner. He scarcely knew what he was eating feeling her beside him alone, at night, in the sleeping house. And her thoughtfulness! If the night was anyway cold or wet or windy there was sure to be a little tumbler of punch ready for him. Perhaps they could be happy together. . . .

They used to go upstairs together on tiptoe, each with a candle, and on the third landing exchange reluctant goodnights. They used to kiss. He remembered well her eyes, the touch of her hand and his delirium. . . .

But delirium passes. He echoed her phrase, applying it to himself: *"What am I to do?"* The instinct of the celibate warned him to hold back. But the sin was there; even his sense of honour told him that reparation must be made for such a sin.

While he was sitting with her on the side of the bed Mary came to the door and said that the missus wanted to see him in the parlour. He stood up to put on his coat and waistcoat, more helpless than ever. When he was dressed he went over to her to comfort her. It would be all right, never fear. He left her crying on the bed and moaning softly: *"O my God!"*

Going down the stairs his glasses became so dimmed with moisture that he had to take them off and polish them. He longed to ascend through the roof and fly away to another country where he would never hear again of his trouble, and yet a force pushed him downstairs step by step. The implacable faces of his employer and of the Madam stared upon his discomfiture. On the last flight of stairs he passed Jack Mooney who was coming up from the pantry nursing two bottles of *Bass*. They saluted coldly; and the lover's eyes rested for a second or two on a thick bulldog face and a pair of thick short arms. When he reached the foot of the staircase he glanced up and saw Jack regarding him from the door of the return-room.

Suddenly he remembered the night when one of the music-hall *artistes*, a little blond Londoner, had made a rather free allusion to Polly. The reunion had been almost broken up on account of Jack's violence. Everyone tried to quiet him. The music-hall *artiste*, a little paler than usual, kept smiling and saying that there was no harm meant: But Jack kept shouting at him that if any fellow tried that sort of a game on with his sister he'd bloody well put his teeth down his throat, so he would.

Polly sat for a little time on the side of the bed, crying. Then she dried her eyes and went over to the looking-glass. She dipped the end of the towel in the water-jug and refreshed her eyes with the cold water. She looked at herself in profile and readjusted a hairpin above her ear. Then she went back to the bed again and sat at the foot. She regarded the pillows for a long time and the sight of them awakened in her mind secret, amiable memories. She rested the nape of her neck against the cool iron bed-rail and fell into a reverie. There was no longer any perturbation visible on her face.

She waited on patiently, almost cheerfully, without alarm, her memories gradually giving place to hopes and visions of the future. Her hopes and visions were so intricate that she no longer saw the white pillows on which her gaze was fixed or remembered that she was waiting for anything.

At last she heard her mother calling. She started to her feet and ran to the banisters.

"Polly! Polly!"

"Yes, mamma?"

"Come down, dear. Mr. Doran wants to speak to you."

Then she remembered what she had been waiting for.

The Boarding House

For Analysis

1. Is Mrs. Mooney's action in removing her daughter from the corn-factor's office consistent with her character? Why or why not? Did Mr. Mooney love his daughter?

2. The principal characters in "The Boarding House" are Roman Catholics. What is the relationship of each to the Church, in terms of his or her adherence to its principles and teaching?

3. The narrator describes Polly as looking like "a little perverse madonna." Does this image accurately describe a facet of her character? Why or why not?

4. Is Polly passive or active in relation to her mother? Justify your
   answer by reference to the story.
5. Why was Mrs. Mooney "sure she could win" in her confrontation
   with Mr. Doran?

Katherine Mansfield

The Fly

"Y'are very snug in here," piped old Mr. Woodifield, and he
peered out of the great, green leather armchair by his friend the
boss's desk as a baby peers out of its pram. His talk was over; it was
time for him to be off. But he did not want to go. Since he had retired, since his . . . stroke, the wife and the girls kept him boxed up
in the house every day of the week except Tuesday. On Tuesday he
was dressed up and brushed and allowed to cut back to the City for
the day. Though what he did there the wife and girls couldn't imagine. Made a nuisance of himself to his friends, they supposed.
. . . Well, perhaps so. All the same, we cling to our last pleasures as
the tree clings to its last leaves. So there sat old Woodifield, smoking
a cigar and staring almost greedily at the boss, who rolled in his
office chair, stout, rosy, five years older then he, and still going strong,
still at the helm. It did one good to see him.

Wistfully, admiringly, the old voice added, "It's snug in here, upon
my word!"

"Yes, it's comfortable enough," agreed the boss, and he flipped
The Financial Times with a paperknife. As a matter of fact he was
proud of his room; he liked to have it admired, especially by old
Woodifield. It gave him a feeling of deep, solid satisfaction to be
planted there in the midst of it in full view of that frail old figure in
the muffler.

"I've had it done up lately," he explained, as he had explained for
the past—how many?—weeks. "New carpet," and he pointed to the
bright red carpet with a pattern of large white rings. "New furniture," and he nodded towards the massive bookcase and the table
with legs like twisted treacle. "Electric heating!" He waved almost
exultantly towards the five transparent, pearly sausages glowing so
softly in the tilted copper pan.

But he did not draw old Woodifield's attention to the photograph
over the table of a grave-looking boy in uniform standing in one of
those spectral photographers' parks with photographers' storm clouds
behind him. It was not new. It had been there for over six years.

"There was something I wanted to tell you," said old Woodifield,
and his eyes grew dim remembering. "Now what was it? I had it in
my mind when I started out this morning." His hands began to tremble and patches of red showed above his beard.

Poor old chap, he's on his last pins, thought the boss. And, feeling kindly, he winked at the old man, and said jokingly, "I tell you
what. I've got a little drop of something here that'll do you good before you go out into the cold again. It's beautiful stuff. It wouldn't
hurt a child." He took a key off his watch chain, unlocked a cupboard
below his desk, and drew forth a dark, squat bottle. "That's the medicine," said he. "And the man from whom I got it told me on the strict
Q.T. it came from the cellars at Windsor Cassel."

Old Woodifield's mouth fell open at the sight. He couldn't have
looked more surprised if the boss had produced a rabbit.

"It's whisky, ain't it?" he piped, feebly.

The boss turned the bottle and lovingly showed him the label.
Whisky it was.

"D'you know," said he, peering up at the boss wonderingly, "they
won't let me touch it at home." And he looked as though he was
going to cry.

"Ah, that's where we know a bit more than the ladies," cried the
boss, swooping across for two tumblers that stood on the table with
the water bottle, and pouring a generous finger into each. "Drink it
down. It'll do you good. And don't put any water with it. It's sac-
rilege to tamper with stuff like this. Ah!" He tossed off his, pulled
out his handkerchief, hastily wiped his moustaches, and cocked an
eye at old Woodifield, who was rolling his in his chaps.

The old man swallowed, was silent a moment, and then said
faintly, "It's nutty!"

But, it warmed him; it crept into his chill old brain—he remembered.

"That was it," he said, heaving himself out of his chair. "I thought you'd like to know. The girls were in Belgium last week having a look at poor Reggie's grave, and they happened to come across your boy's. They're quite near each other, it seems."

Old Woodifield paused, but the boss made no reply. Only a quiver in his eyelids showed that he heard.

"The girls were delighted with the way the place is kept." piped the old voice. "Beautifully looked after. Couldn't be better if they were at home. You've not been across, have yer?"

"No, no!" For various reasons the boss had not been across.

"There's miles of it," quavered old Woodifield, "and it's all as neat as a garden. Flowers growing on all the graves. Nice broad paths." It was plain from his voice how much he liked a nice broad path.

The pause came again. Then the old man brightened wonderfully.

"D'you know what the hotel made the girls pay for a pot of jam?" he piped. "Ten francs! Robbery, I call it. It was a little pot, so Gertrude says, no bigger than a half crown. And she hadn't taken more than spoonful when they charged her ten francs. Gertrude brought the pot away with her to teach 'em a lesson. Quite right, too; it's trading on our feelings. They think because we're over there having a look around we're ready to pay anything. That's what it is." And he turned towards the door.

"Quite right, quite right!" cried the boss, though what was quite right he hadn't the least idea. He came round by his desk, followed the shuffling footsteps to the door, and saw the old fellow out. Woodifield was gone.

For a long moment the boss stayed, staring at nothing, while the gray-haired office messenger, watching him, dodged in and out of his cubbyhole like a dog that expects to be taken for a run. Then: "I'll see nobody for half an hour, Macey," said the boss. "Understand? Nobody at all."

"Very good, sir."

The door shut, the firm heavy steps recrossed the bright carpet, the fat body plumped down in the spring chair, and leaning forward, the boss covered his face with his hands. He wanted, he intended, he had arranged to weep. . . .

It had been a terrible shock to him when old Woodifield sprang that remark upon him about the boy's grave. It was exactly as though

the earth had opened and he had seen the boy lying there with Woodifield's girls staring down at him. For it was strange. Although over
six years had passed away, the boss never thought of the boy except
as lying unchanged, unblemished in his uniform, asleep for ever. "My
son!" groaned the boss. But no tears came yet. In the past, in the
first months and even years after the boy's death, he had only to say
those words to be overcome by such grief that nothing short of a violent fit of weeping could relieve him. Time, he had declared then,
he had told everybody, could make no difference. Other men perhaps
might recover, might live their loss down, but not he. How was it
possible? His boy was an only son. Ever since his birth the boss had
worked at building up this business for him; it had no other meaning
if it was not for the boy. Life itself had come to have no other meaning. How on earth could he have slaved, denied himself, kept going
all those years without the promise forever before him of the boy's
stepping into his shoes and carrying on where he left off?

And that promise had been so near being fulfilled. The boy had been
in the office learning the ropes for a year before the war. Every morning they had started off together; they had come back by the same
train. And what congratulations he had received as the boy's father!
No wonder; he had taken to it marvellously. As to his popularity with
the staff, every man jack of them down to old Macey couldn't make
enough of the boy. And he wasn't in the least spoilt. No, he was just
his bright, natural self, with the right word for everybody, with that
boyish look and his habit of saying, "Simply splendid!"

But all that was over and done with as though it never had been.
The day had come when Macey had handed him the telegram that
brought the whole place crashing about his head. "Deeply regret to
inform you. . . ." And he had left the office a broken man, his life
in ruins.

Six years ago, six years. . . . How quickly time passed! It might
have happened yesterday. The boss took his hands from his face;
he was puzzled. Something seemed to be wrong with him. He wasn't
feeling as he wanted to feel. He decided to get up and have a look at
the boy's photograph. But it wasn't a favorite photograph of his; the
expression was unnatural. It was cold, even stern-looking. The boy
had never looked like that.

At that moment the boss noticed that a fly had fallen into his broken inkpot, and was trying feebly but desperately to clamber out again. Help! help! said those struggling legs. But the sides of the inkpot were wet and slippery; it fell back again and began to swim. The boss took up a pen, picked the fly out of the ink, and shook it onto a piece of blotting paper. For a fraction of a second it lay still on the dark patch that oozed round it. Then the front legs waved, took hold, and, pulling its small sodden body up, it began the immense task of cleaning the ink from its wings. Over and under, over and under, went a leg along a wing, as the stone goes over and under the scythe. Then there was a pause, while the fly, seeming to stand on the tips of its toes, tried to expand first one wing and then the other. It succeeded at last, and, sitting down, it began, like a minute cat, to clean its face. Now one could imagine that the little front legs rubbed against each other lightly, joyfully. The horrible danger was over; it had escaped; it was ready for life again.

But just then the boss had an idea. He plunged his pen back into the ink, leaned his thick wrist on the blotting paper, and as the fly tried its wings down came a great heavy blot. What would it make of that? What indeed! The little beggar seemed absolutely cowed, stunned, and afraid to move because of what would happen next. But then, as if painfully, it dragged itself forward. The front legs waved, caught hold and, more slowly this time, the task began from the beginning.

"He's a plucky little devil," thought the boss, and he felt a real admiration for the fly's courage. That was the way to tackle things; that was the right spirit. Never say die; it was only a question of. . . . But the fly had again finished its laborious task, and the boss had just time to refill his pen, to shake fair and square on the new-cleaned body yet another dark drop. What about it this time? A painful moment of suspense followed. But behold, the front legs were again waving; the boss felt a rush of relief. He leaned over the fly and said to it tenderly, "You artful little b. . . ." And he actually had the brilliant notion of breathing on it to help the drying process. All the same, there was something timid and weak about its efforts now, and the boss decided that this time should be the last, as he dipped the pen into the inkpot.

It was. The last blot fell on the soaked blotting paper, and the draggled fly lay in it and did not stir. The back legs were stuck to the body; the front legs were not to be seen.

"Come on," said the boss. "Look sharp!" And he stirred it with his pen—in vain. Nothing happened or was likely to happen. The fly was dead.

The boss lifted the corpse on the end of the paper knife and flung it into the waste-paper basket. But such a grinding feeling of wretchedness seized him that he felt positively frightened. He started forward and pressed the bell for Macey.

"Bring me some fresh blotting paper," he said, sternly, "and look sharp about it." And while the old dog padded away he fell to wondering what it was he had been thinking about before. What was it? It was . . . . He took out his handkerchief and passed it inside his collar. For the life of him he could not remember.

The Fly

For Analysis

1. Twice old Macey is described as a dog by the narrator. What does this image tell one about Macey's relationship to the boss?
2. Does the fact that the boss is never specifically named have any symbolic significance?
3. Was the boss's son unspoiled? How do you know?
4. Near the end of the story the boss tells both the fly and old Macey to "look sharp." What significance does this repetitious command have?
5. What symbolic meanings may one finally attach to the fly?

D. H. Lawrence

The Horse Dealer's
Daughter

"Well, Mabel, and what are you going to do with yourself?" asked
Joe, with foolish flippancy. He felt quite safe himself. Without listening for an answer, he turned aside, worked a grain of tobacco to the
tip of his tongue, and spat it out. He did not care about anything,
since he felt safe himself.

The three brothers and the sister sat round the desolate breakfast
table, attempting some sort of desultory consultation. The morning's
post had given the final tap to the family fortunes, and all was over.
The dreary dining room itself, with its heavy mahogany furniture,
looked as if it were waiting to be done away with.

But the consultation amounted to nothing. There was a strange
air of ineffectuality about the three men, as they sprawled at the
table, smoking and reflecting vaguely on their own condition. The
girl was alone, a rather short, sullen-looking young woman of twenty-
seven. She did not share the same life as her brothers. She would have
been good-looking, save for the impassive fixity of her face, "bulldog," as her brothers called it.

There was a confused tramping of horses' feet outside. The three
men all sprawled round in their chairs to watch. Beyond the dark
holly bushes that separated the strip of lawn from the highroad, they
could see a cavalcade of shire horses swinging out of their own yard,
being taken for exercise. This was the last time. These were the last
horses that would go through their hands. The young men watched
with critical, callous look. They were all frightened at the collapse of

their lives, and the sense of disaster in which they were involved left them no inner freedom.

Yet they were three fine, well-set fellows enough. Joe, the eldest, was a man of thirty-three, broad and handsome in a hot, flushed way. His face was red, he twisted his black moustache over a thick finger, his eyes were shallow and restless. He had a sensual way of uncovering his teeth when he laughed, and his bearing was stupid. Now he watched the horses with a glazed look of helplessness in his eyes, a certain stupor of downfall.

The great draught-horses swung past. They were tied head to tail, four of them, and they heaved along to where a lane branched off from the highroad, planting their great hoofs floutingly in the fine black mud, swinging their great rounded haunches sumptuously, and trotting a few sudden steps as they were led into the lane, round the corner. Every movement showed a massive, slumbrous strength, and a stupidity which held them in subjection. The groom at the head looked back, jerking the leading rope. And the cavalcade moved out of sight up the lane, the tail of the last horse, bobbed up tight and stiff, held out taut from the swinging great haunches as they rocked behind the hedges in a motion like sleep.

Joe watched with glazed hopeless eyes. The horses were almost like his own body to him. He felt he was done for now. Luckily he was engaged to a woman as old as himself, and therefore her father, who was steward of a neighboring estate, would provide him with a job. He would marry and go into harness. His life was over, he would be a subject animal now.

He turned uneasily aside, the retreating steps of the horses echoing in his ears. Then, with foolish restlessness, he reached for the scraps of bacon rind from the plates, and making a faint whistling sound, flung them to the terrier that lay against the fender. He watched the dog swallow them, and waited till the creature looked into his eyes. Then a faint grin came on his face, and in a high, foolish voice he said:

"You won't get much more bacon, shall you, you little b——?"

The dog faintly and dismally wagged its tail, then lowered its haunches, circled round, and lay down again.

There was another helpless silence at the table. Joe sprawled uneasily in his seat, not willing to go till the family conclave was dissolved. Fred Henry, the second brother, was erect, clean-limbed, alert. He had watched the passing of the horses with more *sangfroid*. If he was an animal, like Joe, he was an animal which controls, not one which is controlled. He was master of any horse, and he carried himself with a well-tempered air of mastery. But he was not master of the situations of life. He pushed his coarse brown moustache upwards, off his lip, and glanced irritably at his sister, who sat impassive and inscrutable.

"You'll go and stop with Lucy for a bit, shan't you?" he asked. The girl did not answer.

"I don't see what else you can do," persisted Fred Henry.

"Go as a skivvy," Joe interpolated laconically.

The girl did not move a muscle.

"If I was her, I should go in for training for a nurse," said Malcolm, the youngest of them all. He was the baby of the family, a young man of twenty-two, with a fresh, jaunty *museau*.

But Mabel did not take any notice of him. They had talked at her and round her for so many years, that she hardly heard them at all.

The marble clock on the mantelpiece softly chimed the half hour, the dog rose uneasily from the hearthrug and looked at the party at the breakfast table. But still they sat on in ineffectual conclave.

"Oh, all right," said Joe suddenly, *á propos* of nothing. "I'll get a move on."

He pushed back his chair, straddled his knees with a downward jerk, to get them free, in horsey fashion, and went to the fire. Still he did not go out of the room; he was curious to know what the others would do or say. He began to charge his pipe, looking down at the dog and saying, in a high, affected voice:

"Going wi' me? Going wi' me are ter? Tha'rt goin' further than tha counts on just now, dost hear?"

The dog faintly wagged its tail, the man stuck out his jaw and covered his pipe with his hands, and puffed intently, losing himself in the tobacco, looking down all the while at the dog with an absent brown eye. The dog looked up at him in mournful distrust. Joe stood with his knees stuck out, in real horsey fashion.

"Have you had a letter from Lucy?" Fred Henry asked of his sister.

"Last week," came the neutral reply.

"And what does she say?"

There was no answer.

"Does she *ask* you to go and stop there?" persisted Fred Henry.

"She says I can if I like."

"Well, then, you'd better. Tell her you'll come on Monday."

This was received in silence.

"That's what you'll do then, is it?" said Fred Henry, in some exasperation.

But she made no answer. There was a silence of futility and irritation in the room. Malcolm grinned fatuously.

"You'll have to make up your mind between now and next Wednesday," said Joe loudly, "or else find yourself lodgings on the kerbstone."

The face of the young woman darkened, but she sat on immutable.

"Here's Jack Fergusson!" exclaimed Malcolm, who was looking aimlessly out of the window.

"Where?" exclaimed Joe, loudly.

"Just gone past."

"Coming in?"

Malcolm craned his neck to see the gate.

"Yes," he said.

There was a silence. Mabel sat on like one condemned, at the head of the table. Then a whistle was heard from the kitchen. The dog got up and barked sharply. Joe opened the door and shouted:

"Come on."

After a moment a young man entered. He was muffled up in overcoat and a purple woollen scarf, and his tweed cap, which he did not remove, was pulled down on his head. He was of medium height, his face was rather long and pale, his eyes looked tired.

"Hello, Jack! Well, Jack!" exclaimed Malcolm and Joe. Fred Henry merely said, "Jack."

"What's doing?" asked the newcomer, evidently addressing Fred Henry.

"Same. We've got to be out by Wednesday.—Got a cold?"

"I have—got it bad, too."

"Why don't you stop in?"

"*Me* stop in? When I can't stand on my legs, perhaps I shall have a chance." The young man spoke huskily. He had a slight Scotch accent.

"It's a knock-out, isn't it," said Joe, boisterously, "if a doctor goes round croaking with a cold. Looks bad for the patients, doesn't it?"

The young doctor looked at him slowly.

"Anything the matter with *you*, then?" he asked sarcastically.

"Not as I know of. Damn your eyes, I hope not. Why?"

"I thought you were very concerned about the patients, wondered if you might be one yourself."

"Damn it, no, I've never been patient to no flaming doctor, and hope I never shall be," returned Joe.

At this point Mabel rose from the table, and they all seemed to become aware of her existence. She began putting the dishes together. The young doctor looked at her, but did not address her. He had not greeted her. She went out of the room with the tray, her face impassive and unchanged.

"When are you off then, all of you?" asked the doctor.

"I'm catching the eleven-forty," replied Malcolm. "Are you goin' down wi' th' trap, Joe?"

"Yes, I've told you I'm going down wi' th' trap, haven't I?"

"We'd better be getting her in then.—So long, Jack, if I don't see you before I go," said Malcolm, shaking hands.

He went out, followed by Joe, who seemed to have his tail between his legs.

"Well, this is the devil's own," exclaimed the doctor, when he was left alone with Fred Henry. "Going before Wednesday, are you?"

"That's the orders," replied the other.

"Where, to Northampton?"

"That's it."

"The devil!" exclaimed Fergusson, with quiet chagrin.

And there was silence between the two.

"All settled up, are you?" asked Fergusson.

"About."

There was another pause.

"Well, I shall miss yer, Freddy, boy," said the young doctor.

"And I shall miss thee, Jack," returned the other.

"Miss you like hell," mused the doctor.

Fred Henry turned aside. There was nothing to say. Mabel came in again, to finish clearing the table.

"What are *you* going to do, then, Miss Pervin?" asked Fergusson. "Going to your sister's, are you?"

Mabel looked at him with her steady, dangerous eyes, that always made him uncomfortable, unsettling his superficial ease.

"No," she said.

"Well, what in the name of fortune *are* you going to do? Say what you mean to do," cried Fred Henry, with futile intensity.

But she only averted her head and continued her work. She folded the white tablecloth and put on the chenille cloth.

"The sulkiest bitch that ever trod!" muttered her brother.

But she finished her task with perfectly impassive face, the young doctor watching her interestedly all the while. Then she went out.

Fred Henry stared after her, clenching his lips, his blue eyes fixing in sharp antagonism, as he made a grimace of sour exasperation.

"You could bray her into bits, and that's all you'd get out of her," he said, in a small, narrowed tone.

The doctor smiled faintly.

"What's she *going* to do, then?" he asked.

"Strike me if *I* know!" returned the other.

There was a pause. Then the doctor stirred.

"I'll be seeing you tonight, shall I?" he said to his friend.

"Ay—where's it to be? Are we going over to Jessdale?"

"I don't know. I've got such a cold on me. I'll come round to the Moon and Stars, anyway."

"Let Lizzie and May miss their night for once, eh?"

"That's it—if I feel as I do now."

"All's one—"

The two young men went through the passage and down to the back door together. The house was large, but it was servantless now, and desolate. At the back was a small bricked houseyard, and beyond that a big square, gravelled fine and red, and having stables on two sides. Sloping, dank, winter-dark fields stretched away on the open sides.

But the stables were empty. Joseph Pervin, the father of the family, had been a man of no education, who had become a fairly large horse dealer. The stables had been full of horses, there was a great turmoil and come-and-go of horses and of dealers and grooms. Then the kitchen was full of servants. But of late things had declined. The old man had married a second time, to retrieve his fortunes. Now he was dead and everything was gone to the dog, there was nothing but debt and threatening.

For months, Mabel had been servantless in the big house, keeping the home together in penury for her ineffectual brothers. She had kept house for ten years. But previously, it was with unstinted means.

Then, however brutal and coarse everything was, the sense of money had kept her proud, confident. The men might be foulmouthed, the women in the kitchen might have bad reputations, her brothers might have illegitimate children. But so long as there was money, the girl felt herself established, and brutally proud, reserved.

No company came to the house, save dealers and coarse men. Mabel had no associates of her own sex, after her sister went away. But she did not mind. She went regularly to church, she attended to her father. And she lived in the memory of her mother, who had died when she was fourteen, and whom she had loved. She had loved her father, too, in a different way, depending upon him, and feeling secure in him, until at the age of fifty-four he married again. And then she had set hard against him. Now he had died and left them all hopelessly in debt.

She had suffered badly during the period of poverty. Nothing, however, could shake the curious sullen, animal pride that dominated each member of the family. Now, for Mabel, the end had come. Still she would not cast about her. She would follow her own way just the same. She would always hold the keys of her own situation. Mindless and persistent, she endured from day to day. Why should she think? Why should she answer anybody? It was enough that this was the end, and there was no way out. She need not pass any more darkly along the main street of the small town, avoiding every eye. She need not demean herself any more, going into the shops and buying the cheapest food. This was at an end. She thought of nobody, not even of herself. Mindless and persistent, she seemed in a sort of ecstasy to be coming nearer to her fulfilment, her own glorification, approaching her dead mother, who was glorified.

In the afternoon she took a little bag, with shears and sponge and a small scrubbing brush, and went out. It was a gray, wintry day, with saddened, dark-green fields and an atmosphere blackened by the smoke of foundries not far off. She went quickly, darkly along the causeway, heeding nobody, through the town to the churchyard.

There she always felt secure, as if no one could see her, although as a matter of fact she was exposed to the stare of everyone who passed along under the churchyard wall. Nevertheless, once under the shadow of the great looming church, among the graves, she felt immune from the world, reserved within the thick churchyard wall as in another country.

Carefully she clipped the grass from the grave, and arranged the pinky-white, small chrysanthemums in the tin cross. When this was done, she took an empty jar from a neighboring grave, brought water, and carefully, most scrupulously sponged the marble headstone and the coping-stone.

It gave her sincere satisfaction to do this. She felt in immediate contact with the world of her mother. She took minute pains, went through the park in a state bordering on pure happiness, as if in performing this task she came into a subtle, intimate connection with her mother. For the life she followed here in the world was far less real than the world of death she inherited from her mother.

The doctor's house was just by the church. Fergusson, being a mere hired assistant, was slave to the countryside. As he hurried now to attend to the outpatients in the surgery, glancing across the graveyard with his quick eye, he saw the girl at her task at the grave. She seemed so intent and remote, it was like looking into another world. Some mystical element was touched in him. He slowed down as he walked, watching her as if spellbound.

She lifted her eyes, feeling him looking. Their eyes met. And each looked again at once, each feeling, in some way, found out by the other. He lifted his cap and passed on down the road. There remained distinct in his consciousness, like a vision, the memory of her face, lifted from the tombstone in the churchyard, and looking at him with slow, large, portentous eyes. It *was* portentous, her face. It seemed to mesmerize him. There was a heavy power in her eyes which laid hold of his whole being, as if he had drunk some powerful drug. He had been feeling weak and done before. Now the life came back into him, he felt delivered from his own fretted, daily self.

He finished his duties at the surgery as quickly as might be, hastily filling up the bottles of the waiting people with cheap drugs. Then, in perpetual haste, he set off again to visit several cases in another part of his round, before teatime. At all times he preferred to walk, if he could, but particularly when he was not well. He fancied the motion restored him.

The afternoon was falling. It was grey, deadened, and wintry, with a slow, moist, heavy coldness sinking in and deadening all the faculties. But why should he think or notice? He hastily climbed the hill and turned across the dark-green fields, following the black cindertrack. In the distance, across a shallow dip in the country, the small town was clustered like smouldering ash, a tower, a spire, a heap of low, raw, extinct houses. And on the nearest fringe of the town, sloping into the dip, was Oldmeadow, the Pervins's house. He could see the stables and the outbuildings distinctly, as they lay towards him on the slope. Well, he would not go there many more times! Another resource would be lost to him, another place gone: the only company he cared for in the alien, ugly little town he was losing. Nothing but work, drudgery, constant hastening from dwelling to dwelling among the colliers and the ironworkers. It wore him out, but at the same time he had a craving for it. It was a stimulant to him to be in the homes of the working people, moving as it were through the innermost body of their life. His nerves were excited and gratified. He could come so near, into the very lives of the rough, inarticulate, powerfully emotional men and women. He grumbled, he said he hated the hellish hole. But as a matter of fact it excited him, the contact with the rough, strongly-feeling people was a stimulant applied direct to his nerves.

Below Oldmeadow, in the green, shallow, soddened hollow of fields, lay a square, deep pond. Roving across the landscape, the doctor's quick eye detected a figure in black passing through the gate of the field, down towards the pond. He looked again. It would be Mabel Pervin. His mind suddenly became alive and attentive.

Why was she going down there? He pulled up on the path on the slope above and stood staring. He could just make sure of the small black figure moving in the hollow of the failing day. He seemed to see her in the midst of such obscurity, that he was like a clairvoyant, seeing rather with the mind's eye that with ordinary sight. Yet he could see her positively enough, whilst he kept his eye attentive. He felt, if he looked away from her, in the thick, ugly falling dusk, he would lose her altogether.

He followed her minutely as she moved, direct and intent, like something transmitted rather than stirring in voluntary activity, straight down the field towards the pond. There she stood on the bank for a moment. She never raised her head. Then she waded slowly into the water.

He stood motionless as the small black figure walked slowly and deliberately towards the center of the pond, very slowly, gradually moving deeper into the motionless water, and still moving forward as the water got up to her breast. Then he could see her no more in the dusk of the dead afternoon.

"There!" he exclaimed. "Would you believe it?"

And he hastened straight down, running over the wet, soddened fields, pushing through the hedges, down into the depression of callous wintry obscurity. It took him several minutes to come to the pond. He stood on the bank, breathing heavily. He could see nothing. His eyes seemed to penetrate the dead water. Yes, perhaps that was the dark shadow of her black clothing beneath the surface of the water.

He slowly ventured into the pond. The bottom was deep, soft clay, he sank in, and the water clasped dead cold round his legs. As he stirred he could smell the cold, rotten clay that fouled up into the water. It was objectionable in his lungs. Still, repelled and yet not heeding, he moved deeper into the pond. The cold water rose over his thighs, over his loins, upon his abdomen. The lower part of his body was all sunk in the hideous cold element. And the bottom was so deeply soft and uncertain, he was afraid of pitching with his mouth underneath. He could not swim and was afraid.

He crouched a little, spreading his hands under the water and moving them round, trying to feel for her. The dead cold pond swayed upon his chest. He moved again, a little deeper, and again, with his hands underneath, he felt all around under the water. And he touched her clothing. But it evaded his fingers. He made a desperate effort to grasp it.

And so doing he lost his balance and went under, horribly, suffocating in the foul earthy water, struggling madly for a few moments. At last, after what seemed an eternity, he got his footing, rose again into the air and looked around. He gasped and knew he was in the world. Then he looked at the water. She had risen near him. He grasped her clothing, and drawing her nearer, turned to take his way to land again.

He went very slowly, carefully, absorbed in the slow progress. He rose higher, climbing out of the pond. The water was now only about his legs; he was thankful, full of relief to be out of the clutches of the pond. He lifted her and staggered on to the bank, out of the horror of wet, gray clay.

He laid her down on the bank. She was quite unconscious and running with water. He made the water come from her mouth, he worked to restore her. He did not have to work very long before he could feel the breathing begin again in her; she was breathing naturally. He worked a little longer. He could feel her live beneath his hands; she was coming back. He wiped her face, wrapped her in his overcoat, looked round into the dim, dark-gray world, then lifted her and staggered down the bank and across the fields.

It seemed an unthinkably long way, and his burden so heavy he felt he would never get to the house. But at last he was in the stable-yard, and then in the house-yard. He opened the door and went into the house. In the kitchen he laid her down on the hearthrug and called. The house was empty. But the fire was burning in the grate.

Then again he kneeled to attend to her. She was breathing regularly, her eyes were wide open and as if conscious, but there seemed something missing in her look. She was conscious in herself, but unconscious of her surroundings.

He ran upstairs, took blankets from a bed, and put them before the fire to warm. Then he removed her saturated, earthy-smelling clothing, rubbed her dry with a towel, and wrapped her naked in the blankets. Then he went into the dining room, to look for spirits. There was a little whiskey. He drank a gulp himself and put some into her mouth.

The effect was instantaneous. She looked full into his face, as if she had been seeing him for some time, and yet had only just become conscious of him.

"Dr. Fergusson?" she said.

"What?" he answered.

He was divesting himself of his coat, intending to find some dry clothing upstairs. He could not bear the smell of the dead, clayey water, and he was mortally afraid for his own health.

"What did I do?" she asked.

"Walked into the pond," he replied. He had begun to shudder like one sick and could hardly attend to her. Her eyes remained full on him, he seemed to be going dark in his mind, looking back at her helplessly. The shuddering became quieter in him, his life came back in him, dark and unknowing, but strong again.

"Was I out of my mind?" she asked, while her eyes were fixed on him all the time.

"Maybe, for the moment," he replied. He felt quiet, because his strength had come back. The strange fretful strain had left him.

"Am I out of my mind now?" she asked.

"Are you?" he reflected a moment. "No," he answered truthfully,

"I don't see that you are." He turned his face aside. He was afraid now, because he felt dazed, and felt dimly that her power was stronger than his, in this issue. And she continued to look at him fixedly all the time. "Can you tell me where I shall find some dry things to put on?" he asked.

"Did you dive into the pond for me?" she asked.

"No," he answered. "I walked in. But I went in overhead as well."

There was silence for a moment. He hesitated. He very much wanted to go upstairs to get into dry clothing. But there was another desire in him. And she seemed to hold him. His will seemed to have gone to sleep, and left him standing there slack before her. But he felt warm inside himself. He did not shudder at all, though his clothes were sodden on him.

"Why did you?" she asked.

"Because I didn't want you to do such a foolish thing," he said.

"It wasn't foolish," she said, still gazing at him as she lay on the floor, with a sofa cushion under her head. "It was the right thing to do. *I* knew best, then."

"I'll go and shift these wet things," he said. But still he had not the power to move out of her presence, until she sent him. It was as if she had the life of his body in her hands, and he could not extricate himself. Or perhaps he did not want to.

Suddenly she sat up. Then she became aware of her own immediate condition. She felt the blankets about her, she knew her own limbs. For a moment it seemed as if her reason were going. She looked round, with wild eye, as if seeking something. He stood still with fear. She saw her clothing lying scattered.

"Who undressed me?" she asked, her eyes resting full and inevitable on his face.

"I did," he replied, "to bring you round."

For some moments she sat and gazed at him awfully, her lips parted.

"Do you love me then?" she asked.

He only stood and stared at her, fascinated. His soul seemed to melt.

She shuffled forward on her knees, and put her arms round him, round his legs, as he stood there, pressing her breasts against his knees and thighs, clutching him with strange, convulsive certainty, pressing his thighs against her, drawing him to her face, her throat, as she looked up at him with flaring, humble eyes of transfiguration, triumphant in first possession.

"You love me," she murmured, in strange transport, yearning and triumphant and confident. "You love me. I know you love me, I know."

And she was passionately kissing his knees, through the wet clothing, passionately and indiscriminately kissing his knees, his legs, as if unaware of everything.

He looked down at the tangled wet hair, the wild, bare, animal shoulders. He was amazed, bewildered, and afraid. He had never thought of loving her. He had never wanted to love her. When he rescued her and restored her, he was a doctor, and she was a patient. He had had no single personal thought of her. Nay, this introduction of the personal element was very distasteful to him, a violation of his professional honor. It was horrible to have her there embracing his knees. It was horrible. He revolted from it, violently. And yet—and yet—he had not the power to break away.

She looked at him again, with the same supplication of powerful love, and that same transcendent, frightening light of triumph. In view of the delicate flame which seemed to come from her face like a light, he was powerless. And yet he had never intended to love her. He had never intended. And something stubborn in him could not give way.

"You love me," she repeated, in a murmur of deep, rhapsodic assurance. "You love me."

Her hands were drawing him, drawing him down to her. He was afraid, even a little horrified. For he had, really, no intention of loving her. Yet her hands were drawing him towards her. He put out his hand quickly to steady himself and grasped her bare shoulder. A flame seemed to burn the hand that grasped her soft shoulder. He had no intention of loving her: His whole will was against his yielding. It was horrible. And yet wonderful was the touch of her shoulders, beautiful the shining of her face. Was she perhaps mad? He had a horror of yielding to her. Yet something in him ached also.

He had been staring away at the door, away from her. But his hand remained on her shoulder. She had gone suddenly very still. He looked down at her. Her eyes were now wide with fear, with doubt, the light was dying from her face, a shadow of terrible greyness was returning. He could not bear the touch of her eyes' question upon him and the look of death behind the question.

With an inward groan he gave way and let his heart yield towards her. A sudden gentle smile came on his face. And her eyes, which never left his face, slowly, slowly filled with tears. He watched the strange water rise in her eyes, like some slow fountain coming up. And his heart seemed to burn and melt away in his breast.

He could not bear to look at her any more. He dropped on his knees and caught her head with his arms and pressed her face against his throat. She was very still. His heart, which seemed to have broken, was burning with a kind of agony in his breast. And he felt her slow, hot tears wetting his throat. But he could not move.

He felt the hot tears wet his neck and the hollows of his neck, and he remained motionless, suspended through one of man's eternities. Only now it had become indispensible to him to have her face pressed close to him; he could never let her go again. He could never let her head go away from the close clutch of his arm. He wanted to remain like that for ever, with his heart hurting him in pain that was also life to him. Without knowing, he was looking down on her damp, soft brown hair.

Then, as it were suddenly, he smelt the horrid stagnant smell of that water. And at the same moment she drew away from him and looked at him. Her eyes were wistful and unfathomable. He was afraid of them, and he fell to kissing her, not knowing what he was doing. He wanted her eyes not to have that terrible, wistful, unfathomable look.

When she turned her face to him again, a faint delicate flush was glowing, and there was again dawning that terrible shining of joy in her eyes, which really terrified him, and yet which he now wanted to see, because he feared the look of doubt still more.

"You love me?" she said, rather faltering.

"Yes." The word cost him a painful effort. Not because it wasn't true. But because it was too newly true, the *saying* seemed to tear open again his newly torn heart. And he hardly wanted it to be true, even now.

She lifted her face to him, and he bent forward and kissed her on the mouth, gently, with the one kiss that is an eternal pledge. And as he kissed her his heart strained again in his breast. He never intended to love her. But now it was over. He had crossed over the gulf to her, and all that he had left behind had shriveled and become void.

After the kiss, her eyes again slowly filled with tears. She sat still, away from him, with her face drooped aside, and her hands folded in her lap. The tears fell very slowly. There was complete silence.

He too sat there motionless and silent on the hearthrug. The strange pain of his heart that was broken seemed to consume him. That he should love her? That this was love! That he should be ripped open in this way!—Him, a doctor—How they would all jeer if they knew!—It was agony to him to think they might know.

In the curious naked pain of the thought he looked again to her. She was sitting there drooped into a muse. He saw a tear fall, and his heart flared hot. He saw for the first time that one of her shoulders was quite uncovered, one arm bare, he could see one of her small breasts; dimly, because it had become almost dark in the room.

"Why are you crying?" he asked, in an altered voice.

She looked up at him, and behind her tears the consciousness of her situation for the first time brought a dark look of shame to her eyes.

"I'm not crying, really," she said, watching him half frightened.

He reached his hand, and softly closed it on her bare arm.

"I love you! I love you!" he said in a soft, low vibrating voice, unlike himself.

She shrank and dropped her head. The soft, penetrating grip of his hand on her arm distressed her. She looked up at him.

"I want to go," she said. "I want to go and get you some dry things."

"Why?" he said. "I'm all right."

"But I want to go," she said. "And I want you to change your things."

He released her arm, and she wrapped herself in the blanket, looking at him rather frightened. And still she did not rise.

"Kiss me," she said wistfully.

He kissed her, but briefly, half in anger.

Then, after a second, she rose nervously, all mixed up in the blanket. He watched her in her confusion, as she tried to extricate herself and wrap herself up so that she could walk. He watched her relentlessly, as she knew. And as she went, the blanket trailing, and as he saw a glimpse of her feet and her white leg, he tried to remember her as she was when he had wrapped her in the blanket. But then he didn't want to remember, because she had been nothing to him then, and his nature revolted from remembering her as she was when she was nothing to him.

A tumbling, muffled noise from within the dark house startled him. Then he heard her voice:—"There are clothes." He rose and went to the foot of the stairs, and gathered up the garments she had thrown down. Then he came back to the fire, to rub himself down and dress. He grinned at his own appearance when he had finished.

The fire was sinking, so he put on coal. The house was now quite dark, save for the light of a street lamp that shone in faintly from beyond the holly trees. He lit the gas with matches he found on the mantelpiece. Then he emptied the pockets of his own clothes, and threw all his wet things in a heap into the scullery. After which he gathered up her sodden clothes, gently, and put them in a separate heap on the coppertop in the scullery.

It was six o'clock on the clock. His own watch had stopped. He ought to go back to the surgery. He waited, and still she did not come down. So he went to the foot of the stairs and called:

"I shall have to go."

Almost immediately he heard her coming down. She had on her best dress of black voile, and her hair was tidy, but still damp. She looked at him—and in spite of herself, smiled.

"I don't like you in those clothes," she said.

"Do I look a sight?" he answered.

They were shy of one another.

"I'll make you some tea," she said.

"No, I must go."

"Must you?" And she looked at him again with the wide, strained, doubtful eyes. And again, from the pain of his breast, he knew how he loved her. He went and bent to kiss her, gently, passionately, with his heart's painful kiss.

"And my hair smells so horrible," she murmured in distraction. "And I'm so awful, I'm so awful! Oh, no, I'm too awful." And she broke into bitter, heartbroken sobbing. "You can't want to love me, I'm horrible."

"Don't be silly, don't be silly," he said, trying to comfort her, kissing her, holding her in his arms. "I want you, I want to marry you, we're going to be married, quickly, quickly—tomorrow if I can."

But she only sobbed terribly, and cried:

"I feel awful. I feel awful. I feel I'm horrible to you."

"No, I want you, I want you," was all he answered, blindly, with that terrible intonation which frightened her almost more than her horror lest he should *not* want her.

The Horse Dealer's Daughter

For Analysis

1. Lawrence repeats that Mabel is "mindless and persistent." How is this a key to her survival? What is it that Mabel needs to survive? Is she like the other people in the community?

2. What is it that the doctor needs to survive? He knows he is a slave, working too long and too hard for little reward. But he feels that he has to be where he is. (Don't confuse this with devotion to duty or a doctor's high calling.) Why? What do these people have? What is this "power" Lawrence keeps mentioning that they have, personified in Mabel, that Fergusson lacks and is therefore drawn to?

3. Fergusson does not capitulate and pretend to love Mabel; he capitulates and does love her. Reread the section which describes his internal turmoil. What is Lawrence saying there about the nature of love?

Conrad Aiken

Silent Snow,
Secret Snow

I

Just why it should have happened, or why it should have happened just when it did, he could not, of course, possibly have said; nor perhaps would it even have occurred to him to ask. The thing was above all a secret, something to be preciously concealed from Mother and Father; and to that very fact it owed an enormous part of its delicious-

SILENT SNOW, SECRET SNOW: Reprinted by permission of The World Publishing Company from THE COLLECTED SHORT STORIES OF CONRAD AIKEN, by Conrad Aiken. Copyright © 1932, 1959 by Conrad Aiken.

ness. It was like a peculiarly beautiful trinket to be carried unmentioned in one's trouser pocket—a rare stamp, an old coin, a few tiny gold links found trodden out of shape on the path in the park, a pebble of carnelian, a seashell distinguishable from all others by an unusual spot or stripe—and, as if it were any one of these, he carried around with him everywhere a warm and persistent and increasingly beautiful sense of possession. Nor was it only a sense of possession —it was also a sense of protection. It was as if, in some delightful way, his secret gave him a fortress, a wall behind which he could retreat into heavenly seclusion. This was almost the first thing he had noticed about it—apart from the oddness of the thing itself—and it was this that now again, for the fiftieth time, occurred to him, as he sat in the little schoolroom. It was the half hour for geography. Miss Buell was revolving with one finger, slowly, a huge terrestrial globe which had been placed on her desk. The green and yellow continents passed and repassed, questions were asked and answered, and now the little girl in front of him, Deirdre, who had a funny little constellation of freckles on the back of her neck, exactly like the Big Dipper, was standing up and telling Miss Buell that the equator was the line that ran round the middle.

Miss Buell's face, which was old and grayish and kindly, with gray stiff curls beside the cheeks, and eyes that swam very brightly, like little minnows, behind thick glasses, wrinkled itself into a complication of amusements.

"Ah! I see. The earth is wearing a belt, or a sash. Or someone drew a line round it!"

"Oh no—not that—I mean—"

In the general laughter, he did not share, or only a very little. He was thinking about the Arctic and Antarctic regions, which of course, on the globe, were white. Miss Buell was now telling them about the tropics, the jungles, the steamy heat of equatorial swamps, where the birds and butterflies, and even the snakes, were like living jewels. As he listened to these things, he was already, with a pleasant sense of half-effort, putting his secret between himself and the words. Was it really an effort at all? For effort implied something voluntary, and perhaps even something one did not especially want; whereas this was distinctly pleasant, and came almost of its own accord. All he needed to do was to think of that morning, the first one, and then of all the others—

But it was all so absurdly simple! It had amounted to so little. It was nothing, just an idea—and just why it should have become so wonderful, so permanent, was a mystery—a very pleasant one, to be sure, but also, in an amusing way, foolish. However, without ceasing to listen to Miss Buell, who had now moved up to the north temperate zones, he deliberately invited his memory of the first morning. It was only a moment or two after he had waked up—or perhaps the moment itself. But was there, to be exact, an exact moment? Was one awake all at once? or was it gradual? Anyway, it was after he had stretched a lazy hand up toward the headrail, and yawned, and then relaxed again among his warm covers, all the more grateful on a December morning, that the thing had happened. Suddenly, for no reason, he had thought of the postman, he remembered the postman. Perhaps there was nothing so odd in that. After all, he heard the postman almost every morning in his life—his heavy boots could be heard clumping round the corner at the top of the little cobbled hill-street, and then, progressively nearer, progressively louder, the double knock at each door, the crossings and recrossings of the street, till finally the clumsy steps came stumbling across to the very door, and the tremendous knock came which shook the house itself.

(Miss Buell was saying, "Vast wheat-growing areas in North America and Siberia."

Deirdre had for the moment placed her left hand across the back of her neck.)

But on this particular morning, the first morning, as he lay there with his eyes closed, he had for some reason *waited* for the postman. He wanted to hear him come round the corner. And that was precisely the joke—he never did. He never came. He never had come—*round the corner*—again. For when at last the steps *were* heard, they had already, he was quite sure, come a little down the hill, to the first house; and even so, the steps were curiously different—they were softer, they had a new secrecy about them, they were muffled and indistinct; and while the rhythm of them was the same, it now said a new thing—it said peace, it said remoteness, it said cold, it said sleep. And he had understood the situation at once—nothing could have seemed simpler—there had been snow in the night, such as all winter he had been longing for; and it was this which had rendered the postman's first footsteps inaudible, and the later ones faint. Of course! How lovely! And even now it must be snowing—it was going to be a snowy day—the long white ragged lines were drifting and sifting across the street, across the faces of the old houses, whispering and hushing, making little triangles of white in the corners between cobblestones, seething a little when the wind blew them over the ground to a drifted corner; and so it would be all day, getting deeper and deeper and silenter and silenter.

(Miss Buell was saying, "Land of perpetual snow.")

All this time, of course (while he lay in bed), he had kept his eyes closed, listening to the nearer progress of the postman, the muffled footsteps thumping and slipping on the snow-sheathed cobbles; and all the other sounds—the double knocks, a frosty far-off voice or two, a bell ringing thinly and softly as if under a sheet of ice—had the same slightly abstracted quality, as if removed by one degree from actuality—as if everything in the world had been insulated by snow. But when at last, pleased, he opened his eyes, and turned them toward the window, to see for himself this long-desired and now so clearly imagined miracle—what he saw instead was brilliant sunlight on a roof; and when, astonished, he jumped out of bed and stared down into the street, expecting to see the cobbles obliterated by snow, he saw nothing but the bare bright cobbles themselves.

Queer, the effect this extraordinary surprise had had upon him—all the following morning he had kept with him a sense as of snow falling about him, a secret screen of new snow between himself and the world. If he had not dreamed such a thing—and how could he have dreamed it while awake—how else could one explain it? In any case, the delusion had been so vivid as to affect his entire behavior. He could not now remember whether it was on the first or the second morning—or was it even the third?—that his mother had drawn attention to some oddness in his manner.

"But my darling"—she had said at the breakfast table—"what has come over you? You don't seem to be listening. . . ."

And how often that very thing had happened since!

(Miss Buell was now asking if anyone knew the difference between the North Pole and the Magnetic Pole. Deirdre was holding up her flickering brown hand, and he could see the four white dimples that marked the knuckles.)

Perhaps it hadn't been either the second or third morning—or even the fourth or fifth. How could he be sure? How could he be sure just when the delicious *progress* had become clear? Just when it had really *begun?* The intervals weren't very precise. . . . All he now knew was, that at some point or other—perhaps the second day, perhaps the sixth —he had noticed that the presence of the snow was a little more insistent, the sound of it clearer; and, conversely, the sound of the postman's footsteps more indistinct. Not only could he not hear the steps come round the corner, he could not even hear them at the first house. It was below the first house that he heard them; and then, a few days later, it was below the second house that he heard them; and a few days later again, below the third. Gradually, gradually, the snow was becoming heavier, the sound of its seething louder, the cobblestones more and more mufflled. When he found, each morning, on going to the window, after the ritual of listening, that the roofs and cobbles were as bare as ever, it made no difference. This was, after all, only what he had expected. It was even what pleased him, what rewarded him: The thing was his own, belonged to no one else. No one else knew about it, not even his mother and father. There, outside, were the bare cobbles; and here, inside, was the snow. Snow growing heavier each day, muffling the world, hiding the ugly, and deadening increasingly—above all—the steps of the postman.

"But, my darling"—she had said at the luncheon table—"what has come over you? You don't seem to listen when people speak to you. That's the third time I've asked you to pass your plate. . . ."

How was one to explain this to Mother? or to Father? There was, of course, nothing to be done about it: nothing. All one could do was to laugh embarrassedly, pretend to be a little ashamed, apologize, and take a sudden and somewhat disingenuous interest in what was being done or said. The cat had stayed out all night. He had a curious swelling on his left cheek—perhaps somebody had kicked him, or a stone had struck him. Mrs. Kempton was or was not coming to tea. The house was going to be housecleaned, or "turned out," on Wednesday instead of Friday. A new lamp was provided for his evening work—perhaps it was eyestrain which accounted for this new and so peculiar vagueness of his—Mother was looking at him with amusement as she said this, but with something else as well. A new lamp? A new lamp. Yes, Mother, No, Mother, Yes, Mother, School is going very well. The geometry is very easy. The history is very dull. The geography is very interesting—particularly when it takes one to the North Pole. Why the North Pole? Oh, well, it would be fun to be an explorer. Another Peary or Scott or Shackleton. And then abruptly he found his interest in the talk at an end, stared at the pudding on his plate, listened, waited, and began once more—ah, how heavenly, too, the first beginnings—to hear or feel—for could he actually hear it?—the silent snow, the secret snow.

(Miss Buell was telling them about the search for the Northwest Passage, about Hendrik Hudson, the *Half Moon*.)

This had been, indeed, the only distressing feature of the new experience; the fact that it so increasingly had brought him into a kind of mute misunderstanding, or even conflict, with his father and mother. It was as if he were trying to lead a double life. On the one hand, he had to be Paul Hasleman and keep up the appearance of being that person—dress, wash, and answer intelligently when spoken to—; on the other, he had to explore this new world which had been opened to him. Nor could there by the slightest doubt—not the slightest—that the new world was the profounder and more wonderful of the two. It was irresistible. It was miraculous. Its beauty was simply beyond anything—beyond speech as beyond thought—utterly incommunicable. But how then, between the two worlds, of which he was thus constantly aware, was he to keep a balance? One must get up, one must go to breakfast, one must talk with Mother, go to school, do one's lessons—and, in all this, try not to appear too much of a fool. But if all the while one was also trying to extract the full deliciousness of another and quite separate existence, one which could not easily (if at all) be spoken of—how was one to manage? How was one to explain? Would it be safe to explain? Would it be absurd? Would it merely mean that he would get into some obscure kind of trouble?

These thoughts came and went, came and went, as softly and secretly as the snow; they were not precisely a disturbance, perhaps they were even a pleasure; he liked to have them; their presence was something almost palpable, something he could stroke with his hand, without closing his eyes, and without ceasing to see Miss Buell and the schoolroom and the globe and the freckles on Deirdre's neck; nevertheless he did in a sense cease to see, or to see the obvious external world, and substituted for this vision the vision of snow, the sound of snow, and the slow, almost soundless, approach of the postman. Yesterday, it had been only at the sixth house that the postman had become audible; the snow was much deeper now, it was falling more swiftly and heavily, the sound of its seething was more distinct, more soothing, more persistent. And this morning, it had been—as nearly as he could figure—just above the seventh house —perhaps only a step or two above; at most, he had heard two or three footsteps before the knock had sounded. . . . And with each such narrowing of the sphere, each nearer approach of the limit at which the postman was first audible, it was odd how sharply was increased the amount of illusion which had to be carried into the ordinary business of daily life. Each day, it was harder to get out of bed, to go to the window, to look out at the—as always— perfectly empty and snowless street. Each day it was more difficult to go through the perfunctory motions of greeting Mother and Father at breakfast, to reply to their questions, to put his books together and go to school. And at school, how extraordinarily hard to conduct with success simultaneously the public life and the life that was secret! There were times when he longed—positively ached—to tell everyone about it —to burst out with it—only to be checked almost at once by a far-off feeling as of some faint absurdity which was inherent in it—but *was* it absurd?—and more importantly by a sense of mysterious power in his very secrecy. Yes; it must be kept secret. That, more and more, became clear. At whatever cost to himself, whatever pain to others—

(Miss Buell looked straight at him, smiling, and said, "Perhaps we'll ask Paul. I'm sure Paul will come out of his daydream long enough to be able to tell us. Won't you Paul?" He rose slowly from his chair, resting one hand on the brightly varnished desk, and deliberately stared through the snow toward the blackboard. It was an effort, but it was amusing to make it. "Yes," he said slowly, "it was what we now call the Hudson River. This he thought to be the Northwest Passage. He was disappointed." He sat down again, and as he did so Deirdre half turned in her chair and gave him a shy smile of approval and admiration.)

At whatever pain to others.

This part of it was very puzzling, very puzzling. Mother was very nice, and so was Father. Yes, that was all true enough. He wanted to be nice to them, to tell them everything—and yet, was it really wrong of him to want to have a secret place of his own?

At bedtime, the night before, Mother had said, "If this goes on, my lad, we'll have to see a doctor, we will! We can't have our boy—" But what was it she had said? "Live in another world"? "Live so far away"? The word "far" had been in it, he was sure, and then Mother had taken up a magazine again and laughed a little, but with an expression which wasn't mirthful. He had felt sorry for her. . . .

The bell rang for dismissal. The sound came to him through long curved parallels of falling snow. He saw Deirdre rise, and had himself risen almost as soon—but not quite as soon—as she.

II

On the walk homeward, which was timeless, it pleased him to see through the accompaniment, or counterpoint, of snow, the items of mere externality on his way. There were many kinds of brick in the sidewalks and laid in many kinds of pattern. The garden walls, too, were various, some of wooden palings, some of plaster, some of stone. Twigs of bushes leaned over the walls: the little hard green winter-buds of lilac, on gray stems, sheathed and fat; other branches very thin and fine and black and desiccated. Dirty sparrows huddled in the bushes, as dull in color as dead fruit left in leafless trees. A single starling creaked on a weather vane. In the gutter, beside a drain, was a scrap of torn and dirty newspaper, caught in a little delta of filth; the word ECZEMA appeared in large capitals, and below it was a letter from Mrs. Amelia D. Cravath, 2100 Pine Street, Fort Worth, Texas, to the effect that after being a sufferer for years she had been cured by Caley's Ointment. In the little delta, beside the fanshaped and deeply runneled continent of brown mud, were lost twigs, descended from their parent trees, dead matches, a rusty horse chestnut burr, a small concentration of eggshell, a streak of yellow sawdust which had been wet and now was dry and congealed, a brown pebble, and a broken feather. Farther on was a cement sidewalk, ruled into geometrical parallelograms, with a brass inlay at one end commemorating the contractors who had laid it, and, halfway across, an irregular and random series of dog tracks, immortalized in synthetic stone. He knew these well, and always stepped on them; to cover the little hollows with his own foot had always been a queer pleasure; today he did it once more, but perfunctorily and detachedly, all the while thinking of something else. That was a dog, a long time ago, who had made a mistake and walked on the cement while it was still wet. He had probably wagged his tail, but that hadn't been recorded. Now, Paul Hasleman, aged twelve, on his way home from school crossed the same river, which in the meantime had frozen into rock. Homeward through the snow, the snow falling in bright sunshine. Homeward?

Then came the gateway with the two posts surmounted by egg-shaped stones which had been cunningly balanced on their ends, as if by Columbus, and mortared in the very act of balance; a source of perpetual wonder. On the brick wall just beyond, the letter H had been stenciled, presumably for some purpose. H? H.

The green hydrant, with a little green-painted chain attached to the brass screw-cap.

The elm tree, with the great gray wound in the bark, kidney-shaped, into which he always put his hand—to feel the cold but living wood. The injury, he had been sure, was due to the gnawings of a tethered horse. But now it deserved only a passing palm, a merely tolerant eye. There were more important things. Miracles. Beyond the thoughts of trees, mere elms. Beyond the thoughts of sidewalks, mere stone, mere brick, mere cement. Beyond the thoughts even of his own shoes, which trod these sidewalks obediently, bearing a burden—far above—of elaborate mystery. He watched them. They were not very well polished; he had neglected them, for a very good reason: They were one of the many parts of the increasing difficulty of the daily return to daily life, the morning struggle. To get up, having at last opened one's eyes, to go to the window, and discover no snow, to wash, to dress, to descend the curving stairs to breakfast—

At whatever pain to others, nevertheless, one must persevere in severance, since the incommunicability of the experience demanded it. It was desirable, of course, to be kind to Mother and Father, especially as they seemed to be worried, but it was also desirable to be resolute. If they should decide—as appeared likely—to consult the doctor, Doctor Howells, and have Paul inspected, his heart listened to through a kind of dictaphone, his lungs, his stomach—well, that was all right. He would go through with it. He would give them answer for question, too—perhaps such answers as they hadn't expected? No. That would never do. For the secret world must, at all costs, be preserved.

The birdhouse in the apple tree was empty—it was the wrong time of year for wrens. The little round black door had lost its pleasure. The wrens were enjoying other houses, other nests, remoter trees.

But this too was a notion which he only vaguely and grazingly entertained—as if, for the moment, he merely touched an edge of it; there was something further on, which was already assuming a sharper importance; something which already teased at the corners of his eyes, teasing also at the corner of his mind. It was funny to think that he so wanted this, so awaited it—and yet found himself enjoying this momentary dalliance with the birdhouse, as if for a quite deliberate postponement and enhancement of the approaching pleasure. He was aware of his delay, of his smiling and detached and now almost uncomprehending gaze at the little birdhouse; he knew what he was going to look at next: It was his own little cobbled hill-street, his own house, the little river at the bottom of the hill, the grocer's shop with the cardboard man in the window—and now, thinking of all this, he turned his head, still smiling, and looking quickly right and left through the snow-laden sunlight.

And the mist of snow, as he had foreseen, was still on it—a ghost of snow falling in the bright sunlight, softly and steadily floating and turning and pausing, soundlessly meeting the snow that covered, as with a transparent mirage, the bare bright cobbles. He loved it—he stood still and loved it. Its beauty was paralyzing—beyond all words, all experience, all dream. No fairy story he had ever read could be compared with it—none had ever given him this extraordinary combination of ethereal loveliness with a something else, unnameable, which was just faintly and deliciously terrifying. What was this thing? As he thought of it, he looked upward toward his own bedroom window, which was open—and it was as if he looked straight into the room and saw himself lying half awake in his bed. There he was—at this very instant he was still perhaps actually there—more truly there than standing here at the edge of the cobbled hill-street, with one hand lifted to shade his eyes against the snow-sun. Had he indeed ever left his room, in all this time? since that very first morning? Was the whole progress still being enacted there, was it still the same morning, and himself not yet wholly awake? And even now, had the postman not yet come round the corner?. . .

This idea amused him, and automatically as he thought of it, he turned his head and looked toward the top of the hill. There was, of course, nothing there—nothing and no one. The street was empty and quiet. And all the more because of its emptiness it occurred to him to count the houses— a thing which, oddly enough, he hadn't before thought of doing. Of course, he had known there weren't many—many, that is, on his own side of the street, which were the ones that figured in the postman's progress—but nevertheless it came as something of a shock to find that there were precisely *six*, above his own house—his own house was the seventh.

Six!

Astonished, he looked at his own house—looked at the door, on which was the number thirteen—and then realized that the whole thing was exactly and logically and absurdly what he ought to have known. Just the same, the realization gave him abruptly, and even a little frighteningly, a sense of hurry. He was being hurried—he was being rushed. For—he knit his brow—he couldn't be mistaken—it was just above the *seventh* house, his *own* house, that the postman had first been audible this very morning. But in that case—in that case—did it mean that tomorrow he would hear nothing? The knock he had heard must have been the knock of their own door. Did it mean—and this was an idea which gave him a really extraordinary feeling of surprise—that he would never hear the postman again?—that tomorrow morning the postman would already have passed the house, in a snow so deep as to render his footsteps completely inaudible? That he would have made his approach down the snow-filled street so soundlessly, so secretly, that he, Paul Haselman, there lying in bed, would not have waked in time, or waking, would have heard nothing?

But how could that be? Unless even the knocker should be muffled in the snow—frozen tight, perhaps? . . . But in that case—

A vague feeling of disappointment came over him; a vague sadness as if he felt himself deprived of something which he had long looked forward to, something much prized. After all this, all this beautiful progress, the slow delicious advance of the postman through the silent and secret snow, the knock creeping closer each day, and the footsteps nearer, the audible compass of the world thus daily narrowed, narrowed, narrowed, as the snow soothingly and beautifully encroached and deepened, after all this, was he to be defrauded of the one thing he had so wanted—to be able to count, as it were, the last two or three solemn footsteps, as they finally approached his own door? Was it all going to happen, at the end, so suddenly? or indeed, had it already happened? with no slow and subtle graduations of menace, in which he could luxuriate.

He gazed upward again, toward his own window which flashed in the sun; and this time almost with a feeling that it would be better if he *were* still in bed, in that room; for in that case this must still be the first morning, and there would be six more mornings to come— or, for that matter, seven or eight or nine—how could he be sure? —or even more.

III

After supper, the inquisition began. He stood before the doctor, under the lamp, and submitted silently to the usual thumpings and tappings.

"Now will you please say 'Ah!'?"

"Ah!"

"Now again, please if you don't mind."

"Ah."

"Say it slowly, and hold it if you can—"

"Ah-h-h-h-h-h—"

"Good."

How silly all this was. As if it had anything to do with his throat! Or his heart, or lungs!

Relaxing his mouth, of which the corners, after all this absurd stretching, felt uncomfortable, he avoided the doctor's eyes, and stared toward the fireplace, past his mother's feet (in gray slippers) which projected from the green chair, and his father's feet (in brown slippers) which stood neatly side by side on the hearth rug.

"Hm. There is certainly nothing wrong there . . . ?"

He felt the doctor's eyes fixed upon him, and, as if merely to be polite, returned the look, but with a feeling of justifiable evasiveness.

"Now, young man, tell me—do you feel all right?"

"Yes, sir, quite all right."

"No headaches? no dizziness?"

"No, I don't think so."

"Let me see. Let's get a book, if you don't mind—yes, thank you, that will do splendidly—and now, Paul, if you'll just read it, holding it as you would normally hold it—"

He took the book and read:

"And another praise have I to tell for this the city our mother, the gift of a great god, a glory of the land most high; the might of horses, the might of young horses, the might of the sea. . . . For thou, son of Cronus, our lord Poseidon, hath throned herein this pride, since in these roads first thou didst show forth the curb that cures the rage of steeds. And the shapely oar, apt to men's hands, hath a wondrous speed on the brine, following the hundred-footed Nereids. . . . O land that art praised above all lands, now is it for thee to make those bright praises seen in deeds."

He stopped, tentatively, and lowered the heavy book.

"No—as I thought—there is certainly no superficial sign of eye-strain."

Silence thronged the room, and he was aware of the focused scrutiny of the three people who confronted him. . . .

"We could have his eyes examined—but I believe it is something else."

"What could it be?" That was his father's voice.

"It's only this curious absent mindedness—" This was his mother's voice.

In the presence of the doctor, they both seemed irritatingly apologetic.

"I believe it is something else. Now Paul—I would like very much to ask you a question or two. You will answer them, won't you—you know I'm an old, old friend of yours, eh? That's right! . . .

His back was thumped twice by the doctor's fat fist—then the doctor was grinning at him with false amiability, while with one fingernail he was scratching the top button of his waistcoat. Beyond the doctor's shoulder was the fire, the fingers of flame making light prestidigitation against the sooty fireback, the soft sound of their random flutter the only sound.

"I would like to know—is there anything that worries you?"

The doctor was again smiling, his eyelids low against the little black pupils, in each of which was a tiny white bead of light. Why answer him? why answer him at all? "At whatever pain to others"— but it was all a nuisance, this necessity for resistance, this necessity for attention; it was as if one had been stood up on a brilliantly lighted stage, under a great round blaze of spotlight; as if one were merely a trained seal, or a performing dog, or a fish, dipped out of an aquarium and held up by the tail. It would serve them right if he were merely to bark or growl. And meanwhile, to miss these last few precious hours, these hours of which each minute was more beautiful than the last, more menacing—! He still looked, as if from a great distance, at the beads of light in the doctor's eyes, at the fixed false smile, and then, beyond, once more at his mother's slippers, his father's slippers, the soft flutter of the fire. Even here, even amongst these hostile presences, and in this arranged light, he could see the snow, he could hear it—it was in the corners of the room, where the shadow was deepest, under the sofa, behind the half-opened door which led to the dining room. It was gentler here, softer, its seethe the quietest of whispers, as if, in deference to a drawing room, it had quite deliberately put on its "manners"; it kept itself out of sight, obliterated itself, but distinctly with an air of saying, "Ah, but just wait! Wait till we are alone together! Then I will begin to tell you something new! Something white! something cold! something sleepy! something of cease, and peace, and the long bright curve of space! Tell them to go away. Banish them. Refuse to speak. Leave them, go upstairs to your room, turn out the light and get into bed—I will go with you, I will be waiting for you, I will tell you a better story than Little Kay of the Skates, or The Snow Ghost—I will surround your bed, I will close the windows, pile a deep drift against the door, so that none will ever again be able to enter. Speak to them! . . ." It seemed as if the little hissing voice came from a slow white spiral of falling flakes in the corner by the front window— but he could not be sure. He felt himself smiling, then, and said to the doctor, but without looking at him, looking beyond him still—

"Oh no, I think not—"

"But are you sure, my boy?"

His father's voice came softly and coldly then—the familiar voice of silken warning.

"You needn't answer at once, Paul—remember we're trying to help you—think it over and be quite sure, won't you?"

He felt himself smiling again, at the notion of being quite sure. What a joke! As if he weren't so sure that reassurance was no longer necessary, and all this cross-examination a ridiculous farce, a grotesque parody! What could they know about it? these gross intelligences, these humdrum minds so bound to the usual, the ordinary? Impossible to tell them about it! Why, even now, even now, with the proof so abundant, so formidable, so imminent, so appallingly present here in this very room, could they believe it?—could even his mother believe it? No—it was only too plain that if anything were said about it, the merest hint given, they would be incredulous—they would laugh—they would say "Absurd!"—think things about him which weren't true. . . .

"Why no, I'm not worried—why should I be?"

He looked then straight at the doctor's low-lidded eyes, looked from one of them to the other, from one bead of light to the other, and gave a little laugh.

The doctor seemed to be disconcerted by this. He drew back in his chair, resting a fat white hand on either knee. The smile faded slowly from his face.

"Well, Paul!" he said, and paused gravely, "I'm afraid you don't take this quite seriously enough. I think you perhaps don't quite realize—don't quite realize—" He took a deep quick breath and turned, as if helplessly, at a loss for words, to the others. But Mother and Father were both silent—no help was forthcoming.

"You must surely know, be aware, that you have not been quite yourself, of late? Don't you know that? . . ."

It was amusing to watch the doctor's renewed attempt at a smile, a queer disorganized look, as of confidential embarrassment.

"I feel all right, sir," he said, and again gave the little laugh.

"And we're trying to help you." The doctor's tone sharpened.

"Yes, sir, I know. But why? I'm all right. I'm just *thinking*, that's all."

His mother made a quick movement forward, resting a hand on the back of the doctor's chair.

"Thinking?" she said. "But my dear, about what?"

This was a direct challenge—and would have to be directly met. But before he met it, he looked again into the corner by the door, as if for reassurance. He smiled again at what he saw, at what he heard. The little spiral was still there, still softly whirling, like the ghost of a white kitten chasing the ghost of a white tail, and making as it did so the faintest of whispers. It was all right! If only he could remain firm, everything was going to be all right.

"Oh, about anything, about nothing—*you* know the way you do!"

"You mean—daydreaming?"

"Oh, no—thinking!"

"But thinking about *what*?"

"Anything."

He laughed a third time—but this time, happening to glance upward toward his mother's face, he was appalled at the effect his
laughter seemed to have upon her. Her mouth had opened in an expression of horror. . . . This was too bad! Unfortunate! He had
known it would cause pain, of course—but he hadn't expected it to
be quite so bad as this. Perhaps—perhaps if he just gave them a tiny
gleaming hint—?

"About the snow," he said.

"What on earth?" This was his father's voice. The brown slippers
came a step nearer on the hearthrug.

"But my dear, what do you mean?" This was his mother's voice.
The doctor merely stared.

"Just *snow*, that's all. I like to think about it."

"Tell us about it, my boy."

"But that's all it is. There's nothing to tell. *You* know what snow
is?"

This he said almost angrily, for he felt that they were trying to
corner him. He turned sideways so as no longer to face the doctor, and
the better to see the inch of blackness between the windowsill and
the lowered curtain—the cold inch of beckoning and delicious night.
At once he felt better, more assured.

"Mother—can I go to bed, now, please? I've got a headache."

"But I thought you said—"

"It's just come. It's all these questions—! Can I, Mother?"

"You can go as soon as the doctor has finished."

"Don't you think this thing ought to be gone into thoroughly, and
now?" This was Father's voice. The brown slippers again came a step
nearer, the voice was the well-known "punishment" voice, resonant
and cruel.

"Oh, what's the use, Norman—"

Quite suddenly, everyone was silent. And without precisely facing
them, nevertheless he was aware that all three of them were watching
him with an extraordinary intensity—staring hard at him—as if he
had done something monstrous, or was himself some kind of monster.
He could hear the soft irregular flutter of the flames; the cluck-click-
cluck-click of the clock; far and faint, two sudden spurts of laughter
from the kitchen, as quickly cut off as begun; a murmur of water in
the pipes; and then, the silence seemed to deepen, to spread out, to
become world-long and world-wide, to become timeless and shapeless,

and to center inevitably and rightly, with a slow and sleepy but enormous concentration of all power, on the beginning of a new sound. What this new sound was going to be, he knew perfectly well. It might begin with a hiss, but it would end with a roar—there was no time to lose—he must escape. It mustn't happen here—

Without another word, he turned and ran up the stairs.

IV

Not a moment too soon. The darkness was coming in long white waves. A prolonged sibilance filled the night—a great seamless seethe of wild influence went abruptly across it—a cold low humming shook the windows. He shut the door and flung off his clothes in the dark. The bare black floor was like a little raft tossed in waves of snow, almost overwhelmed, washed under whitely, up again, smothered in curled billows of feather. The snow was laughing; it spoke from all sides at once; it pressed closer to him as he ran and jumped exulting into his bed.

"Listen to us!" it said. "Listen! We have come to tell you the story we told you about. You remember? Lie down. Shut your eyes, now —you will no longer see much—in this white darkness who could see, or want to see? We will take the place of everything. . . . Listen —"

A beautiful varying dance of snow began at the front of the room, came forward and then retreated, flattened out toward the floor, then rose fountain-like to the ceiling, swayed, recruited itself from a new stream of flakes which poured laughing in through the humming window, advanced again, lifted long white arms. It said peace, it said remoteness, it said cold—it said—

But then a gash of horrible light fell brutally across the room from the opening door—the snow drew back hissing—something alien had come into the room—something hostile. This thing rushed at him, clutched at him, shook him—and he was not merely horrified, he was filled with such a loathing as he had never known. What was this? this cruel disturbance? this act of anger and hate? It was as if he had to reach up a hand toward another world for any understanding of it—an effort of which he was only barely capable. But of that other world he still remembered just enough to know the exorcising words. They tore themselves from his other life suddenly—

"Mother! Mother! Go away! I hate you!"

And with that effort, everything was solved, everything became all right: The seamless hiss advanced once more, the long white wavering lines rose and fell like enormous whispering sea-waves, the whisper becoming louder, the laughter more numerous.

"Listen!" it said. "We'll tell you the last, the most beautiful and secret story—shut your eyes—it is a very small story—a story that gets smaller and smaller—it comes inward instead of opening like a flower—it is a flower becoming a seed—a little cold seed—do you hear? we are leaning closer to you—"

The hiss was now becoming a roar—the whole world was a vast moving screen of snow—but even now it said peace, it said remoteness, it said cold, it said sleep.

Silent Snow, Secret Snow

For Analysis

1. What is the major conflict in this story?
2. A clinical psychologist would probably call this story a study in schizophrenia; Paul begins to live in two worlds, and finally the illusory world overwhelms the real world. Why should it be snow that he hallucinates? What does snow symbolize to him? What does it symbolize to the reader?
3. Is there any hint in the story of the cause of Paul's sickness?
4. Why the author chose this particular point of view is obvious. But why did he choose to begin the story where he did? Why not earlier? Why not later?

W. Somerset Maugham

The
Outstation

The new assistant arrived in the afternoon. When the Resident, Mr. Warburton, was told that the prahu was in sight he put on his solar topee and went down to the landing-stage. The guard, eight little Dyak soldiers, stood to attention as he passed. He noted with satisfaction that their bearing was martial, their uniforms neat and clean, and their guns shining. They were a credit to him. From the landing-stage he watched the bend of the river round which in a moment the boat would sweep. He looked very smart in his spotless ducks and white shoes. He held under his arm a gold-headed Malacca cane which had been given him by the Sultan of Perak. He awaited the newcomer with mingled feelings. There was more work in the district than one man could properly do, and during his periodical tours of the country under his charge it had been inconvenient to leave the station in the hands of a native clerk, but he had been so long the only white man there that he could not face the arrival of another without misgiving. He was accustomed to loneliness. During the war he had not seen an English face for three years; and once when he was instructed to put up an afforestation officer he was seized with panic, so that when the stranger was due to arrive, having arranged everything for his reception, he wrote a note telling him he was obliged to go up-river, and fled; he remained away till he was informed by a messenger that his guest had left.

Now the prahu appeared in the broad reach. It was manned by

THE OUTSTATION: By W. Somerset Maugham, copyright 1924 by W. Somerset Maugham, from the book THE CASUARINA TREE. Reprinted by permission of Doubleday & Company, Inc., The Literary Executor of W. Somerset Maugham, and William Heinemann Ltd.

prisoners, Dyaks under various sentences, and a couple of warders were waiting on the landing-stage to take them back to jail. They were sturdy fellows, used to the river, and they rowed with a powerful stroke. As the boat reached the side a man got out from under the attap awning and stepped on shore. The guard presented arms.

"Here we are at last. By God, I'm as cramped as the devil. I've brought you your mail."

He spoke with exuberant joviality. Mr. Warburton politely held out his hand.

"Mr. Cooper, I presume?"

"That's right. Were you expecting anyone else?"

The question had a facetious intent, but the Resident did not smile.

"My name is Warburton. I'll show you your quarters. They'll bring your kit along."

He preceded Cooper along the narrow pathway, and they entered a compound in which stood a small bungalow.

"I've had it made as habitable as I could, but of course no one has lived in it for a good many years."

It was built on piles. It consisted of a long living room which opened on to a broad verandah, and behind, on each side of a passage, were two bedrooms.

"This'll do me all right," said Cooper.

"I daresay you want to have a bath and a change. I shall be very much pleased if you'll dine with me tonight. Will eight o'clock suit you?"

"Any old time will do for me."

The Resident gave a polite, but slightly disconcerted, smile and withdrew. He returned to the Fort where his own residence was. The impression which Allen Cooper had given him was not very favorable, but he was a fair man, and he knew that it was unjust to form an opinion on so brief a glimpse. Cooper seemed to be about thirty. He was a tall, thin fellow, with a sallow face in which there was not a spot of color. It was a face all in one tone. He had a large, hooked nose and blue eyes. When, entering the bungalow, he had taken off his topee and flung it to a waiting boy, Mr. Warburton noticed that his large skull, covered with short, brown hair, contrasted somewhat oddly with a weak, small chin. He was dressed in khaki shorts and a khaki shirt, but they were shabby and soiled; and his battered topee had not been cleaned for days. Mr. Warburton reflected that the young man had spent a week on a coasting steamer and had passed the last forty-eight hours lying in the bottom of a prahu.

"We'll see what he looks like when he comes in to dinner."

He went into his room where his things were as neatly laid out as if he had an English valet, undressed, and walking down the stairs to the bathhouse, sluiced himself with cool water. The only concession he made to the climate was to wear a white dinner-jacket; but otherwise, in a boiled shirt and a high collar, silk socks and patent-leather shoes, he dressed as formally as though he were dining at his club in Pall Mall. A careful host, he went into the dining room to see that the table was properly laid. It was gay with orchids and the silver shone brightly. The napkins were folded into elaborate shapes. Shaded candles in silver candlesticks shed a soft light. Mr. Warburton smiled his approval and returned to the sitting room to await his guest. Presently he appeared. Cooper was wearing the khaki shorts, the khaki shirt, and the ragged jacket in which he had landed. Mr. Warburton's smile of greeting froze on his face.

"Hulloa, you're all dressed up," said Cooper, "I didn't know you were going to do that. I very nearly put on a sarong."

"It doesn't matter at all. I daresay your boys were busy."

"You needn't have bothered to dress on my account, you know."

"I didn't. I always dress for dinner."

"Even when you're alone?"

"Especially when I'm alone," replied Mr. Warburton, with a frigid stare.

He saw a twinkle of amusement in Cooper's eyes, and he flushed an angry red. Mr. Warburton was a hot-tempered man; you might have guessed that from his red face with its pugnacious features and from his red hair, now growing white; his blue eyes, cold as a rule and observing, could flush with sudden wrath; but he was a man of the world and he hoped a just one. He must do his best to get on with this fellow.

"When I lived in London I moved in circles in which it would have been just as eccentric not to dress for dinner every night as not to have a bath every morning. When I came to Borneo I saw no reason to discontinue so good a habit. For three years, during the war, I never saw a white man. I never omitted to dress on a single occasion on which I was well enough to come in to dinner. You have not been very long in this country; believe me, there is no better way to maintain the proper pride which you should have in yourself. When a white man surrenders in the slightest degree to the influences that surround him he very soon loses his self-respect and when he loses his self-respect you may be quite sure that the natives will soon cease to respect him."

"Well, if you expect me to put on a boiled shirt and a stiff collar in this heat I'm afraid you'll be disappointed."

"When you are dining in your own bungalow you will, of course, dress as you think fit, but when you do me the pleasure of dining with me, perhaps you will come to the conclusion that it is only polite to wear the costume usual in civilized society."

Two Malay boys, in sarongs and songkoks, with smart white coats and brass buttons; came in, one bearing gin pahits, and the other a tray on which were olives and anchovies. Then they went in to dinner, Mr. Warburton flattered himself that he had the best cook, a Chinese, in Borneo, and he took great trouble to have as good food as in the difficult circumstances was possible. He exercised much ingenuity in making the best of his materials.

"Would you care to look at the menu?" he said, handing it to Cooper.

It was written in French and the dishes had resounding names. They were waited on by the two boys. In opposite corners of the room two more waved immense fans, and so gave movement to the sultry air. The fare was sumptuous and the champagne excellent.

"Do you do yourself like this every day?" said Cooper. Mr. Warburton gave the menu a careless glance.

"I have not noticed that the dinner is any different from usual," he said. "I eat very little myself, but I make a point of having a proper dinner served to me every night. It keeps the cook in practice, and it's good discipline for the boys."

The conversation proceeded with effort. Mr. Warburton was elaborately courteous, and it may be that he found a slightly malicious amusement in the embarrassment which he thereby occasioned in his companion. Cooper had not been more than a few months in Sembulu, and Mr. Warburton's enquiries about friends of his in Kuala Solor were soon exhausted.

"By the way," he said presently, "did you meet a lad called Hennerley? He's come out recently, I believe."

"Oh, yes, he's in the police. A rotten bounder."

"I should hardly have expected him to be that. His uncle is my friend Lord Barraclough. I had a letter from Lady Barraclough only the other day asking me to look out for him."

"I heard he was related to somebody or other. I suppose that's how he got the job. He's been to Eton and Oxford and he doesn't forget to let you know it."

"You surprise me," said Mr. Warburton. "All his family have been at Eton and Oxford for a couple of hundred years. I should have expected him to take it as a matter of course."

"I thought him a damned prig."

"To what school did you go?"

"I was born in Barbadoes. I was educated there."

"Oh, I see."

Mr. Warburton managed to put so much offensiveness into his brief reply that Cooper flushed. For a moment he was silent.

"I've had two or three letters from Kuala Solor," continued Mr. Warburton, "and my impression was that young Hennerley was a great success. They say he's a first-rate sportsman."

"Oh, yes, he's very popular. He's just the sort of fellow they would like in K.S. I haven't got much use for the first-rate sportsman myself. What does it amount to in the long run that a man can play golf and tennis better than other people? And who cares if he can make a break of seventy-five at billiards? They attach a damned sight too much importance to that sort of thing in England."

"Do you think so? I was under the impression that the first-rate sportsman had come out of the war certainly no worse than any one else."

"Oh, if you're going to talk of the war then I do know what I'm talking about. I was in the same regiment as Hennerley and I can tell you that the men couldn't stick him at any price."

"How do you know?"

"Because I was one of the men."

"Oh, you hadn't got a commission."

"A fat chance I had of getting a commission. I was what was called a Colonial. I hadn't been to a public school and I had no influence. I was in the ranks the whole damned time."

Cooper frowned. He seemed to have difficulty in preventing himself from breaking into violent invective. Mr Warburton watched him, his little blue eyes narrowed, watched him and formed his opinion. Changing the conversation, he began to speak to Cooper about the work that would be required of him, and as the clock struck ten he rose.

"Well, I won't keep you any more. I daresay you're tired by your journey."

They shook hands.

"Oh, I say, look here," said Cooper, "I wonder if you can find me a boy. The boy I had before never turned up when I was starting from K.S. He took my kit on board and all that and then disappeared. I didn't know he wasn't there till we were out of the river."

"I'll ask my head boy. I have no doubt he can find you someone."

"All right. Just tell him to send the boy along, and if I like the look of him I'll take him."

There was a moon, so that no lantern was needed. Cooper walked across from the Fort to his bungalow.

"I wonder why on earth they've sent me a fellow like that?" reflected Mr. Warburton. "If that's the kind of man they're going to get out now I don't think much of it."

He strolled down his garden. The Fort was built on the top of a little hill and the garden ran down to the river's edge; on the bank was an arbor, and hither it was his habit to come after dinner to smoke a cheroot. And often from the river that flowed below him a voice was heard, the voice of some Malay too timorous to venture into the light of day, and a complaint or an accusation was softly wafted to his ears, a piece of information was whispered to him or a useful hint, which otherwise would never have come into his official ken. He threw himself heavily into a long rattan chair. Cooper! An envious, ill-bred fellow, bumptious, self-assertive and vain. But Mr. Warburton's irritation could not withstand the silent beauty of the night. The air was scented with the sweet-smelling flowers of a tree that grew at the entrance to the arbour, and the fireflies, sparkling dimly, flew with their slow and silvery flight. The moon made a pathway on the broad river for the light feet of Siva's bride, and on the further bank a row of palm trees was delicately silhouetted against the sky. Peace stole into the soul of Mr. Warburton.

He was a queer creature, and he had had a singular career. At the age of twenty-one he had inherited a considerable fortune, a hundred thousand pounds, and when he left Oxford he threw himself into the gay life which in those days (now Mr. Warburton was a man of four and fifty) offered itself to the young man of good family. He had his flat in Mount Street, his private hansom, and his hunting-box in Warwickshire. He went to all the places where the fashionable congregate. He was handsome, amusing and generous. He was a figure in the society of London in the early nineties, and society then had not lost its exclusiveness nor its brilliance. The Boer War which shook it was unthought of; the Great War which destroyed it was prophesied only by the pessimists. It was no unpleasant thing to be a rich young man in those days, and Mr. Warburton's chimney piece during the season was packed with cards for one great function after another. Mr. Warburton displayed them with complacency. For Mr. Warburton was a snob. He was not a timid snob, a little ashamed of being impressed by his betters, nor a snob who sought the intimacy of persons who had acquired celebrity in politics or notoriety in the arts, nor the snob who was dazzled by riches; he was the naked, unadulterated common snob who dearly loved a lord. He was touchy and quick-tempered, but he would much rather have been snubbed by a person of quality than flattered by a commoner. His name figured insignificantly in Burke's Peerage, and it was marvelous to watch the ingenuity he used to mention his distant relationship to the noble family he belonged to; but never a word did he say of the honest Liverpool manufacturer from whom, through his mother, Miss Gubbins, he had come by his fortune. It was the terror of his fashionable life that at Cowes, maybe, or at Ascot, when he was with a duchess or even with a prince of the blood, one of these relatives would claim acquaintance with him.

His failing was too obvious not soon to become notorious, but its extravagance saved it from being merely despicable. The great whom he adored laughed at him, but in their hearts felt his adoration not unnatural. Poor Warburton was a dreadful snob, of course, but after all he was a good fellow. He was always ready to back a bill for an impecunious nobleman, and if you were in a tight corner you could safely count on him for a hundred pounds. He gave good dinners. He played whist badly, but never minded how much he lost if the company was select. He happened to be a gambler, an unlucky one, but he was a good loser, and it was impossible not to admire the coolness with which he lost five hundred pounds at a sitting. His passion for cards, almost as strong as his passion for titles, was the cause of his undoing. The life he led was expensive and his gambling losses were formidable. He began to plunge more heavily, first on horses, and then on the Stock Exchange. He had a certain simplicity of character and the unscrupulous found him an ingenuous prey. I do not know if he ever realized that his smart friends laughed at him behind his back, but I think he had an obscure instinct that he could not afford to appear other than careless of his money. He got into the hands of money lenders. At the age of thirty-four he was ruined.

He was too much imbued with the spirit of his class to hesitate in the choice of his next step. When a man in his set had run through his money he went out to the colonies. No one heard Mr. Warburton repine. He made no complaint because a noble friend had advised a disastrous speculation, he pressed nobody to whom he had lent money to repay it, he paid his debts (if he had only known it, the despised blood of the Liverpool manufacturer came out in him there), sought help from no one, and, never having done a stroke of work in his life, looked for a means of livelihood. He remained cheerful, unconcerned and full of humor. He had no wish to make anyone with whom he happened to be uncomfortable by the recital of his misfortune. Mr. Warburton was a snob, but he was also a gentleman.

The only favor he asked of any of the great friends in whose daily company he had lived for years was a recommendation. The able man who was at the time Sultan of Sembulu took him into his service. The night before he sailed he dined for the last time at his club.

"I hear you're going away, Warburton," the old Duke of Hereford said to him.

"Yes, I'm going to Borneo."

"Good God, what are you going there for?"

"Oh, I'm broke."

"Are you? I'm sorry. Well, let us know when you come back. I hope you have a good time."

"Oh yes. Lots of shooting, you know."

The Duke nodded and passed on. A few hours later Mr. Warburton watched the coast of England recede into the mist, and he left behind everything which to him made life worth living.

Twenty years had passed since then. He kept up a busy correspondence with various great ladies and his letters were amusing and chatty. He never lost his love for titled persons and paid careful attention to the announcements in The Times (which reached him six

weeks after publication) of their comings and goings. He perused
the column which records births, deaths, and marriages, and he was
always ready with his letter of congratulation or condolence. The
illustrated papers told him how people looked and on his periodical
visits to England, able to take up the threads as though they had
never been broken, he knew all about any new person who might
have appeared on the social surface. His interest in the world of fashion was as vivid as when himself had been a figure in it. It still
seemed to him the only thing that mattered.

But insensibly another interest had entered into his life. The position he found himself in flattered his vanity; he was no longer the
sycophant craving the smiles of the great, he was the master whose
word was law. He was gratified by the guard of Dyak soldiers who presented arms as he passed. He liked to sit in judgment on his fellow
men. It pleased him to compose quarrels between rival chiefs. When
the headhunters were troublesome in the old days he set out to
chastise them with a thrill of pride in his own behavior. He was too
vain not to be of dauntless courage, and a pretty story was told of
his coolness in adventuring single-handed into a stockaded village
and demanding the surrender of a bloodthirsty pirate. He became
a skillful administrator. He was strict, just and honest.

And little by little he conceived a deep love for the Malays. He
interested himself in their habits and customs. He was never tired
of listening to their talk. He admired their virtues, and with a smile
and a shrug of the shoulders condoned their vices.

"In my day," he would say, "I have been on intimate terms with
some of the greatest gentlemen in England, but I have never known
finer gentlemen than some well-born Malays whom I am proud to
call my friends."

He liked their courtesy and their distinguished manners, their
gentleness and their sudden passions. He knew by instinct
exactly how to treat them. He had a genuine tenderness for them.
But he never forgot that he was an English gentleman and he had
no patience with the white men who yielded to native customs. He
made no surrenders. And he did not imitate so many of the white
men in taking a native woman to wife, for an intrigue of this nature,
however sanctified by custom, seemed to him not only shocking but
undignified. A man who had been called George by Albert Edward,
Prince of Wales, could hardly be expected to have any connection

with a native. And when he returned to Borneo from his visits to England it was now with something like relief. His friends, like himself, were no longer young, and there was a new generation which looked upon him as a tiresome old man. It seemed to him that the England of today had lost a good deal of what he had loved in the England of his youth. But Borneo remained the same. It was home to him now. He meant to remain in the service as long as was possible, and the hope in his heart was that he would die before at last he was forced to retire. He had stated in his will that wherever he died he wished his body to be brought back to Sembulu and buried among the people he loved within sound of the softly flowing river.

But these emotions he kept hidden from the eyes of men; and no one, seeing this spruce, stout, well-set-up man, with his clean-shaven strong face and his whitening hair, would have dreamed that he cherished so profound a sentiment.

He knew how the work of the station should be done, and during the next few days he kept a suspicious eye on his assistant. He saw very soon that he was painstaking and competent. The only fault he had to find with him was that he was brusque with the natives.

"The Malays are shy and very sensitive," he said to him. "I think you will find that you will get much better results if you take care always to be polite, patient and kindly."

Cooper gave a short, grating laugh.

"I was born in Barbadoes and I was in Africa in the war. I don't think there's much about niggers that I don't know."

"I know nothing," said Mr. Warburton acidly. "But we were not talking of them. We were talking of Malays."

"Aren't they niggers?"

"You are very ignorant," replied Mr. Warburton.

He said no more.

On the first Sunday after Cooper's arrival he asked him to dinner. He did everything ceremoniously, and though they had met on the previous day in the office and later, on the Fort verandah where they drank a gin and bitters together at six o'clock, he sent a polite note across to the bungalow by a boy. Cooper, however unwillingly, came in evening dress and Mr. Warburton, though gratified that his wish was respected, noticed with disdain that the young man's clothes were badly cut and his shirt ill-fitting. But Mr. Warburton was in a good temper that evening.

"By the way," he said to him, as he shook hands, "I've talked to my head boy about finding you someone and he recommends his nephew. I've seen him and he seems a bright and willing lad. Would you like to see him?"

"I don't mind."

"He's waiting now."

Mr. Warburton called his boy and told him to send for his nephew. In a moment a tall, slender youth of twenty appeared. He had large dark eyes and a good profile. He was very neat in his sarong, a little white coat and a fez, without a tassel, of plum-colored velvet. He answered to the name of Abas. Mr. Warburton looked on him with approval, and his manner insensibly softened as he spoke to him in fluent and idiomatic Malay. He was inclined to be sarcastic with white people, but with the Malays he had a happy mixture of condescension and kindliness. He stood in the place of the Sultan. He knew perfectly how to preserve his own dignity, and at the same time put a native at his ease.

"Will he do?" said Mr. Warburton, turning to Cooper.

"Yes, I daresay he's no more of a scoundrel than any of the rest of them."

Mr. Warburton informed the boy that he was engaged and dismissed him.

"You're very lucky to get a boy like that," he told Cooper. "He belongs to a very good family. They came over from Malacca nearly a hundred years ago."

"I don't much mind if the boy who cleans my shoes and brings me a drink when I want it has blue blood in his veins or not. All I ask is that he should do what I tell him and look sharp about it."

Mr. Warburton pursed his lips, but made no reply.

They went in to dinner. It was excellent, and the wine was good. Its influence presently had its effect on them and they talked not only without acrimony, but even with friendliness. Mr. Warburton liked to do himself well, and on Sunday night he made it a habit to do himself even a little better than usual. He began to think he was unfair to Cooper. Of course he was not a gentleman, but that was not his fault, and when you got to know him it might be that he would turn out a very good fellow. His faults, perhaps, were faults of manner. And he was certainly good at his work, quick, conscientious and thorough. When they reached the dessert Mr. Warburton was feeling kindly disposed towards all mankind.

"This is your first Sunday and I'm going to give you a very special glass of port. I've only got about two dozen of it left and I keep it for special occasions."

He gave his boy instructions and presently the bottle was brought. Mr. Warburton watched the boy open it.

"I got this port from my old friend Charles Hollington. He'd had it for forty years and I've had it for a good many. He was well-known to have the best cellar in England."

"Is he a wine merchant?"

"Not exactly," smiled Mr. Warburton. "I was speaking of Lord Hollington of Castle Reagh. He's one of the richest peers in England. A very old friend of mine. I was at Eton with his brother."

This was an opportunity that Mr. Warburton could never resist and he told a little anecdote of which the only point seemed to be that he knew an earl. The port was certainly very good; he drank a glass and then a second. He lost all caution. He had not talked to a white man for months. He began to tell stories. He showed himself in the company of the great. Hearing him you would have thought that at one time ministries were formed and policies decided on his suggestion whispered into the ear of a duchess or thrown over the dinner table to be gratefully acted on by the confidential adviser of the sovereign. The old days at Ascot, Goodwood, and Cowes lived again for him. Another glass of port. There were the great house parties in Yorkshire and in Scotland to which he went every year.

"I had a man called Foreman then, the best valet I ever had, and why do you think he gave me notice? You know in the Housekeeper's Room the ladies' maids and the gentlemen's gentlemen sit according to the precedence of their masters. He told me he was sick of going to party after party at which I was the only commoner. It meant that he always had to sit at the bottom of the table and all the best bits were taken before a dish reached him. I told the story to the old Duke of Hereford and he roared. 'By God, sir,' he said, 'if I were King of England I'd make you a viscount just to give your man a chance.' 'Take him yourself, Duke,' I said. 'He's the best valet I've ever had.' 'Well, Warburton,' he said, 'if he's good enough for you he's good enough for me. Send him along.' "

Then there was Monte Carlo where Mr. Warburton and the Grand Duke Fyodor, playing in partnership, had broken the bank one evening; and there was Marienbad. At Marienbad Mr. Warburton had played baccarat with Edward VII.

"He was only Prince of Wales then, of course. I remember him saying to me, 'George, if you draw on a five you'll lose your shirt.' He was right; I don't think he ever said a truer word in his life. He was a wonderful man. I always said he was the greatest diplomatist in Europe. But I was a young fool in those days, I hadn't the sense to take his advice. If I had, if I'd never drawn on a five, I daresay I shouldn't be here today."

Cooper was watching him. His blue eyes, deep in their sockets, were hard and supercilious, and on his lips was a mocking smile. He had heard a good deal about Mr. Warburton in Kuala Solor. Not a bad sort, and he ran his district like clockwork, they said, but by heaven, what a snob! They laughed at him good-naturedly, for it was impossible to dislike a man who was so generous and so kindly, and Cooper had already heard the story of the Prince of Wales and the game of baccarat. But Cooper listened without indulgence. From the beginning he had resented the Resident's manner. He was very sensitive and he writhed under Mr. Warburton's polite sarcasms. Mr. Warburton had a knack of receiving a remark of which he disapproved with a devastating silence. Cooper had lived little in England, and he had a peculiar dislike of the English. He resented especially the public-school boy since he always feared that he was going to patronize him. He was so much afraid of others putting on airs with him that, in order as it were to get in first, he put on such airs as to make every one think him insufferably conceited.

"Well, at all events the war has done one good thing for us," he said at last. "It's smashed up the power of the aristocracy. The Boer War started it, and 1914 put the lid on."

"The great families of England are doomed," said Mr. Warburton with the complacent melancholy of an *émigré* who remembered the court of Louis XV. "They cannot afford any longer to live in their splendid palaces, and their princely hospitality will soon be nothing but a memory."

"And a damned good job too in my opinion."

"My poor Cooper, what can you know of the glory that was Greece and the grandeur that was Rome?"

Mr. Warburton made an ample gesture. His eyes for an instant grew dreamy with a vision of the past.

"Well, believe me, we're fed up with all that rot. What we want is a business government by business men. I was born in a Crown

Colony, and I've lived practically all my life in the colonies. I don't give a row of pins for a lord. What's wrong with England is snobbishness. And if there's anything that gets my goat it's a snob."

A snob! Mr. Warburton's face grew purple and his eyes blazed with anger. That was a word that had pursued him all his life. The great ladies whose society he had enjoyed in his youth were not inclined to look upon his appreciation of themselves as unworthy, but even great ladies are sometimes out of temper and more than once Mr. Warburton had had the dreadful word flung in his teeth. He knew, he could not help knowing, that there were odious people who called him a snob. How unfair it was! Why, there was no vice he found so detestable as snobbishness. After all, he liked to mix with people of his own class, he was only at home in their company, and how in heaven's name could any one say that was snobbish? Birds of a feather.

"I quite agree with you," he answered. "A snob is a man who admires or despises another because he is of a higher social rank than his own. It is the most vulgar failing of our English middle class."

He saw a flicker of amusement in Cooper's eyes. Cooper put up his hand to hide the broad smile that rose to his lips, and so made it more noticeable. Mr. Warburton's hands trembled a little.

Probably Cooper never knew how greatly he had offended his chief. A sensitive man himself he was strangely insensitive of the feelings of others.

Their work forced them to see one another for a few minutes now and then during the day, and they met at six to have a drink on Mr. Warburton's verandah. This was an old-established custom of the country which Mr. Warburton would not for the world have broken. But they ate their meals separately, Cooper in his bungalow and Mr. Warburton at the Fort. After the office work was over they walked till dusk fell, but they walked apart. There were but few paths in this country, where the jungle pressed close upon the plantations of the village, and when Mr. Warburton caught sight of his assistant passing along with his loose stride, he would make a circuit in order to avoid him. Cooper, with his bad manners, his conceit in his own judgment and his intolerance, had already got on his nerves; but it was not till Cooper had been on the station for a couple of months that an incident happened which turned the Resident's dislike into bitter hatred.

Mr. Warburton was obliged to go up-country on a tour of inspection, and he left the station in Cooper's charge with more confidence, since he had definitely come to the conclusion that he was a capable fellow. The only thing he did not like was that he had no indulgence. He was honest, just and painstaking, but he had no sympathy for the natives. It bitterly amused Mr. Warburton to observe that this man, who looked upon himself as every man's equal, should look upon so many men as his own inferiors. He was hard, he had no patience with the native mind, and he was a bully. Mr. Warburton very quickly realized that the Malays disliked and feared him. He was not altogether displeased. He would not have liked it very much if his assistant had enjoyed a popularity which might rival his own. Mr. Warburton made his elaborate preparations, set out on his expedition, and in three weeks returned. Meanwhile the mail had arrived. The first thing that struck his eyes when he entered his sitting room was a great pile of open newspapers. Cooper had met him, and they went into the room together. Mr. Warburton turned to one of the servants who had been left behind and sternly asked him what was the meaning of those open papers. Cooper hastened to explain.

"I wanted to read all about the Wolverhampton murder and so I borrowed your Times. I brought them back again. I knew you wouldn't mind."

Mr. Warburton turned on him, white with anger.

"But I do mind. I mind very much."

"I'm sorry," said Cooper, with composure. "The fact is, I simply couldn't wait till you came back."

"I wonder you didn't open my letters as well."

Cooper, unmoved, smiled at his chief's exasperation.

"Oh, that's not quite the same thing. After all, I couldn't imagine you'd mind my looking at your newspapers. There's nothing private in them."

"I very much object to any one reading my paper before me." He went up to the pile. There were nearly thirty numbers there. "I think it extremely impertinent of you. They're all mixed up."

"We can easily put them in order," said Cooper, joining him at the table.

"Don't touch them," cried Mr. Warburton.

"I say, it's childish to make a scene about a little thing like that."

"How dare you speak to me like that?"

"Oh, go to hell," said Cooper, and he flung out of the room.

Mr. Warburton, trembling with passion, was left contemplating his papers. His greatest pleasure in life had been destroyed by those callous, brutal hands. Most people living in out-of-the-way places when the mail comes tear open impatiently their papers and taking the last ones first glance at the latest news from home. Not so Mr. Warburton. His newsagent had instructions to write on the outside of the wrapper the date of each paper he despatched and when the great bundle arrived Mr. Warburton looked at these dates and with his blue pencil numbered them. His head boy's orders were to place one on the table every morning in the verandah with the early cup of tea, and it was Mr. Warburton's especial delight to break the wrapper as he sipped his tea, and read the morning paper. It gave him the illusion of living at home. Every Monday morning he read the Monday Times of six weeks back and so went through the week. On Sunday he read The Observer. Like his habit of dressing for dinner it was a tie to civilization. And it was his pride that no matter how exciting the news was he had never yielded to the temptation of opening a paper before its allotted time. During the war the suspense sometimes had been intolerable, and when he read one day that a push was begun he had undergone agonies of suspense which he might have saved himself by the simple expedient of opening a later paper which lay waiting for him on a shelf. It had been the severest trial to which he had ever exposed himself, but he victoriously surmounted it. And that clumsy fool had broken open those neat tight packages because he wanted to know whether some horrid woman had murdered her odious husband.

Mr. Warburton sent for his boy and told him to bring wrappers. He folded up the papers as neatly as he could, placed a wrapper round each and numbered it. But it was a melancholy task.

"I shall never forgive him," he said. "Never."

Of course his boy had been with him on his expedition; he never travelled without him, for his boy knew exactly how he liked things, and Mr. Warburton was not the kind of jungle traveller who was prepared to dispense with his comforts; but in the interval since their arrival he had been gossiping in the servants' quarters. He had learnt that Cooper had had trouble with his boys. All but the youth Abas had left him. Abas had desired to go too, but his uncle had placed him there on the instructions of the Resident, and he was afraid to leave without his uncle's permission.

"I told him he had done well, Tuan," said the boy. "But he is unhappy. He says it is not a good house and he wishes to know if he may go as the others have gone."

"No, he must stay. The tuan must have servants. Have those who went been replaced?"

"No, Tuan, no one will go."

Mr. Warburton frowned. Cooper was an insolent fool, but he had an official position and must be suitably provided with servants. It was not seemly that his house should be improperly conducted.

"Where are the boys who ran away?"

"They are in the kampong, Tuan."

"Go and see them tonight and tell them that I expect them to be back at Tuan Cooper's house at dawn tomorrow."

"They say they will not go, Tuan."

"On my order?

The boy had been with Mr. Warburton for fifteen years, and he knew every intonation of his master's voice. He was not afraid of him, they had gone through too much together, once in the jungle the Resident had saved his life and once, upset in some rapids, but for him the Resident would have been drowned; but he knew when the Resident must be obeyed without question.

"I will go to the kampong," he said.

Mr. Warburton expected that his subordinate would take the first opportunity to apologize for his rudeness, but Cooper had the ill-bred man's inability to express regret; and when they met next morning in the office he ignored the incident. Since Mr. Warburton had been away for three weeks it was necessary for them to have a somewhat prolonged interview. At the end of it Mr. Warburton dismissed him.

"I don't think there's anything else, thank you." Cooper turned to go but Mr. Warburton stopped him. "I understand you've been having some trouble with your boys."

Cooper gave a harsh laugh.

"They tried to blackmail me. They had the damned cheek to run away, all except that incompetent fellow Abas—he knew when he was well off—but I just sat tight. They've all come to heel again."

"What do you mean by that?"

"This morning they were all back on their jobs, the Chinese cook and all. There they were, as cool as cucumbers; you would have thought they owned the place. I suppose they'd come to the conclusion that I wasn't such a fool as I looked."

"By no means. They came back on my express order."

Cooper flushed slightly.

"I should be obliged if you wouldn't interfere with my private concerns."

"They're not your private concerns. When your servants run away it makes you ridiculous. You are perfectly free to make a fool of yourself, but I cannot allow you to be made a fool of. It is unseemly that your house should not be properly staffed. As soon as I heard that your boys had left you, I had them told to be back in their place at dawn. That'll do."

Mr. Warburton nodded to signify that the interview was at an end. Cooper took no notice.

"Shall I tell you what I did? I called them and gave the whole bally lot the sack. I gave them ten minutes to get out of the compound."

Mr. Warburton shrugged his shoulders.

"What makes you think you can get others?"

"I've told my own clerk to see about it."

Mr. Warburton reflected for a moment.

"I think you behaved very foolishly. You will do well to remember in future that good masters make good servants."

"Is there anything else you want to teach me?"

"I should like to teach you manners, but it would be an arduous task, but I have not the time to waste. I will see that you get boys."

"Please don't put yourself to any trouble on my account. I'm quite capable of getting them for myself."

Mr. Warburton smiled acidly. He had an inkling that Cooper disliked him as much as he disliked Cooper, and he knew that nothing is more galling than to be forced to accept the favors of a man you detest.

"Allow me to tell you that you have no more chance of getting Malay or Chinese servants here now than you have of getting an English butler or a French chef. No one will come to you except on an order from me. Would you like me to give it?"

"No."

"As you please. Good morning."

Mr. Warburton watched the development of the situation with acrid humor. Cooper's clerk was unable to persuade Malay, Dyak, or Chinese to enter the house of such a master. Abas, the boy who remained faithful to him, knew how to cook only native food, and Cooper, a coarse feeder, found his gorge rise against the everlasting rice. There was no water-carrier, and in that great heat he needed several baths a day. He cursed Abas, but Abas opposed him with sullen resistance and would not do more than he chose. It was galling to know that the lad stayed with him only because the Resident insisted. This went on for a fortnight and then, one morning, he found in his house the very servants whom he had previously dismissed. He fell into a violent rage, but he had learnt a little sense, and this time, without a word, he let them stay. He swallowed his humiliation, but the impatient contempt he had felt for Mr. Warburton's idiosyncrasies changed into a sullen hatred; the Resident with this malicious stroke had made him the laughing stock of all the natives.

The two men now held no communication with one another. They broke the time-honored custom of sharing, notwithstanding personal dislike, a drink at six o'clock with any white man who happened to be at the station. Each lived in his own house as though the other did not exist. Now that Cooper had fallen into the work, it was necessary for them to have little to do with one another in the office. Mr. Warburton used his orderly to send any message he had to give his assistant, and his instructions he sent by formal letter. They saw one another constantly, that was inevitable, but did not exchange half a dozen words in a week. The fact that they could not avoid catching sight of one another got on their nerves. They brooded over their antagonism and Mr. Warburton, taking his daily walk, could think of nothing but how much he detested his assistant.

And the dreadful thing was that in all probability they would remain thus, facing each other in deadly enmity, till Mr. Warburton went on leave. It might be three years. He had no reason to send in a complaint to headquarters: Cooper did his work very well, and at that time men were hard to get. True, vague complaints reached him and hints that the natives found Cooper harsh. There was certainly a feeling of dissatisfaction among them. But when Mr. Warburton looked into specific cases, all he could say was that Cooper had shown severity where mildness would not have been misplaced and had been unfeeling when himself would have been sympathetic. He had done nothing for which he could be taken to task. But Mr.

Warburton watched him. Hatred will often make a man clear-sighted, and he had a suspicion that Cooper was using the natives without consideration, yet keeping within the law, because he felt that thus he could exasperate his chief. One day perhaps he would go too far. None knew better than Mr. Warburton how irritable the incessant heat could make a man and how difficult it was to keep one's self-control after a sleepless night. He smiled softly to himself. Sooner or later Cooper would deliver himself into his hand.

When at last the opportunity came Mr. Warburton laughed aloud. Cooper had charge of the prisoners; they made roads, built sheds, rowed when it was necessary to send the prahu up- or down-stream, kept the town clean and otherwise usefully employed themselves. If well-behaved they even on occasion served as houseboys. Cooper kept them hard at it. He liked to see them work. He took pleasure in devising tasks for them; and seeing quickly enough that they were being made to do useless things the prisoners worked badly. He punished them by lengthening their hours. This was contrary to the regulations, and as soon as it was brought to the attention of Mr. Warburton, without referring the matter back to his subordinate, he gave instructions that the old hours should be kept; Cooper, going out for his walk, was astounded to see the prisoners strolling back to the jail; he had given instructions that they were not to knock off till dusk. When he asked the warder in charge why they had left off work he was told that it was the Resident's bidding.

White with rage he strode to the Fort. Mr. Warburton, in his spotless white ducks and his neat topee, with a walking stick in his hand, followed by his dogs, was on the point of starting out on his afternoon stroll. He had watched Cooper go and knew that he had taken the road by the river. Cooper jumped up the steps and went straight up to the Resident.

"I want to know what the hell you mean by countermanding my order that the prisoners were to work till six," he burst out, beside himself with fury.

Mr. Warburton opened his cold blue eyes very wide and assumed an expression of great surprise.

"Are you out of your mind? Are you so ignorant that you do not know that that is not the way to speak to your official superior?"

"Oh, go to hell. The prisoners are my pidgin, and you've got no right to interfere. You mind your business, and I'll mind mine. I want to know what the devil you mean by making a damned fool of me. Every one in the place will know that you've countermanded my order."

Mr. Warburton kept very cool.

"You had no power to give the order you did. I countermanded it because it was harsh and tyrannical. Believe me, I have not made half such a damned fool of you as you have made of yourself."

"You disliked me from the first moment I came here. You've done everything you could to make the place impossible for me because I wouldn't lick your boots for you. You got your knife into me because I wouldn't flatter you."

Cooper, spluttering with rage, was nearing dangerous ground, and Mr. Warburton's eyes grew on a sudden colder and more piercing.

"You are wrong. I thought you were a cad, but I was perfectly satisfied with the way you did your work."

"You snob. You damned snob. You thought me a cad because I hadn't been to Eton. Oh, they told me in K.S. what to expect. Why, don't you know that you're the laughing stock of the whole country? I could hardly help bursting into a roar of laughter when you told your celebrated story about the Prince of Wales. My God, how they shouted at the club when they told it. By God, I'd rather be the cad I am than the snob you are."

He got Mr. Warburton on the raw.

"If you don't get out of my house this minute I shall knock you down," he cried.

The other came a little closer to him and put his face in his.

"Touch me, touch me," he said. "By God, I'd like to see you hit me. Do you want me to say it again? Snob. Snob."

Cooper was three inches taller than Mr. Warburton, a strong, muscular young man. Mr. Warburton was fat and fifty-four. His clenched fist shot out. Cooper caught him by the arm and pushed him back.

"Don't be a damned fool. Remember I'm not a gentleman, I know how to use my hands."

He gave a sort of hoot, and, grinning all over his pale, sharp face, jumped down the verandah steps. Mr. Warburton, his heart in his anger pounding against his ribs, sank exhausted into a chair. His body tingled as though he had prickly heat. For one horrible moment he thought he was going to cry. But suddenly he was conscious that his head boy was on the verandah and instinctively regained control of himself. The boy came forward and filled him a glass of whisky and soda. Without a word Mr. Warburton took it and drank it to the dregs.

"What do you want to say to me?" asked Mr. Warburton, trying to force a smile on to his strained lips.

"Tuan, the assistant tuan is a bad man. Abas wishes again to leave him."

"Let him wait a little. I shall write to Kuala Solor and ask that Tuan Cooper should go elsewhere."

"Tuan Cooper is not good with the Malays."

"Leave me."

The boy silently withdrew. Mr. Warburton was left alone with his thoughts. He saw the club at Kuala Solor, the men sitting round the table in the window in their flannels, when the night had driven them in from golf and tennis, drinking whiskies and gin pahits and laughing when they told the celebrated story of the Prince of Wales and himself at Marienbad. He was hot with shame and misery. A snob! They all thought him a snob. And he had always thought them very good fellows, he had always been gentleman enough to let it make no difference to him that they were of very second-rate position. He hated them now. But his hatred for them was nothing compared with his hatred for Cooper. And if it had come to blows Cooper could have thrashed him. Tears of mortification ran down his red, fat face. He sat there for a couple of hours smoking cigarette after cigarette, and he wished he were dead.

At last the boy came back and asked him if he would dress for dinner. Of course! He always dressed for dinner. He rose wearily from his chair and put on his stiff shirt and the high collar. He sat down at the prettily decorated table and was waited on as usual by the two boys while two others waved their great fans. Over there in the bungalow, two hundred yards away, Cooper was eating a filthy meal clad only in a sarong and a baju. His feet were bare and while he ate he probably read a detective story. After dinner Mr. Warburton sat down to write a letter. The Sultan was away, but he wrote, privately and confidentially, to his representative. Cooper did his work very well, he said, but the fact was that he couldn't get on with him. They were getting dreadfully on each other's nerves, and he would look upon it as a very great favour if Cooper could be transferred to another post.

He despatched the letter next morning by special messenger. The answer came a fortnight later with the month's mail. It was a private note and ran as follows:

My dear Warburton:—

    I do not want to answer your letter officially and so I am writing you a few lines myself. Of course if you insist I will put the matter up to the Sultan, but I think you would be much wiser to drop it. I know Cooper is a rough diamond, but he is capable, and he had a pretty thin time in the war, and I think he should be given every chance. I think you are a little too much inclined to attach importance to a man's social position. You must remember that times have changed. Of course it's a very good thing for a man to be a gentleman, but it's better that he should be competent and hardworking. I think if you'll exercise a little tolerance you'll get on very well with Cooper.

Yours very sincerely
Richard Temple

The letter dropped from Mr. Warburton's hand. It was easy to read between the lines. Dick Temple, whom he had known for twenty years, Dick Temple, who came from quite a good county family, thought him a snob and for that reason had no patience with his request. Mr. Warburton felt on a sudden discouraged with life. The world of which he was a part had passed away, and the future belonged to a meaner generation. Cooper represented it, and Cooper he hated with all his heart. He stretched out his hand to fill his glass and at the gesture his head boy stepped forward.

"I didn't know you were there."

The boy picked up the official letter. Ah, that was why he was waiting.

"Does Tuan Cooper go, Tuan?"

"No."

"There will be a misfortune."

For a moment the words conveyed nothing to his lassitude. But only for a moment. He sat up in his chair and looked at the boy. He was all attention.

"What do you mean by that?"

"Tuan Cooper is not behaving rightly with Abas."

Mr. Warburton shrugged his shoulders. How should a man like Cooper know how to treat servants? Mr. Warburton knew the type:

He would be grossly familiar with them at one moment and rude and inconsiderate the next.

"Let Abas go back to his family."

"Tuan Cooper holds back his wages so that he may not run away. He has paid him nothing for three months. I tell him to be patient. But he is angry, he will not listen to reason. If the tuan continues to use him ill there will be a misfortune."

"You were right to tell me."

The fool! Did he know so little of the Malays as to think he could safely injure them? It would serve him damned well right if he got a kris in his back. A kris. Mr. Warburton's heart seemed on a sudden to miss a beat. He had only to let things take their course and one fine day he would be rid of Cooper. He smiled faintly as the phrase, a masterly inactivity, crossed his mind. And now his heart beat a little quicker, for he saw the man he hated lying on his face in a pathway of the jungle with a knife in his back. A fit end for the cad and the bully. Mr. Warburton sighed. It was his duty to warn him, and of course he must do it. He wrote a brief and formal note to Cooper asking him to come to the Fort at once.

In ten minutes Cooper stood before him. They had not spoken to one another since the day when Mr. Warburton had nearly struck him. He did not now ask him to sit down.

"Did you wish to see me?" Cooper asked.

He was untidy and none too clean. His face and hands were covered with little red blotches where mosquitoes had bitten him and he had scratched himself till the blood came. His long, thin face bore a sullen look.

"I understand that you are again having trouble with your servants. Abas, my head boy's nephew, complains that you have held back his wages for three months. I consider it a most arbitrary proceeding. The lad wishes to leave you, and I certainly do not blame him. I must insist on your paying what is due to him."

"I don't choose that he should leave me. I am holding back his wages as a pledge of his good behavior."

"You do not know the Malay character. The Malays are very sensitive to injury and ridicule. They are passionate and revengeful. It is my duty to warn you that if you drive this boy beyond a certain point you run a great risk."

Cooper gave a contemptuous chuckle.

"What do you think he'll do?"

"I think he'll kill you."

"Why should you mind?"

"Oh, I wouldn't," replied Mr. Warburton, with a faint laugh. "I should bear it with the utmost fortitude. But I feel the official obligation to give you a proper warning."

"Do you think I'm afraid of a damned nigger?"

"It's a matter of entire indifference to me."

"Well, let me tell you this, I know how to take care of myself; that boy Abas is a dirty, thieving rascal, and if he tries any monkey tricks on me, by God, I'll wring his bloody neck."

"That was all I wished to say to you," said Mr. Warburton. "Good evening."

Mr. Warburton gave him a little nod of dismissal. Cooper flushed, did not for a moment know what to say or do, turned on his heel and stumbled out of the room. Mr. Warburton watched him go with an icy smile on his lips. He had done his duty. But what would he have thought had he known that when Cooper got back to his bungalow, so silent and cheerless, he threw himself down on his bed and in his bitter loneliness on a sudden lost all control of himself? Painful sobs tore his chest and heavy tears rolled down his thin cheeks.

After this Mr. Warburton seldom saw Cooper, and never spoke to him. He read his Times every morning, did his work at the office, took his exercise, dressed for dinner, dined and sat by the river smoking his cheroot. If by chance he ran across Cooper he cut him dead. Each, though never for a moment unconscious of the propinquity, acted as though the other did not exist. Time did nothing to assuage their animosity. They watched one another's actions and each knew what the other did. Though Mr. Warburton had been a keen shot in his youth, with age he had acquired a distaste for killing the wild things of the jungle, but on Sundays and holidays Cooper went out with his gun: If he got something it was a triumph over Mr. Warburton; if not, Mr. Warburton shrugged his shoulders and chuckled. These counter-jumpers trying to be sportsmen! Christmas was a bad time for both of them: They ate their dinners alone, each in his own quarters, and they got deliberately drunk. They were the only white men within two hundred miles, and they lived within shouting distance of each other. At the beginning of the year Cooper went down with fever, and when Mr. Warburton caught sight of him again he was surprised to see how thin he had grown. He looked ill and worn. The solitude, so much more unnatural because it was due to no necessity, was getting on his nerves. It was getting on Mr. Warburton's too, and often he could not sleep at night. He lay awake brooding. Cooper was drinking heavily and surely the breaking point was near; but in his dealings with the natives he took care to do nothing that might expose him to his chief's rebuke. They fought a grim and silent battle with one another. It was a test of endurance. The months passed, and neither gave sign of weakening. They were like men dwelling in regions of eternal night, and their souls were oppressed with the knowledge that never would the day dawn for them. It looked as though their lives would continue forever in this dull and hideous monotony of hatred.

And when at last the inevitable happened it came upon Mr. Warburton with all the shock of the unexpected. Cooper accused the boy Abas of stealing some of his clothes, and when the boy denied the theft took him by the scruff of the neck and kicked him down the steps of the bungalow. The boy demanded his wages, and Cooper flung at his head every word of abuse he knew. If he saw him in the compound in an hour he would hand him over to the police. Next morning the boy waylaid him outside the Fort when he was walking over to his office, and again demanded his wages. Cooper struck him in the face with his clenched fist. The boy fell to the ground and got up with blood streaming from his nose.

Cooper walked on and set about his work. But he could not attend to it. The blow had calmed his irritation, and he knew that he had gone too far. He was worried. He felt ill, miserable, and discouraged. In the adjoining office sat Mr. Warburton, and his impulse was to go and tell him what he had done; he made a movement in his chair, but he knew with what icy scorn he would listen to the story. He could see his patronizing smile. For a moment he had an uneasy fear of what Abas might do. Warburton had warned him all right. He sighed. What a fool he had been! But he shrugged his shoulders impatiently. He did not care; a fat lot he had to live for. It was all Warburton's fault; if he hadn't put his back up nothing like this would have happened. Warburton had made life a hell for him from the start. The snob. But they were all like that: It was because he was a Colonial. It was a damned shame that he had never got his commission in the war; he was as good as anyone else. They were a lot of dirty snobs. He was damned if he was going to knuckle under now. Of course Warburton would hear of what had happened; the old devil knew everything. He wasn't afraid. He wasn't afraid of any Malay in Borneo, and Warburton could go to blazes.

He was right in thinking that Mr. Warburton would know what had happened. His head boy told him when he went in to tiffin.

"Where is your nephew now?"

"I do not know, Tuan. He has gone."

Mr. Warburton remained silent. After luncheon as a rule he slept a little, but today he found himself very wide awake. His eyes involuntarily sought the bungalow where Cooper was now resting.

The idiot! Hesitation for a little was in Mr. Warburton's mind. Did the man know in what peril he was? He supposed he ought to send for him. But each time he had tried to reason with Cooper, Cooper had insulted him. Anger, furious anger welled up suddenly in Mr. Warburton's heart, so that the veins on his temples stood out and he clenched his fists. The cad had had his warning. Now let him take what was coming to him. It was no business of his and if anything happened it was not his fault. But perhaps they would wish in Kuala Solor that they had taken his advice and transferred Cooper to another station.

He was strangely restless that night. After dinner he walked up and down the verandah. When the boy went away to his own quarters, Mr. Warburton asked him whether anything had been seen of Abas.

"No, Tuan, I think maybe he has gone to the village of his mother's brother."

Mr. Warburton gave him a sharp glance, but the boy was looking down and their eyes did not meet. Mr. Warburton went down to the river and sat in his arbor. But peace was denied him. The river flowed ominously silent. It was like a great serpent gliding with sluggish movement towards the sea. And the trees of the jungle over the water were heavy with a breathless menace. No bird sang. No breeze ruffled the leaves of the cassias. All around him it seemed as though something waited.

He walked across the garden to the road. He had Cooper's bungalow in full view from there. There was a light in his sitting room and across the road floated the sound of ragtime. Cooper was playing his gramophone. Mr. Warburton shuddered; he had never got over his instinctive dislike of that instrument. But for that he would have gone over and spoken to Cooper. He turned and went back to his own house. He read late into the night, and at last he slept. But he did not sleep very long, he had terrible dreams, and he seemed to be awakened by a cry. Of course that was a dream too, for no cry— from the bungalow for instance—could be heard in his room. He lay awake till dawn. Then he heard hurried steps and the sound of voices, his head boy burst suddenly into the room without his fez, and Mr. Warburton's heart stood still.

"Tuan, Tuan."

Mr. Warburton jumped out of bed.

"I'll come at once."

He put on his slippers, and in his sarong and pyjama jacket walked across his compound and into Cooper's. Cooper was lying in bed, with his mouth open, and a kris sticking in his heart. He had been killed in his sleep. Mr. Warburton started, but not because he had not expected to see just such a sight, he started because he felt in himself a sudden glow of exultation. A great burden had been lifted from his shoulders.

Cooper was quite cold. Mr. Warburton took the kris out of the wound, it had been thrust in with such force that he had to use an effort to get it out, and looked at it. He recognized it. It was a kris that a dealer had offered him some weeks before and which he knew Cooper had bought.

"Where is Abas?" he asked sternly.

"Abas is at the village of his mother's brother."

The sergeant of the native police was standing at the foot of the bed.

"Take two men and go to the village and arrest him."

Mr. Warburton did what was immediately necessary. With set face he gave orders. His words were short and peremptory. Then he went back to the Fort. He shaved and had his bath, dressed and went into the dining room. By the side of his plate The Times in its wrapper lay waiting for him. He helped himself to some fruit. The head boy poured out his tea while the second handed him a dish of eggs. Mr. Warburton ate with a good appetite. The head boy waited.

"What is it?" asked Mr. Warburton.

"Tuan, Abas, my nephew, was in the house of his mother's brother all night. It can be proved. His uncle will swear that he did not leave the kampong."

Mr. Warburton turned upon him with a frown.

"Tuan Cooper was killed by Abas. You know it as well as I know. Justice must be done."

"Tuan, you would not hang him?"

Mr. Warburton hesitated an instant, and though his voice remained set and stern a change came into his eyes. It was a flicker which the Malay was quick to notice and across his own eyes flashed an answering look of understanding.

"The provocation was very great. Abas will be sentenced to a term of imprisonment." There was a pause while Mr. Warburton helped himself to marmalade. "When he has served a part of his sentence in prison I will take him into this house as a boy. You can train him in his duties. I have no doubt that in the house of Tuan Cooper he got into bad habits."

"Shall Abas give himself up, Tuan?"

"It would be wise of him."

The boy withdrew. Mr. Warburton took his Times and neatly slit the wrapper. He loved to unfold the heavy, rustling pages. The morning, so fresh and cool, was delicious and for a moment his eyes wandered out over his garden with a friendly glance. A great weight had been lifted from his mind. He turned to the columns in which were announced the births, deaths, and marriages. That was what he always looked at first. A name he knew caught his attention. Lady Ormskirk had had a son at last. By George, how pleased the old dowager must be! He would write her a note of congratulation by the next mail.

Abas would make a very good house boy.

That fool Cooper!

The Outstation

For Analysis

1. Warburton is spoken of as loving the Malayans. What form does this love take? How does Warburton's relationship to his head servant illustrate the deficiency of such love?
2. Do you think Cooper deserved a service commission? Why or why not?

3. What is the difference between the motives of Abas and Warburton for wanting Cooper dead? Which has the more valid motive?
4. What is the difference between Warburton and his fellow administrators at Kuala Solor? Is Cooper's lumping them together as snobs justified?
5. Why is Warburton uneasy in the presence of whites?

Eudora Welty

Death of a Travelling Salesman

R. J. Bowman, who for fourteen years had travelled for a shoe company through Mississippi, drove his Ford along a rutted dirt path. It was a long day! The time did not seem to clear the noon hurdle and settle into soft afternoon. The sun, keeping its strength here even in winter, stayed at the top of the sky, and every time Bowman stuck his head out of the dusty car to stare up the road, it seemed to reach a long arm down and push against the top of his head, right through his hat—like the practical joke of an old drummer, long on the road. It made him feel all the more angry and helpless. He was feverish, and he was not quite sure of the way.

This was his first day back on the road after a long seige of influenza. He had had very high fever, and dreams, and had become weakened and pale, enough to tell the difference in the mirror, and he could not think clearly. . . . All afternoon, in the midst of his anger, and for no reason, he had thought of his dead grandmother. She had been a comfortable soul. Once more Bowman wished he could fall into the big feather bed that had been in her room. . . . Then he forgot her again.

This desolate hill country! And he seemed to be going the wrong way—it was as if he were going back, far back. There was not a house in sight. . . . There was no use wishing he were back in bed, though. By paying the hotel doctor his bill he had proved his recovery. He had not even been sorry when the pretty trained nurse said good-bye. He did not like illness, he distrusted it, as he distrusted the road without signposts. It angered him. He had given the nurse a really expensive bracelet, just because she was packing up her bag and leaving.

But now—what if in fourteen years on the road he had never been ill before and never had an accident? His record was broken, and he had even begun almost to question it. . . . He had gradually put up at better hotels, in the bigger towns, but weren't they all, eternally, stuffy in summer and draughty in winter? Women? He could only remember little rooms within little rooms, like a nest of Chinese paper boxes, and if he thought of one woman he saw the worn loneliness that the furniture of that room seemed built of. And he himself—he was a man who always wore rather wide-brimmed black hats, and in the wavy hotel mirrors had looked something like a bullfighter, as he paused for that inevitable instant on the landing, walking downstairs to supper. . . . He leaned out of the car again, and once more the sun pushed at his head.

Bowman had wanted to reach Beulah by dark, to go to bed and sleep off his fatigue. As he remembered, Beulah was fifty miles away from the last town, on a graveled road. This was only a cow trail. How had he ever come to such a place? One hand wiped the sweat from his face, and he drove on.

He had made the Beulah trip before. But he had never seen this hill or this petering-out path before—or that cloud, he thought shyly, looking up and then down quickly—any more than he had seen this day before. Why did he not admit he was simply lost and had been for miles? . . . He was not in the habit of asking the way of strangers, and these people never knew where the very roads they lived on went to; but then he had not even been close enough to anyone to call out. People standing in the fields now and then, or on top of the haystacks, had been too far away, looking like leaning sticks or weeds, turning a little at the solitary rattle of his car across their countryside, watching the pale sobered winter dust where it chunked out behind like big squashes down the road. The stares of these distant people had followed him solidly like a wall, impenetrable, behind which they turned back after he had passed.

The cloud floated there to one side like the bolster on his grandmother's bed. It went over a cabin on the edge of a hill, where two bare chinaberry trees clutched at the sky. He drove through a heap of dead oak leaves, his wheels stirring their weightless sides to make a silvery melancholy whistle as the car passed through their bed. No car had been along this way ahead of him. Then he saw that he was on the edge of a ravine that fell away, a red erosion, and that this was indeed the road's end.

He pulled the brake. But it did not hold, though he put all his strength into it. The car, tipped toward the edge, rolled a little. Without doubt, it was going over the bank.

He got out quietly, as though some mischief had been done him and he had his dignity to remember. He lifted his bag and sample case out, set them down, and stood back and watched the car roll over the edge. He heard something—not the crash he was listening for, but a slow unuproarious crackle. Rather distastefully he went to look over, and he saw that his car had fallen into a tangle of immense grape vines as thick as his arm, which caught it and held it, rocked it like a grotesque child in a dark cradle, and then, as he watched, concerned somehow that he was not still inside it, released it gently to the ground.

He sighed.

Where am I? he wondered with a shock. Why didn't I do something? All his anger seemed to have drifted away from him. There was the house, back on the hill. He took a bag in each hand and with almost childlike willingness went toward it. But his breathing came with difficulty, and he had to stop to rest.

It was a shotgun house, two rooms and an open passage between, perched on the hill. The whole cabin slanted a little under the heavy heaped-up vine that covered the roof, light and green, as though forgotten from summer. A woman stood in the passage.

He stopped still. Then all of a sudden his heart began to behave strangely. Like a rocket set off, it began to leap and expand into uneven patterns of beats which showered into his brain, and he could not think. But in scattering and falling it made no noise. It shot up with great power, almost elation, and fell gently, like acrobats into nets. It began to pound profoundly, then waited irresponsibly, hitting in some sort of inward mockery first at his ribs, then against his eyes, then under his shoulder blades, and against the roof of his mouth when he tried to say, "Good afternoon, madam." But he could not hear his heart—it was as quiet as ashes falling. This was rather comforting; still, it was shocking to Bowman to feel his heart beating at all.

Stockstill in his confusion, he dropped his bags, which seemed to drift in slow bulks gracefully through the air and to cushion themselves on the gray prostrate grass near the doorstep.

As for the woman standing there, he saw at once that she was old. Since she could not possibly hear his heart, he ignored the pounding and now looked at her carefully, and yet in his distraction dreamily, with his mouth open.

She had been cleaning the lamp, and held it, half blackened, half clear, in front of her. He saw her with the dark passage behind her. She was a big woman with a weather beaten but unwrinkled face; her lips were held tightly together, and her eyes looked with a curious dulled brightness into his. He looked at her shoes, which were like bundles. If it were summer she would be barefoot. . . . Bowman, who automatically judged a woman's age on sight, set her age at fifty. She wore a formless garment of some gray coarse material, rough-dried from a washing, from which her arms appeared pink and unexpectedly round. When she never said a word, and sustained her quiet pose of holding the lamp, he was convinced of the strength in her body.

"Good afternoon, madam," he said.

She stared on, whether at him or at the air around him he could not tell, but after a moment she lowered her eyes to show that she would listen to whatever he had to say.

"I wonder if you would be interested—" He tried once more. "An accident—my car. . . ."

Her voice emerged low and remote, like a sound across a lake. "Sonny he ain't here."

"Sonny?"

"Sonny ain't here now."

Her son—a fellow able to bring my car up, he decided in blurred relief. He pointed down the hill. "My car's in the bottom of the ditch. I'll need help."

"Sonny ain't here, but he'll be here."

She was becoming clearer to him and her voice stronger, and Bowman saw that she was stupid.

He was hardly surprised at the deepening postponement and tedium of his journey. He took a breath, and heard his voice speaking over the silent blows of his heart. "I was sick. I am not strong yet. . . . May I come in?"

He stooped and laid his big black hat over the handle on his bag. It was a humble motion, almost a bow, that instantly struck him as absurd and betraying of all his weakness. He looked up at the woman, the wind blowing his hair. He might have continued for a long time in this unfamiliar attitude; he had never been a patient man, but when he was sick he had learned to sink submissively into the pillows, to wait for his medicine. He waited on the woman.

Then she, looking at him with blue eyes, turned and held open the door, and after a moment Bowman, as if convinced in his action, stood erect and followed her in.

Inside, the darkness of the house touched him like a professional hand, the doctor's. The woman set the half-cleaned lamp on a table in the center of the room and pointed, also like a professional person, a guide, to a chair with a yellow cowhide seat. She herself crouched on the hearth, drawing her knees up under the shapeless dress.

At first he felt hopefully secure. His heart was quieter. The room was enclosed in the gloom of yellow pine boards. He could see the other room, with the foot of an iron bed showing, across the passage. The bed had been made up with a red-and-yellow pieced quilt that looked like a map of a picture, a little like his grandmother's girlhood painting of Rome burning.

He had ached for coolness, but in this room it was cold. He stared at the hearth with dead coals lying on it and iron pots in the corners. The hearth and smoked chimney were of the stone he had seen ribbing the hills, mostly slate. Why is there no fire? he wondered.

And it was so still. The silence of the fields seemed to enter and move familiarly through the house. The wind used the open hall. He felt that he was in a mysterious, quiet, cool danger. It was necessary to do what? . . . To talk.

"I have a nice line of women's low priced shoes . . ." he said.

But the woman answered, "Sonny'll be here. He's strong. Sonny'll move your car."

"Where is he now?"

"Farms for Mr. Redmond."

Mr. Redmond. Mr. Redmond. That was someone he would never

have to encounter, and he was glad. Somehow the name did not appeal to him. . . . In a flare of touchiness and anxiety, Bowman wished to avoid even mention of unknown men and their unknown farms.

"Do you two live here alone?" He was surprised to hear his old voice, chatty, confidential, inflected for selling shoes, asking a question like that—a thing he did not even want to know.

"Yes. We are alone."

He was surprised at the way she answered. She had taken a long time to say that. She had nodded her head in a deep way too. Had she wished to affect him with some sort of premonition? he wondered unhappily. Or was it only that she would not help him, after all, by talking with him? For he was not strong enough to receive the impact of unfamiliar things without a little talk to break their fall. He had lived a month in which nothing had happened except in his head and his body—an almost inaudible life of heartbeats and dreams that came back, a life of fever and privacy, a delicate life which had left him weak to the point of—what? Of begging. The pulse in his palm leapt like a trout in a brook.

He wondered over and over why the woman did not go ahead with cleaning the lamp. What prompted her to stay there across the room, silently bestowing her presence upon him? He saw that with her it was not a time for doing little tasks. Her face was grave; she was feeling how right she was. Perhaps it was only politeness. In docility he held his eyes stiffly wide; they fixed themselves on the woman's clasped hands as though she held the cord they were strung on.

Then, "Sonny's coming," she said.

He himself had not heard anything, but there came a man passing the window and then plunging in at the door, with two hounds beside him. Sonny was a big enough man, with his belt slung low about his hips. He looked at least thirty. He had a hot, red face that was yet full of silence. He wore muddy blue pants and an old military coat stained and patched. World War? Bowman wondered. Great God, it was a Confederate coat. On the back of his light hair he had a wide filthy black hat which seemed to insult Bowman's own. He pushed down the dogs from his chest. He was strong with dignity and heaviness in his way of moving. . . . There was the resemblance to his mother.

They stood side by side. . . . He must account again for his presence here.

"Sonny, this man, he had his car to run off over the prec'pice an' wants to know if you will git it out for him," the woman said after a few minutes.

Bowman could not even state his case.

Sonny's eyes lay upon him.

He knew he should offer explanations and show money—at least appear either penitent or authoritative. But all he could do was to shrug slightly.

Sonny brushed by him going to the window, followed by the eager dogs, and looked out. There was effort even in the way he was looking, as if he could throw his sight out like a rope. Without turning Bowman felt that his own eyes could have seen nothing: It was too far.

"Got me a mule out there an' got me a block an' tackle," said Sonny meaningfully. "I *could* catch me my mule an' get me my ropes, an' before long I'd git your car out the ravine."

He looked completely round the room, as if in meditation, his eyes roving in their own distance. Then he pressed his lips firmly and yet shyly together, and with the dogs ahead of him this time, he lowered his head and strode out. The hard earth sounded, cupping to his powerful way of walking—almost a stagger.

Mischievously, at the suggestion of those sounds, Bowman's heart leapt again. It seemed to walk about inside him.

"Sonny's goin' to do it," the woman said. She said it again, singing it almost, like a song. She was sitting in her place by the hearth.

Without looking out, he heard some shouts and the dogs barking and the pounding of hoofs in short runs on the hill. In a few minutes Sonny passed under the window with a rope, and there was a brown mule with quivering, shining, purple-looking ears. The mule actually looked in the window. Under its eyelashes it turned targetlike eyes into his. Bowman averted his head and saw the woman looking serenely back at the mule, with only satisfaction in her face.

She sang a little more, under her breath. It occurred to him, and it seemed quite marvelous, that she was not really talking to him, but rather following the thing that came about with words that were unconscious and part of her looking.

So he said nothing, and this time when he did not reply he felt a curious and strong emotion, not fear, rise up in him.

This time, when his heart leapt, something—his soul—seemed to leap too, like a little colt invited out of a pen. He stared at the woman while the frantic nimbleness of his feeling made his head sway. He could not move; there was nothing he could do, unless perhaps he might embrace this woman who sat there growing old and shapeless before him.

But he wanted to leap up, to say to her, I have been sick and I found out then, only then, how lonely I am. Is it too late? My heart puts up a struggle inside me, and you may have heard it, protesting against emptiness. . . . It should be full, he would rush on to tell her, thinking of his heart now as a deep lake, it should be holding love like other hearts. It should be flooded with love. There would be a warm spring day. . . . Come and stand in my heart, whoever you are, and a whole river would cover your feet and rise higher and take your knees in whirlpools, and draw you down to itself, your whole body, your heart too.

But he moved a trembling hand across his eyes, and looked at the placid crouching woman across the room. She was still as a statue. He felt ashamed and exhausted by the thought that he might, in one more moment, have tried by simple words and embraces to communicate some strange thing—something which seemed always to have just escaped him. . . .

Sunlight touched the farthest pot on the hearth. It was late afternoon. This time tomorrow he would be somewhere on a good graveled road, driving his car past things that happened to people, quicker than their happening. Seeing ahead to the next day, he was glad, and knew that this was no time to embrace an old woman. He could feel in his pounding temples the readying of his blood for motion and for hurrying away.

"Sonny's hitched up your car by now," said the woman. "He'll git it out the ravine right shortly."

"Fine!" he cried with his customary enthusiasm.

Yet it seemed a long time that they waited. It began to get dark. Bowman was cramped in his chair. Any man should know enough to get up and walk around while he waited. There was something like guilt in such stillness and silence.

But instead of getting up, he listened. . . . His breathing restrained, his eyes powerless in the growing dark, he listened uneasily for a warning sound, forgetting in wariness what it would be. Before long he heard something—soft, continuous, insinuating.

"What's the noise?" he asked, his voice jumping into the dark.

Then wildly he was afraid it would be his heart beating so plainly in the quiet room, and she would tell him so.

"You might hear the stream," she said grudgingly.

Her voice was closer. She was standing by the table. He wondered why she did not light the lamp. She stood there in the dark and did not light it.

Bowman would never speak to her now, for the time was past. I'll sleep in the dark, he thought, in his bewilderment pitying himself.

Heavily she moved on to the window. Her arm, vaguely white, rose straight from her full side, and she pointed out into the darkness.

"That white speck's Sonny," she said, talking to herself.

He turned unwillingly and peered over her shoulder; he hesitated to rise and stand beside her. His eyes searched the dusky air. The white speck floated smoothly toward her finger, like a leaf on a river, growing whiter in the dark. It was as if she had shown him something secret, part of her life, but had offered no explanation. He looked away. He was moved almost to tears, feeling for no reason that she had made a silent declaration equivalent to his own. His hand waited upon his chest.

Then a step shook the house, and Sonny was in the room. Bowman felt how the woman left him there and went to the other man's side.

"I done got your car out, mister," said Sonny's voice in the dark. "She's settin' a-waitin' in the road, turned to go back where she came from."

"Fine!" said Bowman, projecting his own voice to loudness. "I'm surely much obliged—I could never have done it myself—I was sick. . . ."

"I could do it easy," said Sonny.

Bowman could feel them both waiting in the dark, and he could hear the dogs panting out in the yard, waiting to bark when he should go. He felt strangely helpless and resentful. Now that he could go, he longed to stay. From what was he being deprived? His chest was rudely shaken by the violence of his heart. These people cherished something here that he could not see, they withheld some ancient promise of food and warmth and light. Between them they had a conspiracy. He thought of the way she had moved away from him and gone to Sonny, she had flowed toward him. He was shaking with cold, he was tired, and it was not fair. Humbly and yet angrily he stuck his hand into his pocket.

"Of course I'm going to pay you for everything."

"We don't take money for such," said Sonny's voice belligerently.

"I want to pay. But do something more. . . . Let me stay—tonight.
. . ." He took another step toward them. If only they could see him,
they would know his sincerity, his real need! His voice went on,
"I'm not very strong yet, I'm not able to walk far, even back to my
car, maybe, I don't know—I don't know exactly where I am—"

He stopped. He felt as if he might burst into tears. What would
they think of him!

Sonny came over and put his hands on him. Bowman felt
them pass (they were professional too) across his chest, over his hips.
He could feel Sonny's eyes upon him in the dark.

"You ain't no revenuer come sneakin' here, mister, ain't got no
gun?"

To this end of nowhere! And yet *he* had come. He made a grave
answer. "No."

"You can stay."

"Sonny," said the woman, "you'll have to borry some fire."

"I'll go git it from Redmond's," said Sonny.

"What?" Bowman strained to hear their words to each other.

"Our fire, it's out, and Sonny's got to borry some, because it's dark
an' cold," she said.

"But matches—I have matches—"

"We don't have no need for 'em," she said proudly. "Sonny's goin'
after his own fire."

"I'm goin' to Redmond's," said Sonny with an air of importance,
and he went out.

After they had waited a while, Bowman looked out the window
and saw a light moving over the hill. It spread itself out like a little
fan. It zigzagged along the field, darting and swift, not like Sonny at
all. . . . Soon enough, Sonny staggered in, holding a burning stick
behind him in tongs, fire flowing in his wake, blazing light into the
corners of the room.

"We'll make a fire now," the woman said, taking the brand.

When that was done she lit the lamp. It showed its dark and light.
The whole room turned golden-yellow like some sort of flower, and
the walls smelled of it and seemed to tremble with the quiet rushing
of the fire and the waving of the burning lampwick in its funnel of
light.

The woman moved among the iron pots. With the tongs she dropped hot coals on top of the iron lids. They made a set of soft vibrations, like the sound of a bell far away.

She looked up and over at Bowman, but he could not answer. He was trembling. . . .

"Have a drink, mister?" Sonny asked. He had brought in a chair from another room and sat astride it with his folded arms across the back. Now we are all visible to one another, Bowman thought, and cried, "Yes, sir, you bet, thanks!"

"Come after me and do just what I do," said Sonny.

It was another excursion into the dark. They went through the hall, out to the back of the house, past a shed and a hooded well. They came to a wilderness of thicket.

"Down on your knees," said Sonny.

"What?" Sweat broke out on his forehead.

He understood when Sonny began to crawl through a sort of tunnel that the bushes made over the ground. He followed, startled in spite of himself when a twig or a thorn touched him gently without making a sound, clinging to him and finally letting him go.

Sonny stopped crawling and, crouched on his knees, began to dig with both his hands into the dirt. Bowman shyly struck matches and made a light. In a few minutes Sonny pulled up a jug. He poured out some of the whisky into a bottle from his coat pocket, and buried the jug again. "You never know who's liable to knock at your door," he said, and laughed. "Start back," he said, almost formally. "Ain't no need for us to drink outdoors like hogs."

At the table by the fire, sitting opposite each other in their chairs, Sonny and Bowman took drinks out of the bottle, passing it across. The dogs slept; one of them was having a dream.

"This is good," said Bowman. "That is what I needed." It was just as though he were drinking the fire off the hearth.

"He makes it," said the woman with quiet pride.

She was pushing the coals off the pots, and the smells of corn bread and coffee circled the room. She set everything on the table before the men, with a bone-handled knife stuck into one of the potatoes, splitting out its golden fiber. Then she stood for a minute looking at them, tall and full above them where they sat. She leaned a little toward them.

"You-all can eat now," she said, and suddenly smiled.

Bowman had just happened to be looking at her. He set his cup back on the table in unbelieving protest. A pain pressed at his eyes. He saw that she was not an old woman. She was young, still young. He could think of no number of years for her. She was the same age as Sonny, and she belonged to him. She stood with the deep dark corner of the room behind her, the shifting yellow light scattering over her head and her gray formless dress, trembling over her tall body when it bent over them in its sudden communication. She was young. Her teeth were shining and her eyes glowed. She turned and walked slowly and heavily out of the room, and he heard her sit down on the cot and then lie down. The pattern on the quilt moved.

"She goin' to have a baby," said Sonny, popping a bite into his mouth.

Bowman could not speak. He was shocked with knowing what was really in this house. A marriage, a fruitful marriage. That simple thing. Anyone could have had that.

Somehow he felt unable to be indignant or protest, although some sort of joke had certainly been played upon him. There was nothing remote or mysterious here—only something private. The only secret was the ancient communication between two people. But the memory of the woman's waiting silently by the cold hearth, of the man's stubborn journey a mile away to get fire and how they finally brought out their food and drink and filled the room proudly with all they had to show, was suddenly too clear and too enormous within him for response. . . .

"You ain't as hungry as you look," said Sonny.

The woman came out of the bedroom as soon as the men finished, and ate her supper while her husband stared peacefully into the fire.

Then they put the dogs out, with the food that was left.

"I think I'd better sleep here by the fire, on the floor," said Bowman.

He felt that he had been cheated, and that he could afford now to be generous. Ill though he was, he was not going to ask them for their bed. He was through with asking favors in this house, now that he understood what was there.

"Sure, mister."

But he had not known yet how slowly he understood. They had not meant to give him their bed. After a little interval they both rose and looking at him gravely went into the other room.

He lay stretched by the fire until it grew low and dying. He watched

every tongue of blaze lick out and vanish. "There will be special reduced prices on all footwear during the month of January," he found
himself repeating quietly, and then he lay with his lips tight shut.

How many noises the night had! He heard the stream running, the
fire dying, and he was sure now that he heard his heart beating, too,
the sound it made under his ribs. He heard breathing, round and deep,
the man and his wife in the room across the passage. And that was
all. But emotion swelled patiently within him, and he wished that
the child were his.

He must get back to where he had been before. He stood weakly
before the red coals, and put on his overcoat. It felt too heavy on his
shoulders. As he started out he looked and saw that the woman had
never got through with cleaning the lamp. On some impulse he put all
the money from his billfold under its fluted glass base, almost osten-
tatiously.

Ashamed, shrugging a little, and then shivering, he took his bags
and went out. The cold of the air seemed to lift him bodily. The moon
was in the sky.

On the slope he began to run, he could not help it. Just as he
reached the road, where his car seemed to sit in the moonlight like a
boat, his heart began to give off tremendous explosions like a rifle,
bang bang bang.

He sank in fright on to the road, his bags falling about him. He felt
as if all this had happened before. He covered his heart with both
hands to keep anyone from hearing the noise it made.

But nobody heard it.

Death of a Travelling Salesman

For Analysis

1. What is Bowman's attitude toward women when the story opens?
    How does this attitude change as the story progresses?
2. What is Bowman's relationship to his employer? Sonny's relationship
    to his?
3. What is the significance of Bowman's desire at one point to get back
    on a paved road in his automobile? What do the paved road and
    automobile come to symbolize?

4. Why is Sonny "belligerent" when Bowman attempts to pay him for recovering the car?
5. In what way is Bowman's "heart attack" symbolic?

James Thurber

The Secret Life
of Walter Mitty

"We're going through!" The Commander's voice was like thin ice breaking. He wore his full-dress uniform, with the heavily braided white cap pulled down rakishly over one cold gray eye. "We can't make it, sir. It's spoiling for a hurricane, if you ask me." "I'm not asking you, Lieutenant Berg," said the Commander. "Throw on the power light! Rev her up to 8,500! We're going through!" The pounding of the cylinders increased: ta-pocketa-pocketa-pocketa-*pocketa-pocketa*. The Commander stared at the ice forming on the pilot window. He walked over and twisted a row of complicated dials. "Switch on No. 8 auxiliary!" he shouted. "Switch on No. 8 auxiliary!" repeated Lieutenant Berg. "Full strength in No. 3 turret!" shouted the Commander. "Full strength in No. 3 turret!" The crew, bending to their various tasks in the huge, hurtling eight-engined Navy hydroplane, looked at each other and grinned. "The Old Man'll get us through," they said to one another. "The Old Man ain't afraid of Hell!" . . .

"Not so fast! You're driving too fast!" said Mrs. Mitty. "What are you driving so fast for?"

"Hmm?" said Walter Mitty. He looked at his wife, in the seat beside him, with shocked astonishment. She seemed grossly unfamiliar, like a strange woman who had yelled at him in a crowd. "You were up to fifty-five," she said. "You know I don't like to go more than forty. You were up to fifty-five." Walter Mitty drove on toward Waterbury in silence, the roaring of the SN202 through the worst storm in twenty years of Navy flying fading in the remote, intimate airways of his mind. "You're tensed up again," said Mrs. Mitty. "It's one of your days. I wish you'd let Dr. Renshaw look you over."

Walter Mitty stopped the car in front of the building where his wife went to have her hair done. "Remember to get those overshoes while I'm having my hair done," she said. "I don't need overshoes," said Mitty. She put her mirror back into her bag. "We've been all through that," she said, getting out of the car. "You're not a young man any longer." He raced the engine a little. "Why don't you wear your gloves? Have you lost your gloves?" Walter Mitty reached in a pocket and brought out the gloves. He put them on, but after she had turned and gone into the building and he had driven on to a red light, he took them off again. "Pick it up, brother!" snapped a cop as the light changed, and Mitty hastily pulled on his gloves and lurched ahead. He drove around the streets aimlessly for a time, and then he drove past the hospital on his way to the parking lot.

. . . "It's the millionaire banker, Wellington McMillan," said the pretty nurse. "Yes?" said Walter Mitty, removing his gloves slowly. "Who has the case?" "Dr. Renshaw and Dr. Benbow, but there are two specialists here, Dr. Remington from New York and Mr. Pritchard-Mitford from London. He flew over." A door opened down a long, cool corridor and Dr. Renshaw came out. He looked distraught and haggard. "Hello, Mitty," he said. "We're having the devil's own time with McMillan, the millionaire banker and close personal friend of Roosevelt. Obstreosis of the ductal tract. Tertiary. Wish you'd take a look at him." "Glad to," said Mitty.

In the operating room there were whispered introductions: "Dr. Remington, Dr. Mitty. Mr. Pritchard-Mitford, Dr. Mitty." "I've read your book on streptothricosis," said Pritchard-Mitford, shaking hands. "A brilliant performance, sir." "Thank you," said Walter Mitty. "Didn't know you were in the States, Mitty," grumbled Remington. "Coals to Newcastle, bringing Mitford and me up here for a tertiary." "You are very kind," said Mitty. A huge, complicated machine, connected to the operating table, with many tubes and wires, began at this moment to go pocketa-pocketa-pocketa. "The new anesthetizer is giving way!" shouted an intern. "There is

no one in the East who knows how to fix it!" "Quiet, man!" said
Mitty, in a low, cool voice. He sprang to the machine, which was
now going pocketa-pocketa-queep-pocketa-queep. He began fingering delicately a row of glistening dials.

"Give me a fountain pen!" he snapped. Someone handed him
a fountain pen. He pulled a faulty piston out of the machine and
inserted the pen in its place. "That will hold for ten minutes," he said.
"Get on with the operation." A nurse hurried over and whispered to
Renshaw, and Mitty saw the man turn pale. "Coreopsis has set in,"
said Renshaw nervously. "If you would take over, Mitty?" Mitty
looked at him and at the craven figure of Benbow, who drank, and
at the grave, uncertain faces of the two great specialists. "If you wish,"
he said. They slipped a white gown on him; he adjusted a mask and
drew on thin gloves; nurses handed him shining. . . .

"Back it up, Mac! Look out for that Buick!" Walter Mitty jammed
on the brakes. "Wrong lane, Mac," said the parking lot attendant,
looking at Mitty closely. "Gee. Yeh," muttered Mitty. He began cautiously to back out of the lane marked "Exit Only." "Leave her sit
there," said the attendant. "I'll put her away." Mitty got out of the
car. "Hey, better leave the key." "Oh" said Mitty, handing the man
the ignition key. The attendant vaulted into the car, backed it up
with insolent skill, and put it where it belonged.

They're so damn cocky, thought Walter Mitty, walking along Main
Street; they think they know everything. Once he had tried to take
his chains off, outside New Milford, and he had got them wound
around the axles. A man had had to come out in a wrecking car and
unwind them, a young, grinning garageman. Since then Mrs. Mitty
always made him drive to a garage to have the chains taken off. The
next time, he thought, I'll wear my right arm in a sling; they won't
grin at me then. I'll have my right arm in a sling and they'll see I
couldn't possibly take the chains off myself. He kicked at the slush on
the sidewalk. "Overshoes," he said to himself, and he began looking for a shoe store.

When he came out into the street again, with the overshoes in a
box under his arm, Walter Mitty began to wonder what the other
thing was his wife had told him to get. She had told him twice, before
they set out from their house for Waterbury. In a way he hated these
weekly trips to town—he was always getting something wrong.
Kleenex, he thought, Squibb's, razor blades? No. Toothpaste, tooth-

brush, bicarbonate, carborundum, initiative and referendum? He gave it up. But she would remember it. "Where's the what's-its-name?" she would ask. "Don't tell me you forgot the what's-its-name." A newsboy went by shouting something about the Water-bury trial.

. . . "Perhaps this will refresh your memory." The District At-torney suddenly thrust a heavy automatic at the quiet figure on the witness stand. "Have you ever seen this before?" Walter Mitty took the gun and examined it expertly. "This is my Webley-Vickers 50.80," he said calmly. An excited buzz ran around the courtroom. The judge rapped for order. "You are a crack shot with any sort of fire-arms, I believe?" said the District Attorney, insinuatingly. "Objec-tion!" shouted Mitty's attorney. "We have shown that the de-fendant could not have fired the shot. We have shown that he wore his right arm in a sling on the night of the fourteenth of July." Walter Mitty raised his hand briefly and the bickering attorneys were stilled. "With any known make of gun," he said evenly, "I could have killed Gregory Fitzhurst at three hundred feet *with my left hand*." Pande-monium broke loose in the courtroom. A woman's scream rose above the bedlam and suddenly a lovely, dark-haired girl was in Walter Mitty's arms. The District Attorney struck at her savagely. Without rising from his chair, Mitty let the man have it on the point of the chin. "You miserable cur!" . . .

"Puppy biscuit," said Walter Mitty. He stopped walking and the buildings of Waterbury rose up out of the misty courtroom and sur-rounded him again. A woman who was passing laughed. "He said 'Puppy biscuit,' " she said to her companion. "That man said 'Puppy biscuit' to himself." Walter Mitty hurried on. He went into an A. & P., not the first one he came to but a smaller one farther up the street. "I want some biscuit for small, young dogs," he said to the clerk. "Any special brand, sir?" The greatest pistol shot in the world thought a moment. "It says 'Puppies Bark for It' on the box," said Walter Mitty.

His wife would be through at the hairdresser's in fifteen minutes, Mitty saw in looking at his watch, unless they had trouble drying it; sometimes they had trouble drying it. She didn't like to get to the hotel first; she would want him to be there waiting for her as usual. He found a big leather chair in the lobby, facing a window, and he put the overshoes and the puppy biscuit on the floor beside it. He picked up an old copy of *Liberty* and sank down into the chair. "Can Germany Conquer the World Through the Air?" Walter Mitty looked at the pictures of bombing planes and of ruined streets.

. . ."The cannonading has got the wind up in young Raleigh, sir," said the sergeant. Captain Mitty looked up at him through tousled hair. "Get him to bed," he said wearily. "With the others. I'll fly alone." "But you can't, sir," said the sergeant anxiously. "It takes two men to handle that bomber and the Archies are pounding hell out of the air. Von Richtman's circus is between here and Saulier." "Somebody's got to get that ammunition dump," said Mitty. "I'm going over. Spot of brandy?" He poured a drink for the sergeant and one for himself. War thundered and whined around the dugout and battered at the door. There was a rending of wood and splinters flew through the room. "A bit of a near thing," said Captain Mitty carelessly. "The box barrage is closing in," said the sergeant. "We only live once, Sergeant," said Mitty, with his faint, fleeting smile. "Or do we?" He poured another brandy and tossed it off. "I never see a man could hold his brandy like you, sir," said the sergeant. "Begging your pardon, sir." Captain Mitty stood up and strapped on his huge Webley-Vickers automatic. "It's forty kilometers through hell, sir," said the sergeant. Mitty finished one last brandy. "After all," he said softly, "What isn't?" The pounding of the cannon increased; there was the rat-tat-tatting of machine guns, and from somewhere came the menacing pocketa-pocketa-pocketa of the new flamethrowers. Walter Mitty walked to the door of the dugout humming "Auprés de Ma Blonde." He turned and waved to the sergeant. "Cheerio!" he said. . . .

Something struck his shoulder. "I've been looking all over this hotel for you," said Mrs. Mitty. "Why do you have to hide in this old chair? How did you expect me to find you?" "Things close in," said Walter Mitty vaguely. "What?" Mrs. Mitty said. "Did you get the what's-its-name? The puppy biscuit? What's in that box?" "Overshoes," said Mitty. "Couldn't you have put them on in the store?" "I was thinking," said Walter Mitty. "Does it ever occur to you that I am sometimes thinking?" She looked at him. "I'm going to take your temperature when I get you home," she said.

They went out through the revolving doors that made a faintly derisive whistling sound when you pushed them. It was two blocks to the parking lot. At the drugstore on the corner she said, "Wait here for me. I forgot something. I won't be a minute." She was more than a minute. Walter Mitty lighted a cigarette. It began to rain, rain with sleet in it. He stood up against the wall of the drugstore, smoking. . . . He put his shoulders back and his heels together. "To hell with the handkerchief," said Walter Mitty scornfully. He took one last drag on his cigarette and snapped it away. Then, with that faint, fleeting smile playing about his lips, he faced the firing squad; erect and motionless, proud and disdainful, Walter Mitty the Undefeated, inscrutable to the last.

The Secret Life of Walter Mitty

For Analysis

1. What are the common characteristics of Mitty's fantasies? How do they define an image of masculinity?
2. Does Mitty's wife understand his mental processes? How would you describe the type of control she has over him?
3. Some concepts, such as a hospital, dog, and sling, figure both in Mitty's normal existence and in his secret life. How does Mitty's process of association relate them on the two levels?
4. The last sentence in the story describes Mitty as "the Undefeated, inscrutable to the last." What meanings can you derive from this statement?
5. How do the secret lives of Walter Mitty and Paul Haselman of "Silent Snow, Secret Snow" compare?

Wilbur Daniel Steele

The Man Who Saw
Through Heaven

People have wondered (there being obviously no question of romance involved) how I could ever have allowed myself to be let in
for the East African adventure of Mrs. Diana in search of her husband. There were several reasons. To begin with, the time and effort
and money weren't mine; they were the property of the wheel of
which I was but a cog, the Society through which Diana's life had
been insured, along with the rest of that job-lot of missionaries. The
"letting in" was the firm's. In the second place, the wonderers have
not counted on Mrs. Diana's capacity for getting things done for her.
Meek and helpless. Yes, but God was on her side. Too meek, too
helpless to move mountains herself, if those who happened to be
handy didn't move them for her then her God would know the reason
why. Having dedicated her all to making straight the Way, why
should her neighbor cavil at giving a little? The writer for one,
a colonial governor general for another, railway magnates, insurance managers, *safari* leaders, the ostrich-farmer of Ndua, all these
and a dozen others in their turns have felt the hundred-ton weight of
her thin-lipped meekness—have seen her in metaphor sitting grimly
on the doorsteps of their souls.

A third reason lay in my own troubled conscience. Though I did
it in innocence, I can never forget that it was I who personally conducted Diana's party to the observatory on that fatal night in Boston
before it sailed. Had it not been for that kindly intentioned "hunch"
of mine, the astounded eye of the Reverend Hubert Diana would
never have gazed through the floor of Heaven, he would never have
undertaken to measure the Infinite with the footrule of his mind.

It all started so simply. My boss at the shipping-and-insurance office gave me the word in the morning. "Bunch of missionaries for the *Platonic* tomorrow. They're on our hands in a way. Show 'em the town." It wasn't so easy when you think of it; one male and seven females on their way to the heathen; though it was easier in Boston than it might have been in some other towns. The evening looked the simplest. My friend Krum was at the Observatory that semester; there at least I was sure their sensibilities would come to no harm.

On the way out in the street car, seated opposite to Diana and having to make conversation, I talked of Krum and of what I knew of his work with the spiral nebulae. Having to appear to listen, Diana did so (as all day long) with a vaguely indulgent smile. He really hadn't time for me. That night his life was exalted as it had never been and would perhaps never be again. Tomorrow's sailing, the actual fact of leaving all to follow Him, held his imagination in thrall. Moreover, he was a bridegroom of three days with his bride beside him, his nerves at once assuaged and thrilled. No, but more. As if a bride were not enough, arrived in Boston, he had found himself surrounded by a very galaxy of womanhood gathered from the four corners; already within hours one felt the chaste tentacles of their feminine dependence curling about the party's unique man; already their contacts with the world of their new lives began to be made through him; already they saw in part through his eyes. I wonder what he would have said if I had told him he was a little drunk.

In the course of the day I think I had got him fairly well. As concerned his Church he was at once an asset and a liability. He believed its dogma as few still did, with a simplicity, "the old-time religion." He was born that kind. Of the stuff of the fanatic, the reason he was not a fanatic was that, curiously impervious to little questionings, he had never been aware that his faith was anywhere attacked. A self-educated man, he had accepted the necessary smattering facts of science with a serene indulgence, as simply so much further proof of what the Creator could do when He put His Hand to it. Nor was he conscious of any conflict between these facts and the fact that there existed a substantial Heaven, geographically up, and a substantial Hot Place, geographically down.

So, for his Church, he was an asset in these days. And so, and for the same reason, he was a liability. The Church must after all keep abreast of the times. For home consumption, with modern congregations, especially urban ones, a certain streak of "healthy" skepticism is no longer amiss in the pulpit; it makes people who read at all more comfortable in their pews. A man like Hubert Diana is more for the cause than a hundred. But what to do with him? Well, such things arrange themselves. There's the Foreign Field. The blacker the heathen the whiter the light they'll want, and the solider the conception of a God, the Father enthroned in a Heaven of which the sky above them is the visible floor.

And that, at bottom, was what Hubert Diana believed. Accept as he would with the top of his brain the fact of a spherical earth zooming through space, deep in his heart he knew that the world lay flat from modern Illinois to Ancient Palestine, and that the sky above it, blue by day and by night festooned with guiding stars for wise men, was the nether side of a floor on which the resurrected trod. . . .

I shall never forget the expression of his face when he realized he was looking straight through it that night. In the quiet dark of the dome I saw him remove his eye from the eyepiece of the telescope up there on the staging and turn it in the ray of a hooded bulb on the demon's keeper, Krum.

"What's that, Mr. Krum? I didn't get you!"

"I say, that particular cluster you're looking at—"

"This star, you mean?"

"You'd have to count a while to count the stars describing their orbits in that 'star,' Mr. Diana. But what I was saying—have you ever had the wish I used to have as a boy—that you could actually look back into the past? With your own two eyes?"

Diana spoke slowly. He didn't know it, but it had already begun to happen; he was already caught. "I have often wished, Mr. Krum, that I might actually look back into the time of our Lord. Actually. Yes."

Krum grunted. He was young. "We'd have to pick a nearer neighbor than *Messier 79* then. The event you see when you put your eye to that lens is happening much too far in the past. The light-waves thrown off by that particular cluster on the day, say, of the Crucifixion—*you* won't live to see them. They've hardly started yet—a mere twenty centuries on their way—leaving them something like eight hundred and thirty centuries yet to come before they reach the earth."

Diana laughed the queerest catch of a laugh. "And—and there— there won't be any earth here, then, to welcome them."

"*What?*" It was Krum's turn to look startled. So for a moment the two faces remained in confrontation, the one, as I say, startled, the other exuding visibly little sea-green globules of sweat. It was Diana that caved in first, his voice hardly louder than a whisper.

"W-w-will there?"

None of us suspected the enormousness of the thing that had happened in Diana's brain. Krum shrugged his shoulders and snapped his fingers. Deliberately. *Snap!* "What's a thousand centuries or so in the cosmic reckoning?" He chuckled. "We're just beginning to get out among 'em with *Messier*, you know. In the print room, Mr. Diana, I can show you photographs of clusters to which, if you cared to go, travelling at the speed of light—"

The voice ran on; but Diana's eye had gone back to the eyepiece, and his affrighted soul had reentered the big black tube sticking its snout out of the slit in the iron hemisphere. . . . "At the speed of light!" . . . That unsuspected, that wildly chance-found chink in the armor of his philosophy! The body is resurrected and it ascends to Heaven instantaneously. At what speed must it be borne to reach instantaneously that city beyond the ceiling of the sky? At a speed inconceivable, mystical. At, say (as he had often said to himself) *the speed of light*. . . . And now, hunched there in the trap that had caught him, black rods, infernal levers and wheels, he was aware of his own eye passing vividly through unpartitioned emptiness, *eight hundred and fifty centuries at the speed of light!*

"And still beyond these," Krum was heard, "we begin to come into the regions of the spiral nebulae. We've some interesting photographs in the print room, if you've the time."

The ladies below were tired of waiting. One had "lots of packing to do." The bride said, "Yes, I do think we should be getting along. Hubert, dear; if you're ready—"

The fellow actually jumped. It's lucky he didn't break anything. His face looked greener and dewier than ever amid the contraptions above. "If you—you and the ladies, Cora—wouldn't mind—if Mr.—Mr.—(he'd mislaid my name) would see you back to the hotel—" Meeting silence, he began to expostulate. "I feel that this is a rich experience. I'll follow shortly; I know the way."

In the car going back into the city Mrs. Diana set at rest the flut-

terings of six hearts. Being unmarried, they couldn't understand men
as she did. When I think of that face of hers, to which I was to grow
only too accustomed in the weary, itchy days of the trek into Kavirondoland, with its slightly tilted nose, its irregular pigmentation,
its easily inflamed lids, and the long moist cheeks, like a hunting
dog, glorying in weariness, it seems incredible that a light of coyness
could have found lodgment there. But that night it did. She sat serene
among her virgins.

"You don't know Bert. You wait; he'll get a perfectly wonderful
sermon out of that tonight, Bert will."

Krum was having a grand time with his neophyte. He would have
stayed up all night. Immured in the little print room covered with
files and redolent of acids, he conducted his disciple "glassy-eyed"
through the dim frontiers of space, holding before him one after
another the likenesses of universes sister to our own, islanded in
immeasurable vacancy, curled like glimmering crullers on their private Milky Ways, and hiding in their wombs their myriad "coal-
pockets," stardust fetuses of which—their quadrillion years accomplished—their litters of new suns would be born, to bear their
planets, to bear their moons in turn.

"And beyond these?"

Always, after each new feat of distance, it was the same. "And
beyond?" Given an ell, Diana surrendered to a popeyed lust for
nothing less than light-years. "And still beyond?"

"Who knows?"

"The mind quits. For if there's no end to these nebulae—"

"But supposing there is?"

"An end? But Mr. Krum, the very idea of an ending—"

"An end to what we might call this particular category of magnitudes. Eh?"

"I don't get that."

"Well, take this—take the opal in your ring there. The numbers
and distances inside that stone may conceivably be to themselves as
staggering as ours to us in our own system. Come! that's not so far-
fetched. What are we learning about the structure of the atom? A
nucleus (call it a sun) revolved about in eternal orbits by electrons
(call them planets, worlds). Infinitesimal; but after all what are
bigness and littleness but matters of comparison? To eyes on one of
those electrons (don't be too sure there aren't any) its tutelary sun

may flame its way across a heaven a comparative ninety million miles away. Impossible for them to conceive of a boundary to their billions of atomic systems, molecular universes. In that category of magnitudes its diameter is infinity; once it has made the leap into our category and become an opal it is merely a quarter of an inch. That's right, Mr. Diana, you may well stare at it: Between *now* and *now* ten thousand histories may have come and gone down there. . . . And just so the diameter of our own cluster of universes, going over into another category, may be—"

"May be a—ring—a little stone—in a—a—a—ring."

Krum was tickled by the way the man's imagination jumped and engulfed it.

"Why not? That's as good a guess as the next. A ring, let's say, worn carelessly on the—well, say the tentacle—of some vast organism —some inchoate creature hobnobbing with its cloudy kind in another system of universes—which in turn—"

It is curious that none of them realized next day that they were dealing with a stranger, a changed man. Why he carried on, why he capped that night of cosmic debauch by shaving, eating an unre-markable breakfast, packing his terrestrial toothbrush and collars, and going up the gangplank in tow of his excited convoy to sail away, is beyond explanation—unless it was simply that he was in a daze.

It wasn't until four years later that I was allowed to know what had happened on that ship, and even then the tale was so disjointed, warped, and opinionated, so darkly seen in the mirror of Mrs. Diana's orthodoxy, that I had almost to guess what it *really* was all about.

"When Hubert turned irreligious. . . . " That phrase, recurrent on her tongue in the meanderings of the East African quest to which we were by then committed, will serve to measure her understand-ing. Irreligious! Good Lord! But from that sort of thing I had to re-construct the drama. Evening after evening beside her camp fire (appended to the Mineral Survey Expedition Toward Uganda through the kindness—actually the worn-down surrender—of the Protectorate government) I lingered a while before joining the merrier engineers, watched with fascination the bumps growing under the mosquitoes on her forehead, and listened to the jargon of her mortified meekness and her scandalized faith.

There had been a fatal circumstance, it seems, at the very outset.

If Diana could but have been seasick, as the rest of them were (horribly), all might still have been well. In the misery of desired death, along with the other contents of a heaving midriff, he might have brought up the assorted universes of which he had been led too rashly to partake. But he wasn't. As if his wife's theory was right, as if Satan was looking out for him, he was spared to prowl the swooping decks immune. Four days and nights alone. Time enough to digest and assimilate into his being beyond remedy that lump of whirling magnitudes and to feel himself surrendering with a strange new ecstasy to the drunkenness of liberty.

Such liberty! Given Diana's type, it is hard to imagine it adequately. The abrupt, complete removal of the toils of reward and punishment; the withdrawal of the surveillance of an all-seeing, all-knowing Eye; the windy assurance of being responsible for nothing, important to no one, no longer (as the police say) "wanted!" It must have been beautiful in those few days of its first purity, before it began to be discolored by his contemptuous pity for others, the mask of his inevitable loneliness and his growing fright.

The first any of them knew of it—even his wife—was in midvoyage, the day the sea went down and the seven who had been sick came up. There seemed an especial Providence in the calming of the waters; it was Sunday morning and Diana had been asked to conduct the services.

He preached on the text: "For of such is the kingdom of Heaven."

"If our concept of God means anything it means a God *all*-mighty, Creator of *all* that exists, Director of the *infinite,* cherishing in His Heaven the saved souls of *all space and all time*."

Of course; amen. And wasn't it nice to feel like humans again, and real sunshine pouring up through the lounge ports from an ocean suddenly grown kind. . . . But—then—*what* was Diana *saying?*

Mrs. Diana couldn't tell about it coherently even after a lapse of fifty months. Even in a setting as remote from that steamer's lounge as the equatorial bush, the ember-reddened canopy of thorn trees, the meandering camp fires, the chant and tramp somewhere away of Kikuyu porters dancing in honor of an especial largesse of fat zebra meat—even here her memory of that impious outburst was too vivid, too aghast.

"It was Hubert's look! The way he stared at us! As if you'd said he was licking his chops! . . . That *Heaven* of his."

It seems they hadn't waked up to what he was about until he had the dimensions of his sardonic Paradise irreparably drawn in. The final haven of all right souls. Not alone the souls released from this our own tiny earth. In the millions of solar systems we see as stars how many millions of satellites must there be upon which at some time in their histories conditions suited to organic life subsist? Uncounted hordes of wheeling populations! Of men? God's creatures at all events, a portion of them reasoning. Weirdly shaped perhaps, but what of that? And that's only to speak of our own inconsiderable cluster of universes. That's to say nothing of other systems of magnitudes, where God's creatures are to our world what we are to the world's in the atoms in our finger rings. (He had shaken *his,* here, in their astounded faces.) And all these, all the generations of these enormous and microscopic beings harvested through a time beside which the life-span of our earth is as a second in a million centuries: All these brought to rest for an eternity to which time itself is a watchtick—all crowded to rest pell-mell, thronged, serried, packed, packed to suffocation in layers unnumbered light-years deep. This must needs to be our concept of Heaven if God is the God of the Whole. If, on the other hand—

The other hand was the hand of the second officer, the captain's delegate at divine worship that Sabbath day. He at last had "come to."

I don't know whether it was the same day or the next; Mrs. Diana was too vague. But here's the picture. Seven women huddled in the large stateroom on B-deck, conferring in whispers, aghast, searching one another's eyes obliquely even as they bowed their heads in prayer for some light—and of a sudden the putting back of the door and the inmarching of the Reverend Hubert. . . .

As Mrs. Diana tried to tell me, "You understand, don't you, he had just taken a bath? And he hadn't—he had forgotten to—"

Adam-innocent there he stood. Not a stitch. But I don't believe for a minute it was a matter of forgetting. In the high intoxication of his soul-release, already crossed (by the second officer) and beginning to show his zealot claws, he needed some gesture stunning enough to witness to his separation, his unique rightness, his contempt of match-flare civilizations and infinitesimal taboos.

But I can imagine that stateroom scene: The gasps, the heads colliding in aversion, and Diana's six weedy feet of birthday-suit towering in the shadows, and ready to sink through the deck I'll warrant, now the act was irrevocable, but still grimly carrying if off.

"And if, on the other hand, you ask me to bow down before a God peculiar to this one earth, this one grain of dust lost among the giants of space, watching its sparrows fall, profoundly interested in a speck called Palestine no bigger than the quadrillionth part of one of the atoms in the ring here on my finger—"

Really scared by this time, one of the virgins shrieked. It was altogether too close quarters with a madman.

Mad? Of course there was the presumption: "Crazy as a loon." Even legally it was so adjudged at the *Platonic's* first port-of-call, Algiers, where, when Diana escaped ashore and wouldn't come back again, he had to be given over to the workings of the French Law. I talked with the magistrate myself some forty months later, when, "let in" for the business as I have told, I stopped there on my way out.

"But what would you?" were his words. "We must live in the world as the world lives, is it not? Sanity? Sanity is what? Is it, for example, an intellectual clarity, a balanced perception of the realities? Naturally, speaking out of court, your friend was of a sanity—of a sanity, sir—" Here the magistrate made with thumb and fingers the gesture only the French can make for a thing that is matchless, a beauty, a transcendent instance of any kind. He himself was Gallic, rational. Then, with a lift of shoulder, "But what would you? We must live in the world that seems."

Diana, impounded in Algiers for deportation, escaped. What after all are the locks and keys of this pinchbeck category of magnitudes? More remarkable still, there in Arab Africa, he succeeded in vanishing from the knowledge and pursuit of men. And of women. His bride, now that their particular mission had fallen through, was left to decide whether to return to America or to go on with two of the company, the Misses Brookhart and Smutts, who were bound for a school in Smyrna. In the end she followed the latter course. It was there, nearly four years later, that I was sent to join her by an exasperated and worn-out Firm.

But that time she knew again where her husband-errant was—or where at least, from time to time in his starry dartings over this our mote of dust, he had been heard of, spoken to, seen.

Could we but have a written history of those years of his apostolic vagabondage, a record of the towns in which he was jailed or from which he was kicked out, of the ports in which he stowed away, presently to reveal himself in proselyting ardor, denouncing the earthlings, the fatelings, the dupes of bugaboo, meeting scoff with scoff, preaching the new revelation red-eyed, like an angry prophet. Or was it, more simply, like a man afraid?

Was that the secret, after all, of his prodigious restlessness? Had it anything in common with the swarming of those pale worms that flee the Eye of the Infinite around the curves of the stone you pick up in a field? Talk of the man without a country! What of the man without a universe?

It is curious that I never suspected his soul's dilemma until I saw the first of his mud-sculptures in the native village of Ndua in the province of Kasuma in British East. Here it was, our objective attained, we parted company with the government *safari* and shifted the burden of Way-straightening to the shoulders of Major Wyeside, the ostrich farmer of the neighborhood.

While still on the *safari* I had put to Mrs. Diana a question that had bothered me: "Why on earth should your husband ever have chosen this particular neck of the woods to land up in? Why Kavirondoland?"

"It was here we were coming at the time Hubert turned irreligious, to found a mission. It's a coincidence, isn't it?"

And yet I would have sworn Diana hadn't a sense of humor about him anywhere. But perhaps it *wasn't* an ironic act. Perhaps it was simply that, giving up the struggle with a society blinded by "a little learning" and casting about for a virgin field, he had remembered this.

"I supposed he was a missionary," Major Wyeside told us with a flavor of indignation. "I went on that. I let him live here—six or seven months of it—while he was learning the tongue. I was a bit nonplused, to put it mildly, when I discovered what he was up to."

What things Diana had been up to the Major showed us in one of the huts in the native kraal—a round dozen of them, modeled in mud and baked. Blackened blobs of mud, that's all. Likenesses of nothing under the sun, fortuitous masses sprouting haphazard tentacles, only two among them showing postules that might have been experimental heads. . . . The ostrich farmer saw our faces.

"Rum, eh? Of course I realized the chap was anything but fit. A walking skeleton. Nevertheless, whatever it is about these beasties, there's not a nigger in the village has dared set foot inside this hut since Diana left. You can see for yourselves its about to crash.

There's another like it he left at Suki, above here. Taboo, no end!"

So Diana's "hunch" had been right. He had found his virgin field indeed, fit soul for his cosmic fright. A religion in the making, here before our eyes.

"This was at the very last before he left," Wyeside explained. "He took to making these mudpies quite of a sudden; the whole lot within a fortnight's time. Before that he had simply talked, harangued. He would sit here in the doorway of an evening with the niggers squatted around and harangue 'em by the hour. I knew something of it through my houseboys. The most amazing rot. All about the stars to begin with, as if these black baboons could half grasp *astronomy!* But that seemed all proper. Then there was talk about a something a hundred times as big and powerful as the world, sun, moon, and stars put together—some perfectly enormous stupendous awful being—but knowing how mixed the boys can get, it still seemed all regular—simply the parson's way of getting at the notion of an Almighty God. But no, they insisted, there wasn't any God. That's the point, they said; there *is no* God. . . . Well, that impressed me as a go. That's when I decided to come down and get the rights of this star-swallowing monstrosity the beggar was feeding my labor on. And here he sat in the doorway with one of these beasties—here it is, this one—waving it furiously in the niggers' benighted faces. And do you know what he'd done?—you can see the mark here still on this wabble-leg, this tentacle-business—he had taken off a ring he had and screwed it on just here. His finger ring, my word of honor! And still, if you believe it, I didn't realize he was just daft. Not until he spoke to me. 'I find,' he was good enough to enlighten me, 'I find I have to make it somehow concrete.' . . . 'Make what?' . . . 'Our wearer' . . . 'Our *what, where?*' . . . 'In the following category.' . . . His actual words, honor bright. I was going to have him sent down-country where he could be looked after. He got ahead of me though. He cleared out. When I heard he'd turned up at Suki I ought, I suppose, to have attended to it. But I was having trouble with leopards. And you know how things go."

From there we went to Suki, the Major accompanying me. It was as like Ndua as one flea to its brother, a stockade inclosing round houses of mud, wattles, and thatch, and full of naked heathen. The Kavirondo are the nakedest of all African peoples and, it is said, the most moral. It put a great strain on Mrs. Diana; all that whole

difficult anxious time, as it were detachedly, I could see her itching
to get them into Mother Hubbards and cast-off Iowa pants.

Here too, as the Major had promised, we found a holy of holies,
rather a dreadful of dreadfuls, "taboo no end." Its shadows cluttered
with the hurlothrumbos of Diana's artistry. What puzzled me was
their number. Why this appetite for experimentation? There was
an uncertainty; one would think its effect on potential converts would
be bad. Here, as in Ndua, Diana had contented himself at first with
words and skyward gesticulations. Not for so long however. Feeling
the need of giving his concept of the cosmic "wearer" a substance
much earlier, he had shut himself in with the work, literally—a fever
of creation. We counted seventeen of the nameless "blobs," all done,
we were told, in the seven days and nights before their maker had
again cleared out. The villagers would hardly speak of him; only after
spitting, their eyes averted, and in an undertone, would they mention
him: "He of the Ring." Thereafter we were to hear of him only as
"He of the Ring."

Leaving Suki, Major Wyeside turned us over (thankfully, I warrant) to a native who told us his name was Charlie Kamba. He had
spent some years in Nairobi, running for an Indiana outfitter, and
spoke English remarkably well. It was from him we learned, quite
casually, when our modest eight-load *safari* was some miles on its way,
that the primary object of our coming was nonexistent. Hubert Diana
was dead.

Dead nearly five weeks—a moon and a little—and buried in the
mission church of Tara Hill.

Mission church! There was a poser for us. *Mission church?*

Well then, Charlie Kamba gave us to know that he was paraphras-
ing in a large way suitable to our habits of thought. We shouldn't have
understood *his* informant's "wizard house" or "house of the effigy."

I will say for Mrs. Diana that in the course of our halt of lugu-
brious amazement she shed tears. That some of them were not tears
of unrealized relief it would be hardly natural to believe. She had
desired loyally to find her husband, but when she should have found
him—what? This problem, sturdily ignored so long, was now removed.

Turn back? Never! Now it would seem the necessity for pressing
forward was doubled. In the scrub-fringed ravine of our halt the
porters resumed their loads, the dust stood up again, the same
caravan moved on. But how far it was now from being the same.

From that moment it took on, for me at least, a new character. It wasn't the news especially; the fact that Diana was dead had little to do with it. Perhaps it was simply that the new sense of something aimfully and cumulatively dramatic in our progress had to have a beginning, and that moment would do as well as the next.

Six villages: M'nann, Leika, Leikapo, Shamba, Little Tara, and Tara, culminating in the apotheosis of Tara Hill. Six stops for the night on the road it had cost Diana as many months to cover in his singular pilgrimage to his inevitable goal. Or in his flight to it. Yes, his stampede. Now the pipers at that four-day orgy of liberty on the *Platonic's* decks were at his heels for their pay. Now that his strength was failing, the hosts of loneliness were after him, creeping out of their dreadful magnitudes, hounds of space. Over all that ground it seemed to me we were following him not by the word of hearsay but, as one follows a wounded animal making for its earth, by the droppings of his blood.

Our progress had taken on a pattern; it built itself with a dramatic artistry; it gathered suspense. As though it were a story at its most breathless places "continued in our next," and I a reader forgetting the road's weariness, the dust, the torment of insects never escaped, the inadequate food, I found myself hardly able to keep from running on ahead to reach the evening's village, to search out the inevitable repository of images left by the white stranger who had come and tarried there awhile and gone again.

More concrete and ever more concrete. The immemorial compromise with the human hunger for a symbol to see with the eyes, touch with the hands. Hierarchy after hierarchy of little mud effigies —one could see the necessity pushing the man. Out of the protoplasmic blobs of Ndua, Suki, even M'nann, at Leikapo Diana's concept of infinity (so pure in that halcyon epoch at sea), of categories nested within categories like Japanese boxes, of an over-creature wearing our cosmos like a trinket, unawares, had become a mass with legs to stand on and a real head. The shards scattered about in the filth of the hut there (as if in violence of despair) were still monstrosities, but with a sudden stride of concession their monstrousness was the monstrousness of lizard and turtle and crocodile. At Shamba there were dozens of huge-footed birds.

It is hard to be sure in retrospect, but I do believe that by the time we reached Little Tara I began to see the thing as a whole—the fetus, working out slowly, blindly, but surely, its evolution in the womb of fright. At Little Tara there was a change in the character of the exhibits; their numbers had diminished, their size had grown. There was a boar with tusks and a bull the size of a dog with horns, and on a tusk and on a horn an indentation left by a ring.

I don't believe Mrs. Diana got the things at all. Toward the last she wasn't interested in the huts of relics; at Little Tara she wouldn't go near the place; she was "too tired." It must have been pretty awful, when you think of it, even if all she saw in them was the mud-pie play of a man reverted to a child.

There was another thing at Little Tara quite as momentous as the jump to boar and bull. Here at last a mask had been thrown aside. Here there had been no pretense of proselyting, no astronomical lectures, no doorway harangues. Straightway he had arrived (a fabulous figure already, long heralded) he had commandeered a house and shut himself up in it and there, mysterious assiduous, he had remained three days and nights, eathing nothing, but drinking gallons of the foul water they left in gourds outside his curtain of reeds. No one in the village had ever seen what he had done and left there. Now, candidly, those labors were for himself alone.

Here at last in Tara the moment of that confession had overtaken the fugitive. It was he, ill with fever and dying of nostalgia—not these naked black baboon men seen now as little more than blurs—who had to give the Beast of the Infinite a name and a shape. And more and more, not only a shape, but a *shapeliness*. From the instant when, no longer able to live alone with nothingness, he had given it a likeness in Ndua mud, and perceived that it was intolerable and fled its face, the turtles and distorted crocodiles of Leikapo and the little birds of Shamba had become inevitable, and no less inevitable the Little Tara boar and bull. Another thing grows plain in retrospect: the reason why, done to death (as all the way they reported him) he couldn't die. He didn't dare to. Didn't dare to close his eyes.

It was at Little Tara we first heard of him as "Father Witch," a name come back, we were told, from Tara, where he had gone. I had heard it pronounced several times before it suddenly obtruded from the native context as actually two English words. That was what made it queer. It was something they must have picked up by rote, uncomprehending; something then they could have had from no lips but his own. When I repeated it after them with a better accent they pointed up toward the north, saying "Tara! Tara!" their eagerness mingled with awe.

I shall never forget Tara as we saw it, after our last blistering scramble up a gorge, situated in the clear air on a slope belted with cedars. A mid-African stockade left by some blunder in an honest Colorado landscape, or a newer and bigger Vermont. Here at the top of our journey, black savages, their untidy *shambas,* the very Equator, all these seemed as incongruous as a Gothic cathedral in a Congo marsh. I wonder if Hubert Diana knew whither his instinct was guiding him on the long road of his journey here to die. . . .

He had died and he was buried, not in the village, but about half a mile distant, on the ridge; this we were given to know almost before we had arrived. There was no need to announce ourselves, the word of our coming had outrun us; the populace was at the gates.

"Our Father Witch! Our Father Witch!" They knew what we were after; the funny parrot-wise English stood out from the clack and clatter of their excited speech. "Our Father Witch! Ay! Ay!" With a common eagerness they gesticulated at the hilltop beyond the cedars.

Certainly here was a change. No longer the propitiatory spitting, the averted eyes, the uneasy whispering allusion to him who had passed that way: Here in Tara they would shout him from the housetops, with a kind of civic pride.

We learned the reason for this on our way up the hill. It was because they were his chosen, the initiate.

We made the ascent immediately, against the village's advice. It was near evening; the return would be in the dark; it was bad lion country; wouldn't tomorrow morning do? . . . No, it wouldn't do the widow. Her face was set. . . . And so, since we were resolved to go, the village went with us, armed with spears and rattles and drums. Charlie Kamba walked beside us, sifting the information a hundred were eager to give.

These people were proud, he said, because their wizard was more powerful than all the wizards of all the other villages "in the everywhere together." If he cared to he could easily knock down all the other villages in the "everywhere," destroying all the people and all the cattle. If he dared to he could open his mouth and swallow the sky and the stars. But Tara he had chosen. Tara he would protect. He made their mealies to grow and their cattle to multiply.

I protested, "But he is *dead* now!"

Charlie Kamba made signs of deprecation. I discerned that he was far from clear about the thing himself.

Yes, he temporized, this Father Witch was dead, quite dead. On the other hand he was up there. On the other hand he would never die. He was longer than forever. Yes, quite true, he was dead and buried under the pot.

I gave it up. "How did he die?"

Well, he came to this village of Tara very suffering, very sick. The dead man who walked. His face was very sad. Very eaten. Very frightened. He came to this hill. So he lived here for two full moons, very hot, very eaten, very dead. These men made him a house as he commanded them, also a stockade. In the house he was very quiet, very dead, making magic two full moons. Then he came out and they that were waiting saw him. He had made the magic, and the magic had made him well. His face was kind. He was happy. He was full fed. He was full fed, these men said, without any eating. Yes, they carried up to him very fine food, because they were full of wonder and some fear, but he did not eat any of it. Some water he drank. So, for two days and the night between them, he continued sitting in the gate of the stockade, very happy, very full fed. He told these people very much about their wizard, who is bigger than everywhere and longer than forever and can, if he cares to, swallow the sky and stars. From time to time however, ceasing to talk to these people, he got to his knees and talked in his own strange tongue to Our Father Witch, his eyes held shut. When he had done this just at sunset of the second day he fell forward on his face. So he remained that night. The next day these men took him into the house and buried him under the pot. On the other hand Our Father Witch is longer than forever. He remains there still. . . .

The first thing I saw in the hut's interior was the earthen pot at the northern end, wrong-side-up on the ground. I was glad I had preceded Mrs. Diana. I walked across and sat down on it carelessly, hoping so that her afflicted curiosity might be led astray. It gave me the oddest feeling, though, to think of what was there beneath my nonchalant sitting-portion—aware as I was of the Kavirondo burial of a great man—up the neck in mother earth, and the rest of him left out in the dark of the pot for the undertakings of the ants. I hoped his widow wouldn't wonder about that inverted vessel of clay.

I needn't have worried. Her attention was arrested otherwheres.

I shall not forget the look of her face, caught above me in the red shaft of the sundown entering the western door, as she gazed at the last and the largest of the Reverend Hubert Diana's gods. That long, long cheek of hers, buffeted by sorrow, startled now, and mortified. Not till that moment, I believe, had she comprehended the steps of mud images she had been following for what they were, the steps of idolatry.

For my part, I wasn't startled. Even before we started up the hill, knowing that her husband had dared to die here. I could have told her pretty much what she would find.

This overlord of the cosmic categories that he had fashioned (at last) in his own image sat at the other end of the red-streaked house upon a bench—a throne?—of mud. Diana had been no artist. An ovoid two-eyed head, a cylindrical trunk, two arms, two legs, that's all. But indubitably man, man size. Only one finger of one of the hands had been done with much care. It wore an opal, a two-dollar stone from Mexico, set in a silver ring. This was the hand that was lifted and over it the head was bent.

I've said Diana was no artist. I'll take back the words. The figure was crudeness itself, but in the relation between that bent head and that lifted hand there was something which was something else. A sense of scrutiny one would have said no genius of mud could ever have conveyed. An attitude of interest centered in that bauble, intense and static, breathless and eternal all in one—penetrating to its bottom atom, to the last electron, to a hill upon it, and to a two-legged mite about to die. Marking (yes, I'll swear to the incredible) the sparrow's fall.

The magic was made. The road that had commenced with the blobs of Ndua—the same that commenced with our hairy ancestors listening to the nightwind in their caves—was run.

And from here Diana, of a sudden happy, of a sudden looked after, "Full fed," had walked out—

But no; I couldn't stand that mortified sorrow on the widow's face any longer. She had to be made to see. I said it aloud:

"From here, Mrs. Diana, your husband walked out—"

"He had sunk to idolatry. *Idolatry!*"

"To the bottom, yes. And come up its whole history again. And from here he walked out into the sunshine to kneel and talk with Our Father Which—"

She got it. She caught it. I wish you could have seen the light going up those long, long cheeks as she got it:

"Our Father which art in Heaven, Hallowed be Thy Name!"

We went down hill in the darkness, convoyed by a vast rattling of gourds and beating of goat-hide drums.

The Man Who Saw Through Heaven

For Analysis

1. Near the beginning of the story the narrator says Diana undertook "to measure the Infinite with the footrule of his mind." How does this statement sum up both the Reverend's failures in the statuary and his ultimate success?

2. What does the narrator think about Mrs. Diana's religious sensibilities? Do her spiritual perceptions change?

3. What is the natives' understanding of the Reverend Diana's final sculpture and message? In what sense is the description of the whites' descent from the tomb symbolic? Does its symbolism have a wider application than only to the natives?

4. In what sense is this statement of the narrator's concerning the Reverend's experience true: "The magic was made. The road that had commenced with the blobs of Ndua—the same that commenced with our hairy ancestors listening to the nightwind in their caves—was run."

Walter Van Tilburg Clark

The Wind and the
Snow of Winter

It was near sunset when Mike Braneen came onto the last pitch of the old wagon road which had led into Gold Rock from the east since the Comstock days. The road was just two ruts in the hard earth with sagebrush growing between them, and was full of steep pitches and sharp turns. From the summit it descended even more steeply into Gold Rock, in a series of short switchbacks down the slope of the canyon. There was a paved highway on the other side of the pass now, but Mike never used that. Cars coming from behind made him uneasy, so that he couldn't follow his own thoughts long, but had to keep turning around every few minutes, to see that his burro, Annie, was staying out on the shoulder of the road, where she would be safe. Mike didn't like cars anyway, even and on the old road he could forget about them and feel more like himself. He could forget about Annie too, except when the light, quick tapping of her hoofs behind him stopped. Even then he didn't really break his thoughts. It was more as if the tapping were another sound from his own inner machinery, and when it stopped he stopped too, and turned around to see what she was doing. When he began to walk ahead again at the same slow, unvarying pace, his arms scarcely swinging at all, his body bent a little forward from the waist, he would not be aware that there had been any interruption of the memory or the story that was going on in his head. Mike did not like to have his stories interrupted except by an idea of his own, something to do with his prospecting, or the arrival of his story at an actual memory which warmed him to closer recollection or led into a new and more attractive story.

THE WIND AND THE SNOW OF WINTER: From THE WATCHFUL GODS AND OTHER STORIES by Walter Van Tilburg Clark. Reprinted by permission of International Famous Agency, Inc. Copyright © 1944 by Walter Van Tilburg Clark.

An intense, golden light, almost liquid, fanned out from the peaks above him and reached eastward under the gray sky, and the snow which occasionally swarmed across this light was fine and dry. Such little squalls had been going on all day, and still there was nothing like real snow down, but only a fine powder which the wind swept along until it caught under the brush, leaving the ground bare. Yet Mike Braneen was not deceived. This was not just a flurrying day; it was the beginning of winter. If not tonight, then tomorrow, or the next day, the snow would begin which shut off the mountains, so that a man might as well be on a great plain for all he could see, perhaps even the snow which blinded a man at once and blanketed the desert in an hour. Fifty-two years in this country had made Mike Braneen sure about such things, although he didn't give much thought to them but only to what he had to do because of them. Three nights before he had been awakened by a change in the wind. It was no longer a wind born in the near mountains, cold with night and altitude, but a wind from far places, full of a damp chill which got through his blankets and into his bones. The stars had still been clear and close above the dark humps of the mountains, and overhead the constellations had moved slowly in full panoply, unbroken by any invisible lower darkness; yet he had lain there half awake for a few minutes, hearing the new wind beat the brush around him, hearing Annie stirring restlessly and thumping in her hobble. He had thought drowsily, "Smells like winter this time," and then, "It's held off a long time this year, pretty near the end of December." Then he had gone back to sleep, mildly happy because the change meant he would be going back to Gold Rock. Gold Rock was the other half of Mike Braneen's life. When the smell of winter came he always started back for Gold Rock. From March or April until the smell of winter he wandered slowly about among the mountains, anywhere between the White Pines and the Virginias, with only his burro for company. Then there would come the change, and they would head back for Gold Rock.

Mike had traveled with a good many burros during that time, eighteen or twenty, he thought, although he was not sure. He could not remember them all, but only those he had had first, when he was a young man and always thought most about seeing women when he got back to Gold Rock, or those with something queer about them, like Baldy, who'd had a great pale patch, like a bald spot, on one side of his belly, or those who'd had something queer happen to them, like Maria. He could remember just how it had been that night. He could remember it as if it were last night. It had been in Hamilton. He had felt unhappy, because he could remember Hamilton when the whole hollow was full of people and buildings, and everything was new and active. He had gone to sleep in the hollow shell of the Wells Fargo Building, hearing an old iron shutter banging against the wall in the wind. In the morning Maria had been gone. He had followed the scuffing track she made on account of her loose hobble, and it had led far up the old snow gullied road to Treasure Hill, and then ended at one of the black shafts that opened like mouths right at the edge of the road. A man remembered a thing like that. There weren't many burros that foolish. But burros with nothing particular about them were hard to remember—especially those he'd had in the last twenty years or so, when he had gradually stopped feeling so personal about them and had begun to call all the jennies Annie and all the burros Jack.

The clicking of the little hoofs behind him stopped, and Mike stopped too, and turned around. Annie was pulling at a line of yellow grass along the edge of the road.

"Come on, Maria." Mike said patiently. The burro at once stopped pulling at the dead grass and came on up toward him, her small black nose working, the ends of the grass standing out on each side of it like whiskers. Mike began to climb again, ahead of her.

It was a long time since he had been caught by a winter, too. He could not remember how long. All the beginnings ran together in his mind, as if they were all the beginning of one winter so far back that he had almost forgotten it. He could still remember clearly, though, the winter he had stayed out on purpose, clear into January. He had been a young man then, thirty-five or forty or forty-five, somewhere in there. He would have to stop and try to bring back a whole string of memories about what had happened just before, in order to remember just how old he had been, and it wasn't worth the trouble. Besides, sometimes even that system didn't work. It would lead him into an old camp where he had been a number of times, and the dates would get mixed up. It was impossible to remember any other way, because all his comings and goings had been so much alike. He had been young, anyhow, and not much afraid of anything except running out of water in the wrong place;

not even afraid of the winter. He had stayed out because he'd thought he had a good thing, and he had wanted to prove it. He could remember how it felt to be out in the clear winter weather on the mountains, the piñon trees and the junipers weighted down with feathery snow, and making sharp blue shadows on the white slopes. The hills had made blue shadows on one another too, and in the still air his pick had made the beginning of a sound like a bell's. He knew he had been young, because he could remember taking a day off now and then, just to go tramping around those hills, up and down the white and through the blue shadows, on a kind of holiday. He had pretended to his common sense that he was seriously prospecting, and had carried his hammer and even his drill along, but he had really just been gallivanting, playing colt. Maybe he had been even younger than thirty-five, though he could still be stirred a little, for that matter, by the memory of the kind of weather which had sent him gallivanting. High-blue weather, he called it. There were two kinds of high-blue weather, besides the winter kind, which didn't set him off very often, spring and fall. In the spring it would have a soft, puffy wind and soft, puffy white clouds which made separate shadows that travelled silently across hills that looked soft too. In the fall it would be still, and there would be no clouds at all in the blue, but there would be something in the golden air and the soft, steady sunlight on the mountains that made a man as uneasy as the spring blowing, though in a different way, more sad and not so excited. In the spring high-blue a man had been likely to think about women he had slept with, or wanted to sleep with, or imaginary women made up with the help of newspaper pictures of actresses or young society matrons, or of the old oil paintings in the Lucky Boy Saloon, which showed pale, almost naked women against dark, sumptuous backgrounds— women with long hair or braided hair, calm, virtuous faces, small hands and feet, and ponderous limbs, breasts, and buttocks. In the fall high-blue, though it had been much longer since he had seen a woman, or heard a woman's voice, he was more likely to think about old friends, men, or places he had heard about, or places he hadn't seen for a long time. He himself thought most often about Goldfield the way he had last seen it in the summer in 1912. That was as far south as Mike had ever been in Nevada. Since then he had never been south of Tonopah. When the high-blue weather was past, though, and the season worked toward winter, he began to think about Gold

Rock. There were only three or four winters out of the fifty-two when he hadn't gone home to Gold Rock, to his old room at Mrs. Wright's, up on Fourth Street, and to his meals in the dining room at the International House, and to the Lucky Boy, where he could talk to Tom Connover and his other friends, and play cards, or have a drink to hold in his hand while he sat and remembered.

This journey had seemed a little different from most, though. It had started the same as usual, but as he had come across the two vast valleys, and through the pass in the low range between them, he hadn't felt quite the same. He'd felt younger and more awake, it seemed to him, and yet, in a way, older too, suddenly older. He had been sure that there was plenty of time, and yet he had been a little afraid of getting caught in the storm. He had kept looking ahead to see if the mountains on the horizon were still clearly outlined, or if they had been cut off by a lowering of the clouds. He had thought more than once how bad it would be to get caught out there when the real snow began, and he had been disturbed by the first flakes. It had seemed hard to him to have to walk so far too. He had kept thinking about distance. Also the snowy cold had searched out the regions of his body where old injuries had healed. He had taken off his left mitten a good many times, to blow on the fingers which had been frosted the year he was sixty-three, so that now it didn't take much cold to turn them white and stiffen them. The queer tingling, partly like an itch and partly like a pain, in the patch on his back that had been burned in that old powder blast was sharper than he could remember its ever having been before. The rheumatism in his joints, which was so old a companion that it usually made him feel no more than tight-knit and stiff, and the place where his leg had been broken and torn when the ladder broke in '97 ached and had a pulse he could count. All this made him believe that he was walking more slowly than usual, although nothing, probably not even a deliberate attempt, could actually have changed his pace. Sometimes he even thought, with a moment of fear, that he was getting tired.

On the other hand, he felt unusually clear and strong in his mind. He remembered things with a clarity which was like living them again—nearly all of them events from many years back, from the time when he had been really active and fearless and every burro had had its own name. Some of these events, like the night he had spent in Eureka with the little brown-haired whore, a night in the fall in 1888 or '89, somewhere in there, he had not once thought of for years. Now he could remember even her name. Armandy, she had called herself: a funny name. They all picked names for their business, of course, romantic names like Cecily or Rosamunde or Belle or Claire, or hard names like Diamond Gert or Horseshoe Sal, or names that were pinned on them, like Indian Kate or Roman Mary, but Armandy was different.

He could remember Armandy as if he were with her now, not the way she had behaved in bed; he couldn't remember anything particular about that. In fact he couldn't be sure that he remembered anything about that at all. There were others he could remember more clearly for the way they had behaved in bed, women he had been with more often. He had been with Armandy only that one night. He remembered little things about being with her, things that made it seem good to think of being with her again. Armandy had a room upstairs in a hotel. They could hear a piano playing in a club across the street. He could hear the tune, and it was one he knew, although he didn't know its name. It was a gay tune that went on and on the same, but still it sounded sad when you heard it through the hotel window, with the lights from the bars and hotels shining on the street, and the people coming and going through the lights, and then, beyond the lights, the darkness where the mountains were. Armandy wore a white silk dress with a high waist, and a locket on a gold chain. The dress made her look very brown and like a young girl. She used a white powder on her face, that smelled like violets, but this could not hide her brownness. The locket was heart-shaped, and it opened to show a cameo of a man's hand holding a woman's hand very gently, just their fingers laid out long together, and the thumbs holding, the way they were sometimes on tombstones. There were two little gold initials on each hand, but Armandy would never tell what they stood for, or even if the locket was really her own. He stood in the window, looking down at the club from which the piano music was coming, and Armandy stood beside him, with her shoulder against his arm, and a glass of wine in her hand. He could see the toe of her white satin slipper showing from under the edge of her skirt. Her big hat, loaded with black and white plumes, lay on the dresser behind them. His own leather coat, with the sheepskin lining, lay across the foot of the bed. It was a big bed, with a knobby brass foot and head. There was one oil lamp burning in the chandelier in the middle of the room. Armandy was soft-spoken, gentle, and a little fearful, always looking at him to see what he was thinking. He stood with his arms folded. His arms felt big and strong upon his heavily muscled chest. He stood there, pretending to be in no hurry, but really thinking eagerly about what he could do with Armandy, who had something about her which tempted him to be cruel. He stood there, with his chin down into his heavy, dark beard, and watched a man come riding down the middle of the street from the west. The horse was a fine black, which lifted its head and feet with pride. The man sat very straight, with a high rein, and something about his clothes and hat made him appear to be in uniform, although it wasn't a uniform he was wearing. The man also saluted friends upon the sidewalks like an officer, bending his head just slightly, and touching his hat instead of lifting it. Mike Braneen asked Armandy who the man was, and then felt angry because she could tell him, and because he was an important man who owned a mine that was in bonanza. He mocked the airs with which the man rode, and his princely greetings. He mocked the man cleverly, and Armandy laughed and repeated what he said, and made him drink a little of her wine as a reward. Mike had been drinking whisky, and he did not like wine anyway, but this was not the moment in which to refuse such an invitation.

Old Mike remembered all this, which had been completely forgotten for years. He could not remember what he and Armandy had said, but he remembered everything else, and he felt very lonesome for Armandy, and for the room with the red, figured carpet and the brass chandelier with oil lamps in it, and the open window with the long tune coming up through it, and the young summer night outside on the mountains. This loneliness was so much more intense than his familiar loneliness that it made him feel very young. Memories like this had come up again and again during these three days. It was like beginning life over again. It had tricked him into thinking, more than once, "Next summer I'll make the strike, and this time I'll put it into something safe for the rest of my life, and stop this fool wandering around while I've still got some time left"—a way of thinking which he had really stopped a long time before.

It was getting darker rapidly in the pass. When a gust of wind brought the snow against Mike's face so hard that he noticed the flakes felt larger, he looked up. The light was still there, although the fire was dying out of it, and the snow swarmed across it more thickly. Mike remembered God. He did not think anything exact. He did not think about his own relationship to God. He merely felt the idea as a comforting presence. He'd always had a feeling about God whenever he looked at a sunset, especially a sunset which came through under a stormy sky. It had been the strongest feeling left in him until these memories like the one about Armandy had begun. Even in this last pass his strange fear of the storm had come on him again a couple of times, but now that he had looked at the light and thought of God it was gone. In a few minutes he would come to the summit and look down into his lighted city. He felt happily hurried by this anticipation.

He would take the burro down and stable her in John Hammersmith's shed, where he always kept her. He would spread fresh straw for her, and see that the shed was tight against the wind and snow, and get a measure of grain for her from John. Then he would go up to Mrs. Wright's house at the top of Fourth Street, and leave his things in the same room he always had, the one in front, which looked down over the roofs and chimneys of his city, and across at the east wall of the canyon, from which the sun rose late. He would trim his beard with Mrs. Wright's shears, and shave the upper part of his cheeks. He would bathe out of the blue bowl and pitcher, and wipe himself with the towel with yellow flowers on it, and dress in the good dark suit and the good black shoes with the gleaming box toes, and the good black hat which he had left in the chest in his room. In this way he would perform the ceremony which ended the life of the desert and began the life of Gold Rock. Then he would go down to the International House, and greet Arthur Morris in the gleaming bar, and go into the dining room and eat the best supper they had, with fresh meat and vegetables, and new-made pie, and two cups of hot clear coffee. He would be served by the plump blond waitress who always joked with him, and gave him many little extra things with his first supper, including the drink which Arthur Morris always sent in from the bar.

At this point Mike Braneen stumbled in his mind, and his anticipation wavered. He could not be sure that the plump blond waitress would serve him. For a moment he saw her in a long skirt, and the dining room of the International House, behind her, had potted palms standing in the corners, and was full of the laughter and loud, manly talk of many customers who wore high vests and mustaches and beards. These men leaned back from tables covered with empty dishes. They patted their tight vests and lighted expensive cigars. He knew all their faces. If he were to walk down the aisle between the tables on his side they would all speak to him. But he also seemed to remember the dining room with only a few tables, with oilcloth on them instead of linen, and with moody young men sitting at them in their work clothes—strangers who worked for the highway department, or were just passing through, or talked mining in terms which he did not understand or which made him angry.

No, it would not be the plump blond waitress. He did not know who it would be. It didn't matter. After supper he would go up Canyon Street under the arcade to the Lucky Boy Saloon, and there it would be the same as ever. There would be the laurel wreaths on the frosted glass panels of the doors, and the old sign upon the window, the sign that was older than Tom Connover, almost as old as Mike Braneen himself. He would open the door and see the bottles and the white women in the paintings, and the card table in the back corner and the big stove and the chairs along the wall. Tom would look around from his place behind the bar.

"Well, now," he would roar, "look who's here, boys. Now will you believe it's winter?" he would roar at them.

Some of them would be the younger men, of course, and there might even be a few strangers, but this would only add to the dignity of his reception, and there would also be his friends. There would be Henry Bray with the gray walrus mustache, and Mark Wilton and Pat Gallagher. They would all welcome him loudly.

"Mike, how are you, anyway?" Tom would roar, leaning across the bar to shake hands with his big, heavy, soft hand with the diamond ring on it. "And what'll it be, Mike? The same?" he'd ask, as if Mike had been in there no longer ago than the night before.

Mike would play that game too. "The same," he would say.

Then he would really be back in Gold Rock; never mind the plump blond waitress.

Mike came to the summit of the old road and stopped and looked down. For a moment he felt lost again, as he had when he'd thought about the plump blond waitress. He had expected Canyon Street to look much brighter. He had expected a log of orange windows close together on the other side of the canyon. Instead there were only a few scattered lights across the darkness, and they were white. They made no communal glow upon the steep slope, but gave out only single white needles of light, which pierced the darkness secretly and lonesomely, as if nothing could ever pass from one house to another over there. Canyon street was very dark too. There it went, the street he loved, steeply down into the bottom of the canyon, and down its length there were only the few street lights, more than a block apart, swinging in the wind and darting about that cold, small light. The snow whirled and swooped under the nearest street light below.

"You are getting to be an old fool," Mike Braneen said out loud to himself, and felt better. This was the way Gold Rock was now, of course, and he loved it all the better. It was a place that grew old with a man, that was going to die sometime too. There could be an understanding with it.

He worked his way slowly down into Canyon Street, with Annie slipping and checking behind him. Slowly, with the blown snow behind them, they came to the first built-up block and passed the first dim light showing through a smudged window under the arcade. They passed the dark places after it, and the second light. Then Mike Braneen stopped in the middle of the street, and Annie stopped beside him, pulling her rump in and turning her head away from the snow. A highway truck, coming down from the head of the canyon, had to get way over onto the wrong side of the street to pass them. The driver leaned out as he went by, and yelled, "Pull over, Pop. You're in town now."

Mike Braneen didn't hear him. He was staring at the Lucky Boy. The Lucky Boy was dark, and there were boards nailed across the big window that had shown the sign. At last Mike went over onto the boardwalk to look more closely. Annie followed him but stopped at the edge of the walk and scratched her neck against a post of the arcade. There was the other sign, hanging crossways under the arcade, and even in that gloom Mike could see that it said Lucky Boy and had a Jack of Diamonds painted on it. There was no mistake. The Lucky Boy sign, and others like it under the arcade, creaked and rattled in the wind.

There were footsteps coming along the boards. The boards sounded hollow, and sometimes one of them rattled. Mike Braneen looked down slowly from the sign and peered at the approaching figure. It was a man wearing a sheepskin coat with the collar turned up around his head. He was walking quickly, like a man who knew where he was going, and why, and where he had been. Mike almost let him pass. Then he spoke.

"Say, fella—"

He even reached out a hand as if to catch hold of the man's sleeve, though he didn't touch it. The man stopped and asked, impatiently, "Yeah?" and Mike let the hand down again slowly.

"Well, what is it?" the man asked.

"I don't want anything," Mike said. "I got plenty."

"Okay, okay," the man said. "What's the matter?"

Mike moved his hand toward the Lucky Boy. "It's closed," he said.

"I see it is, Dad," the man said. He laughed a little. He didn't seem to be in quite so much of a hurry now.

"How long has it been closed?" Mike asked.

"Since about June, I guess," the man said. "Old Tom Connover, the guy that ran it, died last June."

Mike waited for a moment. "Tom died?" he asked.

"Yup. I guess he'd just kept it open out of love of the place anyway. There hasn't been any real business for years. Nobody cared to keep it open after him."

The man started to move on, but then he waited, peering, trying to see Mike better.

"This June?" Mike asked finally.

"Yup. This last June."

"Oh," Mike said. Then he just stood there. He wasn't thinking anything. There didn't seem to be anything to think.

"You knew him?" the man asked.

"Thirty years," Mike said. "No, more'n that," he said, and started to figure out how long he had known Tom Connover, but lost it, and said, as if it would do just as well, "He was a lot younger than I am, though."

"Hey," said the man, coming closer, and peering again. "You're Mike Braneen, aren't you?"

"Yes," Mike said.

"Gee, I didn't recognize you at first. I'm sorry."

"That's all right," Mike said. He didn't know who the man was, or what he was sorry about.

He turned his head slowly and looked out into the street. The snow was coming down heavily now. The street was all white. He saw Annie with her head and shoulders in under the arcade but the snow settling on her rump.

"Well, I guess I'd better get Molly under cover," he said. He moved toward the burro a step, but then halted.

"Say, fella—"

The man had started on, but he turned back. He had to wait for Mike to speak.

"I guess this about Tom's mixed me up."

"Sure," the man said. "It's tough, an old friend like that."

"Where do I turn up to get to Mrs. Wright's place?"

"Mrs. Wright?"

"Mrs. William Wright," Mike said. "Her husband used to be a foreman in the Aztec. Got killed in the fire."

"Oh," the man said. He didn't say anything more, but just stood there, looking at the shadowy bulk of old Mike.

"She's not dead too, is she?" Mike asked slowly.

"Yeah, I'm afraid she is, Mr. Braneen," the man said. "Look," he said more cheerfully. "It's Mrs. Branley's house you want right now, isn't it? Place where you stayed last winter?"

Finally Mike said, "Yeah. Yeah, I guess it is."

"I'm going up that way. I'll walk up with you," the man said.

After they had started Mike thought that he ought to take the burro down to John Hammersmith's first, but he was afraid to ask about it. They walked on down Canyon Street, with Annie walking along beside them in the gutter. At the first side street they turned right and began to climb the steep hill toward another of the little street lights dancing over a crossing. There was no sidewalk here, and Annie followed right at their heels. That one street light was the only light showing up ahead.

When they were halfway up to the light Mike asked, "She die this summer too?"

The man turned his body half around, so that he could hear inside his collar.

"What?"

"Did she die this summer too?"

"Who?"

"Mrs. Wright," Mike said.

The man looked at him, trying to see his face as they came up toward the light. Then he turned back again, and his voice was muffled by the collar.

"No, she died quite a while ago, Mr. Braneen."

"Oh," Mike said finally.

They came up onto the crossing under the light, and the snow-laden wind whirled around them again. They passed under the light, and their three lengthening shadows before them were obscured by the innumerable tiny shadows of the flakes.

The Wind and the Snow of Winter

For Analysis

1. What is Mike's sense of his identity, his personality? How does he construct it?
2. What is significant to Mike in his remembrance of Armandy? How is his relationship to her related to his life in Gold Rock?
3. What is Mike's feeling toward nature? How is his relationship to it different than that of the highway crews that come to Gold Rock?
4. Do the approaching winter and the snow have a symbolic value? If so, what is it?

William Faulkner

Pantaloon
in Black

I

He stood in the worn, faded clean overalls which Mannie herself had washed only a week ago and heard the first clod stride the pine box. Soon he had one of the shovels himself, which in his hands (he was better than six feet and weighed better than two hundred pounds) resembled the toy shovel a child plays with at the shore, its half cubic foot of flung dirt no more than the light gout of sand the child's shovel would have flung. Another member of his sawmill gang touched his arm and said, "Lemme have hit, Rider." He didn't even falter. He released one hand in midstroke and flung it backward, striking the other across the chest, jolting him back a step, and restored the hand to the moving shovel, flinging the dirt with that effortless fury so that the mound seemed to be rising of its own volition, not built up from above but thrusting visibly upward out of the earth itself, until at last the grave, save for its rawness, resembled any other marked off without order about the barren plot by shards of pottery and broken bottles and old brick and other objects insignificant to sight but actually of a profound meaning and fatal to touch, which no white man could have read. Then he straightened up and with one hand flung the shovel quivering upright in the mound like a javelin and turned and began to walk away, walking on even when an old woman came out of the meager clump of his kin and friends and a few old people who had known him and his dead wife both since they were born, and grasped his forearm. She was his aunt. She had raised him. He could not remember his parents at all.

"Whar you gwine?" she said.

"Ah'm goan home," he said.

"You dont wants ter go back dar by yoself," she said. "You needs to eat. You come on home and eat."

"Ah'm goan home," he repeated, walking out from under her hands, his forearm like iron, as if the weight on it were no more than that of a fly, the other members of the mill gang whose head he was giving way quietly to let him pass. But before he reached the fence one of them overtook him; he did not need to be told it was his aunt's messenger.

"Wait, Rider," the other said. "We gots a jug in de bushes—" Then the other said what he had not intended to say, what he had never conceived of himself saying in circumstances like these, even though everybody knew it—the dead who either will not or cannot quit the earth yet although the flesh they once lived in has been returned to it, let the preachers tell and reiterate and affirm how they left it not only without regret but with joy, mounting toward glory: "You dont wants ter go back dar. She be wawkin yit."

He didn't pause, glancing down at the other, his eyes red at the inner corners in his high, slightly backtilted head. "Lemme lone, Acey," he said. "Doan mess wid me now," and went on, stepping over the three-strand wire fence without even breaking his stride, and crossed the road and entered the woods. It was middle dusk when he emerged from them and crossed the last field, stepping over that fence too in one stride, into the lane. It was empty at this hour of Sunday evening—no family in wagon, no rider, no walkers church-ward to speak to him and carefully refrain from looking after him when he had passed—the pale, powder-light, powder-dry dust of August from which the long week's marks of hoof and wheel had been blotted by the strolling and unhurried Sunday shoes, with some-where beneath them, vanished but not gone, fixed and held in the annealing dust, the narrow, splay-toed prints of his wife's bare feet where on Saturday afternoons she would walk to the commissary to buy their next week's supplies while he took his bath; himself, his own prints, setting the period now as he strode on, moving almost as fast as a smaller man could have trotted, his body breasting the air her body had vacated, his eyes touching the objects—post and tree and field and house and hill—her eyes had lost.

The house was the last one in the lane, not his but rented from Carothers Edmonds, the local white landowner. But the rent was paid promptly in advance, and even in just six months he had refloored the porch and rebuilt and roofed the kitchen, doing the work himself on Saturday afternoon and Sunday with his wife helping him, and bought the stove. Because he made good money: sawmilling ever since he began to get his growth at fifteen and sixteen and now, at twenty-four, head of the timber gang itself because the gang he headed moved a third again as much timber between sunup and sundown as any other moved, handling himself at times out of the vanity of his own strength logs which ordinarily two men would have handled with cant hooks; never without work even in the old days when he had not actually needed the money, when a lot of what he wanted, needed perhaps, didn't cost money—the women bright and dark and for all purposes nameless he didn't need to buy and it didn't matter to him what he wore and there was always food for him at any hour of day or night in the house of his aunt who didn't even want to take the two dollars he gave her each Saturday—so there had been only the Saturday and Sunday dice and whiskey that had to be paid for until that day six months ago when he saw Mannie, whom he had known all his life, for the first time and said to himself: "Ah'm thu wid all dat," and they married and he rented the cabin from Carothers Edmonds and built a fire on the hearth on their wedding night as the tale told how Uncle Lucas Beauchamp, Edmonds' oldest tenant, had done on his forty-five years ago and which had burned ever since; and he would rise and dress and eat his breakfast by lamplight to walk the four miles to the mill by sunup, and exactly one hour after sundown he would enter the house again, five days a week, until Saturday. Then the first hour would not have passed noon when he would mount the steps and knock, not on post or doorframe but on the underside of the gallery roof itself, and enter and ring the bright cascade of silver dollars onto the scrubbed table in the kitchen where his dinner simmered on the stove and the galvanized tub of hot water and the baking powder can of soft soap and the towel made of scalded flour sacks sewn together and his clean overalls and shirt waited, and Mannie would gather up the money and walk the half-mile to the commissary and buy their next week's supplies and bank the rest of the money in Edmonds' safe and return and they would eat once again without haste or hurry after five days—the sidemeat, the greens, the cornbread, the buttermilk from the well-house, the cake which she baked every Saturday now that she had a stove to bake in.

But when he put his hand on the gate it seemed to him suddenly that there was nothing beyond it. The house had never been his anyway, but now even the new planks and sills and shingles, the hearth and stove and bed, were all a part of the memory of somebody else, so that he stopped in the half-open gate and said aloud, as though he had gone to sleep in one place and then waked suddenly to find himself in another: "Whut's Ah doing hyar?" before he went on. Then he saw the dog. He had forgotten it. He remembered neither seeing nor hearing it since it began to howl just before dawn yesterday— a big dog, a hound with a strain of mastiff from somewhere (he had told Mannie a month after they married: "Ah needs a big dawg. You's de onliest least thing whut ever kep up wid me one day, leff alone fo weeks.") coming out from beneath the gallery and approaching, not running but seeming rather to drift across the dusk until it stood lightly against his leg, its head raised until the tips of his fingers just touched it, facing the house and making no sound; whereupon, as if the animal controlled it, had lain guardian before it during his absence and only this instant relinquished, the shell of planks and shingles facing him solidified, filled, and for the moment he believed that he could not possibly enter it. "But Ah needs to eat," he said. "Us bofe needs to eat," he said, moving on though the dog did not follow until he turned and cursed it. "Come on hyar!" he said. "Whut you skeered of? She lacked you too, same as me," and they mounted the steps and crossed the porch and entered the house—the dusk-filled single room where all those six months were now crammed and crowded into one instant of time until there was no space left for air to breathe, crammed and crowded about the hearth where the fire which was to have lasted to the end of them, before which in the days before he was able to buy the stove he would enter after his four-mile walk from the mill and find her, the shape of her narrow back and haunches squatting, one narrow spread hand shielding her face from the blaze over which the other hand held the skillet, had already fallen to a dry, light soilure of dead ashes when the sun rose yesterday—and himself standing there while the last of light died about the strong and indomitable beating of his heart and the deep steady arch and collapse of his chest which walking fast over the rough going of woods and fields had not increased and standing still in the quiet and fading room had not slowed down.

Then the dog left him. The light pressure went off his flank; he heard the click and hiss of its claws on the wooden floor as it surged away and he thought at first that it was fleeing. But it stopped just outside the front door, where he could see it now, and the upfling of its head as the howl began, and then he saw her too. She was standing in the kitchen door, looking at him. He didn't move. He didn't breathe nor speak until he knew his voice would be all right, his face fixed too not to alarm her. "Mannie," he said. "Hit's awright. Ah aint afraid." Then he took a step toward her slow, not even raising his hand yet, and stopped. Then he took another step. But this time as soon as he moved she began to fade. He stopped at once, not breathing again, motionless, willing his eyes to see that she had stopped too. But she had not stopped. She was fading, going. "Wait," he said, talking as sweet as he had ever heard his voice speak to a woman: "Den lemme go wid you honey." But she was going. She was going fast now, he could actually feel between them the insuperable barrier of that very strength which could handle alone a log which would have taken any two other men to handle, of the blood and bones and flesh too strong, invincible for life, having learned at least once with his own eyes how tough, even in sudden and violent death, not a young man's bones and flesh perhaps but the will of that bone and flesh to remain alive, actually was.

Then she was gone. He walked through the door where she had been standing, and went to the stove. He did not light the lamp. He needed no light. He had set the stove up himself and built the shelves for the dishes, from among which he took two plates by feel and from the pot sitting cold on the cold stove he ladled onto the plates the food which his aunt had brought yesterday and of which he had eaten yesterday though now he did not remember when he had eaten it nor what it was, and carried the plates to the scrubbed bare table beneath the single small fading window and drew two chairs up and sat down, waiting again until he knew his voice would be what he wanted it to be. "Come on hyar, now," he said roughly. "Come on hyar and eat yo supper. Ah aint gonter have no—" and ceased, looking down at his plate, breathing the strong, deep pants, his chest arching and collapsing until he stopped it presently and held himself motionless for perhaps a half minute, and raised a spoonful of the cold and glutinous peas to his mouth. The congealed and lifeless mass seemed to bounce on contact with his lips. Not even warmed from mouth-heat, peas and spoon spattered and rang upon the plate; his chair crashed backward and he was standing, feeling the muscles of his jaw beginning to drag his mouth open, tugging upward the top half of his head. But he stopped that too before it became sound, holding himself again while he rapidly scraped the food from his plate onto the other and took it up and left the kitchen, crossed the other room and the gallery and set the plate on the bottom step and went on toward the gate.

The dog was not there, but it overtook him within the first half mile. There was a moon then, their two shadows flitting broken and intermittent among the trees or slanted long and intact across the slope of pasture or old abandoned fields upon the hills, the man moving almost as fast as a horse could have moved over the ground, altering his course each time a lighted window came in sight, the dog trotting at heel while their shadows shortened to the moon's curve until at last they trod them and the last far lamp had vanished and the shadows began to lengthen on the other hand, keeping to heel even when a rabbit burst from almost beneath the man's foot, then lying in the gray of dawn beside the man's prone body, beside the labored heave and collapse of the chest, the loud harsh snoring which sounded not like groans of pain but like someone engaged without arms in prolonged single combat.

When he reached the mill there was nobody there but the fireman—an older man just turning from the woodpile, watching quietly as he crossed the clearing, striding as if he were going to walk not only through the boiler shed but through (or over) the boiler too, the overalls which had been clean yesterday now draggled and soiled and drenched to the knees with dew, the cloth cap flung onto the side of his head, hanging peak downward over his ear as he always wore it, the whites of his eyes rimmed with red and with something urgent and strained about them. "Whar yo bucket?" he said. But before the fireman could anwer he had stepped past him and lifted the polished lard pail down from a nail in a post. "Ah just wants a biscuit," he said.

"Eat hit all," the fireman said. "Ah'll eat outen de yuthers' buckets at dinner. Den you gawn home and go to bed. You dont looks good."

"Ah aint come hyar to look," he said, sitting on the ground, his back against the post, the open pail between his knees, cramming the food into his mouth with his hands, wolfing it—peas again, also gelid and cold, a fragment of yesterday's Sunday fried chicken, a few rough chunks of this morning's fried sidemeat, a biscuit the size of a child's cap—indiscriminate, tasteless. The rest of the crew was gathering now, with voices and sounds of movement outside the boiler shed; presently the white foreman rode into the clearing on a horse. He did not look up, setting the empty pail aside, rising, looking at no one, and went to the branch and lay on his stomach and lowered his face to the water, drawing the water into himself with the same deep, strong, troubled inhalations that he had snored with, or as when he had stood in the empty house at dusk yesterday, trying to get air.

Then the trucks were rolling. The air pulsed with the rapid beating of the exhaust and the whine and clang of the saw, the trucks rolling one by one up to the skidway, he mounting the trucks in turn, to stand balanced on the load he freed, knocking the chocks out and casting loose the shackle chains and with his cant hook squaring the sticks of cypress and gum and oak one by one to the incline and holding them until the next two men of his gang were ready to receive and guide them, until the discharge of each truck became one long rumbling roar punctuated by grunting shouts and, as the morning grew and the sweat came, chanted phrases of song tossed back and forth. He did not sing with them. He rarely ever did, and this morning might have been no different from any other—himself man-height again above the heads which carefully refrained from looking at him, stripped to the waist now, the shirt removed and the overalls knotted about his hips by the suspender straps, his upper body bare except for the handkerchief about his neck and the cap clapped and clinging somehow over his right ear, the mounting sun sweat-glinted steel-blue on the midnight-colored bunch and slip of muscles until the whistle blew for noon and he said to the two men at the head of the skidway: "Look out. Git out de way," and rode the log down the incline, balanced erect upon it in short rapid backward-running steps above the headlong thunder.

His aunt's husband was waiting for him—an old man, as tall as he was, but lean, almost frail, carrying a tin pail in one hand and a covered plate in the other; they too sat in the shade beside the branch a short distance from where the others were opening their dinner pails. The bucket contained a fruit jar of buttermilk packed in a clean damp towsack. The covered dish was a peach pie, still warm. "She baked hit fer you dis mawin," the uncle said. "She say fer you to come home." He didn't answer, bent forward a little, his elbows on his knees, holding the pie in both hands, wolfing at it, the syrupy filling smearing and trickling down his chin, blinking rapidly as he chewed, the whites of his eyes covered a little more by the creeping red. "Ah went to yo house last night, but you want dar. She sont me. She wants you to come on home. She kept de lamp burnin all last night fer you."

"Ah'm awright," he said.

"You aint awright. De Lawd guv, and He tuck away. Put yo faith and trust in Him. And she kin help you."

"Whut faith and trust?" he said. "Whut Mannie ever done ter Him? Whut He wanter come messin wid me and ——"

"Hush!" the old man said. "Hush!"

Then the trucks were rolling again. Then he could stop needing to invent to himself reasons for his breathing, until after a while he began to believe he had forgot about breathing since now he could not hear it himself above the steady thunder of the rolling logs; whereupon as soon as he found himself believing he had forgotten it, he knew that he had not, so that instead of tipping the final log onto

the skidway he stood up and cast his cant hook away as if it were a
burnt match and in the dying reverberation of the last log's rumbling descent he vaulted down between the two slanted tracks of the
skid, facing the log which still lay on the truck. He had done it before
—taken a log from the truck onto his hands, balanced, and turned
with it and tossed it onto the skidway, but never with a stick of this
size, so that in a complete cessation of all sound save the pulse of
the exhaust and the light free-running whine of the disengaged saw
since every eye there, even that of the white foreman, was upon him,
he nudged the log to the edge of the truckframe and squatted and
set his palms against the underside of it. For a time there was no movement at all. It was as if the unrational and inanimate wood had in-
vested, mesmerized the man with some of its own primal inertia.
Then a voice said quietly: "He got hit. Hit's off de truck," and they
saw the crack and gap of air, watching the infinitesimal straightening
of the braced legs until the knees locked, the movement mounting
infinitesimally through the belly's insuck, the arch of the chest, the
neck cords, lifting the lip from the white clench of teeth in passing,
drawing the whole head backward and only the bloodshot fixity of
the eyes impervious to it, moving on up the arms and the straightening elbows until the balanced log was higher than his head. "Only
he aint gonter turn wid dat un," the same voice said. "And when he
try to put hit back on de truck, hit gonter kill him." But none of
them moved. Then—there was no gathering of supreme effort—the
log seemed to leap suddenly backward over his head of its own
volition, spinning, crashing, and thundering down the incline; he
turned and stepped over the slanting track in one stride and walked
through them as they gave way and went on across the clearing toward the woods even though the foreman called after him: "Rider!"
and again: "You, Rider!"

At sundown he and the dog were in the river swamp four miles
away—another clearing, itself not much larger than a room, a hut,
a hovel partly of planks and partly of canvas, an unshaven white
man standing in the door beside which a shotgun leaned, watching
him as he approached, his hand extended with four silver dollars on
the palm. "Ah wants a jug," he said.

"A jug?" the white man said. "You mean a pint. This is Monday.
Aint you all running this week?"

"Ah laid off," he said. "Whar's my jug?" waiting, looking at nothing apparently, blinking his bloodshot eyes rapidly in his high, slightly back-tilted head, then turning, the jug hanging from his crooked middle finger against his leg, at which moment the white man looked suddenly and sharply at his eyes as though seeing them for the first time—the eyes which had been strained and urgent this morning and which now seemed to be without vision too and in which no white showed at all—and said,

"Here. Gimme that jug. You dont need no gallon. I'm going to give you that pint, give it to you. Then you get out of here and stay out. Don't come back until—" Then the white man reached and grasped the jug, whereupon the other swung it behind him, sweeping his other arm up and out so that it struck the white man across the chest.

"Look out, white folks," he said. "Hit's mine. Ah done paid you."

The white man cursed him. "No you aint. Here's your money. Put that jug down, nigger."

"Hit's mine," he said, his voice quiet, gentle even, his face quiet save for the rapid blinking of the red eyes. "Ah done paid for hit," turning on, turning his back on the man and the gun both, and re-crossed the clearing to where the dog waited beside the path to come to heel again. They moved rapidly on between the close walls of impenetrable cane stalks which gave a sort of blondness to the twilight and possessed something of that oppression, that lack of room to breathe in, which the walls of his house had had. But this time, instead of fleeing it, he stopped and raised the jug and drew the cob stopper from the fierce duskreek of uncured alcohol and drank, gulping the liquid solid and cold as ice water, without either taste or heat until he lowered the jug and the air got in. "Hah," he said. "Dat's right. Try me. Try me, big boy. Ah gots something hyar now dat kin whup you."

And, once free of the bottom's unbreathing blackness, there was the moon again, his long shadow and that of the lifted jug slanting away as he drank and then held the jug poised, gulping the silver air into his throat until he could breathe again, speaking to the jug: "Come on now. You always claim you's a better man den me. Come on now. Prove it." He drank again, swallowing the chill liquid tamed of taste or heat either while the swallowing lasted, feeling it flow solid and cold with fire, past then enveloping the strong steady panting of his lungs until they too ran suddenly free as his moving body ran in the silver solid wall of air he breasted. And he was all right, his striding shadow and the trotting one of the dog travelling swift as those of two clouds along the hill; the long cast of his motionless shadow and that of the lifted jug slanting across the slope as he watched the frail figure of his aunt's husband toiling up the hill.

"Dey tole me at de mill you was gone," the old man said. "Ah knowed whar to look. Come home, son. Dat ar cant help you."

"Hit done awready hope me," he said. "Ah'm awready home. Ah'm snakebit now and pizen cant hawm me."

"Den stop and see her. Leff her look at you. Dat's all she axes: just leff her look at you—" But he was already moving. "Wait!" the old man cried. "Wait!"

"You cant keep up," he said, speaking into the silver air, breasting aside the silver solid air which began to flow past him almost as fast as it would have flowed past a moving horse. The faint frail voice was already lost in the night's infinitude, his shadow and that of the dog scudding the free miles, the deep strong panting of his chest running free as air now because he was all right.

Then, drinking, he discovered suddenly that no more of the liquid was entering his mouth. Swallowing, it was no longer passing down his throat, his throat and mouth filled now with a solid and unmoving column which without reflex or revulsion sprang, columnar and intact and still retaining the mold of his gullet, outward glinting in the moonlight, splintering, vanishing into the myriad murmur of the dewed grass. He drank again. Again his throat merely filled solidly until two icy rills ran from his mouth-corners; again the intact column sprang silvering, glinting, shivering, while he panted the chill of air into his throat, the jug poised before his mouth while he spoke to it: "Awright. Ah'm ghy try you again. Soon as you makes up yo mind to stay whar I puts you, Ah'll leff you alone." He drank, filling his gullet for the third time and lowered the jug one instant ahead of the bright intact repetition, panting, indrawing the cool of air until he could breathe. He stoppered the cob carefully back into the jug and stood, panting, blinking, the long cast of his solitary shadow slanting away across the hill and beyond, across the mazy infinitude of all the night-bound earth. "Awright," he said. "Ah just misread de sign wrong. Hit's done done me all de help Ah needs. Ah'm awright now. Ah doan needs no mo of hit."

He could see the lamp in the window as he crossed the pasture, passing the black-and-silver yawn of the sandy ditch where he had played as a boy with empty snuff-tins and rusted harness-buckles and fragments of trace-chains and now and then an actual wheel, passing the garden patch where he had hoed in the spring days while his aunt stood sentry over him from the kitchen window, crossing the grassless yard in whose dust he had sprawled and crept before he learned to walk. He entered the house, the room, the light itself, and stopped in the door, his head backtilted a little as if he could not see, the jug hanging from his crooked finger, against his leg. "Unc Alec say you wanter see me," he said.

"Not just to see you," his aunt said. "To come home, whar we can help you."

"Ah'm awright," he said. "Ah doan needs no help."

"No," she said. She rose from the chair and came and grasped his arm as she had grasped it yesterday at the grave. Again, as on yesterday, the forearm was like iron under her hand. "No! When Alec come back and tole me how you had wawked off de mill and de sun not half down, Ah knowed why and whar. And dat cant help you."

"Hit done awready hope me. Ah'm awright now."

"Dont lie to me," she said. "You aint never lied to me. Dont lie to me now."

Then he said it. It was his own voice, without either grief or amazement, speaking quietly out of the tremendous panting of his chest which in a moment now would begin to strain at the walls of this room too. But he would be gone in a moment.

"Nome," he said, "Hit aint done me no good."

"And hit cant! Cant nothing help you but Him! Ax Him! Tole Him about hit! He wants to hyar you and help you!"

"Efn He God, Ah dont needs to tole Him. Efn He God, He awready know hit. Awright. Hyar Ah is. Leff Him come down hyar and do me some good."

"On yo knees!" she cried. "On yo knees and ax Him!" But it was not his knees on the floor, it was his feet. And for a space he could hear her feet too on the planks of the hall behind him and her voice crying after him from the door: "Spoot! Spoot!"—crying after him across the moon-dappled yard the name he had gone by in his childhood and adolescence, before the men he worked with and the bright dark nameless women he had taken in course and forgotten until he saw Mannie that day and said, "Ah'm thu wid all dat," began to call him Rider.

It was just after midnight when he reached the mill. The dog was gone now. This time he could not remember when nor where. At first he seemed to remember hurling the empty jug at it. But later the jug was still in his hand and it was not empty, although each time he drank now the two icy runnels streamed from his mouth-corners, sopping his shirt and overalls until he walked constantly in the fierce chill of the liquid tamed now of flavor and heat and odor too even when the swallowing ceased. "Sides that," he said, "Ah wouldn't thow nothin at him. Ah mout kick him efn he needed hit and was close enough. But Ah wouldn't ruint no dog chunkin hit."

The jug was still in his hand when he entered the clearing and paused among the mute soaring of the moon-blond lumber-stacks. He stood in the middle now of the unimpeded shadow which he was treading again as he had trod it last night, swaying a little, blinking about at the stacked lumber, the skidway, the piled logs waiting for tomorrow, the boiler-shed all quiet and blanched in the moon. And then it was all right. He was moving again. But he was not moving, he was drinking, the liquid cold and swift and tasteless and requiring no swallowing, so that he could not tell if it were going down inside or outside. But it was all right. And now he was moving, the jug gone now and he didn't know the when or where of that either. He crossed the clearing and entered the boiler shed and went on through it, crossing the junctureless backloop of time's trepan, to the door of the tool-room, the faint glow of the lantern beyond the plank-joints, the surge and fall of living shadow, the mutter of voices, the mute click and scutter of the dice, his hand loud on the barred door, his voice loud too: "Open hit. Hit's me. Ah'm snakebit and bound to die."

Then he was through the door and inside the tool-room. They were the same faces—three members of his timber gang, three or four others of the mill crew, the white nightwatchman with the heavy pistol in his hip pocket and the small heap of coins and worn bills on the floor before him, one who was called Rider and was Rider standing above the squatting circle, swaying a little, blinking, the dead muscles of his face shaped into smiling while the white man stared up at him. "Make room, gamblers," he said. "Make room. Ah'm snakebit and de pizen cant hawm me."

"You're drunk," the white man said. "Get out of here. One of you niggers open the door and get him out of here."

"Dass awright, boss-man," he said, his voice equable, his face still fixed in the faint rigid smiling beneath the blinking of the red eyes; "Ah aint drunk. Ah just cant wawk straight fer dis yar money weighin me down."

Now he was kneeling too, the other six dollars of his last week's pay on the floor before him, blinking, still smiling at the face of the white man opposite, then, still smiling, he watched the dice pass from hand to hand around the circle as the white man covered the bets, watching the soiled and palm-worn money in front of the white man gradually and steadily increase, watching the white man cast and win two doubled bets in succession then lose on for twenty-five cents, the dice coming to him at last, the cupped snug clicking of them in his fist. He spun a coin into the center.

"Shoots a dollar," he said, and cast, and watched the white man pick up the dice and flip them back to him. "Ah lets hit lay," he said. "Ah'm snakebit. Ah kin pass wid anything," and cast, and this time one of the Negroes flipped the dice back. "Ah lets hit lay," he said, and cast, and moved as the white man moved, catching the white man's wrist before his hand reached the dice, the two of them squatting, facing each other above the dice and the money, his left hand grasping the white man's wrist, his face still fixed in the rigid and deadened smiling, his voice equable, almost deferential: "Ah kin pass even wid miss-outs. But dese hyar yuther boys—" until the white man's hand sprang open and the second pair of dice clattered onto the floor beside the first two and the white man wrenched free and sprang up and back and reached the hand backward toward the pocket where the pistol was.

The razor hung between his shoulder blades from a loop of cotton string round his neck inside his shirt. The same motion of the hand which brought the razor forward over his shoulder flipped the blade open and freed it from the cord, the blade opening on until the back edge of it lay across the knuckles of his fist, his thumb pressing the handle into his closing fingers, so that in the second before the half-drawn pistol exploded he actually struck at the white man's throat not with the blade but with a sweeping blow of his fist, following through in the same motion so that not even the first jet of blood touched his hand or arm.

II

After it was over—it didn't take long; they found the prisoner on the following day, hanging from the bell rope in a negro schoolhouse about two miles from the sawmill, and the coroner had pronounced his verdict of death at the hands of a person or persons unknown and surrendered the body to its next of kin all within five minutes— the sheriff's deputy who had been officially in charge of the business was telling his wife about it. They were in the kitchen. His wife was cooking supper. The deputy had been out of bed and in motion ever since the jail delivery shortly before midnight of yesterday and had covered considerable ground since, and he was spent now from lack of sleep and hurried food at hurried and curious hours and, sitting in a chair beside the stove, a little hysterical too.

"Them damn niggers," he said "I swear to godfrey, it's a wonder we have as little trouble with them as we do. Because why? Because they aint human. They look like a man and they walk on their hind legs like a man, and they can talk and you can understand them and you think they are understanding you, at least now and then. But when it comes to the normal human feelings and sentiments of human beings, they might just as well be a damn herd of wild buffaloes. Now you take this one today——"

"I wish you would," his wife said harshly. She was a stout woman, handsome once, graying now and with a neck definitely too short, who looked not harried at all but composed in fact, only choleric. Also, she had attended a club rook-party that afternoon and had won the first, the fifty-cent, prize until another member had insisted on a recount of the scores and the ultimate throwing out of one entire game. "Take him out of my kitchen, anyway. You sheriffs! Sitting around that courthouse all day long, talking. It's no wonder two or three men can walk in and take prisoners out from under your very noses. They would take your chairs and desks and window sills too if you ever got your feet and backsides off of them that long."

"It's more of them Birdsongs than just two or three," the deputy said. "There's forty-two active votes in that connection. Me and Maydew taken the poll-list and counted them one day. But listen——" The wife turned from the stove, carrying a dish. The deputy snatched his feet rapidly out of the way as she passed him, passed almost over him, and went into the dining room. The deputy raised his voice a little to carry the increased distance: "His wife dies on him. All right. But does he grieve? He's the biggest and busiest man at the funeral. Grabs a shovel before they even got the box into the grave they tell me, and starts throwing dirt onto her faster than a slip scraper could have done it. But that's all right——" His wife came back. He moved his feet again and altered his voice again to the altered range: "—maybe that's how he felt about her. There aint any law against a man rushing his wife into the ground, provided he never had nothing to do with rushing her to the cemetery too. But here the next day he's the first man back at work except the fireman, getting back to the mill before the fireman had his fire going, let alone steam up; five minutes earlier and he could even have helped the fireman wake Birdsong up so Birdsong could go home and go back to bed again, or he could even have cut Birdsong's throat then and saved everybody trouble.

"So he comes to work, the first man on the job, when McAndrews and everybody else expected him to take the day off since even a nigger couldn't want no better excuse for a holiday than he had just buried his wife, when a white man would have took the day off out of pure respect no matter how he felt about his wife, when even a little child would have had sense enough to take a day off when he would still get paid for it too. But not him. The first man there, jumping from one log truck to another before the starting whistle quit blowing even, snatching up ten-foot cypress logs by himself and throwing them around like matches. And then, when everybody had finally decided that that's the way to take him, the way he wants to be took, he walks off the job in the middle of the afternoon without by-your-leave or much obliged or goodbye to McAndrews or nobody else, gets himself a whole gallon of bust-skull white-mule whisky, comes straight back to the mill and to the same crap game where Birdsong has been running crooked dice on them mill niggers for fifteen years, goes straight to the same game where he has been peacefully losing a probably steady average ninety-nine per cent of his pay ever since he got big enough to read the spots on them miss-out dice, and cuts Birdsong's throat clean to the neckbone five minutes later." The wife passed him again and went to the dining room. Again he drew his feet back and raised his voice:

"So me and Maydew go out there. Not that we expected to do any good, as he had probably passed Jackson, Tennessee, about daylight; and besides, the simplest way to find him would be just to stay close behind them Birdsong boys. Of course there wouldn't be nothing hardly worth bringing back to town after they did find him, but it would close the case. So it's just by the merest chance that we go by his house; I dont even remember why we went now, but we did; and there he is. Sitting behind the barred front door with a open razor on one knee and a loaded shotgun on the other? No. He was asleep. A big pot of field peas et clean empty on the stove, and him laying in the back yard asleep in the broad sun with just his head under the edge of the porch in the shade and a dog that looked like a cross between a bear and a Polled Angus steer yelling fire and murder from the back door. And we wake him and he sets up and says, 'Awright, white folks. Ah done it. Jest dont lock me up,' and Maydew says, 'Mr. Birdsong's kinfolks aint going to lock you up neither. You'll have plenty of fresh air when they get hold of you,' and he says, 'Ah done it. Jest dont lock me up'—advising, instructing the sheriff not to lock him up; he done it all right and it's too bad but it aint convenient for him to be cut off from the fresh air at the moment. So we loaded him into the car, when here come the old woman—his ma or aunt or something—panting up the road at a dog-trot, wanting to come with us too, and Maydew trying to explain to her what would maybe happen to her too if them Birdsong kin catches us before we can get him locked up, only she is coming anyway, and like Maydew says, her being in the car too might be a good thing if the Birdsongs did happen to run into us, because after all interference with the law cant be condoned even if the Birdsong connection did carry that beat for Maydew last summer.

"So we brought her along too and got him to town and into the jail all right and turned him over to Ketcham and Ketcham taken him on up stairs and the old woman coming too, right on up to the cell, telling Ketcham, 'Ah tried to raise him right. He was a good boy. He aint never been in no trouble till now. He will suffer for what he done. But dont let the white folks get him,' until Ketcham says, 'You and him ought to thought of that before he started barbering white men without using no later first.' So he locked them both up in the cell because he felt like Maydew did, that her being in there with him might be a good influence on the Birdsong boys if anything started if he should happen to be running for sheriff or something when Maydew's term was up. So Ketcham come on back down stairs and pretty soon the chain gang come in and went on up to the bull pen and he thought things had settled down for a while when all of a sudden he begun to hear the yelling not howling: yelling, though there wasn't no words in it, and he grabbed his pistol and run back up stairs to the bull pen where the chain gang was and Ketcham could see into the cell where the old woman was kind of squinched down in one corner and where that nigger had done tore that iron cot clean out of the floor it was bolted to and was standing in the middle of the cell, holding the cot over his head like it was a baby's cradle, yelling, and says to the old woman, 'Ah aint goan hurt you,' and throws the cot against the wall and comes and grabs holt of that steel barred door and rips it out of the wall, bricks hinges and all, and walks out of the cell toting the door over his head like it was a gauze window-screen, hollering, "It's awright. It's awright. Ah aint trying to git away.'

"Of course Ketcham could have shot him right there, but like he said, if it wasn't going to be the law, then them Birdsong boys ought to have the first lick at him. So Ketcham dont shoot. Instead, he jumps in behind where them chain gang niggers was kind of backed off from that steel door, hollering, 'Grab him! Throw him down!' except the niggers hung back at first too until Ketcham gets in where he can kick the ones he can reach, batting at the others with the flat of the pistol until they rush him. And Ketcham says that for a full minute that nigger would grab them as they come in and fling then clean across the room like they was rag dolls, saying, 'Ah aint trying to git out. Ah aint trying to git out,' until at last they pulled him down—a big mass of nigger heads and arms and legs boiling around on the floor and even then Ketcham says every now and then a nigger would come flying out and go sailing through the air across the room, spraddled out like a flying squirrel and with his eyes sticking out like car headlights, until at last they had him down and Ketcham went in and begun peeling away niggers until he could see him laying there under the pile of them, laughing, with tears big as glass marbles running across his face and down past his ears and making a kind of popping sound on the floor like somebody dropping bird eggs, laughing and laughing and saying, 'Hit look lack Ah just cant quit thinking. Look lack Ah just cant quit.' And what do you think of that?"

"I think if you eat any supper in this house you'll do it in the next five minutes," his wife said from the dining room. "I'm going to clear this table then and I'm going to the picture show."

Pantaloon in Black

For Analysis

1. What is a pantaloon? In what sense is Rider a pantaloon? Is the title of this story ironic?

2. There are three marriages in this story (Rider and Mannie, Rider's
    Uncle and Aunt, the deputy and his wife). How does the quality of
    the Negroes' marriages compare to that of the deputy?
3. What is the significance of Rider's red eyes and labored breathing?
4. Is the deputy's interpretation of Rider's behavior correct? How does
    the deputy's attitude toward Negroes determine his interpretation?

John Collier

The
Chaser

Alan Austen, as nervous as a kitten, went up certain dark and
creaky stairs in the neighborhood of Pell Street and peered about for
a long time on the dim landing before he found the name he wanted
written obscurely on one of the doors.

He pushed open this door, as he had been told to do, and found
himself in a tiny room, which contained no furniture but a plain
kitchen table, a rocking chair, and an ordinary chair. On one of the
dirty buff-colored walls were a couple of shelves, containing in all
perhaps a dozen bottles and jars.

An old man sat in the rocking chair, reading a newspaper. Alan,
without a word, handed him the card he had been given. "Sit down,
Mr. Austen," said the old man very politely. "I am glad to make
your acquaintance."

"Is it true," asked Alan, "that you have a certain mixture that has
—er—quite extraordinary effects?"

"My dear sir," replied the old man, "my stock in trade is not very
large—I don't deal in laxatives and teething mixtures—but such as
it is, it is varied. I think nothing I sell has effects which could be precisely described as ordinary."

"Well, the fact is—" began Alan.

"Here, for example," interrupted the old man, reaching for a bottle from the shelf. "Here is a liquid as colorless as water, almost tasteless, quite imperceptible in coffee, milk, wine, or any other beverage. It is also quite imperceptible to any known method of autopsy."

"Do you mean it is a poison?" cried Alan, very much horrified.

"Call it a glove-cleaner if you like," said the old man indifferently. "Maybe it will clean gloves. I have never tried. One might call it a life-cleaner. Lives need cleaning sometimes."

"I want nothing of that sort," said Alan.

"Probably it is just as well," said the old man. "Do you know the price of this? For one teaspoonful, which is sufficient, I ask five thousand dollars. Never less. Not a penny less."

"I hope all your mixtures are not as expensive," said Alan apprehensively.

"Oh dear, no," said the old man. "It would be no good charging that sort of price for a love potion, for example. Young people who need a love potion very seldom have five thousands dollars. Otherwise they would not need a love potion."

"I am glad to hear that," said Alan.

"I look at it like this," said the old man. "Please a customer with one article, and he will come back when he needs another. Even if it *is* more costly. He will save up for it, if necessary."

"So," said Alan, "you really do sell love potions?"

"If I did not sell love potions," said the old man, reaching for another bottle, "I should not have mentioned the other matter to you. It is only when one is in a position to oblige that one can afford to be so confidential."

"And these potions," said Alan. "They are not just—just—er—"

"Oh, no," said the old man. "Their effects are permanent and extend far beyond casual impulse. But they include it. Bountifully, insistently. Everlastingly."

"Dear me!" said Alan, attempting a look of scientific detachment. "How very interesting!"

"But consider the spiritual side," said the old man.

"I do, indeed," said Alan.

"For indifference," said the old man, "they substitute devotion. For scorn, adoration. Give one tiny measure of this to the young lady—its flavor is imperceptible in orange juice, soup, or cocktails— and however gay and giddy she is, she will change altogether. She will want nothing but solitude, and you."

"I can hardly believe it," said Alan. "She is so fond of parties."

"She will not like them any more," said the old man. "She will be afraid of the pretty girls you may meet."

"She will actually be jealous?" cried Alan in a rapture. "Of me?"

"Yes, she will want to be everything to you."

"She is, already. Only she doesn't care about it."

"She will, when she has taken this. She will care intensely. You will be her sole interest in life."

"Wonderful!" cried Alan.

"She will want to know all you do," said the old man. "All that happened to you during the day. Every word of it. She will want to know what you are thinking about, why you smile suddenly, why you are looking sad."

"That is love!" cried Alan.

"Yes," said the old man. "How carefully she will look after you! She will never allow you to be tired, to sit in a draught, to neglect your food. If you are an hour late, she will be terrified. She will think you are killed, or that some siren has caught you."

"I can hardly imagine Diana like that!" cried Alan, overwhelmed with joy.

"You will not have to use your imagination," said the old man. "And, by the way, since there are always sirens, if by any chance you *should*, later on, slip a little, you need not worry. She will forgive you, in the end. She will be terribly hurt, of course, but she will forgive you—in the end."

"That will not happen," said Alan fervently.

"Of course not," said the old man. "But, if it did, you need not worry. She would never divorce you. Oh, no! And, of course, she herself will never give you the least, the very least, grounds for—uneasiness."

"And how much," said Alan, "is this wonderful mixture?"

"It is not as dear," said the old man, "as the glove-cleaner, or life-cleaner, as I sometimes call it. No. That is five thousand dollars, never a penny less. One has to be older than you are, to indulge in that sort of thing. One has to save up for it."

"But the love potion?" said Alan.

"Oh, that," said the old man, opening the drawer in the kitchen table, and taking out a tiny, rather dirty-looking phial. "That is just a dollar."

"I can't tell you how grateful I am," said Alan, watching him fill it.

"I like to oblige," said the old man. "Then customers come back, later in life, when they are rather better off, and want more expensive things. Here you are. You will find it very effective."

"Thank you again," said Alan. "Good-bye."

"*Au revoir,*" said the old man.

The Chaser

For Analysis

1. What is the old man's theory of marketing? How does he put it into effect on Alan?
2. What will Alan's relationship to Diana be after their marriage? How does the old man expect to benefit from their marriage?
3. Why is *au revoir* a perfect concluding line for the story?

James Baldwin

Sonny's Blues

I read about it in the paper, in the subway, on my way to work. I read it, and I couldn't believe it, and I read it again. Then perhaps I just stared at it, at the newsprint spelling out his name, spelling out the story. I stared at it in the swinging lights of the subway car, and in the faces and bodies of the people, and in my own face, trapped in the darkness which roared outside.

It was not to be believed, and I kept telling myself that as I walked from the subway station to the high school. And at the same time I couldn't doubt it. I was scared, scared for Sonny. He became real to me again. A great block of ice got settled in my belly and kept melting there slowly all day long, while I taught my classes algebra. It was a special kind of ice. It kept melting, sending trickles of ice water all up and down my veins, but it never got less. Sometimes it hardened and seemed to expand until I felt my guts were going to come spilling out or that I was going to choke or scream. This would always be at a moment when I was remembering some specific thing Sonny had once said or done.

When he was about as old as the boys in my classes, his face had been bright and open, there was a lot of copper in it; and he'd had wonderfully direct brown eyes, and great gentleness and privacy. I wondered what he looked like now. He had been picked up, the evening before, in a raid on an apartment downtown, for peddling and using heroin.

I couldn't believe it: But what I mean by that is that I couldn't find any room for it anywhere inside me. I had kept it outside me for a long time. I hadn't wanted to know. I had had suspicions, but I didn't name them, I kept putting them away. I told myself that Sonny was wild, but he wasn't crazy. And he'd always been a good boy, he hadn't ever turned hard or evil or disrespectful, the way kids can, so quick, so quick, especially in Harlem. I didn't want to believe that I'd ever see my brother going down, coming to nothing, all that light in his face gone out, in the condition I'd already seen so many others. Yet it had happened and here I was, talking about algebra to a lot of boys who might, every one of them for all I knew, be popping off needles every time they went to the head. Maybe it did more for them than algebra could.

I was sure that the first time Sonny had ever had horse, he couldn't have been much older than these boys were now. These boys, now, were living as we'd been living then, they were growing up with a rush and their heads bumped abruptly against the low ceiling of their actual possibilities. They were filled with rage. All they really knew were two darknesses, the darkness of their lives, which was now closing in on them, and the darkness of the movies, which had blinded them to that other darkness, and in which they now, vindictively, dreamed, at once more together than they were at any other time, and more alone.

When the last bell rang, the last class ended, I let out my breath. It seemed I'd been holding it for all that time. My clothes were set— I may have looked as though I'd been sitting in a steam bath, all dressed up, all afternoon. I sat alone in the classroom a long time. I listened to the boys outside, downstairs, shouting and cursing and laughing. Their laughter struck me for perhaps the first time. It was not the joyous laughter which—God knows why—one associates with children. It was mocking and insular, its intent was to denigrate. It was disenchanted, and in this, also, lay the authority of their curses. Perhaps I was listening to them because I was thinking about my brother and in them I heard my brother. And myself.

One boy was whistling a tune, at once very complicated and very simple, it seemed to be pouring out of him as though he were a bird, and it sounded very cool and moving through all that harsh, bright air, only just holding its own through all those other sounds.

I stood and walked over to the window and looked down into the courtyard. It was the beginning of the spring, and the sap was rising in the boys. A teacher passed through them every now and again, quickly, as though he or she couldn't wait to get out of that courtyard to get those boys out of their sight and off their minds. I started collecting my stuff. I thought I'd better get home and talk to Isabel.

The courtyard was almost deserted by the time I got downstairs. I saw this boy standing in the shadow of a doorway, looking just like Sonny. I almost called his name. Then I saw it wasn't Sonny but somebody we used to know, a boy from around our block. He'd been Sonny's friend. He'd never been mine, having been too young for me, and, anyway, I'd never liked him. And now, even though he was a grown-up man, he still hung around that block, still spent hours on the street corner, was always high and raggy. I used to run into him from time to time, and he'd often work around to asking me for a quarter or fifty cents. He always had some real good excuse, too, and I always gave it to him, I don't know why.

But now, abruptly, I hated him. I couldn't stand the way he looked at me, partly like a dog, partly like a cunning child. I wanted to ask him what the hell he was doing in the school courtyard.

He sort of shuffled over to me, and he said, "I see you got the papers. So you already know about it."

"You mean about Sonny?" Yes, I already know about it. How come they didn't get you?"

He grinned. It made him repulsive and it also brought to mind what he'd looked like as a kid. "I wasn't there. I stay away from them people."

"Good for you." I offered him a cigarette and I watched him through the smoke. "You come all the way down here just to tell me about Sonny?"

"That's right." He was sort of shaking his head and his eyes looked strange, as though they were about to cross. The bright sun deadened his damp dark brown skin and it made his eyes look yellow and showed up the dirt in his conked hair. He smelled funky. I moved a little away from him and I said, "Well thanks. But I already know about it and I got to get home."

"I'll walk you a little ways," he said. We started walking. There were a couple of kids still loitering in the courtyard and one of them said good night to me and looked strangely at the boy beside me.

"What're you going to do?" he asked me. "I mean, about Sonny?"

"Look. I haven't seen Sonny for over a year, I'm not sure I'm going to do anything. Anyway, what the hell *can* I do?"

"That's right," he said quickly, "ain't nothing you can do. Can't much help old Sonny no more, I guess."

It was what I was thinking and so it seemed to me he had no right to say it.

"I'm surprised at Sonny, though," he went on—he had a funny way of talking, he looked straight ahead as though he were talking to himself—"I thought Sonny was a smart boy, I thought he was too smart to get hung."

"I guess he thought so, too," I said sharply, "and that's how he got hung. And how about you? You're pretty goddamn smart, I bet."

Then he looked directly at me, just for a minute. "I ain't smart," he said. "If I was smart, I'd have reached for a pistol a long time ago."

"Look. Don't tell *me* your sad story, if it was up to me, I'd give you one." Then I felt guilty—guilty probably, for never having supposed that the poor bastard *had* a story of his own, much less a sad one, and I asked, quickly, "What's going to happen to him now?"

He didn't answer this. He was off by himself someplace. "Funny thing," he said, and from his tone we might have been discussing the quickest way to get to Brooklyn, "when I saw the papers this morning, the first thing I asked myself was if I had anything to do with it. I felt sort of responsible."

I began to listen more carefully. The subway station was on the corner, just before us, and I stopped. He stopped, too. We were in front of a bar and he ducked slightly, peering in, but whoever he was looking for didn't seem to be there. The juke box was blasting away with something black and bouncy, and I half watched the barmaid as she danced her way from the juke box to her place behind the bar. And I watched her face as she laughingly responded to something someone said to her, still keeping time to the music. When she smiled one saw the little girl, one sensed the doomed, still-struggling woman beneath the battered face of the semi-whore.

"I never *give* Sonny nothing," the boy said finally, "but a long time ago I come to school high and Sonny asked me how it felt." He paused, I couldn't bear to watch him, I watched the barmaid, and I listened to the music which seemed to be causing the pavement to shake. "I told him it felt great." The music stopped, the barmaid paused and watched the juke box until the music began again. "It did."

All this was carrying me someplace I didn't want to go. I certainly didn't want to know how it felt. It filled everything, the people, the houses, the music, the dark, quick-silver barmaid, with menace; and this menace was their reality.

"What's going to happen to him now?" I asked again.

"They'll send him away someplace and they'll try to cure him." he shook his head. "Maybe he'll even think he's kicked the habit. Then they'll let him loose"—He gestured, throwing his cigarette into the gutter. "That's all."

"What do you mean, that's *all?*"

But I knew what he meant.

"I *mean,* that's *all.*" He turned his head and looked at me, pulling down the corners of his mouth. "Don't you know what I mean?" he asked, softly.

"How the hell *would* I know what you mean?" I almost whispered it, I don't know why.

"That's right," he said to the air, "how would *he* know what I mean?" He turned toward me again, patient and calm, and yet I somehow felt him shaking, shaking as though he were going to fall apart. I felt that ice in my guts again, the dread I'd felt all afternoon; and again I watched the barmaid, moving about the bar, washing glasses, and singing. "Listen. They'll let him out and then it'll just start over again. That's what I mean."

"You mean—they'll let him out. And then he'll just start working his way back in again. You mean he'll never kick the habit. Is that what you mean?"

"That's right," he said, cheerfully. "*You* see what I mean."

"Tell me," I said at last, "why does he want to die? He must want to die, he's killing himself, why does he want to die?"

He looked at me in surprise. He licked his lips. "He don't want to die. He wants to live. Don't nobody want to die, ever."

Then I wanted to ask him—too many things. He could not have answered, or if he had, I could not have borne the answers. I started walking. "Well, I guess it's none of my business."

"It's going to be rough on old Sonny," he said. We reached the subway station. "This is your station?" he asked. I nodded. I took one step down. "Damn!" he said, suddenly. I looked up at him. He grinned again. "Damn if I didn't leave all my money home. You ain't got a dollar on you, have you? Just for a couple of days, is all."

All at once something inside gave and threatened to come pouring out of me. I didn't hate him any more. I felt that in another moment I'd starting crying like a child.

"Sure," I said. "Don't sweat." I looked in my wallet and didn't have a dollar, I only had a five. "Here," I said. "That hold you?"

He didn't look at it—he didn't want to look at it. A terrible, closed look came over his face, as though he were keeping the number on the bill a secret from him and me. "Thanks," he said, and now he was dying to see me go. "Don't worry about Sonny. Maybe I'll write him or something."

"Sure," I said. "You do that. So long."

"Be seeing you," he said. I went on down the steps.

And I didn't write Sonny or send him anything for a long time. When I finally did, it was just after my little girl died, he wrote me back a letter which made me feel like a bastard.

Here's what he said:

Dear brother,
    You don't know how much I needed to hear from you. I wanted to write you many a time but I dug how much I must have hurt you and so I didn't write. But now I feel like a man who's been

trying to climb up out of some deep, real deep and funky hole and just saw the sun up there, outside. I got to get outside.

I can't tell you much about how I got here. I mean I don't know how to tell you. I guess I was afraid of something or I was trying to escape from something and you know I have never been very strong in the head (smile). I'm glad Mama and Daddy are dead and can't see what's happened to their son and I swear if I'd known what I was doing I would never have hurt you so, you and a lot of other fine people who were nice to me and who believed in me.

I don't want you to think it had anything to do with me being a musician. It's more than that. Or maybe less than that. I can't get anything straight in my head down here and I try not to think about what's going to happen to me when I get outside again. Sometime I think I'm going to flip and *never* get outside and sometime I think I'll come straight back. I tell you one thing, though, I'd rather blow my brains out than go through this again. But that's what they all say, so they tell me. If I tell you when I'm coming to New York and if you could meet me, I sure would appreciate it. Give my love to Isabel and the kids and I was sure sorry to hear about little Gracie. I wish I could be like Mama and say the Lord's will be done, but I don't know it seems to me that trouble is the one thing that never does get stopped and I don't know what good it does to blame it on the Lord. But maybe it does some good if you believe it.

Your brother,

SONNY

Then I kept in constant touch with him and I sent him whatever I could and I went to meet him when he came back to New York. When I saw him, many things I thought I had forgotten came flooding back to me. This was because I had begun, finally, to wonder about Sonny, about the life that Sonny lived inside. This life, whatever it was, had made him older and thinner and it had deepened the distant stillness in which he had always moved. He looked very unlike my baby brother. Yet, when he smiled, when we shook hands, the baby brother I'd never known looked out from the depths of his private life, like an animal waiting to be coaxed into the light.

"How you been keeping?" he asked me.

"All right. And you?"

"Just fine." He was smiling all over his face. "It's good to see you again."

"It's good to see you."

The seven years' difference in our ages lay between us like a chasm: I wondered if these years would ever operate between us as a bridge.

I was remembering, and it made it hard to catch my breath, that I had been there when he was born; and I had heard the first words he had ever spoken. When he started to walk, he walked from our mother straight to me. I caught him just before he fell when he took the first steps he ever took in this world.

"How's Isabel?"

"Just fine. She's dying to see you."

"And the boys?"

"They're fine too. They're anxious to see their uncle."

"Oh, come on. You know they don't remember me."

"Are you kidding? Of course they remember you."

He grinned again. We got into a taxi. We had a lot to say to each other, far too much to know how to begin.

As the taxi began to move, I asked, "You still want to go to India?"

He laughed. "You still remember that. Hell, no. This place is Indian enough for me."

"It used to belong to them," I said.

And he laughed again. "They damn sure knew what they were doing when they got rid of it."

Years ago, when he was around fourteen, he'd been all hipped on the idea of going to India. He read books about people sitting on rocks, naked, in all kinds of weather, but mostly bad, naturally, and walking barefoot through hot coals and arriving at wisdom. I used to say that it sounded to me as though they were getting away from wisdom as fast as they could. I think he sort of looked down on me for that.

"Do you mind," he asked, "If we have the driver drive alongside the park? On the west side—I haven't seen the city in so long."

"Of course not," I said. I was afraid that I might sound as though I were humoring him, but I hoped he wouldn't take it that way.

So we drove along, between the green of the park and the stony, lifeless elegance of hotels and apartment buildings, toward the vivid, killing streets of our childhood. These streets hadn't changed, though housing projects jutted up out of them now like rocks in the middle of a boiling sea. Most of the houses in which we had grown up had vanished, as had the stores from which we had stolen, the basements in which we had first tried sex, the rooftops from which we had hurled tin cans and bricks. But houses exactly like the houses of our past yet dominated the landscape, boys exactly like the boys we once had been found themselves smothering in these houses, came down into the streets for light and air and found themselves encircled by disaster. Some escaped the trap, most didn't. Those who got out always left something of themselves behind, as some animals amputate a leg and leave it in the trap. It might be said, perhaps, that I had escaped, after all, I was a schoolteacher; or that Sonny had, he hadn't lived in Harlem for years. Yet as the cab moved uptown through streets which seemed, with a rush, to darken with dark people, and as I covertly studied Sonny's face, it came to me that what we both were seeking through our separate cab windows was that part of ourselves which had been left behind. It's always at the hour of trouble and confrontation that the missing member aches.

We hit 110th Street and started rolling up Lenox Avenue. And I'd known this avenue all my life, but it seemed to me again, as it had seemed on the day I'd first heard about Sonny's trouble, filled with a hidden menace which was its very breath of life.

"We almost there," said Sonny.

"Almost." We were both too nervous to say anything more.

We live in a housing project. It hasn't been up long. A few days after it was up it seemed uninhabitably new, now, of course, it's already rundown. It looked like a parody of the good, clean, faceless life—God knows the people who live in it do their best to make it a parody. The beat-looking grass lying around isn't enough to make their lives green, the hedges will never hold out the streets, and they know it. The big windows fool no one, they aren't big enough to make space out of no space. They don't bother with the windows, they watch the TV screen instead. The playground is most popular with the children who don't play at jacks, or skip rope, or roller skate, or swing, and they can be found in it after dark. We moved in partly because it's not too far from where I teach, and partly for the kids; but it's really just like the houses in which Sonny and I grew up. The same things happen, they'll have the same things to remember. The moment Sonny and I started into the house I had the feeling that I was simply bringing him back into the danger he had almost died trying to escape.

Sonny has never been talkative. So I don't know why I was sure he'd be dying to talk to me when supper was over the first night. Everything went fine, the oldest boy remembered him, and the youngest boy liked him, and Sonny had remembered to bring something for each of them; and Isabel, who is really much nicer than I am, more open and giving, had gone to a lot of trouble about dinner and was genuinely glad to see him. And she'd always been able to tease Sonny in a way that I haven't. It was nice to see her face so vivid again and to hear her laugh and watch her make Sonny laugh. She wasn't, or, anyway, she didn't seem to be, at all uneasy or embarrassed. She chatted as though there were no subject which had to be avoided and she got Sonny past his first, faint stiffness. And thank God she was there, for I was filled with that icy dread again. Everything I did seemed awkward to me, and everything I said sounded freighted with hidden meaning. I was trying to remember everything I'd heard about dope addiction and I couldn't help watching Sonny for signs. I wasn't doing it out of malice. I was trying to find out something about my brother. I was dying to hear him tell me he was safe.

"Safe!" my father grunted, whenever Mama suggested trying to move to a neighborhood which might be safer for children. "Safe, hell! Ain't no place safe for kids, nor nobody."

He always went on like this, but he wasn't, ever, really as bad as he sounded, not even on weekends, when he got drunk. As a matter of fact, he was always on the lookout for "something a little better," but he died before he found it. He died suddenly, during a drunken weekend in the middle of the war, when Sonny was fifteen. He and Sonny hadn't ever got on too well. And this was partly because Sonny was the apple of his father's eye. It was because he loved Sonny so much and was frightened for him, that he was always fighting with him. It doesn't do any good to fight with Sonny. Sonny just moves back, inside himself, where he can't be reached. But the principal reason that they never hit it off is that they were so much alike. Daddy was big and rough and loud-talking, just the opposite of Sonny, but they both had—that same privacy.

Mama tried to tell me something about this, just after Daddy died. I was home on leave from the army.

This was the last time I ever saw my mother alive. Just the same, this picture gets all mixed up in my mind with pictures I had of her when she was younger. The way I always see her is the way she used to be on Sunday afternoon, say, when the old folks were talking after the big Sunday dinner. I always see her wearing pale blue. She'd be sitting on the sofa. And my father would be sitting in the easy chair, not far from her. And the living room would be full of church folks and relatives. There they sit, in chairs all around the living room, and the night is creeping up outside, but nobody knows it yet. You can see the darkness growing against the windowpanes and you hear the street noises every now and again, or maybe the jangling beat of a tambourine from one of the churches close by, but it's real quiet in the room. For a moment nobody's talking, but every face looks darkening, like the sky outside. And my mother rocks a little from the waist, and my father's eyes are closed. Everyone is looking at something a child can't see. For a minute they've forgotten the children. Maybe a kid is lying on the rug, half asleep. Maybe somebody's got a kid in his lap and is absent-mindedly stroking the kid's head. Maybe there's a kid, quiet and big-eyed, curled up in a big chair in the corner. The silence, the darkness coming, and the darkness in the faces frighten the child obscurely. He hopes that the hand which strokes his forehead will never stop—will never die. He hopes that there will never come a time when the old folks won't be sitting around the living room, talking about where they've come from, and what they've seen, and what's happened to them and their kinfolk.

But something deep and watchful in the child knows that this is bound to end, is already ending. In a moment someone will get up and turn on the light. Then the old folks will remember the children and they won't talk any more that day. And when light fills the room, the child is filled with darkness. He knows that every time this happens he's moved just a little closer to that darkness outside. The darkness outside is what the old folks have been talking about. It's what they've come from. It's what they endure. The child knows that they won't talk any more because if he knows too much about what's happened to *them*, he'll know too much too soon, about what's going to happen to *him*.

The last time I talked to my mother, I remember I was restless. I wanted to get out and see Isabel. We weren't married then and we had a lot to straighten out between us.

There Mama sat, in black, by the window. She was humming an old church song, *Lord, you brought me from a long ways off*. Sonny was out somewhere. Mama kept watching the streets.

"I don't know," she said, "if I'll ever see you again, after you go off from here. But I hope you'll remember the things I tried to teach you."

"Don't talk like that," I said, and smiled. "You'll be here a long time yet."

She smiled, too, but she said nothing. She was quiet for a long time. And I said, "Mama, don't you worry about nothing. I'll be writing all the time, and you be getting the checks. . . ."

"I want to talk to you about your brother," she said, suddenly. "If anything happens to me, he ain't going to have nobody to look out for him."

"Mama," I said, "ain't nothing going to happen to you *or* Sonny. Sonny's all right. He's a good boy and he's got good sense."

"It ain't a question of his being a good boy," Mama said, "nor of his having good sense. It ain't only the bad ones, nor yet the dumb ones that gets sucked under." She stopped, looking at me. "Your Daddy once had a brother," she said, and she smiled in a way that made me feel she was in pain. "You didn't never know that, did you?"

"No," I said. "I never knew that," and I watched her face.

"Oh, yes," she said, "your Daddy had a brother." She looked out of the window again. "I know you never saw your Daddy cry. But *I* did—many a time, through all these years."

I asked her, "What happened to his brother? How come nobody's ever talked about him?"

This was the first time I ever saw my mother look old.

"His brother got killed," she said, "when he was just a little younger than you are now. I knew him. He was a fine boy. He was maybe a little full of the devil, but he didn't mean nobody no harm."

Then she stopped, and the room was silent, exactly as it had sometimes been on those Sunday afternoons. Mama kept looking out into the streets.

"He used to have a job in the mill," she said, "and, like all young folks, he just liked to perform on Saturday nights. Saturday nights, him and your father would drift around to different places, go to dances and things like that, or just sit around with people they knew, and your father's brother would sing, he had a fine voice, and play along with himself on his guitar. Well, this particular Saturday night, him and your father was coming home from some place, and they were both a little drunk and there was a moon that night, it was bright like day. Your father's brother was feeling kind of good, and he was whistling to himself, and he had his guitar slung over his shoulder. They was coming down a hill, and beneath them was a road that turned off from the highway. Well, your father's brother, being always kind of frisky, decided to run down this hill, and he did, with that guitar banging and clanging behind him, and he ran across the road, and he was making water behind a tree. And your father was sort of amused at him and he was still coming down the hill, kind of slow. Then he heard a car motor and that same minute his brother stepped from behind the tree, into the road, in the moonlight. And he started to cross the road. And your father started to run down the hill, he says he don't know why. This car was full of white men. They was all drunk, and when they seen your father's brother they let out a great whoop and holler and they aimed the car straight at him. They was having fun, they just wanted to scare him, the way they do sometimes, you know. But they was drunk. And I guess the boy, being drunk, too, and scared, kind of lost his head. By the time he jumped it was too late. Your father says he heard his brother scream when the car rolled over him, and he heard the wood of that guitar when it give, and he heard them strings go flying, and he heard them white men shouting, and the car kept on a-going and it ain't stopped till this day. And, time your father got down the hill, his brother weren't nothing but blood and pulp."

Tears were gleaming on my mother's face. There wasn't anything I could say.

"He never mentioned it," she said, "because I never let him mention it before you children. Your Daddy was like a crazy man that night and for many a night thereafter. He says he never in his life seen anything as dark as that road after lights of that car had gone away. Weren't nothing, weren't nobody on that road, just your Daddy and his brother and that busted guitar. Oh, yes. Your Daddy never did really get right again. Till the day he died he weren't sure but that every white man he saw was the man that killed his brother."

She stopped and took out her hankerchief and dried her eyes and looked at me.

"I ain't telling you all this," she said, "to make you scared or bitter or to make you hate nobody. I'm telling you this because you got a brother. And the world ain't changed."

I guess I didn't want to believe this. I guess she saw this in my face. She turned away from me, toward the window again, searching those streets.

"But I praise my Redeemer," she said at last, "that he called your Daddy home before me. I ain't saying it to throw no flowers at myself, but, I declare, it keeps me from feeling too cast down to know I helped your father get safely through this world. Your father always acted like he was the roughest, strongest man on earth. And everybody took him to be like that. But if he hadn't had *me* there— to see his tears!"

She was crying again. Still, I couldn't move. I said, "Lord, Lord, Mama, I didn't know it was like that."

"Oh, honey," she said, "there's a lot that you don't know. But you are going to find it out." She stood up from the window and came over to me. "You got to hold on to your brother," she said, "and don't let him fall, no matter what it looks like is happening to him and no matter how evil you gets with him. You going to be evil with him many a time. But don't you forget what I told you, you hear?"

"I won't forget," I said. "Don't you worry, I won't forget. I won't let nothing happen to Sonny."

My mother smiled as though she was amused at something she saw in my face. Then, "You may not be able to stop nothing from happening. But you got to let him know you's *there*.

Two days later I was married, and then I was gone. And I had a lot of things on my mind and I pretty well forgot my promise to Mama until I got shipped home on a special furlough for her funeral.

And, after the funeral, with just Sonny and me alone in the empty kitchen, I tried to find out something about him.

"What do you want to do?" I asked him.

"I'm going to be a musician," he said.

For he had graduated, in the time I had been away, from dancing to the juke box to finding out who was playing what, and what they were doing with it, and he had bought himself a set of drums.

"You mean, you want to be a drummer?" I somehow had the feeling that being a drummer might be all right for other people but not for my brother Sonny.

"I don't think," he said, looking at me very gravely, "that I'll ever be a good drummer. But I think I can play a piano."

I frowned. I'd never played the role of the older brother quite so seriously before, had scarcely ever, in fact, *asked* Sonny a damn thing. I sensed myself in the presence of something I didn't really know how to handle, didn't understand. So I made my frown a little deeper as I asked: "What kind of musician do you want to be?"

He grinned. "How many kinds do you think there are?"

"Be *serious*," I said.

He laughed, throwing his head back, and then looked at me. "I *am* serious."

"Well, then, for Christ's sake, stop kidding around and answer a serious question. I mean, do you want to be a concert pianist, you want to play classical music and all that, or—or, what?" Long before I finished he was laughing again. "For Christ's *sake*, Sonny!"

He sobered, but with difficulty. "I'm sorry. But you sound so— *scared!*" And he was off again.

"Well, you may think it's funny now, baby, but it's not going to be so funny when you have to make your living at it, let me tell you *that*." I was furious because I knew he was laughing at me and I didn't know why.

"No," he said, very sober now, and afraid, perhaps, that he'd hurt me," "I don't want to be a classical pianist. That isn't what interests me. I mean"—he paused, looking hard at me, as though his eyes would help me to understand, and then gestured helplessly, as though perhaps his hand would help—"I mean, I'll have a lot of studying to do, and I'll have to study *everything*, but, I mean, I want to play *with*—jazz musicians." He stopped. "I want to play jazz," he said.

Well, the word had never before sounded as heavy, as real, as it sounded that afternoon in Sonny's mouth. I just looked at him and I was probably frowning a real frown by this time. I simply couldn't see why on earth he'd want to spend his time hanging around night clubs, clowning around on bandstands, while people pushed each other around a dance floor. It seemed—beneath him, somehow. I had never thought about it before, had never been forced to, but I suppose I had always put jazz musicians in a class with what Daddy called "good-time people."

"Are you *serious?*"

"Hell, *yes,* I'm serious."

He looked more helpless than ever, and annoyed, and deeply hurt. I suggested, helpfully: "You mean—like Louis Armstrong?"

His face closed as though I'd struck him. "No. I'm not talking about none of that old-time, down home crap."

"Well, look, Sonny, I'm sorry, don't get mad. I just don't altogether get it, that's all. Name somebody—you know, a jazz musician you admire."

"Bird."

"Who?"

"Bird! Charlie Parker! Don't they teach you nothing in the god-damn army?"

I lit a cigarette. I was surprised and then a little amused to dis-cover that I was trembling. "I've been out of touch," I said. "You'll have to be patient with me. Now. Who's this Parker character?"

"He's just one of the greatest jazz musicians alive," said Sonny, sullenly, his hands in his pockets, his back to me. "Maybe *the* great-est," he added, bitterly, "that's probably why *you* never heard of him."

"All right," I said, "I'm ignorant. I'm sorry. I'll go out and buy all the cat's records right away, all right?"

"It don't," said Sonny, with dignity, "make any difference to me. I don't care what you listen to. Don't do me no favors."

I was beginning to realize that I'd never seen him so upset before. With another part of my mind I was thinking that this would probably turn out to be one of those things kids go through and that I shouldn't make it seem important by pushing it too hard. Still, I didn't think it would do any harm to ask: "Doesn't all this take a lot of time? Can you make a living at it?"

He turned back to me and half leaned, half sat, on the kitchen table. "Everything takes time," he said, "and—well, yes, sure, I can make a living at it. But what I don't seem to be able to make you understand is that it's the only thing I want to do."

"Well, Sonny," I said gently, "you know people can't always do exactly what they want to do—"

"*No*, I don't know that," said Sonny, surprising me. "I think people *ought* to do what they want to do, what else are they alive for?"

"You getting to be a big boy," I said desperately, "it's time you started thinking about your future."

"I'm thinking about my future," said Sonny, grimly. "I think about it all the time."

I gave up. I decided, if he didn't change his mind, that we could always talk about it later. "In the meantime," I said, "you got to finish school." We had already decided that he'd have to move in with Isabel and her folks. I knew this wasn't the ideal arrangement because Isabel's folks are inclined to be dicty and they hadn't especially wanted Isabel to marry me. But I didn't know what else to do. "And we have to get you fixed up at Isabel's."

There was a long silence. He moved from the kitchen table to the window. "That's a terrible idea. You know it yourself."

"Do you have a *better* idea?"

He just walked up and down the kitchen for a minute. He was as tall as I was. He had started to shave. I suddenly had the feeling that I didn't know him at all.

He stopped at the kitchen table and picked up my cigarettes. Looking at me with a kind of mocking, amused defiance, he put one between his lips. "You mind?"

"You smoking already?"

He lit the cigarette and nodded, watching me through the smoke. "I just wanted to see if I'd have the courage to smoke in front of you." He grinned and blew a great cloud of smoke to the ceiling. "It was easy." He looked at my face. "Come on, now. I bet you was smoking at my age, tell the truth."

I didn't say anything but the truth was on my face, and he laughed. But now there was something very strained in his laugh. "Sure. And I bet that ain't all you was doing."

He was frightening me a little. "Cut the crap," I said. "We already decided that you was going to go and live at Isabel's. Now what's got into you all of a sudden?"

"*You* decided it," he pointed out. "*I* didn't decide nothing." He stopped in front of me, leaning against the stove, arms loosely folded. "Look, brother. I don't want to stay in Harlem no more, I really don't." He was very earnest. He looked at me, then over toward the kitchen window. There was something in his eyes I'd never seen before, some thoughtfulness, some worry all his own. He rubbed the muscle of one arm. "It's time I was getting out of here."

"Where do you want to *go* Sonny?"

"I want to join the army. Or the navy, I don't care. If I say I'm old enough, they'll believe me."

Then I got mad. It was because I was so scared. "You must be crazy. You goddamn fool, what the hell do you want to go and join the *army* for?"

"I just told you. To get out of Harlem."

"Sonny, you haven't even finished *school*. And if you really want to be a musician, how do you expect to study if you're in the *army?*"

He looked at me, trapped, and in anguish. "There's ways. I might be able to work out some kind of deal. Anyway, I'll have the G.I. Bill when I come out."

"*If* you come out." We stared at each other. "Sonny, please. Be reasonable. I know the setup is far from perfect. But we got to do the best we can."

"I ain't learning nothing in school," he said. "Even when I go." He turned away from me and opened the window and threw his cigarette out into the narrow alley. I watched his back. "At least, I ain't learning nothing you'd want me to learn." He slammed the window so hard I thought the glass would fly out, and turned back to me. "And I'm sick of the stink of these garbage cans!"

"Sonny," I said, "I know how you feel. But if you don't finish school now, you're going to be sorry later that you didn't." I grabbed him by the shoulders. "And you only got another year. It ain't so bad. And I'll come back and I swear I'll help you do *whatever* you want to do. Just try to put up with it till I come back. Will you please do that? For me?"

He didn't answer and he wouldn't look at me.

"Sonny. You hear me?"

He pulled away. "I hear you. But you never hear anything *I* say."

I didn't know what to say to that. He looked out of the window and then back at me. "OK," he said, and sighed. "I'll try."

Then I said, trying to cheer him up a little, "They got a piano at Isabel's. You can practice on it."

And as a matter of fact, it did cheer him up for a minute. "That's right," he said to himself. "I forgot that." His face relaxed a little. But the worry, the thoughtfulness, played on it still, the way shadows play on a face which is staring into the fire.

But I thought I'd never hear the end of that piano. At first, Isabel would write me, saying how nice it was that Sonny was so serious about his music and how, as soon as he came in from school, or wherever he had been when he was supposed to be at school, he went straight to that piano and stayed there until suppertime. And, after supper, he went back to that piano and stayed there until everybody went to bed. He was at that piano all day Saturday and all day

Sunday. Then he bought a record player and started playing records. He'd play one record over and over again, all day long sometimes, and he'd improvise along with it on the piano. Or he'd play one section of the record, one chord, one change, one progression, then he'd do it on the piano. Then back to the record. Then back to the paino.

Well, I really don't know how they stood it. Isabel finally confessed that it wasn't like living with a person at all, it was like living with sound. And the sound didn't make any sense to her, didn't make any sense to any of them—naturally. They began, in a way, to be afflicted by this presence that was living in their home. It was as though Sonny were some sort of god, or monster. He moved in an atmosphere which wasn't like theirs at all. They fed him and he ate, he washed himself, he walked in and out of their door; he certainly wasn't nasty or unpleasant or rude, Sonny isn't any of those things; but it was as though he were all wrapped up in some cloud, some fire, some vision all his own; and there wasn't any way to reach him.

At the same time, he wasn't really a man yet, he was still a child, and they had to watch out for him in all kinds of ways. They certainly couldn't throw him out. Neither did they dare to make a great scene about that piano because even they dimly sensed, as I sensed, from so many thousands of miles away, that Sonny was at that piano playing for his life.

But he hadn't been going to school. One day a letter came from the school board, and Isabel's mother got it—there had, apparently, been other letters but Sonny had torn them up. This day, when Sonny came in, Isabel's mother showed him the letter and asked where he'd been spending his time. And she finally got it out of him that he'd been down in Greenwich Village, with musicians and other characters, in a white girl's apartment. And this scared her and she started to scream at him, and what came up, once she began—though she denies it to this day—was what sacrifices they were making to give Sonny a decent home and how little he appreciated it.

Sonny didn't play the piano that day. By evening, Isabel's mother had calmed down but then there was the old man to deal with, and Isabel herself. Isabel says she did her best to be calm but she broke down and started crying. She says she just watched Sonny's face. She could tell, by watching him, what was happening with him. And what was happening was that they penetrated his cloud, they had reached him. Even if their fingers had been a thousand times more gentle than human fingers ever are, he could hardly help feeling that they had stripped him naked and were spitting on that nakedness. For he also had to see that his presence, that music, which was life or death to him, had been torture for them and that they had endured it, not at all for his sake, but only for mine. And Sonny couldn't take that. He can take it a little better today than he could then but he's still not very good at it and, frankly, I don't know anybody who is.

The silence of the next few days must have been louder than the sound of all the music ever played since time began. One morning, before she went to work, Isabel was in his room for something and she suddenly realized that all of his records were gone. And she knew for certain that he was gone. And he was. He went as far as the Navy could carry him. He finally sent me a postcard from someplace in Greece, and that was the first I knew that Sonny was still alive. I didn't see him any more until we were both back in New York and the war had long been over.

He was a man by then, of course, but I wasn't willing to see it. He came by the house from time to time, but we fought almost every time we met. I didn't like the way he carried himself, loose and dreamlike all the time, and I didn't like his friends, and his music seemed to be merely an excuse for the life he led. It sounded just that weird and disordered.

Then we had a fight, a pretty awful fight, and I didn't see him for months. By and by I looked him up, where he was living, in a furnished room in the Village, and I tried to make it up. But there were lots of other people in the room, and Sonny just lay on his bed, and he wouldn't come downstairs with me, and he treated these other people as though they were his family and I weren't. So I got mad and then he got mad, and then I told him that he might just as well be dead as live the way he was living. Then he stood up and he told me not to worry about him any more in life, that he *was* dead as far as I was concerned. Then he pushed me to the door, and the other people looked on as though nothing were happening, and he slammed the door behind me. I stood in the hallway, staring at the door. I heard somebody laugh in the room and then the tears came to my eyes. I started down the steps, whistling to keep from crying, I kept whistling to myself, *You going to need me, baby, one of these cold, rainy days.*

I read about Sonny's trouble in the spring. Little Grace died in the fall. She was a beautiful little girl. But she only lived a little over two years. She died of polio and she suffered. She had a slight fever for a couple of days, but it didn't seem like anything and we just kept her in bed. And we would certainly have called the doctor, but the fever dropped, she seemed to be all right. So we thought it had just been a cold. Then, one day, she was up, playing, Isabel was in the kitchen fixing lunch for the two boys when they'd come in from school, and she heard Grace fall down in the living room. When you have a lot of children you don't always start running when one of them falls, unless they start screaming or something. And, this time, Grace was quiet. Yet, Isabel says that when she heard that *thump* and then that silence, something happened in her to make her afraid. And she ran to the living room and there was little Grace on the floor, all twisted up, and the reason she hadn't screamed was that she couldn't get her breath. And when she did scream, it was the worst sound, Isabel says, that she'd ever heard in all her life, and she still hears it sometimes in her dreams. Isabel will sometimes wake me up with a low, moaning, strangled sound, and I have to be quick to awaken her and hold her to me and where Isabel is weeping against me seems a mortal wound.

I think I may have written Sonny the very day that little Grace was buried. I was sitting in the living room in the dark, by myself, and I suddenly thought of Sonny. My trouble made his real.

One Saturday afternoon, when Sonny had been living with us, or, anyway, been in our house, for nearly two weeks, I found myself wandering aimlessly about the living room, drinking from a can of beer, and trying to work up the courage to search Sonny's room. He was out, he was usually out whenever I was home, and Isabel had taken the children to see their grandparents. Suddenly I was standing still in front of the living-room window, watching Seventh Avenue. The idea of searching Sonny's room made me still. I scarcely dared to admit to myself what I'd be searching for. I didn't know what I'd do if I found it. Or if I didn't.

On the sidewalk across from me, near the entrance to a barbecue joint, some people were holding an old-fashioned revival meeting. The barbecue cook, wearing a dirty white apron, his conked hair reddish and metallic in the pale sun, and a cigarette between his lips, stood in the doorway, watching them. Kids and older people paused in their errands and stood there, along with some older men and a couple of very tough-looking women who watched everything that happened on the avenue, as though they owned it, or were maybe owned by it. Well, they were watching this, too. The revival was being carried on by three sisters in black, and a brother. All they had were their voices and their Bibles and a tambourine. The brother was testifying and while he testified two of the sisters stood together, seeming to say, Amen, and the third sister walked around with the tambourine outstretched and a couple of people dropped coins into it. Then the brother's testimony ended, and the sister who had been taking up the collection dumped the coins into her palm and transferred them to the pocket of her long black robe. Then she raised both hands, striking the tambourine against the air, and then against one hand, and she started to sing. And the two other sisters and the brother joined in.

It was strange, suddenly, to watch, though I had been seeing these street meetings all my life. So, of course, had everybody else down there. Yet, they paused and watched and listened and I stood still at the window. "'*Tis the old ship of Zion*,'" they sang, and the sister with the tambourine kept a steady, jangling beat, "*it has rescued many a thousand!*" Not a soul under the sound of their voices was hearing this song for the first time, not one of them had been rescued. Nor had they seen much in the way of rescue work being done around them. Neither did they especially believe in the holiness of the three sisters and the brother, they knew too much about them, knew where they lived and how. The woman with the tambourine, whose voice dominated the air, whose face was bright with joy, was divided by very little from the woman who stood watching her, a cigarette between her heavy, chapped lips, her hair a cuckoo's nest, her face scarred and swollen from many beatings, and her black eyes glittering like coal. Perhaps they both knew this, which was why, when, as rarely, they addressed each other, they addressed each other as Sister. As the singing filled the air, the watching, listening faces underwent a change, the eyes focusing on something within; the music seemed to soothe a poison out of them; and

time seemed, nearly, to fall away from the sullen, belligerent, battered faces, as though they were fleeing back to their first condition,
while dreaming of their last. The barbecue cook half shook his head
and smiled, and dropped his cigarette and disappeared into his joint.
A man fumbled in his pockets for change and stood holding it in
his hand impatiently, as though he had just remembered a pressing
appointment further up the avenue. He looked furious. Then I saw
Sonny, standing on the edge of the crowd. He was carrying a wide, flat
notebook with a green cover, and it made him look, from where I
was standing, almost like a schoolboy. The coppery sun brought
out the copper in his skin, he was very faintly smiling, standing very
still. Then the singing stopped, the tambourine turned into a collection plate again. The furious man dropped in his coins and vanished,
so did a couple of the women, and Sonny dropped some change in
the plate, looking directly at the woman with a little smile. He started
across the avenue, toward the house. He has a slow, loping walk, something like the way Harlem hipsters walk, only he's imposed on this
his own half-beat. I had never really noticed it before.

I stayed at the window, both relieved and apprehensive. As Sonny
disappeared from my sight, they began singing again. And they were
still singing when his key turned in the lock.

"Hey," he said.

"Hey, yourself. You want some beer?"

"No. Well, maybe." But he came up to the window and stood beside me, looking out. "What a warm voice," he said.

They were singing *If I could only hear my mother pray again!*

"Yes," I said, "and she can sure beat that tambourine."

"But what a terrible song," he said, and laughed. He dropped his
notebook on the sofa and disappeared into the kitchen. "Where's
Isabel and the kids?"

"I think they went to see their grandparents. You hungry?"

"No." He came back into the living room with his can of beer. "You
want to come someplace with me tonight?"

I sensed, I don't know how, that I couldn't possibly say no. "Sure.
Where?"

He sat down on the sofa and picked up his notebook and started
leafing through it. "I'm going to sit in with some fellows in a joint
in the Village."

"You mean, you're going to play, tonight?"

"That's right." He took a swallow of his beer and moved back to the window. He gave me a sidelong look. "If you can stand it."

"I'll try," I said.

He smiled to himself, and we both watched as the meeting across the way broke up. The three sisters and the brother, heads bowed, were singing *God be with you till we meet again*. The faces around them were very quiet. Then the song ended. The small crowd dispersed. We watched the three women and the lone man walk slowly up the avenue.

"When she was singing before," said Sonny, abruptly, "her voice reminded me for a minute of what heroin feels like sometimes—when it's in your veins. It makes you feel sort of warm and cool at the same time. And distant. And—and sure." He sipped his beer, very deliberately not looking at me. I watched his face. "It makes you feel—in control. Sometimes you've got to have that feeling."

"Do you?" I sat down slowly in the easy chair.

"Sometimes." He went to the sofa and picked up his notebook again. "Some people do."

"In order," I asked, "to play?" And my voice was very ugly, full of contempt and anger.

"Well"—he looked at me with great, troubled eyes, as though, in fact, he hoped his eyes would tell me things he could never otherwise say—"they *think* so. And *if* they think so—!"

"And what do *you* think?" I asked.

He sat on the sofa and put his can of beer on the floor. "I don't know," he said, and I couldn't be sure if he were answering my question or pursuing his thoughts. His face didn't tell me. "It's not so much to *play*. It's to *stand* it, to be able to make it at all. On any level." He frowned and smiled: "In order to keep from shaking to pieces."

"But these friends of yours," I said, "they seem to shake themselves to pieces pretty goddamn fast."

"Maybe." He replied with the notebook. And something told me that I should curb my tongue, that Sonny was doing his best to talk, that I should listen. "But of course you only know the ones that've gone to pieces. Some don't—or at least they haven't *yet* and that's just about all *any* of us can say." He paused. "And then there are some who just live, really, in hell, and they know it and they see what's happening and they go right on. I don't know." He sighed, dropped the notebook, folded his arms. "Some guys, you can tell from the way they play, they on something *all* the time. And you can see that, well, it makes something real for them. But of course," he picked up his beer from the floor and sipped it and put the can down again, "they *want* to, too, you've got to see that. Even some of them that say they don't—*some*, not all."

"And what about you?" I asked—I couldn't help it. "What about you? Do *you* want to?"

He stood up and walked to the window and remained silent for a long time. Then he sighed. "Me," he said. Then: "While I was downstairs before, on my way here, listening to that woman sing, it struck me all of a sudden how much suffering she must have had to go through—to sing like that. It's *repulsive* to think you have to suffer that much."

I said: "But there's no way not to suffer—is there, Sonny?"

"I believe not," he said, and smiled, "but that's never stopped anyone from trying." He looked at me. "Has it?" I realized, with this mocking look, that there stood between us, forever, beyond the power of time or forgiveness, the fact that I had held silence—so long!—when he had needed human speech to help him. He turned back to the window. "No, there's no way not to suffer. But you try all kinds of ways to keep from drowning in it, to keep on top of it, and to make it seem—well, like *you*. Like you did something, all right, and now you're suffering for it. You know?" I said nothing. "Well you know," he said, impatiently, "why *do* people suffer? Maybe it's better to do something to give it a reason, *any* reason."

"But we just agreed," I said, "that there's no way not to suffer. Isn't it better, then, just to —take it?"

"But nobody just takes it," Sonny cried, "that's what I'm telling you! *Everybody* tries not to. You're just hung up on the *way* some people try—it's not *your* way!"

The hair on my face began to itch, my face felt wet. "That's not true," I said, "that's not true. I don't give a damn what other people do, I don't even care how they suffer. I just care how *you* suffer." And he looked at me. "Please believe me," I said, "I don't want to see you—die—trying not to suffer."

"I won't," he said, flatly, "die trying not to suffer. At least, not any faster than anybody else."

"But there's no need," I said, trying to laugh, "is there, in killing yourself?"

I wanted to say more, but I couldn't. I wanted to talk about will power and how life could be—well, beautiful. I wanted to say that it was all within; but was it? Or, rather, wasn't that exactly the trouble? And I wanted to promise that I would never fail him again. But it would all have sounded—empty words and lies.

So I made the promise to myself and prayed that I would keep it.

"It's terrible sometimes, inside," he said, "that's what's the trouble. You walk these streets, black and funky and cold, and there's not really a living ass to talk to, and there's nothing shaking, and there's no way of getting it out—that storm inside. You can't talk it and you can't make love with it, and when you finally try to get with it and play it, you realize *nobody's* listening. So *you've* got to listen. You got to find a way to listen."

And then he walked away from the window and sat on the sofa again, as though all the wind had suddenly been knocked out of him. "Sometimes you'll do *anything* to play, even cut your mother's throat." He laughed and looked at me. "Or your brother's." Then he sobered. "Or your own." Then: "Don't worry. I'm all right now and I think I'll *be* all right. But I can't forget—where I've been. I don't mean just the physical place I've been, I mean where I've *been*. And *what* I've been."

"What have you been, Sonny?" I asked.

He smiled—but sat sideways on the sofa, his elbow resting on the back, his fingers playing with his mouth and chin, not looking at me. "I've been something I didn't recognize, didn't know I could be. Didn't know anybody could be." He stopped, looking inward, looking helplessly young, looking old. "I'm not talking about it now because I feel *guilty* or anything like that—maybe it would be better if I did, I don't know. Anyway, I can't really talk about it. Not to you, not to anybody." And now he turned and faced me. "Sometimes, you know, and it was actually when I was most out of the world, I felt that I was in it, that I was *with* it, really, and I could play or I didn't really have to *play*, it just came out of me, it was there. And I don't know how I played, thinking about it now, but I know I did awful things, those times, sometimes, to people. Or it wasn't that I *did* anything to them—it was that they weren't real." He picked up the beer can; it was empty; he rolled it between his palms: "And other times—well, I needed a fix, I needed to find a place to lean, I needed to clear a space to *listen*—and I couldn't find it, and I—went crazy, I did terrible things to *me*, I was terrible *for* me." He began pressing the beer can between his hands, I watched the metal begin to give. It glittered, as he played with it, like a knife, and I was afraid he would cut himself, but I said nothing. "Oh well. I can never tell you. I was all by myself at the bottom of something, stinking and sweating and crying and shaking, and I smelled it, you know? *My* stink, and I thought I'd die if I couldn't get away from it and yet, all the same, I knew that everything I was doing was just locking me in with it. And I didn't know," he paused, still flattening the beer can, "I didn't know, I still *don't* know, something kept telling me that maybe it was good to smell your own stink, but I didn't think that *that* was what I'd been trying to do—and—who can stand it?" And he abruptly dropped the ruined beer can, looking at me with a small, still smile, and then rose, walking to the window as though it were the lodestone rock. I watched his face, he watched the avenue. "I couldn't tell you when Mama died—but the reason I wanted to leave Harlem so bad was to get away from drugs. And then, when I ran away, that's what I was running from —really. When I came back, nothing had changed, *I* hadn't changed, I was just—older." And he stopped, drumming with his fingers on the windowpane. The sun had vanished, soon darkness would fall. I watched his face. "It can come again," he said, almost as though speaking to himself. Then he turned to me. "It can come again," he repeated. "I just want you to know that."

"All right," I said at last. "So it can come again. All right."

He smiled, but the smile was sorrowful. "I had to try to tell you," he said.

"Yes," I said. "I understand that."

"You're my brother," he said, looking straight at me, and not smiling at all.

"Yes," I repeated, "yes. I understand that."

He turned back to the window, looking out. "All that hatred down there," he said, "all that hatred and misery and love. It's a wonder it doesn't blow the avenue apart."

We went to the only night club on a short, dark street, downtown. We squeezed through the narrow, chattering, jam-packed bar to the entrance of the big room, where the bandstand was. And we stood there for a moment, for the lights were very dim in this room and we couldn't see. Then, "Hello, boy," said a voice, and an enormous black man, much older than Sonny or myself, erupted out of all that atmospheric lighting and put an arm around Sonny's shoulder. "I been sitting right here," he said, "waiting for you."

He had a big voice, too, and heads in the darkness turned toward us.

Sonny grinned and pulled a little away, and said, "Creole, this is my brother. I told you about him."

Creole shook my hand. "I'm glad to meet you, son," he said, and it was clear that he was glad to meet me *there,* for Sonny's sake. And he smiled. "You got a real musician in *your* family," and he took his arm from Sonny's shoulder and slapped him, lightly, affectionately, with the back of his hand.

"Well. Now I've heard it all," said a voice behind us. This was another musician, and a friend of Sonny's, a coal-black, cheerful-looking man, built close to the ground. He immediately began con-fiding to me, at the top of his lungs, the most terrible things about Sonny, his teeth gleaming like a lighthouse and his laugh coming up out of him like the beginning of an earthquake. And it turned out that everyone at the bar knew Sonny, or almost everyone; some were musicians, working there, or nearby, or not working, some were simply hangers-on, and some were there to hear Sonny play. I was introduced to all of them and they were all very polite to me. Yet, it was clear that, for them, I was only Sonny's brother. Here, I was in Sonny's world. Or, rather: his kingdom. Here, it was not even a question that his veins bore royal blood.

They were going to play soon, and Creole installed me, by myself, at a table in a dark corner. Then I watched them, Creole, and the little black man, and Sonny, and the others, while they horsed around, standing just below the bandstand. The light from the bandstand spilled just a little short of them and, watching them laughing and gesturing and moving about, I had the feeling that they, nevertheless, were being most careful not to step into that circle of light too sud-denly: That if they moved into the light too suddenly, without think-ing, they would perish in flame. Then, while I watched, one of them, the small black man, moved into the light and crossed the bandstand and started fooling around with his drums. Then—being funny and being, also, extremely ceremonious—Creole took Sonny by the arm and led him to the piano. A woman's voice called Sonny's name, and a few hands started clapping. And Sonny, also being funny and being ceremonious, and so touched, I think, that he could have cried, but neither hiding it nor showing it, riding it like a man, grinned, and put both hands to his heart and bowed from the waist.

Creole then went to the bass fiddle and a lean, very bright-skinned brown man jumped up on the bandstand and picked up his horn. So there they were, and the atmosphere on the bandstand and in the room began to change and tighten. Someone stepped up to the microphone and announced them. Then there were all kinds of murmurs. Some people at the bar shushed others. The waitress ran around, frantically getting in the last orders, guys and chicks got closer to each other, and the lights on the bandstand, on the quartet, turned to a kind of indigo. Then they all looked different there. Creole looked about him for the last time, as though he were making certain that all his chickens were in the coop, and then he—jumped and struck the fiddle. And there they were.

All I know about music is that not many people ever really hear it. And even then, on the rare occasions when something opens within, and the music enters, what we mainly hear, or hear corroborated, are personal, private, vanishing evocations. But the man who creates the music is hearing something else, is dealing with the roar rising from the void and imposing order on it as it hits the air. What is evoked in him, then, is of another order, more terrible because it has no words, and triumphant, too, for that same reason. And his triumph, when he triumphs, is ours. I just watched Sonny's face. His face was troubled, he was working hard, but he wasn't with it. And I had the feeling that, in a way, everyone on the bandstand was waiting for him, both waiting for him and pushing him along. But as I began to watch Creole, I realized that it was Creole who held them all back. He had them on a short rein. Up there, keeping the beat with his whole body, wailing on the fiddle, with his eyes half closed, he was listening to everything, but he was listening to Sonny. He was having a dialogue with Sonny. He wanted Sonny to leave the shore line and strike out for the deep water. He was Sonny's witness that deep water and drowning were not the same thing—he had been there, and he knew. And he wanted Sonny to know. He was waiting for Sonny to do the things on the keys which would let Creole know that Sonny was in the water.

And, while Creole listened, Sonny moved, deep within, exactly like someone in torment. I had never before thought of how awful the relationship must be between the musician and his instrument. He has to fill it, this instrument, with the breath of life, his own. He has to make it do what he wants it to do. And a piano is just a piano. It's made out of so much wood and wires and little hammers and big ones, and ivory. While there's only so much you can do with it, the only way to find this out is to try to try and make it do everything.

And Sonny hadn't been near a piano for over a year. And he wasn't on much better terms with his life, not the life that stretched before him now. He and the piano stammered, started one way, got scared, stopped; started another way, panicked, marked time, started again; then seemed to have found a direction, panicked again, got stuck. And the face I saw on Sonny I'd never seen before. Everything had been burned out of it, and, at the same time, things usually hidden were being burned in, by the fire and fury of the battle which was occurring in him up there.

Yet, watching Creole's face as they neared the end of the first set, I had the feeling that something had happened, something I hadn't heard. Then they finished, there was scattered applause, and then, without an instant's warning, Creole started into something else, it was almost sardonic, it was *Am I Blue*. And, as though he commanded, Sonny began to play. Something began to happen. And Creole let out the reins. The dry, low, black man said something awful on the drums, Creole answered, and the drums talked back. Then the horn insisted, sweet and high, slightly detached perhaps, and Creole listened, commenting now and then, dry, and driving, beautiful and calm and old. Then they all came together again, and Sonny was part of the family again. I could tell this from his face. He seemed to have found, right there beneath his fingers, a damn brand-new piano. I seemed that he couldn't get over it. Then, for a while, just being happy with Sonny, they seemed to be agreeing with him that brand-new pianos certainly were a gas.

Then Creole stepped forward to remind them what they were playing was the blues. He hit something in all of them, he hit something in me, myself, and the music tightened and deepened, apprehension began to beat the air. Creole began to tell us what the blues were all about. They were not about anything very new. He and his boys up there were keeping it new, at the risk of ruin, destruction, madness, and death, in order to find new ways to make us listen. For, while the tale of how we suffer, and how we are delighted, and how we may triumph is never new, it always must be heard. There isn't any other tale to tell, it's the only light we've got in all this darkness.

And this tale, according to that face, that body, those strong hands on those strings, has another aspect in every country, and a new depth in every generation. Listen, Creole seemed to be saying, listen. Now these are Sonny's blues. He made the little black man on the drums know it, and the bright, brown man on the horn. Creole wasn't trying any longer to get Sonny in the water. He was wishing him Godspeed. Then he stepped back, very slowly, filling the air with the immense suggestion that Sonny speak for himself.

Then they all gathered around Sonny, and Sonny played. Every now and again one of them seemed to say, Amen. Sonny's fingers filled the air with life, his life. But that life contained so many others. And Sonny went all the way back, he really began with the spare, flat statement of the opening phrase of the song. Then he began to make it his. It was very beautiful because it wasn't hurried and it was no longer a lament. I seemed to hear with what burning he had made it his, with what burning we had yet to make it ours, how we could cease lamenting. Freedom lurked around us and I understood, at last, that he could help us to be free if we would listen, that he would never be free until we did. Yet there was no battle in his face now. I heard what he had gone through, and would continue to go through until he came to rest in earth. He had made it his: that long line, of which we knew only Mama and Daddy. And he was giving it back, as everything must be given back, so that, passing through death, it can live forever. I saw my mother's face again, and felt, for the first time, how the stones of the road she had walked on must have bruised her feet. I saw the moonlit road where my father's brother died. And it brought something else back to me, and carried me past it. I saw my little girl again and felt Isabel's tears again, and I felt my own tears begin to rise. And I was aware that this was only a moment, that the world waited outside, as hungry as a tiger, and that trouble stretched above us, longer than the sky.

Then it was over. Creole and Sonny let out their breath, both soaking wet, and grinning. There was a lot of applause and some of it was real. In the dark, the girl came by and I asked her to take drinks to the bandstand. There was a long pause, while they talked up there in the indigo light and after a while I saw the girl put a Scotch and milk on top of the piano for Sonny. He didn't seem to notice it, but just before they started playing again, he sipped from it and looked toward me, and nodded. Then he put it back on top of the piano. For me, then, as they began to play again, it glowed and shook above my brother's head like the very cup of trembling.

Sonny's Blues

For Analysis

1. Why did Baldwin choose first-person restricted as his narrative point of view in telling this story?
2. How does the narrator's relationship to his brother change in the course of the story?
3. What is the significance of the narrator's feeling "for the first time, how the stones of the road she [his mother] had walked on must have bruised her feet"?

might be on exam   starts changing when his brother child die.

John Updike

A & P

In walks these three girls in nothing but bathing suits, I'm in the third checkout slot, with my back to the door, so I don't see them until they're over by the bread. The one that caught my eye first was the one in the plaid green two-piece. She was a chunky kid, with a good tan and a sweet broad soft-looking can with those two crescents of white just under it, where the sun never seems to hit, at the top of the backs of her legs. I stood there with my hand on a box of HiHo

A & P: © Copyright 1962 by John Updike. Reprinted from PIGEON FEATHERS AND OTHER STORIES, by John Updike, by permission of Alfred A. Knopf, Inc. Originally appeared in *The New Yorker*.

crackers trying to remember if I rang it up or not. I ring it up again and the customer starts giving me hell. She's one of these cash-register-watchers, a witch about fifty with rouge on her cheekbones and no eyebrows, and I know it made her day to trip me up. She'd been watching cash registers for fifty years and probably never seen a mistake before.

By the time I got her feathers smoothed and her goodies into a bag—she gives me a little snort in passing, if she'd been born at the time they would have burned her over in Salem—by the time I get her on her way the girl had circled around the bread and were coming back, without a pushcart, back my way along the counters, in the aisle between the checkouts and the Special bins. They didn't even have shoes on. There was this chunky one, with the two-piece—it was bright green and the seams on the bra were still sharp and her belly was still pretty pale so I guessed she just got it (the suit)—there was this one, with one of those chubby berry-faces, the lips all bunched together under her nose, this one, and a tall one, with black hair that hadn't quite frizzed right, and one of these sunburns right across under the eyes, and a chin that was too long—you know, the kind of girl other girls think is very "striking" and "attractive" but never quite makes it, as they very well know, which is why they like her so much—and then the third one, that wasn't quite so tall. She was the queen. She kind of led them, the other two peeking around and making their shoulders round. She didn't look around, not this queen, she just walked straight on slowly, on these long white prima-donna legs. She came down a little hard on her heels, as if she didn't walk in her bare feet that much, putting down her heels and then letting the weight move along to her toes as if she was testing the floor with every step, putting a little deliberate extra action into it. You never know for sure how girls' minds work (do you really think it's a mind in there or just a little buzz like a bee in a glass jar?) but you got the idea she had talked the other two into coming in here with her, and now she was showing them how to do it, walk slow and hold yourself straight.

She had on a kind of dirty-pink—beige maybe, I don't know—bathing suit with a little nubble all over it and, what got me, the straps were down. They were off her shoulders looped loose around the cool tops of her arms, and I guess as a result the suit had slipped a little on her, so all around the top of the cloth there was this shining rim. If it hadn't been there you wouldn't have known there could have been anything whiter than those shoulders. With the straps pushed off, there was nothing between the top of the suit and the top of her head except just *her*, this clean bare plane of the top of her chest down from the shoulder bones like a dented sheet of metal tilted in the light. I mean, it was more than pretty.

She had sort of oaky hair that the sun and salt had bleached, done up in a bun that was unraveling, and a kind of prim face. Walking into the A & P with your straps down, I suppose it's the only kind of face you *can* have. She held her head so high her neck, coming up out of those white shoulders, looked kind of stretched, but I didn't mind. The longer her neck was, the more of her there was.

She must have felt in the corner of her eye me and over my shoulder Stokesie in the second slot watching, but she didn't tip. Not this queen. She kept her eyes moving across the racks, and stopped, and turned so slow it made my stomach rub the inside of my apron, and buzzed to the other two, who kind of huddled against her for relief, and then they all three of them went up the cat-and-dog-food-breakfast-cereal-macaroni-rice-raisins-seasonings-spreads spaghetti-soft-drinks-crackers and cookies aisle. From the third slot I look straight up this aisle to the meat counter, and I watched them all the way. The fat one with the tan sort of fumbled with the cookies, but on second thought she put the package back. The sheep pushing their carts down the aisle—the girls were walking against the usual traffic (not that we have one-way signs or anything)—were pretty hilarious. You could see them, when Queenie's white shoulders dawned on them, kind of jerk, or hop, or hiccup, but their eyes snapped back to their own baskets and on they pushed. I bet you could set off dynamite in an A & P and the people would by and large keep reaching and checking oatmeal off their lists and muttering "Let me see, there was a third thing, began with A, asparagus, no, ah, yes, applesauce!" or whatever it is they do mutter. But there was no doubt, this jiggled them. A few houseslaves in pin curlers even looked around after pushing their carts past to make sure what they had seen was correct.

You know, it's one thing to have a girl in a bathing suit down on the beach, where what with the glare nobody can look at each other much anyway, and another thing in the cool of the A & P, under the fluorescent lights, against all those stacked packages, with her feet paddling along naked over our checkerboard green-and-cream rubber-tile floor.

"Oh Daddy," Stokesie said beside me. "I feel so faint."

"Darling," I said. "Hold me tight," Stokesie's married, with two babies chalked up on his fuselage already, but as far as I can tell that's the only difference. He's twenty-two, and I was nineteen this April.

"Is it done?" he asks, the responsible married man finding his voice. I forgot to say he thinks he's going to be manager some sunny day, maybe in 1990 when it's called the Great Alexandrov and Petrooshki Tea Company or something.

What he meant was, our town is five miles from a beach, with a big summer colony out on the Point, but we're right in the middle of town, and the women generally put on a shirt or shorts or something before they get out of the car into the street. And anyway these are usually women with six children and varicose veins mapping their legs and nobody, including them, could care less. As I say, we're right in the middle of town, and if you stand at our front doors you can see two banks and the Congregational church and the newspaper store and three real-estate offices and about twenty-seven old freeloaders tearing up Central Street because the sewer broke again. It's not as if we're on the Cape; we're north of Boston and there's people in this town haven't seen the ocean for twenty years.

The girls had reached the meat counter and were asking McMahon something. He pointed, they pointed, and they shuffled out of sight behind a pyramid of Diet Delight peaches. All that was left for us to see was old McMahon patting his mouth and looking after them sizing up their joints. Poor kids, I began to feel sorry for them, they couldn't help it.

Now here comes the sad part of the story, at least my family says it's sad, but I don't think it's so sad myself. The store's pretty empty, it being Thursday afternoon, so there was nothing much to do except lean on the register and wait for the girls to show up again. The whole store was like a pinball machine and I didn't know which tunnel they'd come out of. After a while they come around out of the far aisle, around the light bulbs, records at discount of the Caribbean Six or Tony Martin Sings or some such gunk you wonder they waste the wax on, sixpacks of candy bars, and plastic toys done up in cellophane that fall apart when a kid looks at them anyway. Around they come, Queenie still leading the way, and holding a little gray jar in her hand. Slots Three through Seven are unmanned and I could

see her wondering between Stokes and me, but Stokesie with his usual luck draws an old party in baggy gray pants who stumbles up with
four giant cans of pineapple juice (what do these bums *do* with
all that pineapple juice? I've often asked myself) so the girls come
to me. Queenie puts down the jar and I take it into my fingers icy
cold. Kingfish Fancy Herring Snacks in Pure Sour Cream: 49¢. Now
her hands are empty, not a ring or a bracelet, bare as God made
them, and I wonder where the money's coming from. Still with that
prim look she lifts a folded dollar bill out of the hollow at the center
of her nubbled pink top. The jar went heavy in my hand. Really, I
thought that was so cute.

Then everybody's luck begins to run out. Lengel comes in from
haggling with a truck full of cabbages on the lot and is about to scuttle into the door marked MANAGER behind which he hides all day when
the girls touch his eye. Lengel's pretty dreary, teaches Sunday school
and the rest, but he doesn't miss that much. He comes over and says,
"Girls, this isn't the beach."

Queenie blushes, though maybe it's just a brush of sunburn I
was noticing for the first time, now that she was so close. "My mother
asked me to pick up a jar of herring snacks." Her voice kind of
startled me, the way voices do when you see the people first, coming
out so flat and dumb yet kind of tony, too, the way it tickled over
"pick up" and "snacks." All of a sudden I slid right down her voice
into her living room. Her father and the other men were standing
around in ice-cream coats and bow ties and the women were in sandals picking up herring snacks on toothpicks off a big glass plate and
they were all holding drinks the color of water with olives and sprigs
of mint in them. When my parents have somebody over they get
lemonade and if it's a real racy affair Schlitz in tall glasses with
"They'll Do It Every Time" cartoons stenciled on.

"That's all right," Lengel said. "But this isn't the beach." His repeating this struck me as funny, as if it had just occurred to him,
and he had been thinking all these years the A & P was a great big
dune and he was the head lifeguard. He didn't like my smiling—as I
say he doesn't miss much—but he concentrates on giving the girls
that sad Sunday-school-superintendent stare.

Queenie's blush is no sunburn now, and the plump one in plaid,
that I liked better from the back—a really sweet can—pipes up,
"We weren't doing any shopping. We just came in for the one thing."

"That makes no difference," Lengel tells her, and I could see from the way his eyes went that he hadn't noticed she was wearing a two-piece before. "We want you decently dressed when you come in here."

"We *are* decent," Queenie says suddenly, her lower lip pushing, getting sore now that she remembers her place, a place from which the crowd that runs the A & P must look pretty crummy. Fancy Herring Snacks flashed in her very blue eyes.

"Girls, I don't want to argue with you. After this come in here with your shoulders covered. It's our policy." He turns his back. That's policy for you. Policy is what the kingpins want. What the others want is juvenile delinquency.

All this while, the customers had been showing up with their carts but, you know, sheep, seeing a scene, they had all bunched up on Stokesie, who shook open a paper bag as gently as peeling a peach, not wanting to miss a word. I could feel in the silence everybody getting nervous, most of all Lengel, who asks me, "Sammy, have you rung up their purchase?"

I thought and said "No" but it wasn't about that I was thinking. I go through the punches, 4, 9, GROC, TOT—it's more complicated than you think, and after you do it often enough, it begins to make a little song, that you hear words to, in my case "Hello (bing) there, you (*gung*) hap-py *pee*-pul (*splat*)!"—the *splat* being the drawer flying out. I uncrease the bill tenderly as you may imagine, it just having come from between the two smoothest scoops of vanilla I had ever known were there, and pass a half and a penny into her narrow pink palm, and nestle the herrings in a bag and twist its neck and hand it over, all the time thinking.

The girls, and who'd blame them, are in a hurry to get out, so I say "I quit" to Lengel quick enough for them to hear, hoping they'll stop and watch me, their unsuspected hero. They keep right on going, into the electric eye; the door flies open and they flicker across the lot to their car, Queenie and Plaid and Big Tall Goony-Goony (not that as raw material she was so bad), leaving me with Lengel and a kink in his eyebrow.

"Did you say something, Sammy?"

"I said I quit."

"I thought you did."

"You didn't have to embarrass them."

"It was they who were embarrassing us."

I started to say something that came out "Fiddle-de-doo." It's a saying of my grandmother's, and I know she would have been pleased.

"I don't think you know what you're saying," Lengel said.

"I know you don't," I said. "But I do." I pull the bow at the back
of my apron and start shrugging it off my shoulders. A couple customers that had been heading for my slot begin to knock against
each other, like scared pigs in a chute.

Lengel sighs and begins to look very patient and old and gray. He's
been a friend of my parents for years. "Sammy, you don't want to
do this to your Mom and Dad," he tells me. It's true, I don't. But it
seems to me that once you begin a gesture it's fatal not to go through
with it. I fold the apron, "Sammy" stitched in red on the pocket,
and put it on the counter, and drop the bow tie on top of it. The bow
tie is theirs, if you've ever wondered. "You'll feel this for the rest
of your life," Lengel says, and I know that's true, too, but remembering how he made that pretty girl blush makes me so scrunchy inside
I punch the No Sale tab and the machine whirs "pee-pul" and the
drawer splats out. One advantage to this scene taking place in summer, I can follow this up with a clean exit, there's no fumbling around
getting your coat and galoshes, I just saunter into the electric eye
in my white shirt that my mother ironed the night before, and the
door heaves itself open, and outside the sunshine is skating around
on the asphalt.

I look around for my girls, but they're gone, of course. There
wasn't anybody but some young married screaming with her children about some candy they didn't get by the door of a powder-blue
Falcon station wagon. Looking back in the big windows, over the
bags of peat moss and aluminum lawn furniture stacked on the
pavement, I could see Lengel in my place in the slot, checking the
sheep through. His face was dark gray and his back stiff, as if he'd
just had an injection of iron, and my stomach kind of fell as I felt
how hard the world was going to be to me hereafter.

A & P

For Analysis

1.   What do the images Sammy uses to describe the customers in the
     A & P indicate about the quality of their consciousnesses?
2.   What does the girls' purchase of "Kingfish Fancy Herring in Pure

Sour Cream" indicate about their life-style? How is it different from
that of Lengel and the social class he represents?

3. Is Sammy's name for the prettiest girl significant? What is its symbolic
value?

4. Why does Sammy feel that the world will be hard to him after his
decision to quit the A & P?

Ernest Hemingway

A Clean
Well-Lighted Place

It was late and everyone had left the café except an old man who
sat in the shadow the leaves of the tree made against the electric
light. In the day time the street was dusty, but at night the dew settled the dust and the old man liked to sit late because he was deaf
and now at night it was quiet and he felt the difference. The two waiters
inside the café knew that the old man was a little drunk, and while
he was a good client they knew that if he became too drunk he would
leave without paying, so they kept watch on him.

"Last week he tried to commit suicide," one waiter said.

"Why?"

"He was in despair."

"What about?"

"Nothing."

"How do you know it was nothing?"

"He has plenty of money."

They sat together at a table that was close against the wall near the
door of the café and looked at the terrace where the tables were all

empty except where the old man sat in the shadow of the leaves of the tree that moved slightly in the wind. A girl and a soldier went by in the street. The street light shone on the brass number on his collar. The girl wore no head covering and hurried beside him.

"The guard will pick him up," one waiter said.

"What does it matter if he gets what he's after?"

"He had better get off the street now. The guard will get him. They went by five minutes ago."

The old man sitting in the shadow rapped on his saucer with his glass. The younger waiter went over to him.

"What do you want?"

The old man looked at him. "Another brandy," he said.

"You'll be drunk," the waiter said. The old man looked at him. The waiter went away.

"He'll stay all night," he said to his colleague. "I'm sleepy now. I never get into bed before three o'clock. He should have killed himself last week."

The waiter took the brandy bottle and another saucer from the counter inside the café and marched out to the old man's table. He put down the saucer and poured the glass full of brandy.

"You should have killed yourself last week," he said to the deaf man. The old man motioned with his finger. "A little more," he said. The waiter poured on into the glass so that the brandy slopped over and ran down the stem into the top saucer of the pile. "Thank you," the old man said. The waiter took the bottle back inside the café. He sat down at the table with his colleague again.

"He's drunk now," he said.

"He's drunk every night."

"What did he want to kill himself for?"

"How should I know?"

"How did he do it?"

"He hung himself with a rope."

"Who cut him down?"

"His niece."

"Why did they do it?"

"Fear for his soul."

"How much money has he got?"

"He's got plenty."

"He must be eighty years old."

"Anyway I should say he was eighty."

"I wish he would go home. I never get to bed before three o'clock. What kind of hour is that to go to bed?"

"He stays up because he likes it."

"He's lonely. I'm not lonely. I have a wife waiting in bed for me."

"He had a wife once too."

"A wife would be no good to him now."

"You can't tell. He might be better with a wife."

"His niece looks after him."

"I know. You said she cut him down."

"I wouldn't want to be that old. An old man is a nasty thing."

"Not always. This old man is clean. He drinks without spilling. Even now, drunk. Look at him."

"I don't want to look at him. I wish he would go home. He has no regard for those who must work."

The old man looked from his glass across the square, then over at the waiters.

"Another brandy," he said, pointing to his glass. The waiter who was in a hurry came over.

"Finished," he said, speaking with that omission of syntax stupid people employ when talking to drunken people or foreigners. "No more tonight. Close now."

"Another," said the old man.

"No. Finished." The waiter wiped the edge of the table with a towel and shook his head.

The old man stood up, slowly counted the saucers, took a leather coin purse from his pocket and paid for the drinks, leaving half a peseta tip.

The waiter watched him go down the street, a very old man walking unsteadily but with dignity.

"Why didn't you let him stay and drink?" the unhurried waiter asked. They were putting up the shutters. "It is not half past two."

"I want to go home to bed."

"What is an hour?"

"More to me than to him."

"An hour is the same."

"You talk like an old man yourself. He can buy a bottle and drink at home."

"It's not the same."

"No, it is not," agreed the waiter with a wife. He did not wish to be unjust. He was only in a hurry.

"And you? You have no fear of going home before your usual hour?"

"Are you trying to insult me?"

"No, hombre, only to make a joke."

"No," the waiter who was in a hurry said, rising from pulling down the metal shutters. "I have confidence. I am all confidence."

"You have youth, confidence, and a job," the older waiter said. "You have everything."

"And what do you lack"

"Everything but work."

"You have everything I have."

"No. I have never had confidence and I am not young."

"Come on. Stop talking nonsense and lock up."

"I am of those who like to stay late at the café," the older waiter said. "With all those who do not want to go to bed. With all those who need a light for the night."

"I want to go home and into bed."

"We are of two different kinds," the older waiter said. He was now dressed to go home. "It is not only a question of youth and confidence although those things are very beautiful. Each night I am reluctant to close up because there may be someone who needs the café."

"Hombre, there are bodegas open all night long."

"You do not understand. This is a clean and pleasant café. It is well-lighted. The light is very good and also, now, there are shadows of the leaves."

"Good night," said the younger waiter.

"Good night," the other said. Turning off the electric light he continued the conversation with himself. It is the light of course but it is necessary that the place be clean and pleasant. You do not want music. Certainly you do not want music. Nor can you stand before a bar with dignity although that is all that is provided for these hours. What did he fear? It was not fear or dread. It was a nothing that he knew too well. It was all a nothing and a man was nothing too. It was only that and light was all it needed and a certain cleanness and order. Some lived in it and never felt it but he knew it all was nada y pues nada y nada y pues nada. Our nada who art in nada,

nada by thy name thy kingdom nada thy will be nada in nada as it is in nada. Give us this nada our daily nada and nada us out nada as we nada our nadas and nada us not into nada but deliver us from nada; pues nada. Hail nothing full of nothing, nothing is with thee. He smiled and stood before a bar with a shining steam pressure coffee machine.

"What's yours?" asked the barman.

"Nada."

"Otro loco mas," said the barman and turned away.

"A little cup," said the waiter.

The barman poured it for him.

"The light is very bright and pleasant but the bar is unpolished," the waiter said.

The barman looked at him but did not answer. It was too late at night for conversation.

"You want another copita?" the barman asked.

"No, thank you," said the waiter and went out. He disliked bars and bodegas. A clean, well-lighted café was a very different thing. Now, without thinking further, he would go home to his room. He would lie in the bed and finally, with daylight, he would go to sleep. After all, he said to himself, it is probably only insomnia. Many must have it.

A Clean Well-Lighted Place

For Analysis

1. The young waiter has "confidence" whereas the old waiter does not. What does "confidence" mean in the context of the story?

2. Note the places where the word "nothing" is used. What does "nothing" mean to the old waiter? How is the young waiter's statement that the old man has "nothing" to fear because he has money ironic from the old waiter's point of view?

3. What is the old waiter's concept of dignity? How does it relate to his concept of nothingness?

4. What is the significance of the young waiter's act of pouring brandy until it sloshes over the side of the old man's cup?

Daniel Keyes

Flowers for
Algernon

progris riport 2—martch 6

Dr. Strauss says I shud rite down what I think and evrey thing
that happins to me from now on. I dont know why but he says its
importint so they will see if they will use me. I hope they use me.
Miss Kinnian says maybe they can make me smart. I want to be
smart. My name is Charlie Gordon. I am 37 years old and 2 weeks
ago was my birthday. I have nuthing more to rite now so I will close
for today.

progress riport 1—martch 5 1965

I had a test today. I think I faled it. and I think that maybe now
they wont use me. What happind is a nice young man was in the
room and he had some white cards with ink spilled all over them.
He sed Charlie what do you see on this card. I was very skared even
tho I had my rabits foot in my pockit because when I was a kid I
always faled tests in school and I spillled ink to.

I told him I saw a inkblot. He said yes and it made me feel good.
I thot that was all but when I got up to go he stopped me. He said
now sit down Charlie we are not thru yet. Then I dont remember
so good but he wantid me to say what was in the ink. I dint see nuthing in the ink but he said there was picturs there other pepul saw
some picturs. I couldnt see any picturs. I reely tryed to see. I held

the card close up and then far away. Then I said if I had my glases I coud see better I usually only ware my glases in the movies or TV but I said they are in the closit in the hall. I got them. Then I said let me see that card agen I bet Ill find it now.

I tryed hard but I still coudnt find the picturs I only saw the ink. I told him maybe I need new glases. He rote somthing down on a paper and I got skared of faling the test. I told him it was a very nice inkblot with little points all around the eges. He looked very sad so that wasnt it. I said please let me try agen. Ill get it in a few minits becaus Im not so fast sometimes. Im a slow reeder too in Miss Kinnians class for slow adults but I'm trying very hard.

He gave me a chance with another card that had 2 kinds of ink spillled on it red and blue.

He was very nice and talked slow like Miss Kinnian does and he explaned it to me that it was a *raw shok*. He said pepul see things in the ink. I said show me where. He said think. I told him I think a inkblot but that wasnt rite eather. He said what does it remind you— pretend something. I closd my eyes for a long time to pretend. I told him I pretned a fowntan pen with ink leeking all over a table cloth. Then he got up and went out.

I dont think I passd the *raw shok* test.

progris report 3—martch 7

Dr Strauss and Dr Nemur say it dont matter about the inkblots. I told them I dint spill the ink on the cards and I couldn't see anything in the ink. They said that maybe they will still use me. I said Miss Kinnian never gave me tests like that one only spellin and reading. They said Miss Kinnian told that I was her bestist pupil in the adult nite school becaus I tryed the hardist and I reely wanted to lern. They said how come you went to the adult nite school all by yourself Charlie. How did you find it. I said I askd pepul and sumbody told me where I shud go to lern to read and spell good. They said why did you want to. In told them becaus all my life I wantid to be smart and not dumb. But its very hard to be smart. They said you know it will probly be tempirery. I said yes. Miss Kinnian told me. I dont care if it herts.

Later I had more crazy tests today. The nice lady who gave it me told me the name and I asked her how do you spellit so I can rite it in my progris report. THEMATIC APPERCEPTION TEST. I don't know the frist 2 words but I know what *test* means. You got to pass it or you get bad marks. This test lookd easy becaus I coud see the picturs. Only this time she dint want me to tell her the picturs. That mixd me up. I said the man yesterday said I shoud tell him what I saw in the ink she said that dont make no difrence. She said make up storys about the pepul in the picturs.

I told her how can you tell storys about pepul you never met. I said why shud I make up lies. I never tell lies any more becaus I always get caut.

She told me this test and the other one the raw shok was for getting personalty. I laffed so hard. I said how can you get that thing from inkblots and fotos. She got sore and put her picturs away. I dont care. It was sily. I gess I faled that test too.

Later some men in white coats took me to a difernt part of the hospitil and gave me a game to play. It was like a race with a white mouse. They called the mouse Algernon. Algernon was in a box with a lot of twists and turns like all kinds of walls and they gave me a pencil and paper with lines and lots of boxes. On one side it said START and on the other end it said FINISH. They said it was *amazed* and that Algernon and me had the same *amazed* to do. I dint see how we could have the same *amazed* if Algernon had a box and I had a paper but I dint say nothing. Anyway there wasnt time because the race started.

One of the men had a watch he was trying to hide so I wouldnt see it so I tred not to look and that made me nervus.

Anyway that test made me feel worser than all the others because they did it over 10 times with difernt *amazeds* and Algernon won every time. I dint know that mice were so smart. Maybe thats because Algernon is a white mouse. Maybe white mice are smarter then other mice.

progris riport 4—*Mar 8*

Their going to use me! Im so exited I can hardly write. Dr Nemur and Dr Strauss had a argament about it first. Dr Nemur was in the office when Dr Strauss brot me in. Dr Nemur was worryed about using me but Dr Strauss told him Miss Kinnian rekemmended me the best from all the people who she was teaching. I like Miss Kinnian becaus shes a very smart teacher. And she said Charlie your going to have a second chance. If you volenteer for this experament you mite get smart. They dont know if it will be perminint but theirs a chance. Thats why I said ok even when I was scared because she said it was an operashun. She said dont be scared Charlie you done so much with so little I think you deserv it most of all.

So I got scaird when Dr. Nemur and Dr Strauss argud about it. Dr Strauss said I had something that was very good. He said I had a good *motor-vation*. I never even knew I had that. I felt proud when he said that not every body with an eye-q of 68 had that thing. I dont know what it is or where I got it but he said Algernon had it too. Algernons *motor-vation* is the cheese they put in his box. But it cant be that because I didnt eat any cheese this week.

Then he told Dr Nemur something I dint understand so while they were talking I wrote down some of the words.

He said Dr Nemur I know Charlie is not what you had in mind as the first of your new brede of intelek** (coudnt get the word) superman. But most people of his low men** are host** and un-coop** they are usualy dull apath** and hard to reach. He has a good natcher hes intristed and eager to please.

Dr Nemur said remember he will be the first human beeng ever to have his intelijence trippled by surgicle meens.

Dr Strauss said exakly. Look at how well hes lerned to read and write for his low mentel age its as grate an acheve** as you and I lerning einstines therey of **vity without help. That shows the intenss motor-vation. Its comparat** a tremen** achev** I say we use Charlie.

I dint get all the words and they were talking to fast but it sounded like Dr. Strauss was on my side and like the other one wasnt.

Then Dr Nemur nodded he said all right maybe your right. We will use Charlie. When he said that I got so exited I jumped up and shook his hand for being so good to me. I told him thank you doc you wont be sorry for giving me a second chance. And I mean it like I told him. After the operashun Im gonna try to be smart. Im gonna try awful hard.

progris ript 5—Mar 10

Im skared. Lots of people who work here and the nurses and the people who gave me the tests came to bring me candy and wish me luck. I hope I have luck. I got my rabits foot and my lucky penny and my horse shoe. Only a black cat crossed me when I was comming to the hospitil. Dr Strauss says dont be supersitis Charlie this is sience. Anyway Im keeping my rabits foot with me.

I asked Dr Strauss if Ill beat Algernon in the race after the operashun and he said maybe. If the operashun works Ill show that mouse I can be as smart as he is. Maybe smarter. Then Ill be abel to read better and spell the words good and know lots of things and be like other people. I want to be smart like other people. If it works perminint they will make everybody smart all over the wurld.

They dint give me anything to eat this morning. I dont know what that eating has to do with getting smart. Im very hungry and Dr Nemur took away my box of candy. That Dr Nemur is a grouch. Dr Strauss says I can have it back after the operashun. You cant eat befor a operashun. . . .

Progress Report 6—Mar 15

The operashun dint hurt. He did it while I was sleeping. They took off the bandijis from my eyes and my head today so I can make a PROGRESS REPORT. Dr Nemur who looked at some of my other ones says I spell PROGRESS wrong and he told me how to spell it and REPORT too. I got to try and remember that.

I have a very bad memary for spelling. Dr Strauss says its ok to tell about all the things that happin to me but he says I should tell more about what I feel and what I think. When I told him I dont know how to think he said try. All the time when the bandijis were on my eyes I tryed to think. Nothing happened. I don't know what to think about. Maybe if I ask him he will tell me how I can think now that Im suppose to get smart. What do smart people think about. Fancy things I suppose. I wish I knew some fancy things alredy.

Progress Report 7—mar 19

Nothing is happining. I had lots of tests and different kinds of races with Algernon. I hate that mouse. He always beats me. Dr Strauss said I got to play those games. And he said some time I got to take those tests over again. Thse inkblots are stupid. And those pictures are stupid too. I like to draw a picture of a man and a woman but I wont make up lies about people.

I got a headache from trying to think so much. I thot Dr Stauss was my frend but he dont help me. He don't tell me what to think or when Ill get smart. Miss Kinnian dint come to see me. I think writing these progress reports are stupid too.

Progress Report 8—Mar 23

Im going back to work at the factery. They said it was better I shud go back to work but I cant tell anyone what the operashun was for and I have to come to the hospitil for an hour evry night after work. They are gonna pay me mony every month for lerning to be smart.

Im glad Im going back to work because I miss my job and all my frends and all the fun we have there.

Dr Strauss says I shud keep writing things down but I dont have to do it every day just when I think of something or something speshul happins. He says dont get discoridged because it takes time and it happins slow. He says it took a long time with Algernon before he got 3 times smarter then he was before. Thats why Algernon beats me all the time because he had that operashun too. That makes me feel better. I coud probly do that *amazed* faster than a reglar mouse. Maybe some day Ill beat Algernon. Boy that would be something. So far Algernon looks like he mite be smart perminent.

Mar 25 (I dont have to write PROGRESS REPORT *on top any more* just when I hand it in once a week for Dr Nemur to read. I just have to put the date on. That saves time)

We had a lot of fun at the factery today. Joe Carp said hey look where Charlie had his operashun what did they do Charlie put some brains in. I was going to tell him but I remembered Dr Strauss said no. Then Frank Reilly said what did you do Charlie forget your key and open your door the hard way. That made me laff. Their really my friends and they like me.

Sometimes somebody will say hey look at Joe or Frank or George he really pulled a Charlie Gordon. I don't know why they say that but they always laff. This morning Amos Borg who is the 4 man at Donnegans used my name when he shouted at Ernie the office boy. Ernie lost a packige. He said Ernie for godsake what are you trying to be a Charlie Gordon. I dont understand why he said that. I never lost any packiges.

Mar 28   Dr Strauss came to my room tonight to see why I dint come in like I was suppose to. I told him I dont like to race with Algernon any more. He said I dont have to for a while but I shud come in. He had a present for me only it wasnt a present but just for lend. I thot it was a little television but it wasnt. He said I got to turn it on when I go to sleep. I said your kidding why shud I turn it on when Im going to sleep. Who ever herd of a thing like that. But he said if I want to get smart I got to do what he says. I told him I dint think I was going to get smart and he put his hand on my sholder and said Charlie you dont know it yet but your getting smarter all the time. You wont notice for a while. I think he was just being nice to make me feel good because I dont look any smarter.

Oh yes I almost forgot. I asked him when I can go back to the class at Miss Kinnians school. He said I wont go their. He said that soon Miss Kinnian will come to the hospital to start and teach me speshul. I was mad at her for not comming to see me when I got the operashun but I like her so maybe we will be frends again.

Mar 29   That crazy TV kept me up all night. How can I sleep with something yelling crazy things all night in my ears. And the nutty pictures. WOW. I dont know what it says when Im up so how am I going to know when Im sleeping.

Dr Strauss says its ok. He says my brains are lerning when I sleep and that will help me when Miss Kinnian starts my lessons in the hopitl (only I found out it isnt a hospitil its a labatory). I think its all crazy. If you can get smart when your sleeping why do people go to school. That thing I dont think will work. I use to watch the late show and the late late show on TV all the time and it never made me smart. Maybe you have to sleep while you watch it.

PROGRESS REPORT 9—April 3

Dr Strauss showed me how to keep the TV turned low so now I can sleep. I dont hear a thing. And I still dont understand what it says. A few times I play it over in the morning to find out what I lerned when I was sleeping and I dont think so. Miss Kinnian says Maybe its another langwidge or something. But most times it sounds american. It talks so fast faster then even Miss Gold who was my teacher in 6 grade and I remember she talked so fast I coudnt understand her.

I told Dr Strauss what good is it to get smart in my sleep. I want to be smart when Im awake. He says its the same thing and I have two minds. Theres the *subconscious* and the *conscious* (thats how you spell it.) And one dont tell the other one what its doing. They don't even talk to each other. Thats why I dream. And boy have I been having crazy dreams. Wow. Ever since that night TV. The late late late late late show.

I forgot to ask him if it was only me or if everybody had those two minds.

(I just looked up the word in the dictionary Dr Strauss gave me. The word is *subconscious adj. Of the nature of mental operations yet not present in consciousness; as, subconscious conflict of desires.)* Theres more but I still dont know what it means. This isnt a very good dictionary for dumb people like me.

Anyway the headache is from the party. My frends from the factery Joe Carp and Frank Reilly invited me to go with them to Muggsys Saloon for some drinks. I dont like to drink but they said we will have lots of fun. I had a good time.

Joe Carp said I shoud show the girls how I mop out the toilet in the factory and he got me a mop. I showed them and everyone laffed when I told that Mr Donnegan said I was the best janiter he ever had because I like my job and do it good and never come late or or miss a day except for my operashun.

I said Miss Kinnian always said Charlie be proud of your job because you do it good.

Everybody laffed and we had a good time and they gave me lots of drinks and Joe said Charlie is a card when hes potted. I dont know what that means but everybody likes me and we have fun. I cant wait to be smart like my best frends Joe Carp and Frank Reilly.

I dont remember how the party was over but I think I went out to buy a newspaper and coffe for Joe and Frank and when I came back there was no one their. I looked for them all over till late. Then I dont remember so good but I think I got sleepy or sick. A nice cop brot me back home. Thats what my landlady Mrs. Flynn says.

But I got a headache and a big lump on my head and black and blue all over. I think maybe I fell but Joe Carp says it was the cop they beat up drunks some times. I don't think so. Miss Kinnian says cops are to help people. Anyway I got a bad headache and Im sick and hurt all over. I dont think Ill drink anymore.

April 6   I beat Algernon! I dint even know I beat him until Burt the tester told me. Then the second time I lost because I got so exited I fell off the chair before I finished. But after that I beat him 8 more times. I must be getting smart to beat a smart mouse like Algernon. But I dont *feel* smarter.

I wanted to race Algernon some more but Burt said thats enough for one day. They let me hold him for a minit. Hes not so bad. Hes soft like a ball of cotton. He blinks and when he opens his eyes their black and pink on the eges.

I said can I feed him because I felt bad to beat him and I wanted to be nice and make frends. Burt said no Algernon is a very specshul mouse with an operashun like mine, and he was the first of all the animals to stay smart so long. He told me Algernon is so smart that every day he has to solve a test to get his food. Its a thing like a lock on a door that changes every time Algernon goes in to eat so he has to lern something new to get his food. That made me sad because if he couldnt lern he would be hungry.

I dont think its right to make you pass a test to eat. How woud Dr Nemur like it to have to pass a test every time he wants to eat. I think Ill be frends with Algernon.

April 9   Tonight after work Miss Kinnian was at the laboratory. She looked like she was glad to see me but scared. I told her dont worry Miss Kinnian Im not smart yet and she laffed. She said I have confidence in you Charlie the way you struggled so hard to read and right better than all the others. At werst you will have it for a little wile and your doing something for sience.

We are reading a very hard book. I never read such a hard book before. Its called *Robinson Crusoe* about a man who gets merooned on a dessert Iland. Hes smart and figers out all kinds of things so he can have a house and food and hes a good swimmer. Only I feel sorry because hes all alone and has no frends. But I think their must be somebody else on the iland because theres a picture with his funny umbrella looking at footprints. I hope he gets a frend and not be lonely.

April 10   Miss Kinnian teaches me to spell better. She says look at a word close your eyes and say it over and over until you remember. I have lots of truble with *through* that you say *threw* and *enough*

and *tough* that you dont say *enew* and *tew*. You got to say *enuff* and
tuff. Thats how I use to write it before I started to get smart. Im confused but Miss Kinnian says theres no reason in spelling.

Apr 14   Finished *Robinson Crusoe*. I want to find out more about
what happens to him but Miss Kinnian says thats all there is. *Why*.

Apr 15 Miss Kinnian says Im learning fast. She read some of the Progress Reports and she looked at me kind of funny. She says Im a fine
person and Ill show them all. I asked her why. She said never mind but
I shoudnt feel bad if I find out that everybody isnt nice like I think.
She said for a person who god gave so little to you done more then
a lot of people with brains they never even used. I said all my frends
are smart people but there good. They like me and they never did
anything that wasnt nice. Then she got something in her eye and she
had to run out to the ladys room.

Apr 16 Today, I lerned, the *comma,* this is a comma (,) a period, with
a tail, Miss Kinnian, says its importent, because, it makes writing better, she said, somebeody, coud lose, a lot of money, if a comma, isnt,
in the, right place, I dont have, any money, and I dont see, how a
comma, keeps you from losing it.
    But she says, everybody, uses commas, so Ill use, them too,

Apr 17   I used the comma wrong. Its punctuation. Miss Kinnian told
me to look up long words in the dictionary to lern to spell them. I
said whats the difference if you can read it anyway. She said its part
of your education so now on I'll look up all the words Im not sure
how to spell. It takes a long time to write that way but I think Im
remembering. I only have to look up once and after that I get it right.
Anyway thats how come I got the word *punctuation* right. (its that
way in the dictionary.) Miss Kinnian says a period is punctuation too,
and there are lots of other marks to lern. I told her I thot all the
periods had to have tails but she said no.
    You got to mix them up, she showed? me" how. to mix! them (up,.
and now; I can! mix up all kinds" of punctuation, in! my writing?
There, are lots! of rules? to lern; but Im gettin'g them in my head.
    One thing I? like about, Dear Miss Kinnian: (thats the way it goes
in a business letter if I ever go into business) is she, always gives

me' a reason" when—I ask. She's a gen'ius! I wish! I cou'd be smart'
like, her;

   (Punctuation, is; fun!)

April 18   What a dope I am! I didn't even understand what she was
talking about. I read the grammar book last night and it explanes
the whole thing. Then I saw it was the same way as Miss Kinnian
was trying to tell me, but I didn't get it. I got up in the middle of
the night, and the whole thing straightened out in my mind.

   Miss Kinnian said that the TV working in my sleep helped out.
She said I reached a plateau. Thats like the flat top of a hill.

   After I figgered out how punctuation worked, I read over all my
old Progress Reports from the beginning. Boy, did I have crazy
spelling and punctuation! I told Miss Kinnian I ought to go over
the pages and fix all the mistakes but she said, "No, Charlie, Dr.
Nemur wants them just as they are. That's why he let you keep
them after they were photostated, to see your own progress. You're
coming along fast, Charlie."

   That made me feel good. After the lesson I went down and played
with Algernon. We don't race any more.

April 20   I feel sick inside. Not sick like for a doctor, but inside my
chest it feels empty like getting punched and a heartburn at the
same time.

   I wasn't going to write about it, but I guess I got to, because it's important. Today was the first time I ever stayed home from work.

   Last night Joe Carp and Frank Reilly invited me to a party. There
were lots of girls and some men from the factory. I remembered
how sick I got last time I drank too much, so I told Joe I didn't want
anything to drink. He gave me a plain Coke instead. It tasted funny,
but I thought it was just a bad taste in my mouth.

   We had a lot of fun for a while. Joe said I should dance with Ellen
and she would teach me the steps. I fell a few times and I couldn't
understand why because no one else was dancing besides Ellen and
me. And all the time I was tripping because somebody's foot was always sticking out.

   Then when I got up I saw the look on Joe's face and it gave me
a funny feeling in my stomack. "He's a scream," one of the girls said.
Everybody was laughing.

Frank said, "I ain't laughed so much since we sent him off for the newspaper that night at Muggsy's and ditched him."

"Look at him. His face is red."

"He's blushing. Charlie is blushing."

"Hey, Ellen, what'd you do to Charlie? I never saw him act like that before."

I didn't know what to do or where to turn. Everyone was looking at me and laughing and I felt naked. I wanted to hide myself. I ran out into the street and I threw up. Then I walked home. It's a funny thing I never knew that Joe and Frank and the others liked to have me around all the time to make fun of me.

Now I know what it means when they say "to pull a Charlie Gordon."

I'm ashamed.

PROGRESS REPORT 11

April 21   Still didn't go into the factory. I told Mrs. Flynn my landlady to call and tell Mr. Donnegan I was sick. Mrs. Flynn looks at me very funny lately like she's scared of me.

I think it's a good thing about finding out how everybody laughs at me. I thought about it a lot. It's because I'm so dumb and I don't even know when I'm doing something dumb. People think it's funny when a dumb person can't do things the same way they can.

Anyway, now I know I'm getting smarter every day. I know punctuation and I can spell good. I like to look up all the hard words in the dictionary and I remember them. I'm reading a lot now, and Miss Kinnian says I read very fast. Sometimes. I even understand what I'm reading about, and it stays in my mind. There are times when I can close my eyes and think of a page and it all comes back like a picture.

Besides history, geography, and arithmetic, Miss Kinnian said I should start to learn a few foreign languages. Dr. Strauss gave me some more tapes to play while I sleep. I still don't understand how that conscious and unconscious mind works, but Dr. Strauss says not to worry yet. He asked me to promise that when I start learning college subjects next week I wouldn't read any books on psychology—that is, until he gives me permission.

I feel a lot better today, but I guess I'm still a little angry that all the time people were laughing and making fun of me because I wasn't so smart. When I become intelligent like Dr. Strauss says, with three times my I.Q. of 68, then maybe I'll be like everyone else and people will like me and be friendly.

I'm not sure what an I.Q. is. Dr. Nemur said it was something that measured how intelligent you were—like a scale in the drugstore weighs pounds. But Dr. Strauss had a big argument with him and said an I.Q. didn't weigh intelligence at all. He said an I.Q. showed how much intelligence you could get, like the numbers on the outside of a measuring cup. You still had to fill the cup up with stuff.

Then when I asked Burt, who gives me my intelligence tests and works with Algernon, he said that both of them were wrong (only I had to promise not to tell them he said so). Burt says that the I.Q. measures a lot of different things including some of the things you learned already, and it really isn't any good at all.

So I still don't know what I.Q. is except that mine is going to be over 200 soon. I didn't want to say anything, but I don't see how if they don't know *what* it is, or *where* it is—I don't see how they know *how much* of it you've got.

Dr. Nemur says I have to take a *Rorchach Test* tomorrow. I wonder what *that* is.

April 27   I found out what a *Rorshach* is. It's the test I took before the operation—the one with the inkblots on the pieces of cardbord. The man who gave me the test was the same one.

I was scared to death of those inkblots. I knew he was going to ask me to find the pictures and I knew I wouldn't be able to. I was thinking to myself, if only there was some way of knowing what kind of pictures were hidden there. Maybe there weren't any pictures at all. Maybe it was just a trick to see if I was dumb enough to look for something that wasn't there. Just thinking about that made me sore at him.

"All right, Charlie," he said, "you've seen these cards before, remember?"

"Of course I remember."

The way I said it, he knew I was angry, and he looked surprised. "Yes, of course. Now I want you to look at this one. What might this be? What do you see on this card? People see all sorts of things in these inkblots. Tell me what it might be for you—what it makes you think of."

I was shocked. That wasn't what I had expected him to say at all. "You mean there are no pictures hidden in those inkblots?"

He frowned and took off his glasses. "What?"

"Pictures. Hidden in the inkblots. Last time you told me that everyone could see them and you wanted me to find them too."

He explained to me that the last time he had used almost the exact same words he was using now. I didn't believe it, and I still have the suspicion that he misled me at the time just for the fun of it. Unless—I don't know any more—could I have been *that* feeble-minded?

We went through the cards slowly. One of them looked like a pair of bats tugging at something. Another one looked like two men fencing with swords. I imagined all sorts of things. I guess I got carried away. But I didn't trust him any more, and I kept turning them around and even looking on the back to see if there was anything there I was supposed to catch. While he was making his notes, I peeked out of the corner of my eye to read it. But it was all in code that looked like this:

WF + A   DdF—Ad orig.   WF—A   SF + obj

The test still doesn't make sense to me. It seems to me that anyone could make up lies about things that they didn't really see. How could he know I wasn't making a fool of him my mentioning things that I didn't really imagine? Maybe I'll understand it when Dr. Strauss lets me read up on psychology.

April 25   I figured out a new way to line up the machines in the factory, and Mr. Donnegan says it will save him ten thousand dollars a year in labor and increased production. He gave me a twenty-five dollar bonus.

I wanted to take Joe Carp and Frank Reilly out to lunch to celebrate, but Joe said he had to buy some things for his wife, and Frank said he was meeting his cousin for lunch. I guess it'll take a little time for them to get used to the changes in me. Everybody seems to be frightened of me. When I went over to Amos Borg and tapped him on the shoulder, he jumped up in the air.

People don't talk to me much any more or kid around the way they used to. It makes the job kind of lonely.

April 27   I got up the nerve today to ask Miss Kinnian to have dinner with me tomorrow night to celebrate my bonus.

At first she wasn't sure it was right, but I asked Dr. Strauss and he said it was okay. Dr. Strauss and Dr. Nemur don't seem to be getting along so well. They're arguing all the time. This evening when I came in to ask Dr. Strauss about having dinner with Miss Kinnian, I heard them shouting. Dr. Nemur was saying that it was *his* experiment and *his* research, and Dr. Strauss was shouting back that he contributed just as much, because he found me through Miss Kinnian and he performed the operation. Dr. Strauss said that someday thousands of neurosurgeons might be using his technique all over the world.

Dr. Nemur wanted to publish the results of the experiment at the end of this month. Dr. Strauss wanted to wait a while longer to be sure. Dr. Strauss said that Dr. Nemur was more interested in the Chair of Psychology at Princeton than he was in the experiment. Dr. Nemur said that Dr. Strauss was nothing but an opportunist who was trying to ride to glory on *his* coattails.

When I left afterwards, I found myself trembling. I don't know why for sure, but it was as if I'd seen both men clearly for the first time. I remember hearing Burt say that Dr. Nemur had a shrew of a wife who was pushing him all the time to get things published so that he could become famous. Burt said that the dream of her life was to have a big-shot husband.

Was Dr. Strauss really trying to ride on his coattails?

April 28   I don't understand why I never noticed how beautiful Miss Kinnian really is. She has brown eyes and feathery brown hair that comes to the top of her neck. She's only thirty-four! I think from the beginning I had the feeling that she was an unreachable genius— and very, very old. Now, every time I see her she grows younger and more lovely.

We had dinner and a long talk. When she said that I was coming along so fast that soon I'd be leaving her behind, I laughed.

"It's true, Charlie. You're already a better reader than I am. You can read a whole page at a glance while I can take in only a few lines at a time. And you remember every single thing you read. I'm lucky if I can recall the main thoughts and the general meaning."

"I don't feel intelligent. There are so many things I don't understand."

She took out a cigarette and I lit it for her. "You've got to be a *little* patient. You're accomplishing in days and weeks what it takes normal people to do in half a lifetime. That's what makes it so amazing. You're like a giant sponge now, soaking things in. Facts, figures, general knowledge. And soon you'll begin to connect them, too. You'll see how the different branches of learning are related. There are many levels, Charlie, like steps on a giant ladder that take you up higher and higher to see more and more of the world around you.

"I can see only a little bit of that, Charlie, and I won't go much higher than I am now, but you'll keep climbing up and up, and see more and more, and each step will open new worlds that you never even knew existed." She frowned. "I hope . . . I just hope to God—"

"What?"

"Never mind, Charles. I just hope I wasn't wrong to advise you to go into this in the first place."

I laughed. "How could that be? It worked, didn't it? Even Algernon is still smart."

We sat there silently for a while and I knew what she was thinking about as she watched me toying with the chain of my rabbit's foot and my keys. I didn't want to think of that possibility any more than elderly people want to think of death. I *knew* that this was only the beginning. I knew what she meant about levels because I'd seen some of them already. The tought of leaving her behind made me sad.

I'm in love with Miss Kinnian.

PROGRESS REPORT 12

April 30   I've quit my job with Donnegan's Plastic Box Company. Mr. Donnegan insisted that it would be better for all concerned if I left. What did I do to make them hate me so?

The first I knew of it was when Mr. Donnegan showed me the petition. Eight hundred and forty names, everyone connected with the factory, except Fanny Girden. Scanning the list quickly, I saw at once that hers was the only missing name. All the rest demanded that I be fired.

Joe Carp and Frank Reilly wouldn't talk to me about it. No one else would either, except Fanny. She was one of the few people I'd known who set her mind to something and believed it no matter what the rest of the world proved, said, or did—and Fanny did not believe that I should have been fired. She had been against the petition on principle and despite the pressure and threats she'd held out.

"Which don't mean to say," she remarked, "that I don't think there's something mighty strange about you, Charlie. Them changes. I don't know. You used to be a good, dependable, ordinary man—not too bright maybe, but honest. Who knows what you done to yourself to get so smart all of a sudden. Like everybody around here's saying, Charlie, it's not right."

"But how can you say that, Fanny? What's wrong with a man becoming intelligent and wanting to acquire knowledge and understanding of the world around him?"

She stared down at her work and I turned to leave. Without looking at me, she said: "It was evil when Eve listened to the snake and ate from the tree of knowledge. It was evil when she saw that she was naked. If not for that none of us would ever have to grow old and sick, and die."

Once again now I have the feeling of shame burning inside me. This intelligence has driven a wedge between me and all the people I once knew and loved. Before, they laughed at me and despised me for my ignorance and dullness; now, they hate me for my knowledge and understanding. What in God's name do they want of me?

They've driven me out of the factory. Now I'm more alone than ever before. . . .

May 15 Dr. Strauss is very angry at me for not having written any progress reports in two weeks. He's justified because the lab is now paying me a regular salary. I told him I was too busy thinking and reading. When I pointed out that writing was such a slow process that it made me impatient with my poor handwriting, he suggested that I learn to type. It's much easier to write now because I can type nearly seventy-five words a minute. Dr. Trauss continually reminds me of the need to speak and write simply so that people will be able to understand me.

I'll try to review all the things that happened to me during the last two weeks. Algernon and I were presented to the American

Psychological Association sitting in convention with the World Psychological Association last Tuesday. We created quite a sensation. Dr. Nemur and Dr. Strauss were proud of us.

I suspect that Dr. Nemur, who is sixty—ten years older than Dr. Strauss—finds it necessary to see tangible results of his work. Undoubtedly the result of pressure by Mrs. Nemur.

Contrary to my earlier impressions of him, I realize that Dr. Nemur is not at all a genius. He has a very good mind, but it struggles under the specter of self-doubt. He wants people to take him for a genius. Therefore, it is important for him to feel that his work is accepted by the world. I believe that Dr. Nemur was afraid of further delay because he worried that someone else might make a discovery along these lines and take the credit from him.

Dr. Strauss on the other hand might be called a genius, although I feel that his areas of knowledge are too limited. He was educated in the tradition of narrow specialization; the broader aspects of background were neglected far more than necessary—even for a neurosurgeon.

I was shocked to learn that the only ancient languages he could read were Latin, Greek, and Hebrew, and that he knows almost nothing of mathematics beyond the elementary levels of the calculus of variations. When he admitted this to me, I found myself almost annoyed. It was is if he'd hidden this part of himself in order to deceive me, pretending—as do many people I've discovered—to be what he is not. No one I've ever known is what he appears to be on the surface.

Dr. Nemur appears to be uncomfortable around me. Sometimes when I try to talk to him, he just looks at me strangely and turns away. I was angry at first when Dr. Strauss told me I was giving Dr. Nemur an inferiority complex. I thought he was mocking me and I'm oversensitive at being made fun of.

How was I to know that a highly respected psychoexperimentalist like Nemur was unacquainted with Hindustani and Chinese? It's absurd when you consider the work that is being done in India and China today in the very field of his study.

I asked Dr. Strauss how Nemur could refute Rahajamati's attack on his method and results if Nemur couldn't even read them in the first place. That strange look on Dr. Strauss's face can mean only one of two things. Either he doesn't want to tell Nemur what they're saying in India, or else—and this worries me—Dr. Strauss doesn't know either. I must be careful to speak and write clearly and simply so that people won't laugh.

May 18   I am very disturbed. I saw Miss Kinnian last night for the first time in over a week. I tried to avoid all discussions of intellectual concepts and to keep the conversation on a simple, everyday level, but she just stared at me blankly and asked me what I meant about the mathematical variance equivalent in Dorbermann's *Fifth Concerto*.

When I tried to explain she stopped me and laughed. I guess I got angry, but I suspect I'm approaching her on the wrong level. No matter what I try to discuss with her, I am unable to communicate. I must review Vrostadt's equations on *Levels of Semantic Progression*. I find that I don't communicate with people much any more. Thank God for books and music and things I can think about. I am alone in my apartment at Mrs. Flynn's boardinghouse most of the time and seldom speak to anyone.

May 20   I would not have noticed the new dishwasher, a boy of about sixteen, at the corner diner where I take my evening meals if not for the incident of the broken dishes.

They crashed to the floor, shattering and sending bits of white china under the tables. The boy stood there, dazed and frightened, holding the empty tray in his hand. The whistles and catcalls from the customers (the cries of "hey, there go the profits!" . . . "*Mazeltov!*" . . . and "well, *he* didn't work here very long . . ." which invariably seems to follow the breaking of glass or dishware in a public restaurant) all seemed to confuse him.

When the owner came to see what the excitement was about, the boy cowered as if he expected to be struck and threw up his arms as if to ward off the blow.

"All right! All right, you dope," shouted the owner, "Don't just stand there! Get the broom and sweep that mess up. A broom . . . a broom, you idiot! It's in the kitchen. Sweep up all the pieces."

The boy saw that he was not going to be punished. His frightened expression disappeared and he smiled and hummed as he came back with the broom to sweep the floor. A few of the rowdier customers kept up the remarks, amusing themselves at his expense.

"Here, sonny, over here there's a nice piece behind you. . . ."

"C'mon, do it again. . . ."

"He's not so dumb. It's easier to break 'em than to wash 'em. . . ."

As his vacant eyes moved across the crowd of amused onlookers, he slowly mirrored their smiles and finally broke into an uncertain grin at the joke which he obviously did not understand.

I felt sick inside as I looked at his dull, vacuous smile, the wide, bright eyes of a child, uncertain but eager to please. They were laughing at him because he was mentally retarded.

And I had been laughing at him too.

Suddenly, I was furious at myself and all those who were smirking at him. I jumped up and shouted, "Shut up! Leave him alone! It's not his fault he can't understand! He can't help what he is! But for God's sake . . . he's still a human being!"

The room grew silent. I cursed myself for losing control and creating a scene. I tried not to look at the boy as I paid my check and walked out without touching my food. I felt ashamed for both of us.

How strange it is that people of honest feelings and sensibility, who would not take advantage of a man born without arms or legs or eyes—how such people think nothing of abusing a man born with low intelligence. It infuriated me to think that not too long ago, I, like this boy, had foolishly played the clown.

And I had almost forgotten.

I'd hidden the picture of the old Charlie Gordon from myself because now that I was intelligent it was something that had to be pushed out of my mind. But today in looking at that boy, for the first time I saw what I had been. *I was just like him!*

Only a short time ago, I learned that people laughed at me. Now I can see that unknowingly I joined with them in laughing at myself. That hurts most of all.

I have often reread my progress reports and seen the illiteracy, the childish naïveté, the mind of low intelligence peering from a dark room, through the keyhole, at the dazzling light outside. I see that even in my dullness I knew that I was inferior, and that other people had something I lacked—something denied me. In my mental blindness, I thought that it was somehow connected with the ability to read and write, and I was sure that if I could get those skills I would automatically have intelligence too.

Even a feeble-minded man wants to be like other men.

A child may not know how to feed itself, or what to eat, yet it knows of hunger.

This then is what I was like, I never knew. Even with my gift of intellectual awareness, I never really knew.

This day was good for me. Seeing the past more clearly, I have decided to use my knowledge and skills to work in the field of increasing human intelligence levels. Who is better equipped for this work? Who else has lived in both worlds? These are my people. Let me use my gift to do something for them.

Tomorrow, I will discuss with Dr. Strauss the manner in which I can work in this area. I may be able to help him work out the problems of widespread use of the technique which was used on me. I have several good ideas of my own.

There is so much that might be done with this technique. If I could be made into a genius, what about thousands of others like myself? What fantastic levels might be achieved by using this technique on normal people? On *geniuses?*

There are so many doors to open. I am impatient to begin.

PROGRESS REPORT   13

May 23   It happened today. Algernon bit me. I visited the lab to see him as I do occasionally, and when I took him out of his cage, he snapped at my hand. I put him back and watched him for a while. He was unusually disturbed and vicious.

May 24   Burt, who is in charge of the experimental animals, tells me that Algernon is changing. He is less cooperative, he refuses to run the maze any more; general motivation has decreased. And he hasn't been eating. Everyone is upset about what this may mean.

May 25   They've been feeding Algernon, who now refuses to work the shifting-lock problem. Everyone identifies me with Algernon. In a way we're both the first of our kind. They're all pretending that Algernon's behavior is not necessarily significant for me. But it's hard to hide the fact that some of the other animals who were used in this experiment are showing strange behavior.

Dr. Strauss and Dr. Nemur have asked me not to come to the lab any more. I know what they're thinking but I can't accept it. I am going ahead with my plans to carry their research forward. With all due respect to both of these fine scientists, I am well aware of their limitations. If there is an answer, I'll have to find it out for myself. Suddenly, time has become very important to me.

May 29   I have been given a lab of my own and permission to go ahead with the research. I'm on to something. Working day and night. I've had a cot moved into the lab. Most of my writing time is spent on the notes which I keep in a separate folder, but from time to time I feel it necessary to put down my moods and my thoughts out of sheer habit.

I find the *calculus of intelligence* to be a fascinating study. Here is the place for the application of all the knowledge I have acquired. In a sense it's the problem I've been concerned with all my life.

May 31   Dr. Strauss thinks I'm working too hard. Dr. Nemur says I'm trying to cram a lifetime of research and thought into a few weeks. I know I should rest, but I'm driven on by something inside that won't let me stop. I've got to find the reason for the sharp regression in Algernon. I've got to know *if* and *when* it will happen to me.

June 4

LETTER TO DR. STRAUSS (*copy*)
Dear Dr. Strauss:

Under separate cover I am sending you a copy of my report entitled, "The Algernon-Gordon Effect: A Study of Structure and Function of Increased Intelligence," which I would like to have you read and have published.

As you see, my experiments are completed. I have included in my report all of my formulae, as well as mathematical analysis in the appendix. Of course, these should be verified.

Because of its importance to both you and Dr. Nemur (and need I say to myself, too?) I have checked and rechecked my results a dozen times in the hope of finding an error. I am sorry to say the results must stand. Yet for the sake of science, I am grateful for the little bit that I here add to the knowledge of the function of the human mind and of the laws governing the artificial increase of human intelligence.

I recall your once saying to me that an experimental *failure* or the *disproving* of a theory was as important to the advancement of learning as a success would be. I know now that this is true. I am sorry, however, that my own contribution to the field must rest upon the ashes of the work of two men I regard so highly.

Yours truly,
Charles Gordon

encl.: rept.

June 5   I must not become emotional. The facts and the results of my experiments are clear, and the more sensational aspects of my own rapid climb cannot obscure the fact that the tripling of intelligence by the surgical technique developed by Drs. Strauss and Nemur must be viewed as having little or no practical applicability (at the present time) to the increase of human intelligence.

As I review the records and data on Algernon, I see that although he is still in his physical infancy, he has regressed mentally. Motor activity is imparied; there is a general reduction of glandular activity; there is an accelerated loss of coordination.

There are also strong indications of progressive amnesia.

As will be seen by my report, these and other physical mental deterioration syndromes can be predicted with statistically significant results by the application of my formula.

The surgical stimulus to which we were both subjected has resulted in an intensification and acceleration of all mental processes. The unforeseen development, which I have taken the liberty of calling the *Algernon-Gordon Effect,* is the logical extension of the entire intelligence speed-up. The hypothesis here proven may be described simply in the following terms: Artificially increased intelligence deteriorates at a rate of time directly proportional to the quantity of the increase.

I feel that this, in itself, is an important discovery.

As long as I am able to write, I will continue to record my thoughts in these progress reports. It is one of my few pleasures. However, by all indications, my own mental deterioration will be very rapid.

I have already begun to notice signs of emotional instability and forgetfulness, the first symptoms of the burnout.

June 10   Deterioration progressing. I have become absentminded. Algernon died two days ago. Dissection shows my predictions were right. His brain had decreased in weight and there was a great smoothing out of cerebral convolutions as well as a deepening and broadening of brain fissures.

I guess the same thing is or will soon be happening to me. Now that it's definite, I don't want it to happen.

I put Algernon's body in a cheese box and buried him in the back yard. I cried.

June 15 Dr. Strauss came to see me again. I wouldn't open the door and I told him to go away. I want to be left to myself. I have become touchy and irritable. I feel the darkness closing in. It's hard to throw off the thoughts of suicide. I keep telling myself how important this introspective journal will be.

It's a strange sensation to pick up a book that you've read and enjoyed just a few months ago and discover that you don't remember it. I remembered how great I thought John Milton was, but when I picked up *Paradise Lost* I couldn't understand it at all. I got so angry I threw the book across the room.

I've got to try to hold on to some of it. Some of the things I've learned. Oh, God, please don't take it all away.

June 19 Sometimes, at night, I go out for a walk. Last night I couldn't remember where I lived. A policeman took me home. I have the strange feeling that this has all happened to me before—a long time ago. I keep telling myseslf I'm the only person in the world who can describe what's happening to me.

June 21 Why can't I remember? I've got to fight. I lie in bed for days and I don't know who or where I am. Then it all comes back to me in a flash. Fugues of amnesia. Symptoms of senility—second childhood. I can watch them coming on. It's so cruelly logical. I learned so much and so fast. Now my mind is deteriorating rapidly. I won't let it happen. I'll fight it. I can't help thinking of the boy in the restaurant, the blank expression, the silly smile, the people laughing at him. No—please—not that again. . . .

June 22 I'm forgetting things that I learned recently. It seems to be following the classic pattern—the last things learned are the first things forgotten. Or is that the pattern? I'd better look it up again. . . .

I reread my paper on the *Algernon-Gordon Effect* and I get the strange feeling that it was written by someone else. There are parts I don't even understand.

Motor activity impaired. I keep tripping over things, and it becomes increasingly difficult to type.

June 23 I've given up using the typewriter completely. My coordination is bad. I feel that I'm moving slower and slower. Had a terrible shock today. I picked up a copy of an article I used in my research, Krueger's *Uber psychische Ganzheit,* to see if it would help me understand what I had done. First I thought there was something wrong with my eyes. Then I realized I could no longer read German. I tested myself in other languages. All gone.

June 30 A week since I dare to write again. It's slipping away like sand through my fingers. Most of the books I have are too hard for me now. I get angry with them because I know that I read and understood them just a few weeks ago.

I keep telling myself I must keep writing these reports so that somebody will know what is happening to me. But it gets harder to form the words and remember spellings. I have to look up even simple words in the dictionary now and it makes me impatient with myself.

Dr. Strauss comes around almost every day, but I told him I wouldn't see or speak to anybody. He feels guilty. They all do. But I don't blame anyone. I knew what might happen. But how it hurts.

July 7 I don't know where the week went. Todays Sunday I know because I can see through my window people going to church. I think I stayed in bed all week but I remember Mrs. Flynn bringing food to me a few times. I keep saying over and over I've got to do something but then I forget or maybe its just easier not to do what I say Im going to do.

I think of my mother and father a lot these days. I found a picture of them with me taken at a beach. My father has a big ball under his arm and my mother is holding me by the hand. I dont remember them the way they are in the picture. All I remember is my father drunk most of the time and arguing with mom about money.

He never shaved much and he used to scratch my face when he hugged me. My mother said he died but Cousin Miltie said he heard his mom and dad say that my father ran away with another woman.

When I asked my mother she slapped my face and said my father was dead. I dont think I ever found out which was true but I don't care much. (He said he was going to take me to see cows on a farm once but he never did. He never kept his promises. . . .)

July 10   My landlady Mrs. Flynn is very worried about me. She says the way I lay around all day and dont do anything I remind her of her son before she threw him out of the house. She said she doesnt like loafers. If Im sick its one thing, but if Im a loafer thats another thing and she wont have it. I told her I think Im sick.

I try to read a little bit every day, mostly stories, but sometimes I have to read the same thing over and over again because I dont know what it means. And its hard to write. I know I should look up all the words in the dictionary but its so hard and Im so tired all the time.

Then I got the idea that I would only use the easy words instead of the long hard ones. That saves time. I put flowers on Algernons grave about once a week. Mrs Flynn thinks Im crazy to put flowers on a mouses grave but I told her that Algernon was special.

July 14   Its sunday again. I don't have anything to do to keep me busy now because my television set is broke and I don't have any money to get it fixed. (I think I lost this months check from the lab. I dont remember)

I get awful headaches and asperin doesnt help me much. Mrs. Flynn knows Im really sick and she feels very sorry for me. Shes a wonderful woman whenever someone is sick.

July 22   Mrs. Flynn called a strange doctor to see me. She was afraid I was going to die. I told the doctor I wasn't too sick and that I only forget sometimes. He asked me did I have any friends or relatives and I said no I dont have any. I told him I had a friend called Algernon once but he was a mouse and we used to run races together. He looked at me kind of funny like he thought I was crazy.

He smiled when I told him I used to be a genius. He talked to me like I was a baby and he winked at Mrs. Flynn. I got mad and chased him out because he was making fun of me the way they all used to.

July 24   I have no more money and Mrs Flynn says I got to go to work somewhere and pay the rent because I havent paid for over two months. I dont know any work but the job I used to have at

Donnegans Plastic Box Company. I dont want to go back there because they all knew me when I was smart and maybe they'll laugh at me. But I don't know what else to do to get money.

July 25   I was looking at some of my old progress reports and its very funny but I cant read what I wrote. I can make out some of the words but they dont make sense.

Miss Kinnian came to the door but I said go away I dont want to see you. She cried and I cried too but I wouldnt let her in because I didn't want her to laugh at me. I told her I didn't like her any more. I told her I didnt want to be smart any more. Thats not true. I still love her and I still want to be smart but I had to say that so shed go away. She gave Mrs Flynn money to pay the rent. I dont want that. I got to get a job.

Please . . . please let me not forget how to read and write . . .

July 27   Mr. Donnegan was very nice when I came back and asked him for my old job of janitor. First he was very suspicious but I told him what happened to me then he looked very sad and put his hand on my shoulder and said Charlie Gordon you got guts.

Everybody looked at me when I came downstairs and started working in the toilet sweeping it out like I used to. I told myself Charlie if they make fun of you dont get sore because you remember their not so smart as you once thot they were. And besides they were once your friends and if they laughed at you that doesnt mean anything because they like you too.

One of the new men who came to work there after I went away made a nasty crack he said hey Charlie I hear your a very smart fella a real quiz kid. Say something intelligent. I felt bad but Joe Carp came over and grabbed him by the shirt and said leave him alone you lousy cracker or Ill break your neck. I didn't expect Joe to take my part so I guess hes really my friend.

Later Frank Reilly came over and said Charlie if anybody bothers you or trys to take advantage you call me or Joe and we will set em straight. I said thanks Frank and I got choked up so I had to turn around and go into the supply room so he wouldn't see me cry. Its good to have friends.

July 28   I did a dumb thing today I forgot I wasnt in Miss Kinnians class at the adult center any more like I use to be. I went in and sat down in my old seat in the back of the room and she looked at me funny and she said Charles. I dint remember she ever called me that before only Charlie so I said hello Miss Kinnian Im redy for my lesin today only I lost my reader that we was using. She startid to cry and run out of the room and everybody looked at me and I saw they wasnt the same pepul who used to be in my class.

Then all of a suddin I remembered some things about the operashun and me getting smart and I said holy smoke I reely pulled a Charlie Gordon that time. I went away before she come back to the room.

Thats why I'm going away from New York for good. I dont want to do nothing like that agen. I dont want Miss Kinnian to feel sorry for me. Evry body feels sorry at the factery and I dont want that eather so Im going someplace where nobody knows that Charlie Gordon was once a genus and now he cant even reed a book or rite good.

Im taking a cuple of books along and even if I cant reed them Ill practise hard and maybe I wont forget every thing I lerned. If I try reel hard maybe Ill be a little bit smarter then I was before the operashun. I got my rabits foot and my luky penny and maybe they will help me.

If you ever reed this Miss Kinnian dont be sorry for me Im glad I got a second chanse to be smart becaus I lerned a lot of things that I never even new were in this world and Im grateful that I saw it all for a little bit. I dont know why Im dumb agen or what I did wrong maybe its becaus I dint try hard enuff. But if I try and practis very hard maybe Ill get a littl smarter and know what all the words are. I remember a littel bit how nice I had a feeling with the blue book that has the torn cover when I red it. Thats why Im gonna keep trying to get smart so I can have that feeling agen. Its a good feeling to know things and be smart. I wish I had it rite now if I did I would sit down and reed all the time. Anyway I bet Im the first dumb person in the world who ever found out somthing important for sience. I remember I did something but I dont remember what. So I gess its like I did it for all the dumb pepul like me.

Good-by Miss Kinnian and Dr. Strauss and evreybody. And P.S. please tell Dr. Nemur not to be such a grouch when pepul laff at him and he would have more frends. Its easy to make frends if you let pepul laff at you. Im going to have lots of frends where I go.

P.P.S. Please if you get a chanse put some flowers on Algernons grave in the bak yard. . . .

Flowers for Algernon

For Analysis

1. What is the significance of Charlie's exchange with Fanny Girden? What might his later allusion to *Paradise Lost* have to do with their conversation?
2. Are the results of Charlie's operation good, bad, or both? Justify your answer by recourse to the text.
3. Why does Charlie leave New York? What is his attitude toward others at this point?

Poetry

AN INTRODUCTION

Poetry is the most highly organized and compressed form of expression. Because every word in a poem must contribute a greater weight of meaning than in prose, a poet must always assume that what does not positively add to his effect detracts from it. Therefore, every word in a poem must justify its existence or be eliminated.

Because a poem must be so compact, it is very dependent upon conventions. The following poem, a highly organized experience, illustrates how poetic conventions help to satisfy the reader's need for order. *and the reader expectation*

John Keats

On First Looking
into Chapman's Homer

Much have I travelled in the realms of gold,	*a*
And many goodly states and kingdoms seen;	*b*
Round many western islands have I been	*b*
Which bards in fealty to Apollo hold.	*a*
Oft of one wide expanse had I been told	*a*
That deep-browed Homer ruled as his demesne;	*b*
Yet did I never breathe its pure serene	*b*
Till I heard Chapman speak out loud and bold:	*a*
Then felt I like some watcher of the skies	*c*
When a new planet swims into his ken;	*d*

301

Or like stout Cortez when with eagle eyes   *c*
    He stared at the Pacific—and all his men   *d*
Looked at each other with a wild surmise—   *c*
    Silent, upon a peak in Darien.   *d*

This poem, written by John Keats when he was twenty-one, expresses his surprise and delight at first reading George Chapman's translation of Homer's *Iliad*. Keats could not read Greek; other translations of Homer had not inspired him. Chapman's translation illuminated for him the greatness and the beauty of Homer. There is the real experience, which sounds flat, badly stated, as do all summaries or paraphrases of works of art. It is Keats's problem to communicate that experience so that it seems urgent and important. He does this by organizing it. To organize, the writer must arrange the subject matter in a certain order, compare it with something else, or use both methods. (Notice how the methods of the scientist and the artist are identical in this respect.) Keats does both.

First, he employs several conventions. He chooses a highly organized and very familiar form for his poem—the Italian sonnet, a poem composed of fourteen lines which divide into two units of eight (the octave) and six (the sestet). The first eight lines rhyme always the same way, *abba, abba* (see marginal notes), whereas the sestet may rhyme any of several ways so long as it includes no more than three (*c, d, e*) new rhymes. Because of its two-part division, the Italian form, as opposed to the four-part English or Shakespearean form, is ideally adapted to dealing with an experience that involves describing an experience and commenting on it, asking a question and answering it, or posing a problem and solving it. Many readers will be familiar with this pattern. Thus, Keats establishes an expectation in the reader by deciding to use this form and then satisfies that expectation by using the form conventionally.

Next, he uses a metaphor, a figure of comparison, to describe his experience, since it is almost impossible to state emotion and emotional experience directly and flatly. He portrays himself as a traveller, and explorer: The *Iliad* and the *Odyssey* deal often with the experience of Odysseus—one of the great travellers and explorers in literature. This figure of speech is maintained throughout the poem; all the references are to actions of some kind of traveller or explorer. Again Keats has satisfied the desire for order and symmetry.

Then Keats organizes the experience chronologically and spatially.

Notice that the octave, while maintaining the explorer image, becomes increasingly specific with each line. The first two lines tell us that the poet has travelled much "in the realms of gold"—that is, he has read widely in literature—and has found many great books there— "goodly states and kingdoms." Then he narrows his compass. Apollo was the god of, among other things, poetry; therefore, in lines three and four Keats says that he has read a large amount of poetry. Becoming more specific, in lines five and six he says that he had been told of "one wide expanse" that Homer ruled. The reference here is to epic poetry. Finally, narrowing even farther, he tells us that he never really read Homer until he read Chapman's translation of Homer. This account has been expertly organized.

    lines 1 and 2—literature as a whole
    lines 3 and 4—poetry, one branch of literature
        line 5—epic poetry, one branch of poetry
        line 6—Homer, the greatest epic poet
    lines 7 and 8—Chapman's translation of Homer

The octave is built like a pyramid standing on its apex. But the experience is incomplete. Thus far Keats has told us what he did but not how he felt about it. He does this in the sestet. Keeping the same figure, Keats says he felt like an astronomer who discovers a new planet (the only kind of space explorer possible in Keats's preastronaut days) or like Cortez when, first seeing the Pacific, he and his men were awed by the realization that here at last was the greatest body of water in the world. (Many readers will be bothered by the fact that Balboa, not Cortez, discovered the Pacific, but the lines, after all, do not say that Cortez discovered the Pacific, just as Keats was not the first discoverer of Chapman.) At that moment, Keats, like Cortez, stood alone on a peak of experience, seeing what few other men had seen.

Our account is still flat and stale because it is still paraphrase. No summary of a work of art ever approximates the experience of art. The paraphrase has not described the reader's pleasure of discovery as he recreates the experience line by line. Nor has it even mentioned the melody and the rhythm in the lines. It is not necessary to do those things here to illustrate how an experience is organized. A satisfactory account of the poem as a whole would certainly include these matters. Yet even such an account would not explain the experience fully because it would describe how all these elements appear separately when what is important—but impossible to communicate—is how all the elements work together simultaneously. This is one reason why poetry must be read, rather than discussed, to be appreciated. We will talk about it as briefly as possible.

We have remarked how Keats establishes an expectation in the reader and satisfies it. Any artist—painter, composer, sculptor, writer—establishes such a pattern. It works for him and the reader in two ways: by satisfying the expectation he appeals to the sense of order, symmetry, unity in all of us; by breaking the pattern he stops the reader momentarily, that is, he emphasizes whatever happens at the break in the pattern. Let us illustrate how this works in poetry.

1. A poet may break his rhythm and meter. When Shakespeare writes "To be or not to be, that is the question" he has taken a perfectly regular iambic line, that is, one in which each unaccented syllable is followed by an accented syllable ˣ'ˣ'ˣ', and broken the pattern. The phrase "that is" is trochaic: It is made up of an accented syllable followed by an unaccented syllable, so that the meter goes this way ˣ'ˣ'ˣ''ˣˣ'ˣ. The word that stands out is the one that first breaks the meter. That is the one Shakespeare wants to emphasize.

2. A poet may break his diction or vocabulary. Every poet in any specific poem writes on a certain level of usage in a fairly limited vocabulary. Emily Dickinson, for example, has a habit of breaking out of her vocabulary with the last word of the first line of a poem to arrest the reader and shock him into attention. She begins one poem (we omit the last word) "I heard a fly buzz when I _____." What word is expected? The rest of the words lead one to expect "opened the door" or "sat down." But her word is "died." The pattern is broken and the reader's attention has been focused. Another Dickinson poem begins "Because I could not stop for _____." The reader expects "coffee" or something innocuous. Dickinson's word is "death."

3. A poet may break his image pattern. Keats maintains the image of the explorer throughout his sonnet. However, Shakespeare wants to emphasize an idea when he has Macbeth say, "Tomorrow, and tomorrow, and tomorrow,/Creeps in this petty pace from day to day,/To the last syllable . . . ." The word "syllable" is attention-getting because "creeps" and "pace" have led the reader to expect something physical, something snail-like. But

"syllable" establishes a new line of thought: "to the last syllable of recorded time." It doesn't break the *sense* of the passage (it makes excellent sense) but it does command attention. Similarly, in the "Garden of Proserpine," after the poet Swinburne has almost soothed the reader to sleep with long, drowsy pictures of the underworld as a place of slow-growing, peaceful gardens, he suddenly interjects "Time stoops to no man's lure." This is an image from falconry, where the hawk is recalled by whirling a lure that the hawk "stoops" to, enabling the falconer to recapture him. This violent image, coming in the midst of the somnolent pattern, breaks that pattern and awakens the reader. Why? Because the idea in it—that no man controls time and therefore can never recapture the past—is central to the poem and the poet wants you to notice it.

4. A poet may shift his tone. When a serious poem shifts to sarcasm or a satirical poem becomes solemn, the reader is immediately aware of the shift. This device is perhaps best illustrated in comic verse:

> There's the wonderful love of a beautiful maid,
>   And the love of a staunch true man,
> And the love of a baby that's unafraid—
>   All have existed since time began.
> But the most wonderful love, the Love of all loves,
>   Even greater than the love for Mother,
> Is the infinite, tenderest, passionate love
>   Of one dead drunk for another.

Any writer who does not pay attention to his patterns and to his departures from them is usually unsuccessful. Max Shulman parodies the bad modern poet when he writes:

> Tread quietly, Al,
> For the moon
> Is a half-slice of lemon
> On the teacup of the world.

The result here is that the reader is continually off balance—no pattern is ever established. The whole "poem" is a series of breaks. "Tread quietly" does not fit "Al," the "moon" doesn't fit "a half-slice of lemon/ On the teacup of the world." "Tread quietly" and "moon" go together. Nothing else does.

The point of this discussion is that the ability to distinguish pattern in a poem is the first step toward understanding the manipulated experience, the work itself.

Because poetry is compressed rather than diffuse, the poet must choose words that have the largest number of meanings. In practice, this means that he wants the word with the greatest number of relevant overtones to it. As a result, although a poet can achieve great precision of statement, he also often achieves ambiguity— multiple meanings. A discussion of the causes of ambiguity follows.

Metaphor

Metaphor, in poetry, generally refers to any figure of comparison. It may be a metaphor proper ("There is a garden in her face"), a simile ("Her cheeks were like roses"), or even an analogy ("Her face was a storm cloud; and when the angry rain began to fall, lightning flashed from her eyes").

Metaphors are figurative, not literal, which means simply that their meaning consists largely of their overtones. Thomas Campion, for example, wrote:

> There is a garden in her face,
> Where roses and white lilies grow.

Obviously the reader is not meant to envision dirt and wheelbarrows. What the translated metaphor says is that the lady's cheeks are red and her skin is white. But the overtones suggest much more. "Garden," "roses," and "lilies" imply youth and health and natural, not artificial, loveliness. And they further suggest the temporary nature of that loveliness. Consider, for instance, the difference between the garden metaphor and:

> A face from alabaster carved
> That glowing rubies frame.

These two seventeenth-century poets have opposing ideas about how long beauty will endure. They may also be suggesting different degrees of accessibility in the lady, since the garden metaphor is in its overtones familiar and sweet, the statue metaphor, cold and rather distant.

Metaphoric ambiguity of this kind creates no special difficulties for the careful reader. And it enhances the pleasure of reading, since it provokes the reader's imagination, adds emotional coloring to intellectual perception, and makes sensuous what otherwise would be abstract.

But many ambiguities are more complex than these, and the reader grows uneasy because he feels he must make a choice between possible meanings. When Shakespeare, for example, in "Sonnet 75" writes that his love is to his thoughts as "sweet season'd showers are to the ground," "sweet season'd" can mean two things: "sweet scented" and "in the sweet season," that is, springtime. Both meanings are correct. They are complementary; the phrase has two parallel overtones instead of one.

Of course this is not to say that any random overtone sensed by any reader is legitimate. The overtone can usually be validated by the poem itself—the nature of the poem determines its relevance or irrelevance. For example, Shakespeare's "Sonnet 66" begins, "Tir'd with all these for restful death I cry." Now "Tir'd," that is, exhausted, gives the line a perfectly clear meaning. But Elizabethan English was a very flexible instrument, and "tir'd" is often a clipped form of a longer word, frequently of "attired" and "retired." Moreover, to twentieth-century ears, "with" seems at first an odd appendage to "tir'd"; one expects "of." Both "retired with" and "attired with" are linguistically proper, and used in the line, they make sensible metaphoric statements that in no way clash with the idea of exhaustion. But are they valid? Here is the total poem:

Tir'd with all these for restful death I cry,
As to behold desert a beggar borne,
And needy Nothing trim'd in jollitie,
And purest faith unhappily forsworn,
And gilded honor shamefully misplaced,   5
And maiden virtue rudely strumpeted,
And right perfection wrongfully disgraced,
And strength by limping sway disabled,
And art made tongue-tied by authority,
And Folly (Doctor-like) controlling skill,   10
And simple Truth miscalled Simplicity,
And captive good attending Captain ill.
　Tir'd with all these, from these would I be gone,
　Save that to die, I leave my love alone.

Even a quick reading reveals that "retired" will not do. Of all possibilities, the speaker here definitely is not retired. His complaint is that he is too entangled in the hurly-burly of a dishonest and distasteful life. What about "attired"? There is validation for this metaphor in line 3: "needy Nothing trim'd in jollitie," that is, dressed in finery. The social evils he describes are then to be seen as a burdensome suit of clothes he would throw off in order to be again the natural man.

Thus overtones are accepted or rejected because they do or do not fit the facts of the poem.

Symbols

Symbols were explored briefly in the discussion of the short story (pp. 21–22). A symbol is an emblem; it represents something else without ever announcing that an identification or a comparison is being made, as the metaphor does.

As in dealing with metaphor, the reader must exercise discretion in recognizing and accepting symbolic meaning. Again, the total poem must be the basis for accepting or rejecting symbolic meaning. One of the best known poetic symbols occurs in the concluding lines of Browning's "My Last Duchess" (pp. 362–3). Because of what the reader knows of the Duke by the time he reaches these lines, he sees that, whatever the conscious reason for the Duke's mention of the statue of Neptune taming a sea horse, the statue symbolizes his cast of mind. The Duke is a man whose pride of ownership leads him to regard everything in his area of influence, including people, as property to be handled as he pleases. If these possessions do not conform to his desires, they must be "tamed."

Paradox

A paradox is an apparent contradiction, a true statement that is made up of seemingly incompatible elements. Richard Lovelace's "I could not love thee dear so much/Loved I not honour more" is a paradox. Paradoxes are always emphatic because they demand inspection. Thus, John Donne concludes a sonnet with the striking paradox, "Death, thou shalt die," and Shakespeare with

> To give away your self, keeps your self still,
> And you must live drawn by your own sweet skill.

Many poetic paradoxes are far more complex than these. Probably the best known example in English literature is John Donne's "The Canonization," in which Donne proves the paradox that fleshly lovers are heavenly lovers, that is, saints. The same poet's "A Valediction Forbidding Mourning" (p. 333–4) argues that when lovers part, they do not part, another paradox.

Irony

Irony is the use of words that say one thing and mean another. It can occur variously in poetry. Occasionally, irony is a trick of phrasing, as when Byron in the *Don Juan* speaks of Coleridge:

> Explaining metaphysics to the nation—
> I wish he would explain his Explanation.

Sometimes it is a result of a situation, as in Housman's "Is My Team Ploughing" (p. 353–4). In that poem, the questioner does not understand the significance of the answers he receives from his former friend, who is the one man who can, but who ought not, answer the questions truthfully. This is "dramatic irony," irony that evolves from a character's ignorance of the significance of what he is saying. "My Last Duchess" is a thoroughly ironic poem, in that the Duke never realizes the terrible portrait he draws of himself in his own words.

A more difficult kind of irony to explain is that appearing, for example, in John Crowe Ransom's "Bells for John Whiteside's Daughter" (pp. 457–8). The speaker seems vexed at the little girl for not running and playing and refers to her present disposition as a "brown study," although both he and the reader know perfectly well that the little girl is dead. The mind of the speaker simply cannot assimilate this tragic fact, and he therefore uses logically inappropriate language in speaking of the child. He cannot say what he means.

Allusion

Like all writers, poets compress and add overtones by alluding, that is, referring, to facts outside the poem proper. Allusions are meant to deepen and illuminate a poem, but the careless reader may overlook them and therefore misread the poem. The impact of Yeats's "The Second Coming" (pp. 424–5) depends partly on the

reader's knowledge of the Nativity. No one is likely to misread this
allusion. Part of the force and much of the logic of Milton's sonnet,
"On His Blindness," (pp. 414-15) depends on recognizing the allusion
in the third line to the parable of the talents (*Matthew* 25:26). Not
many will miss this reference either. But many readers may pass over
the significance of the allusions to Lazarus, Hamlet, and John
the Baptist in Eliot's "The Love Song of J. Alfred Prufrock"
(pp. 364–7). If so, the reader won't fully understand the character
of Prufrock, since his comparisons of himself with these men illuminate his weaknesses.

Close-Packed Imagery

An image in literature is a word or phrase that evokes a response
in a reader by appealing to one or more of his five senses. It therefore arouses him physically and mentally. In the following example,
which is the first thirteen lines of "Preludes" by T. S. Eliot, many
senses are appealed to:

The winter evening settles down	
With *smell of steaks* in passageways.	smell
Six o'clock.	
The *burnt-out ends of smoky days.*	smell and sight (the im-age is of a cigarette or cigar)
And now a *gusty shower* wraps	sight and touch
The *grimy scraps*	touch
Of *withered leaves* about your feet	sight
And *newspapers from vacant lots;*	sight and touch
The *showers* beat	sight and sound
On *broken blinds and chimney-pots,*	sight
And at the corner of the street	
A *lonely cab-horse steams and stamps.*	sight, smell, and sound
And then the *lighting of the lamps.*	sight

Many of these are arguable—the newspapers blown about your
feet could include sound imagery—but only the most obvious are
mentioned. The reader's senses have a thorough exercise, which will
probably create a reaction to the passage. But the passage hasn't
said anything, that is, it contains no statement except the descriptive

generalization in the first line. The images here create any feeling
the reader may have, and they are able to do this because they are
concrete. The more vague and abstract imagery becomes, the less
effect it can produce. Compare, for example, the two following poems:

O wind, come soon   Western Wind, when wilt thou blow
Bringing rain from the sea;   So the small rain down can rain?
Then will the time arrive   Christ, that I were in my bed
When my love returns to me.   And my love in my arms again!

The poem on the left is a very poor twentieth-century imitation of
the very good sixteenth-century poem on the right. The older poem
is specific and concrete: The west wind (not just wind) brings the
spring showers (not just rain); the love the speaker longs for is made
real by a series of specific images: *Christ, bed, arms*—whereas the
version on the left is vague and therefore unconvincing and lackluster.
Literature, as defined before, is a manipulation of experience, and
human beings experience things first through the five physical senses.
Imagery, therefore, is an important device, so important that one
school of poetry in America—the Imagist school—devoted itself
to writing poems entirely in images, without any comment by the
poet. The popularity of the Japanese *haiku* today (a three-line picture
poem, the first line having five syllables, the second seven, and
the third five, with the point of the poem growing out of the picture
presented) is further evidence of the importance attached to imagery:

Blossoms on the pear—
a woman in the moonlight
reads a letter there.

CONVENTIONS OF DICTION

Since every poem in a sense establishes its own vocabulary and
since fashions in poetic diction have changed so often in literary
history, conventions of diction are fluid. The history of British poetry,
for example, has been a series of reactions against the "poetic diction" of a preceding age, and each new school of poetry has claimed
that it was restoring "natural" language to poetry. In fact, none of
them did that; they simply replaced one set of conventions with
another. The early nineteenth-century Romantics said they were returning to nature and natural language in opposition to the highly

artificial diction of the eighteenth-century Neoclassical school. The Neoclassicists had argued that they were restoring natural language to poetry as a reaction against the rough, over-specialized language of the seventeenth-century Metaphysical school. In turn, the Metaphysicals were reacting against the artificial diction of the sixteenth-century sonneteers. This constant shift in diction makes a brief discussion of conventions of diction difficult. It is easier to give some examples and generalize from them.

Older conventions sometimes trouble present-day readers. In much pretwentieth-century poetry, for example, the "neither . . . nor" construction familiar to us in prose was a "nor . . . nor" construction:

> Nor Mars his sword nor war's quick fire

The original reason for the use of this odd construction is lost; probably it was designed to produce metrical regularity, a balance, and a sonority that is lacking in the long *e* of *neither* but is supplied by the long *o* of *nor*. This minor example is representative of many conventional constructions that should cause no real difficulty once the convention is noted.

Other conventions are not so easily explained and accepted. Much eighteenth-century verse, for example, sounds to modern ears excessively wordy. Few nouns, so it seems, appear without adjectives, and often the same noun is linked to the same adjective. What the modern reader must realize is that the eighteenth-century poet was following a convention now discarded: The English construction was often a translation of a Latin construction. Its constant use was a kind of poetic shorthand peculiar to a society of writers and readers that set a high value on the classics. With second-rate poets the shorthand degenerated into an irritating mannerism that even at its best displeases readers today. For example, a section of Gray's "Elegy Written in a Country Churchyard":

> Now fades the glimmering landscape on the sight,
>   And all the air a solemn stillness holds,
> Save where the beetle wheels his droning flight,
>   And drowsy tinklings lull the distant folds.

Today this might be called uneconomical diction because the four lines contain five nouns paired with adjectives for no apparent reason.

An inventive reader can rewrite the lines for himself by leaving out
an adjective in each line:

> Now fades the landscape on the sight,
> And all the air a stillness holds,
> Save where the beetle wheels his flight,
> And tinklings lull the distant folds.

Many readers will feel that the poem is not harmed by this editing.
But they should also realize that it has now lost one of its conventions, one of the things that ties it to its period—that it is not the
same poem reedited but an entirely different poem.

The poetic diction of the eighteenth century looks peculiar today
because we have virtually eliminated conventions of diction in our
time by eliminating restrictions on subject matter. Present-day dogma
could probably be stated thus: *Any word or phase is poetic if it is
appropriate to the subject matter; any subject matter is appropriate
if it renders a significant experience vividly and concretely.* It is hard
to imagine a twentieth-century reader objecting to a "low" subject
in the manner of eighteenth- or nineteenth-century readers. It is
equally hard to imagine another century writing about many of the
subjects we deal with today. When the seventeenth-century poet
John Donne, probably the most modern poet writing before our day,
wrote poems that contained references to flies, he used the fly as a
symbol of fleshly love (since the fly is short-lived and filthy); but
several twentieth-century poets have written poems about flies simply
as dirty little beasts.

If the present-day reader is irritated by the habits of diction of a
previous century, he ought to reflect for a moment on how modern
habits of diction would irritate readers of the past. In a very real
sense, the absence of conventional diction is in itself a convention,
probably no better and no worse than previous conventions. Taste
does not improve; it only changes.

The responsibility of the reader, then, is to acclimate himself to
the vocabulary the poet is using. *A good poem is one that is compatible with its own logic.* If the diction of the poem harmonizes
with the subject matter and theme, it is probably appropriate. A very
crude example of this could be a seventeenth-century poem that
begins with an invocation to Apollo. Surely no reader will object
to the passage simply because Apollo was a mythical figure and

therefore could not possibly help the poet. The invocation was a convention and Apollo, as the god of poetry, was a conventional figure to be invoked; both were parts of the frame of reference of the past. Furthermore, if the passage begins, "O Apollo, on the wings of morning . . ." the reader has reason to dislike the phrase but not to condemn it entirely, since it is again part of an established convention and *it is compatible with the logic of invocation.* However, if the poet were to begin, "Hey, Apollo . . . ," then the diction is obviously not compatible with the logic of the poem (unless it is a burlesque) and deserves condemnation.

CONVENTIONS OF RHYTHM AND METER

We are all rhythmical creatures: Our pulse beats to a rhythm, we breathe in rhythm, we brush our teeth in rhythm. The poet takes natural rhythm and conventionalizes it; that is, he builds it into different artificial rhythms that we call *meter.* As we have said before, he establishes a pattern of regularity and then breaks the pattern for emphasis.

The study of meter is called prosody. Different kinds of poetry use different prosodic systems. Most systems rest on the counting of recurring sounds or stresses. A few do not: Syllabic verse, for example, is built on similar line length, as in the haiku. Marianne Moore, the American poet, writes syllabic verse; you cannot hear one sound recurring regularly in a line nor can you count a recurring number of stresses in a line, but you can count a recurring number of syllables in the line. This prosodic system, however, is unusual.

Most English verse is based on accentual-syllabic prosody, that is, on recurring stresses in combinations of two or three syllables. In English, it is difficult to pronounce three syllables successively without stressing ("accenting") one syllable more than the others. Thus stresses can be counted in units of two or three syllables. In English, four degrees of stress are possible, but in the interests of simplicity, let's limit our consideration to two possibilities—stress or no stress— and designate those two by ′ for stress and ˣ for no stress. A word such as *undo* has two syllables, the first unstressed, the second stressed (ŭndó). A word like *taken* reverses the pattern (tákĕn). *Unaware* is

a three-syllable word stressed in this fashion: unǎwáre. *Sickening,*
also three syllables, is stressed this way: síckěnǐng.

The patterns in *undo, taken, unaware,* and *sickening* are the most
common in English verse; each of these words is a natural foot—
it contains in itself the smallest prosodic unit of measurement, the
foot. A foot is a unit containing at least one stressed syllable and one
or two unstressed syllables. The four feet illustrated above have
these names:

x ′	(undo)	iambic foot
′ x	(taken)	trochaic foot
x x ′	(unaware)	anapestic foot
′ x x	(sickening)	dactylic foot

A good poet never composes a poem using only one kind of foot
because it becomes monotonous and dead; the reader gets so hyp-
notized by the sing-song of the meter that he can pay no attention to
anything else. However, in most poems one foot pattern predominates.
The most common foot is the iambic; it occurs in natural speech
more often than any other, and the poet who wants a conversational
realism often adopts this one as the dominant foot. The trochaic foot
sounds a little odd to English ears if it is repeated regularly, but it
is a very emphatic foot because of the location of its stress ("Nó, Ǐ
críed, aňd . . ."). The anapest is a very rapid foot, useful in speed-
ing up a line; when anapests are combined, they often result in a
marching meter ("The Stars and Stripes Forever" begins with a strong
trochaic foot and then shifts immediately into the marching anapest).
The dactylic foot is the least common of the four; it is used chiefly
for emphasis (it is simply a long trochaic foot) or for a galloping,
lunging rhythm (in reading aloud Browning's "I galloped, Dirck
galloped, we galloped all three" one can hear the horses' hooves).

There are also terms that describe the number of feet in a line.

one foot	monometer	"Ǐ dó"	(iambic monometer)
two feet	dimeter	"Tǒ thís wě cáme"	(iambic dimeter)
three feet	trimeter	"Aňd óne ǔpón thě ráck"	(iambic trimeter)

four feet	tetrameter	"Sing no great songs of the bold and the brave" (dactylic tetrameter [last foot shortened])
five feet	pentameter	"Was this the face that launched a thousand ships?" (iambic pentameter)
six feet	hexameter	"Where are Elmer, Herman, Bert, Tom, and Charley" (trochaic hexameter)
seven feet	heptameter	"Dying, dying, dying, singing dirges for a sinking soul" (trochaic heptameter)

The commonest line in English verse is the iambic pentameter, probably because an adult male can pronounce that many syllables comfortably in one breath. Nursery rhymes are generally in dimeter or trimeter because a child can sustain that many syllables and no more comfortably in one breath. Hexameter and heptameter lines tend to be too long for one breath and too short for two and are therefore unpopular. But poets choose different line lengths for many other reasons. Short lines have a snap and sparkle that appeal to the poet who wants to write epigrams. Long iambic or trochaic lines, because they have a breath break in them, lend themselves to reflective utterances. Long anapestic lines have a dash and speed that work equally well for narrative or comic verse. The possible combinations of feet and line length for different effects are virtually inexhaustible.

After some practice in listening to verse, a reader begins to hear the music that an expert builds into his lines. For example, a poet sometimes syncopates a line: He plays off a natural rhythm against a metrical pattern. Take the following line:

A whirling, dipping, dancing, prancing girl.

In most aspects, this is probably an undistinguished line except for the fact that it moves and twists as you read it, not just because of the meaning of the words, but because of the syncopation. The four middle words are all natural trochaic feet: whirling, dipping, dancing, prancing. But the meter is not trochaic—it is iambic. The poet has placed one unaccented syllable at the beginning of the line and an accented monosyllable at the end so that in a line composed chiefly of natural trochees, there is an overriding iambic pattern; the ear hears the two rhythms going at the same time.

A poet can employ many rhythmic devices besides those already mentioned:

1. Alliteration: the repetition of initial consonants to tie phrases and ideas together ("When to the sessions of sweet silent thought")

2. Assonance: the repetition of vowel sounds ("Nor let the beetle nor the deathmoth be")

3. Consonance: the repetition of consonant patterns ("Loving and living, I could not leave")

Rhyme is also a rhythmic device, basically the repetition of a similar vowel sound at the end of successive lines. A great deal of poetry does not rhyme. Many poets have felt that rhyme restricts them or destroys a natural sentence effect; they have therefore turned to unrhymed forms such as blank verse (unrhymed iambic pentameter) or free verse (unmetered verse). On the other hand, rhyme has great advantages to offer the poet: It appeals to the rhythmic demand in each of us; it organizes a poem in that rhyme is the basis of stanza forms; it offers a frame for a poem in much the same way that a picture frame enhances a portrait; and it is an effective mnemonic device.

Furthermore, the poet can use various kinds of rhyme.

1. Slant rhyme: repetition of a similar but not identical vowel and an identical consonant: heel/ still

2. Light rhyme: repetition of identical vowel sounds but with varying stress on the vowel: be/ silly

3. Eye rhyme: repetition of different vowel sounds that appear identical to the eye: sentry/comply

4. Full rhyme: repetition of an identical vowel sound and identical following consonants: hope/ scope

Rhyme and meter are the basis of stanza form. Like many formal conventions, stanza form can best be studied in the poems themselves.

The poems that follow are organized on a double principle. After an introduction, poems that are alike in form appear—ballad, sonnet, ode, and so on. Following those poems, a theme or topic common to that form is announced, and a longer selection of poems—in a variety of forms but developing the same topic—appears.

THE BALLAD   *on exam*

Folk ballads are the popular music of bygone days. How they came to be composed, who composed them, under what circumstances —these things are not known. Theoretically, they could have been composed by a group gathered around a campfire; practically, they were probably composed by individual authors and then passed through many hands and many voices until they were finally written down and solidified. The same ballad has usually many variant forms: "Lord Randal" in England may become "John Randal" in New England, "Johnnie Randolph" in the South, and "Jamie Rambo" in the Southwest. The basic story line is usually the same in all versions, but the special events are changed to fit the region.

From some of the more obvious conventions in the ballads, one can make additional inferences about their development. Many ballads, for example, have a refrain, sometimes a nonsense refrain: "with a hey and ho/ and a hey-nonny-no!" At other times the refrain changes slightly each time to make use of *incremental repetition*, that is, each time the refrain repeats, it adds a little more to the narrative as a kind of progress report. Simply changing one word in a refrain can accomplish this. For example, in a ballad about a young man who goes to his wedding only to find his bride has died in the night (a common ballad theme), a refrain might in successive stanzas go like this:

1. And onward he did go, oh!
2. And quickly he did go, oh!
3. And gladly he did go, oh!
4. And sadly he did go, oh!
5. And madly he did go, oh!

The change in the adverb reflects the change of mind in the main character.

This habitual use of a refrain implies two things: First, the ballad is basically an oral form; the refrain is used as a summary to pull together divisions of the story in a fashion that would not be necessary if the ballad were a printed form. Second, many ballads probably were dance forms: The nonsense refrain suggests that it allowed the dancers to regroup for the next "set" or pattern.

It is easy to see why the ballad is defined as the popular music of bygone days. Like most popular forms, its appeal rests largely on using material and techniques familiar to the audience: familiar themes, images, characters, phrases, actions—in other words, conventional material and methods. Following is a list of conventional folk ballad elements:

1. Stanza form: usually iambic quatrains (four-line stanzas) with alternating lines of four feet and three feet—an abbreviated speech rhythm.
2. Themes: the death of the young, the innocent, the beautiful, the good, often through no fault of their own.
3. Images: stock figures, often connected by alliteration (hounds and hawks, dale and down, heath and hollow), sometimes alone (nut-brown maid, snow-white steed).

The literary ballad differs from the folk ballad: One author alone creates and edits the poem, and the first form is generally printed, not oral. This means that the literary ballad is often more sophisticated; close inspection of the printed form will reveal touches by the author that would go unnoticed in oral presentation (and therefore probably would not be present in the folk ballad). If, for example, you examine the organization of detail in "La Belle Dame Sans Merci," you will discover a tightness of structure uncharacteristic of the folk ballad. Examination of the language will likewise show a heightened form of diction.

Anonymous

Edward

"Why dois your brand sae drap wi bluid,
      Edward, Edward,
Why dois your brand sae drap wi bluid,
  And why sae sad gang yee O?"
"O I hae killed my hauke sae guid,   5
      Mither, mither,
O I hae killed my hauke sae guid,
  And I had nae mair bot hee O."

"Your haukis bluid was nevir sae reid,
      Edward, Edward,   10
Your haukis bluid was nevir sae reid,
  My deir son I tell thee O."
"O I hae killed my reid-roan steid,
      Mither, mither,
O I hae killed my reid-roan steid,   15
  That erst was sae fair and frie O."

"Your steid was auld, and ye hae gat mair,
      Edward, Edward,
Your steid was auld, and ye hae gat mair,
  Sum other dule ye drie O."
"O I hae killed my fadir deir,   20
      Mither, mither,
O I hae killed my fadir deir,
  Alas, and wae is mee O!"

"And whatten penance wul ye drie for that,   25
      Edward, Edward?
And whatten penance will ye drie for that?
  My deir son, now tell me O."
"Ile set my feit in yonder boat,
      Mither, mither,   30

Ile set my feit in yonder boat,
   And Ile fare ovir the sea O."

"And what wul ye doe wi your towirs and your ha,
      Edward, Edward?
And what wul ye doe wi your towirs and your ha,   35
   That were sae fair to see O?"
"Ile let thame stand tul they doun fa,
      Mither, mither,
Ile let thame stand tul they doun fa,
   For here nevir mair maun I bee O."   40

"And what wul ye leive to your bairns and your wife,
      Edward, Edward?
And what wul ye leive to your bairns and your wife,
   Whan ye gang ovir the sea O?"
"The warldis room, late them beg thrae life,   45
      Mither, mither,
The warldis room, late them beg thrae life,
   For thame nevir mair wul I see O."

"And what wul ye leive to your ain mither deir,
      Edward, Edward?
And what wul ye leive to your ain mither deir?   50
   My deir son, now tell me O."
"The curse of hell frae me sall ye beir,
      Mither, mither,
The curse of hell frae me sall ye beir,   55
   Sic counseils ye gave to me O."

Edward

For Analysis

1. How does "Edward" fulfill the conventions of the folk ballad?
2. What aspect of the poem's structure gives it such dramatic power?

John Keats

[handwritten: beautiful woman without mercy]

La Belle Dame
Sans Merci

"O what can ail thee, knight-at-arms,
  Alone and palely loitering?
The sedge has wither'd from the lake,
  And no birds sing.

"O what can ail thee, knight-at-arms, 5
  So haggard and so woe-begone?
The squirrel's granary is full, *[handwritten: in the fall]*
  And the harvest's done.

[handwritten: lily a symbol of death]
"I see a lily on thy brow
  With anguish moist and fever dew; *[handwritten: the knight is answering question]* 10
And on thy cheek a fading rose
  Fast withereth too.'

"I met a lady in the meads,
  Full beautiful—a faery's child,
Her hair was long, her foot was light, 15
  And her eyes were wild.

"I made a garland for her head,
  And bracelets too, and fragrant zone;
She look'd at me as she did love,
  And made sweet moan. 20

"I set her on my pacing steed,
  And nothing else saw all day long,
For sidelong would she bend, and sing
  A faery's song.

"She found me roots of relish sweet, 25
  And honey wild, and manna dew,

And sure in language strange she said—
  'I love thee true.'

"She took me to her elfin grot,
  And there she wept, and sigh'd full sore;   30
And there I shut her wild wild eyes
  With kisses four.

"And there she lullèd me asleep,
  And there I dream'd—Ah! woe betide!
The latest dream I ever dream'd   35
  On the cold hill's side.

"I saw pale kings and princes too,
  Pale warriors, death-pale were they all;
They cried—'La Belle Dame Sans Merci
  Hath thee in thrall!'   40

"I saw their starv'd lips in the gloom,
  With horrid warning gapèd wide,
And I awoke and found me here,
  On the cold hill's side.

"And this is why I sojourn here,   45
  Alone and palely loitering,
Though the sedge is wither'd from the lake,   *under the*
  And no birds sing."   *the knight is in the*
                               spell of the beautiful
                                           woman

La Belle Dame Sans Merci

For Analysis

1. What are the standard ballad elements in this poem? What features
    make it as a literary ballad, as opposed to a folk ballad?
2. Of what is the lily a symbol? The lady?

Anonymous

Lord Randal

"O where hae ye been, Lord Randal, my son?
O where hae ye been, my handsome young man?"
"I hae been to the wild wood; mother, make my bed soon,
Fir I'm weary wi hunting, and fain wald lie down."

"Where gat ye your dinner, Lord Randal, my son?   5
Where gat ye your dinner, my handsome young man?"
"I dined wi my true-love; mother, make my bed soon,
For I'm weary wi hunting, and fain wald lie down."

"What gat ye to your dinner, Lord Randal, my son?
What gat ye to your dinner, my handsome young man?"   10
"I gat eels boiled in broo; mother, make my bed soon,
For I'm weary wi hunting, and fain wald lie down."

"What became of your bloodhounds, Lord Randal, my son?
What became of your bloodhounds, my handsome young man?"
"O they swelled and they died; mother, make my bed soon, 15
For I'm weary wi hunting, and fain wald lie down."

"O I fear ye are poisond, Lord Randal, my son!
O I fear ye are poisond, my handsome young man!"
"O yes! I am poisond; mother, make my bed soon,
For I'm sick at the heart and I fain wald lie down."   20

Lord Randal

For Analysis

1. This typical ballad uses two kinds of repetition:
   a. *simple*, as in the first two lines of each stanza;
   b. *incremental*, as in the last two lines of each stanza.
   What "increment" do you find in each set of concluding lines? How does this make the ballad "sing itself"?
2. What double meaning do you find in the last increment, "For I'm sick at the heart"?
3. Why is Lord Randal unwilling to tell the story so that his mother must pry it out of him? What in the ballad tells you that he is unwilling?

Anonymous

The Demon
Lover

1

"O where have you been, my long, long love,
  This long seven years and mair?"
"O I'm come to seek my former vows
  Ye granted me before."

2

"O hold your tongue of your former vows,
  For they will breed sad strife;
O hold your tongue of your former vows,
  For I am become a wife."   5

3

He turned him right and round about,
    And the tear blinded his ee: 10
"I wad never hae trodden on Irish ground,
    If it had not been for thee.

4

"I might hae had a king's daughter,
    Far, far beyond the sea;
I might have had a king's daughter,   15
    Had it not been for love o thee."

5

"If ye might have had a king's daughter,
    Yer sel ye had to blame;
Ye might have taken the king's daughter,
    For ye kend that I was nane.   20

6

"If I was to leave my husband dear,
    And my two babes also,
O what have you to take me to,
    If with you I should go?"

7

"I hae seven ships upon the sea—   25
    The eighth brought me to land—
With four-and-twenty bold mariners,
    And music on every hand."

8

She has taken up her two little babes,
    Kiss'd them baith cheek and chin:
"O fair ye weel, my ain two babes,   30
    For I'll never see you again."

9

She set her foot upon the ship,
    No mariners could she behold;
But the sails were o the taffetie,   35
    And the masts o the beaten gold.

10

They had not sailed a league, a league,
   A league but barely three,
When dismal grew his countenance,
   And drumlie grew his ee.   40

11

They had not sailed a league, a league,
   A league but barely three,
Until she espied his cloven foot,
   And she wept right bitterlie.

12

"O hold your tongue of your weeping," says he,   45
   "Of your weeping now let me be;
I will shew you how the lilies grow
   On the banks of Italy."

13

"O what hills are yon, yon pleasant hills,
   That the sun shines sweetly on?"
"O yon are the hills of heaven," he said,   50
   "Where you will never win."

14

"O whaten mountain is yon," she said,
   "All so dreary wi frost and snow?"
"O yon is the mountain of hell," he cried,   55
   "Where you and I will go."

15

He strack the tap-mast wi his hand,
   The fore-mast wi his knee,
And he brake that gallant ship in twain,
   And sank her in the sea.   60

The Demon Lover

For Analysis

1. Is the woman's sudden decision to leave with her former lover adequately explained? Are ballads usually concerned with motive or action?
2. Is the supernatural element in this ballad present for ethical reasons, because of the surprise and awe it evokes in the reader, or both?

Anonymous

Thomas Rymer

True Thomas lay oer yon grassy bank,
   And he beheld a ladie gay,
A ladie that was brisk and bold,
   Come riding oer the fernie brae.

Her skirt was of the grass-green silk,   5
   Her mantel of the velvet fine,
And ilka tett of her horse's mane
   Hung fifty silver bells and nine.

True Thomas he took off his hat,
   And bowed him low down till his knee: 10
"All hail, thou mighty Queen of Heaven!
   For your peer on earth I never did see."

"O no, O no, True Thomas," she says,
   "That name does not belong to me;
I am but the queen of fair Elfland,   15
   And I'm come here for to visit thee.

"But ye maun go wi me now, Thomas,
   True Thomas, ye maun go wi me,
For ye maun serve me seven years,
   Thro weel or wae as may chance to be."   20

She turned about her milk-white steed,
    And took True Thomas up behind,
And aye wheneer her bridle rang,
    The steed flew swifter than the wind.

For forty days and forty nights   25
    He wade thro red blude to the knee,
And he saw neither sun nor moon,
    But heard the roaring of the sea.

O they rade on, and further on,
    Until they came to a garden green:
"Light down, light down, ye ladie free,   30
    Some of that fruit let me pull to thee."

"O no, O no, True Thomas," she says,
    "That fruit maun mot to be touched by thee,
For a' the plagues that are in hell   35
    Light on the fruit of this countrie.

"But I have a loaf here in my lap,
    Likewise a bottle of claret wine,
And now ere we go farther on,
    We'll rest a while, and ye may dine."   40

When he had eaten and drunk his fill,
    "Lay down your head upon my knee,"
The lady sayd, "ere we climb yon hill,
    And I will show you fairlies three.

"O see not ye yon narrow road,   45
    So thick beset wi thorns and briers?
That is the path of righteousness,
    Tho after it but few enquires.

"And see not ye that braid braid road,
    That lies across yon lillie leven?
That is the path of wickedness,
    Tho some call it the road to heaven.

"And see not ye that bonny road,
    Which winds about the fernie brae?
That is the road to fair Elfland,
    Where you and I this night maun gae.   55

"But Thomas, ye maun hold your tongue,
    Whatever you may hear or see,

For gin ae word you should chance to speak,
　　You will neer get back to your ain countrie."   60

He has gotten a coat of the even cloth,
　' And a pair of shoes of velvet green,
And till seven years were past and gone
　　True Thomas on earth was never seen.

Thomas Rhymer

For Analysis

1.　The Queen of Elfland is not concerned with the paths of wickedness
or righteousness but with the road to fairyland. What does this tell
you about how this poem is to be read?

Sir Walter Raleigh

In the Grace of Wit,
of Tongue and Face

Your face	Your tongue	Your wit
So fair	So sweet	So sharp
First bent	Then drew	So hit
Mine eye	Mine ear	My heart
Mine eye	Mine ear	My heart
To like	To learn	To love
Your face	Your tongue	Your wit
Doth lead	Doth teach	Doth move
Your face	Your tongue	Your wit
With beams	With sound	With art
Doth blind	Doth charm	Doth rule
Mine eye	Mine ear	My heart

5

10

Mine eye	My ear	My heart
With life	With hope	With skill
Your face	Your tongue	Your wit
Doth feed	Doth feast	Doth fill

15

Oh face	O tongue	O wit
With frowns	With checks	With smart
Wrong not	Vex not	Wound not
Mine eye	My ear	My heart

20

This eye	This ear	This heart
Shall joy	Shall bend	Shall swear
Your face	Your tongue	Your wits
To serve	To trust	To fear

In the Grace of Wit, of Tongue and Face

For Analysis

1. What features of the poem's structure produce the ritualistic, measured effect that counterpoints the emotion inherent in the subject matter?
2. What is the full meaning of "wit" in this context?

17 century poet

John Donne

Song

Go and catch a falling star,
   Get with child a mandrake root,
Tell me where all past years are,
   Or who cleft the devil's foot;
Teach me to hear mermaids singing,
   To keep off envy's stinging,
      And find
      What wind
Serves to advance an honest mind.

do all these impossible things

5

If thou be'st born to strange sights,   10
   Things invisible to see,
Ride ten thousand days and nights
   Till Age snow white hairs on thee;
Thou, when thou return'st, wilt tell me
All strange wonders that befell thee,   15
      And swear
      No where
Lives a woman true and fair.

If thou find'st one, let me know;
   Such a pilgrimage were sweet.   20
Yet do not; I would not go,
   Though at next door we might meet.
Though she were true when you met her,
And last till you write your letter,
      Yet she   25
      Will be
False, ere I come, to two or three.

Song

For Analysis

1. This is a remarkably strong and emphatic poem to be entitled "Song."
    What in the verbs particularly gives the poem this strength?
2. What do catching a falling star, impregnating a mandrake root,
    finding all past years, and the other things have in common? What
    does this imply about the possibility of any task or the validity of
    any belief raised later in the poem?
3. This poem is heavily rhymed but it has the ring of the spoken word
    at the same time. How does the poet get that seemingly contradictory
    effect?

John Donne

a bidding of farewell

A Valediction
Forbidding Mourning

As virtuous men pass mildly away,
  And whisper to their souls to go,
Whilst some of their sad friends do say,
  "The breath goes now," and some say, "No,"

As people die

So let us melt and make no noise,
  No tear-floods nor sigh-tempests move;
'Twere profanation of our joys
  To tell the laity our love.

two people melt together   **5**

Moving of th' earth brings harms and fears;
  Men reckon what it did and meant,
But trepidation of the spheres,
  Though greater far, is innocent.

movement   **10**

Dull sublunary lovers' love,
  Whose soul is sense, cannot admit
Absence, because it doth remove
  Those things which elemented it.

physical love

sensuous   **15**

But we by a love so much refin'd
  That ourselves know not what it is,
Interassurèd of the mind,
  Care less eyes, lips, and hands to miss.

love based not on physical contact love much deeper   **20**

Our two souls, therefore, which are one,
  Though I must go, endure not yet
A breach, but an expansion,
  Like gold to airy thinness beat.

If they be two, they are two so
  As stiff twin compasses are two;

souls   **25**

333

Thy soul, the fix'd foot, makes no show
    To move, but doth if th' other do.

And though it in the center sit,
    Yet when the other far doth roam,   30
It leans and hearkens after it,
    And grows erect as that comes home.

Such wilt thou be to me, who must,
    Like th' other foot, obliquely run;
Thy firmness makes my circle just,   35
    And makes me end where I begun.

A Valediction Forbidding Mourning

For Analysis

1. Metaphysical poetry abounds in strange and unusual metaphors. In this poem, the narrator tells his loved one why she should not grieve when he must leave her. What things are the two lovers compared to in successive stanzas? You should find at least five different metaphorical comparisons.
2. Now that you have isolated the metaphors, consider how they are related. Do they all have something in common? Does one generate another?

Robert Herrick

Upon Julia's Clothes

Whenas in silks my Julia goes,
    Then, then, methinks, how sweetly flows
    The liquefaction of her clothes.

Next, when I cast mine eyes, and see
That brave vibration, each way free,   5
Oh, how that glittering taketh me!

Upon Julia's Clothes

For Analysis

1. How do the meter and rhyme scheme of this poem enable the poet's tone to be exuberant but decorous?
2. What quality does Herrick attribute to Julia's walk by using the "liquefaction" image?

Leigh Hunt

Jenny Kissed Me

Jenny kissed me when we met,
   Jumping from the chair she sat in;
Time, you thief, who love to get
   Sweets into your list, put that in:

Say I'm weary, say I'm sad,   5
   Say that health and wealth have missed me,
Say I'm growing old, but add,
   Jenny kissed me.

Jenny Kissed Me

For Analysis

1. This poem originally appeared under the title "Rondeau." This is a conventional French verse pattern. What does a rondeau usually

consist of? How does "Jenny Kissed Me" depart from the standard
rondeau pattern?

2. How does the meter of this poem contribute to its lilting, buoyant
tone?

Percy Bysshe Shelley

Lines

When the lamp is shattered,
The light in the dust lies dead—
    When the cloud is scattered,
The rainbow's glory is shed.
    When the lute is broken,   5
Sweet tones are remembered not;
    When the lips have spoken,
Loved accents are soon forgot.

    As music and splendor
Survive not the lamp and the lute,   10
    The heart's echoes render
No song when the spirit is mute—
    No song but sad dirges,
Like the wind through a ruined cell,
    Or the mournful surges   15
That ring the dead seaman's knell.

    When hearts have once mingled
Love first leaves the well-built nest;
    The weak one is singled
To endure what it once possessed.   20
    O Love! who bewailest
The frailty of all things here,
    Why choose you the frailest
For your cradle, your home, and your bier?

    Its passions will rock thee   25
As the storms rock the ravens on high;
    Bright reason will mock thee,

> Like the sun from a wintry sky.
>   From thy nest every rafter
> Will rot, and thine eagle home
>   Leave thee naked to laughter,
> When leaves fall and cold winds come.

30

Lines

For Analysis

1. What metric pattern and rhyme scheme are followed in this poem?
2. Analyze the analogies developed in the first two stanzas. Do they fail to develop consistently?

John Keats *a romantic poet*

The Eve of
St. Agnes

the legend of St. Agnes was to find who there (the woman's) true love was going to be

madeline and her lover elope and live happily everafter.

1

> St. Agnes' Eve—Ah, bitter chill it was!
> The owl, for all his feathers, was a-cold;
> The hare limped trembling through the frozen grass,
> And silent was the flock in woolly fold:
> Numb were the Beadsman's fingers, while he told
> His rosary, and while his frosted breath,
> Like pious incense from a censer old,
> Seemed taking flight for heaven, without a death,
> Past the sweet Virgin's picture, while his prayer he saith.

5

2

> His prayer he saith, this patient, holy man;
> Then takes his lamp, and riseth from his knees,
> And back returneth, meager, barefoot, wan,

10

Along the chapel aisle by slow degrees:
The sculptured dead, on each side, seem to freeze,
Emprisoned in black, purgatorial rails: 15
Knights, ladies, praying in dumb orat'ries,
He passeth by; and his weak spirit fails
To think how they may ache in icy hoods and mails.

3

Northward he turneth through a little door,
And scarce three steps, ere Music's golden tongue   20
Flattered to tears this aged man and poor;
But no—already had his deathbell rung:
The joys of all his life were said and sung:
His was harsh penance on St. Agnes' Eve:
Another way he went, and soon among   25
Rough ashes sat he for his soul's reprieve,
And all night kept awake, for sinner's sake to grieve.

4

That ancient Beadsman heard the prelude soft;
And so it chanced, for many a door was wide,
From hurry to and fro. Soon, up aloft,   30
The silver, snarling trumpets 'gan to chide:
The level chambers, ready with their pride,
Were glowing to receive a thousand guests:
The carvèd angels, ever eager-eyed,
Stared, where upon their heads the cornice rests,   35
With hair blown back, and wings put cross-wise on their breasts.

5

At length burst in the argent revelry,
With plume, tiara, and all rich array,
Numerous as shadows haunting fairily
The brain, new stuffed, in youth, with triumphs gay   40
Of old romance. These let us wish away,
And turn, sole-thoughted, to one Lady there,
Whose heart had brooded, all that wintry day,
On love, and winged St. Agnes' saintly care,
As she had heard old dames full many times declare.   45

6

They told her how, upon St. Agnes' Eve,
Young virgins might have visions of delight,
And soft adorings from their loves receive
Upon the honeyed middle of the night,

If ceremonies due they did aright;   50
As, supperless to bed they must retire,
And couch supine their beauties, lily white;
Nor look behind, nor sideways, but require
Of Heaven with upward eyes for all that they desire.

7

Full of this whim was thoughtful Madeline: 55
The music, yearning like a god in pain,
She scarcely heard: her maiden eyes divine,
Fixed on the floor, saw many a sweeping train
Pass by—she heeded not at all: in vain
Came many a tiptoe, amorous cavalier,   60
And back retired; not cooled by high disdain,
But she saw not: her heart was otherwhere:
She sighed for Agnes' dreams, the sweetest of the year.

8

She danced along with vague, regardless eyes,
Anxious her lips, her breathing quick and short: 65
The hallowed hour was near at hand: she sighs
Amid the timbrels, and the thronged resort
Of whispers in anger, or in sport;
'Mid looks of love, defiance, hate, and scorn,
Hoodwinked with faery fancy; all amort,   70
Save to St. Agnes and her lambs unshorn,
And all the bliss to be before tomorrow morn.

9

So, purposing each moment to retire,
She lingered still. Meantime, across the moors,
Had come young Porphyro, with heart on fire   75
For Madeline. Beside the portal doors,
Buttressed from moonlight, stands he, and implores
All saints to give him sight of Madeline,
But for one moment in the tedious hours,
That he might gaze and worship all unseen;   80
Perchance speak, kneel, touch, kiss—in sooth such things have been.

10

He ventures in: let no buzzed whisper tell:
All eyes be muffled, or a hundred swords
Will storm his heart, Love's fev'rous citadel:
For him, those chambers held barbarian hordes,   85

Hyena foemen, and hot-blooded lords,
Whose very dogs would execrations howl
Against his lineage; not one breast affords
Him any mercy, in that mansion foul,
Save one old beldame, weak in body and in soul.   90

11

Ah, happy chance! the aged creature came,
Shuffling along with ivory-headed wand,
To where he stood, hid from the torch's flame,
Behind a broad hall-pillar, far beyond
The sound of merriment and chorus bland: 95
He startled her: but soon she knew his face,
And grasped his fingers in her palsied hand,
Saying, "Mercy, Porphyro! hie thee from this place;
They are all here to-night, the whole blood-thirsty race!

12

"Get hence! get hence! there's dwarfish Hildebrand;   100
He had a fever late, and in the fit
He cursèd thee and thine, both house and land:
Then there's that old Lord Maurice, not a whit
More tame for his gray hairs—Alas me! flit!
Flit like a ghost away."—"Ah, Gossip dear,   105
We're safe enough; here in this arm-chair sit,
And tell me how"—"Good Saints! not here, not here;
Follow me, child, or else these stones will be thy bier."

13

He followed through a lowly arched way,
Brushing the cobwebs with his lofty plume,   110
And as she muttered "Well-a—well-a-day!"
He found him in a little moonlight room,
Pale, latticed, chill, and silent as a tomb.
"Now tell me where is Madeline," said he,
"O tell me, Angela, by the holy loom   115
Which none but secret sisterhood may see,
When they St. Agnes' wool are weaving piously."

14

St. Agnes! Ah! it is St. Agnes' Eve—
Yet men will murder upon holy days:
Thou must hold water in a witch's sieve,   120
And be liege-lord of all the Elves and Fays,

To venture so: it fills me with amaze
To see thee, Porphyro!—St. Agnes' Eve!
God's help! my lady fair the conjuror plays
This very night: good angels her deceive!   125
But let me laugh awhile, I've mickle time to grieve."

15

Feebly she laugheth in the languid moon,
While Porphyro upon her face doth look,
Like puzzled urchin on an aged crone
Who keepeth closed a wondrous riddlebook,   130
As spectacled she sits in chimney nook.
But soon his eyes grew brilliant when she told
His lady's purpose; and he scarce could brook
Tears, at the thought of those enchantments cold,
And Madeline asleep in lap of legends old.   135

16

Sudden a thought came like a full-blown rose,
Flushing his brow, and in his painèd heart
Made purple riot: then doth he propose
A stratagem, that makes the beldame start:
"A cruel man and impious thou art: 140
Sweet lady, let her pray, and sleep, and dream
Alone with her good angels, far apart
From wicked men like thee. Go, go!—I deem
Thou canst not surely be the same that thou didst seem."

17

"I will not harm her, by all saints I swear,"   145
Quoth Porphyro: "O may I ne'er find grace
When my weak voice shall whisper its last prayer,
If one of her soft ringlets I displace,
Or look with ruffian passion in her face:
Good Angela, believe me by these tears;   150
Or I will, even in a moment's space,
Awake, with horrid shout, my foemen's ears,
And beard them, though they be more fanged than wolves and bears."

18

"Ah! why wilt thou affright a feeble soul?
A poor, weak, palsy-stricken, churchyard thing,   155
Whose passing-bell may ere the midnight toll;
Whose prayers for thee, each morn and evening,

Were never missed."—Thus plaining, doth she bring
A gentler speech from burning Porphyro;
So woeful, and of such deep sorrowing,   160
That Angela gives promise she will do
Whatever he shall wish, betide her weal or woe.

19

Which was, to lead him, in close secrecy,
Even to Madeline's chamber, and there hide
Him in a closet, of such privacy   165
That be might see her beauty unespied,
And win perhaps that night a peerless bride,
While legioned faeries paced the coverlet,
And pale enchantment held her sleepy-eyed.
Never on such a night have lovers met,   170
Since Merlin paid his Demon all the monstrous debt.

20

"It shall be as thou wishest," said the Dame:
"All cates and dainties shall be storèd there
Quickly on this feast-night: by the tambour frame
Her own lute thou wilt see: no time to spare,   175
For I am slow and feeble, and scarce dare
On such a catering trust my dizzy head.
Wait here, my child, with patience; kneel in prayer
The while: Ah! thou must needs the lady wed,
Or may I never leave my grave among the dead."   180

21

So saying, she hobbled off with busy fear.
The lover's endless minutes slowly passed:
The dame returned, and whispered in his ear
To follow her; with aged eyes aghast
From fright of dim espial. Safe at last,   185
Through many a dusky gallery, they gain
The maiden's chamber, silken, hushed, and chaste;
Where Porphyro took covert, pleased amain.
His poor guide hurried back with agues in her brain.

22

Her falt'ring hand upon the balustrade,   190
Old Angela was feeling for the stair,
When Madeline, St. Agnes' charmèd maid,
Rose, like a missioned spirit, unaware:

With silver taper's light, and pious care,
She turned, and down the aged gossip led   195
To a safe level matting. Now prepare,
Young Porphyro, for gazing on that bed;
She comes, she comes again, like ring-dove frayed and fled.

23

Out went the taper as she hurried in;
Its little smoke, in pallid moonshine, died: 200
She closed the door, she panted, all akin
To spirits of the air, and visions wide:
No uttered syllable, or, woe betide!
But to her heart, her heart was voluble,
Paining with eloquence her balmy side;   205
As though a tongueless nightingale should swell
Her throat in vain, and die, heart-stifled, in her dell.

24

A casement high and triple-arched there was,
All garlanded with carven imag'ries
Of fruits, and flowers, and bunches of knotgrass,   210
And diamonded with panes of quaint device,
Innumerable of stains and splendid dyes,
As are the tiger-moth's deep-damasked wings;
And in the midst, 'mong thousand heraldries,
And twilight saints, and dim emblazonings,   215
A shielded scutcheon blushed with blood of queens and kings.

25

Full on this casement shone the wintry moon,
And threw warm gules on Madeline's fair breast,
As down she knelt for heaven's grace and boon;
Rose-bloom fell on her hands, together pressed,   220
And on her silver cross soft amethyst,
And on her hair a glory, like a saint:
She seemed a splendid angel, newly dressed,
Save wings, for heaven:—Porphyro grew faint:
She knelt, so pure a thing, so free from mortal taint.   225

26

Anon his heart revives: her vespers done,
Of all its wreathèd pearls her hair she frees;
Unclasps her warmèd jewels one by one;
Loosens her fragrant bodice; by degrees

Her rich attire creeps rustling to her knees: 230
Half-hidden, like a mermaid in sea-weed,
Pensive awhile she dreams awake, and sees,
In fancy, fair St. Agnes in her bed,
But dares not look behind, or all the charm is fled.

27

Soon, trembling in her soft and chilly nest,   235
In sort of wakeful swoon, perplexed she lay,
Until the poppied warmth of sleep oppressed
Her soothèd limbs, and soul fatigued away;
Flown, like a thought, until the morrow-day;
Blissfully havened both from joy and pain;   240
Clasped like a missal where swart Paynims pray;
Blinded alike from sunshine and from rain,
As though a rose should shut, and be a bud again.

28

Stol'n to this paradise, and so entranced,
Porphyro gazed upon her empty dress,   245
And listened to her breathing, if it chanced
To wake into a slumberous tenderness;
Which when he heard, that minute did he bless,
And breathed himself: then from the closet crept,
Noiseless as fear in a wide wilderness,   250
And over the hushed carpet, silent, stepped,
And 'tween the curtains peeped, where, lo!—how fast she slept.

30

Then by the bed-side, where the faded moon
Made a dim, silver twilight, soft he set
A table, and, half anguished, threw thereon   255
A cloth of woven crimson, gold, and jet:—
O for some drowsy Morphean amulet!
The boisterous, midnight, festive clarion,
The kettle-drum, and far-heard clarinet,
Affray his ears, though but in dying tone:—   260
The hall door shuts again, and all the noise is gone.

30

And still she slept an azure-lidded sleep,
In blanchèd linen, smooth, and lavendered,
While he from forth the closet brought a heap
Of candied apple, quince, and plum, and gourd;   265

With jellies soother than the creamy curd,
And lucent syrops, tinct with cinnamon;
Manna and dates, in argosy transferred
From Fez; and spicèd dainties, every one,
From silken Samarkand to cedared Lebanon.   270

31

These delicates he heaped with glowing hand
On golden dishes and in baskets bright
Of wreathèd silver: sumptuous they stand
In the retired quiet of the night,
Filling the chilly room with perfume light.—   275
"And now, my love, my seraph fair, awake!
Thou art my heaven, and I thine eremite:
Open thine eyes, for meek St. Agnes' sake,
Or I shall drowse beside thee, so my soul doth ache."

32

Thus whispering, his warm, unnerved arm   280
Sank in her pillow. Shaded was her dream
By the dusk curtains:—'twas a midnight charm
Impossible to melt as icèd stream:
The lustrous salvers in the moonlight gleam;
Broad golden fringe upon the carpet lies: 285
It seemed he never, never could redeem
From such a stedfast spell his lady's eyes;
So mused awhile, entoiled in woofèd phantasies.

33

Awakening up, he took her hollow lute—
Tumultuous—and, in chords that tenderest be,
He played an ancient ditty, long since mute,   290
In Provence called, "La belle dame sans merci":
Close to her ear touching the melody;—
Wherewith disturbed, she uttered a soft moan:
He ceased—she panted quick—and suddenly   295
Her blue affrayèd eyes wide open shone:
Upon his knees he sank, pale as smooth-sculptured stone.

34

Her eyes were open, but she still beheld,
Now wide awake, the vision of her sleep:
There was a painful change, that nigh expelled   300
The blisses of her dream so pure and deep

At which fair Madeline began to weep,
And moan forth witless words with many a sigh;
While still her gaze on Porphyro would keep;
Who knelt, with joinèd hands and piteous eye,   305
Fearing to move or speak, she looked so dreamingly.

35

"Ah, Porphyro!" said she, "but even now
Thy voice was at sweet tremble in mine ear,
Made tuneable with every sweetest vow;
And those sad eyes were spiritual and clear: 310
How changed thou art! how pallid, chill, and drear!
Give me that voice again, my Porphyro,
Those looks immortal, those complainings dear!
Oh leave me not in this eternal woe,
For if thou diest, my Love, I know not where to go."   315

36

Beyond a mortal man impassioned far
At these voluptuous accents, he arose,
Ethereal, flushed, and like a throbbing star
Seen mid the sapphire heaven's deep repose;
Into her dream he melted, as the rose   320
Blended its odor with the violet—
Solution sweet: meantime the frost-wind blows
Like Love's alarum pattering the sharp sleet
Against the window-panes; St. Agnes' moon hath set.

37

'Tis dark: quick pattereth the flaw-blown sleet: 325
"This is no dream, my bride, my Madeline!"
'Tis dark: the icèd gusts still rave and beat:
"No dream, alas! alas! and woe is mine!
Porphyro will leave me here to fade and pine.—
Cruel! what traitor could thee hither bring?   330
I curse not, for my heart is lost in thine,
Though thou forsakest a deceivèd thing;—
A dove forlorn and lost with sick unprunèd wing."

38

"My Madeline! sweet dreamer! lovely bride!
Say, may I be for aye thy vassal blest?   335
Thy beauty's shield, heart-shaped and vermeil dyed?
Ah, silver shrine, here will I take my rest

After so many hours of toil and quest,
A famished pilgrim—saved by miracle.
Though I have found, I will not rob thy nest   340
Saving of thy sweet self; if thou think'st well
To trust, fair Madeline, to no rude infidel.

39

"Hark! 'tis an elfin-storm from faery land,
Of haggard seeming, but a boon indeed:
Arise—arise! the morning is at hand;—   345
The bloated wassailers will never heed:—
Let us away, my love, with happy speed;
There are no ears to hear, or eyes to see—
Drowned all in Rhenish and the sleepy mead:
Awake! arise! my love, and fearless be,   350
For o'er the southern moors I have a home for thee."

40

She hurried at his words, beset with fears,
For there were sleeping dragons all around,
At glaring watch, perhaps, with ready spears—
Down the wide stairs a darkling way they found.—   355
In all the house was heard no human sound.
A chain-drooped lamp was flickering by each door;
The arras, rich with horseman, hawk, and hound,
Fluttered in the besieging wind's uproar;
And the long carpets rose along the gusty floor.   360

41

They glide, like phantoms, into the wide hall;
Like phantoms, to the iron porch, they glide;
Where lay the Porter, in uneasy sprawl,
With a huge empty flagon by his side:
The wakeful bloodhound rose, and shook his hide,   365
But his sagacious eye an inmate owns:
By one, and one, the bolts full easy slide:—
The chains lie silent on the footworn stones;—
The key turns, and the door upon its hinges groans.

42

And they are gone: aye, ages long ago   370
These lovers fled away into the storm.
That night the Baron dreamt of many a woe,
And all his warrior-guests, with shade and form

Of witch, and demon, and large coffin-worm,
Were long be-nightmared. Angela the old   375
Died palsy-twitched, with meager face deform;
The Beadsman, after thousands aves told,
For aye unsought-for slept among his ashes cold.

The Eve of St. Agnes

For Analysis

1. The poem is based on the ancient legend that on St. Agnes's Eve, January 20, traditionally the coldest night of the year, a virgin can see in a vision her future husband if she performs a stipulated ritual. How does this legend furnish a plot for the poem?

2. Imagery may appeal to sight, touch, taste, hearing, and smell. Examine stanzas twenty-six, thirty, and thirty-one. What senses does Keats appeal to in these stanzas? What does this analysis tell you about the way he achieves his effects?

3. What values does the Beadsman embody? Is his appearance at the beginning and end of the poem significant? Are the words addressed to Madeline in stanza thirty-one—"Thou art my Heaven, and I thine eremite"—comic, absurd? Does Porphyro use these terms in the same sense that the Beadsman would?

4. In an early version of the poem, Keats had Porphyro and Madeline actually consummate their visionary marriage in her room. His friends objected strenuously, and he changed the poem. What would this episode do to the poem as it now stands?

5. What colors dominate the early part of the poem?

6. What colors are associated with Porphyro and Madeline? How do they contrast with the other colors?

7. Besides color imagery, what other sensuous appeal has Keats built into the poem? Take lines 262–271, for example. What sense impressions are heaped up there? Then consider just line 262. Notice the sound pattern of the vowels:

> And still she slept an azure-lidded sleep
>   *a   i   e   a   i   e*

Now take lines 98 and 99 and see how the vowels make a much more complicated pattern.

William Morris

The Haystack
in the Floods

Had she come all the way for this,
To part at last without a kiss?
Yea, had she borne the dirt and rain
That her own eyes might see him slain
Beside the haystack in the floods?   5

Along the dripping leafless woods,
The stirrup touching either shoe,
She rode astride as troopers do,
With kirtle kilted to her knee,
To which the mud splash'd wretchedly;   10

And the wet dripp'd from every tree
Upon her head and heavy hair,
And on her eyelids broad and fair;
The tears and rain ran down her face.
By fits and starts they rode apace,   15
And very often was his place
Far off from her; he had to ride
Ahead, to see what might betide
When the roads cross'd; and sometimes, when
There rose a murmuring from his men,   20
Had to turn back with promises;
Ah me! she had but little ease;
And often for pure doubt and dread
She sobb'd, made giddy in the head
By the swift riding; while, for cold,   25
Her slender fingers scarce could hold
The wet reins; yea, and scarcely, too,
She felt the foot within her shoe
Against the stirrup: all for this,
To part at last without a kiss   30
Beside the haystack in the floods.

For when they near'd that old soak'd hay,
They saw across the only way
That Judas, Godmar, and the three
Red running lions dismally   35
Grinn'd from his pennon, under which,
In one straight line along the ditch,
They counted thirty heads.

                              So then,
While Robert turn'd round to his men,
She saw at once the wretched end,
And, stooping down, tried hard to rend   40
Her coif the wrong way from her head,
And hid her eyes; while Robert said:
"Nay, love, 'tis scarcely two to one,
At Poictiers where we made them run   45
So fast—why, sweet my love, good cheer,
The Gascon frontier is so near,
Nought after this."

                    But, "O," she said,
"My God! my God! I have to tread
The long way back without you; then   50
The court at Paris; those six men;
The gratings of the Chatelet;
The swift Seine on some rainy day
Like this, and people standing by,
And laughing, while my weak hands try   55
To recollect how strong men swim.
All this, or else a life with him,
For which I should be damned at last,
Would God that this next hour were past!"

He answer'd not, but cried his cry,   60
"St. George for Marny!" cheerily;
And laid his hand upon her rein.
Alas! no man of all his train
Gave back that cheery cry again;
And, while for rage his thumb beat fast   65
Upon his sword-hilt, someone cast
About his neck a kerchief long,
And bound him.

                    Then they went along
To Godmar; who said: "Now, Jehane,
Your lover's life is on the wane   70

So fast, that, if this very hour
You yield not as my paramour,
He will not see the rain leave off—
Nay, keep your tongue from gibe and scoff,
Sir Robert, or I slay you now."   75

She laid her hand upon her brow,
Then gazed upon the palm, as though
She thought her forehead bled, and—"No!"
She said, and turn'd her head away,
As there were nothing else to say,   80
And everything were settled; red
Grew Godmar's face from chin to head:
"Jehane, on yonder hill there stands
My castle, guarding well my lands:
What hinders me from taking you,   85
And doing that I list to do
To your fair wilful body, while
Your knight lies dead?"

                              A wicked smile
Wrinkled her face, her lips grew thin,
A long way out she thrust her chin: 90
"You know that I should strangle you
While you were sleeping; or bite through
Your throat, by God's help—ah!" she said,
"Lord Jesus, pity your poor maid!
For in such wise they hem me in,   95
I cannot choose but sin and sin,
Whatever happens: yet I think
They could not make me eat or drink,
And so should I just reach my rest."
"Nay, if you do not my behest,   100
O Jehane! though I love you well,"
Said Godmar, "would I fail to tell
All that I know?" "Foul lies," she said.
"Eh? lies my Jehane? by God's head,
At Paris folks would deem them true!   105
Do you know, Jehane, they cry for you:
'Jehane the brown! Jehane the brown!
Give us Jehane to burn or drown!'—
Eh—gag me Robert!—sweet my friend,
This were indeed a piteous end   110
For those long fingers, and long feet,
And long neck, and smooth shoulders sweet:
An end that few men would forget

That saw it—So, an hour yet:
Consider, Jehane, which to take   115
Of life or death!"

                So, scarce awake,
Dismounting, did she leave that place,
And totter some yards: with her face
Turn'd upward to the sky she lay,
Her head on a wet heap of hay,   120
And fell asleep: and while she slept
And did not dream, the minutes crept
Round to the twelve again; but she,
Being waked at last, sigh'd quietly,
And strangely childlike came, and said: 125
"I will not." Straightway Godmar's head,
As though it hung on strong wires, turn'd
Most sharply round, and his face burn'd.

For Robert—both his eyes were dry,
He could not weep, but gloomily   130
He seem'd to watch the rain; yea, too,
His lips were firm; he tried once more
To touch her lips; she reach'd out, sore
And vain desire so tortured them,
The poor grey lips, and now the hem   135
Of his sleeve brush'd them.

                With a start
Up Godmar rose, thrust them apart;
From Robert's throat he loosed the bands
Of silk and mail; with empty hands
Held out, she stood and gazed, and saw,   140
The long bright blade without a flaw
Glide out from Godmar's sheath, his hand
In Robert's hair; she saw him bend
Back Robert's head; she saw him send
The thin steel down; the blow told well,   145
Right backward the knight Robert fell,
And moan'd as dogs do, being half dead,
Unwitting, as I deem: so then
Godmar turn'd grinning to his men,
Who ran, some five or six, and beat   150
His head to pieces at their feet.

Then Godmar turn'd again and said:
"So, Jehane, the first fitte is read!
Take note, my lady, that your way

Lies backward to the Chatelet!"   155
She shook her head and gazed awhile
At her cold hands with a rueful smile,
As though this thing had made her mad.

This was the parting that they had
Beside the haystack in the floods.   160

The Haystack in the Floods

For Analysis

1. How does Morris create the impression that physical factors and
   animal passions are more important than spiritual ideals in determining the behavior of the characters in "The Haystack in the
   Floods"?
2. Does the objective, dispassionate mode of narration heighten or
   lessen the horror of the tale?
3. What narrative tone does the question posed in the first stanza—
   "Had she come all the way for this,/To part at last without a kiss?"
   —lead one to expect? Is the rest of the poem narrated in a tone
   consistent with that suggested by the question?

A. E. Housman

Is My Team Ploughing

"Is my team ploughing,
    That I was used to drive
And hear the harness jingle
    When I was man alive?"

Ay, the horses trample,   5
   The harness jingle now;
No change though you lie under
   The land you used to plough.

"Is football playing
   Along the river shore,   10
With lads to chase the leather,
   Now I stand up no more?"

Ay, the ball is flying,
   The lads play heart and soul;
The goal stands up, the keeper   15
   Stands up to keep the goal.

"Is my girl happy,
   That I thought hard to leave,
And has she tired of weeping
   As she lies down at eve?"   20

Ay, she lies down lightly,
   She lies not down to weep:
Your girl is well-contented.
   Be still, my lad, and sleep.

"Is my friend hearty,   25
   Now I am thin and pine,
And has he found to sleep in
   A better bed than mine?"

Yes, lad, I lie easy,
   I lie as lads would choose;   30
I cheer a dead man's sweetheart,
   Never ask me whose.

Is My Team Ploughing

For Analysis

1. How does Housman break the pattern of expectation (and therefore attract attention and get emphasis) in the first line of the last stanza?
2. How has Housman made the reader's suspicions grow as the poem progresses so that the outcome is no surprise? For example, how does the reply to the third question differ from that to the first and second?

William Butler Yeats

The Folly of
Being Comforted

One that is ever kind said yesterday:
"Your well-beloved's hair has threads of gray,
And little shadows come about her eyes;
Time can but make it easier to be wise
Though now it seem impossible, and so   5
Patience is all that you have need of."
                                        No,
I have not a crumb of comfort, not a grain,
Time can but make her beauty over again:
Because of that great nobleness of hers
The fire that stirs about her, when she stirs   10
Burns but more clearly. O she had not these ways,
When all the wild summer was in her gaze.
O heart! O heart! if she'd but turn her head,
You'd know the folly of being comforted.

The Folly of Being Comforted

For Analysis

1. Who is the "one that is ever kind?"
2. Paraphrase the poet's argument that illustrates the folly of being comforted.

E. E. Cummings

if everything happens
that can't be done

if everything happens that can't be done
(and anything's righter
than books
could plan)
the stupidest teacher will almost guess   5
(with a run
skip
around we go yes)
there's nothing as something as one

one hasn't a why or because or although   10
(and buds know better
than books
don't grow)
one's anything old being everything new
(with a what   15
which
around we come who)
one's everyanything so

so world is a leaf so tree is a bough
(and birds sing sweeter   20
than books
tell how)
so here is away and so your is a my
(with a down
up   25
around again fly)
forever was never till now

now i love you and you love me
(and books are shuter
than books   30
can be)
and deep in the high that does nothing but fall
(with a shout
each
around we go all)   35
there's somebody calling who's we

we're anything brighter than even the sun
(we're everything greater
than books
might mean)   40
we're everyanything more than believe
(with a spin
leap
alive we're alive)
we're wonderful one times one   45

if everything happens that can't be done

For Analysis

Cummings used capital letters, he said, only for important things; he
constructed, in other words, his own conventions of typography.
1. Read this poem aloud for its rhythm. What is this young girl, now
    in love for the first time, doing as she sings this poem? The rhythm
    will tell you.
2. What besides the recurring rhythm pattern holds this poem together?
    Notice, for example, the last word of each stanza and the first word
    of the text.
3. After reading this poem, do you think that disrupting natural syntax
    necessarily blocks meaning?

if i

if i

or anybody don't
know where it her his

my next meal's coming from
i say to hell with that   5
that doesn't matter (and if

he she it or everybody gets a
bellyful without
lifting my finger i say to hell
with that i   10

say that doesn't matter) but
if somebody
or you are beautiful or

not superficial

deep or generous what
i say is   15

whistle that
sing that yell that spell
that out big (bigger than cosmic
rays war earthquakes famine or the ex

prince of whoses diving into   20
a whatses to rescue miss nobody's
probably handbag) because i say that's not

swell (get me) babe not (understand me) lousy

kid that's something else my sweet (i feel that's true)   25 *if i*

For Analysis

1. What are the important and valuable things that human beings ought to celebrate, according to this poem?
2. What is the narrator parodying when he talks of the rescue of the handbag?

Tuli Kupferberg

Morning, Morning

Morning morning
Feel so lonesome in the morning
Morning morning
Morning brings me grief

Sunshine sunshine 5
Sunshine laughs upon my face
And the glory of the growing
Puts me in my rotting place

Evening evening
Feel so lonesome in the evening 10
Evening evening
Evening brings me grief

Moonshine moonshine
Moonshine drugs the hills with grace
And the secret of the shining 15
Seeks to break my simple face

MORNING, MORNING: Reprinted by permission of ESP Disc Ltd.

Nighttime nighttime
Kills the blood upon my cheek
Nighttime nighttime
Does not bring me to relief   20

Starshine starshine
Feel so loving in the starshine
Starshine starshine
Darling kiss me as I weep.

Morning, Morning

For Analysis

1. What part does nature play in this lyric? Are there any clichés in it? What do the answers to these two questions taken together tell you about the tradition the writer has drawn on?
2. Might this lyric be a successful song when performed? Why or why not?

THE DRAMATIC MONOLOGUE

Narrowly defined, a dramatic poem is a play in verse. But today the dramatic monologue is usually included in this category because it is sometimes much like a condensed play. In the monologue, a single speaker, having reached a crucial point in his life, reveals his character by speaking to a listener or listeners whose presence and characteristics we know only through signs the speaker gives us. Every word in the poem belongs to the single speaker.

The monologue, then, is like a compressed play in that it requires a dramatic situation and an invented speaker who is not the poet. It differs from a play in that only one character speaks and from a soliloquy in that the speaker in the monologue does address a specific audience.

The popularity of the dramatic monologue is attributed to its "reality," its concentration on a single, vivid, human character, and its complexity. The reader is able to see the character as he sees himself, as we see him, and by implication, as others, usually the listeners, see him.

This implies that we do not see the character undergoing change: He remains throughout the poem what he is. What he reveals he reveals largely to the reader, not to himself. The reader knows the character fully; the character knows himself only in part.

The dramatic monologue is not a narrative form; hence one does not expect a fully developed plot nor does one expect to be able to answer finally questions of action, place, date, and event that bear on past events. It is, for example, important to note that in "My Last Duchess" the Duke has had the Duchess either shut away or killed. But in the end it is impossible to say exactly what was done with her, nor does it make any difference: Either action would imply the same thing about the Duke.

had wealthy family

Robert Browning

not as poetic as others

My Last Duchess

That's my last Duchess painted on the wall,
Looking as if she were alive. I call
That piece a wonder, now: Frà Pandolf's hands
Worked busily a day, and there she stands.
Will 't please you sit and look at her? I said   5
"Frà Pandolf" by design, for never read
Strangers like you that pictured countenance,
The depth and passion of its earnest glance,
But to myself they turned (since none puts by
The curtain I have drawn for you, but I)   10
And seemed as they would ask me, if they durst,
How such a glance came there; so, not the first
Are you to turn and ask thus. Sir, 't was not
Her husband's presence only, called that spot
Of joy into the Duchess' cheek; perhaps   15
Frà Pandolf chanced to say, "Her mantle laps
Over my lady's wrist too much," or "Paint
Must never hope to reproduce the faint
Half-flush that dies along her throat:" such stuff
Was courtesy, she thought, and cause enough   20
For calling up that spot of joy. She had
A heart—how shall I say?—too soon made glad,
Too easily impressed; she liked whate'er
She looked on, and her looks went everywhere.
Sir, 't was all one! My favor at her breast,   25
The dropping of the daylight in the West,
The bough of cherries some officious fool
Broke in the orchard for her, the white mule
She rode with round the terrace—all and each
Would draw from her alike the approving speech,   30
Or blush, at least. She thanked men,—good! but thanked
Somehow—I know not how—as if she ranked

My gift of a nine-hundred-years-old name
With anybody's gift. Who'd stoop to blame
This sort of trifling? Even had you skill   35
In speech—(which I have not)—to make your will
Quite clear to such an one, and say, "Just this
Or that in you disgusts me; here you miss,
Or there exceed the mark"—and if she let
Herself be lessoned so, nor plainly set   40
Her wits to yours, forsooth, and made excuse,
—E'en then would be some stooping; and I choose
Never to stoop. Oh, sir, she smiled, no doubt,
Whene'er I passed her; but who passed without
Much the same smile? This grew; I gave commands;   45
Then all smiles stopped together. There she stands
As if alive. Will 't please you rise? We'll meet
The company below then. I repeat,
The Count your master's known munificence
Is ample warrant that no just pretense   50
Of mine for dowry will be disallowed;
Though his fair daughter's self, as I avowed
At starting, is my object. Nay, we'll go
Together down, sir. Notice Neptune, though,
Taming a sea-horse, thought a rarity,   55
Which Claus of Innsbruck cast in bronze for me!

My Last Duchess

For Analysis

1. What is the significance of the title? Is that the way one normally speaks of his wife? What does "Last" imply? What does this tell you about the Duke's attitude toward his wife—or wives?

2. The dramatic monologue allows the reader to see the character from several points of view. How do the following views of the character differ?
   a. The Duke as he sees himself and the Duke as the reader sees him.
   b. The Duchess as the Duke sees her and the Duchess as the reader sees her.

3. The Duke is possessive. He is also an extreme aesthete, one who values art more than life. How is this developed in the poem? What is the source of his dissatisfaction for example, with Frà Pandolf, since he seems to admire the painting Pandolf produced?

4.   Notice that although this poem sounds as if it were in blank verse, it is really written in couplets. How does Browning achieve this blend of conventions—maintaining a strict form while getting a conversational naturalness at the same time? Is there some connection between this marriage of naturalness and strictness and the situation and characters in the poem?

T. S. Eliot   *become a british subject*
lived in london

The Love Song of
J. Alfred Prufrock

S'io credesse che mia risposta fosse
A persona che mai tornasse al mondo,
Questa fiamma staria senza piu scosse.
Ma perciocche giammai di questo fondo
Non torno vivo alcun, s'i'odo il vero,
*Senza tema d'infamia ti rispondo.**

Let us go then, you and I,
When the evening is spread out against the sky
Like a patient etherized upon a table;
Let us go, through certain half-deserted streets,
The muttering retreats
Of restless nights in one-night cheap hotels

And sawdust restaurants with oyster-shells:
Streets that follow like a tedious argument
Of insidious intent

*S'io . . . rispondo. If I could believe that my answer might be to a person who should ever return into the world, this flame would stand without more quiverings; but inasmuch as, if I hear the truth, never from this depth did any living man return, without fear of infamy I answer thee (from Dante's *Inferno,* Canto XXVII, ll. 61–66).

To lead you to an overwhelming question . . .
Oh, do not ask, "What is it?"
Let us go and make our visit.

In the room the women come and go
Talking of Michelangelo.

The yellow fog that rubs its back upon the window-panes,   15
The yellow smoke that rubs its muzzle on the window-panes
Licked its tongue into the corners of the evening,
Lingered upon the pools that stand in drains,
Let fall upon its back that soot that falls from chimneys,
Slipped by the terrace, made a sudden leap,   20
And seeing that it was a soft October night,
Curled once about the house, and fell asleep.

And indeed there will be time
For the yellow smoke that slides along the street,
Rubbing its back upon the window-panes;   25
There will be time, there will be time
To prepare a face to meet the faces that you meet;
There will be time to murder and create,
And time for all the works and days of hands
That lift and drop a question on your plate;   30
Time for you and time for me,
And time yet for a hundred indecisions,
And for a hundred visions and revisions,
Before the taking of a toast and tea.
In the room the women come and go   35
Talking of Michelangelo.

And indeed there will be time
To wonder, "Do I dare?" and, "Don't I dare?"
Time to turn back and descend the stair,
With a bald spot in the middle of my hair—   40
(They will say: "How his hair is growing thin!")
My morning coat, my collar mounting firmly to the chin,
My necktie rich and modest, but asserted by a simple pin—
(They will say: "But how his arms and legs are thin!")
Do I dare   45
Disturb the universe?
In a minute there is time
For decisions and revisions which a minute will reverse.

For I have known them all already, known them all:—
Have known the evenings, mornings, afternoons,
I have measured out my life with coffee spoons;   50

I know the voices dying with a dying fall
Beneath the music from a farther room.
  So how should I presume?

And I have known the eyes already, known them all—   55
The eyes that fix you in a formulated phrase,
And when I am formulated, sprawling on a pin,
When I am pinned and wriggling on the wall,
Then how should I begin
To spit out all the butt-ends of my days and ways?   60
  And how should I presume?

And I have known the arms already, known them all—
Arms that are braceleted and white and bare
(But in the lamplight, downed with light brown hair!)
Is it perfume from a dress   65
That makes me so digress?
Arms that lie along a table, or wrap about a shawl.
  And should I then presume?
  And how should I begin?

         .   .   .   .   .   .

Shall I say, I have gone at dusk through narrow streets   70
And watched the smoke that rises from the pipes
Of lonely men in shirt-sleeves, leaning out of windows? . . .
I should have been a pair of ragged claws
Scuttling across the floors of silent seas.

         .   .   .   .   .   .

And the afternoon, the evening, sleeps so peacefully!   75
Smoothed by long fingers,
Asleep . . . tired . . . or it malingers,
Stretched on the floor, here beside you and me.
Should I, after tea and cakes and ices,
Have the strength to force the moment to its crisis?   80
But though I have wept and fasted, wept and prayed,

Though I have seen my head (grown slightly bald)
      brought in upon a platter,
I am no prophet—and here's no great matter;
I have seen the moment of my greatness flicker,
And I have seen the eternal Footman hold my coat, and snicker,   85
And in short, I was afraid.

And would it have been worth it, after all,
After the cups, the marmalade, the tea,
Among the porcelain, among some talk of you and me,
Would it have been worth while,   90
To have bitten off the matter with a smile,

To have squeezed the universe into a ball
To roll it toward some overwhelming question,
To say: "I am Lazarus, come from the dead,
Come back to tell you all, I shall tell you all"— 95
If one, settling a pillow by her head,
    Should say: "That is not what I meant at all,
    That is not it, at all."

        .   .   .   .   .

And would it have been worth it, after all,
Would it have been worth while, 100
And the sunsets and the dooryards and the sprinkled streets,
After the novels, after the teacups, after the skirts that trail along the
    floor—
And this, and so much more?—
It is impossible to say just what I mean!
But as if a magic lantern threw the nerves in patterns on a screen: 105
Would it have been worth while
If one, settling a pillow or throwing off a shawl,
And turning toward the window, should say:
    "That is not it at all,
    That is not what I meant, at all." 110

        .   .   .   .   .

No! I am not Prince Hamlet, nor was meant to be;
Am an attendant lord, one that will do
To swell a progress, start a scene or two,
Advise the prince; no doubt, any easy tool,
Deferential, glad to be of use, 115
Politic, cautious, and meticulous;
Full of high sentence, but a bit obtuse;
At times, indeed, almost ridiculous—
Almost, at times, the Fool.

I grow old . . . I grow old . . . 120
I shall wear the bottoms of my trousers rolled.

Shall I part my hair behind? Do I dare to eat a peach?
I shall wear white flannel trousers, and walk upon the beach.
I have heard the mermaids singing, each to each.

I do not think that they will sing to me. 125

I have seen them riding seaward on the waves
Combing the white hair of the waves blown back
When the wind blows the water white and black.
We have lingered in the chambers of the sea
By sea-girls wreathed with seaweed red and brown 130
Till human voices wake us, and we drown.

The Love Song of J. Alfred Prufrock

For Analysis

The "I" and "you" of the poem are simply two sides of the same man, Prufrock, a prototype of frustrated twentieth-century man. If the poem seems difficult, it is partly because Prufrock is afraid to admit even to himself the extent of his own frustration. Thus, it is important for the reader to answer to his own satisfaction at least three basic questions about Prufrock:

a. What is Prufrock afraid of?
b. What kind of frustration does Prufrock suffer from?
c. The conclusion says that "human voices wake us, and we drown." In what way are the characters in the poem not human?

The questions that follow attempt to guide you to the answers to the three questions above.

1. In the first ten lines we learn that Prufrock is going to a rendezvous where he intends to ask someone a question. In what way do the figures of speech that Prufrock uses to describe the evening and the streets tell us that he is burdened by the thought of asking the question and apprehensive of the answer he may receive?

2. Prufrock reviews at length, in indirect fashion, his own real or imagined shortcomings. In what way does the chorus, "In the room the women come and go/ Talking of Michelangelo," describe the kind of life he leads? In what way does his remark, "I have measured out my life with coffee spoons," sum up both his past and present existence? How does his remark, "I should have been a pair of ragged claws/ Scuttling across the floors of silent seas," summarize Prufrock's reaction to his review of his past and present existence?

3. What does the repeated "And would it have been worth it, after all" tell us of his intention to ask the question?

4. By line 110, the reader should understand what question Prufrock intended to ask, of whom he intended to ask it, and why he did not do so. The remainder of the poem explores the consequences of his not asking the question. What will his future life be like?

5. In the first half of the poem, Prufrock thinks chiefly of what he is and has been. In the second half he suggests what he has not been, is not, and will not be. His method in the latter half is that of allusive comparison. In what way is Prufrock not like John the Baptist (lines

81–83) or the lover of Marvell's "To His Coy Mistress" (lines 91–92) or Lazarus (lines 94–95) or Hamlet (line 111)? What resemblances, then, does Prufrock see between himself and these characters that cause him to introduce them for contrast?

INTEGRITY AND ISOLATION, AS SEEN IN THE DRAMATIC MONOLOGUE AND OTHER FORMS

Alfred Lord Tennyson

Ulysses

It little profits that an idle king,
By this still hearth, among these barren crags,
Match'd with an aged wife, I mete and dole
Unequal laws unto a savage race,
That hoard, and sleep, and feed, and know not me.   5
I cannot rest from travel; I will drink
Life to the lees. All times I have enjoy'd
Greatly, have suffer'd greatly, both with those
That loved me, and alone; on shore, and when
Thro' scudding drifts the rainy Hyades   10
Vext the dim sea. I am become a name;
For always roaming with a hungry heart
Much have I seen and known,—cities of men
And manners, climates, councils, governments,
Myself not least, but honor'd of them all,—
And drunk delight of battle with my peers,
Far on the ringing plains of windy Troy.
I am a part of all that I have met;
Yet all experience is an arch wherethro,
Gleams that untravel'd world whose margin fades   20
For ever and for ever when I move.
How dull it is to pause, to make an end,

To rust unburnish'd, not to shine in use!
As tho' to breathe were life! Life piled on life
Were all too little, and of one to me   25
Little remains; but every hour is saved
From that eternal silence, something more,
A bringer of new things; and vile it were
For some three suns to store and hoard myself,
And this gray spirit yearning in desire   30
To follow knowledge like a sinking star,
Beyond the utmost bound of human thought.
    This is my son, mine own Telemachus,
To whom I leave the scepter and the isle,—
Well-loved of me, discerning to fulfill   35
This labor, by slow prudence to make mild
A rugged people, and thro' soft degrees
Subdue them to the useful and the good.
Most blameless is he, centered in the sphere
Of common duties, decent not to fail   40
In offices of tenderness, and pay
Meet adoration to my household gods,
When I am gone. He works his work, I mine.
    There lies the port; the vessel puffs her sail;
There gloom the dark, broad seas. My mariners,   45
Souls that have toil'd, and wrought, and thought with me,—
That ever with a frolic welcome took
The thunder and the sunshine, and opposed
Free hearts, free foreheads,—you and I are old;
Old age hath yet his honor and his toil.   50
Death closes all; but something ere the end,
Some work of noble note, may yet be done,
Not unbecoming men that strove with Gods.
The lights begin to twinkle from the rocks;
The long day wanes; the slow moon climbs; the deep   55
Moans round with many voices. Come, my friends,
'Tis not too late to seek a newer world.
Push off, and sitting well in order smite
The sounding furrows; for my purpose holds
To sail beyond the sunset, and the baths   60
Of all the western stars, until I die.
It may be that the gulfs will wash us down;
It may be we shall touch the Happy Isles,
And see the great Achilles, whom we knew.
Tho' much is taken, much abides; and tho'   65
We are not now that strength which in old days
Moved earth and heaven, that which we are, we are,—
One equal temper of heroic hearts,
Made weak by time and fate, but strong in will
To strive, to seek, to find, and not to yield.   70

Ulysses

For Analysis

1. Tennyson's Ulysses is the Ulysses of Dante, not the Ulysses of Homer. Dante put Ulysses in the eighth circle of Hell. One expects, therefore, some signs of an unheroic Ulysses.
    a. What is the attitude of Ulysses toward his people, the Ithacans?
    b. What is his attitude toward his wife, Penelope, a paragon of faithfulness?
    c. What is his attitude toward his son, Telemachus? What does Ulysses's use of modifying words (*slow* prudence, *soft* degrees, *common* duties) tell you of his attitude toward Telemachus? Toward himself?
2. Careless readers often think that "Ulysses" is a strong statement of courage, determination, and hope. Probably they are concentrating on the last lines of the poem, which contain a typical, crashing, Tennysonian conclusion. Does the fact that no matter how hard you try to do otherwise, you have to read most of the poem in a slow, almost dragging rhythm suggest something about the Ulysses of this poem? This is the aged Ulysses. What is the actual destination of his voyage? (Look, for example, at lines 30–31.)
3. What is it that Ulysses wants? He says "to follow knowledge." But how would he define "knowledge"? What do lines such as the following tell you?

   "Life piled on life/ Were all too little, and of one to me/ Little remains"
   "I will drink/Life to the lees."
   "For always roaming with a hungry heart"
   "And drunk delight of battle with my peers"

What do all these appetite metaphors suggest?
4. If, ten years after the Trojan War, he thinks he may "see the great Achilles," what would have to happen to him? Does Ulysses simply want to die with his boots—sandals, rather—on?
5. Does it aid in reading the poem to know that the first line echoes the biblical, "What shall it profit a man if he gain the whole world and lose his own life" and that the last two lines, so often taken as a statement of moral courage, echo Satan's famous speech in *Paradise Lost*, wherein he resolves never to give in to God's commands?

Robert Browning

Andrea del Sarto

But do not let us quarrel any more,
No, my Lucrezia; bear with me for once:
Sit down and all shall happen as you wish.
You turn your face, but does it bring your heart?
I'll work then for your friend's friend, never fear,   5
Treat his own subject after his own way,
Fix his own time, accept too his own price,
And shut the money into this small hand
When next it takes mine. Will it? tenderly?
Oh, I'll content him,—but tomorrow, Love!   10
I often am much wearier than you think,
This evening more than usual, and it seems
As if—forgive now—should you let me sit
Here by the window with your hand in mine
And look a half-hour forth on Fiesole,   15
Both of one mind, as married people use,
Quietly, quietly the evening through,
I might get up tomorrow to my work
Cheerful and fresh as ever. Let us try.
Tomorrow, how you shall be glad for this!   20
Your soft hand is a woman of itself,
And mine the man's bared breast she curls inside.
Don't count the time lost, neither you must serve
For each of the five pictures we require:
It saves a model. So! keep looking so—   25
My serpentining beauty, rounds on rounds!
—How could you ever prick those perfect ears,
Even to put the pearl there! oh, so sweet—
My face, my moon, my everybody's moon,
Which everybody looks on and calls his,   30
And, I suppose, is looked on by in turn,
While she looks—no one's: very dear, no less.

15 *Fiesole*: a suburb of Florence.

You smile? why, there's my picture ready made,
There's what we painters call our harmony!
A common grayness silvers everything,—   35
All in a twilight, you and I alike
—You, at the point of your first pride in me
(That's gone you know),—but I, at every point;
My youth, my hope, my art, being all toned down
To yonder sober pleasant Fiesole.   40
There's the bell clinking from the chapel-top;
That length of convent-wall across the way
Holds the trees safer, huddled more inside;
The last monk leaves the garden; days decrease,
And autumn grows, autumn in everything.   45
Eh? the whole seems to fall into shape
As if I saw alike my work and self
And all that I was born to be and do,
A twilight-piece. Love, we are in God's hand.
How strange now looks the life he makes us lead;   50
So free we seem, so fettered fast we are!
I feel he laid the fetter: let it lie!
This chamber for example—turn your head—
All that's behind us! You don't understand
Nor care to understand about my art,   55
But you can hear at least when people speak:
And that cartoon, the second from the door
—It is the thing, Love! so such things should be—
Behold Madonna!—I am bold to say.
I can do with my pencil what I know,   60
What I see, what at bottom of my heart
I wish for, if I ever wish so deep—
Do easily, too—when I say, perfectly,
I do not boast, perhaps: yourself are judge,
Who listened to the Legate's talk last week,   65
And just as much they used to say in France.
At any rate 'tis easy, all of it!
No sketches first, no studies, that's long past:
I do what many dream of all their lives,
—Dream? strive to do, and agonize to do,   70
And fail in doing. I could count twenty such
On twice your fingers, and not leave this town,
Who strive—you don't know how the others strive
To paint a little thing like that you smeared
Carelessly passing with your robes afloat,—   75
Yet do much less, so much less, Someone says,

65 *Legate's*: a delegate of the Pope. 93 *Morello's*: a mountain near
Florence.

(I know his name, no matter)—so much less!
Well, less is more, Lucrezia: I am judged.
There burns a truer light of God in them,
In their vexed beating stuffed and stopped-up brain,   80
Heart, or whate'er else, than goes on to prompt
This low-pulsed forthright craftsman's hand of mine.
Their works drop groundward, but themselves, I know,
Reach many a time a heaven that's shut to me,
Enter and take their place there sure enough,   85
Though they come back and cannot tell the world.
My works are nearer heaven, but I sit here.
The sudden blood of these men! at a word—
Praise them, it boils, or blame them, it boils too.
I, painting from myself and to myself,   90
Know what I do, am unmoved by men's blame
Or their praise either. Somebody remarks
Morello's outline there is wrongly traced,
His hue mistaken; what of that? or else,
Right traced and well ordered; what of that?   95
Speak as they please, what does the mountain care?
Ah, but a man's reach should exceed his grasp,
Or what's a heaven for? All is silver-gray
Placid and perfect with my art: the worse!
I know both what I want and what might gain,   100
And yet how profitless to know, to sigh
"Had I been two, another and myself,
Our head would have o'erlooked the world!" No doubt.
Yonder's a work now, of that famous youth
The Urbinate who died five years ago.   105
('Tis copied, George Vasari sent it me.)
Well, I can fancy how he did it all,
Pouring his soul, with kings and popes to see,
Reaching, that heaven might so replenish him,
Above and through his art—for it gives way;   110
That arm is wrongly put—and there again—
A fault to pardon in the drawing's lines,
Its body, so to speak: its soul is right,
He means right—that, a child may understand.
Still, what an arm! and I could alter it: 115
But all the play, the insight, and the stretch—
Out of me! out of me! And wherefore out?
Had you enjoined them on me, given me soul,
We might have risen to Rafael, I and you!
Nay, Love, you did give all I asked, I think—   120

105 *The Urbinate*: Raphael Sanzio (1483–1520). 106 *George Vasari*: **a**
student of Andrea del Sarto. 130 *Agnolo*: Michelangelo (1475–1564).

More than I merit, yes, by many times.
But had you—oh, with the same perfect brow,
And perfect eyes, and more than perfect mouth,
And the low voice my soul hears, as a bird
The fowler's pipe, and follows to the snare—   125
Had you, with these the same, but brought a mind!
Some women do so. Had the mouth there urged,
"God and the glory! never care for gain.
The present by the future, what is that?
Live for fame, side by side with Agnolo!   130
Rafael is waiting: up to God all three!"
I might have done it for you. So it seems—
Perhaps not. All is as God overrules.
Beside, incentives come from the soul's self;
The rest avail not. Why do I need you?   135
What wife had Rafael, or has Agnolo?
In this world, who can do a thing, will not;
And who would do it, cannot, I perceive:
Yet the will's somewhat—somewhat, too, the power—
And thus we half-men struggle. At the end,   140
God, I conclude, compensates, punishes.
'Tis safer for me, if the award be strict,
That I am something underrated here,
Poor this long while, despised, to speak the truth.
I dared not, do you know, leave home all day,   145
For fear of chancing on the Paris lords.
The best is when they pass and look aside;
But they speak sometimes; I must bear it all.
Well may they speak! That Francis, that first time,
And that long festal year at Fontainebleau!   150
I surely then could sometimes leave the ground,
Put on the glory, Rafael's daily wear,
In that humane great monarch's golden look,—
One finger in his beard or twisted curl
Over his mouth's good mark that made the smile,   155
One arm about my shoulder, round my neck,
The jingle of his gold chain in my ear,
I painting proudly with his breath on me,
All his court round him, seeing with his eyes,
Such frank French eyes, and such a fire of souls   160
Profuse, my hand kept plying by those hearts,—
And, best of all, this, this, this face beyond,
This in the background, waiting on my work,
To crown the issue with a last reward!
A good time, was it not, my kingly days?   165

149 *Francis*: King Francis I of France.

And had you not grown restless . . . but I know—
'Tis done and past; 'twas right, my instinct said;
Too live the life grew, golden and not gray,
And I'm the weak-eyed bat no sun should tempt
Out of the grange whose four walls make his world.   170
How could it end in any other way?
You called me, and I came home to your heart.
The triumph was—to reach and stay there; since
I reached it ere the triumph, what is lost?
Let my hands frame your face in your hair's gold,   175
You beautiful Lucrezia that are mine!
"Rafael did this, Andrea painted that;
The Roman's is the better when you pray,
But still the other's Virgin was his wife"—
Men will excuse me, I am glad to judge   180
Both pictures in your presence; clearer grows
My better fortune, I resolve to think.
For, do you know, Lucrezia, as God lives,
Said one day Agnolo, his very self,
To Rafael . . . I have known it all these years . . .   185
(When the young man was flaming out his thoughts
Upon a palace-wall for Rome to see,
Too lifted up in heart because of it)
"Friend, there's a certain sorry little scrub
Goes up and down our Florence, none cares how,   190
Who, were he set to plan and execute
As you are, pricked on by your popes and kings,
Would bring the sweat into that brow of yours!"
To Rafael's!—And indeed the arm is wrong.
I hardly dare . . . yet, only you to see,   195
Give the chalk here—quick, thus the line should go!
Ay, but the soul! he's Rafael! rub it out!
Still, all I care for, if he spoke the truth,
(What he? why, who but Michel Agnolo?
Do you forget already words like those?)   200
If really there was such a chance, so lost,—
Is, whether you're—not grateful—but more pleased.
Well, let me think so. And you smile indeed!
This hour has been an hour! Another smile?
If you would sit thus by me every night   205
I should work better, do you comprehend?
I mean that I should earn more, give you more.
See, it is settled dusk now; there's a star;
Morello's gone, the watch-lights show the wall,
The cue-owls speak the name we call them by.   210
Come from the window, love,—come in, at last,

Inside the melancholy little house
We built to be so gay with. God is just.
King Francis may forgive me: oft at nights
When I look up from painting, eyes tired out,   215
The walls become illumined, brick from brick
Distinct, instead of mortar, fierce bright gold,
That gold of his I did cement them with!
Let us but love each other. Must you go?
That Cousin here again? he waits outside?   220
Must see you—you, and not with me? Those loans?
More gaming debts to pay? you smiled for that?
Well, let smiles buy me! have you more to spend?
While hand and eye and something of a heart
Are left me, work's my ware, and what's it worth?   225
I'll pay my fancy. Only let me sit
The gray remainder of the evening out,
Idle, you call it, and muse perfectly
How I could paint, were I but back in France,
One picture, just one more—the Virgin's face,   230
Not yours this time! I want you at my side
To hear them—that is, Michel Agnolo—
Judge all I do and tell you of its worth.
Will you? Tomorrow, satisfy your friend.
I take the subjects for his corridor,   235
Finish the portrait out of hand—there, there,
And throw him in another thing or two
If he demurs; the whole should prove enough
To pay for this same Cousin's freak. Beside,
What's better and what's all I care about,   240
Get you the thirteen scudi for the ruff!
Love, does that please you? Ah, but what does he,
The Cousin! what does he to please you more?
    I am grown peaceful as old age tonight.
I regret little, I would change still less.   245
Since there my past life lies, why alter it?
The very wrong to Francis!—it is true
I took his coin, was tempted and complied,
And built this house and sinned, and all is said.
My father and my mother died of want.   250
Well, had I riches of my own? you see
How one gets rich! Let each one bear his lot.
They were born poor, lived poor, and poor they died:
And I have labored somewhat in my time

241 *scudi*: gold coins; *ruff*: perch. 262 *angel's reed*: measuring rod. 263
Leonard: Leonardo da Vinci (1452–1519).

And not been paid profusely. Some good son   255
Paint my two hundred pictures—let him try!
No doubt, there's something strikes a balance. Yes,
You loved me quite enough, it seems tonight.
This must suffice me here. What would one have?
In heaven, perhaps, new chances, one more chance—   260
Four great walls in the New Jerusalem,
Much as one holds a spider, will destroy,
For Leonard, Rafael, Agnolo and me
To cover—the three first without a wife,
While I have mine! So—still they overcome   265
Because there's still Lucrezia—as I choose.
Again the Cousin's whistle! Go my Love.

Andrea del Sarto

For Analysis

The facts about Andrea del Sarto are that he was once a painter of great
promise; he was and still is a superb draftsman; he has ruined his career
by both painting for only money and by promising to paint for money
and to buy paintings and then not painting or buying; his lust for money
is a facet of his need to keep his model-wife, Lucrezia; Lucrezia finds
more pleasure now in other men—the "cousin" is clearly no relative.
1. Andrea might have been a great painter, but he isn't. On whom
    does he blame his failure? Consider lines such as
       . . "My serpentining beauty"
       . . "Love, we are in God's hand.
       How strange now, looks the life he makes us lead;
       So free we seem, so fettered fast we are!
       I feel he laid the fetter: let it lie!"
       . . "You don't understand
       Now care to understand about my art"
       . . "Had you, with these the same, but brought a mind!"
       . . "All is as God over-rules."
       . . "And had you not grown restless"
Is there ambivalence here? Does he ever say plainly that Lucrezia is
to blame? Why?
2. At the same time, Andrea seems to want to prove to Lucrezia what
    a great artist he is. See lines 60–71. Note also his recounting of
    his popularity in Paris and his account of what Michelangelo said
    about him to Raphael. Something is basically wrong in the reason-

ing of the poem: He was once a promising artist, as he boasts. He is now a second-rate artist, as he admits. In the middle comes the question, Why? He has not blamed Lucrezia openly, and blaming God is silly since Andrea is obviously no fatalist, no determinist, not even a moralist. Who caused his failure? In what way is the key to Andrea's failure his line, "Ah, but a man's reach should exceed his grasp,/ Or what's a heaven for?" What is it that he lacks?

3.   The supposed praise and the supposed blame in Andrea's mind come together finally when he envisions (lines 260ff.) another chance, this time in open and even competition with Michelangelo and Raphael. "So" he concludes, "still they overcome/ Because there's still Lucrezia—as I choose." On whom does the ultimate blame for failure lie?

4.   What, then, is the significance of the final line? Andrea sends Lucrezia to her lover, knowing full well what he is. What does this say of Andrea?

Robert Lowell

Mr. Edwards

and the Spider

I saw the spiders marching through the air,
Swimming from tree to tree that mildewed day
   In latter August when the hay
   Came creaking to the barn. But where
      The wind is westerly,   5
Where gnarled November makes the spiders fly.
Into the apparitions of the sky,
   They purpose nothing but their ease and die
Urgently beating east to sunrise and the sea;

What are we in the hands of the great God?   10
It was in vain you set up thorn and briar

In battle array against the fire
And treason crackling in your blood;
   For the wild thorns grow tame
And will do nothing to oppose the flame;   15
Your lacerations tell the losing game
You play against a sickness past your cure.
How will the hands be strong? How will the heart endure?

A very little thing, a little worm,
Or hourglass-blazoned spider, it is said,   20
   Can kill a tiger. Will the dead
   Hold up his mirror and affirm
   To the four winds the smell
And flash of his authority? It's well
If God who holds you to the pit of hell,   25
Much as one holds a spider, will destroy,
Baffle and dissipate your soul. As a small boy

On Windsor Marsh, I saw the spider die
When thrown into the bowels of fierce fire:
   There's no long struggle, no desire
   To get up on its feet and fly—
   It stretches out its feet
And dies. This is the sinner's last retreat;
Yes, and no strength exerted on the heat
Then sinews the abolished will, when sick   35
And full of burning, it will whistle on a brick.

But who can plumb the sinking of that soul?
Josiah Hawley, picture yourself cast
   Into a brick-kiln where the blast
   Fans your quick vitals to a coal—   40
   If measured by a glass,
How long would it seem burning! Let there pass
A minute, ten, ten trillion, but the blaze
Is infinite, eternal: this is death,
To die and know it. This is the Black Widow, death.   45

Mr. Edwards and the Spider

For Analysis

The Mr. Edwards of the title is Jonathan Edwards, the early American
Puritan minister, whose most famous sermon, *Sinners in the Hands of an*

Angry God, pictures the sinner as a spider hung over the fires of hell. As a young man, Edwards had seen on the New England coast spiders spinning out a filament of web and then floating into the air; many of them were blown out to sea where they perished. The young Edwards wrote two essays on the beauty and the end of these spiders. The Josiah Hawley of the poem is a relative of Edwards who committed suicide.

1. Only the second stanza contains no reference to spiders. It is a dogmatic statement by Edwards of his view of human nature. Satisfy yourself that you understand that view.

2. Spiders appear variously in the poem: the pleasure-bound spiders of August; the doomed spiders of November in the first stanza alone. How does this combination lead to Edwards's outburst in stanza two?

3. In stanza three, the spider is the deadly black widow, then a simile for a sinner. Do these two references relate back to stanza two?

4. In stanza four, the spider is both a spider sizzling on a red-hot brick and a sinner. How can Edwards possibly know how the spider feels at that moment? See also stanza one: "They purpose nothing but their ease and die." How does he know what they purpose? Is he talking from observation or from a theological position?

5. Is this aspect intensified in the last stanza? How, for example, can he know what Hawley would feel, and for how long he would feel, after being cast into the flames?

6. What is the meaning of "This is death,/ To die and know it"? Who is the one man in the poem who seems to know all about death?

7. If the spider references seem to shift, their common denominator comes out in the last line. Edwards is not obsessed with spiders or God or Josiah Hawley but something else. What is it?

8. Obviously Edwards hates Josiah Hawley, since he is singled out as the prime example of a tortured soul. Is there a resemblance between Edwards's conception of God and his own attitude toward Hawley? In what way is stanza two a description of Edwards himself?

Horace Gregory

Longface Mahoney
Discusses Heaven

If someone said, *Escape,*
let's get away from here,
you'd see snow mountains thrown
against the sky,
cold, and you'd draw your breath and feel   5
air like cold water going through your veins.
but you'd be free, up so high,
or you'd see a row of girls dancing on a beach
with tropic trees and a warm moon
and warm air floating under your clothes   10
and through your hair.
Then you'd think of heaven
where there's peace, away from here
and you'd go someplace unreal
where everybody goes after something happens,
set up in the air, safe, a room in a hotel.
A brass bed, military hair brushes,
a couple of coats, trousers, maybe a dress
on a chair or draped on the floor.
This room is not on earth, feel the air,   20
warm like heaven and far away.

This is a place
where marriage nights are kept
and sometimes here you say, Hello
to a neat girl with you   25
and sometimes she laughs
because she thinks it's funny to be sitting here
for no reason at all, except perhaps,
she likes you daddy.

Maybe this isn't heaven but near   30
to something like it,
more like love coming up in elevators
and nothing to think about, except, o god,
you love her now and it makes no difference
if it isn't spring. All seasons are warm   35
in the warm air
and the brass bed is always there.

If you've done something
and the cops get you afterwards, you
can't remember the place again,   40
away from cops and streets—
it's all unreal—
the warm air, a dream
that couldn't save you now.
No one would care   45
to hear about it,
it would be heaven
far away, dark and no music,
not even a girl there.

Longface Mahoney Discusses Heaven

For Analysis

The references to "Escape" and "the cops get you afterwards" and "cops
and streets" indicate what Longface Mahoney does for a living. If
Mahoney discusses heaven, he can only discuss it in on the basis of his
experience. Heaven, to him, equals freedom. But freedom from what?
1. How do warmth and cold in Mahoney's perception tell you something of his perception of freedom? When someone mentions achiev-
   ing freedom, he feels cold, but he associates freedom itself with
   warmth.
2. What has apparently been the only "peace" and "freedom" Mahoney
   has known, if he associates both with a girl and a hotel room?
3. Mahoney's heaven, even to him, is "someplace unreal"—a hotel room
   equipped with a brass bed and military hairbrushes and clothes
   strewn about where "marriage nights are kept." In what way would
   this be unreal to Mahoney?
4. In what way is a girl coming up to this room because "she likes
   you daddy" closer to Mahoney's experience?

5. How does this jarring note explain Mahoney's retreat from heaven ("Maybe this isn't heaven but near/to something like it")?

6. What is the meaning of the mechanical metaphor, "more like love coming up in elevators?" How is this truer to Mahoney's probable experience?

7. If Mahoney fails to conceive Heaven but adds, "o god,/ you love her now and it makes no difference/ if it isn't spring," how does this define what Mahoney's life has been? What is it he lacks and wants?

8. In what way does Mahoney's life destroy even his poor dream? He began by thinking of escape and moved to defining heaven, and then fell off to admitting that his idea probably wasn't heaven, and then settled for something less. But in the end he can't be sure even of that—if "The cops get you afterwards" the whole thing is unreal, "a dream/ that couldn't save you now."

9. Where does he imagine he is at this moment of loss of his vision of heaven? (See "No one would care to hear about it,/ it would be heaven/ far away, dark and no music,/ not even a girl there.") Put that another way: Where would Longface and his peers be, without music, in the dark, with no girls, after the "cops get you?"

10. Now define the character of Longface Mahoney.

 Matthew Arnold

Dover Beach

Ebb —the flow of water
back toward the
sea.
2. weakening decl...

       The sea is calm tonight,
The tide is full, the moon lies fair
Upon the Straits;—on the French coast, the light
Gleams, and is gone; the cliffs of England stand,
Glimmering and vast, out in the tranquil bay.   5
Come to the window, sweet is the night air!
   Only, from the long line of spray
Where the ebb meets the moon-blanched sand,
Listen! you hear the grating roar
Of pebbles which the waves suck back, and fling,   10
At their return, up the high strand,
Begin, and cease, and then again begin,
With tremulous cadence slow, and bring
The eternal note of sadness in.

         Sophocles long ago   15
Heard it on the Ægean, and it brought
Into his mind the turbid ebb and flow
         Of human misery; we
Find also in the sound a thought,
Hearing it by this distant northern sea.   20

         The sea of faith
Was once, too, at the full, and round earth's shore
Lay like the folds of a bright girdle furled;
         But now I only hear
Its melancholy, long, withdrawing roar,   25
         Retreating to the breath
Of the night-wind down the vast edges drear
And naked shingles of the world.

         Ah, love let us be true
To one another! for the world, which seems   30
To lie before us like a land of dreams,
So various, so beautiful, so new,
Hath really neither joy, nor love, nor light,
Nor certitude, nor peace, nor help for pain;
And we are here as on a darkling plain   35
Swept with confused alarms of struggle and flight,
Where ignorant armies clash by night.

Arthur Hugh Clough

Say Not the Struggle
Nought Availeth

Say not the struggle nought availeth,
    The labor and the wounds are vain,
The enemy faints not, nor faileth,
    And as things have been they remain.

If hopes were dupes, fears may be liars;   5
    It may be, in yon smoke concealed,

Your comrades chase e'en now the fliers,
   And, but for you, possess the field.

For while the tired waves, vainly breaking,
   Seem here no painful inch to gain,   10
Far back, through creeks and inlets making,
   Comes silent, flooding in, the main.

And not by eastern windows only,
   When daylight comes, comes in the light,
In front, the sun climbs slow, how slowly,   15
   But westward, look, the land is bright.

Archibald MacLeish

"Dover Beach"
—A Note to That Poem

The Wave Withdrawing
Withers with seaward rustle of flimsy water
Sucking the sand down: dragging at empty shells:
The roil after it settling: too smooth: smothered. . . .

After forty a man's a fool to wait in the   5
Sea's face for the full force and the roaring of
Surf to come over him: droves of careening water.
After forty the tug's out and the salt and the
Sea follow it: less sound and violence:
Nevertheless the ebb has its own beauty   10
Shells sand and all the whispering rustle.
There's earth in it then and the bubbles of foam gone.

Moreover—and this too has its lovely uses—
It's the outward wave that spills the inward forward

[handwritten margin note: to make a liquid cloudy, muddy, unsettled]

Tripping the proud piled mute virginal   15
Mountain of water in wallowing welter of light and
Sound enough—thunder for miles back: it's a fine and a
Wild smother to vanish in: pulling down—
Tripping with outward ebb the urgent inward.

Speaking alone for myself it's the steep hill and the   20
Toppling lift of the young men I am toward now—
Waiting for that as the wave for the next wave.
Let them go over us all I say with the thunder of
What's to be next in the world. It's we will be under it!

Three Poems

For Analysis

"Dover Beach" is a famous statement of a universal problem: That things
in this world are not what they seem and solutions to that problem are
hard to find. Consider these questions about the three poems:

1. What solution does "Dover Beach" propose to the problem of illusion
   (what we see) versus reality (what is)? How are the images of
   sight and sound arranged to show this conflict?
2. MacLeish disagrees with Arnold. Does he disagree with Arnold's
   solution or with Arnold's statement of the problem? Consider what
   single image from "Dover Beach" he has selected as the basis of his
   poem.
3. Clough and Arnold were close friends in their youth; Arnold's
   "Thyrsis" is an elegy on Clough. But they differed on many things.
   Construct a detailed comparison and contrast of Clough's poem and
   Arnold's. What do they share? How do they differ?

Samuel Taylor Coleridge

Kubla Khan

In Xanadu did Kubla Khan
A stately pleasure-dome decree;
Where Alph, the sacred river, ran
Through caverns measureless to man
Down to a sunless sea.   5

So twice five miles of fertile ground
With walls and towers were girdled round:
And here were gardens bright with sinuous rills,
Where blossomed many an incense-bearing tree;
And here were forests ancient as the hills   10
Enfolding sunny spots of greenery.

But oh! that deep romantic chasm which slanted
Down the green hill athwart a cedarn cover!
A savage place! as holy and enchanted
As e'er beneath a waning moon was haunted   15
By woman wailing for her demon-lover!
And from this chasm, with ceaseless turmoil seething,
As if this earth in fast thick pants were breathing
A mighty fountain momently was forced:
Amid whose swift half-intermitted burst   20
Huge fragments vaulted like rebounding hail,
Or chaffy grain beneath the thresher's flail:
And 'mid these dancing rocks at once and ever
It flung up momently the sacred river.
Five miles meandering with a mazy motion   25
Through wood and dale the sacred river ran,
Then reached the caverns measureless to man,
And sank in tumult to a lifeless ocean:
And 'mid this tumult Kubla heard from far
Ancestral voices prophesying war!   30

    The shadow of the dome of pleasure
    Floated midway on the waves;
    Where was heard the mingled measure
    From the fountain and the caves.

It was a miracle of rare device,   35
A sunny pleasure-dome with caves of ice!

A damsel with a dulcimer
In a vision once I saw:
It was an Abyssinian maid,
And on her dulcimer she played,   40
Singing of Mount Abora.
Could I revive with me
Her symphony and song,
To such a deep delight 'twould win me,
That with music loud and long,   45
I would build that dome in air,
That sunny dome! those caves of ice!
And all who heard should see them there,—
And all should cry, Beware! Beware!—
His flashing eyes, his floating hair!   50
Weave a circle round him thrice,
And close your eyes with holy dread,
For he on honey-dew hath fed,
And drunk the milk of Paradise.

Kubla Khan

For Analysis

1. The first thirty-six lines deal with the Khan and his pleasure dome.
    The Khan has ordered built an earthly paradise, lush, exotic, and
    at the same time including in its precincts high religious overtones
    ("Where Alph, the sacred river, ran"). The Khan has tried to bring
    together in harmony the best of beauty and pleasure with man's
    highest metaphysical yearnings. But this paradise is threatened by
    forces beneath that throw up a fountain and "Huge fragments."
    What sign is there that the Khan has failed to create the perfect
    synthesis of beauty and pleasure and metaphysics?
2. The last stanza deals with the speaker, the poet. Like the Khan,
    the poet has had a vision of a created paradise. He thinks he can
    build it, if he can recall the vision clearly enough. But notice the
    difference between his pleasure dome and the Khan's. His will come
    out of "symphony and song," built with "music" and existing in
    "air." What fits this description? Does it help to remember that
    Coleridge defined the creation of poetry as the reconciliation of op-
    posites? Notice that his pleasure dome is to be "heard," not seen.
3. What does the poem say about poetry and the nature of the poet?

Gerard Manley Hopkins

Spring and Fall

To a Young Child

    Márgarét, are you griéving
    Over Goldengrove unleaving?
    Leáves, like the things of man, you
    With your fresh thoughts care for can you?
    Ah! ás the heart grows older   5
    It will come to such sights colder
    By and by, nor spare a sigh
    Though worlds of wanwood leafmeal lie;
    And yet you wíll weep and know why.
    Now no matter, child, the name: 10
    Sórrow's spríngs áre the same.
    Nor mouth had, no nor mind, expressed
    What heart heard of, ghost guessed:
    It ís the blight man was born for,
    It is Margaret you mourn for.   15

Spring and Fall

For Analysis

1. As you read this poem, be sure to stress whatever words the poet has marked as stressed. In line 9, should the stress fall on "will" or on "weep"?
2. "Goldengrove," "unleaving," "wanwood," and "leafmeal" won't be found in a dictionary. They are both images and coined words. But they aren't difficult to interpret. Consider that the young girl is standing in a grove of trees and that "leafmeal" is coined by analogy with "piecemeal." Now what do the other coined words mean?
3. Consider the stanzaic structure of the poem. It is written in couplets,

Spring and Fall: From POEMS OF GERARD MANLEY HOPKINS, third edition, edited by W. H. Gardner. Copyright 1948 by Oxford University Press. Reprinted by permission.

EMILY DICKINSON

and it has fifteen lines. Yet is resembles a sonnet—notic
divisions. What is the pivotal line in the poem—the one that adds
one more line than a conventional sonnet contains, the one that
stands alone, the one that swings the thought of the poem?

4. Why, according to the speaker, is Margaret crying? What is "the
blight man was born for" that Margaret shares? Don't immediately
conclude that it is death. The trees don't die when the leaves fall.
What is it that Margaret will lose as she grows older?

Emily Dickinson

Tell All the Truth
but Tell It Slant

to turn a direct course

Tell all the truth but tell it slant,
Success in circuit lies,
Too bright for our infirm delight
The truth's superb surprise;

As lightning to the children eased   5
With explanation kind,
The truth must dazzle gradually
Or every man be blind.

Tell All the Truth
but Tell It Slant

For Analysis

The "advice" the poem gives is easily discovered: The truth is too blinding to be given all at once; it must therefore be given in small glimpses.

TELL ALL THE TRUTH BUT TELL IT SLANT: Reprinted by permission of the publishers and the Trustees of Amherst College from Thomas H. Johnson, Editor, THE POEMS OF EMILY DICKINSON, Cambridge, Mass.: The Belknap Press of Harvard University Press, Copyright, 1951, 1955, by The President and Fellows of Harvard College.

1. What is the major image in the poem? What do words such as "circuit," "bright," "lighting," "dazzle," and "blind' suggest?
2. In the second quatrain, the poet compares telling the truth slant with explaining lightning to children that it frightens. Since she plays on the meaning of 'circuit,' she may be playing on the meaning of "kind." Consult your dictionary. What sort of explanation would be "kind" in a sense other than "gentle"? Would there be any surprise" in that explanation?
3. What is the difference between being dazzled and being blind? Consider, in line 3, "our infirm delight." What are the possible meanings of "infirm"? Does it mean "unstable" or "ill" or both? How does the word help you with the meanings of "dazzle" and 'blind"?
4. What, finally, is the difference between being dazzled gradually and being blinded? What is the end result in each case?

Emily Dickinson

A Bird Came
Down the Walk

A Bird came down the Walk—
He did not know I saw—
He bit an Angleworm in halves
And ate the fellow, raw,

And then he drank a Dew   5
From a convenient Grass—
And then hopped sidewise to the Wall
To let a Beetle pass—

He glanced with rapid eyes
That hurried all around—   10

A BIRD CAME DOWN THE WALK: Reprinted by permission of the publishers and the Trustees of Amherst College from Thomas H. Johnson, Editor, THE POEMS OF EMILY DICKINSON, Cambridge, Mass.: The Belknap Press of Harvard University Press, Copyright, 1951, 1955, by The President and Fellows of Harvard College.

They looked like frightened Beads, I thought—
He stirred his Velvet Head

Like one in danger, Cautious,
I offered him a Crumb
And he unrolled his feathers   15
And rowed him softer home—

Than Oars divide the Ocean,
Too silver for a seam—
Or Butterflies, off Banks of Noon
Leap, plashless as they swim.   20

A Bird Came Down the Walk

For Analysis

Wallace Stevens wrote a poem called "Thirteen Ways of Looking at a
Blackbird"; this poem might be called "Five Ways of Looking at a Bird."
To perceive the experience Miss Dickinson is recreating, one must pay
careful attention to the shifting *tones* in the poem caused by the changes
in diction.

1. The first two lines are flat statement. But then the tone shifts in lines
   3 and 4. What sort of tone is created by calling the worm a "fellow"
   and remarking that the bird ate him, in halves, "raw"? (After all,
   how else could a bird eat a worm?)
2. Lines 5 and 6 are in a slightly different tone; there is not the slightest
   hint of repulsion. What is the poet's attitude here? Notice that the
   bird drinks not dew but "a Dew/ From a convenient Grass"—
   much as a rakish fellow would toss off a drink in a convenient pub.
3. What change appears in lines 7 and 8?
4. Lines 9–13 show a quite different aspect of the bird—what the speaker
   takes to be fear and attendant caution. Then she offers him a
   crumb—which may seem a little stupid since he just ate an angleworm, washed him down with dew, and sidestepped a beetle—and
   he flies away. At that moment the most striking aspect of the bird
   appears. To this point in the poem he has been treated in a somewhat
   condescending, although affectionate fashion. But now the bird
   moves—and not just in space—far beyond the speaker, and the diction changes radically to show the difference in perception.
   a. What motion of the bird is suggested in "unrolled his feathers"?

    b. The air is conceived of as water, by analogy with the motion of the bird's wings. The bird is said to move more softly than a boat through water or even butterflies. What are butterflies being compared to, if they "Leap, plashless as they swim"? What is the meaning of "Banks of Noon"? One fishes, of course, off "Banks." Does the extraordinarily short life of the butterfly have some bearing on the meaning?

5. Having answered these questions, can you see a progressive change in the speaker's attitude toward the bird?

January 1940
Survey of Literature

The following two poems contain similar subject matter, similar arrangement, but quite different themes.

Some biographical details are necessary. Jonathan Swift died of a brain tumor; Samuel Johnson tried to ease the dropsy by himself draining the excess water accumulation; William Blake had visions that included the supernatural and minute natural objects; Tennyson had extraordinary hearing and sight; Pope was a tubercular, hunchbacked dwarf; Emily Dickinson lived like a hermit; Hart Crane and Percy Shelley died by drowning; Coleridge was addicted to opium; Robert Southwell was hanged; Byron was reputed to have a clubfoot; Christopher Smart and William Cowper had bouts of insanity; D. H. Lawrence was neurotic; John Donne preached a sermon in his own death shroud; Shakespeare is sometimes thought to have predicted his own end, particularly in *The Tempest*; Keats was scarcely five feet tall.

1. Their "talents" are unquestionable. What is meant by their "fertile lack of balance"?

2. What does the "appearance of choice" mean in the penultimate line? In reality, Pope didn't choose to be crippled, Shelley to drown, and so on. It is the appearance of choice in "Their sad and fatal voice"—in their poetry—that the poet envies. Then he must envy what they said *despite* their circumstances. What did they choose to say?

3. Why should Fuller, who has none of the infirmities of these poets, envy them? Consider the title. How might a young poet in January, 1940, envy bygone poets who knew how they would die, or chose how they would die (Crane, for example, committed suicide), and yet wrote the kind of poetry they did?

Roy Fuller

January 1940

Swift had pains in his head.
Johnson dying in bed
Tapped the dropsy himself.
Blake saw a flea and an elf.
Tennyson could hear the shriek   5
Of a bat. Pope was a freak.
Emily Dickinson stayed
Indoors for a decade.
Water inflated the belly
Of Hart Crane, and of Shelley.   10
Coleridge was a dope.
Southwell died on a rope.
Byron had a round white foot.
Smart and Cowper were put
Away. Lawrence was a fidget.   15
Keats was almost a midget.
Donne, alive in his shroud,
Shakespeare, in the coil of a cloud,
Saw death very well as he
Came crab-wise, dark and massy.   20
I envy not only their talents
And fertile lack of balance
But the appearance of choice
In their sad and fatal voice.

Janaury 1940: From THE MIDDLE OF A WAR 1940 by Roy Fuller. Reprinted by permission of Curtis Brown Ltd.

John Crowe Ransom

Survey of
Literature

In all the good Greek of Plato
I lack my roast beef and potato.

A better man was Aristotle
Pulling steady on the bottle.

I dip my hat to Chaucer   5
Swilling soup from his saucer,

And to Master Shakespeare
Who wrote big on small beer.

The abstemious Wordsworth
Subsisted on a curd's-worth.   10

But a slick one was Tennyson,
Putting gravy on his venison.

What these men had to eat and drink
Is what we say and what we think.

The flatulence of Milton   15
Came out of wry Stilton.

Sing a song for Percy Shelley,
Drowned in pale lemon jelly,

And for precious John Keats,
Dripping blood of pickled beets.   20

Then there was poor Willie Blake,
He foundered on sweet cake.

God have mercy on the sinner
Who must write with no dinner,

No gravy and no grub,   25
No pewter and no pub,

No belly and no bowels,
Only consonants and vowels.

For Analysis

Ransom, unlike Fuller, makes up biographical details. They are true, in a metaphorical sense—for example, "John Keats,/Dripping blood of pickled beets" does harmonize with the fact that Keats died of a tubercular hemorrhage. Shelley, as a man, was "Drowned," but only as a poet "in pale lemon jelly." Ransom is chiefly concerned with defining the kind of poetry and criticism he admires; his focus differs from Fuller's.

1. Two kinds of poets and critics are distinguished here: Plato, Wordsworth, Tennyson, Shelley, Keats, and Blake on the one hand; Aristotle, Chaucer, Shakespeare, and possibly Milton on the other. The difference between the two groups lies not in what they ate but in what they fed on. What does the first group have in common? (Consider, for example, that in Plato, the Idealist, Ransom misses "my roast beef and potato.") What does the second group have in common?

2. This poem demands more knowledge of past literature than Fuller's poem, because in Fuller's poem, only one aspect of each poet is emphasized, and it is an aspect that all the named poets share. In this poem, for example, the sixth couplet seems to require that one know that Tennyson's natural, wild, lyric talent ("venison") was buried under his decorative catering to the Victorian reading public ("gravy"). But the poem can still be read and enjoyed without all this specialized information. What does Ransom admire in a poet or critic and what does he not admire?

3. For which group of poets is God's mercy asked?

4. How does the last couplet sum up the poet's judgment? Which group has "belly and bowels"? Which group has only "consonants and vowels" to work with?

5. Milton is a pivotal case here. In literary history, he is the precursor of Wordsworth and Keats and Tennyson—the "sublime tradition." Does Ransom put him on the other side? If he is plagued with "flatulence," what does that say about his possession of "belly and bowels"?

Robert Frost

satire on educational bureacrasy

Departmental

An ant on the table cloth
Ran into a dormant moth
Of many times his size.
He showed not the least surprise.
His business wasn't with such. 5
He gave it scarcely a touch,
And was off on his duty run.
Yet if he encountered one
Of the hive's enquiry squad
Whose work is to find out God 10
And the nature of time and space,
He would put him onto the case.
Ants are a curious race;
One crossing with hurried tread
The body of one of their dead 15
Isn't given a moment's arrest—
Seems not even impressed.
But he no doubt reports to any
With whom he crosses antennae,
And they no doubt report 20
To the higher up at court.
Then word goes forth in Formic:
"Death's come to Jerry McCormic,
Our selfless forager Jerry,
Will the special Janizary 25
Whose office it is to bury
The dead of the commissary
Go bring him home to his people.
Lay him in state on a sepal.

Wrap him for shroud in a petal.   30
Embalm him with ichor of nettle. —
This is the word of your Queen."
And presently on the scene
Appears a solemn mortician;
And taking formal position   35
With feelers calmly atwiddle,
Seizes the dead by the middle,
And heaving him high in air,
Carries him out of there.
No one stands round to stare.   40
It is nobody else's affair.

it is ungentle

It couldn't be called ungentle.
But how thoroughly departmental.

Departmental

For Analysis

1. Through the first seven lines, the poem seems destined to deal with the curious habits of ants. But what do lines 8–12 suggest about the central subject matter of the poem?

2. Note that the first seven lines are based on a simple observation of what one ant did. From there on, everything is based on speculation (for example, "he no doubt reports"). What is the basis of the speculation, that is, what is the species that the speaker has in mind that allows him to imagine ants doing these odd things?

3. What two meanings of the word "curious" are possible in line 13? If a species seeks out the nature of God, time, and space, in what sense is it "curious"? If it does that, but at the same time its members are indifferent to their own dead and to other phenomena (such as the dormant moth) that relate to God, time, and space, in what sense is the species "curious"?

4. Is there a discrepancy between what is said of Jerry McCormic and what is done with him? Consider the difference between the elaborate *formal* procedure that is ordered and what the "solemn mortician" actually does.

5. The short couplets, the odd rhymes, and the unusual words keep the poem from being solemn; that doesn't mean it isn't serious. What is the absurdity inherent in a species that departmentalizes questions of life and death to the point where "It is nobody else's affair"?

400

Langston Hughes

Deferred

This year, maybe, do you think I can graduate?
I'm already two years late.
Dropped out six months when I was seven,
a year when I was eleven,
then got put back when we come North.   5
To get through high school at twenty's kind of late—
But maybe this year I can graduate.

Maybe now I can have that white enamel stove
I dreamed about when we first fell in love
eighteen years ago.   10
But you know,
rooming and everything
then kids,
cold-water flat and all that.
But now my daughter's married   15
And my boy's most grown—
quit school to work—
and where we're moving
there ain't no stove—
Maybe I can buy that white enamel stove!   20

Me, I always did want to study French.
It don't make sense—
I'll never go to France,
but night schools teach French.
Now at last I've got a job   25
where I get off at five,
in time to wash and dress,
so, s'il-vous plait, I'll study French!
Someday,
I'm gonna buy two new suits   30
at once!

DEFERRED: From MONTAGE OF A DREAM DEFERRED. Reprinted by permission of Harold Ober Associates Incorporated. Copyright © 1951 by Langston Hughes.

All I want is
one more bottle of gin.

All I want is to see
my furniture paid for.   35

All I want is a wife who will
work with me and not against me. Say,
baby, could you see your way clear?

Heaven, heaven, is my home!
This world I'll leave behind.   40
When I set my feet in glory
I'll have a throne for mine!

I want to pass the civil service.

I want a television set.

You know, as old as I am,   45
I ain't never
owned a decent radio yet?

I'd like to take up Bach.

   Montage
   of a dream   50
   deferred.
Buddy, have you heard?

Deferred

For Analysis

This poem, from *Montage of a Dream Deferred*, provides the epigraph,
title, and theme of *A Raisin in the Sun* later in this text.

1. Is there one speaker in the poem or several? Is this the same speaker
    carried through several ages or several speakers of several ages? If
    several speakers, what do they have in common?
2. Where does the poet's voice intrude?
3. What does the last line mean? What is it the audience is supposed
    to have heard?

David Meltzer

15th Raga/
For Bela Lugosi

Sir, when you say
Transylvania or wolfbane
or
I am Count Dracula,
your eyes become wide   5
&, for the moment, pure
white marble.

It is no wonder that
you were so long a junkie.

It's in the smile. The way   10
you drifted into Victorian bedrooms
holding up your cape like skirts,

then covering her face
as you bent over her to kiss
into her neck & sup.   15

It is no wonder & it was
in good taste too.

15th Raga/For Bela Lugosi

For Analysis

A raga is a traditional form of music developed in India. It seems to
have no function in the poem beyond indicating that the poet is at home
with gurus and other popular manifestations of Indian metaphysics.

1. What is the difference between what Bela Lugosi, the film vampire, does and the manner in which he does it?
2. In what sense is Lugosi an "addict"?
3. What pun occurs in "in good taste"?
4. What is being made fun of in the poem?

Gabriel Okara

Were I
to Choose

When Adam broke the stone
and red streams raged down to
gather in the womb,
an angel calmed the storm;

And I, the breath mewed   5
in Cain, unblinking gaze
at the world without
from the brink of an age

That draws from the groping lips
a breast-muted cry   10
to thread the years.
(O were I to choose)

And now the close of one
and thirty turns, the world
of bones in Babel, and   15
the different tongues within
are flames the head
continually burning.

And O of this dark halo
were the tired head free.   20
And when the harmattan
of days has parched the throat
and skin, and sucked the fever
of the head away,

WERE I TO CHOOSE: From AFRICAN-ENGLISH LITERATURE by Anne Tibble published by Peter Owen Ltd. London. Reprinted by permission.

Then the massive dark   25
descends, and flesh and bone
are razed. And (O were I
to choose) I'd cheat the worms
and silence seek in stone.

Were I to Choose

For Analysis

Rather than give a series of questions on this poem, below is a series of
notes that allows the reader to supply his own questions and answers.
1. Gabriel Okara is an African poet.
2. The *harmattan* of the penultimate stanza is a wind blowing off the
    Sahara in the winter, bringing a dense haze of sand and dirt to lands
    below the desert.
3. The stone that Adam broke is (despite chronology) one of the stone
    tablets on which the ten commandments were engraved. (Adam had
    a choice.)
4. Cain, one product of the "red streams [that] raged down to/ gather
    in the womb" broke another "stone" by killing his brother, Abel.
5. The mark of Cain has come to mean any group or race that, with-
    out and beyond any choice of its own, has been damned and
    demeaned by others.
6. The destruction of the tower of Babel resulted in all languages
    being confused so that no group could understand another.
7. The refrain occurs twice; in neither case is the speaker able to choose
    since history and death ("the massive dark") leave no choice.

Edward Lucie-Smith

The Lesson

"Your father's gone," my bald headmaster said.
His shiny dome and brown tobacco jar
Splintered at once in tears. It wasn't grief.

I cried for knowledge which was bitterer
Than any grief. For there and then I knew   5
That grief has uses—that a father dead
Could bind the bully's fist a week or two;
And then I cried for shame, then for relief.

I was a month past ten when I learnt this:
I still remember how the noise was stilled   10
In school-assembly when my grief came in.
Some goldfish in a bowl quietly sculled
Around their shining prison on its shelf.
They were indifferent. All the other eyes
Were turned towards me. Somewhere in myself   15
Pride, like a goldfish, flashed a sudden fin.

THE LESSON: From A TROPICAL CHILDHOOD AND OTHER POEMS, by
Edward Lucie-Smith, published by the Oxford University Press.

The Lesson

For Analysis

1. What happened, physically, when the dome and the jar "Splintered at once in tears"?
2. What is the connection between the goldfish in their "prison" and the situation of this boy who speaks the poem? Is it that because of his father's death the bullies in the school, this "prison," will not bother him? Or that because he will not cry in front of the boys this toughness will cause the bullies to respect him and therefore leave him alone? Who is indifferent to whom in the poem?
3. "Grief has uses," the speaker says. How many different uses is grief put to in the poem, and by how many people?
4. "Pride, like a goldfish, flashed a sudden fin," the speaker states. What is the source of his pride? That he cried for shame? That he cried for relief? That he kept off the bullies? That he learned that "grief has uses"?

Paul Simon

The Sound
of Silence

Hello darkness my old friend,
I've come to talk with you again,
Because a vision softly creeping,
Left its seeds while I was sleeping
And the vision that was planted in my brain   5
Still remains within the sound of silence.

In restless dreams I walked alone,
Narrow streets of cobble stone
'Neath the halo of a street lamp,
I turned my collar to the cold and damp   10
When my eyes were stabbed by the flash of a neon light
That split the night, and touched the sound of silence.

And in the naked light I saw
Ten thousand people maybe more,
People talking without speaking,   15
People hearing without listening,
People writing songs that voices never share
And no one dares disturb the sound of silence.

"Fools!" said I, "You do not know
Silence like a cancer grows.   20
Hear my words that I might teach you
Take my arms that I might reach you."
But my words like silent raindrops fell
And echoed, in the wells of silence.

And the people bowed and prayed   25
To the neon God they made,
And the sign flashed out its warning

In the words that it was forming,
And the sign said:
   "The words of the prophets are written
   on the subway walls and tenement halls"   30
And whispered in the sounds of silence.

The Sound of Silence

For Analysis

1. In the opening stanza the narrator states that the drama he recounts came to him in a dream; what aspects of the lyric justify ascribing to it the character of a dream?
2. What is the relationship defined among man, city, and technology? How do verbal signs enter into this relationship?

THE SONNET

A conventional sonnet is a fourteen-line poem dealing with a single subject, usually weighty in nature.

The convention of length varies. Some of the earliest sonnets in English (for example, Thomas Watson's "Hecatompathia" or "The Passionate Century of Love" [1582]) had eighteen lines; some more recent sonnets (George Meredith's "Modern Love" sequence) have sixteen lines. These exceptions are really not departures—basically, sonnet form is more a method of development than a stipulated length. Critics sometimes apply the term "sonnet structure" or "sonnet development" to a poem shorter or much longer than fourteen lines. They are referring, first, to the convention of the single weighty subject, and, second, to the pattern of discussion in the poem. This pattern may take either of two forms:

1. Italian (or Petrarchan) form: a two-part development, consisting of an octave (eight lines) and a sestet (six lines). The octave of the Italian sonnet rhymes *abba abba*; the sestet may rhyme in almost any way (*cde cde; cdc dcd, and so forth.*)
2. English (or Shakespearean) form: a four-part development, consisting of three quatrains (rhyming *abab cdcd efef*) and a closing couplet (*gg*).

Spenserian form has the same development as the English form, except that the rhyme scheme is interlocked (for instance, *abab bcbc cdcd ee*). This form is sometimes regarded as having more continuity than the English form because of its interlocked rhymes, but it has never been used much by British and American poets. It can be considered simply a variant of the English form.

The conventions of each form offer special advantages to the poet and reader. The Italian form has several advantages:

1. The two-part form of the Italian form is ideal for a pattern that involves asking a question and answering it, posing a problem and solving it, or describing an experience and commenting on it. A vast number of sonnets are argumentative; two-part development is the basic structure of argument.
2. Italian form enables the poet to change direction easily (at the end of the octave) without changing his subject matter.
3. Although the poet may have difficulty in composing enough rhymes, it is sufficient in a sonnet based on metaphorical comparison for him to use one metaphor for both the octave and sestet or a different one for each. The English form, however, requires *three* cogent metaphors for the three quatrains. This difficulty often causes a weakness that appears in the third quatrain —the point where the poet's inspiration has lapsed and he is merely completing the form.

The English form has these advantages:

1. The concluding couplet offers an opportunity for a neat, concise conclusion or summary, sometimes in epigrammatic form, of the whole sonnet. In the couplet, the poet can emphasize his main point, thus aiding the reader's comprehension.
2. English is a difficult language for rhyming compared to, for example, French, Italian, and Spanish. Because the English form uses more varied rhymes, the poet is less handicapped by the resources of the language.
3. The English form is a more complete unit than the Italian form since the three quatrains develop parallel or succeeding aspects of a single subject; in a sense, the English form uses a pattern of reinforcement.

These are generalizations, of course, and individual poets change conventions to avail themselves of the advantages and avoid the disadvantages of each form. For example, to create a more unified poem, Milton and Wordsworth often separated the Italian sonnet in the middle of the eighth or ninth line, rather than at the end of the eighth line. The outstanding innovator was probably Keats, who was dissatisfied with both forms. After much experimenting, he invented a ten-line sonnet stanza to use in his Odes, which consisted of a quatrain and a sestet—an English beginning and an Italian conclusion.

Edmund Spenser

Sonnet

One day I wrote her name upon the strand,
But came the waves and washèd it away:
Again I wrote it with a second hand,
But came the tide, and made my pains his prey,
Vain man, said she, that dost in vain essay   5
A mortal thing so to immortalize;
For I myself shall like to this decay,
And eke my name by wiped out likewise.
Not so, (quod I) let baser things devise,
To die in dust, but you shall live by fame;   10
My verse your virtues rare shall eternize,
And in the heavens write your glorious name:
Where, whenas death shall all the world subdue,
Our love shall live, and later life renew.

Sonnet 75

For Analysis

1. How does the Spenserian sonnet differ from the Shakespearean?
2. What relationship does the concluding couplet bear to the last quatrain? How does it sum up the poet's argument against his lady's skepticism?

married at early age 19 or 20

William Shakespeare

attached to london where the actor in

was an actor to support himself and after some success, returned home. was married and a mistress as well which he has written sonnets to her.

Sonnet 29

When in disgrace with fortune and men's eyes,
I all alone beweep my outcast state   *useless*
And trouble deaf heaven with my bootless cries
And look upon myself and curse my fate,   *showing someone*
Wishing me like to one more rich in hope,   *sexually*   5
Featured like him, like him with friends possessed,
Desiring this man's art and that man's scope,
With what I most enjoy contented least;
Yet in these thoughts myself almost despising,
Haply I think on thee, and then my state,   10
Like to the lark at break of day arising
From sullen earth, sings hymns at heaven's gate;
For thy sweet love remembered such wealth brings
That then I scorn to change my state with kings.

when one is down and out I think of you and one feels better.

Sonnet 29

For Analysis

1. This poem uses the English sonnet rhyme scheme. What is the pattern developed by the thought structure?
2. What is the primary metaphor of this sonnet? Where is it used?

the image of wealth.

Sonnet 130

My mistress' eyes are nothing like the sun;
Coral is far more red than her lips' red;
If snow be white, why then her breasts are dun;   *grayish brow*

a typographical Rose

If hairs be wires, black wires grow on her head.
I have seen roses damasked, red and white, 5
But no such roses see I in her cheeks;
And in some perfumes is there more delight
Than in the breath that from my mistress reeks.
I love to hear her speak, yet well I know
That music hath a far more pleasing sound; 10
I grant I never saw a goddess go;
My mistress, when she walks, treads on the ground:
And yet, by heaven, I think my love as rare
As any she belied with false compare.

Sonnet 130

For Analysis

1. What is Shakespeare satirizing in this poem?
2. The reversal of attitude in the concluding couplet gains its impact from the preceding comparisons; would Shakespeare have been able to achieve a comparable climax using the Italian form?

a Romantic poet

William Wordsworth

graduated from Cambridge with BA in literature

1800 —

involved in napoleonic wars, had a illigitamate child in france and wrote of the experience.

Composed Upon Westminster Bridge September 3, 1802

this poem is about or describes the beauty of the city in the morning light

Earth has not anything to show more fair:
Dull would he be of soul who could pass by
A sight so touching in its majesty:
This city now doth like a garment wear
The beauty of the morning; silent, bare, 5
Ships, towers, domes, theaters, and temples lie
Open unto the fields, and to the sky;
All bright and glittering in the smokeless air.

Never did sun more beautifully steep
In his first splendor valley, rock, or hill;   10
Ne'er saw I, never felt, a calm so deep!
The river glideth at his own sweet will:
Dear God! the very houses seem asleep;
And all that mighty heart is lying still!

heart of the city

***Composed Upon Westminster
Bridge September 3, 1802***

For Analysis

1.   Are the form and content of this sonnet at odds?
2.   What is the controlling metaphor in this sonnet?

Gerard Manley Hopkins

Felix Randal

Felix Randal the farrier, O he is dead then? my duty all ended,
Who have watched his mold of man, big-boned and hardy-handsome
Pining, pining, till time when season rambled in it and some
Fatal four disorders, fleshed there, all contended?

Sickness broke him. Impatient he cursed at first, but mended   5
Being anointed and all; though a heavenlier heart began some
Months earlier, since I had our sweet reprieve and ransom
Tendered to him. Ah, well, God rest him all road ever he offended!

This seeing the sick endears them to us, us too it endears.
My tongue had taught thee comfort, touch had quenched thy tears,   10
Thy tears that touched my heart, child, Felix, poor Felix Randal;

FELIX RANDAL: From POEMS OF GERARD MANLEY HOPKINS, third
edition, edited by W. H. Gardner. Copyright 1948 by Oxford University Press,
Inc. Reprinted by permission.

How far from then forethought of, all thy more boisterous years,
When thou at the random grim forge, powerful amidst peers,
Didst fettle for the great gray drayhorse his bright and battering sandal!

Felix Randal

For Analysis

1. The persona of this poem is a Roman Catholic priest. In what ways does this information clarify the meaning of the poem?
2. What is the meaning of "all road ever," "random," and "fettle"?
3. This poem is written in sprung rhythm, that is, there are a fixed number of accented syllables in each line and an indefinite number of unaccented syllables. How many accented syllables are there in each line?
4. In the octave the poet receives the news of Felix Randal's death and recounts his relationship with the farrier. How is the information given in the octave related to the thoughts conveyed in the sestet?

RELIGION AND THE WORLD, AS SEEN IN THE SONNET AND OTHER FORMS

John Donne

Holy Sonnet

Batter my heart, three personed God; for you
As yet but knock, breathe, shine, and seek to mend;
That I may rise and stand, o'erthrow me and bend
Your force to break, blow, burn and make me new.
I, like an usurped town, to another due,

5

Representation

Labor to admit you, but Oh, to no end, *b*
Reason, your viceroy in me, me should defend, *b*
But is captived, and proves weak or untrue. *a*
Yet dearly I love you, and would be loved fain,
But am betrothed unto your enemy: 10
Divorce me, untie or break that knot again,
Take me to you, imprison me, for I
Except you enthrall me, never shall be free,
Nor ever chaste, except you ravish me.

Holy Sonnet 14

For Analysis

1. In what traditional sense is God "three personed"?
2. In the first quatrain of the sonnet, what is the conception of God? (What kind of artisan batters, knocks, bends, breaks, blows, burns, breathes on, and shines his work?)
3. In what shape is God conceived of in the second quatrain? In the third?
4. What paradox, common in Christian doctrine, is expressed in sexual terms in the concluding couplet?
5. How, then, does the phrase "three personed God" forecast and order the development of the sonnet?

John Milton

On His Blindness

When I consider how my light is spent
Ere half my days in this dark world and wide,
And that one talent which is death to hide
Lodged with me useless, though my soul more bent
To serve therewith my Maker, and present   5

My true account, lest he returning chide,
"Doth God exact day-labor, light denied?"
I fondly ask. But Patience, to prevent
That murmur, soon replies, "God doth not need
Either man's work or his own gifts. Who best   10
Bear his mild yoke, they serve him best. His state
Is kingly: thousands at his bidding speed,
And post o'er land and ocean without rest;
They also serve who only stand and wait."

On His Blindness

For Analysis

1. How does Milton give unusual unity to the Italian sonnet form here?
2. What is the "talent" of line three? What other talent, besides his own, is Milton referring to? (See *Matthew* 25:26.)

William Wordsworth

The World Is Too Much with Us

The world is too much with us: late and soon,
Getting and spending, we lay waste our powers:
Little we see in Nature that is ours;
We have given our hearts away, a sordid boon!
This sea that bares her bosom to the moon;   5
The winds that will be howling at all hours,
And are up-gathered now like sleeping flowers;
For this, for everything, we are out of tune;
It moves us not.—Great God! I'd rather be
A pagan suckled in a creed outworn.   10
So might I, standing on this pleasant lea,
Have glimpses that would make me less forlorn;
Have sight of Proteus rising from the sea;
Or hear old Triton blow his wreathèd horn.

The World Is Too Much with Us

For Analysis

1. How does the poet utilize the octave-sestet division of the Italian
    sonnet?
2. What do Proteus and Triton symbolize?
3. Are there thematic resemblances between this poem and "if every-
    thing happens"?

Gerard Manley Hopkins

The Windhover

To Christ Our Lord

I caught this morning morning's minion, king-
   dom of daylight's dauphin, dapple-dawn-drawn Falcon, in his riding
   Of the rolling level underneath him steady air, and striding
High there, how he rung upon the rein of a wimpling wing
In his ecstasy! then off, off forth on swing,
   As a skate's heel sweeps smooth on a bow-bend: the hurl and gliding
   Rebuffed the big wind. My heart in hiding
Stirred for a bird,—the achieve of, the mastery of the thing!

Brute beauty and valor and act, oh, air, pride, plume, here
   Buckle! AND the fire that breaks from thee then, a billion   10
Times told lovelier, more dangerous, O my chevalier!

   No wonder of it: shéer plód makes plough down sillion
Shine, and blue-bleak embers, ah my dear,
   Fall, gall themselves, and gash gold-vermilion.

The Windhover: From POEMS OF GERARD MANLEY HOPKINS, third
edition, edited by W. H. Gardner. Copyright 1948 by Oxford University Press,
Inc. Reprinted by permission.

The Windhover

For Analysis

1. A windhover is a small hawk, seen flying in the turbulent early
    morning air currents. In what figurative sense did the narrator
    "catch" the windhover? In what two senses is the hawk "drawn" by
    the dappled dawn? What is the hawk doing that so stirs the narrator?
2. The narrator is at first surprised by the hawk's mastery of and de-
    light in the turbulent currents and asks that this same courage and
    joy be given to him. But then he says that he should not have been
    surprised: Simply plodding down a field behind a plow reveals a
    similar beauty—the plow and the sillion (the turned-back soil of
    the furrow) shine as the plowing goes on. Finally, he says, even the
    dying embers of a fire reveal a similar beauty, as in their last moment
    they collapse and throw a gold-vermilion flash of final fire. What
    do all these things—the flying hawk, the plodding plowman and
    plow, the falling embers—have in common? Why, therefore, should
    he not have been surprised by the hawk's beauty?

As Kingfishers
Catch Fire

> As kingfishers catch fire, dragonflies draw flame;
> As tumbled over rim in roundy wells
> Stones ring; like each tucked string tells, each hung bell's
> Bow swung finds tongue to fling out broad its name;
> Each mortal thing does one thing and the same;   5
> Deals out that being indoors each one dwells;
> Selves—goes itself; *myself*, it speaks and spells,
> Crying *What I do is me; for that I came.*

AS KINGFISHERS CATCH FIRE: From POEMS OF GERARD MANLEY
HOPKINS, third edition, edited by W. H. Gardner. Copyright 1948 by Oxford
University Press, Inc. Reprinted by permission.

I say more: the just man justices;
Keeps grace: that keeps all his goings graces;   10
Acts in God's eye what in God's eye he is—
Christ—for Christ plays in ten thousand places,
Lovely in limbs, and lovely in eyes not his
To the father through the features of men's faces.

As Kingfishers Catch Fire

For Analysis

Hopkins is a difficult poet to read at first because, although he was a
nineteenth-century poet, he wrote in the fashion of some of the most
adventurous twentieth-century poets. He omits simple connectives and
runs words together for economy, borrows words from vocabularies old
and new, coins words when he feels the need.

1. What do kingfishers catching fire, dragonflies drawing flame, stones
   ringing as they fall down a well, bells tolling as they swing, strings
   on instruments sounding as they are plucked, all have in common?
   What are they doing in terms of what they are? What are they doing
   in terms of what created them? (A kingfisher does not literally catch
   fire and a dragonfly does not literally draw flame; when the kingfisher dives, light reflects from his feathers and flashes, and as the
   dragonfly darts about the rays of the sun reflect on his wings.)
2. How does man share in this process of doing something that is
   uniquely his and yet is the same as all the rest? How does what a
   man does show what he is?

Edwin Arlington Robinson

Credo

I cannot find my way: there is no star
In all the shrouded heavens anywhere;

CREDO: "Credo" is reprinted with the permission of Charles Scribner's Sons
from THE CHILDREN OF THE NIGHT by Edwin Arlington Robinson
(1897).

And there is not a whisper in the air
Of any living voice but one so far
That I can hear it only as a bar   5
Of lost, imperial music, played when fair
And angel fingers wove, and unaware,
Dead leaves to garlands where no roses are.

No, there is not a glimmer, nor a call,
For one that welcomes, welcomes when he fears,   10
The black and awful chaos of the night;
For through it all—above, beyond it all—
I know the far-sent message of the years,
I feel the coming glory of the Light.

Credo

For Analysis

1. What do the star and voice symbolize?
2. What is a credo?
3. At what point does the tone of the poem shift from pessimism to optimism?

John Ciardi

A Sonnet for
Robert Frost
but Not About Him

He'd heard in school about the Constitution
and what he thought he'd heard, or what he got
of what was said, and claimed he had been taught,
was that free government's an institution
for making all men equal. So equated   5
he set up an opinion, good as any,

on anything that didn't have too many
bunglesome facts about it. So he waited
for what was his by law of equal state.
It came to very few cents on the dollar.   10
Somehow his equalness kept getting smaller.
He died firmly bewildered by his fate.
Confusion's bound to be the mortal sequel
to letting children think they'll grow up equal.

A Sonnet for Robert Frost but Not About Him

For Analysis

1. What is the form of this sonnet?
2. Thematically, this poem presents a bit of conservative political
   wisdom of the type Frost deals out. How does it imitate Frost stylis-
   tically?

Kenneth Fearing

Art Review

Recently displayed at the Times Square Station, a new Vandyke on
    the face-cream girl,
(Artist unknown. Has promise, but lacks the brilliance shown by
    the great masters of the Elevated age)
That latest wood carving in a Whelan telephone booth, titled
    "O Mortal Fools WA 9–5090," shows two winged hearts above
    an ace of spades.
(His meaning is not entirely clear, but this man will go far)
A charcoal nude in the rear of Flatbush Ahearn's Bar & Grill,   5
    "Forward to the Brotherhood of Man," has been boldly conceived
    in the great tradition.

(We need more, much more of this)
Then there is the chalk portrait, on the walls of a waterfront
    warehouse, of a gentleman wearing a derby hat: "Bleecker
    Street Mike is a double-crossing rat."
(Morbid, but powerful. Don't miss)

Know then by these presents, know all men by these signs
    and omens, by these simple thumbprints on the throat of time,
Know that Pete, the people's artist, is ever watchful,   10
That Tuxedo Jim has passed among us, and was much displeased,
    as always,
That George the Ghost (no man has ever seen him) and Billy the
    Bicep boy will neither bend nor break,
That Mr. Harkness of Sunnyside still hopes for the best, and
    has not lost his human touch,
That Phantom Phil, the master of them all, has come and gone,
    but will return, and all is well.

Art Review

For Analysis

1. What is Fearing satirizing here? Conventional art reviewing? Or is it more involved than that? Consider, for example, the change in tone at the beginning of the sestet.
2. Ambiguity is a chief ingredient in this sonnet. "Elevated age" is obviously a humorous reference to the days when the elevated railway was an important means of transportation in New York, but has it also a more serious reference? The phrase, "thumbprints on the throat of time," is a parody of Longfellow's sententious "footprints on the sands of time," but it has another significance. What would one be doing, figuratively speaking, to "time" if he left thumbprints on time's throat?
3. In what sense is the conclusion, "and all is well," ironic, in what sense straightforward?

George Herbert

The Collar

I struck the board, and cried, "No more;
  I will abroad!
What! shall I ever sigh and pine?
  My lines and life are free; free as the road,
Loose as the wind, as large as store.   5
  Shall I be still in suit?
 Have I no harvest but a thorn
To let me blood, and not restore
  What I have lost with cordial fruit?
    Sure there was wine   10
 Before my sighs did dry it; there was corn
  Before my tears did drown it;
 Is the year only lost to me?
  Have I no bays to crown it,
No flowers, no garlands gay? all blasted,   15
   All wasted?
 Not so, my heart, but there is fruit,
  And thou hast hands.
 Recover all thy sigh-blown age
On double pleasures; leave thy cold dispute   20
Of what is fit and not; forsake thy cage,
  Thy rope of sands
Which petty thoughts have made; and made to thee
 Good cable, to enforce and draw,
   And be thy law,   25
 While thou didst wink and wouldst not see.
   Away! take heed;
   I will abroad.
Call in thy death's head there, tie up thy fears:
  He that forbears   30
  To suit and serve his need
  Deserves his load."
But as I raved, and grew more fierce and wild
   At every word,
 Methought I heard one calling, "Child";   35
  And I replied, "My Lord."

The Collar

For Analysis

1. What is the significance of the title?
2. Notice the metrical difference between lines 1–31 and lines 32–35. Line 1 has at least six feet, line 2 only four, line 3 five, and so on, and each of them breaks somewhere into at least two pieces. Now scan the last two lines. What effect is the poet aiming at with these different metrical arrangements?
3. Why are there so many questions in the early part of the poem? Are they rhetorical questions? What answer to all of them is given later in the poem?

John Donne

A Hymn to
God the Father

Wilt thou forgive that sin where I begun,
    Which was my sin, though it were done before?
Wilt thou forgive that sin through which I run,
    And do run still, though still I do deplore?
When thou hast done, thou hast not done;   5
      For I have more.

Wilt thou forgive that sin which I have won
    Others to sin, and made my sins their door?
Wilt thou forgive that sin which I did shun
    A year or two, but wallowed in a score?   10
When thou hast done, thou hast not done;
      For I have more.

I have a sin of fear, that when I've spun
    My last thread, I shall perish on the shore;

But swear by thyself that at my death thy Son   15
   Shall shine as he shines now and heretofore;
And having done that, thou hast done;
      I fear no more.

A Hymn to God the Father

For Analysis

1. What pun is Donne repeating throughout this poem? Can you find other puns in the poem?
2. The seventeenth century would have found pleasure in these puns. Has our attitude toward the punning convention changed since Donne's day?

William Butler Yeats

The Second
Coming

Turning and turning in the widening gyre
The falcon cannot hear the falconer;
Things fall apart; the center cannot hold;
Mere anarchy is loosed upon the world,
The blood-dimmed tide is loosed, and everywhere   5
The ceremony of innocence is drowned;
The best lack all conviction, while the worst
Are full of passionate intensity.

Surely some revelation is at hand;
Surely the Second Coming is at hand.   10
The Second Coming! Hardly are those words out
When a vast image out of *Spiritus Mundi**

THE SECOND COMING: Reprinted with permission of The Macmillan Company from COLLECTED POEMS by William Butler Yeats. Copyright 1924 by The Macmillan Company, renewed 1952 by Bertha Georgie Yeats. Reprinted with permission of A. P. Watt & Son Ltd.

Troubles my sight: somewhere in sands of the desert
A shape with lion body and the head of a man,
A gaze blank and pitiless as the sun,   15
Is moving its slow thighs, while all about it
Reel shadows of the indignant desert birds.
The darkness drops again; but now I know
That twenty centuries of stony sleep
Were vexed to nightmare by a rocking cradle,   20
And what rough beast, its hour come round at last,
Slouches towards Bethlehem to be born?

*For Yeats, a collective unconscious, a racial memory.

The Second Coming

For Analysis

1. A cyclical but not necessarily repetitive theory of history is imbedded in the poem. Consider, for example, the commonly accepted meaning of the phrase, "Second Coming," and compare it with what Yeats suggests it may mean. How do the two concepts differ?
2. Why does Yeats choose to cast the "beast" in the form of a sphinx?
3. Justify the phrase, "Mere anarchy." Identify the "tide" and then explain in what sense it can be said to be "blood-dimmed."

Jewish gal saw truth toward must hypocracy.

Janis Ian

New Christ
Cardiac Hero

Yesterday's preacher, today's bikini beacher,
They've stolen your clerical robes and your Bible's been thrown.
Your virgin red crown of thorns has turned to ivory horns
And your corner throne it has become a coroner's stone.
The crucifix you prayed on turned to jailhouse bars;   5
Its silver chain you left out in the rain to glow with dust.

And turned to seaweed tangled in your heart.
Now how does it feel to pull out the nails and find you still can walk?
Oh, you can't feel at all from your self-imposed rack on the wall.
The tighter you drive the nails, oh, the harder you'll fall.   10
So come on down, come off it, Sir, before you get hurt.

The holy water you bathe in mingles with the sewer,
All your disciples have reclaimed their rifles and taken the cure.
Your lectures of ways are only today's poolroom jokes
Scrawled on the walls of tenement halls and bathroom bowls.   15
As jingle bells cry pay us well or you'll go to hell.
Freedom's chains bind your pain and tie you well,
But how could you know the gallows you hold weighs you down?
Now isn't it boss, you don't need a cross to get around.
The eyes that cried for mankind's pride are covered with shades   20
As the children of God trample unshod past your mindly grave.
And the new Christ hipster cardiac hero of 2,000 years past your mind
Spits at your feet, crying "We have no need of God, each of us is his own."

Yesterday's preacher, today's bikini beacher,
They've stolen your clerical robes, your Bible's been thrown.   25
You must have a cross, but they've taken you, God, and shot you filled
    with dead,
So following new Christ pick up on a cycle instead.

New Christ Cardiac Hero

For Analysis

1. Analyze the symbolic value of Jesus in this lyric. Is he meant to be more than the historical Jesus? How is the concept of Christ separated from Jesus as man? How are the two Christs projected by institutional Christianity and the hipster different, according to the narrator?
2. What does the narrator mean when he implores Jesus to "pull out the nails" and find that He "still can walk"?

THE ODE

A coventional ode is an elaborate lyrical poem of praise, elevated in tone and intricate in form. Once popular, the form has been used very little during the past hundred years.

The Pindaric ode is characterized by sets of three stanzas (strophe, antistrophe, epode); the strophe and antistrophe are metrically identical, and the epode different. It largely disappeared in the seventeenth century, perhaps partly because the original reason for the three-part division became meaningless: a Greek chorus moving to the left while chanting the strophe, to the right for the antistrophe, and then remaining still to recite the epode.

Since the seventeenth century, the most frequently used form has been the irregular ode, first written by Abraham Cowley. It retains the previous tone and form, but it abandons the three-part organization and metrical repetition. See, for an example of the irregular ode, Wordsworth's "Ode: Intimations of Immortality" (pp. 432–7).

Finally, the Horatian ode, an irregular ode with a less elevated tone and less intricate form, has attracted the talents of many excellent English and American poets. For an example, see Keats's "Ode on a Grecian Urn" (pp. 438–9).

About the only thing the different kinds of odes have in common is that they praise something or someone, and they do so openly. Odes are public poetry.

Percy Bysshe Shelley

Ode to the West Wind

I

O wild west wind, thou breath of Autumn's being,
Thou, from whose unseen presence the leaves dead
Are driven, like ghosts from an enchanter fleeing,

Yellow, and black, and pale, and hectic red,
Pestilence-stricken multitudes: O thou,
Who chariotest to their dark wintry bed   5

The wingéd seeds, where they lie cold and low,
Each like a corpse within its grave, until
Thine azure sister of the Spring shall blow

Her clarion o'er the dreaming earth, and fill   10
(Driving sweet buds like flocks to feed in air)
With living hues and odors plain and hill:

Wild Spirit, which art moving everywhere;
Destroyer and preserver; hear, oh, hear!

                                  II

Thou on whose stream, mid the steep sky's commotion,   15
Loose clouds like earth's decaying leaves are shed,
Shook from the tangled boughs of Heaven and Ocean,

Angels of rain and lightning: there are spread
On the blue surface of thine aëry surge,
Like the bright hair uplifted from the head   20

Of some fierce Maenad, even from the dim verge
Of the horizon to the zenith's height,
The locks of the approaching storm. Thou dirge

Of the dying year, to which this closing night
Will be the dome of a vast sepulcher,   25
Vaulted with all thy congregated might

Of vapors, from whose solid atmosphere
Black rain, and fire, and hail will burst: oh, hear!

                                  III

Thou who didst waken from his summer dreams
The blue Mediterranean, where he lay,   30
Lulled by the coil of his crystalline streams,

Beside a pumice isle in Baiae's bay,
And saw in sleep old palaces and towers
Quivering within the wave's intenser day,

All overgrown with azure moss and flowers   35
So sweet, the sense faints picturing them! Thou
For whose path the Atlantic's level powers

Cleave themselves into chasms, while far below
The sea-blooms and the oozy woods which wear
The sapless foliage of the ocean, know   40

Thy voice, and suddenly grow gray with fear,
And tremble and despoil themselves: oh, hear!

IV

If I were a dead leaf thou mightest bear,
If I were a swift cloud to fly with thee;
A wave to pant beneath thy power, and share   45

The impulse of thy strength, only less free
Than thou, O uncontrollable! If even
I were as in my boyhood, and could be

The comrade of thy wanderings over Heaven,
As then, when to outstrip thy skyey speed   50
Scarce seemed a vision; I would ne'er have striven

As thus with thee in prayer in my sore need.
Oh, lift me as a wave, a leaf, a cloud!
I fall upon the thorns of life! I bleed!

A heavy weight of hours has chained and bowed   55
One too like thee: tameless, and swift, and proud.

V

Make me thy lyre, even as the forest is:
What if my leaves are falling like its own!
The tumult of thy mighty harmonies

Will take from both a deep, autumnal tone,   60
Sweet though in sadness. Be thou, Spirit fierce,
My spirit! Be thou me, impetuous one!

Drive my dead thoughts over the universe
Like withered leaves to quicken a new birth!
And, by the incantation of this verse,   65

Scatter, as from an unextinguished hearth
Ashes and sparks, my words among mankind!
Be through my lips to unawakened earth

The trumpet of a prophecy! O Wind,
If Winter comes, can Spring be far behind?   70

Ode to the West Wind

For Analysis

1. This poem is written in *terza rima,* a form that achieves continuity
    by interlocking rhymes—*aba bcb cdc.* But does Shelley seem to
    have some other form also in mind? Consider the way he blocks
    the lines into larger units.
2. This poem is both an invocation and an incantation. Why does
    Shelley pick the West Wind as his object of supplication? What par-
    ticularly does that wind do that makes it suitable? What similarities
    does Shelley see in himself and the West Wind?
3. The "statement" that the poem makes is obviously metaphorical:
    The poet could not actually become the wind or even use the wind.
    What, then, is Shelley saying in the poem?

Adrian Mitchell

Ode to
Money

somewhat satirical

Man-eater, woman-eater, brighter than tigers,
Lover and killer in my pocket,
In your black sack I'm one of the vipers.
Golden-eyed mother of suicide,
Your photo's in my heart's gold locket.   5

Capitalistic love of money

You make me warm, you keep me cool,
You cure the terrifying dream.
Nature and art await your call.
Money, don't lead me to milk and honey
But a land of Drambuie and icebergs of cream.   10

ODE TO MONEY: From POEMS by Adrian Mitchell. Reprinted by permission
of Jonathan Cape Ltd.

The Palm Court Planet's orchestra whines
The Money Spangled Money
And The Red Money. In my silver chains
I always stand when I hear the band
Play Money Save the Money.   15

Ode to Money

For Analysis

1. Abstract the rhyme scheme and meter of this ode. Are they in the tradition of the conventional ode?
2. The conventional ode is elevated in tone. Is Mitchell's ode elevated in tone? What does he accomplish by the tone?
3. What does stanza two say about the source of money's attraction? What is the significance of the contrast drawn at the end of the stanza?
4. What does the parody of national anthems communicate in stanza three?
5. How does the image of the silver chain function as metaphor?
6. Both Shelley and Mitchell utilize the conventions of the conventional ode. How do their purposes in using these conventions differ?

William Wordsworth

Ode: Intimations of Immortality from Recollections of Early Childhood

I

There was a time when meadow, grove, and stream,
    The earth, and every common sight,
      To me did seem
    Appareled in celestial light,
The glory and the freshness of a dream.   5
It is not now as it hath been of yore;—
    Turn wheresoe'er I may,
      By night or day,
The things which I have seen I now can see no more.

II

    The Rainbow comes and goes,   10
    And lovely is the Rose;
    The Moon doth with delight
Look round her when the heavens are bare;
    Waters on a starry night
    Are beautiful and fair;   15
  The sunshine is a glorious birth;
  But yet I know, where'er I go,
That there hath passed away a glory from the earth.

III

Now, while the birds thus sing a joyous song,
        And while the young lambs bound   20
            As to the tabor's sound,
To me alone there came a thought of grief:
A timely utterance gave that thought relief,
        And I again am strong:
The cataracts blow their trumpets from the steep;   25
No more shall grief of mine the season wrong;
I hear the Echoes through the mountains throng,
The Winds come to me from the fields of sleep,
        And all the earth is gay;
            Land and sea   30
        Give themselves up to jollity,
            And with the heart of May
            Doth every Beast keep holiday;—
                Thou Child of Joy,
Shout round me, let me hear thy shouts, thou happy Shepherd-boy! 35

IV

Ye blessèd Creatures, I have heard the call
        Ye to each other make; I see
The heavens laugh with you in your jubilee;
        My heart is at your festival,
        My head hath its coronal,   40
The fullness of your bliss, I feel—I feel it all.
        Oh, evil day! if I were sullen
        While Earth herself is adorning,
            This sweet May-morning,
        And the Children are culling   45
            On every side,
        In a thousand valleys far and wide,
Fresh flowers; while the sun shines warm,
And the Babe leaps up on his Mother's arm—
        I hear, I hear, with joy I hear!   50
        —But there's a Tree, of many, one,
A single Field which I have looked upon,
Both of them speak of something that is gone:
        The Pansy at my feet
        Doth the same tale repeat: 55
Whither is fled the visionary gleam?
Where is it now, the glory and the dream?

V

Our birth is but a sleep and a forgetting:
The Soul that rises with us, our life's Star,

    Hath had elsewhere its setting,   60
      And cometh from afar:
    Not in entire forgetfulness,
    And not in utter nakedness,
But trailing clouds of glory do we come
    From God, who is our home: 65
Heaven lies about us in our infancy!
Shades of the prison-house begin to close
    Upon the growing Boy,
But he beholds the light, and whence it flows
    He sees it in his joy;   70
The Youth, who daily farther from the east
    Must travel, still is Nature's priest,
    And by the vision splendid
    Is on his way attended;
At length the Man perceives it die away,   75
And fade into the light of common day.

VI

Earth fills her lap with pleasures of her own;
Yearnings she hath in her own natural kind,
And even with something of a Mother's mind,
    And no unworthy aim,   80
    The homely Nurse doth all she can
To make her Foster-child, her Inmate Man,
    Forget the glories he hath known,
And that imperial palace whence he came.

VII

Behold the Child among his new-born blisses,   85
A six years' Darling of a pigmy size!
See, where 'mid work of his own hand he lies,
Fretted by sallies of his mother's kisses,
With light upon him from his father's eyes!
See, at his feet, some little plan or chart,   90
Some fragment from his dream of human life,
Shaped by himself with newly-learnéd art;
    A wedding or a festival,
    A mourning or a funeral,
    And this hath now his heart,   95
    And unto this he frames his song:
    Then will he fit his tongue
To dialogues of business, love, or strife;
    But it will not be long
    Ere this be thrown aside,   100

     And with new joy and pride
The little Actor cons another part;
Filling from time to time his "humorous stage"
With all the Persons, down to palsied Age,
That Life brings with her in her equipage;   105
       As if his whole vocation
       Were endless imitation.

VIII

Thou, whose exterior semblance doth belie
       Thy Soul's immensity;
Thou best Philosopher, who yet dost keep   110
Thy heritage, thou Eye among the blind,
That, deaf and silent, read'st the eternal deep,
Haunted forever by the eternal mind—
       Mighty Prophet! Seer blest!
       On whom those truths do rest,   115
Which we are toiling all our lives to find,
In darkness lost, the darkness of the grave;
Thou, over whom thy Immortality
Broods like the Day, a Master o'er a Slave,
A Presence which is not to be put by;   120
Thou little Child, yet glorious in the might
Of heaven-born freedom on thy being's height,
Why with such earnest pains dost thou provoke
The years to bring the inevitable yoke,
Thus blindly with thy blessedness at strife?   125
Full soon thy Soul shall have her earthly freight,
And custom lie upon thee with a weight,
Heavy as frost, and deep almost as life!

IX

     Oh, joy! that in our embers
     Is something that doth live,   130
     That nature yet remembers
     What was so fugitive!
The thought of our past years in me doth breed
Perpetual benediction: not indeed
For that which is most worthy to be blest;   135
Delight and liberty, the simple creed
Of Childhood, whether busy or at rest,
With new-fledged hope still fluttering in his breast—
       Not for these I raise
       The song of thanks and praise;   140
       But for those obstinate questionings

Of sense and outward things,
Falling from us, vanishings;
Blank misgivings of a Creature
Moving about in worlds not realized,   145
High instincts before which our mortal nature
Did tremble like a guilty thing surprised:
But for those first affections,
Those shadowy recollections,
Which, be they what they may,   150
Are yet the fountain light of all our day,
Are yet a master light of all our seeing;
Uphold us, cherish, and have power to make
Our noisy years seem moments in the being
Of the eternal Silence: truths that wake,   155
To perish never;
Which neither listlessness, nor mad endeavor,
Nor Man nor Boy,
Nor all that is at enmity with joy,
Can utterly abolish or destroy!   160
Hence in a season of calm weather
Though inland far we be,
Our Souls have sight of that immortal sea
Which brought us hither,
Can in a moment travel thither,   165
And see the Children sport upon the shore,
And hear the mighty waters rolling evermore.

                                    X

Then sing, ye Birds, sing, sing a joyous song!
And let the young Lambs bound
As to the tabor's sound!   170
We in thought will join your throng,
Ye that pipe and ye that play,
Ye that through your hearts today
Feel the gladness of the May!
What though the radiance which was once so bright   175
Be now forever taken from my sight,
Though nothing can bring back the hour
Of splendor in the grass, of glory in the flower;
We will grieve not, rather find
Strength in what remains behind;   180
In the primal sympathy
Which having been must ever be;
In the soothing thoughts that spring
Out of human suffering;
In the faith that looks through death,   185
In years that bring the philosophic mind.

XI

And O, ye Fountains, Meadows, Hills, and Groves,
Forebode not any severing of our loves!
Yet in my heart of hearts I feel your might;
I only have relinquished one delight   190
To live beneath your more habitual sway.
I love the Brooks which down their channels fret,
Even more than when I tripped lightly as they;
The innocent brightness of a new-born Day
          Is lovely yet;   195
The Clouds that gather round the setting sun
Do take a sober coloring from an eye
That hath kept watch o'er man's mortality.
Another race hath been, and other palms are won.
Thanks to the human heart by which we live,   200
Thanks to its tenderness, its joys, and fears,
To me the meanest flower that blows can give
Thoughts that do often lie too deep for tears.

*Ode: Intimations of Immortality
from Recollections of Early Childhood*

For Analysis

Wordsworth apparently conceives of an ode as being much less stylized than John Dryden does. Both poets observe the same elevation of subject, tone, and language, but where Dryden's ode is public and oratorical, Wordsworth's is personal and reflective, making the "Ode: Intimations of Immortality" a more difficult poem for the reader to deal with. Any serious reader of the poem will eventually have to answer to his own satisfaction such questions as the following:

1. What are the "things" that the poet says "I now can see no more"?
2. What is the "glory" that has passed away?
3. What is the "visionary gleam"?
4. In what way does a child live in a "dream of human life"? How does the dream differ from the reality?
5. What does the adult gain that partially makes up for the loss of the dream?

*keats is looking a Grecian Urn and is
describing the urn
or
about*

Sylvan — to do with forest, tree etc.

Pastoral — a country scene

John Keats

Ode on a
Grecian Urn

Thou still unravished bride of quietness,
  Thou foster-child of silence and slow time,
Sylvan historian, who canst thus express
  A flowery tale more sweetly than our rhyme:
What leaf-fringed legend haunts about thy shape   5
    Of deities or mortals, or of both,
      In Tempe or the dales of Arcady?
    What men or gods are these? What maidens loath?
What mad pursuit? What struggle to escape?
    What pipes and timbrels? What wild ecstasy?   10

Heard melodies are sweet, but those unheard
  Are sweeter; therefore, ye soft pipes, play on:
Not to the sensual ear, but, more endeared,
  Pipe to the spirit ditties of no tone:
Fair youth, beneath the trees, thou canst not leave   15
  Thy song, nor ever can those trees be bare;
    Bold Lover, never, never canst thou kiss
Though winning near the goal—yet, do not grieve;
    She cannot fade, though thou hast not thy bliss,
  For ever wilt thou love, and she be fair!   20

Ah, happy, happy boughs! that cannot shed
  Your leaves, nor ever bid the Spring adieu;
And, happy melodist, unwearièd,
  For ever piping songs for ever new;
More happy love! more happy, happy love!   25
  For ever warm and still to be enjoyed,
    For ever panting, and for ever young;
All breathing human passion far above,
  That leaves a heart high-sorrowful and cloyed,
    A burning forehead, and a parching tongue.   30

Who are these coming to the sacrifice?
    To what green altar, O mysterious priest,
Lead'st thou that heifer lowing at the skies,
    And all her silken flanks with garlands dressed?
What little town by river or sea shore,   35
    Or mountain-built with peaceful citadel,
        Is emptied of this folk, this pious morn?
And, little town, thy streets for evermore
    Will silent be; and not a soul to tell
        Why thou art desolate, can e'er return.   40

O Attic shape! Fair attitude! with brede
    Of marble men and maidens over wrought,
With forest branches and the trodden weed;
    Thou, silent form, dost tease us out of thought
As doth eternity: Cold Pastoral!   45
    When old age shall this generation waste,
        Thou shalt remain, in midst of other woe
    Than ours, a friend to man, to whom thou say'st,
"Beauty is truth, truth beauty,"—that is all
    Ye know on earth, and all ye need to know.   50

Ode on a Grecian Urn

For Analysis

1. This poem attempts to express a basic paradox of life, phrased here in several ways. In what sense are the first two lines of the second stanza true?

2. What dissatisfaction with his own thoughts about the urn is the poet expressing when he calls it a "Cold Pastoral"?

3. There has been endless debate about the meaning of the "Beauty is truth, truth beauty" epigram. Considered by itself, it is not, at a rational level, true. One key to the difficulty lies in the pronoun "that" following the epigram. To what does "that" refer? To the epigram? Or to the whole sentence preceding it, "When old age shall this generation . . ."? Another key is the pronoun ye. To whom does this refer? The figures on the urn? Or the reader generally? Does the second ye refer to the same person as the one signified by the first ye?

William Wordsworth

A Slumber Did
My Spirit Seal

A slumber did my spirit seal;
   I had no human fears;
She seemed a thing that could not feel
   The touch of earthly years.

No motion has she now, no force;   5
   She neither hears nor sees;
Rolled round in earth's diurnal course,
   With rocks, and stones, and trees.

A. E. Housman

The Night Is
Freezing Fast

The night is freezing fast,
   Tomorrow comes December;
      And winterfalls of old
Are with me from the past;
      And chiefly I remember   5
         How Dick would hate the cold.

Fall, winter, fall; for he,
   Prompt hand and headpiece clever,
    Has woven a winter robe,
And made of earth and sea   **10**
   His overcoat for ever,
    And wears the turning globe.

A Slumber Did My Spirit Seal and *The Night Is Freezing Fast*

For Analysis

Both these poems deal with death of a loved one, but they are not elegies because they center not on the qualities of the dead person but on the feelings of the narrator.

1. After reading both stanzas of the Wordsworth poem, what do you think is the "slumber" that Wordsworth says sealed his spirit? What did it seal it off from? What are the "human fears" of line 2?

2. Notice that the first stanza of the Wordsworth poem speaks of the woman in human terms, but the second speaks of her as a thing. Is this last a natural way to speak of a loved one, dead or not? What, then, can you infer about the state of mind of the narrator?

3. The state of mind of the narrator in the Housman poem is more complex than in the Wordsworth poem. You can infer this by considering exactly what he says: that Dick was lucky to die because now he'll never be cold again since in his grave he has the whole world as his overcoat. Again, is this a natural way to speak of a dead loved one? Or is it grotesque? Could the narrator mean literally what he says? Then what is he trying to do? In a similar but longer poem, "To an Athlete Dying Young," Housman says that the athlete was "smart" to die young because now he will never see his records broken, never grow old and lose his fine physical condition. Clearly this is not meant literally; rational creatures do not wish early death to those they love. Housman is trying to do the same thing in both poems.

William Wordsworth

She Dwelt Among
the Untrodden Ways

She dwelt among the untrodden ways
  Beside the springs of Dove,
A Maid whom there were none to praise
  And very few to love:

A violet by a mossy stone
  Half hidden from the eye!
—Fair as a star, when only one
  Is shining in the sky.

She lived unknown, and few could know
  When Lucy ceased to be;
But she is in her grave, and, oh,
  The difference to me!

Hartley Coleridge

He Lived Amidst
th' Untrodden Ways

He lived amidst th' untrodden ways
  To Rydal Lake that lead;
A bard whom there were none to praise,
  And very few to read.

Behind a cloud his mystic sense,   5
  Deep hidden, who can spy?
Bright as the night when not a star
  Is shining in the sky.

Unread his works—his "Milk White Doe"
  With dust is dark and dim;   10
It's still in Longman's shop, and oh!
  The difference to him!

Sue Stites

A Lucy Poem

She dwelt among the untrodden ways,
  Said Charley Brown to me;
A maid whom there were few to praise,
  And we can all agree.

Fair as a dandelion   5
  Hidden from the eye;
Fair as the sun when only one
  Is shining in the sky.

Who could have guessed (he giggled)
  That she'd ever cease to be?   10
But she's erased, and Oh!
  The difference to me!

A LUCY POEM: Printed by permission of the author, Susanne Minter Stites.

Three Poems

For Analysis

"She Dwelt Among the Untrodden Ways" is one of Wordsworth's Lucy
poems, five poems dealing with a girl, real or imaginary, and Wordsworth's deepening relationship with her. Hartley Coleridge's poem is a

good-humored comment on Wordsworth's poetry. (Hartley was the son of Samuel Taylor Coleridge.) Sue Stites gives the poem a contemporary application.

1. In the original, what is Wordsworth communicating about Lucy in his studied use of paradoxes? (For example, how can a "way" be "untrodden"? If there were "none" to praise her, how could there be anyone who loved her? If she "lived unknown," how could anyone "know" when she "ceased to be"?) What does the use of the secluded violet and the eminently visible star as companion descriptions tell you about these paradoxes?

2. Is the concentration in the original on the girl or on the reactions of the poet?

3. In Hartley Coleridge's parody, Rydal Lake is near Wordsworth's home, the "Milk White Doe" is an unpopular work by Wordsworth, and Longman's is a publisher and bookseller. What aspect of Wordsworth's poetry does Coleridge suggest made his poems unpopular?

4. To readers of "Peanuts," "A Lucy Poem" is immediately clear. What qualities of Schulz's Lucy, far different from Wordsworth's, are being outlined in the second stanza?

5. What do all three poems have in common as their focus?

A. E. Housman

Loveliest
of Trees

Loveliest of trees, the cherry now
Is hung with bloom along the bough,
And stands about the woodland ride
Wearing white for Eastertide.

LOVELIEST OF TREES: From "A Shropshire Lad"—Authorised Edition—from THE COLLECTED POEMS OF A. E. HOUSMAN. Copyright 1939, 1940, © 1959 by Holt, Rinehart and Winston, Inc. Copyright © 1967, 1968 by Robert E. Symons. Reprinted by permission of Holt, Rinehart and Winston, Inc., and The Society of Authors.

Now, of my threescore years and ten,   5
Twenty will not come again,
And take from seventy springs a score,
It only leaves me fifty more.

And since to look at things in bloom
Fifty springs are little room,   10
About the woodlands I will go
To see the cherry hung with snow.

Robert Frost

Stopping by Woods
on a Snowy Evening

Whose woods these are I think I know.
His house is in the village though;
He will not see me stopping here
To watch his woods fill up with snow.

My little horse must think it queer   5
To stop without a farmhouse near
Between the woods and frozen lake
The darkest evening of the year.

He gives his harness bells a shake
To ask if there is some mistake.   10
The only other sound's the sweep
Of easy wind and downy flake.

The woods are lovely, dark and deep.
But I have promises to keep,
And miles to go before I sleep,   15
And miles to go before I sleep.

Loveliest of Trees and
Stopping by Woods on a Snowy Evening

For Analysis

1. Although one can explore similarities and differences in these two poems at great length, the greatest difference probably stems from a very simple divergence of association: When Housman looks at a natural scene just coming to life, he thinks of death; and when Frost looks at a dead or dormant natural scene he thinks of life. Both poets feel that demands are being made upon them. What are these demands and which ones do the two poets decide to honor?
2. What does the reference to the cherry blossoms as snow say about Housman's final attitude toward death as contrasted with the one expressed at the beginning of the poem?
3. What is the nature of Frost's reaction to the scene he stops by. Is it simple or complex?
4. In what sense are the woods "lovely, dark and deep"?
5. Compare the use of snow as a symbol in Frost's poem with its use as a symbol in the short story "Silent Snow, Secret Snow."

William Shakespeare

Sonnet 73

That time of year thou mayst in me behold
When yellow leaves, or none, or few, do hang
Upon those boughs which shake against the cold,
Bare ruined choirs, where late the sweet birds sang.
In me thou see'st the twilight of such day   5
As after sunset fadeth in the west,
Which by and by black night doth take away,
Death's second self, that seals up all in rest.
In me thou see'st the glowing of such fire
That on the ashes of his youth doth lie,   10

As the death-bed whereon it must expire,
Consumed with that which it was nourished by.
This thou perceiv'st, which makes thy love more strong,
To love that well which thou must leave ere long.

*his going to leave her and making
her love more strong.*

Sonnet 73

For Analysis

1. This is an example of classic English sonnet development: three separate quatrains using three separate metaphors, with each metaphor related to the others, and all embodying the same idea, commented on in the couplet. What are the three metaphors and their common idea?
2. What color image is shared by each of the three quatrains?
3. Is the concluding couplet ambiguous? Is "thou" a specific person being spoken to? Or is it a general pronoun? What difference would it make to the sense of the sonnet?

Edmund Waller

Go, Lovely Rose

Go, lovely rose!
Tell her that wastes her time and me,
That now she knows,
When I resemble her to thee,
How sweet and fair she seems to be.   5

Tell her that's young,
And shuns to have her graces spied,
That hadst thou sprung
In deserts, where no men abide,
Thou must have uncommended died.   10

Small is the worth
Of beauty from the light retired;
Bid her come forth,
Suffer herself to be desired,
And not blush so to be admired.   15

Then die! that she
The common fate of all things rare
May read in thee;
How small a part of time they share
That are so wondrous sweet and fair!   20

Andrew Marvell

*18ᵗʰ century poet
member of house of Common
"   "   parliment
traveled in Russia*

To His
Coy Mistress

Had we but world enough, and time,
This coyness, Lady, were no crime,
We would sit down and think which way
To walk and pass our long love's day.
Thou by the Indian Ganges' side   5
Shouldst rubies find; I by the tide
Of Humber would complain. I would
Love you ten years before the Flood,
And you should, if you please, refuse
Till the conversion of the Jews.   10
My vegetable love should grow
Vaster than empires, and more slow;
An hundred years should go to praise
Thine eyes and on thy forehead gaze,
Two hundred to adore each breast,   15
But thirty-thousand to the rest;
An age at least to every part,
And the last age should show your heart.
For, Lady, you deserve this state,
Nor would I love at lower rate.   20

ANDREW MARVELL

> But at my back I always hear
> Time's wingèd chariot hurrying near
> And yonder all before us lie
> Deserts of vast eternity.
> Thy beauty shall no more be found,25
> Nor, in thy marble vault, shall sound
> My echoing song; then worms shall try
> That long preserved virginity,
> And your quaint honor turn to dust,
> And into ashes all my lust:30
> The grave's a fine and private place,
> But none, I think, do there embrace.
>
> Now therefore, while the youthful hue
> Sits on thy skin like morning dew,
> And while thy willing soul transpires35
> At every pore with instant fires,
> Now let us sport us while we may,
> And now, like amorous birds of prey,
> Rather at once our time devour
> Than languish in his slow-chapt power.40
> Let us roll all our strength and all
> Our sweetness up into one ball,
> And tear our pleasures with rough strife
> Thorough the iron gates of life:
> Thus, though we cannot make our sun45
> Stand still, yet we will make him run.

Go, Lovely Rose! and *To His Coy Mistress*

For Analysis

1. Are the themes of "Go, Lovely Rose!" and "To His Coy Mistress" similar? What two Latin phrases indicate the basic ingredients of each argument?
2. How and why are the respective tones of the poems different? Does the difference necessarily indicate the superiority of one poem over the other?

Percy Bysshe Shelley

Ozymandias

I met a traveller from an antique land
Who said: Two vast and trunkless legs of stone
Stand in the desert. Near them, on the sand,
Half sunk, a shattered visage lies, whose frown,
And wrinkled lip, and sneer of cold command,   5
Tell that its sculptor well those passions read
Which yet survive, (stamped on these lifeless things),
The hand that mocked them and the heart that fed;
And on the pedestal these words appear:
"My name is Ozymandias, king of kings;   10
Look on my works, ye Mighty, and despair!"
Nothing beside remains. Round the decay
Of that colossal wreck, boundless and bare,
The lone and level sands stretch far away.

Ozymandias

For Analysis

1. How does this fourteen-line poem differ from an ordinary sonnet?
2. The effect of the landscape described in this poem is similar to that achieved by what style of modern painting?
3. What does the narrator gain by reporting the story at secondhand?

Alfred, Lord Tennyson

Tears,
Idle Tears

Tears, idle tears, I know not what they mean;
Tears from the depth of some divine despair
Rise in the heart, and gather to the eyes,
In looking on the happy autumn fields,
And thinking of the days that are no more.   5

Fresh as the first beam glittering on a sail,
That brings our friends up from the underworld,
Sad as the last which reddens over one
That sinks with all we love below the verge;
So sad, so fresh, the days that are no more.   10

Ah, sad and strange as in dark summer dawns
The earliest pipe of half-awakened birds
To dying ears, when unto dying eyes
The casement slowly grows a glimmering square;
So sad, so strange, the days that are no more.   15

Dear as remembered kisses after death,
And sweet as those by hopeless fancy feigned
On lips that are for others; deep as love,
Deep as first love, and wild with all regret;
O Death in Life, the days that are no more!   20

Tears, Idle Tears

For Analysis

1. What three devices does the poet use to unify this blank verse poem in lieu of rhyme?

451

2. This lyric is part of a longer poem entitled *The Princess*. In context it is spoken by a young woman who desires not to isolate herself from men, as the Princess and her female subjects have done. Is this knowledge necessary for the enjoyment of the poem? Does the poem succeed better if the reader doesn't know its original context?

Emily Dickinson

My Life Closed Twice
Before Its Close

> My life closed twice before its close;
> It yet remains to see
> If Immortality unveil
> A third event to me,
>
> So huge, so hopeless to conceive 5
> As these that twice befel.
> Parting is all we know of heaven,
> And all we need of hell.

Exam on these last two lines.

*My Life Closed Twice
Before Its Close*

For Analysis

1. How does the effect of this poem depend on the information conveyed in the last two lines?

Robert Frost

Dust of
Snow

The way a crow
Shook down on me
The dust of snow
From a hemlock tree

Has given my heart   5
A change of mood
And saved some part
Of a day I had rued.

[feared, ~ regret]

Dust of Snow

For Analysis

1. Would this poem be more successful if it utilized figurative language to a greater extent?
2. To what feature of the poem's grammatical structure does the stanzaic division correspond?

DUST OF SNOW: From COMPLETE POEMS OF ROBERT FROST. Copyright 1923 by Holt, Rinehart and Winston, Inc. Copyright 1951 by Robert Frost. Reprinted by permission of Holt, Rinehart and Winston, Inc.

Fire and Ice

love and hate

Some say the world will end in fire,
Some say in ice.
From what I've tasted of desire
I hold with those who favor fire.
But if it had to perish twice,   5
I think I know enough of hate
To say that for destruction ice
Is also great
And would suffice.

John Crowe Ransom

 # Janet Waking

Beautifully Janet slept
Till it was deeply morning. She woke then
And thought about her dainty-feathered hen,
To see how it had kept.

One kiss she gave her mother,   5
Only a small one gave she to her daddy
Who would have kissed each curl of his shining baby;
No kiss at all for her brother.

"Old Chucky, Old Chucky!" she cried,
Running on little pink feet upon the grass   10
To Chucky's house, and listening. But alas,
Her Chucky had died.

454

It was a transmogrifying bee
Came droning down on Chucky's old bald head
And sat and put the poison. It scarcely bled, 15
But how exceedingly

And purply did the knot
Swell with the venom and communicate
Its rigor! Now the poor comb stood up straight
But Chucky did not. 20

So there was Janet
Kneeling on the wet grass, crying her brown hen
(Translated far beyond the daughters of men)
To rise and walk upon it.

And weeping fast as she had breath 25
Janet implored us, "Wake her from her sleep!"
And would not be instructed in how deep
Was the forgetful kingdom of death.

Janet Waking

For Analysis

1. In what two senses is Janet "waking" here?
2. If one assumes that the narrator of the poem is the father (only he could know the psychological fact of his own attitude mentioned early in the poem), how does this explain the odd, stilted words ("transmogrifying") and the bad jokes ("the comb stood up straight/ But Chucky did not") in the poem? What would be the state of mind of the narrator in the situation he outlines in the concluding lines?
3. What details early in the poem lead you to expect Janet's later reaction to the death of her hen?

Paul Simon *a musician*

met garfunkle at a young age
they went to college together

Save the Life
of My Child

"Good God! Don't jump!"
A boy sat on the ledge.
An old man who had fainted was revived.
And everyone agreed it would be a miracle indeed
If the boy survived.   5
"Save the life of my child!"
Cried the desperate mother.
The woman from the supermarket
Ran to call the cops.
"He must be high on something," someone said   10
Though it never made *The New York Times*,
In *The Daily News*, the caption read,
"Save the life of my child!"
Cried the desperate mother.
A patrol car passing by   15
Halted to a stop.
Said officer MacDougal in dismay:
"The force can't do a decent job
'Cause the kids got no respect
For the law today (and blah blah blah)."   20
"Save the life of my child!"
Cried the desperate mother.
"What's becoming of the children?"
People asking each other.
When darkness fell, excitement kissed the crowd   25
And made them wild
In an atmosphere of freaky holiday.
When the spotlight hit the boy,
The crowd began to cheer,
He flew away.   30
"Oh, my Grace, I got no hiding place."

Save the Life of My Child

For Analysis

1. Asuming that it is the boy speaking in the last line, what does his statement indicate about his intentions. Did he want to jump?
2. Is the spotlight symbolic of adult attitudes concerning children? If so, what does it indicate about the nature of those attitudes?

John Crowe Ransom

Bells for John Whiteside's Daughter

There was such speed in her little body,
And such lightness in her footfall,
It is no wonder that her brown study
Astonishes us all.

Her wars were bruited in our high window.   5
We looked among orchard trees and beyond,
Where she took arms against her shadow,
Or harried unto the pond

The lazy geese, like a snow cloud
Dripping their snow on the green grass,   10
Tricking and stopping, sleepy and proud,
Who cried in goose, Alas,

For the tireless heart within the little
Lady with rod that made them rise
From their noon apple-dreams, and scuttle   15
Goose-fashion under the skies!

But now go the bells, and we are ready;
   In one house we are sternly stopped
To say we are vexed at her brown study,
   Lying so primly propped.   20

Eugene Field

Little Boy Blue

The little toy dog is covered with dust,
   But sturdy and staunch he stands;
And the little toy soldier is red with rust,
   And his musket moulds in his hands.
Time was when the little toy dog was new,   5
   And the soldier was passing fair;
And that was the time when our Little Boy Blue
   Kissed them and put them there.

"Now, don't you go till I come," he said,
   "And don't you make any noise!"   10
So, toddling off to his trundle-bed,
   He dreamt of the pretty toys;
And, as he was dreaming, an angel song
   Awakened our Little Boy Blue—
Oh! the years are many, the years are long,   15
   But the little toy friends are true!

Ay, faithful to Little Boy Blue they stand,
   Each in the same old place—
Awaiting the touch of a little hand,
   The smile of a little face;   20
And they wonder, as waiting the long years through
   In the dust of that little chair,
What has become of our Little Boy Blue,
   Since he kissed them and put them there.

LITTLE BOY BLUE: From THE POEMS OF EUGENE FIELD, published by Charles Scribner's Sons.

Bells for John Whiteside's Daughter and *Little Boy Blue*

For Analysis

These two poems deal with the same situation, the death of a young child. There all resemblances stop. Contrast the two poems by answering these questions:

1. What is the state of mind of the narrator in the Ransom poem? What can you infer about that state of mind from the use of the phrase "brown study" in this context? Can the narrator accept the fact of the child's death? What does he recall most about her—her sedateness or her constant vitality? How does this help to explain the odd ending? Is this a special kind of grief?

2. What is the narrator's state of mind in the Field poem? Is he sentimentalizing his recollections of the child? Is the focus of the poem on the child or on the narrator's grief? Is there fiction in this poem created by the narrator?

3. Which of the two poems implies the grief of the narrator more subtly and more exactly? Which of the poems seems sentimental? Which of the poems seems to you more successful?

THE LYRIC VOICE

Lyric originally meant "song"; it got its name from the Greek practice of accompanying a song on the lyre. Through the ages and through all changes, it has meant any short poem in which one hears the voice of a single speaker expressing a state of mind that is private in any of several senses. Either it evidences a highly personal point of view or it deals with events that are not public. Unlike the dramatic monologue, there is no listener nor any setting implicit in the poem; unlike purely narrative verse, the center of interest is not a story but a viewpoint on an event. In reading lyrics, therefore, it is important to concentrate on the *voice* in the poem, a voice that may or may not be the voice of the poet. Only the poem will tell you.

George Gordon, Lord Byron

The Destruction
of Sennacherib

I

The Assyrian came down like the wolf on the fold,
And his cohorts were gleaming in purple and gold;
And the sheen of their spears was like stars on the sea,
When the blue wave rolls nightly on deep Galilee.

II

Like the leaves of the forest when Summer is green,   5
That host with their banners at sunset were seen:
Like the leaves of the forest when Autumn hath blown,
That host on the morrow lay withered and strown.

III

For the angel of Death spread his wings on the blast,
And breathed in the face of the foe as he passed;   10
And the eyes of the sleepers waxed deadly and chill,
And their hearts but once heaved—and forever grew still!

IV

And there lay the steed with his nostril all wide,
But through it there rolled not the breath of his pride;
And the foam of his gasping lay white on the turf,   15
And cold as the spray of the rock-beating surf.

V

And there lay the rider distorted and pale,
With the dew on his brow, and the rust on his mail:
And the tents were all silent—the banners alone—
The lances unlifted—the trumpet unblown.   20

VI

And the widows of Ashur are loud in their wail,
And the idols are broke in the temple of Baal;
And the might of the Gentile, unsmote by the sword,
Hath melted like snow in the glance of the Lord!

The Destruction of Sennacherib

For Analysis

The historical event (c.680 B.C.) the poem deals with is the seige of Jerusalem by the Assyrian king, Sennacherib. The story is told in *II Kings* 18–19. Sennacherib had already conquered one of the Palestinian kingdoms. All that remained was that he crush Jerusalem. Sennacherib sent a messenger to Jerusalem to tell the defenders that they would be fools to depend either on Egypt, their ally, or on their Lord, who he said was on his side. The prophet Isaiah advised the Hebrew king and his people to stand fast and the Lord would deliver them. They did so, and the army of Sennacherib was stricken with a plague that destroyed it. Sennacherib returned to his capital, Nineveh, where his sons killed him.

1. The poem is highly stylized in its meter and its diction. What is the meter? Look, for example, at line 3: "And the sheen of their spears was like stars on the sea." What is unusual about the diction? Thirteen of the twenty-four lines begin with "And." Where have you seen that stylistic habit before?

2. From whose point of view is the story told?

3. "Purple and gold" are the colors of kings and emperors. The Assyrian spears are said to be as numerous and bright as the stars reflected on the incoming waves of the Sea of Galilee. The Assyrian soldiers are said to be as numerous as the green leaves on the trees of summer. How are all these images reversed later in the poem? What holy color replaces purple and gold? What stops the waves? What happens to the green leaves?

4. Is any of this, beyond the reference to "the Angel of Death" attributed
    to supernatural causes? What do the images say about supernatural
    v. natural?
5. Does the defeat of the Assyrians go beyond the seige of Jerusalem?
    Note that Ashur was the chief god of the Assyrians and Baol was
    the chief god of the Phoenicians, the allies of the Assyrians.
6. Bearing in mind the answers to questions 3, 4, and 5, and the last
    lines of the poem, does the speaker of the poem see anything par-
    ticularly startling in the defeat of the Assyrians?

Carl Sandburg

Grass

Pile the bodies high at Austerlitz and Waterloo.
Shovel them under and let me work—
    I am the grass; I cover all.

And pile them high at Gettysburg
And pile them high at Ypres and Verdun.   5
Shovel them under and let me work.
Two year, ten years, and passengers ask the conductor:
    What place is this?
    Where are we now?

    I am the grass.   10
    Let me work.

Grass

For Analysis

Read *Isaiah* 40:7ff. Then comment on the poem.

GRASS: From *CORNHUSKERS* by Carl Sandburg. Copyright 1918 by Holt,
Rinehart and Winston, Inc. Copyright 1946 by Carl Sandburg. Reprinted by
permission of Holt, Rinehart and Winston, Inc.

Siegfried Sassoon

They

The Bishop tells us: "When the boys come back
They will not be the same; for they'll have fought
In a just cause: they lead the last attack
On Anti-Christ; their comrades' blood has bought
New right to breed an honorable race,   5
They have challenged Death and dared him face to face."

"We're none of us the same!" the boys reply.
"For George lost both his legs; and Bill's stone blind;
Poor Jim's shot through the lungs and like to die;
And Bert's gone syphilitic: you'll not find   10
A chap who's served that hasn't found *some* change."
And the Bishop said: "The ways of God are strange!"

They

For Analysis

1. This poem was written in 1917. The heavy irony rests, first of all, on the difference between theories and facts. Note how the optimistic view of the effects of war comes from a man who has not himself "challenged Death and dared him face to face" and who phrases his view in totally abstract language, as opposed to the pessimistic view that comes from those who have been through the experience and cite concrete evidence. But the irony goes deeper than that. How do you know that the "boys" do not succeed in making the Bishop see his error?

2. Is there something more universal in this experience than viewpoints on war? How is a remark such as "The ways of God are strange!" unanswerable? Is it likely that regardless what the subject matter is the Bishop will ever see his error? Whose "ways" seem strange?

THEY: From COLLECTED POEMS, 1908–1956, reprinted by permission of George Sassoon.

W. H. Auden

from
In Time
of War

So from the years the gifts were showered; each
Ran off with his at once into his life:
Bee took the politics that make a hive,
Fish swam as fish, peach settled into peach.

And were successful at the first endeavor;   5
The hour of birth their only time at college,
They were content with their precocious knowledge,
And knew their station and were good forever.

Till finally there came a childish creature
On whom the years could model any feature,   10
And fake with ease a leopard of a dove;

Who by the lightest wind was changed and shaken,
And looked for truth and was continually mistaken,
And envied his few friends and chose his love.

from *In Time of War*

For Analysis

1. This is a twentieth-century sonnet. In what ways does the poet say man differs from the rest of creation?

IN TIME OF WAR: Copyright 1945 by W. H. Auden. Reprinted from COL-LECTED SHORTER POEMS 1927–1957, by W. H. Auden, by permission of Random House, Inc., and Faber & Faber.

2. Is man said to be static? What does the verb in "And fake ease a leopard or a dove" tell you?
3. What is the tone of the last three lines? Is man being condemned? Praised? Notice that he is given six attributes in those three lines. Are the attributes admirable or reprehensible?
4. This is the first sonnet in a sequence entitled "In Time of War." Does the poem begin to explain why men go to war?

californ— poet

Robinson Jeffers

✗ on exam
does not believe in war

Time of
Disturbance

The best is, in war or faction or ordinary vindictive life, not to take
  sides.
Leave it for children, and the emotional rabble of the streets, to
  back their horse or support a brawler.

But if you are forced into it: remember that good and evil are as
  common as air, and like air shared
By the panting belligerents; the moral indignation that hoarsens
  orators is mostly a fool.

Hold your nose and compromise; keep a cold mind. Fight, if needs
  must; hate no one. Do as God does,   5
Or the tragic poets: they crush their man without hating him,
  their Lear or Hitler, and often save without love.

As for these quarrels, they are like the moon, recurrent and
  fantastic. They have their beauty but night's is better.
It is better to be silent than make a noise. It is better to strike dead
  than strike often. It is better not to strike.

TIME OF DISTURBANCE: Copyright 1951 by Robinson Jeffers. Reprinted from HUNGERFIELD AND OTHER POEMS, by Robinson Jeffers, by permission of Random House, Inc.

Time of Disturbance

For Analysis

1. Assume that the central phrase in the poem is "keep a cold mind." Show how all the details in the poem define that phrase.

Randall Jarrell

The Death of the Ball Turret Gunner

From my mother's sleep I fell into the State,
And I hunched in its belly till my wet fur froze.
Six miles from earth, loosed from its dream of life,
I woke to black flak and the nightmare fighters.
When I died they washed me out of the turret with a hose.   5

The Death of the Ball Turret Gunner

For Analysis

1. A ball turret gunner was a small man who fired twin .50 caliber machine guns from a plexiglass bubble in the belly of a B–17 during World War II. Even a small man had to curl up fetus-fashion to fit into a ball turret, which was designed to protect the most vulnerable part of the B–17, the underside. The ball turret gunner was not only small and very busy, but he was extraordinarily exposed to attack. Is the gunner in this poem ever fully born, or does he simply pass from one fetal position to another? Consider, for example, that he falls from his "mother's sleep" into "the State," and that

his vehicle is "loosed from its dream of life" and that the enemy
planes are "nightmare fighters." Did he ever live? What does this
say of the poet's attitude toward war and young people?

Henry Reed

Lessons of
the War

To Alan Mitchell
Vixi duiellis nuper idoneus Et militavi non sine gloria*

I. NAMING OF PARTS

Today we have naming of parts. Yesterday,
We had daily cleaning. And tomorrow morning,
We shall have what to do after firing. But today,
Today we have naming of parts. Japonica
Glistens like coral in all of the neighboring gardens,   5
      And today we have naming of parts.

This is the lower sling swivel. And this
Is the upper sling swivel, whose use you will see,
When you are given your slings. And this is the piling swivel,
Which in your case you have not got. The branches   10
Hold in the gardens their silent, eloquent gestures,
      Which in our case we have not got.

This is the safety-catch, which is always released
With an easy flick of the thumb. And please do not let me

LESSONS OF THE WAR: From A MAP OF VERONA AND OTHER POEMS,
copyright, 1947, by Henry Reed. Reprinted by permission of Harcourt, Brace
& World, Inc., and Jonathan Cape Ltd.

*Epigraph: Horace, *Odes*, III, 26—"I have lived fit for the wars lately and
acted like a soldier not without glory." See last two lines of section IV of this
poem.

See anyone using his finger. You can do it quite easy   15
If you have any strength in your thumb. The blossoms
Are fragile and motionless, never letting anyone see
            Any of them using their finger.

And this you can see is the bolt. The purpose of this
Is to open the breech, as you see. We can slide it   20
Rapidly backwards and forwards: we call this
Easing the spring. And rapidly backwards and forwards
The early bees are assaulting and fumbling the flowers:
            They call it easing the Spring.

They call it easing the Spring: it is perfectly easy   25
If you have any strength in your thumb: like the bolt,
And the breech, and the cocking-piece, and the point of balance,
Which in our case we have not got; and the almond-blossom
Silent in all of the gardens and the bees going backwards and forwards,
            For today we have naming of parts.   30

II. JUDGING DISTANCES

Not only how far away, but the way that you say it
Is very important. Perhaps you may never get
The knack of judging a distance, but at least you know
How to report on a landscape: the central sector,
The right of arc and that, which we had last Tuesday,   5
            And at least you know

That maps are of time, not place, so far as the army
Happens to be concerned—the reason being,
Is one which need not delay us. Again, you know
There are three kinds of tree, three only, the fir and the poplar,   10
And those which have bushy tops to; and lastly
            That things only seem to be things.

A barn is not called a barn, to put it more plainly,
Or a field in the distance, where sheep may be safely grazing.
You must never be over-sure. You must say, when reporting: 15
At five o'clock in the central sector is a dozen
Of what appear to be animals; whatever you do,
            Don't call the bleeders sheep.

I am sure that's quite clear; and suppose, for the sake of example,
The one at the end, asleep endeavors to tell us   20
What he sees over there to the west, and how far away,
After first having come to attention. There to the west,

On the fields of summer the sun and the shadows bestow
        Vestments of purple and gold.

The still white dwellings are like a mirage in the heat,   25
And under the swaying elms a man and a woman
Lie gently together. Which is, perhaps, only to say
That there is a row of houses to the left of arc,
And that under some poplars a pair of what appear to be humans
        Appear to be loving.   30

Well that, for an answer, is what we might rightly call
Moderately satisfactory only, the reason being,
Is that two things have been omitted, and those are important.
The human beings, now: in what direction are they,
And how far away, would you say? And do not forget   35
        There may be dead ground in between.

There may be dead ground in between; and I may not have got
The knack of judging a distance; I will only venture
A guess that perhaps between me and the apparent lovers,
(Who, incidentally, appear by now to have finished,)   40
At seven o'clock from the houses, is roughly a distance
        Of about one year and a half.

III. MOVEMENT OF BODIES

Those of you that have got through the rest, I am going to rapidly
Devote a little time to showing you, those that can master it,
A few ideas about tactics, which must not be confused
With what we call strategy. Tactics is merely
The mechanical movement of bodies, and that is what we mean by it.   5
        Or perhaps I should say: by them.

Strategy, to be quite frank, you will have no hand in.
It is done by those up above, and it merely refers to
The larger movements over which we have no control.
But tactics are also important, together or single.   10
You must never forget that suddenly, in an engagement,
        You may find yourself alone.

This brown clay model is a characteristic terrain
Of a simple and typical kind. Its general character
Should be taken in at a glance, and its general character   15
You can see at a glance it is somewhat hilly by nature,
With a fair amount of typical vegetation
        Disposed at certain parts.

Here at the top of the tray, which we might call the northwards,
Is a wooded headland, with a crown of bushy-topped trees on;   20
And proceeding downwards or south we take in at a glance
A variety of gorges and knolls and plateaus and basins and saddles,
Somewhat symmetrically put, for easy identification.
            And here is our point of attack.

But remember of course it will not be a tray you will fight on,   25
Nor always by daylight. After a hot day, think of the night
Cooling the desert down, and you still moving over it:
Past a ruined tank or a gun, perhaps, or a dead friend,
Lying about somewhere: it might quite well be that.
            It isn't always a tray.   30

And even this tray is different to what I had thought,
These models are somehow never always the same; the reason
I do not know how to explain quite. Just as I do not know
Why there is always someone at this particular lesson
Who always starts crying. Now will you kindly   35
            Empty those blinking eyes?

I thank you. I have no wish to seem impatient.
I know it is all very hard, but you would not like,
To take a simple example, to take for example,
This place we have thought of here, you would not like   40
To find yourself face to face with it, and you not knowing
            What there might be inside?

Very well then: suppose this is what you must capture.
It will not be easy, not being very exposed,
Secluded away like it is, and somewhat protected   45
By a typical formation of what appear to be bushes,
So that you cannot see, as to what is concealed inside,
            As to whether it is friend or foe.

And so, a strong feint will be necessary in this connection.
It will not be a tray, remember. It may be a desert stretch   50
With nothing in sight, to speak of. I have no wish to be inconsiderate,
But I see there are two of you now, commencing to snivel.
I cannot think where such emotional privates can come from.
            Try to behave like men.

I thank you. I was saying: a thoughtful deception   55
Is always somewhat essential in such a case. You can see
That if only the attacker can capture such an emplacement
The rest of the terrain is his: a key-position, and calling
For the most resourceful maneuvers. But that is what tactics is.
            Or I should say rather: are.   60

Let us begin then and appreciate the situation.
I am thinking especially of the point we have been considering,
Though in a sense everything in the whole of the terrain
Must be appreciated. I do not know what I have said
To upset so many of you. I know it is a difficult lesson.   65
        Yesterday a man was sick,

But I have never known as many as *five* in a single intake,
Unable to cope with this lesson. I think you had better
Fall out, all five, and sit at the back of the room,
Being careful not to talk. The rest will close up.   70
Perhaps it was me saying "a dead friend," earlier on?
        Well, some of us live.

And I never know why, whenever we get to tactics,
Men either laugh or cry, though neither being strictly called for.
But perhaps I have started too early with a difficult problem?   75
We will start again, further north, with a simpler assault.
Are you ready? Is everyone paying attention?
        Very well then. Here are two hills.

IV. Unarmed Combat

In due course of course you will all be issued with
Your proper issue; but until tomorrow,
You can hardly be said to need it; and until that time,
We shall have unarmed combat. I shall teach you.
The various holds and rolls and throws and breakfalls   5
        Which you may sometimes meet.

And the various holds and rolls and throws and breakfalls
Do not depend on any sort of weapon,
But only on what I might coin a phrase and call
The ever-important question of human balance,   10
And the ever-important need to be in a strong
        Position at the start.

There are many kinds of weakness about the body,
Where you would least expect, like the ball of the foot.
But the various holds and rolls and throws and breakfalls   15
Will always come in useful. And never be frightened
To tackle from behind: it may not be clean to do so,
        But this is global war.

So give them all you have, and always give them
As good as you get; it will always get you somewhere.   20

(You may not know it, but you can tie a Jerry
Up without rope; it is one of the things I shall teach you.)
Nothing will matter if only you are ready for him.
> The readiness is all.

The readiness is all. How can I help but feel   25
I have been here before? But somehow then,
I was the tied-up one. How to get out
Was always then my problem. And even if I had
A piece of rope I was always the sort of person
> Who threw the rope aside.   30

And in my time I have given them all I had,
Which was never as good as I got, and it got me nowhere.
And the various holds and rolls and throws and breakfalls
Somehow or other I always seemed to put
In the wrong place. And as for war, my wars   35
> Were global from the start.

Perhaps I was never in a strong position,
Or the ball of my foot got hurt, or I had some weakness
Where I had least expected. But I think I see your point.
While awaiting a proper issue, we must learn the lesson   40
Of the ever-important question of human balance.
> It is courage that counts.

Things may be the same again; and we must fight
Not in the hope of winning but rather of keeping
Something alive: so that when we meet our end,   45
It may be said that we tackled wherever we could,
That battle-fit we lived, and though defeated,
> Not without glory fought.

Lessons of War

For Analysis

The epigraph of the poem is from Horace's *Odes*: "I have lived fit for
the wars lately and acted like soldier not without glory." In some Horatian manuscripts, however, the word *duellis* (wars) appears as *puellis*
(girls), yielding the reading, "I have lived fit for the girls lately and
acted like a soldier not without glory." One therefore expects to find
in the poem some opposition between seriousness and humor, war and
love, rigidity and naturalness.

1. In section I, "Naming of Parts," we hear two voices, one of a weapons instructor, one of a recruit. Characterize the two speakers.
2. In section II we hear the two voices again, but this time the voices come into dialogue. How does the conclusion of the section follow the instructor's directions, "maps are of time, not place, so far as the army/ Happens to be concerned"? Has the relationship between the instructor and the recruit deteriorated since section one?
3. In section III, we hear only one voice—the instructor's—and the poem operates by dramatic irony. The instructor does not realize that the relief map is shaped like a woman's body, and therefore he fails to understand either the recruits' reaction or the double meaning of his remarks on tactics. How do you know this is the same instructor as in section II?
4. In section IV the two voices reappear. The phrase that trips off the recruit's voice is a phrase from *Hamlet*, V; ii: "The readiness is all." In this phrase, Hamlet, who also has been through a "global war" and who has failed to "tackle from behind" and who "gave all he had" and who was not "in a strong position at the start" and who has been through the "various holds and rolls and throws and breakfalls," decides what will be his course of action: He will take what comes and do what he can to see justice done. How is this reflected in what the recruit thinks here?
5. What, in the end, is the most important lesson of the war that the recruit learned?

Joe McDonald

I-Feel-Like-I'm-Fixing-to-Die-Rag

Come on, all of you big strong men,
Uncle Sam needs your help again.
He's got himself in a terrible jam
Way down yonder in Viet Nam.

So put down your books and pick up your guns,   5
We're going to have a whole lot of fun.

CHORUS

> And it's one-two-three,
> What're we fighting for?
> Don't ask me,
> I don't give a damn;
> Next stop is Viet Nam.   5
> And it's five-six-seven,
> Open up the Pearly Gates.
> Now ain't no time to wonder why.
> Whoopee! We're all gonna die.

Well, come on, generals, let's move fast,   10
Your big chance has come at last.
Gotta go out and get those Reds,
The only good Commie is one that's dead;
And you know that peace can only be won
When they blow them all to kingdom come.   15

CHORUS

> And it's one-two-three,
> What're we fighting for?
> Don't ask me,
> I don't give a damn;
> Next stop is Viet Nam.   5
> And it's five-six-seven,
> Open up the Pearly Gates.
> Well, ain't no time to wonder why.
> Whoopee! We're all gonna die.

Well, come on, Wall Street, don't move slow,   10
Why, man, this war is a go-go-go!
There's plenty good money to be made
By supplying the Army with the tools of the trade.
Just hope and pray that if they drop the bomb,
They drop it on the Viet Cong.   15

CHORUS

> And it's one-two-three,
> What're we fighting for?
> Don't ask me,
> I don't give a damn;

Next stop is Viet Nam.   5
And it's five-six-seven,
Open up the Pearly Gates.
Well, ain't no time to wonder why.
Whoopee! We're all gonna die.

Well, come on, mothers, throughout the land,   10
Pack your boys off to Viet Nam
Come on, fathers, don't hesitate,
Send them off before it's too late;
Be the first one on the block
To have your boy come home in a box.   15

CHORUS

And it's one-two-three,
What're we fighting for?
Don't ask me,
I don't give a damn;
Next stop is Viet Nam.   5
And it's five-six-seven,
Open up the Pearly Gates.
Well, ain't no time to wonder why.
Whoopee! We're all gonna die.

I-Feel-Like-I'm-Fixing-To-Die-Rag

For Analysis

1. These are lyrics to a popular song by Country Joe and the Fish. What kind of song is a "rag"? Is there irony implicit in putting this kind of subject matter into ragtime?

2. Although a great deal of the irony in the poem exists at the level of statement ("peace can only be won/ When they blow them all to kingdom come"), some of it works by allusion and parody. What familiar slogans are being parodied in
     "Uncle Sam needs your help, again"
     "Be the first one on the block"
     "Now ain't no time to wonder why"
     "The only good Commie is . . ."?

3. If the audience is told, sarcastically, to "put down your books and pick up your guns," the audience must be composed of students. What aspect of campus sports life is being used in "one-two-three/

What're we fighting for? . . . And it's five-six-seven/ Open up the Pearly Gates"? Notice that if you complete the usual sequence (with four and eight), the lines would be complete: They would rhyme. Apparently campus cheers will never be completed. Why not?

FAME AND FORTUNE AS SEEN IN THE LYRIC AND OTHER FORMS

Walt Whitman

When Lilacs Last in the Dooryard Bloom'd

wrote in free verse

O Captain My Captain is a clear departure of Whitman's style.

western star is abraham lincoln

1

When lilacs last in the dooryard bloom'd,
And the great star early droop'd in the western sky in the night,
I mourn'd, and yet shall mourn with ever-returning spring.

Ever-returning spring, trinity sure to me you bring,
Lilac blooming perennial and drooping star in the west,
And thought of him I love.   5

expresses grief

2

over powering grief

O powerful western fallen star!
O shades of night—O moody, tearful night!
O great star disappear'd—O the black murk that hides the star!
O cruel hands that hold me powerless—O helpless soul of me!   10
O harsh surrounding cloud that will not free my soul.

3

In the dooryard fronting an old farmhouse near the white-wash'd palings,
Stands the lilac bush tall-growing with heart-shaped leaves of rich green,
With many a pointed blossom rising delicate, with the perfume strong
    I love,
With every leaf a miracle—and from this bush in the dooryard,   15
With delicate-color'd blossoms and heart-shaped leaves of rich green,
A sprig with its flower I break.

4

In the swamp in secluded recesses,
A shy and hidden bird is warbling a song.
Solitary the thrush,   20
The hermit withdrawn to himself, avoiding the settlements,
Sings by himself a song.

Song of the bleeding throat,
Death's outlet song of life, (for well dear brother I know,
If thou wast not granted to sing thou would'st surely die.)   25

5

Over the breast of the spring, the land, amid cities,
Amid lanes and through old woods, where lately the violets peep'd from
    the ground, spotting the gray debris,
Amid the grass in the fields each side of the lanes, passing the endless
    grass,
Passing the yellow-spear'd wheat, every grain from its shroud in the dark-
    brown fields uprisen,
Passing the apple-tree blows of white and pink in the orchards,   30
Carrying a corpse to where it shall rest in the grave,
Night and day journeys a coffin.

6

Coffin that passes through lanes and streets,
Through day and night with the great cloud darkening the land,
With the pomp of the inloop'd flags with the cities draped in black,   35
With the show of the States themselves as of crape-veil'd women standing,
With processions long and winding and the flambeaus of the night,
With the countless torches lit, with the silent sea of faces and the unbared
    heads,
With the waiting depot, the arriving coffin, and the somber faces,
With dirges through the night, with the thousand voices rising strong and
    solemn,   40
With all the mournful voices of the dirges pour'd around the coffin,
The dim-lit churches and the shuddering organs—where amid these you
    journey,
With the tolling, tolling bells' perpetual clang,
Here, coffin that slowly passes,
I give you my sprig of lilac.   45

7

(Nor for you, for one alone,
Blossoms and branches green to coffins all I bring,

For fresh as the morning, thus would I chant a song for you O sane and
    sacred death.
All over bouquets of roses,
O death, I cover you over with roses and early lilies,   50
But mostly and now the lilac that blooms the first,
Copious I break, I break the sprigs from the bushes,
With loaded arms I come, pouring for you,
For you and the coffins all of you O death.)

8

O western orb sailing the heaven,   55
Now I know what you must have meant as a month since I walk'd,
As I walk'd in silence the transparent shadowy night,
As I saw you had something to tell as you bent to me night after night,
As you droop'd from the sky low down as if to my side, (while the other
    stars all look'd on,)
As we wander'd together the solemn night, (for something I know not
    what kept me from sleep,)   60
As the night advanced, and I saw on the rim of the west how full you
    were of woe,
As I stood on the rising ground in the breeze in the cool transparent night,
As I watch'd where you pass'd and was lost in the netherward black of
    the night,
As my soul in its trouble dissatisfied sank, as where you sad orb,
Concluded, dropt in the night, and was gone.   65

9

Sing on there in the swamp,
O singer bashful and tender, I hear your notes, I hear your call,
I hear, I come presently, I understand you,
But a moment I linger, for the lustrous star has detain'd me,
The star my departing comrade holds and detains me.   70

10

O how shall I warble myself for the dead one there I loved?
And how shall I deck my song for the large sweet soul that has gone?
And what shall my perfume be for the grave of him I love?

Sea-winds blown from east and west,
Blown from the Eastern sea and blown from the Western sea, till there
    on the prairies meeting,   75
These and with these and the breath of my chant,
I'll perfume the grave of him I love.

11

O what shall I hang on the chamber walls?
And what shall the pictures be that I hang on the walls,
To adorn the burial house of him I love?   80

Pictures of growing spring and farms and homes,
With the Fourth-month eve at sundown, and the gray smoke lucid and
  bright,
With floods of the yellow gold of the gorgeous, indolent, sinking sun,
  burning, expanding the air,
With the fresh sweet herbage under foot, and the pale green leaves of the
  trees prolific,
In the distance the flowing glaze, the breast of the river, with a wind-
  dapple here and there,   85
With ranging hills on the banks, with many a line against the sky, and
  shadows,
And the city at hand with dwellings so dense, and stocks of chimneys,
And all the scenes of life and the workshops, and the workmen homeward
  returning.

12

Lo, body and soul—this land,
My own Manhattan with spires, and the sparkling and hurrying tides, and
  the ships,   90
The varied and ample land, the South and the North in the light, Ohio's
  shores and flashing Missouri,
And ever the far-spreading prairies cover'd with grass and corn.

Lo, the most excellent sun so calm and haughty,
The violent and purple morn with just-felt breezes,
The gentle soft-born measureless light,   95
The miracle spreading bathing all, the fulfill'd noon,
The coming eve delicious, the welcome night and the stars,
Over my cities shining all, enveloping man and land.

13

Sing on, sing on you gray-brown bird,
Sing from the swamps, the recesses, pour your chant from the bushes, 100
Limitless out of the dusk, out of the cedars and pines.

Sing on dearest brother, warble your reedy song,
Loud human song, with voice of uttermost woe.
O liquid and free and tender!
O wild and loose to my soul—O wondrous singer!   105

You only I hear—yet the star holds me, (but will soon depart,)
Yet the lilac with mastering odor holds me.

14

Now while I sat in the day and look'd forth
In the close of the day with its light and the fields of spring, and the
    farmers preparing their crops,
In the large unconscious scenery of my land with its lakes and forests, 110
In the heavenly aerial beauty (after the perturb'd winds and the storms,)
Under the arching heavens of the afternoon swift passing, and the voices
    of children and women,
The many-moving sea tides, and I saw the ships how they sail'd,
And the summer approaching with richness, and the fields all busy with
    labor,
And the infinite separate houses, how they all went on, each with its meals
    and minutia of daily usages,   115
And the streets how their throbbings throbb'd, and the cities pent—lo,
    then and there,
Falling upon them all and among them all, enveloping me with the rest,
Appear'd the cloud, appear'd the long black trail,
And I knew death, its thought, and the sacred knowledge of death.

Then with the knowledge of death as walking one side of me,   120
And the thought of death close-walking the other side of me,
And I in the middle as with companions, and as holding the hands of
    companions,
I fled forth to the hiding receiving night that talks not,
Down to the shores of the water, the path by the swamp in the dimness,
To the solemn shadowy cedars and ghostly pines so still.   125

And the singer so shy to the rest receiv'd me,
The gray-brown bird I know receiv'd us comrades three,
And he sang the carol of death, and a verse for him I love.

From deep secluded recesses,
From the fragrant cedars and the ghostly pines so still   130
Came the carol of the bird.
And the charm of the carol rapt me,
As I held as if by their hands my comrades in the night,
And the voice of my spirit tallied the song of the bird.

Come lovely and soothing death,   135
Undulate round the world, serenely arriving, arriving,
In the day, in the night, to all, to each,
Sooner or later delicate death.

Prais'd be the fathomless universe,
For life and joy, and for objects and knowledge curious,   140
And for love, sweet love—but praise! praise! praise!
For the sure-enwinding arms of cool-enfolding death.

Dark mother always gliding near with soft feet,
Have none chanted for thee a chant of fullest welcome?
Then I chant it for thee, I glorify thee above all,   145
I bring thee a song that when thou must indeed come, come unfalteringly.

Approach, strong deliveress,
When it is so, when thou has taken them I joyously sing the dead,
Lost in the loving floating ocean of thee,
Laved in the flood of thy bliss O death.   150

From me to thee glad serenades,
Dances for thee I propose saluting thee, adornments and feastings for thee,
And the sights of the open landscape and the high-spread sky are fitting,
And life and the fields, and the huge and thoughtful night.

The night in silence under many a star,   155
The ocean shore and the husky whispering wave whose voice I know,
And the soul turning to thee O vast and well-veil'd death,
And the body gratefully nestling close to thee.

Over the tree-tops I float thee a song,
Over the rising and sinking waves, over the myriad fields and the prairies
*   wide,*   160
Over the dense-pack'd cities all and the teeming wharves and ways,
I float this carol with joy, with joy to thee O death.

15

To the tally of my soul,
Loud and strong kept up the gray-brown bird,
With pure deliberate notes spreading filling the night.   165

Loud in the pines and cedars dim,
Clear in the freshness moist and the swamp-perfume,
And I with my comrades there in the night.
While my sight that was bound in my eyes unclosed,
As to long panoramas of visions.   170
And I saw askant the armies,
I saw as in noiseless dreams hundreds of battle-flags,
Borne through the smoke of the battles and pierc'd with missiles I saw
   them,

And carried hither and yon through the smoke, and torn and bloody,
And at last but a few shreds left on the staffs, (and all in silence,)   175
And the staffs all splinter'd and broken.

I saw battle corpses, myriads of them,
And the white skeletons of young men, I saw them,
I saw the debris and debris of all the slain soldiers of the war,
But I saw they were not as was thought,   180
They themselves were fully at rest, they suffer'd not,
The living remain'd and suffer'd, the mother suffer'd,
And the wife and the child and the musing comrade suffer'd,
And the armies that remain'd suffer'd.

16

Passing the visions, passing the night,   185
Passing, unloosing the hold of my comrades' hands,
Passing the song of the hermit bird and the tallying song of my soul,
Victorious song, death's outlet song, yet varying ever-altering song,
As low and wailing, yet clear the notes, rising and falling, flooding the
     night,
Sadly sinking and fainting, as warning and warning, and yet again bursting
     joy,   190
Covering the earth and filling the spread of the heaven,
As that powerful psalm in the night I heard from recesses,
Passing, I leave thee lilac with heart-shaped leaves,
I leave thee there in the dooryard, blooming, returning with spring.

I cease from my song for thee,   195
From my gaze on thee in the west, fronting the west, communing with
     thee,
O comrade lustrous with silver face in the night.

Yet each to keep and all, retrievements out of the night,
The song, the wondrous chant of the gray-brown bird,
And the tallying chant, the echo arous'd in my soul,   200
With the lustrous and drooping star with the countenance full of woe,
With the holders holding my hand nearing the call of the bird,
Comrades mine and I in the midst, and their memory ever to keep, for
     the dead I loved so well,
For the sweetest, wisest soul of all my days and lands—and this for his
     dear sake,
Lilac and star and bird twined with the chant of my soul,   205
There in the fragrant pines and the cedars dusk and dim.

When Lilacs Last in the Dooryard Bloom'd

For Analysis

1. Whitman's elegy is on Abraham Lincoln. Whitman's spacious free verse takes some getting used to by anyone weaned on neatly rhymed, strictly metered verse; his exclamations and strong personal intrusions also require adjustment for some readers: One of Whitman's contemporaries, the English critic, Edmund Gosse, wrote that he hoped he would be dead before English poets imitated the "bastard jargon of Walt Whitman." He wasn't. It is a mistake, however, to assume that Whitman is free of convention. The poem makes use of thoroughly traditional symbols—the lilac as a symbol of love; the star as the departed spirit; the bird as the voice of the departed that lingers on. Sections 1–4 are then a kind of table of contents, introducing and establishing these symbols. This being so, what does the second stanza of section 1 say? (Why does Whitman use the word "trinity," which usually refers to the three aspects of the godhead as "one God, world without end"? What are the three-in-one here for Whitman?)

2. Read carefully stanza 2 of section 1. The repeated "O" is a mark of a traditional lament. But is not the mind of the speaker in a state of confusion? Stars show brightly only at night. But if the star has fallen, it would make no difference whether it were night or not. But the "fallen" star changes to a star that has only "disappear'd" behind a "black murk" and that murk becomes a cloud that surrounds not the star but the mind of the speaker. What does this suggest? Is Lincoln really gone forever? How do sections 3 and 4 support your analysis?

3. Sections 5 and 6 record the funeral journey of Lincoln's coffin. How does what the speaker learned in the first part of the poem explain what he means when he says (lines 44–45), "Here, coffin that slowly passes,/ I give you my sprig of lilac"?

4. As in the traditional elegy, section 7 broadens what the speaker perceives about the dead Lincoln to all dead men.

5. Another aspect of the traditional elegy: in sections 8–13 Whitman asks how he can sing a proper song for the dead Lincoln because, although he understands what the star and the bird "meant," he is neither bird nor star, and their message has to be put into words.

Look at the song he does sing in sections 11 and 12. How does a song describing the best aspects of America become a proper song for Abraham Lincoln?

6. In the traditional elegy, the final responsibility of the poet is to make sense of death. That is the subject matter of the last part of the poem. How does Whitman finally reconcile himself to the thought of death—not only the death of Lincoln but of himself and of all men?

O Captain!
My Captain!

O Captain! my Captain! our fearful trip is done,
The ship has weather'd every rack, the prize we sought is won,
The port is near, the bells I hear, the people all exulting,
While follow eyes the steady keel, the vessel grim and daring;
    But O heart! heart! heart!   5
      O the bleeding drops of red,
        Where on the deck my Captain lies,
         Fallen cold and dead.

O Captain! my Captain! rise up and hear the bells;
Rise up—for you the flag is flung—for you the bugle trills,   10
For you bouquets and ribbon'd wreaths—for you the shores a-crowding,
For you they call, the swaying mass, their eager faces turning;
    Here Captain! dear father!
      This arm beneath your head!
        It is some dream that on the deck,   15
         You've fallen cold and dead.

My Captain does not answer, his lips are pale and still,
My father does not feel my arm, he has no pulse nor will,
The ship is anchor'd safe and sound, its voyage closed and done,
From fearful trip the victor ship comes in with object won;   20
    Exult O shores, and ring O bells!
      But I with mournful tread,
        Walk the deck my Captain lies,
         Fallen cold and dead.

Oh Captain! My Captain!

For Analysis

Here Walt Whitman is on the same subject as the preceding poem—the death of Lincoln. Opposed to the freedom of the preceding poem, this selection has a relatively metrical regularity. It is possible, however, that something is seriously wrong with this poem. The framework is traditional, perhaps even trite: The Captain (Lincoln) of the Ship of State (the U.S.) has brought it safely to harbor (the end of the Civil War). Supposing that metaphor, symbol, and analogy require some logic, answer these questions:

1. Does stanza 2 say anything not said in stanza 1?
2. Does stanza 3 say anything not said in stanza 1?
3. Does stanza 3 say anything not said in stanza 2?
4. If the ship has been through the storm and the prize is won, how is it that the ship is not in port but only approaching port?
5. If the basic metaphor is captain-ship-journey, how does "dear father" enter?
6. Why should Lincoln be only Whitman's "father"? Everyone else seems to be celebrating ("Exult O shores, and ring O bells!") but only the speaker mourns ("But I with mournful tread,/ Walk the deck my Captain lies").
7. By the logic of the poem, the speaker must be, metaphorically, a crewman who is also the Captain's son, and the only one aware of the Captain's death. Is this supportable?

Stanley Koehler

In Arlington
Cemetery

In the city of memorials,
among tombstones and small
headstones, I look through the cold
not for a monument
but for a grave with ferns   5
and evergreens lent
from the season past. A flame burns
in the air, not a leaf
to shelter it, blown like our grief,
variable and new, endless and old.   10

Uphill, over open ground,
on the wind's edge are coming
echoes of drummers drumming
on tight-stretched skin,
tatooing the stillness   15
to the funeral sound
of hoofs at the hobble,
unharnessed, held in
to the ritual pace;
and of wheels on the cobble.   20

The carriage circles a green park
with its temple, the dark
porch where the Form in his chair
sheds a marble tear
for what is fated like him: 25
statues for whom
there are robes of stone.
Love waves in her car

In Arlington Cemetery: Reprinted from OF POETRY AND POWER
edited by Erwin A. Glikes and Paul Schwaber, © 1964 by Basic Books, Inc.,
Publishers, New York.

          while Hate takes aim
          through a lens from far-
          off, and History bleeds, an old charade,   30
          and Madmen fly
          the line of parade
          down empty walks, and from the shocked
          stage the Actor's shout   35
          is driven out.
          Still, in those marble eyes
          deepgrained as memory,
          the barns are burning, the streets are blocked,
          while motorcade and obsequies   40

          through iron gates
          to somber guns and the horn's last notes
          continually come.
          For this to end, for the drum
          to be stilled at last,   45
          more than this green bough
          will be cut and cast.

          The flame leaps up. Fresh as our vow,
          it makes a gentle monument at night
          with the simplicity of light.   50

In Arlington Cemetery

For Analysis

An elegy on John F. Kennedy, this poem moves from one death to
another and then contrasts the memorials of those deaths to reach a
generalization.

1. The grave with ferns and the eternal flame, of course, refer to Ken-
    nedy's grave. What other dead man is referred to in "the dark/
    porch where the Form in his chair/sheds a marble tear/for what
    is fated like him"?
2. "Love waves in her car/while Hate takes aim" refers to the assassina-
    tion in Dallas. What two events, widely separated in time, does the
    following passage refer to?

              and Madmen fly
              the line of parade

down empty walks, and from the shocked
stage the Actor's shout
is driven out.

3. To what two events does the following line refer: "the barns are
    burning, the streets are blocked"?
4. What is the "green bough" of the penultimate stanza? This poem
    (that is, a tribute thrown on the grave)? The evergreen on the grave?
    John Kennedy himself? How do you know?
5. The Lincoln Memorial is not "a gentle monument at night" nor
    does it have the "simplicity of light"—it is massive and awesome.
    The eternal flame on the grave of Kennedy, however, has these first
    characteristics. The ending of the poem is quiet. Like "our vow"
    ("What vow would be appropriate to Kennedy's assassination), it
    is fresh and different. But is the poem hopeful? Take into account
    the whole poem.

Richard Frost

On Not Writing
an Elegy

My friend told me about kids in a coffee house
who laughed and celebrated the killing. Another friend
didn't care, sick at his own divorce,
drinking martinis with a delicate hand,
saying he couldn't care when I said I cried   5
like everybody. Still, I am the vain one,
a bullet in my shoulder, six seconds to go
before another burns in my head. Trying
to write about the thing, I always end
by feeling I have been shot. My brain, my spine   10
gone, and with time winding foolishly,
I am raced, tabled, cleaned out, boxed, flown,

ON NOT WRITING AN ELEGY: Reprinted from OF POETRY AND POWER
edited by Erwin A. Glikes and Paul Schwaber, © 1964 by Basic Books, Inc.,
Publishers, New York.

carried and lowered in. I have had this done
on a shiny day with my wife and bodyguards
and everyone there to cry out, and I have cried   15
without trying and without a clear thought.
This death has had me where I cannot write
or hate or love, numb as a coined face
fallen where all flames have only to burn
down. Lost where I must only lose my place,   20
I mourn the glories of our blood and state.

On Not Writing an Elegy

For Analysis

Frost's work is another elegy on the death of John F. Kennedy but much
less direct than the preceding one and certainly less predictable. One is
expected to react negatively to hearing that "kids in a coffee house/
. . . laughed and celebrated the killing" and that someone thought his
own divorce more important than the assassination. "Still," says the poet,
"I am the vain one." Are there two senses of *vain* here? What is his
vanity?

1. Who does he imagine himself to be when he tries to write of the
   assassination?
2. Is he likely to recover from this illusion? (See "numbed as a coined
   face/ fallen where all flames have only to burn down." Whose face
   was coined? Will the flame on the grave "burn down"?)
3. Kennedy lost his life; what is the only thing the speaker can lose?
4. In the end, is the speaker's sympathetic identification with the dead
   president a "vanity" or is it a sign of deep respect and grief?
5. In what way, then, is the title ironic?
6. The last line of this poem is quoted from a stanza of James Shirley's
   seventeenth-century poem, *The Contention of Ajax and Ulysses*:

> The glories of our blood and state
>   Are shadows, not substantial things;
> There is no armor against Fate;
>   Death lays his icy hand on kings:
>   Sceptre and crown
>   Must tumble down,
> And in the dust be equal made
> With the poor crooked scythe and spade.

Does this help to set the tone of the poem?

his critics?

— born in Eng.

A. E. Housman *— attending church regularly.*
— his mother died when he was 12.

his poems speak of sorry, separation and duty.

To an Athlete
Dying Young

theme of poem: how a young athlete when in his death — still he will be remembered for his accomplishments. his winning.

The time you won your town the race
We chaired you through the market-place;
Man and boy stood cheering by,
And home we brought you shoulder-high.

Today, the road all runners come,   5
Shoulder-high we bring you home,
And set you at your threshold down,
Townsman of a stiller town.

Smart lad, to slip betimes away
From fields where glory does not stay,   10
And early though the laurel grows
It withers quicker than the rose.

Eyes the shady night has shut
Cannot see the record cut,
And silence sounds no worse than cheers   15
After earth has stopped the ears.

Now you will not swell the rout
Of lads that wore their honors out,
Runners whom renown outran
And the name died before the man.   20

So set, before its echoes fade,
The fleet foot on the sill of shade,
And hold to the low lintel up
The still-defended challenge-cup.

And round that early-laureled head   25
Will flock to gaze the strengthless dead,
And find unwithered on its curls
The garland briefer than a girl's.

To an Athlete Dying Young

For Analysis

The situation is simple; the reaction of the speaker is not. An athlete, who once was carried on the shoulders of the villagers because he won a race, is now carried, shoulder-high, in his coffin. One assumes he was congratulated on the first victory. Now the speaker congratulates him on his second and greater victory: He was "smart," the speaker says, to die now, because he will not live to see his record broken or to become a has-been ("The name died before the man"). But against that odd reasoning comes another line of reasoning. What is implied, for example, in this?

So set, *before its echoes fade,*
The fleet foot on the sill of shade,
And hold to the *low* lintel up
The still-defended challenge-cup.

The implication of "still-defended" is both "yet defended" and "defended by death." But what value do "before its echoes fade" and "the low lintel" put on this accomplishment?

How does the last stanza reinforce this impression? If the dead are "strengthless" and the garland that the dead athlete wears is "briefer than a girl's" does not this negate the thought of the early stanzas? The garland may be unwithered, but it is still briefer than a girl's.

In the end, do we concentrate on the athlete or on the mind of the narrator? Do the contradictions force us to concentrate on what the narrator sees as achievement, fame, fortune?

If so, what is his view of achievement and fame and fortune?

satire on our organization of a communist state.

W. H. Auden

The Unknown
Citizen

TO JS/07/M/378

THIS MARBLE MONUMENT IS ERECTED BY THE STATE

He was found by the Bureau of Statistics to be
One against whom there was no official complaint,
And all the reports on his conduct agree
That, in the modern sense of an old-fashioned word, he was a saint,
For in everything he did he served the Greater Community. 5
Except for the War till the day he retired
He worked in a factory and never got fired,
But satisfied his employers, Fudge Motors Inc.
Yet he wasn't a scab or odd in his views,
For his Union reports that he paid his dues, 10
(Our report on his Union shows it was sound)
And our Social Psychology workers found
That he was popular with his mates and liked a drink.
The Press are convinced that he bought a paper every day
And that his reactions to advertisements were normal in every way. 15
Policies taken out in his name prove that he was fully insured,
And his Health-card shows he was once in hospital but left it cured.
Both Producers Research and High-Grade Living declare
He was fully sensible to the advantages of the Installment Plan
And had everything necessary to the Modern Man, 20
A gramophone, a radio, a car and a frigidaire.
Our researchers into Public Opinion are content
That he held the proper opinions for the time of year;
When there was peace, he was for peace; when there was war, he went.
He was married and added five children to the population, 25

Expert on genetics, birth and population.

Which our Eugenist says was the right number for a parent of his
    generation,
And our teachers report that he never interfered with their education.
Was he free? Was he happy? The question is absurd:
Had anything been wrong, we should certainly have heard.

The Unknown Citizen

For Analysis

1. What aspects of contemporary society is Auden satirizing?
2. How does the form of the poem, especially the rhymes, enhance the satire?

Kenneth Fearing

Dirge

1-2-3 was the number he played but today the number
     came 3-2-1;
    bought his Carbide at 30 but it went to 29; had the
    favorite at Bowie but the track was slow—

O, executive type, would you like to drive a floating power,
    knee action, silk-upholstered six? Wed a Hollywood star?   5
    Shoot the course in 58? Draw to the ace, king, jack?
O, fellow with a will who won't take no, watch out for three
    cigarettes on the same, single match; O democratic voter
    born in August under Mars, beware of liquidated rails—

Dénouement to dénouement, he took a personal pride in the   10
    certain, certain way he lived his own, private life,
    but nevertheless, they shut off his gas; nevertheless,

the bank foreclosed; nevertheless, the landlord called;
nevertheless, the radio broke,

And twelve o'clock arrived just once too often,   15
   just the same he wore one gray tweed suit, bought one
      straw hat, drank one straight Scotch, walked one short
      step, took one long look, drew one deep breath,
   just one too many,

And wow he died as wow he lived,   20
   going whop to the office and blooie home to sleep and
      biff got married and bam had children and oof got fired,
   zowie did he live and zowie did he die,

With who the hell are you at the corner of his casket,
   and where the hell we going on the right hand silver   25
   knob, and who the hell cares walking second from the
   end with an American Beauty wreath from why the hell
   not.

Very much missed by the circulation staff of the *New York
Evening Post*; deeply, deeply mourned by the B.M.T.,   30

Wham, Mr. Roosevelt; pow, Sears Roebuck; awk, big dipper;
   bop, summer rain;
   bong, Mr., bong, Mr., bong, Mr., bong.

Dylan Thomas

Do Not
Go Gentle

Do not go gentle into that good night,
Old age should burn and rave at close of day;
Rage, rage against the dying of the light.

Though wise men at their end know dark is right,
Because their words had forked no lightning they   5
Do not go gentle into that good night.

Good men, the last wave by, crying how bright
Their frail deeds might have danced in a green bay,
Rage, rage against the dying of the light.

Wild men who caught and sang the sun in flight,   10
And learn, too late, they grieved it on its way,
Do not go gentle into that good night.

Grave men, near death, who see with blinding sight
Blind eyes could blaze like meteors and be gay,
Rage, rage against the dying of the light.   15

And you, my father, there on the sad height,
Curse, bless, me now with your fierce tears, I pray.
Do not go gentle into that good night.
Rage, rage against the dying of the light.

Do Not Go Gentle

For Analysis

Formally, this is a *villanelle*, a poem containing only two rhymes, divided
into tercets, with the first line reappearing as the sixth and twelfth, the
third line as the ninth and fifteenth, and both the first and third appearing
in the final quatrain. Biographically, this is Thomas's poem for his father.
The poem is built on a series of paradoxes. The greatest is that the poet
asks his father not to go easily to death, even while he characterizes
death as "good night." In support of this paradox he cites a series of
paradoxes and ends with paradoxes ("the sad height," "Curse, bless me
now," "fierce tears"). By so doing he not only illuminates his feeling
for his father but says something about the nature of existence.

1. Is there a double meaning to "good night"? Is the phrase to be taken
   as a farewell or as a description of death with "good" as a value
   judgment?
2. If wise men are really wise, they know "dark is right." Why then
   do they not "go gentle"?
3. Why do "good men" "rage against the dying of the light"?

4. Why do "wild men," who celebrated the riotous passing of time, "rage against the dying of the light"?
5. "Grave men" surely ought to know that "dark is right." Why do they "rage against the dying of the light"?
6. Wise, good, wild, and grave men all have what in common?
7. Does the list imply what the poet thinks are the characteristics of his father?
8. In what way would the tears of his father, considering the argument of the whole poem, both curse and bless the son?

THE LIMERICK

British and American poets have generally used stanzaic forms borrowed from other countries: the sonnet, ottava rima, terza rima, villanelle, and so on. One form native to English is the limerick, named after a town in Ireland and originally invented somewhere in the British Isles.

The limerick became popular in the mid-nineteenth century largely through the practice of Edward Lear. The limerick is bound to no limits of subject matter or audience; one difficulty in dealing with limericks is that so many of them are, or were, unprintable. That should say something about their continuing vitality in the oral tradition. Because of what might be called the Obscene Tradition in the limerick, some readers insist on finding that tradition in almost every limerick.

> There was a young lady named Bright
> Whose speed was much faster than light.
>   She went out one day
>   In a relative way,
> And returned on the previous night.

Although the poem is built on the theory of relativity, we know one reader who sees an entirely different poem here: Since the lady is "fast" and "relative" implies "in the family way," he sees in the poem a reference to a clandestine operation. So much for light verse among heavy readers.

There was a young student named Pressah
Whose knowledge grew lessah and lessah.
   It at last grew so small,
   He knew nothing at all,
And was hired as a college professah.

This same upstart, however, got his comeuppance:

Pressah, whose first name was Reese,
Died pursuing M.A.'s, Ph.D.'s.
   The coroner said
   It's plain that he's dead
From killing himself—by degrees.

While alive, Reese Pressah led a pointless existence:

Teaching freshmen only for cash,
Pressah lacked professorial flash.
   His comments on papers
   Were confined to the capers
Of the errant: and —.

Be a poet. Make your own.

The
Drama

AN INTRODUCTION

Drama employs more conventions than any other form of literature because of its two-part nature: It can be read as literature; however its primary purpose is to portray people and events through action and dialogue that are performed. It adds to literary conventions a series of stage conventions. Staging devices—such as lighting, props, costumes—form an integral part of a play. Thus, the playwright includes stage directions not only for staging the play, but to help the reader visualize the scene and action.

Superficially, drama may seem less artificial, less conventional than other literary forms because it involves real people, words, and actions. But drama only seeks—it does not achieve—reality. The people are acting; the situations, conversations, and problems are simulated. Everything in drama is selected and manipulated to compress the experience just as in other literary forms. The physical characteristics of the theater itself create a situation that is vastly unreal—whether it is an open-air Greek stage, an Elizabethan platform stage projecting into the audience, a modern proscenium stage with a curtain, or a theater-in-the-round where the audience surrounds the stage.

The most familiar stage today is the proscenium stage. The audience sees a room with only three sides. People who have assumed personalities are talking to others about contrived problems and situations. Their dress is often affected, their words out of character, and their actions unlikely.

The conventions of the theater, however, provide a context for the action of a play. The audience can overlook departures from actuality that are involved. If conventions were not accepted, the play would not seem plausible to the audience. The conventions of drama are numerous because the dramatist must concern himself with staging—music, costumes, lighting, movement, and so forth. He must be concerned with staging because drama involves a dimension that literature does not: Action has been added to words. One can read a play intelligently only if he considers the acting side along with the printed side; he must consider stage convention along with literary convention.

Conventions and their applications are more easily understood when their function is considered in a specific play. Tennessee Williams's *The Glass Menagerie* is a play about the problems of the Wingfield family and, by extension, of the society they represent. The family lives in a shabby apartment in St. Louis. The father long ago ran away from the family, unable to bear, among other things, his wife Amanda. Amanda, unable to cope with the present, lives in the past; her fondest recollection is of the night when seventeen gentlemen callers courted her. She lives by a code that died with the civilization she grew up in. Her daughter, Laura, is a shy, withdrawn cripple, who like her mother, cannot or will not cope with the outside world, and who retires more and more into herself, spending hours with her collection of glass animals—the glass menagerie. Laura's brother, Tom, "a poet with a job in a warehouse" (says Williams in the stage directions) is torn between wanting to help Laura and needing to salvage his own identity.

The plot is simple: Amanda convinces Tom to invite an acquaintance, Jim O'Connor, to the Wingfield home for supper in hope that he will be attracted to Laura. Jim, a normal but simple-minded young man, comes to supper; however, he is already engaged. Amanda's plan to help Laura only damages her; Laura retreats farther into unreality, and Tom leaves.

Abstracted in this fashion, the play sounds weak. It is not. It had 563 performances on Broadway and won the New York Drama Critics' Circle Award as the best play of 1945. In creating this powerful comment on society and a tragic, touching portrayal of a family, Williams used almost every technique the drama offers.

CONVENTIONS OF SYMBOL

Williams used transparent walls on the set. As the curtain rises, the solid wall of the tenement becomes transparent and then rises slowly out of sight, not to be lowered again until Tom's final speech at the end of the play. This staging device is not a gimmick; Williams is illustrating symbolically the existence of a menagerie within a menagerie. Just as the beautiful glass animals stand imprisoned in their glass case, so these people live within their glass case. When the wall ascends, the menagerie is open for inspection. Here is a kind of symbol available only to the dramatist.

Another symbolic convention is the use of lighting in the play. As Williams says in the stage directions, "The lighting in the play is not realistic." Spotlights focus continually on Laura, even when she is not directly involved in the action. For example, when Tom and his mother argue about Tom's responsibility to Laura, the strong light is not on them but on Laura. Williams is again making a point symbolically: That although Tom has a problem, the central problem in the play is Laura—she is the center of everything.

Music also serves a symbolic purpose—by illustrating Laura's centrality. Williams demanded delicate, sad circus music, suggesting both nostalgia and the menagerie; he called it "Laura's music."

Williams had originally used an old vaudeville technique in the play. He wanted, at the beginning of each scene, a legend shown on a screen to suggest the mood and action of the scene to come. For example, the first scene when Amanda reminisces about her seventeen gentlemen callers was to be preceded by the legend *"Où sont les neiges?"* part of the refrain ("Where are the snows of yesteryear?") of a poem by François Villon, suggesting nostalgic and inevitably pointless recollections of a dead past. The screen device was never used, but it is included in the reading version of the play as another symbolic device.

Other symbolic devices are equally obvious. The animals in Laura's menagerie symbolize something to the audience—they also symbolize something to Laura. When her mother insists that she think of marriage, Laura reaches quickly for a glass animal. The gesture suggests that Laura realizes her retreat into unreality is being threatened. When Jim O'Connor comes to supper, Laura offers him her favorite glass animal to hold—an obvious gesture of love and trust. The animal is a unicorn, an animal traditionally connected with love and virgins. Jim clumsily breaks the horn from the unicorn as he and Laura dance, and Laura remarks that now the unicorn is just like all other horses, just as she is like other girls at the moment. Jim kisses her, then announces that he is engaged, and Laura insists that he take the broken unicorn as a souvenir.

The glass animal symbolism is strengthened by a recurring phrase that Jim uses to describe Laura—Blue Roses. Laura and her beauty have a highly unnatural quality: Roses, delicate and lovely, are not naturally blue.

Still another symbol is the use of candles. In the play Laura is associated with light, specifically with candles. At the end, long after he has fled from his family, Tom says that wherever he travelled, he always felt something pursuing him, especially when he heard music or saw a piece of transparent glass. As he speaks, Laura in the background (that is, in his memory) bends over candles and blows them out. Tom says he runs to movies or to a bar or to a stranger—"anything that can blow your candles out." As Laura blows out the candles, Tom says, "for nowadays the world is lit by lightning! Blow out your candles, Laura—and so, good-bye. . . ."

Tom, feeling guilt about leaving his sister, is here justifying his flight in the candles-lightning image. It's not a complicated image: Lightning is far more powerful and brilliant than candlelight, and Tom is saying that there are more important things for him than Laura's problems, that he must live in the present rather than die in the past. There is also an implication that Laura's problem is unsolvable—she herself blows out her candles, he does not. The basis for this explanation of his flight was developed early in the play when Tom says something that is repeated several times: That although in the U.S. there were labor squabbles and a slowly dissolving economy, "in Spain there was Guernica." The reference is to the Spanish city of Guernica, which was totally destroyed by the Fascists in the Spanish Civil War as a kind of threat to the enemy. However, to the Spanish Communists, Guernica became a battle-cry, a symbol of what they were fighting to overcome—it symbolized a cause to fight for. This is the lightning that lights the world: Tom feels he must face the lightning, not the candles in a St. Louis alley.

CONVENTIONS OF CHARACTER

Characters in plays can serve more functions than can characters in novels, poems, and short stories. Playwrights often use function characters, characters whose major importance is what they do, not what they are.

One of the oldest conventions and the earliest kind of function character is the chorus. A chorus is a group of actors (sometimes a single actor) speaking in unison and functioning as an expository device (for example, to give the audience necessary information that a character could not reveal because of limitations of time, place, or character consistency). Thus a chorus gives background information to the audience, comments on the action, or predicts what will happen. The convention requires that the audience believe what the chorus says—the chorus never lies.

When playwrights grew dissatisfied with the chorus device, they took three other character conventions and expanded them:

1. The confidant—A character whose main function is to carry information to and from the main character and to provide an excuse for self-revelation by the main character. In the western movie, the hero talks to his horse or to a comical sidekick, both of them confidants. Hamlet talks to Horatio, a confidant. Antony talks to Enobarbus, a confidant. Juliet talks to the nurse, a confidant.

2. The soliloquy—A character speaks his inmost thoughts directly to the audience. The chorus convention applies here with one difference: What the character says in soliloquy is what he sees as the truth. He may not, of course, know the truth or he may be deceiving himself.

3. The aside—A character, in the midst of a group scene, suddenly turns to another character or to the audience and says something directed only to them. The convention requires that no one else hear the aside, even though the actor must shout to be heard in the back rows.

Some earlier plays have confidants, choruses, soliloquies, and asides. Modern playwrights have become more selective in using these devices. In *The Glass Menagerie* Williams has condensed all of them into the actions of one figure: Tom Wingfield. Consider what Tom does in this play:

1. He is a character in the play.
2. He is the narrator—the whole play is his memory of the action.
3. He is a chorus. He goes to the front of the stage, speaks directly to the audience, and nobody else hears what he says; he speaks completely free of time and space.

4. He is a confidant—an ironic one sometimes, but still a confidant. When he is with Amanda, he provokes her to reveal her paranoia, obviously not because he really did it in that situation, but because he wants the audience to see these qualities.

Another ancient convention of character, not limited to drama but especially noticeable there, is the use of a foil character. A foil is a function character whose personality contrasts with the main character to offset and clarify his qualities for the audience. In *Hamlet,* for example, Laertes, brother of Ophelia, son of Polonius, enemy of Hamlet, is a foil to Hamlet. Both men are in similar situations: Each is a young student, each loves Ophelia in his own way, each has had a father murdered, each desires revenge. But where Hamlet must be sure that his revenge is just, Laertes resorts to trickery, poison, and possible damnation to achieve his. Thus, the relative nobility of Hamlet is emphasized.

In *The Glass Menagerie*, Jim O'Connor is a foil to Tom. Jim is a success in his own eyes and in Amanda's, a kind of all-American boy, but his own definition of success is stupid and depressing. Tom is a failure to everyone in the play, but unlike Jim, a success to the audience.

CONVENTIONS OF PLOT

Plays often employ a narrative structure similar in some respects to many novels and short stories. But because of its long history, drama is more conventionalized in the kind of plot it uses. Through the years, drama has built its own conventions—some of these have developed into so-called schools of playwriting: sentimental drama, expressionism, impressionism, theater of the absurd, and many others. But basically there are two kinds of plot structures and therefore two kinds of drama: comedy and tragedy.

Comedy is associated with happy endings and tragedy with sad endings—a vaguely correct but nondefinitive description. Comedy is concerned less with individuals than with types, types involved in social situations. Comedy tends to be, then, a heavily plotted (although often episodic) form, since what happens rather than the persons involved is emphasized. A character in a comedy is usually trying desperately to adapt to a social situation; a tragic character is usually trying to establish his own identity or to live his life despite society's demands.

Comedy usually ends happily, with life triumphing over ruin and death—it ends with a beginning, that is, by suggesting a whole new story to come. "And they lived happily ever after" suggests a continuation, another story. Tragedy ends and ends finally, often with the death of the main character.

From these two forms have grown a series of subordinate forms. Each has its special conventions. Farce, for example, is highly exaggerated comedy wherein the playwright does not profess to maintain an illusion of reality. Melodrama is to tragedy what farce is to comedy: an exaggerated and therefore highly unreal rendering of a potentially tragic situation in which characters are so stereotyped and the plot so contrived that tragic characters seem almost funny. This is one of the paradoxes of the derivative forms: When the comic character becomes farcical, he loses much of the humor he would have had, and the audience almost despairs; comedy has taken on overtones of tragedy. When the tragic character becomes melodramatic, he loses much of the dignity he would have had; tragedy has taken on overtones of comedy.

To define tragedy and comedy in such limited fashion is sufficient for the purposes of this book. More specific explanation would involve numerous points that have been debated for two thousand years. For example, different ages have written different kinds of tragedy and have theorized differently about tragedy. The theory has usually been drawn from the practice. Aristotle defined tragedy as the imitation of a serious action of a man of noble but imperfect character, the action complete in itself, written poetically and dramatically, and aimed at arousing pity and fear in the audience so as to purge their emotions. His definition applies very well to the plays of Sophocles and Euripides, because those were the plays he was describing. But it cannot be applied to plays of all other ages. In the Middle Ages, tragedy was generally the case history of a man of high estate who fell from happiness to misery, usually to death. In the Renaissance, preeminently in Shakespeare, tragedy was sometimes Aristotelian (*King Lear*), sometimes not (*Macbeth*). During the late Renaissance, epic somehow became intertwined with tragedy—the characters of tragedy were often "Aristotelian," but the rest of the play's machinery was not. The eighteenth century eliminated even that resemblance by using middle-class heroes and heroines.

It cannot be said that writers since Aristotle have not been writing tragedy—it is just not tragedy as written in ancient Greece.

The same variety is observable in comedy. It is possible to distinguish two general types of comedy: high comedy (highly intellectualized, provoking laughter and scorn at the absurdity of men's conduct); and low comedy (slapstick). But this does not explain the variety of comic forms playwrights have developed through the centuries. Comedy during the Middle Ages mingled with romance and developed into romantic comedy, which involves uniting two (or four or six or eight) confused lovers despite outsiders' objections, tricks of fate, and their own indecisiveness. Whether this is high or low is debatable. Certainly high comedy is the "comedy of manners" developed in the seventeenth century that deals with sophisticated characters and satirizes the absurdities of both fashionable conduct and deliberate violations of decorum. Sentimental comedy, which appeared in the eighteenth century, has elements of high and low comedy in its use of impossibly upright main characters who suffer indignity, embarrassment, and ill-fortune with surprising control that is even more surprising since these characters are not meant to be ridiculous but lovable.

At least two other derivative forms deserve mention. The history play or chronicle is based on an actual historical character or event, and on it is superimposed the form of tragedy or comedy. The problem play deals with a specific, usually contemporary social problem and explores solutions to the problem. By involving a major character in the problem, the playwright often superimposes the form of tragedy, less often comedy, as in the history play. The major difference is that the history play deals with the actual past, the problem play with the fictional present, and that the problem play is always argumentative.

By these definitions, *A Raisin in the Sun* is a problem play. *Antigone* is a tragedy in the Aristotelian sense. *Hamlet* is a special kind of tragedy, a revenge play, that with some straining has been sometimes forced by critics into the Aristotelian framework. (As the questions following the play indicate, we believe this position requires rethinking.)

By these definitions, *The Glass Menagerie* is tragedy. But it also has aspects that require close study before one leaps to definition or assumes that one knows what that definition means in relation to this play. It is true, for example, that the plot line of the play can be condensed in this fashion: With her brother's help, Laura tries to break out of her glass case into the real world and fails. Tom salvages what he can from the ruins of his family life—his own identity. If Tom were trying to adjust to a social situation (the mode of comedy), he would stay with the family through its progressive degeneration. But Tom must be true to his own nature (the mode of tragedy) no matter how callous that action may make him seem. In tragedy, we all stand alone ultimately, as Tom does. Like his father before him, who fled Amanda, Tom flees the hopeless Laura. Tom is not happy in his choice; he has paid a heavy price for his freedom—a continual burden of guilt for what his conscience tells him is desertion.

But like most plot outlines and most statements of the problem in a play, this one leaves out a great deal. It is, for example, an open question at the end of the play whether or not Tom is the hero of the play. We still remember that it was Amanda who held the family together after the father left, who tried to find a normal outlet for Laura's frustrations, who attempted to assure the continuity of the family by prodding Tom, who coped with the economic facts of the Depression, who stayed with Laura when Tom left. Amanda, for all her illusions, is a realist, and Tom is not.

Who is the hero of *The Glass Menagerie?* The boy who ran away and is haunted by his flight? The pasteboard Jim, who gave advice and fled? The father, who also ran away? The center of the play is Laura, but Tom gets all the lines. So far as one can see, Tom, although he talks about lightning, finds none, nor does Jim or the father. What is the lightning that lights the world, and what character does it strike? One must ask himself: Whose play is this, Amanda's or Tom's?

Sophocles

Antigone

The Characters

ANTIGONE, *daughter of Œdipus, former banished king.*

ISMENE, *her elder sister.*

CREON, *their maternal uncle, now King of Thebes.*

HAIMON, *Creon's son, beloved of Antigone.*

EURYDICE, *the Queen, his mother, whose other son has just been killed defending Thebes from attack.*

TEIRESIAS, *the old and blind seer or prophet.*

A SENTRY *and* A MESSENGER

THE CHORUS *of fifteen Thebans, elder citizens, among whom the* CHORAGOS *is the leader.*

TIME.   *The legendary past of Ancient Greece.*

PLACE: *The walled city of Thebes with its seven gates.*

Prologue

(SCENE: *Before the palace of* CREON, *King of Thebes. A central double door and two lateral doors. A platform extends the length of the façade, and from this platform three steps lead down into the "orchestra," or chorus-ground. Time: Dawn of the day after the repulse of the Argive army from the assault on Thebes.*)

(·ANTIGONE *and* ISMENE *enter from the central door of the Palace.*)

ANTIGONE   Ismenê, dear sister,
You would think that we had already suffered enough
For the curse on Œdipus:
I cannot imagine any grief
That you and I have not gone through. And now—
Have they told you of the new decree of our King Creon?

ISMENE.   I have heard nothing: I know
That two sisters lost two brothers, a double death
In a single hour; and I know that the Argive army
Fled in the night; but beyond this, nothing.

ANTIGONE.   I thought so. And that is why I wanted you
To come out here with me. There is something we must do.

ISMENE.   Why do you speak so strangely?

ANTIGONE.   Listen, Ismenê: Creon buried our brother Eteoclês
With military honors, gave him a soldier's funeral,
And it was right that he should; but Polyneicês,
Who fought as bravely and died as miserably,—
They say that Creon has sworn
No one shall bury him, no one mourn for him,
But his body must lie in the fields, a sweet treasure
For carrion birds to find as they search for food.
That is what they say, and our good Creon is coming here
To announce it publicly; and the penalty—
Stoning to death in the public square!

                                                  There   it   is

And now you can prove what you are:
A true sister, or a traitor to your family.

ISMENE.   Antigonê, you are mad! What could I possibly do?

ANTIGONE.   You must decide whether you will help me or not.

ISMENE.   I do not understand you. Help you in what?

ANTIGONE.   Ismenê, I am going to bury him. Will you come?

ISMENE.   Bury him! You have just said the new law forbids it.

ANTIGONE.   He is my brother. And he is your brother, too.

ISMENE.   But think of the danger! Think what Creon will do!

ANTIGONE.   Creon is not strong enough to stand in my way.

ISMENE.   Ah sister!
Œdiput died, everyone hating him
For what his own search brought to light, his eyes
Ripped out by his own hand; and Iocastê died,
His mother and wife at once: she twisted the cords

That strangled her life; and our two brothers died,
Each killed by the other's sword. And we are left:
But oh, Antigonê,
Think how much more terrible than these
Our own death would be if we should go against Creon
And do what he has forbidden! We are only women,
We cannot fight with men, Antigonê!
The law is strong, we must give in to the law
In this thing, and in worse. I beg the Dead
To forgive me, but I am helpless: I must yield
To those in authority. And I think it is dangerous business
To be always meddling.

    ANTIGONE.   If that is what you think,
I should not want you, even if you asked to come.
You have made your choice, you can be what you want to be.
But I will bury him; and if I must die,
I say that this crime is holy: I shall lie down
With him in death, and I shall be as dear
To him as he to me.

                  It is the dead,
Not the living, who make the longest demands:
We die for ever. . . .

                  You may do as you like,
Since apparently the laws of the gods mean nothing to you.

    ISMENE.   They mean a great deal to me; but I have no strength
To break laws that were made for the public good.

    ANTIGONE.   That must be your excuse, I suppose. But as for me,
I will bury the brother I love.

    ISMENE.   Antigonê
I am so afraid for you!

    ANTIGONE.   You need not be:
You have yourself to consider, after all.

    ISMENE.   But no one must hear of this, you must tell no one!
I will keep it a secret, I promise!

    ANTIGONE.   Oh, tell it! Tell everyone!
Think how they'll hate you when it all comes out
If they learn that you knew about it all the time!

    ISMENE.   So fiery! You should be cold with fear.

    ANTIGONE.   Perhaps. But I am doing only what I must.

    ISMENE.   But can you do it? I say that you cannot.

ANTIGONE.   Very well: When my strength gives out, I shall do no
more.

ISMENE.   Impossible things should not be tried at all.

ANTIGONE.   Go away, Ismenê: I shall be hating you soon, and the
dead will too,
For your words are hateful. Leave me my foolish plan:
I am not afraid of the danger; if it means death,
It will not be the worst of deaths—death without honor.

ISMENE.   Go then, if you feel that you must. You are unwise,
But a loyal friend indeed to those who love you.

(*Exit into the Palace.* ANTIGONE *goes off, L.*)

(*Enter the* CHORUS.)

PÁRODOS

CHORUS.   (*strophe 1*)
Now the long blade of the sun, lying
Level east to west, touches with glory
Thebes of the Seven Gates. Open, unlidded
Eye of golden day! O marching light
Across the eddy and rush of Dircê's stream,
Striking the white shields of the enemy
Thrown headlong backward from the blaze of morning!

CHORAGOS.   Polyneicês their commander
Roused them with windy phrases,
He the wild eagle screaming
Insults above our land,
His wings their shields of snow,
His crest their marshalled helms.

CHORUS.   (*antistrophe 1*)
Against our seven gates in a yawning ring
The famished spears came onward in the night;
But before his jaws were sated with our blood,
Or pinefire took the garland of our towers.
He was thrown back; and as he turned, great Thebes—
No tender victim for his noisy power—
Rose like a dragon behind him, shouting war.

CHORAGOS.   For God hates utterly
The bray of bragging tongues;
And when he beheld their smiling,
Their swagger of golden helms,

The frown of his thunder blasted
Their first man from our walls.

    CHORUS.   (*strophe 2*)
We heard his shout of triumph high in the air
Turn to a scream; far out in a flaming arc
He fell with his windy torch, and the earth struck him.
And others storming in fury no less than his
Found shock of death in the dusty joy of battle.

    CHORAGOS.   Seven captains at seven gates
Yielded their clanging arms to the god
That bends the battle line and breaks it.
These two only, brothers in blood,
Face to face in matchless rage,
Mirroring each the other's death,
Clashed in long combat.

    CHORUS   (*antistrophe 2*)
But now in the beautiful morning of victory
Let Thebes of the many chariots sing for joy!
With hearts dancing we'll take leave of war:
Our temples shall be sweet with hymns of praise,
And the long night shall echo with our chorus.

    SCENE 1

    CHORAGOS.   But now at last our new King is coming:
Creon of Thebes, Menoiceus's son.
In this auspicious dawn of his reign
What are the new complexities
That shifting Fate has woven for him?
What is his counsel? Why has he summoned
The old men to hear him?

    (*Enter* CREON *from the Palace, C. He addresses the* CHORUS *from the top step.*)

    CREON.   Gentlemen: I have the honor to inform you that our Ship of State, which recent storms have threatened to destroy, has come safely to harbor at last, guided by the merciful wisdom of Heaven. I have summoned you here this morning because I know that I can depend upon you: Your devotion to King Laïos was absolute; you never hesitated in your duty to our late ruler Œdipus; and when Œdipus died, your loyalty was transferred to his children. Unfortunately, as you know, his two sons, the princes Eteoclês and Polyneicês, have killed each other in battle; and I, as the next in blood, have succeeded to the full power of the throne.

I am aware, of course, that no Ruler can expect complete loyalty from his subjects until he has been tested in office. Nevertheless, I say to you at the very outset that I have nothing but contempt for the kind of Governor who is afraid, for whatever reason, to follow the course that he knows is best for the State; and as for the man who sets private friendship above the public welfare—I have no use for him, either. I call God to witness that if I saw my country headed for ruin, I should not be afraid to speak out plainly; and I need hardly remind you that I would never have any dealings with an enemy of the people. No one values friendship more highly than I; but we must remember that friends made at the risk of wrecking our Ship are not real friends at all.

These are my principles, at any rate, and that is why I have made the following decision concerning the sons of Œdipus: Eteoclês, who died as a man should die, fighting for his country, is to be buried with full military honors, with all the ceremony that is usual when the greatest heroes die; but his brother Polyneicês, who broke his exile to come back with fire and sword against his native city and the shrines of his fathers' gods, whose one idea was to spill the blood of his blood and sell his own people into slavery—Polyneicês, I say, is to have no burial: No man is to touch him or say the least prayer for him; he shall lie on the plain, unburied; and the birds and the scavenging dogs can do with him whatever they like.

This is my command, and you can see the wisdom behind it. As long as I am King, no traitor is going to be honored with the loyal man. But whoever shows by word and deed that he is on the side of the State,—he shall have my respect while he is living, and my reverence when he is dead.

CHORAGOS.   If that is your will, Creon son of Menoiceus,
You have the right to enforce it: We are yours.

CREON.   That is my will. Take care that you do your part.

CHORAGOS.   We are old men: Let the younger ones carry it out.

CREON.   I do not mean that: The sentries have been appointed.

CHORAGOS.   Then what is it that you would have us do?

CREON.   You will give no support to whoever breaks this law.

CHORAGOS.   Only a crazy man is in love with death!

CREON.   And death it is; yet money talks, and the wisest
Have sometimes been known to count a few coins too many.

(*Enter* SENTRY *from L.*)

SENTRY.   I'll not say that I'm out of breath from running, King, because every time I stopped to think about what I have to tell you, I felt like going back. And all the time a voice kept saying, "You fool, don't you know you're walking straight into trouble?" and then another voice: "Yes,

but if you let somebody else get the news to Creon first, it will be even
worse than that for you!" But good sense won out, at least I hope it was
good sense, and here I am with a story that makes no sense at all; but I'll
tell it anyhow, because, as they say, what's going to happen's going to
happen, and—

CREON.   Come to the point. What have you to say?

SENTRY.   I did not do it. I did not see who did it. You must not punish
me for what someone else has done.

CREON.   A comprehensive defense! More effective, perhaps,
If I knew
its purpose. Come: What is it?

SENTRY.   A dreadful thing . . . I don't know how to put it—

CREON.   Out with it!

SENTRY.   Well, then; the dead man—
                                    Polyneicês—

> (*Pause.   The* SENTRY *is overcome, fumbles for words.*   CREON
> *waits impassively.*)

                                                out there—
                                                someone,—

New dust on the slimy flesh!

> (*Pause.   No sign from* CREON.)

Someone has given it burial that way, and
Gone. . . .

> (*Long pause.*   CREON *finally speaks with deadly control.*)

CREON.   And the man who dared do this?

SENTRY   I swear I
Do not know! You must believe me!

                                                Listen:

The ground was dry, not a sign of digging, no,
Not a wheeltrack in the dust, no trace of anyone.
It was when they relieved us this morning: and one of them,
The corporal, pointed to it.
                There it was,
The strangest—
        Look:
The body, just mounded over with light dust: You see?
Not buried really, but as if they'd covered it
Just enough for the ghost's peace. And no sign
Of dogs or any wild animal that had been there.

And then what a scene there was! Every man of us
Accusing the other: We all proved the other man did it,
We all had proof that we could not have done it.
We were ready to take hot iron in our hands,
Walk through fire, swear by all the gods,
It was not I!
I do not know who it was, but it was not I!

(CREON'S *rage has been mounting steadily, but the* SENTRY *is too in-*
tent upon his story to notice it.)

And then, when this came to nothing, someone said
A thing that silenced us and made us stare
Down at the ground: You had to be told the news,
And one of us had to do it! We threw the dice,
And the bad luck fell to me. So here I am,
No happier to be here than you are to have me:
Nobody likes the man who brings bad news.

    CHORAGOS.   I have been wondering, King: can it be that the gods have
done this?

    CREON   (*furiously*).   Stop.
Must you doddering wrecks
Go out of your heads entirely? "The gods!"
Intolerable!
The gods favor this corpse? Why? How had he served them?
Tried to loot their temples, burn their images,
Yes, and the whole State, and its laws with it!
Is it your senile opinion that the gods love to honor bad men?
A pious thought!—

                    No, from the very beginning
There have been those who have whispered together,
Stiff-necked anarchists, putting their heads together,
Scheming against me in alleys. These are the men,
And they have bribed my own guard to do this thing.
(*Sententiously*) Money!
There's nothing in the world so demoralizing as money.
Down go your cities,
Homes gone, men gone, honest hearts corrupted,
Crookedness of all kinds, and all for money!
(*To* SENTRY)

                          But you—!

I swear by God and by the throne of God,

The man who has done this thing shall pay for it!
Find that man, bring him here to me, or your death
Will be the least of your problems: I'll string you up
Alive, and there will be certain ways to make you
Discover your employer before you die;
And the process may teach you a lesson you seem to have missed:
The dearest profit is sometimes all too dear:
That depends on the source. Do you understand me?
A fortune won is often misfortune.

    SENTRY.   King, may I speak?

    CREON.   Your very voice distresses me.

    SENTRY.   Are you sure that it is my voice and not your conscience?

    CREON.   By God, he wants to analyze me now!

    SENTRY.   It is not what I say, but what has been done, that hurts you.

    CREON.   You talk too much.

    SENTRY.   Maybe; but I've done nothing.

    CREON.   Sold your soul for some silver: that's all you've done.

    SENTRY.   How dreadful it is when the right judge judges wrong!

    CREON.   Your figures of speech
May entertain you now; but unless you bring me the man,
You will get little profit from them in the end.

                    (*Exit* CREON *into the Palace.*)

    SENTRY.   "Bring me the man"—!
I'd like nothing better than bringing him the man!
But bring him or not, you have seen the last of me here.
At any rate, I am safe!

                    (*Exit* SENTRY.)

        ODE I

    CHORUS.   (*strophe 1*)
Numberless are the world's wonders, but none
More wonderful than man; the storm-gray sea
Yields to his prows, the huge crests bear him high;
Earth, holy and inexhaustible, is graven
With shining furrows where his plows have gone
Year after year, the timeless labor of stallions.

                            (*antistrophe 1*)
The lightboned birds and beasts that cling to cover,

The lithe fish lighting their reaches of dim water,
All are taken, tamed in the net of his mind;
The lion on the hill, the wild horse windy-maned,
Resign to him; and his blunt yoke has broken
The sultry shoulders of the mountain bull.

(*strophe 2*)

Words also, and thought as rapid as air,
He fashions to his good use; statecraft is his,
And his the skill that deflects the arrows of snow,
The spears of winter rain: From every wind
He has made himself secure—from all but one:
In the late wind of death he cannot stand.

(*antistrophe 2*)

O clear intelligence, force beyond all measure!
O fate of man, working both good and evil!
When the laws are kept, how proudly his city stands!
When the laws are broken, what of his city then?
Never may the anárchic man find rest at my hearth,
Never be it said that my thoughts are his thoughts.

SCENE 2

(*Reenter* SENTRY *leading* ANTIGONE.)

CHORAGOS.   What does this mean? Surely this captive woman
Is the Princess, Antigonê. Why should she be taken?

SENTRY.   Here is the one who did it! We caught her
In the very act of burying him.—Where is Creon?

CHORAGOS.   Just coming from the house.

(*Enter* CREON, *C.*)

CREON.   What has happened?
Why have you come back so soon?

SENTRY (*expansively*).   O King,
A man should never be too sure of anything:
I would have sworn
That you'd not see me here again: Your anger
Frightened me so, and the things you threatened me with;
But how could I tell then
That I'd be able to solve the case so soon?
No dice-throwing this time: I was only too glad to come!

Here is this woman. She is the guilty one:
We found her trying to bury him.
Take her, then; question her; judge her as you will.
I am through with the whole thing now, and glád óf it.

CREON.   But this is Antigonê! Why have you brought her here?

SENTRY.   She was burying him, I tell you!

CREON   (*severely*).   Is this the truth?

SENTRY.   I saw her with my own eyes. Can I say more?

CREON.   The details: Come, tell me quickly!

SENTRY.   It was like this:
After those terrible threats of yours, King,
We went back and brushed the dust away from the body.
The flesh was soft by now, and stinking,
So we sat on a hill to windward and kept guard.
No napping this time! We kept each other awake.
But nothing happened until the white round sun
Whirled in the center of the round sky over us:
Then, suddenly,
A storm of dust roared up from the earth, and the sky
Went out, the plain vanished with all its trees
In the stinging dark. We closed our eyes and endured it.
The whirlwind lasted a long time, but it passed;
And then we looked, and there was Antigonê!
I have seen
A mother bird come back to a stripped nest, heard
Her crying bitterly a broken note or two
For the young ones stolen. Just so, when this girl
Found the bare corpse, and all her love's work wasted,
She wept, and cried on heaven to damn the hands
That had done this thing.
                              And then she brought more dust
And sprinkled wine three times for her brother's ghost.
We ran and took her at once. She was not afraid,
Not even when we charged her with what she had done.
She denied nothing.
                              And this was a comfort to me,
And some uneasiness: For it is a good thing
To escape from death, but it is no great pleasure
To bring death to a friend.
                              Yet I always say
There is nothing so comfortable as your own safe skin!

CREON   (*slowly, dangerously*). And you, Antigonê?

You with your head hanging—do you confess this thing?

    ANTIGONE.   I do. I deny nothing.

    CREON   (*to* SENTRY). You may go.

                                                                 (*Exit* SENTRY.)

(*To* ANTIGONE.)   Tell me, tell me briefly:
Had you heard my proclamation touching this matter?

    ANTIGONE.   It was public. Could I help hearing it?

    CREON.   And yet you dared defy the law.

    ANTIGONE.   I dared.
It was not God's proclamation. That final Justice
That rules the world below makes no such laws.
Your edict, King, was strong,
But all your strength is weakness itself against
The immortal unrecorded laws of God.
They are not merely now: They were, and shall be,
Operative for ever, beyond man utterly.
I knew I must die, even without your decree:
I am only mortal. And if I must die
Now, before it is my time to die,
Surely this is no hardship: Can anyone
Living, as I live, with evil all about me,
Think Death less than a friend? This death of mine
Is of no importance; but if I had left my brother
Lying in death unburied, I should have suffered.
Now I do not.

                    You smile at me. Ah Creon,
Think me a fool, if you like; but it may well be
That a fool convicts me of folly.

    CHORAGOS.   Like father, like daughter: both headstrong, deaf to
    reason!
She has never learned to yield.

    CREON.   She has much to learn.
The inflexible heart breaks first, the toughest iron
Cracks first, and the wildest horses bend their necks
At the pull of the smallest curb.

                          Pride? In a slave?
This girl is guilty of a double insolence,
Breaking the given laws and boasting of it.
Who is the man here,
She or I, if this crime goes unpunished?
Sister's child, or more than sister's child,

Or closer yet in blood—she and her sister
Win bitter death for this!
(*To* SERVANTS.)   Go, some of you,
Arrest Ismenê.   I accuse her equally.
Bring her: You will find her sniffling in the house there.

Her mind's a traitor: crimes kept in the dark
Cry for light, and the guardian brain shudders;
But how much worse than this
Is brazen boasting of barefaced anarchy!

    ANTIGONE.   Creon, what more do you want than my death?

    CREON.   Nothing.
That gives me everything.

    ANTIGONE.   Then I beg you: Kill me.
This talking is a great weariness: Your words
Are distasteful to me, and
I am sure that mine
Seem so to you. And yet they should not seem so:
I should have praise and honor for what I have done.
All these men here would praise me
Were their lips not frozen shut with fear of you.

(*Bitterly*.)   Ah the good fortune of kings,
Licensed to say and do whatever they please!

    CREON.   You are alone here in that opinion.

    ANTIGONE.   No they are with me. But they keep their tongues in leash.

    CREON.   Maybe. But you are guilty, and they are not.

    ANTIGONE.   There is no guilt in reverence for the dead.

    CREON.   But Eteoclês—was he not your brother too?

    ANTIGONE.   My brother too.

    CREON.   And you insult his memory?

    ANTIGONE   (*softly*).   The dead man would not say that I insult it.

    CREON.   He would: For you honor a traitor as much as him.

    ANTIGONE.   His own brother, traitor or not, and equal in blood.

    CREON.   He made war on his country. Eteoclês defended it.

    ANTIGONE.   Nevertheless, there are honors due all the dead.

    CREON.   But not the same for the wicked as for the just.

    ANTIGONE.   Ah Creon, Creon.
Which of us can say what the gods hold wicked?

    CREON.   An enemy is an enemy, even dead.

    ANTIGONE.   It is my nature to join in love, not hate.

CREON   (*finally losing patience*).
Go join them, then; if you must have your love,
Find it in hell!

CHORAGOS.   But see, Ismenê comes:

(Enter ISMENE, *guarded.)*

Those tears are sisterly, the cloud
That shadows her eyes rains down gentle sorrow.

CREON.   You too, Ismenê,
Snake in my ordered house, sucking my blood
Stealthily—and all the time I never knew
That these two sisters were aiming at my throne!

Ismenê,
Do you confess your share in this crime, or deny it?
Answer me.

ISMENE.   Yes, if she will let me say so. I am guilty.

ANTIGONE   (*coldly*).   No, Ismenê. You have no right to say so.
You would not help me, and I will not have you help me.

ISMENE.   But now I know what you meant; and I am here
To join you, to take my share of punishment.

ANTIGONE.   The dead man and the gods who rule the dead
Know whose act this was. Words are not friends.

ISMENE.   Do you refuse me, Antigonê? I want to die with you:
I too have a duty that I must discharge to the dead.

ANTIGONE.   You shall not lessen my death by sharing it.

ISMENE.   What do I care for life when you are dead?

ANTIGONE.   Ask Creon. You're always hanging on his opinions.

ISMENE.   You are laughing at me. Why Antigonê?

ANTIGONE.   It's a joyless laughter, Ismenê.

ISMENE.   But can I do nothing?

ANTIGONE.   Yes. Save yourself. I shall not envy you.
There are those who will praise you; I shall have honor, too.

ISMENE.   But we are equally guilty!

ANTIGONE.   No more, Ismenê.
You are alive, but I belong to Death.

CREON   (*to the* CHORUS).   Gentlemen, I beg you to observe these
     girls:
One has just now lost her mind; the other,
It seems, has never had a mind at all.

ISMENE.   Grief teaches the steadiest minds to waver, King.

CREON.   Yours certainly did, when you assumed guilt with the guilty!

ISMENE.   But how could I go on living without her?

CREON.   You are.
She is already dead.

ISMENE.   But, your own son's bride!

CREON.   There are places enough for him to push his plow.
I want no wicked women for my sons!

ANTIGONE.   O dearest Haimon, how your father wrongs you!

CREON.   I've had enough of your childish talk of marriage!

CHORAGOS.   Do you really intend to steal this girl from your son?

CREON.   No; Death will do that for me.

CHORAGOS.   Then she must die?

CREON   (*ironically*).   You dazzle me.

—But enough of this talk!
(*To* GUARDS.)   You, there, take them away and guard them well:
For they are but women, and even brave men run
When they see Death coming.

(*Exeunt* ISMENE, ANTIGONE, *and* GUARDS.)

ODE II

CHORUS.   (*strophe 1*)
Fortunate is the man who has never tasted God's vengeance!
Where once the anger of heaven has struck, that house is shaken
Forever: Damnation rises behind each child
Like a wave cresting out of the black northeast,
When the long darkness under sea roars up
And bursts drumming death upon the wind-whipped sand.

                                                    (*antistrophe 1*)

I have seen this gathering sorrow from time long past
Loom upon Œdipus's children: generation from generation
Takes the compulsive rage of the enemy god.
So lately this last flower of Œdipus's line
Drank the sunlight! but now a passionate word
And a handful of dust have closed up all its beauty.

                                                    (*strophe 2*)

What mortal arrogance
Transcends the wrath of Zeus?

Sleep cannot lull him, nor the effortless long months
Of the timeless gods: But he is young forever,
And his house is the shining day of high Olympos.
 All that is and shall be,
 And all the past, is his.
No pride on earth is free of the curse of heaven.

(antistrophe 2)

 The straying dreams of men
 May bring them ghosts of joy:
But as they drowse, the waking embers burn them;
Or they walk with fíxed éyes, as blind men walk.
But the ancient wisdom speaks for our own time:
 Fate works most for woe
 With Folly's fairest show.
Man's little pleasure is the spring of sorrow.

 SCENE 3

 CHORAGOS.   But here is Haimon, King, the last of all your sons.
Is it grief for Antigonê that brings him here,
And bitterness at being robbed of his bride?

(Enter HAIMON.*)*

 CREON.   We shall soon see, and no need of diviners.
 —Son,
You have heard my final judgment on that girl:
Have you come here hating me, or have you come
With deference and with love, whatever I do?
 HAIMON.   I am your son, father. You are my guide.
You make things clear for me, and I obey you.
No marriage means more to me than your continuing wisdom.
 CREON.   Good. That is the way to behave: Subordinate
Everything else, my son, to your father's will.
This is what a man prays for, that he may get
Sons attentive and dutiful in his house,
Each one hating his father's enemies,
Honoring his father's friends. But if his sons
Fail him, if they turn out unprofitably,
What has he fathered but trouble for himself
And amusement for the malicious?
 So you are right
Not to lose your head over this woman.

Your pleasure with her would soon grow cold, Haimon,
And then you'd have a hellcat in bed and elsewhere.
Let her find her husband in Hell!
Of all the people in this city, only she
Has had contempt for my law and broken it.

Do you want me to show myself weak before the people?
Or to break my sworn word? No, and I will not.
The woman dies.

I suppose she'll plead "family ties." Well, let her.
If I permit my own family to rebel,
How shall I earn the world's obedience?
Show me the man who keeps his house in hand,
He's fit for public authority.
                                    I'll have no dealings
With law-breakers, critics of the government:
Whoever is chosen to govern should be obeyed—
Must be obeyed, in all things, great and small,
Just and unjust! O Haimon,
The man who knows how to obey, and that man only,
Knows how to give commands when the time comes.
You can depend on him, no matter how fast
The spears come: He's a good soldier, he'll stick it out.

Anarchy, anarchy! Show me a greater evil!
This is why cities tumble and the great houses rain down,
This is what scatters armies!
No, no: Good lives are made so by discipline.
We keep the laws then, and the law-makers,
And no woman shall seduce us. If we must lose,
Let's lose to a man, at least! Is a woman stronger than we?

    CHORAGOS.   Unless time has rusted my wits,
What you say, King, is said with point and dignity.

    HAIMON (*boyishly earnest*).   Father.
Reason is God's crowning gift to man, and you are right
To warn me against losing mine. I cannot say—
I hope that I shall never want to say—that you
Have reasoned badly. Yet there are other men
Who can reason, too; and their opinions might be helpful.
You are not in a position to know everything
That people say or do, or what they feel:

Your temper terrifies them—everyone
Will tell you only what you like to hear.
But I, at any rate, can listen; and I have heard them
Muttering and whispering in the dark about this girl.
They say no woman has ever, so unreasonably,
Died so shameful a death for a generous act:
"She covered her brother's body. Is this indecent?
"She kept him from dogs and vultures. Is this a crime?
"Death?—She should have all the honor that we can give her!"
This is the way they talk out there in the city.
You must believe me:
Nothing is closer to me than your happiness.
What could be closer? Must not any son
Value his father's fortune as his father does his?
I beg you, do not be unchangeable:
Do not believe that you alone can be right.
The man who thinks that,
The man who maintains that only he has the power
To reason correctly, the gift to speak, the soul—
A man like that, when you know him, turns out empty.
It is not reason never to yield to reason!
In flood time you can see how some trees bend,
And because they bend, even their twigs are safe,
While stubborn trees are torn up, roots and all.
And the same thing happens in sailing:
Make your sheet fast, never slacken, and over you go,
Head over heels and under; and there's your voyage.

Forget you are angry! Let yourself be moved!
I know I am young; but please let me say this:
The ideal condition
Would be, I admit, that men should be right by instinct;
But since we are all too likely to go astray,
The reasonable thing is to learn from those who can teach.

    CHORAGOS.   You will do well to listen to him, King,
If what he says is sensible. And you, Haimon,
Must listen to your father. Both speak well.

    CREON.   You consider it right for a man of my years and experience
To go to school to a boy?

    HAIMON.   It is not right
If I am wrong. But if I am young, and right,
What does my age matter?

CREON.   You think it right to stand up for an anarchist?

HAIMON.   Not at all. I pay no respect to criminals.

CREON.   Then she is not a criminal?

HAIMON.   The City would deny it, to a man.

CREON.   And the City proposes to teach me how to rule?

HAIMON.   Ah. Who is it that's talking like a boy now?

CREON.   My voice is the one voice giving orders in this City!

HAIMON.   It is no City if it takes orders from one voice.

CREON.   The State is the King!

HAIMON.   Yes, if the State is a desert.

(*Pause.*)

CREON.   This boy, it seems, has sold out to a woman.

HAIMON.   If you are a woman: My concern is only for you.

CREON.   So? Your "concern"! In a public brawl with your father!

HAIMON.   How about you, in a public brawl with justice?

CREON.   With justice, when all that I do is within my rights?

HAIMON.   You have no right to trample on God's right.

CREON   (*completely out of control*). Fool, adolescent fool! Taken in by a woman!

HAIMON.   You'll never see me taken in by anything vile.

CREON.   Every word you say is for her!

HAIMON   (*quietly, darkly*).   And for you.
And for me. And for the gods under the earth.

CREON.   You'll never marry her while she lives.

HAIMON.   Then she must die. But her death will cause another.

CREON.   Another?
Have you lost your senses? Is this an open threat?

HAIMON.   There is no threat in speaking to emptiness.

CREON.   I swear you'll regret this superior tone of yours!
You are the empty one!

HAIMON.   If you were not my father, I'd say you were perverse.

CREON.   You girlstruck fool, don't play at words with me!

HAIMON.   I am sorry. You prefer silence.

CREON.   Now, by God—!
I swear, by all the gods in heaven above us,
You'll watch it, I swear you shall!

(*To the* SERVANTS)   Bring her out!
Bring the woman out! Let her die before his eyes!
Here, this instant, with her bridegroom beside her!

HAIMON.   Not here, no; she will not die here, King.
And you will never see my face again.
Go on raving as long as you've a friend to endure you.

(*Exit* HAIMON.)

CHORAGOS.   Gone, gone.
Creon, a young man in a rage is dangerous!

CREON.   Let him do, or dream to do, more than a man can.
He shall not save these girls from death.

CHORAGOS.   These girls?
You have sentenced them both?

CREON.   No, you are right.
I will not kill the one whose hands are clean.

CHORAGOS.   But Antigonê?

CREON (*somberly*).   I will carry her far away
Out there in the wilderness, and lock her
Living in a vault of stone. She shall have food,
As the custom is, to absolve the State of her death.
And there let her pray to the gods of hell:
They are her only gods:
Perhaps they will show her an escape from death,
Or she may learn,
                 though late,
That pity shown the dead is pity in vain.

(*Exit* CREON.)

ODE III

CHORUS   (*strophe*)
Love, unconquerable
Waster of rich men, keeper
Of warm lights and all-night vigil
In the soft face of a girl:
Sea-wanderer, forest-visitor!
Even the pure Immortals cannot escape you,
And mortal man, in his one day's dusk,
Trembles before your glory.

(antistrophe)

Surely you swerve upon ruin
The just man's consenting heart,
As here you have made bright anger
Strike between father and son—
And none has conquered but Love!
A girl's glánce wórking the will of heaven:
Pleasure to her alone who mocks us,
Merciless Aphroditê.

SCENE 4

CHORAGOS *(as* ANTIGONE *enters guarded).*
But I can no longer stand in awe of this,
Nor, seeing what I see, keep back my tears.
Here is Antigonê, passing to that chamber
Where all find sleep at last.

ANTIGONE.   *(strophe 1)*
Look upon me, friends, and pity me
Turning back at the night's edge to say
Good-bye to the sun that shines for me no longer;
Now sleepy Death
Summons me down to Acheron, that cold shore:
There is no bridesong there, nor any music.
    CHORUS.   Yet not unpraised, not without a kind of honor,
You walk at last into the underworld;
Untouched by sickness, broken by no sword.
What woman has ever found your way to death?

ANTIGONE.   *(antistrophe 1)*
How often I have heard the story of Niobê,
Tantalos's wretched daughter, how the stone
Clung fast about her, ivy-close: And they say
The rain falls endlessly
And sifting soft snow; her tears are never done.
I feel the loneliness of her death in mine.
    CHORUS.   But she was born of heaven, and you
Are woman, woman-born. If her death is yours,
A mortal woman's, is this not for you
Glory in our world and in the world beyond?

ANTIGONE.   *(strophe 2)*

You laugh at me. Ah, friends, friends,
Can you not wait until I am dead? O Thebes,
O men many-charioted, in love with Fortune,
Dear springs of Dircê, sacred Theban grove,
Be witness for me, denied all pity,
Unjustly judged! and think a word of love
For her whose path turns
Under dark earth, where there are no more tears.

CHORUS.   You have passed beyond human daring and come at last
Into a place of stone where Justice sits.
I cannot tell
What shape of your father's guilt appears in this.

ANTIGONE.   *(antistrophe 2)*

You have touched it at last: that bridal bed
Unspeakable, horror of son and mother mingling:
Their crime, infection of all our family!
O Œdipus, father and brother!
Your marriage strikes from the grave to murder mine.
I have been a stranger here in my own land:
All my life
The blasphemy of my birth has followed me.

CHORUS.   Reverence is a virtue, but strength
Lives in established law: That must prevail.
You have made your choice,
Your death is the doing of your conscious hand.

ANTIGONE.   *(epode)*

Then let me go, since all your words are bitter,
And the very light of the sun is cold to me.
Lead me to my vigil, where I must have
Neither love nor lamentation; no song, but silence.

(CREON interrupts impatiently.)

CREON.   If dirges and planned lamentations could put off death,
Men would be singing for ever.
(To the SERVANTS*)*   Take her, go!
You know your orders: Take her to the vault
And leave her alone there. And if she lives or dies,
That's her affair, not ours: Our hands are clean.

ANTIGONE.   O tomb, vaulted bridebed in eternal rock,

Soon I shall be with my own again
Where Persephonê welcomes the thin ghosts underground:
And I shall see my father again, and you, mother,
And dearest Polyneicês—
                              dearest indeed
To me, since it was my hand
That washed him clean and poured the ritual wine:
And my reward is death before my time!
And yet, as men's hearts know, I have done no wrong,
I have not sinned before God. Or if I have,
I shall know the truth in death. But if the guilt
Lies upon Creon who judged me, then, I pray,
May his punishment equal my own.

    CHORAGOS.   O passionate heart,
Unyielding, tormented still by the same winds!

    CREON.   Her guards shall have good cause to regret their delaying.

    ANTIGONE.   Ah! That voice is like the voice of death!

    CREON.   I can give you no reason to think you are mistaken.

    ANTIGONE.   Thebes, and you my fathers' gods,
And rulers of Thebes, you see me now, the last
Unhappy daughter of a line of kings,
Your kings, led away to death. You will remember
What things I suffer, and at what men's hands,
Because I would not transgress the laws of heaven.
(To the GUARDS, *simply)* Come: Let us wait no longer.

                                  (Exit ANTIGONE, *L., guarded.)*

    ODE IV

    CHORUS.   *(strophe 1)*
All Danaê's beauty was locked away
In a brazen cell where the sunlight could not come:
A small room, still as any grave, enclosed her.
Yet she was a princess too,
And Zeus in a rain of gold poured love upon her.
O child, child,
No power in wealth or war
Or tough sea-blackened ships
Can prevail against untiring Destiny!

(antistrophe 1)

And Dryas's son also, that furious king,
Bore the god's prisoning anger for his bride:
Sealed up by Dionysos in deaf stone,
His madness died among echoes.
So at the last he learned what dreadful power
His tongue had mocked:
For he had profaned the revels,
And fired the wrath of the nine
Implacable Sisters that love the sound of the flute.

(strophe 2)

And old men tell a half-remembered tale
Of horror done where a dark ledge splits the sea
And a double surf beats on the gray shóres:
How a king's new woman, sick
With hatred for the queen he had imprisoned,
Ripped out his two sons' eyes with her bloody hands
While grinning Arês watched the shuttle plunge
Four times: Four blind wounds crying for revenge,

(antistrophe 2)

Crying, tears and blood mingled.—Piteously born,
Those sons whose mother was of heavenly birth!
Her father was the god of the North Wind
And she was cradled by gales,
She raced with young colts on the glittering hills
And walked untrammeled in the open light:
But in her marriage deathless Fate found means
To build a tomb like yours for all her joy.

SCENE 5

(*Enter blind* TEIRESIAS, *led by a boy. The opening speeches of* TEIRESIAS *should be in singsong contrast to the realistic lines of* CREON.)

TEIRESIAS.   This is the way the blind man comes, Princess, Princess, Lock-step, two heads lit by the eyes of one.

CREON.   What new thing have you to tell us, old Teiresias?

TEIRESIAS.   I have much to tell you: Listen to the prophet, Creon.

CREON.   I am not aware that I have ever failed to listen.

TEIRESIAS.   Then you have done wisely, King, and ruled well.

CREON.   I admit my debt to you. But what have you to say?

TEIRESIAS.   This, Creon: You stand once more on the edge of fate.

CREON.   What do you mean? Your words are a kind of dread.

TEIRESIAS.   Listen, Creon:
I was sitting in my chair of augury, at the place
Where the birds gather about me. They were all a-chatter,
As is their habit, when suddenly I heard
A strange note in their jangling, a scream, a
Whirring fury; I knew that they were fighting,
Tearing each other, dying
In a whirlwind of wings clashing. And I was afraid.
I began the rites of burnt-offering at the altar,
But Hephaistos failed me: instead of bright flame,
There was only the sputtering slime of the fat thigh-flesh
Melting: The entrails dissolved in gray smoke,
The bare bone burst from the welter. And no blaze!

This was a sign from heaven. My boy described it,
Seeing for me as I see for others.
I tell you, Creon, you yourself have brought
This new calamity upon us. Our hearths and altars
Are stained with the corruption of dogs and carrion birds
That glut themselves on the corpse of Œdipus's son.
The gods are deaf when we pray to them, their fire
Recoils from our offering, their birds of omen
Have no cry of comfort, for they are gorged
With the thick blood of the dead.
        O my son,
These are no trifles! Think: All men make mistakes,
But a good man yields when he knows his course is wrong,
And repairs the evil. The only crime is pride.
Give in to the dead man, then: Do not fight with a corpse—
What glory is it to kill a man who is dead?
Think, I beg you:
It is for your own good that I speak as I do.
You should be able to yield for your own good.

CREON.   It seems that prophets have made me their especial province.
All my life long
I have been a kind of butt for the dull arrows

Of doddering fortune-tellers!
                              No, Teiresias:
If your birds—if the great eagles of God himself
Should carry him stinking bit by bit to heaven,
I would not yield. I am not afraid of pollution:
No man can defile the gods.
                              Do what you will,
Go into business, make money, speculate
In India gold or that synthetic gold from Sardis,
Get rich otherwise than by my consent to bury him.
Teiresias, it is a sorry thing when a wise man
Sells his wisdom, lets out his words for hire!

    TEIRESIAS.   Ah Creon! Is there no man left
in the world—

    CREON.   To do what—Come, let's have the aphorism!

    TEIRESIAS.   No man who knows that wisdom outweighs any wealth?

    CREON.   As surely as bribes are baser than any baseness.

    TEIRESIAS.   You are sick, Creon! You are deathly sick!

    CREON.   As you say: It is not my place to challenge a prophet.

    TEIRIESIAS.   Yet you have said my prophecy is for sale.

    CREON.   The generation of prophets has always loved gold.

    TEIRESIAS.   The generation of kings has always loved brass.

    CREON.   You forget yourself! You are speaking to your King.

    TEIRESIAS.   I know it. You are a king because of me.

    CREON.   You have a certain skill; but you have sold out.

    TEIRESIAS.   King, you will drive me to words that—

    CREON.   Say them, say them!
Only remember: I will not pay you for them.

    TEIRESIAS.   No, you will find them too costly.

    CREON.   No doubt. Speak:
Whatever you say, you will not change my will.

    TEIRESIAS.   Then take this, and take it to heart!
The time is not far off when you shall pay back
Corpse for corpse, flesh of your own flesh.
You have thrust the child of this world into living night,
You have kept from the gods below the child that is theirs:
The one in a grave before her death, the other,
Dead, denied the grave. This is your crime:
And the Furies and the dark gods of Hell

Are swift with terrible punishment for you.
Do you want to buy me now, Creon?

                                        Not many days,

And your house will be full of men and women weeping,
And curses will be hurled at you from far
Cities grieving for sons unburied, left to rot
Before the walls of Thebes.
These are my arrows, Creon: They are all for you.
(*To* Boy) But come, child: Lead me home.
Let him waste his fine anger upon younger men.
Maybe he will learn at last
To control a wiser tongue in a better head.

                                        (*Exit* TEIRESIAS.)

CHORAGOS.   The old man has gone, King, but his words
Remain to plague us. I am old, too,
But I cannot remember that he was ever false.

CREON.   That is true. . . . It troubles me.
Oh it is hard to give in! but it is worse
To risk everything for stubborn pride.

CHORAGOS.   Creon: Take my advice.

CREON.   What shall I do?

CHORAGOS.   Go quickly: Free Antigonê from her vault
And build a tomb for the body of Polyneicês.

CREON.   You would have me do this?

CHORAGOS.   Creon, yes!
And it must be done at once: God moves
Swiftly to cancel the folly of stubborn men.

CREON.   It is hard to deny the heart! But I
Will do it: I will not fight with destiny.

CHORAGOS.   You must go yourself, you cannot leave it to others.

CREON.   I will go.
                    —Bring axes, servants:
Come with me to the tomb. I buried her, I
Will set her free. Oh, quickly!
My mind misgives—
The laws of the gods are mighty, and a man must serve them
To the last day of his life!

                                        (*Exit* CREON.)

PAEAN

CHORAGOS.   God of many names

CHORUS.   O   Iacchos
                                                                        son

of Cadmeian Sémelê
                         O born of the Thunder!
Guardian of the West
                         Regent
of Eleusis' plain
                         O Prince of Mænad Thebes
and the Dragon Field by rippling Ismenos:

(*antistrophe 1*)

CHORAGOS.   God of many names

CHORUS.   the flame of torches
flares on our hills

                                                  the nymphs of Iacchos

dance at the spring of Castalia:
from the vine-close mountain

                                                  come ah come in ivy:

Evohê evohê! sings through the streets of Thebes

(*strophe 2*)

CHORAGOS.   God of many names

CHORUS.   Iacchos of Thebes
heavenly Child

                                of Sémelê bride of the Thunderer!

The shadow of plague is upon us:

                                                                come

with clement feet

                                oh come from Parnasos

down the long slopes

                                across the lamenting water

(*antistrophe 2*)

CHORAGOS.   Iô Fire! Chorister of the throbbing stars!
O purest among the voices of the night!
Thou son of God, blaze for us!

CHORUS.   Come with choric rapture of circling Mænads
Who cry *Iô Iacche!*

God of many names!

ÉXODUS

(*Enter* MESSENGER, *L.*)

MESSENGER.   Men of the line of Cadmos, you who live
Near Amphion's citadel:

I cannot say
Of any condition of human life "This is fixed,
This is clearly good, or bad." Fate raises up,
And Fate casts down the happy and unhappy alike:
No man can foretell his Fate.

Take the case of Creon:

Creon was happy once, as I count happiness:
Victorious in battle, sole governor of the land,
Fortunate father of children nobly born
And now it has all gone from him! Who can say
That a man is still alive when his life's joy fails?
He is a walking dead man. Grant him rich,
Let him live like a king in his great house:
If his pleasure is gone, I would not give
So much as the shadow of smoke for all he owns.

CHORAGOS.   Your words hint at sorrow: What is your news for us?

MESSENGER.   They are dead. The living are guilty of their death.

CHORAGOS.   Who is guilty? Who is dead? Speak!

MESSENGER.   Haimon.
Haimon is dead; and the hand that killed him
Is his own hand.

CHORAGOS.   His father's or his own?

MESSENGER.   His own, driven mad by the murder his father had
done.

CHORAGOS.   Teiresias, how clearly you saw it all!

MESSENGER.   This is my news: You must draw what conclusions you
can from it.

CHORAGOS.   But look: Eurydicê, our Queen:
Has she overheard us?

(*Enter* EURYDICE *from the Palace, C.*)

EURYDICE.   I have heard something, friends:
As I was unlocking the gate of Pallas's shrine,

For I needed her help today, I heard a voice
Telling of some new sorrow. And I fainted
There at the temple with all my maidens about me.
But speak again: Whatever it is, I can bear it:
Grief and I are no strangers.

    MESSENGER.   Dearest Lady,
I will tell you plainly all that I have seen.
I shall not try to comfort you: What is the use,
Since comfort could lie only in what is not true?
The truth is always best.

                              I went with Creon
To the outer plain where Polyneicês was lying,
No friend to pity him, his body shredded by dogs.
We made our prayers in that place to Hecatê
And Pluto, that they would be merciful. And we bathed
The corpse with holy water, and we brought
Fresh-broken branches to burn what was left of it,
And upon the urn we heaped up a towering barrow
On the earth of his own land.

                              When we were done, we ran
To the vault where Antigonê lay on her couch of stone.
One of the servants had gone ahead,
And while he was yet far off he heard a voice
Grieving within the chamber, and he came back
And told Creon. And as the King went closer,
The air was full of wailing, the words lost,
And he begged us to make all haste. "Am I a prophet?"
He said, weeping, "And must I walk this road,
"The saddest of all that I have gone before?
"My son's voice calls me on. Oh quickly, quickly!
"Look through the crevice there, and tell me
"If it is Haimon, or some deception of the gods!"
We obeyed; and in the cavern's farthest corner
We saw her lying:
She had made a noose of her fine linen veil
And hanged herself. Haimon lay beside her,
His arms about her waist, lamenting her,
His love lost under ground, crying out
That his father had stolen her away from him.
When Creon saw him the tears rushed to his eyes
And he called to him: "What have you done, child? Speak to me.
"What are you thinking that makes your eyes so strange?

"Oh my son, my son, I come to you on my knees!"
But Haimon spat in his face. He said not a word,
Staring—

And suddenly drew his sword
And lunged. Creon shrank back, the blade missed; and the boy,
Desperate against himself, drove it half its length
Into his own side, and fell. And as he died
He gathered Antigonê close in his arms again,
Choking, his blood bright red on her white cheek.
And now he lies dead with the dead, and she is his
At last, his bride in the houses of the dead.

(*Exit* EURYDICE *into the Palace.*)

CHORAGOS.   She has left us without a word. What can this mean?

MESSENGER.   It troubles me, too; yet she knows what is best,
Her grief is too great for public lamentation,
And doubtless she has gone to her chamber to weep
For her dead son, leading her maidens in dirge.

CHORAGOS.   It may be so: But I fear this deep silence.

(*Pause.*)

MESSENGER.   I will see what she is doing. I will go in.

(*Exit* MESSENGER *into the Palace.*)
(*Enter* CREON *with attendants, bearing* HAIMON'S *body.*)

CHORAGOS.   But here is the King himself: Oh look at him,
Bearing his own damnation in his arms.

CREON.   Nothing you say can touch me any more.
My own blind heart has brought me
From darkness to final darkness. Here you see
The father murdering, the murdered son—
And all my civic wisdom!
Haimon my son, so young, so young to die,
I was the fool, not you; and you died for me.

CHORAGOS.   That is the truth; but you were late in learning it.

CREON.   This truth is hard to bear. Surely a god
Has crushed me beneath the hugest weight of heaven,
And driven me headlong a barbaric way
To trample out the thing I held most dear.
The pains that men will take to come to pain!

(*Enter* MESSENGER *from the Palace.*)

MESSENGER.   The burden you carry in your hands is heavy,
But it is not all: You will find more in your house.

CREON.   What burden worse than this shall I find there?

MESSENGER.   The Queen is dead.

CREON.   O port of death, deaf world,
Is there no pity for me? And you, Angel of evil,
I was dead, and your words are death again.
Is it true, boy? Can it be true?
Is my life dead? Has death bred death?

MESSENGER.   You can see for yourself.

(*The doors are opened, and the body of* EURYDICE
is disclosed within.)

CREON.   Oh pity!
All true, all true, and more than I can bear!
O my wife, my son!

MESSENGER.   She stood before the altar, and her heart
Welcomed the knife her own hand guided,
And a great cry burst from her lips for Megareus dead,
And for Haimon dead, her sons; and her last breath
Was a curse for their father, the murderer of her sons.
And she fell, and the dark flowed in through her closing eyes.

CREON.   O God, I am sick with fear.
Are there no swords here? Has no one a blow for me?

MESSENGER.   Her curse is upon you for the deaths of both.

CREON.   It is right that it should be. I alone am guilty.
I know it, and I say it. Lead me in,
Quickly, friends.
I have neither life nor substance. Lead me in.

CHORAGOS.   You are right, if there can be right in so much wrong.
The briefest way is best in a world of sorrow.

CREON.   Let it come,
Let death come quickly, and be kind to me.
I would not ever see the sun again.

CHORAGOS.   All that will come when it will; but we, meanwhile,
Have much to do. Leave the future to itself.

CREON.   All my heart was in that prayer!

CHORAGOS.   Then do not pray any more: The sky is deaf.

CREON.   Lead me away. I have been rash and foolish.
I have killed my son and my wife.
I look for comfort; my comfort lies here dead.
Whatever my hands have touched has come to nothing.
Fate has brought all my pride to a thought of dust.

(*As* CREON *is being led into the house, the* CHORAGOS *advances and
speaks directly to the audience.*)

CHORAGOS.   There is no happiness where there is no wisdom;
No wisdom but in submission to the gods.
Big words are always punished,
And proud men in old age learn to be wise.

Antigone

For Analysis

1. The conflicting forces are introduced immediately in this play.
   Antigone states her position and the reasons for it, the Chorus provides
   a brief exposition of how the situation developed, and Creon states
   his position and the reasons for it. At this point in the play, is it
   possible to say that either Creon or Antigone is wrong?
2. Why is it necessary that Creon not change his order? Why is it
   necessary that Antigone not abandon her resolve?
3. What in the conversation of Creon with the sentry indicates that the
   feelings of Polyneices's family never entered Creon's thoughts when
   he decided to forbid burial?
4. To what does the Chorus attribute the conflict in this play? To two
   strong-minded people? Or to something beyond that? Look carefully
   at the second ode.
5. What secondary conflict of principle springs up between Creon and
   Haimon?
6. What does Creon's releasing Ismene reveal of the effect of Haimon's
   arguments? Does the *way* Antigone is sentenced to die suggest more of
   that effect?
7. In the third ode, love is described in terms usually reserved for
   another emotion. What is that emotion? What does this foreshadow
   in the play?
8. Why does the messenger report the death of Haimon and Antigone?
   What convention of the Greek stage would Sophocles apparently
   violate if he were to show Creon's excavation or the lovers' deaths
   dramatically?
9. At the end, Creon first assumes all the blame himself and then blames
   Fate. Is this a reversal?
10. The play does not seem to be about Antigone or Creon. What is the
    play about?
11. After having read the entire play, go back and look at the choruses.
    What is their function? In what way are they an economical device?
    What would the twentieth-century playwright substitute for them?

William Shakespeare

Hamlet, Prince
of Denmark

Characters

CLAUDIUS, *King of Denmark.*

HAMLET, *son to the former, and nephew of the present King.*

POLONIUS, *lord chamberlain.*

HORATIO, *friend to Hamlet.*

LAERTES, *son to Polonius.*

VOLTIMAND,
CORNELIUS,
ROSENCRANTZ, } *courtiers.*
GUILDENSTERN,
OSRIC,

A GENTLEMAN.

A PRIEST.

MARCELLUS,
BERNARDO, } *officers.*

FRANCISCO, *a soldier.*

REYNALDO, *servant to Polonius.*

PLAYERS.

TWO CLOWNS, *grave-diggers.*

FORTINBRAS, *prince of Norway.*

A CAPTAIN.

ENGLISH AMBASSADORS.

GERTRUDE, *Queen of Denmark, and mother to Hamlet.*

OPHELIA, *daughter of Polonius.*

LORDS, *Ladies, Officers, Soldiers, Sailors, Messengers, and other Attendants.*

GHOST *of Hamlet's Father.*

541

Act I

SCENE I   ELSINORE, A PLATFORM BEFORE THE CASTLE

(FRANCISCO *at his post. Enter to him* BERNARDO.)

BERNARDO.   Who's there?

FRANCISCO.   Nay, answer me: Stand and unfold yourself.

BERNARDO.   Long live the king!

FRANCISCO.   Bernardo?

BERNARDO.   He.   5

FRANCISCO.   You come most carefully upon your hour.

BER.   'Tis now struck twelve; get thee to bed, Francisco.

FRANCISCO.   For this relief much thanks: 'Tis bitter cold,
And I am sick at heart.

BER.   Have you had quiet guard?

FRANCISCO.   Not a mouse stirring.   10

BERNARDO.   Well, good night.
If you do meet Horatio and Marcellus,
The rivals of my watch, bid them make haste.

FRAN.   I think I hear them. Stand, ho! Who is there?

(*Enter* HORATIO *and* MARCELLUS.)

HOR.   Friends to this ground.

MARCELLUS.   And liegemen to the Dane.   15

FRAN.   Give you good night.

MARCELLUS.   O, farewell, honest soldier:
Who hath relieved you?

FRANCISCO.   Bernardo has my place.
Give you good night.   [*Exit.*]

MARCELLUS.   Holla! Bernardo!

BERNARDO.   Say,—
What, is Horatio there?

HORATIO.   A piece of him.

BER.   Welcome, Horatio: welcome, good Marcellus.   20

MAR.   What, has this thing appear'd again tonight?

BERNARDO.   I have seen nothing.

MARCELLUS.   Horatio says 'tis but our fantasy,
And will not let belief take hold of him
Touching this dreaded sight, twice seen of us: 25

Therefore I have entreated him along
With us to watch the minutes of this night;
That, if again this apparition come,
He may approve our eyes and speak to it.

HOR.   Tush, tush, 'twill not appear.

BERNARDO.   Sit down awhile;   30
And let us once again assail your ears,
That are so fortified against our story,
What we two nights have seen.

HORATIO.   Well, sit we down,
And let us hear Bernardo speak of this.

BERNARDO.   Last night of all,   35
When yond same star that's westward from the pole
Had made his course to illume that part of heaven
Where now it burns, Marcellus and myself,
The bell then beating one—

MAR.   Peace, break thee off; look, where it comes again!   40

(*Enter* GHOST.)

BERNARDO.   In the same figure, like the king that's dead.

MARCELLUS.   Thou art a scholar; speak to it, Horatio.

BERNARDO.   Looks it not like the king? Mark it, Horatio.

HORATIO.   Most like: It harrows me with fear and wonder.

BER.   It would be spoke to.

MARCELLUS.   Question it, Horatio.   45

HORATIO.   What art thou that usurp'st this time of night,
Together with that fair and warlike form
In which the majesty of buried Denmark
Did sometimes march? By heaven I charge thee, speak!

MARCELLUS.   It is offended.

BERNARDO.   See, it stalks away!   50

HORATIO.   Stay! speak, speak! I charge thee, speak!

[*Exit* GHOST.]

MARCELLUS.   'Tis gone, and will not answer.

BER.   How now, Horatio! You tremble and look pale:
Is not this something more than fantasy?
What think you on't?   55

HORATIO.   Before my God, I might not this believe
Without the sensible and true avouch
Of mine own eyes.

MARCELLUS.   Is it not like the king?

HORATIO.   As thou art to thyself:
Such was the very armour he had on   60
When he the ambitious Norway combated;
So frown'd he once, when, in an angry parle,
He smote the sledded Polacks on the ice.
'Tis strange.

MAR.   Thus twice before, and jump at this dead hour,   65
With martial stalk hath he gone by our watch.

HOR.   In what particular thought to work I know not;
But, in the gross and scope of my opinion,
This bodes some strange eruption to our state.

MAR.   Good now, sit down, and tell me, he that knows,   70
Why this same strict and most observant watch
So nightly toils the subject of the land;
And why such daily cast of brazen cannon,
And foreign mart for implements of war;
Why such impress of shipwrights, whose sore task   75
Does not divide the Sunday from the week;
What might be toward, that this sweaty haste
Doth make the night joint-labourer with the day:
Who is't that can inform me?

HORATIO.   That can I;
At least, the whisper goes so. Our last king,   80
Whose image even but now appear'd to us,
Was, as you know, by Fortinbras of Norway,
Thereto prick'd on by a most emulate pride,
Dared to the combat; in which our valiant Hamlet—
For so this side of our known world esteem'd him—   85
Did slay this Fortinbras; who, by a seal'd compact,
Well ratified by law and heraldry,
Did forfeit,with his life, all those his lands
Which he stood seized of to the conqueror:
Against the which, a moiety competent   90
Was gaged by our king; which had return'd
To the inheritance of Fortinbras,
Had he been vanquisher; as, by the same covenant,
And carriage of the article design'd,
His fell to Hamlet. Now, sir, young Fortinbras,   95
Of unimproved mettle hot and full,
Hath in the skirts of Norway, here and there,

Shark'd up a list of lawless resolutes,
For food and diet, to some enterprise
That hath a stomach in't: Which is no other—   100
As it doth well appear unto our state—
But to recover of us, by strong hand
And terms compulsatory, those foresaid lands
So by his father lost: And this, I take it,
Is the main motive of our preparations,   105
The source of this our watch, and the chief head
Of this post-haste and romage in the land.

    BERNARDO.   I think it be no other but e'en so:
Well may it sort, that this portentous figure
Comes armed through our watch; so like the king   110
That was and is the question of these wars.

    HORATIO.   A mote it is to trouble the mind's eye
In the most high and palmy state of Rome,
A little ere the mightiest Julius fell,
The graves stood tenantless and the sheeted dead   115
Did squeak and gibber in the Roman streets:
As stars with trains of fire and dews of blood,
Disasters in the sun; and the moist star,
Upon whose influence Neptune's empire stands,
Was sick almost to doomsday with eclipse: 120
And even the like precurse of fierce events,
As harbingers preceding still the fates
And prologue to the omen coming on,
Have heaven and earth together demonstrated
Unto our climatures and countrymen.   125
But, soft, behold! Lo, where it comes again!

                                     (*Reenter* GHOST.)

I'll cross it, though it blast me. Stay, illusion!
If thou hast any sound, or use of voice,
Speak to me:
If there be any good thing to be done,   130
That may to thee do ease and grace to me,
Speak to me:
If thou art privy to thy country's fate,
Which, happily, foreknowing may avoid,
O, speak!   135
Or if thou hast uphoarded in thy life
Extorted treasure in the womb of earth,
For which, they say, you spirits oft walk in death,

[*Cock crows.*]

Speak of it: Stay, and speak! Stop it, Marcellus.

MARCELLUS.   Shall I strike at it with my partisan?   140

HORATIO.   Do, if it will not stand.

BERNARDO.   'Tis here!

HORATIO.   'Tis here!

MARCELLUS.   'Tis gone!   [*Exit* GHOST.]
We do it wrong, being so majestical,
To offer it the show of violence;
For it is, as the air, invulnerable,   145
And our vain blows malicious mockery.

BERNARDO.   It was about to speak when the cock crew.

HORATIO.   And then it started like a guilty thing
Upon a fearful summons. I have heard,
The cock, that is the trumpet to the morn,   150
Doth with his lofty and shrill-sounding throat
Awake the god of day; and at his warning,
Whether in sea or fire, in earth or air,
The extravagant and erring spirit hies
To his confine: And of the truth herein   155
This present object made probation.

MARCELLUS.   It faded on the crowing of the cock.
Some say that ever 'gainst that season comes
Wherein our Saviour's birth is celebrated,
The bird of dawning singeth all night long: 160
And then, they say, no spirit dare stir abroad;
The nights are wholesome; then no planets strike,
No fairy takes, nor witch hath power to charm;
So hallow'd and so gracious is the time.

HORATIO.   So have I heard, and do in part believe it.   165
But, look, the morn, in russet mantle clad,
Walks o'er the dew of yon high eastern hill:
Break we our watch up: And, by my advice,
Let us impart what we have seen tonight
Unto young Hamlet: For, upon my life,   170
This spirit, dumb to us, will speak to him:
Do you consent we shall acquaint him with it,
As needful in our loves, fitting our duty?

MARCELLUS.   Let's do't, I pray; and I this morning know
Where we shall find him most conveniently.   [*Exeunt.*]

175

[handwritten annotation in top margin]

Scene II   A Room of State in the Castle

(*Enter the* King, Queen, Hamlet, Polonius, Laertes, Voltimand, Cornelius, Lords, *and* Attendants.)

King.   Though yet of Hamlet our dear brother's death
The memory be green, and that it us befitted
To bear our hearts in grief, and our whole kingdom
To be contracted in one brow of woe;
Yet so far hath discretion fought with nature,   5
That we with wisest sorrow think on him,
Together with remembrance of ourselves.
Therefore our sometime sister, now our queen,
The imperial jointress to this warlike state,
Have we, as 'twere with a defeated joy,   10
With an auspicious and a dropping eye,
With mirth in funeral and with dirge in marriage,
In equal scale weighing delight and dole—
Taken to wife: Nor have we herein barr'd
Your better wisdoms, which have freely gone   15
With this affair along. For all, our thanks.
Now follows, that you know, young Fortinbras,
Holding a weak supposal of our worth,
Or thinking by our late dear brother's death
Our state to be disjoint and out of frame,   20
Colleagued with the dream of his advantage,
He hath not fail'd to pester us with message,
Importing the surrender of those lands
Lost by his father, with all bonds of law,
To our most valiant brother. So much for him.   25
Now for ourself, and for this time of meeting:
Thus much the business is: We have here writ
To Norway, uncle of young Fortinbras,—
Who, impotent and bed-rid, scarcely hears
Of this his nephew's purpose—to suppress   30
His further gait herein; in that the levies,
The lists and full proportions, are all made
Out of his subject: And we here dispatch
You, good Cornelius, and you, Voltimand,
For bearers of this greeting to old Norway;   35
Giving to you no further personal power
To business with the king, more than the scope

Of these delated articles allow.
Farewell, and let your haste commend your duty.

COR., VOL.   In that and all things will we show our duty.   40

KING.   We doubt it nothing: heartily farewell.

[*Exeunt* VOLTIMAND *and* CORNELIUS.]

And now, Laertes, what's the news with you?
You told us of some suit; what is't, Laertes?
You cannot speak of reason to the Dane,
And lose your voice: What wouldst thou beg, Laertes,   45
That shall not be my offer, not thy asking?
The head is not more native to the heart,
The hand more instrumental to the mouth,
Than is the throne of Denmark to thy father.
What wouldst thou have, Laertes?

LAERTES.   My dread lord,   50
Your leave and favour to return to France;
From whence though willingly I came to Denmark,
To show my duty in your coronation;
Yet now, I must confess, that duty done,
My thoughts and wishes bend again toward France,   55
And bow them to your gracious leave and pardon.

KING.   Have you your father's leave? What says Polonius?

POL.   He hath, my lord, wrung from me my slow leave
By laboursome petition, and at last
Upon his will I seal'd my hard consent: 60
I do beseech you, give him leave to go.

KING.   Take thy fair hour, Laertes; time be thine,
And thy best graces spend it at thy will!
But now, my cousin Hamlet, and my son—

HAM.   [*Aside*]   A little more than kin, and less than kind.   65

KING.   How is it that the clouds still hang on you?

HAMLET.   Not so, my lord; I am too much i' the sun.

QUEEN.   Good Hamlet, cast thy nighted colour off,
And let thine eye look like a friend on Denmark.
Do not forever with thy vailed lids   70
Seek for thy noble father in the dust:
Thou know'st 'tis common; all that live must die,
Passing through nature to eternity.

HAMLET.   Ay, madam, it is common.

QUEEN.   If it be,
Why seems it so particular with thee?   75

    HAMLET.   Seems, madam! nay, it is; I know not "seems."
'Tis not alone my inky cloak, good mother,
Nor customary suits of solemn black,
Nor windy suspiration of forced breath,
No, nor the fruitful river in the eye,   80
Nor the dejected haviour of the visage,
Together with all forms, moods, shapes of grief,
That can denote me truly: These, indeed, seem,
For they are actions that a man might play:
But I have that within which passeth show;   85
These but the trappings and the suits of woe.

    KING.   'Tis sweet and commendable in your nature, Hamlet,
To give these mourning duties to your father:
But, you must know, your father lost a father;
That father lost, lost his, and the survivor bound   90
In filial obligation for some term
To do obsequious sorrow: But to persever
In obstinate condolement, is a course
Of impious stubborness; 'tis unmanly grief:
It shows a will most incorrect to heaven,   95
A heart unfortified, a mind impatient,
An understanding simple and unschool'd:
For what we know must be, and is as common
As any the most vulgar thing to sense,
Why should we in our peevish opposition   100
Take it to heart? Fie! 'tis a fault to heaven,
A fault against the dead, a fault to nature,
To reason most absurd; whose common theme
Is death of fathers, and who still hath cried,
From the first corse till he that died today,   105
"This must be so." We pray you, throw to earth
This unprevailing woe, and think of us
As of a father. For let the world take note,
You are the most immediate to our throne;
And with no less nobility of love   110
Than that which dearest father bears his son,
Do I impart toward you. For your intent
In going back to school in Wittenberg,
It is most retrograde to our desire:

And we beseech you, bend you to remain   115
Here in the cheer and comfort of our eye,
Our chiefest courtier, cousin, and our son.

    QUEEN.   Let not thy mother lose her prayers, Hamlet:
I pray thee, stay with us; go not to Wittenberg.

    HAMLET.   I shall in all my best obey you, madam.   120

    KING.   Why, 'tis a loving and a fair reply:
Be as ourself in Denmark. Madam, come;
This gentle and unforced accord of Hamlet
Sits smiling to my heart: In grace whereof,
No jocund health that Denmark drinks today,   125
But the great cannon to the clouds shall tell,
And the king's rouse the heavens shall bruit again,
Re-speaking earthly thunder. Come away.

                          [Exeunt all except HAMLET.]

    HAMLET.   O, that this too too solid flesh would melt,
Thaw and resolve itself into a dew!   130
Or that the Everlasting had not fix'd
His canon 'gainst self-slaughter! O God! O God!
How weary, stale, flat and unprofitable
Seem to me all the uses of this world!
Fie on't! O, fie! 'Tis an unweeded garden,   135
That grows to seed; things rank and gross in nature
Possess it merely. That it should come to this!
But two months dead! nay, not so much, not two:
So excellent a king; that was, to this,
Hyperion to a satyr. So loving to my mother,   140
That he might not beteem the winds of heaven
Visit her face too roughly. Heaven and earth!
Must I remember? Why, she would hang on him,
as if increase of appetite had grown
By what it fed on: And yet, with a month—   145
Let me not think on't—Frailty, thy name is woman!—
A little month, or ere those shoes were old
With which she follow'd my poor father's body,
Like Niobe, all tears; why she, even she—
O God! a beast, that wants discourse of reason,   150
Would have mourn'd longer—married with my uncle,
My father's brother; but no more like my father
Than I to Hercules: within a month;
Ere yet the salt of most unrighteous tears

Had left the flushing in her galled eyes,   155
She married. O, most wicked speed!
It is not, nor it cannot come to, good:
But break, my heart, for I must hold my tongue!

(*Enter* HORATIO, MARCELLUS *and* BERNARDO.)

HOR.   Hail to your lordship!

HAMLET.   I am glad to see you well:
Horatio, or I do forget myself.   160

HORATIO.   The same, my lord, and your poor servant ever.

HAMLET.   Sir, my good friend; I'll change that name with you:
And what make you from Wittenberg, Horatio?
Marcellus?

MARCELLUS.   My good lord—   165

HAMLET.   I am very glad to see you. Good even, sir.
But what, in faith, make you from Wittenberg?

HORATIO.   A truant disposition, good my lord.

HAMLET.   I would not hear your enemy say so;
Nor shall you do mine ear that violence   170
To make it truster of your own report
Against yourself: I know you are no truant.
But what is your affair in Elsinore?
We'll teach you to drink deep ere you depart.

HORATIO.   My lord, I came to see your father's funeral.   175

HAMLET.   I pray thee, do not mock me, fellow-student;
I think it was to see my mother's wedding.

HORATIO.   Indeed, my lord, it follow'd hard upon.

HAMLET.   Thrift, thrift, Horatio! the funeral baked meats
Did coldly furnish forth the marriage tables.   180
Would I had met my dearest foe in heaven
Or ever I had seen that day, Horatio!
My father—methinks I see my father.

HORATIO.   Where, my lord?

HAMLET.   In my mind's eye, Horatio.

HORATIO.   I saw him once; he was a goodly king.   185

HAMLET.   He was a man, take him for all in all,
I shall not look upon his like again.

HORATIO.   My lord, I think I saw him yesternight.

HAMLET.   Saw who?

HOR.   My lord, the king your father.

HAMLET.   The king my father!   190

HORATIO.   Season your admiration for a while
With an attent ear, till I may deliver,
Upon the witness of these gentlemen,
This marvel to you.

HAMLET.   For God's love, let me hear.

HORATIO.   Two nights together had these gentlemen,   195
Marcellus and Bernardo, on their watch,
In the dead vast and middle of the night,
Been thus encounter'd. A figure like your father,
Armed at point, exactly, cap-a-pe,
Appears before them, and with solemn march   200
Goes slow and stately by them: Thrice he walk'd
By their oppress'd and fear-surprised eyes,
Within his truncheon's length; whilst they, distill'd
Almost to jelly with the act of fear,
Stand dumb, and speak not to him. This to me   205
In dreadful secrecy impart they did;
And I with them the third night kept the watch:
Where, as they had deliver'd, both in time,
Form of the thing, each word made true and good,
The apparition comes: I knew your father;   210
These hands are not more like.

HAMLET.   But where was this?

MARCELLUS.   My lord, upon the platform where we watch'd.

HAMLET.   Did you not speak to it?

HORATIO.   My lord, I did;
But answer made it none: Yet once methought
It lifted up its head, and did address   215
Itself to motion, like as it would speak:
But even then the morning cock crew loud,
And at the sound it shrunk in haste away,
And vanish'd from our sight.

HAMLET.   'Tis very strange.

HORATIO.   As I do live, my honour'd, 'tis true;   220
And we did think it writ down in our duty
To let you know of it.

HAMLET.   Indeed, indeed, sirs, but this troubles me.
Hold you the watch tonight?

MARCELLUS, BERNARDO.   We do, my lord.

HAMLET.   Arm'd, say you?   225

MARCELLUS, BERNARDO.   Arm'd, my lord.

HAMLET.   From top to toe?

MARCELLUS, BERNARDO.   My lord, from head to foot.

HAMLET.   Then saw you not his face?

HORATIO.   O, yes my lord; he wore his beaver up.

HAMLET.   What, look'd he frowningly?   230

HORATIO.   A countenance more in sorrow than in anger.

HAMLET.   Pale or red?

HORATIO.   Nay, very pale.

HAMLET.   And fix'd his eyes upon you?

HORATIO.   Most constantly.

HAMLET.   I would I had been there.

HORATIO.   It would have much amazed you.   235

HAMLET.   Very like, very like. Stay'd it long?

HORATIO.   While one with moderate haste might tell a hundred.

MARCELLUS, BERNARDO.   Longer, longer.

HORATIO.   Not when I saw't.

HAMLET.   His beard was grizzled? no?

HORATIO.   It was, as I have seen it in his life,   240
A sable silver'd.

HAMLET.   I will watch tonight;
Perchance 'twill walk again.

HORATIO.   I warrant it will.

HAMLET.   If it assume my noble father's person,
I'll speak to it, though hell itself should gape
And bid me hold my peace. I pray you all,   245
If you have hitherto conceal'd this sight,
Let it be tenable in your silence still;
And whatsoever else shall hap tonight,
Give it an understanding, but no tongue:
I will requite your loves. So, fare you well: 250
Upon the platform, 'twixt eleven and twelve,
I'll visit you.

ALL.   Our duty to your honour.

HAMLET.   Your loves, as mine to you: Farewell.

[*Exeunt* HORATIO, MARCELLUS, *and* BERNARDO.]

My father's spirit in arms! all is not well;
I doubt some foul play: Would the night were come!   255
Till then sit still my soul: Foul deeds will rise,
Though all the earth o'erwhelm them, to men's eyes.   [*Exit.*]

SCENE III   A ROOM IN POLONIUS'S HOUSE

(*Enter* LAERTES *and* OPHELIA.)

LAERTES.   My necessaries are embark'd: Farewell:
And, sister, as the winds give benefit,
And convoy is assistant, do not sleep,
But let me hear from you.

OPHELIA.   Do you doubt that?

LAERTES.   For Hamlet and the trifling of his favour,   5
Hold it a fashion and a toy in blood;
A violet in the youth of primy nature,
Forward, not permanent, sweet, not lasting,
The perfume and suppliance of a minute;
No more.

OPH.   No more but so?

LAERTES.   Think it no more: 10
For nature, crescent, does not grow alone
In thews and bulk; but, as this temple waxes,
The inward service of the mind and soul
Grows wide withal. Perhaps he loves you now,
And now no soil nor cautel doth besmirch   15
The virtue of his will: But you must fear,
His greatness weigh'd, his will is not his own:
For he himself is subject to his birth:
He may not, as unvalued persons do,
Carve for himself; for on his choice depends   20
The safety and health of this whole state;
And therefore must his choice be circumscribed
Unto the voice and yielding of that body
Whereof he is the head. Then if he says he loves you,
It fits your wisdom so far to believe it,   25
As he in his particular act and place
May give his saying deed; which is no further
Than the main voice of Denmark goes withal.
Then weigh what loss your honour may sustain,
If with too credent ear you list his songs;   30
Or lose your heart.

Fear it. Ophelia, fear it, my dear sister,
And keep you in the rear of your affection,
Out of the shot and danger of desire.
The chariest maid is prodigal enough,   35
If she unmask her beauty to the moon:
Virtue itself scapes not calumnious strokes:
The canker galls the infants of the spring,
Too oft before their buttons be disclosed;
And in the morn and liquid dew of youth   40
Contagious blastments are most imminent.
Be wary, then; best safety lies in fear:
Youth to itself rebels, though none else near.

    OPHELIA.   I shall the effect of this good lesson keep,
As watchman to my heart. But, good my brother,   45
Do not, as some ungracious pastors do,
Show me the steep and thorny way to heaven;
Whiles, like a puff'd and reckless libertine,
Himself the primrose path of dalliance treads,
And recks not his own rede.

    LAERTES.   O, fear me not.   50
I stay too long: But here my father comes.

                        (Enter POLONIUS.*)*

A double blessing is a double grace;
Occasion smiles upon a second leave.

    POLONIUS.   Yet here, Laertes! Aboard, aboard, for shame!
The wind sits in the shoulder of your sail,   55
And you are stay'd for.   There, my blessing with thee!

                    [*Laying his hand on* LAERTES' *head.*]

And these few precepts in thy memory
See thou character. Give thy thoughts no tongue,
Nor any unproportion'd thought his act.
Be thou familiar, but by no means vulgar.   60
The friends thou hast, and their adoption tried,
Grapple them to thy soul with hoops of steel;
But do not dull thy palm with entertainment
Of each new-hatch'd, unfledged comrade. Beware
Of entrance to a quarrel; but being in,   65
Bear't, that the opposed may beware of thee.
Give every man thine ear, but few thy voice:
Take each man's censure, but reserve thy judgment.
Costly thy habit as thy purse can buy,

But not express'd in fancy; rich, not gaudy: 70
For the apparel oft proclaims the man;
And they in France of the best rank and station
Are most select and generous, chief in that.
Neither a borrower nor a lender be:
For loan oft loses both itself and friend,   75
And borrowing dulls the edge of husbandry.
This above all: to thine ownself be true,
And it must follow, as the night the day,
Thou canst not then be faise to any man.
Farewell: my blessing season this in thee!   80

    LAERTES.   Most humbly do I take my leave, my lord.

    POLONIUS.   The time invites you; go, your servants tend.

    LAERTES.   Farewell, Ophelia; and remember well
What I have said to you.

    OPHELIA.   'Tis in my memory lock'd,
And you yourself shall keep the key of it.   85

    LAERTES.   Farewell.   [*Exit.*]

    POLONIUS.   What is't, Ophelia, he hath said to you?

    OPH.   So please you, something touching the Lord Hamlet.

    POLONIUS.   Marry, well bethought:
'Tis told me, he hath very oft of late   90
Given private time to you, and you yourself
Have of your audience been most free and bounteous:
If it be so—as so 'tis put on me,
And that in way of caution—I must tell you,
You do not understand yourself so clearly   95
As it behoves my daughter and your honour.
What is between you? Give me up the truth.

    OPHELIA.   He hath, my lord, of late made many tenders
Of his affection to me.

    POL.   Affection! Pooh! You speak like a green girl,   100
Unsifted in such perilous circumstance.
Do you believe his tenders, as you call them?

    OPHELIA.   I do not know, my lord, what I should think.

    POLONIUS.   Marry, I'll teach you: Think yourself a baby,
That you have ta'en these tenders for true pay,   105
Which are not sterling. Tender yourself more dearly;
Or—not to crack the wind of the poor phrase,
Running it thus—you'll tender me a fool.

OPHELIA.   My lord, he hath importuned me with love
In honourable fashion.   110

POLONIUS.   Ay, fashion you may call it; go to, go to.

OPHELIA.   And hath given countenance to his speech, my lord,
With almost all the holy vows of heaven.

POLONIUS.   Ay, springes to catch woodcocks. I do know,
When the blood burns, how prodigal the soul   115
Lends the tongue vows: These blazes, daughter,
Giving more light than heat, extinct in both,
Even in their promise, as it is a-making,
You must not take for fire. From this time
Be somewhat scanter of your maiden presence;   120
Set your entreatments at a higher rate
Than a command to parley. For Lord Hamlet,
Believe so much in him, that he is young,
And with a larger tether may he walk
Than may be given you: In few, Ophelia,   125
Do not believe his vows; for they are brokers,
Not of that dye which their investments show,
But mere implorators of unholy suits,
Breathing like sanctified and pious bonds,
The better to beguile. This is for all: 130
I would not, in plain terms, from this time forth,
Have you so slander any moment leisure
As to give words or talk with the Lord Hamlet.
Look to't, I charge you: Come your ways.

OPHELIA.   I shall obey, my lord.   135

[*Exeunt.*]

SCENE IV   THE PLATFORM BEFORE THE CASTLE

(*Enter* HAMLET, HORATIO, *and* MARCELLUS.)

HAMLET.   The air bites shrewdly; it is very cold.

HORATIO.   It is a nipping and an eager air.

HAMLET.   What hour now?

HORATIO.   I think it lacks of twelve.

MARCELLUS.   No, it is struck.

HORATIO.   Indeed? I heard it not: Then it draws near the season   5
Wherein the spirit held his wont to walk.

[*A flourish of trumpets, and ordnance shot off, within.*]
What does this mean, my lord?

HAMLET.   The king doth wake tonight and takes his rouse,
Keeps wassail, and the swaggering up-spring reels;
And, as he drains his draughts of Rhenish down,   10
The kettle-drum and trumpet thus bray out
The triumph of his pledge.

HORATIO.   Is it a custom?

HAMLET.   Ay, marry, is't:
But to my mind, though I am native here
And to the manner born, it is a custom   15
More honour'd in the breach than the observance.
This heavy-headed revel east and west
Makes us traduced and tax'd of other nations:
They clepe us drunkards, and with swinish phrase
Soil our addition; and indeed it takes   20
From our achievements, though perform'd at height,
The pith and marrow of our attribute.
So, oft it chances in particular men,
That for some vicious mole of nature in them,
As, in their birth—wherein they are not guilty,   25
Since nature cannot choose his origin—
By the o'ergrowth of some complexion,
Oft breaking down the pales and forts of reason,
Or by some habit that too much o'er-leavens
The form of plausive manners; that these men,   30
Carrying, I say, the stamp of one defect,
Being nature's livery, or fortune's star—
Their virtues else—be they as pure as grace,
As infinite as man may undergo—
Shall in the general censure take corruption   35
From that particular fault: The dram of eale
Doth all the noble substance of a doubt
To his own scandal.

HORATIO.   Look, my lord, it comes!

(*Enter* GHOST.)

HAMLET.   Angels and ministers of grace defend us!
Be thou a spirit of health or goblin damn'd,   40
Bring with thee airs from heaven or blasts from hell,
Be thy intents wicked or charitable,
Thou comest in such a questionable shape,
That I will speak to thee: I'll call thee Hamlet,
King, father, royal Dane: O, answer me!   45

Let me not burst in ignorance; but tell
Why thy canonized bones, hearsed in death,
Have burst their cerements; why the sepulchre,
Wherein we saw thee quietly inurn'd,
Hath oped his ponderous and marble jaws   50
To cast thee up again! What may this mean,
That thou, dead corse, again in complete steel
Revisit'st thus the glimpses of the moon,
Making night hideous; and we fools of nature
So horridly to shake our disposition   55
With thoughts beyond the reaches of our souls?
Say, why is this? Wherefore? What should we do?

[GHOST *beckons* HAMLET.]

HORATIO.   It beckons you to go away with it,
As if it some impartment did desire.
To you alone.

MARCELLUS.   Look, with what courteous action   60
It waves you to a more removed ground:
But do not go with it.

HORATIO.   No, by no means.

HAMLET.   It will not speak; then I will follow it.

HORATIO.   Do not, my lord.

HAMLET.   Why, what should be the fear?   65
I do not set my life at a pin's fee;
And for my soul, what can it do to that,
Being a thing immortal as itself?
It waves me forth again; I'll follow it.

HORATIO.   What if it tempt you toward the flood, my lord,
Or to the dreadful summit of the cliff   70
That beetles o'er his base into the sea,
And there assume some other horrible form,
Which might deprive your sovereignty of reason,
And draw you into madness? Think of it:
The very place puts toys of desperation,   75
Without more motive, into every brain
That looks so many fathoms to the sea
And hears it roar beneath.

HAMLET.   It waves me still.
Go on; I'll follow thee.

MAR.   You shall not go, my lord.

HAMLET. Hold off your hands. 80

HORATIO. Be ruled; you shall not go.

HAMLET. My fate cries out,
And makes each petty artery in this body
As hardy as the Nemean lion's nerve.
Still am I call'd: Unhand me, gentlemen;
By heaven, I'll make a ghost of him that lets me: 85
I say, away! Go on; I'll follow thee.

[*Exeunt* GHOST *and* HAMLET.]

HORATIO. He waxes desperate with imagination.

MARCELLUS. Let's follow; 'tis not fit thus to obey him.

HORATIO. Have after. To what issue will this come?

MAR. Something is rotten in the state of Denmark. 90

HORATIO. Heaven will direct it.

MARCELLUS. Nay, let's follow him.

[*Exeunt.*]

SCENE V   ANOTHER PART OF THE PLATFORM

(*Enter* GHOST *and* HAMLET.)

HAMLET. Where wilt thou lead me? Speak; I'll go no further.

GHOST. Mark me.

HAMLET. I will.

GHOST. My hour is almost come,
When I to sulphurous and tormenting flames
Must render up myself.

HAMLET. Alas, poor ghost!

GHOST. Pity me not, but lend thy serious hearing 5
To what I shall unfold.

HAMLET. Speak; I am bound to hear.

GHOST. So art thou to revenge, when thou shalt hear.

HAMLET. What?

GHOST. I am thy father's spirit;
Doom'd for a certain term to walk the night, 10
And for the day confined to fast in fires,
Till the foul crimes done in my days of nature
Are burnt and purged away. But that I am forbid
To tell the secrets of my prison-house,

I could a tale unfold whose lightest word   15
Would harrow up thy soul, freeze thy young blood,
Make thy two eyes, like stars, start from their spheres,
Thy knotted and combined locks to part,
And each particular hair to stand an end,
Like quills upon the fretful porpentine: 20
But this eternal blazon must not be
To ears of flesh and blood. List, list, O, list!
If thou didst ever thy dear father love—

    HAMLET.   O God!

    GHOST.   Revenge his foul and most unnatural murder.   25

    HAMLET.   Murder!

    GHOST.   Murder most foul, as in the best it is;
But this most foul, strange and unnatural.

    HAMLET.   Haste me to know't, that I, with wings as swift
As meditation or the thoughts of love,   30
May sweep to my revenge.

    GHOST.   I find thee apt;
And duller shouldst thou be than the fat weed
That roots itself in ease on Lethe wharf,
Wouldst thou not stir in this. Now, Hamlet, hear:
'Tis given out that, sleeping in my orchard,   35
A serpent stung me; so the whole ear of Denmark
Is by a forged process of my death
Rankly abused: But know, thou noble youth,
The serpent that did sting thy father's life
Now wears his crown.

    HAMLET.   O my prophetic soul!   40
My uncle!

    GHOST.   Ay, that incestuous, that adulterate beast,
With witchcraft of his wit, with traitorous gifts—
O wicked wit and gifts, that have the power
So to seduce!—won to his shameful lust   45
The will of my most seeming-virtuous queen:
O Hamlet, what a falling-off was there!
From me, whose love was of that dignity,
That it went hand in hand even with the vow
I made to her in marriage; and to decline   50
Upon a wretch, whose natural gifts were poor
To those of mine!
But virtue, as it never will be moved,

Though lewdness court it in a shape of heaven,
So lust, though to a radiant angel link'd,   55
Will sate itself in a celestial bed,
And prey on garbage.
But, soft! Methinks I scent the morning air;
Brief let me be. Sleeping within my orchard,
My custom always in the afternoon,   60
Upon my secure hour thy uncle stole,
With juice of cursed hebenon in a vial,
And in the porches of mine ears did pour
The leperous distilment; whose effect
Holds such an enmity with blood of man,   65
That swift as quicksilver it courses through
The natural gates and alleys of the body,
And with a sudden vigour it doth posset
And curd, like eager droppings into milk,
The thin and wholesome blood: So did it mine;   70
And a most instant tetter bark'd about,
Most lazar-like, with vile and loathsome crust
All my smooth body.
Thus was I, sleeping, by a brother's hand
Of life, of crown, of queen, at once dispatch'd: 75
Cut off even in the blossoms of my sin,
Unhousel'd, disappointed, unaneled;
No reckoning made, but sent to my account
With all my imperfections on my head:
O, horrible! O, horrible! most horrible!   80
If thou hast nature in thee, bear it not;
Let not the royal bed of Denmark be
A couch for luxury and damned incest.
But, howsoever thou pursuest this act,
Taint not thy mind, nor let thy soul contrive   85
Against thy mother aught: Leave her to heaven,
And to those thorns that in her bosom lodge,
To prick and sting her. Fare thee well at once!
The glow-worm shows the matin to be near,
And gins to pale his uneffectual fire: 90
Adieu, adieu, adieu! Remember me.

                                                                    [*Exit.*]

   HAMLET.   O all you host of heaven! O earth! What else?
And shall I couple hell? O, fie! Hold, hold my heart;
And you, my sinews, grow not instant old,
But bear me stiffly up. Remember thee!   95

Ay, thou poor ghost, while memory holds a seat
In this distracted globe. Remember thee!
Yea, from the table of my memory
I'll wipe away all trivial fond records,
All saws of books, all forms, all pressures past,   100
That youth and observation copied there;
And thy commandment all alone shall live
Within the book and volume of my brain,
Unmix'd with baser matter: Yes, by heaven!
O most pernicious woman!   105
O villain, villain, smiling, damned villain!
My tables—meet it is I set it down,
That one may smile, and smile, and be a villain;
At least I'm sure it may be so in Denmark: [*Writing.*]
So, uncle, there you are. Now to my word;   110
It is, "Adieu, adieu! remember me:"
I have sworn't.

Hor. ⎫
Mar. ⎬ [*Within*]   My lord, my lord!

Marcellus.   Lord Hamlet!

Horatio.   Heaven secure him!

Hamlet.   So be it!

Horatio.   Illo, ho, ho, my lord!   115

Hamlet.   Hillo, ho, ho, boy! come, bird, come.

(*Enter* Horatio *and* Marcellus.)

Mar.   How is't, my noble lord?

Horatio.   What news, my lord?

Hamlet.   O, wonderful!

Horatio.   Good my lord, tell it.

Hamlet.   No; you'll reveal it.   120

Horatio.   Not I, my lord, by heaven.

Marcellus.   Nor I, my lord.

Hamlet.   How say you, then; would heart of man once think it?
But you'll be secret?

Horatio, Marcellus.   Ay, by heaven, my lord.

Hamlet.   There's ne'er a villain dwelling in all Denmark
But he's an arrant knave.

Hor.   There needs no ghost, my lord, come from the grave   125
To tell us this.

HAMLET.   Why, right! You are i' the right;
And so, without more circumstance at all,
I hold it fit that we shake hands and part:
You, as your business and desire shall point you,
For every man hath business and desire,   130
Such as it is; and for mine own poor part,
Look you, I'll go pray.

HOR.   These are but wild and whirling words, my lord.

HAMLET.   I'm sorry they offend you, heartily;
Yes, faith, heartily.

HORATIO.   There's no offence, my lord.   135

HAMLET.   Yes, by Saint Patrick, but there is, Horatio,
And much offence too. Touching this vision here,
It is an honest ghost, that let me tell you:
For your desire to know what is between us,
O'ermaster't as you may. And now, good friends,   140
As you are friends, scholars and soldiers,
Give me one poor request.

HORATIO.   What is't, my lord? We will.

HAM.   Never make known what you have seen tonight.

HOT., MAR.   My lord, we will not.

HAMLET.   Nay, but swear't.

HORATIO.   In faith,   145
My lord, not I.

MARCELLUS.   Nor I, my lord, in faith.

HAM.   Upon my sword.

MARCELLUS.   We have sworn, my lord, already.

HAMLET.   Indeed, upon my sword, indeed.

GHOST.   [*Beneath*]   Swear.

HAMLET.   Ah, ha, boy! say'st thou so? art thou there,
true-penny?—   150
Come on—you hear this fellow in the cellarage—
Consent to swear.

HORATIO.   Propose the oath, my lord.

HAMLET.   Never to speak of this that you have seen,
Swear by my sword.

GHOST.   [*Beneath*]   Swear.   155

HAMLET.   *Hic et ubique?* Then we'll shift our ground.
Come hither, gentlemen,

And lay your hands again upon my sword:
Never to speak of this that you have heard,
Swear by my sword.   160

GHOST.   [*Beneath*]   Swear.

HAM.   Well said, old mole! Canst work i' the earth so fast?
A worthy pioner! Once more remove, good friends.

HORATIO.   O day and night, but this is wondrous strange!

HAMLET.   And therefore as a stranger give it welcome.   165
There are more things in heaven and earth, Horatio,
Than are dreamt of in your philosophy.
But come;
Here, as before, never, so help you mercy,
How strange or odd soe'er I bear myself—   170
As I, perchance, hereafter shall think meet
To put an antic disposition on—
That you, at such times seeing me, never shall,
With arms encumber'd thus, or this head-shake,
Or by pronouncing of some doubtful phrase,   175
As 'Well, well, we know," or "We could, an if we would,"
Or "If we list to speak," or "There be, an if they might,"
Or such ambiguous giving out, to note
That you know aught of me: This not to do,
So grace and mercy at your most need help you,   180
Swear.

GHOST.   [*Beneath*]   Swear.

HAMLET.   Rest, rest, perturbed spirit! [*They swear*]   So, gentlemen,
With all my love I do commend me to you:
And what so poor a man as Hamlet is   185
May do to express his love and friending to you,
God willing, shall not lack. Let us go in together;
And still your fingers on your lips, I pray.
The time is out of joint: O cursed spite,
That ever I was born to set it right!   190
Nay, come, let's go together.

                                                        [*Exeunt.*]

Act II

SCENE I   A ROOM IN POLONIUS'S HOUSE

                                        (*Enter* POLONIUS *and* REYNALDO.)

POL.   Give him this money and these notes, Reynaldo.

REYNALDO.   I will, my lord.

POL.   You shall do marvellous wisely, good Reynaldo,
Before you visit him, to make inquiry
Of his behaviour.

REYNALDO.   My lord, I did intend it.   5

POL.   Marry, well said; very well said. Look you, sir,
Inquire me first what Danskers are in Paris;
And how, and who, what means, and where they keep,
What company, at what expense; and finding,
By this encompassment and drift of question,   10
That they do know my son, come you more nearer
Than your particular demands will touch it:
Take you, as 'twere, some distant knowledge of him;
As thus, "I know his father and his friends,
And in part him;" do you mark this, Reynaldo?   15

REYNALDO.   Ay, very well, my lord.

POL.   "And in part him; but," you may say, "not well:
But, if't be he I mean, he's very wild;
Addicted so and so;" and there put on him
What forgeries you please; marry, none so rank   20
As may dishonour him; take heed of that;
But, sir, such wanton, wild and usual slips
As are companions noted and most known
To youth and liberty.

REYNALDO.   As gaming, my lord.

POLONIUS.   Ay, or drinking, fencing, swearing, quarrelling: 25
You may go so far; but breathe his faults so quaintly,
That they may seem the taints of liberty,
The flash and outbreak of a fiery mind,
A savageness in unreclaimed blood,
Of general assault.

REYNALDO.   But, my good lord—   30

POLONIUS.   Wherefore should you do this?

REYNALDO.   Ay, my lord,
I would know that.

POLONIUS.   Marry, sir, here's my drift;
And I believe it is a fetch of warrant:
You laying these slight sullies on my son,
As 'twere a thing a little soil'd i' the working,   35
Mark you,
Your party in converse, him you would sound,

Having ever seen in the prenominate crimes
The youth you breathe of guilty, be assured
He closes with you in this consequence;   40
"Good sir," or so, or "friend," or "gentleman,"
According to the phrase or the addition.
Of man and country.

    REYNALDO.   Very good, my lord.

    POLONIUS.   And then, sir, does he this—he does—
What was I about to say? By the mass, I was   45
About to say something: Where did I leave?

    REYNALDO.   At "closes in the consequence,"
At "friend or so," and "gentleman."

    POLONIUS.   At "closes in the consequence," ay, marry;
He closes with you thus; "I know the gentleman;   50
I saw him yesterday, or t'other day,
Or then, or then; with such, or such; and, as you say.
There was he gaming, there o'ertook in's rouse,
There falling out at tennis." Or perchance,
"I saw him enter such a house of sale."   55
See you now;
Your bait of falsehood takes this carp of truth:
And thus do we of wisdom and of reach,
With windlasses and with assays of bias,
By indirections find directions out: 60
So by my former lecture and advice
Shall you my son. You have me, have you not?

   REY.   My lord, I have.

   POLONIUS.   God be wi' you! fare you well.

   REYNALDO.   Good my lord!

   POLONIUS.   Observe his inclination in yourself.   65

   REYNALDO.   I shall, my lord.

   POLONIUS.   And let him ply his music.

   REYNALDO.   Well, my lord.

  POL.   Farewell!   [*Exit* REYNALDO.]

                                      (*Enter* OPHELIA.)

             How now, Ophelia! what's the matter?

  OPH.   O, my lord, my lord, I have been so affrighted!

  POLONIUS.   With what, i' the name of God?   70

  OPHELIA.   My lord, as I was sewing in my closet,

Lord Hamlet, with his doublet all unbraced,
No hat upon his head, his stockings foul'd,
Ungarter'd and down-gyved to his ankle;
Pale as his shirt, his knees knocking each other;   75
And with a look so piteous in purport
As if he had been loosed out of hell
To speak of horrors—he comes before me.

POLONIUS.   Mad for thy love?

OPHELIA.   My lord, I do not know;
But, truly, I do fear it.

POLONIUS.   What said he?   80

OPHELIA.   He took me by the wrist and held me hard;
Then goes he to the length of all his arm;
And, with his other hand thus o'er his brow,
He falls to such perusal of my face
As he would draw it. Long stay'd he so;   85
At last, a little shaking of mine arm
And thrice his head thus waving up and down,
He raised a sigh so piteous and profound,
As it did seem to shatter all his bulk
And end his being: That done, he lets me go: 90
And, with his head over his shoulder turn'd,
He seem'd to find his way without his eyes;
For out o' doors he went without their help,
And, to the last, bended their light on me.

POLONIUS.   Come, go with me: I will go seek the king.   95
This is the very ecstasy of love,
Whose violent property fordoes itself,
And leads the will to desperate undertakings,
As oft as any passion under heaven
That does afflict our natures. I am sorry.   100
What, have you given him any hard words of late?

OPHELIA.   No, my good lord; but, as you did command,
I did repel his letters, and denied
His access to me.

POLONIUS.   That hath made him mad.
I am sorry that with better heed and judgment   105
I had not quoted him: I fear'd he did but trifle,
And meant to wreck thee; but, beshrew my jealousy!
It seems it is as proper to our age
To cast beyond ourselves in our opinions,

As it is common for the younger sort   110
To lack discretion. Come, go we to the king:
This must be known; which, being kept close, might move
More grief to hide than hate to utter love.
Come.   [*Exeunt.*]

SCENE II   A ROOM IN THE CASTLE

(*Enter* KING, QUEEN, ROSENCRANTZ, GUILDENSTERN, *and*
ATTENDANTS.)

KING.   Welcome, dear Rosencrantz and Guildenstern!
Moreover that we much did long to see you,
The need we have to use you did provoke
Our hasty sending. Something have you heard
Of Hamlet's transformation; so I call it,   5
Sith nor the exterior nor the inward man
Resembles that it was. What it should be,
More than his father's death, that thus hath put him
So much from the understanding of himself,
I cannot dream of: I entreat you both,   10
That, being of so young days brought up with him,
And sith so neighbour'd to his youth and humour,
That you vouchsafe your rest here in our court
Some little time: So by your companies
To draw him on to pleasures, and to gather,   15
So much as from occasion you may glean,
Whether aught, to us unknown, afflicts him thus,
That, open'd, lies within our remedy.

QUEEN.   Good gentlemen, he hath much talk'd of you;
And sure I am two men there are not living   20
To whom he more adheres. If it will please you
To show us so much gentry and good will
As to expend your time with us awhile,
For the supply and profit of our hope,
Your visitation shall receive such thanks   25
As fits a king's remembrance.

ROSENCRANTZ.   Both your majesties
Might, by the sovereign power you have of us,
Put your dread pleasures more into command
Than to entreaty.

GUILDENSTERN.   But we both obey,
And here give up ourselves, in the full bent   30

To lay our service freely at your feet.
To be commanded.

KING.   Thanks, Rosencrantz and gentle Guildenstern.

QUEEN.   Thanks, Guildenstern and gentle Rosencrantz:
And I beseech you instantly to visit   35
My too much changed son. Go, some of you,
And bring these gentlemen where Hamlet is.

GUIL.   Heavens make our presence and our practices
Pleasant and helpful to him!

QUEEN.   Ay, amen!

[*Exeunt* ROSENCRANTZ, GUILDENSTERN, *and* ATTENDANTS.]
(Enter POLONIUS.*)*

POL.   The ambassadors from Norway, my good lord,   40
Are joyfully return'd.

KING.   Thou still hast been the father of good news.

POLONIUS. Have I, my lord? Assure you, my good liege,
I hold my duty, as I hold my soul,
Both to my God and to my gracious king: 45
And I do think, or else this brain of mine
Hunts not the trail of policy so sure
As it hath used to do, that I have found
The very cause of Hamlet's lunacy.

KING.   O, speak of that; that do I long to hear.   50

POLONIUS.   Give first admittance to the ambassadors;
My news shall be the fruit to that great feast.

KING.   Thyself do grace to them, and bring them in.

[*Exit* POLONIUS.]

He tells me, my dear Gertrude, he hath found
The head and source of all your son's distemper.   55

QUEEN.   I doubt it is no other but the main;
His father's death, and our o'erhasty marriage.

KING.   Well, we shall sift him.

(Reenter POLONIUS, *with* VOLTIMAND *and* CORNELIUS.*)*

Welcome, my good friends!
Say, Voltimand, what from our brother Norway?

VOLTIMAND.   Most fair return of greetings and desires.   60
Upon our first, he sent out to suppress
His nephew's levies; which to him appear'd

To be a preparation 'gainst the Polack;
But, better look'd into, he truly found
It was against your highness: Whereat grieved,   65
That so his sickness, age and impotence,
Was falsely borne in hand, sends out arrests
On Fortinbras; which he, in brief, obeys;
Receives rebuke from Norway, and in fine
Makes vow before his uncle never more   70
To give the assay of arms against your majesty.
Whereon old Norway, overcome with joy,
Gives him three thousand crowns in annual fee,
And his commission to employ those soldiers,
So levied as before, against the Polack: 75
With an entreaty, herein further shown,   [*Gives a paper.*]
That it might please you to give quiet pass
Through your dominions for this enterprise,
On such regards of safety and allowance
As therein are set down.

    KING.   It likes us well;   80
And at our more consider'd time we'll read,
Answer, and think upon this business.
Meantime we thank you for your well-took labour:
Go to your rest; at night we'll feast together:
Most welcome home!

                        [*Exeunt* VOLTIMAND *and* CORNELIUS.]

    POLONIUS.   This business is well ended.   85
My liege, and madam, to expostulate
What majesty should be, what duty is,
Why day is day, night night, and time is time,
Were nothing but to waste night, day and time.
Therefore, since brevity is the soul of wit,   90
And tediousness the limbs and outward flourishes,
I will be brief: Your noble son is mad:
Mad call I it; for, to define true madness,
What is't but to be nothing else but mad?
But let that go.

    QUEEN.   More matter, with less art.   95

    POLONIUS.   Madam, I swear I use no art at all.
That he is mad, 'tis true: 'Tis true 'tis pity,
And pity 'tis 'tis true: a foolish figure;
But farewell it, for I will use no art.

Mad let us grant him, then: And now remains   100
That we find out the cause of this effect,
Or rather say, the cause of this defect,
For this effect defective comes by cause:
Thus it remains, and the remainder thus.
Perpend.   105
I have a daughter—have whilst she is mine—
Who, in her duty and obedience, mark,
Hath given me this: Now gather, and surmise.   [*Reads.*]
"To the celestial and my soul's idol, the most beautified
Ophelia,"   110
That's an ill phrase, a vile phrase; "beautified" is a vile
phrase: But you shall hear. Thus: [*Reads.*]
"In her excellent white bosom, these," &c.—

    QUEEN.   Came this from Hamlet to her?

    POLONIUS.   Good madam, stay awhile; I will be faithful.   115

                                 [*Reads.*]

        "Doubt thou the stars are fire;
           Doubt that the sun doth move;
        Doubt truth to be a liar;
           But never doubt I love.

    "O dear Ophelia, I am ill at these numbers; I have not art to reckon
my groans: But that I love thee best, O most best, believe it. Adieu.
                     "Thine evermore, most dear lady, whilst this
                            machine is to him, HAMLET."
This, in obedience, hath my daughter shown me:
And more above, hath his solicitings,   125
As they fell out by time, by means and place,
All given to mine ear.

    KING.   But how hath she
Received his love?

    POLONIUS.   What do you think of me?

    KING.   As of a man faithful and honourable.

    POL.   I would fain prove so. But what might you think,   130
When I had seen this hot love on the wing,
As I perceived it, I must tell you that,
Before my daughter told me, what might you,
Or my dear majesty your queen here, think,
If I had play'd the desk or table-book,   135

Or given my heart a winking, mute and dumb,
Or look'd upon this love with idle sight;
What might you think? No, I went round to work,
And my young mistress thus I did bespeak:
"Lord Hamlet is a prince, out of thy star;   140
This must not be." And then I prescripts gave her,
That she should lock herself from his resort,
Admit no messengers, receive no tokens.
Which done, she took the fruits of my advice;
And he, repulsed—a short tale to make—   145
Fell into a sadness, then into a fast,
Thence to a watch, thence into a weakness,
Thence to a lightness, and by this declension
Into the madness wherein now he raves,
And all we mourn for.

KING.   Do you think 'tis this?   150

QUEEN.   It may be, very likely.

POL.   Hath there been such a time—I'd fain know that—
That I have positively said " 'Tis so,"
When it proved otherwise?

KING.   Not that I know.

POLONIUS.   [*Pointing to his head and shoulder*] Take this from this,
if this be otherwise: 155
If circumstances lead me, I will find
Where truth is hid, though it were hid indeed
Within the centre.

KING.   How may we try it further?

POL.   You know, sometimes he walks four hours together
Here in the lobby.   160

QUEEN.   So he does, indeed.

POL.   At such a time I'll loose my daughter to him:
Be you and I behind an arras then;
Mark the encounter: If he love her not,
And be not from his reason fall'n thereon.   165
Let me be no assistant for a state,
But keep a farm and carters.

KING.   We will try it.

QUEEN.   But, look, where sadly the poor wretch comes reading.

POLONIUS.   Away, I do beseech you, both away: I'll board him
presently.

[*Exeunt* KING, QUEEN, *and* ATTENDANTS.]
(*Enter* HAMLET, *reading.*)

O, give me leave.

How does my good Lord Hamlet?

HAMLET.   Well, God-a-mercy.

POLONIUS.   Do you know me, my lord?

HAMLET.   Excellent well; you are a fishmonger.

POLONIUS.   Not I, my lord.   175

HAMLET.   Then I would you were so honest a man.

POLONIUS.   Honest, my lord!

HAMLET.   Ay, sir; to be honest, as this world goes, is to be one man picked out of ten thousand.

POLONIUS.   That's very true, my lord.   180

HAMLET.   For if the sun breed maggots in a dead dog, being a good kissing carrion—Have you a daughter?

POLONIUS.   I have, my lord.

HAMLET.   Let her not walk i' the sun: Friend, look to't.

POLONIUS.   [*Aside*]   How say you by that? Still harping on my daughter: Yet he knew me not at first; he said I was a fishmonger: He is far gone: And truly in my youth I suffered much extremity for love; very near this. I'll speak to him again. What do you read, my lord?

HAMLET.   Words, words, words.

POLONIUS.   What is the matter, my lord?   190

HAMLET.   Between who?

POLONIUS.   I mean, the matter that you read, my lord.

HAMLET.   Slanders, sir: For the satirical rogue says here, that old men have gray beards; that their faces are wrinkled, their eyes purging thick amber and plum-tree gum; and that they have a plentiful lack of wit, together with most weak hams: All of which, sir, though I most powerfully and potently believe, yet I hold it not honesty to have it thus set down; for you yourself, sir, should be old as I am, if, like a crab, you could go backward.

POLONIUS.   [*Aside*]   Though this be madness, yet there is method in't. Will you walk out of the air, my lord?

HAMLET.   Into my grave?

POLONIUS.   Indeed, that is out o' the air.   [*Aside*]   How pregnant sometimes his replies are! A happiness that often madness hits on, which reason and sanity could not so prosperously be delivered of. I will leave him, and suddenly contrive the means of meeting between him and my daughter. My honourable lord, I will most humbly take my leave of you.

HAMLET.   You cannot, sir, take from me any thing that I will more willingly part withal: except my life, except my life, except my life.

POLONIUS.   Fare you well, my lord.   210

HAMLET.   These tedious old fools!

(*Enter* ROSENCRANTZ *and* GUILDENSTERN.)

POLONIUS.   You go to seek the Lord Hamlet; there he is.

ROS. [*To* POLONIUS]   God save you, sir!   [*Exit* POLONIUS.]

GUILDENSTERN.   My honoured lord!

ROSENCRANTZ.   My most dear lord!   215

HAMLET.   My excellent good friends! How dost thou, Guildenstern? Ah, Rosencrantz! Good lads, how do ye both?

ROSENCRANTZ.   As the indifferent children of the earth.

GUILDENSTERN.   Happy, in that we are not overhappy; On Fortune's cap we are not the very button.   220

HAMLET.   Nor the soles of her shoe?

ROSENCRANTZ.   Neither, my lord.

HAMLET.   Then you live in the middle of her favours. What's the news?

ROS.   None, my lord, but that the world's grown honest.   225

HAMLET.   Then is doomsday near: But your news is not true. Let me question more in particular: What have you, my good friends, deserved at the hands of Fortune, that she sends you to prison hither?

GUILDENSTERN.   Prison, my lord!

HAMLET.   Denmark's a prison.   230

ROSENCRANTZ.   Then is the world one.

HAM.   A goodly one; in which there are many confines, wards and dungeons, Denmark being one o' the worst.

ROSENCRANTZ.   We think not so, my lord.

HAMLET.   Why, then, 'tis none to you: For there is nothing either good or bad, but thinking makes it so: To me it is a prison.

ROSENCRANTZ.   Why, then, your ambition makes it one; 'tis too narrow for your mind.

HAMLET.   O God, I could be bounded in a nut-shell, and count myself a king of infinite space, were it not that I have bad dreams.   240

GUIL.   Which dreams, indeed, are ambition; for the very substance of the ambitious is merely the shadow of a dream.

HAMLET.   A dream itself is but a shadow.

ROSENCRANTZ.   Truly, and I hold ambition of so airy and light a quality, that it is but a shadow's shadow.   245

HAMLET. Then are our beggars bodies, and our monarchs and out-stretched heroes the beggars' shadows. Shall we to the court? For, by my fay, I cannot reason.

ROSENCRANTZ, GUILDENSTERN. We'll wait upon you.

HAMLET. No such matter: I will not sort you with the rest of my servants; for, to speak to you like an honest man, I am most dreadfully attended. But, in the beaten way of friendship, what make you at Elsinore?

ROSENCRANTZ. To visit you, my lord; no other occasion.

HAMLET. Beggar that I am, I am even poor in thanks; but I thank you: And sure, dear friends, my thanks are too dear a halfpenny. Were you not sent for? Is it your own inclining? Is it a free visitation? Come, deal justly with me; come, come; nay, speak.

GUILDENSTERN. What should we say, my lord?

HAMLET. Why, any thing, but to the purpose. You were sent for; and there is a kind of confession in your looks, which your modesties have not craft enough to colour: I know the good king and queen have sent for you.

ROSENCRANTZ. To what end, my lord?

HAMLET. That you must teach me. But let me conjure you, by the rights of our fellowship, by the consonancy of our youth, by the obligation of our ever-preserved love, and by what more dear a better proposer could charge you withal, be even and direct with me, whether you were sent for, or no?

ROSENCRANTZ. [*Aside to* GUILDENSTERN] What say you?

HAMLET. [*Aside*] Nay, then, I have an eye of you. If you love me, hold not off.

GUILDENSTERN. My lord, we were sent for.

HAMLET. I will tell you why; so shall my anticipation prevent your discovery, and your secrecy to the king and queen moult no feather. I have of late—but wherefore I know not—lost all my mirth, forgone all custom of exercises; and indeed it goes so heavily with my disposition, that this goodly frame, the earth, seems to me a sterile promontory; this most excellent canopy, the air, look you, this brave o'erhanging firmament, this majestical roof fretted with golden fire, why, it appears no other thing to me than a foul and pestilent congregation of vapours. What a piece of work is man! how noble in reason! how infinite in faculties! in form and moving how express and admirable! in action how like an angel! in apprehension how like a god! the beauty of the world! the paragon of animals! And yet, to me, what is this quintessence of dust? Man delights not me; no, nor woman neither, though by your smiling you seem to say so.

Ros.   My lord, there was no such stuff in my thoughts.

HAMLET.   Why did you laugh, then, when I said "man delights not me"?

ROSENCRANTZ.   To think, my lord, if you delight not in man, what lenten entertainment the players shall receive from you; we coted them on the way; and hither are they coming, to offer you service.

HAMLET.   He that plays the king shall be welcome; his majesty shall have tribute of me; the adventurous knight shall use his foil and target; the lover shall not sigh gratis; the humorous man shall end his part in peace; the clown shall make those laugh whose lungs are tickle o' the sere; and the lady shall say her mind freely, or the blank verse shall halt for't. What players are they?

ROSENCRANTZ.   Even those you were wont to take such delight in, the tragedians of the city.   305

HAMLET.   How chances it they travel? Their residence, both in reputation and profit, was better both ways.

ROSENCRANTZ.   I think their inhibition comes by the means of the late innovation.

HAMLET.   Do they hold the same estimation they did when I was in the city? are they so followed?

ROSENCRANTZ.   No, indeed, are they not.

HAMLET.   How comes it? do they grow rusty?

ROSENCRANTZ.   Nay, their endeavour keeps in the wonted pace: but there is, sir, an eyrie of children, little eyases, that cry out on the top of question, and are most tyrannically clapped for't: These are now the fashion, and so berattle the common stages—so they call them—that many wearing rapiers are afraid of goose-quills, and dare scarce come thither.

HAMLET.   What, are they children? Who maintains 'em? How are they escoted? Will they pursue the quality no longer than they can sing? Will they not say afterwards, if they should grow themselves to common players—as it is most like, if their means are no better—their writers do them wrong, to make them exclaim against their own succession?

Ros.   Faith, there has been much to do on both sides; and the nation holds it no sin to tarre them to controversy: There was, for a while, no money bid for argument, unless the poet and the player went to cuffs in the question.

HAMLET.   Is't possible?

GUIL.   O, there has been much throwing about of brains.

HAMLET.   Do the boys carry it away?   330

Ros.   Ay, that they do, my lord; Hercules and his load too.

HAMLET.　It is not very strange; for my uncle is king of Denmark, and those that would make mows at him while my father lived, give twenty, forty, fifty, an hundred ducats a-piece for his picture in little. 'Sblood, there is something in this more than natural, if philosophy could find it out.

[Flourish of trumpets within.]

GUILDENSTERN.　There are the players.

HAMLET.　Gentlemen, you are welcome to Elsinore. Your hands, come then: The appurtenance of welcome is fashion and ceremony: Let me comply with you in this garb, lest my extent to the players, which, I tell you, must show fairly outward, should more appear like entertainment than yours. You are welcome: But my uncle-father and aunt-mother are deceived.

GUILDENSTERN.　In what, my dear lord?

HAMLET.　I am but mad north-north-west: When the wind is southerly I know a hawk from a handsaw.

(Enter POLONIUS.)

POLONIUS.　Well be with you, gentlemen!

HAMLET.　Hark you, Guildenstern; and you too; at each ear a hearer: That great baby you see there is not yet out of his swaddling-clouts.

ROSENCRANTZ.　Happily he's the second time come to them; for they say an old man is twice a child.

HAMLET.　I will prophesy he comes to tell me of the players; mark it. You say right, sir: o' Monday morning; 'twas so indeed.

POLONIUS.　My lord, I have news to tell you.

HAMLET.　My lord, I have news to tell you. When Roscius was an actor in Rome—

POLONIUS.　The actors are come hither, my lord.

HAMLET.　Buz, buz!

POLONIUS.　Upon my honour—

HAMLET.　Then came each actor on his ass—　　　　　360

POLONIUS.　The best actors in the world, either for tragedy, comedy, history, pastoral, pastoral-comical, historical-pastoral, tragical-historical, tragical-comical-historical-pastoral, scene individable, or poem unlimited: Seneca cannot be too heavy, nor Plautus too light. For the law of writ and the liberty, these are the only men.　　　　　365

HAMLET.　O Jephthah, judge of Israel, what a treasure hadst thou!

POLONIUS.　What treasure had he, my lord?

HAMLET.   Why,
> "One fair daughter, and no more,
> The which he loved passing well."

POLONIUS.   [*Aside*]   Still on my daughter.   370

HAMLET.   Am I not i' the right, old Jephthah?

POLONIUS.   If you call me Jephthah, my lord, I have a daughter that I love passing well.

HAMLET.   Nay, that follows not.

POLONIUS.   What follows, then, my lord?   375

HAMLET.   Why,
> "As by lot, God wot,"

and then, you know,
> "It came to pass, as most like it was,"

the first row of the pious chanson will show you more; for look, where my abridgment comes.

> (*Enter four or five* PLAYERS.)

You are welcome, masters; welcome, all; I am glad to see thee well. Welcome, good friends. O, my old friend! They face is valanced since I saw thee last; comest thou to beard me in Denmark? What, my young lady and mistress; by'r lady, your ladyship is nearer to heaven than when I saw you last by the altitude of a chopine. Pray God, your voice, like a piece of uncurrent gold, be not cracked within the ring. Masters, you are all welcome. We'll e'en to't like French falconers, fly at any thing we see: We'll have a speech straight: Come, give us a taste of your quality: Come, a passionate speech.   390

FIRST PLAYER.   What speech, my lord?

HAMLET.   I heard thee speak me a speech once, but it was never acted; or, if it was, not above once; for the play, I remember, pleased not the million; 'twas caviare to the general: But it was—as I received it, and others, whose judgments in such matters cried in the top of mine—an excellent play, well digested in the scenes, set down with as much modesty as cunning. I remember, one said there were no sallets in the lines to make the matter savoury, nor no matter in the phrase that might indict the author of affection; but called it an honest method, as wholesome as sweet, and by very much more handsome than fine. One speech in it I chiefly loved: 'twas Æneas' tale to Dido; and thereabout of it especially where he speaks of Priam's slaughter. If it live in your memory, begin at this line: Let me see, let me see;
> "The rugged Pyrrhus, like the Hyrcanian beast,"

—'tis not so:—It begins with Pyrrhus;   405

"The rugged Pyrrhus, he whose sable arms,
Black as his purpose, did the night resemble
When he lay couched in the ominous horse,
Hath now this dread and black complexion smear'd
With heraldry more dismal; head to foot   410
Now is he total gules; horridly trick'd
With blood of fathers, mothers, daughters, sons,
Baked and impasted with the parching streets,
That lend a tyrannous and damned light
To their lord's murder: roasted in wrath and fire,   415
And thus o'er-sized with coagulate gore,
With eyes like carbuncles, the hellish Pyrrus
Old grandsire Priam seeks."
So, proceed you.

POLONIUS.   'Fore God, my lord, well spoken, with good
accent and good discretion.

FIRST PLAYER.   "Anon he finds him   420
Striking too short at Greeks; his antique sword,
Rebellious to his arm, lies where it falls,
Repugnant to command; unequal match'd,
Pyrrhus at Priam drives; in rage strikes wide;
But with the whiff and wind of his fell sword   425
The unnerved father falls. Then senseless Ilium,
Seeming to feel this blow, with flaming top
Stoops to his base, and with a hideous crash
Takes prisoner Pyrrhus' ear: For, lo! his sword,
Which was declining on the milky head   430
Of reverend Priam, seem'd i' the air to stick:
So, as a painted tyrant, Pyrrhus stood,
And, like a neutral to his will and matter,
Did nothing.
But, as we often see, against some storm,   435
A silence in the heavens, the rack stand still,
The bold winds speechless, and the orb below
As hush as death, anon the dreadful thunder
Doth rend the region; so, after Pyrrhus' pause,
Aroused vengeance sets him new a-work;   440
And never did the Cyclops' hammers fall
On Mars's armour, forg'd for proof eterne,
With less remorse than Pyrrhus' bleeding sword
Now falls on Priam. Out, Fortune! All you gods,
In general synod, take away her power;   445

Break all the spokes and fellies from her wheel,
And bowl the round nave down the hill of heaven,
As low as to the fiends!"

POLONIUS.   This is too long.

HAMLET.   It shall to the barber's, with your beard. Prithee, say on: he's for a jig or a tale, or he sleeps: Say on; come to Hecuba.

FIRST PLAYER.   "But who, O, who had seen the mobled queen—"

HAMLET.   "The mobled queen"?

POLONIUS.   That's good; "mobled queen" is good.

FIRST PLAYER.   "Run barefoot up and down, threatening the flames.
With bisson rheum; a clout upon that head
Where late the diadem stood, and for a robe,
About her lank and all o'er-teemed loins,
A blanket, in the alarm of fear caught up,
Who this had seen, with tongue in venom steep'd,   460
'Gainst Fortune's state would treason have pronounced:
But if the gods themselves did see her then,
When she saw Pyrrhus make malicious sport
In mincing with his sword her husband's limbs,
The instant burst of clamour that she made—   465
Unless things mortal move them not at all—
Would have made milch the burning eyes of heaven,
And passion in the gods."

POLONIUS.   Look, whether he has not turned his colour, and has tears in's eyes. Pray you, no more.   470

HAMLET.   'Tis well; I'll have thee speak out the rest soon. Good my lord, will you see the players well bestowed? Do you hear, let them be well used; for they are the abstract and brief chronicles of the time: After your death you were better have a bad epitaph than their ill report while you live.   475

POL.   My lord, I will use them according to their desert.

HAMLET.   God's bodykins, man, much better: Use every man after his desert, and who should scape whipping? Use them after your own honour and dignity: The less they deserve, the more merit is in your bounty. Take them in.   480

POLONIUS.   Come, sirs.

HAM.   Follow him, friends: We'll hear a play tomorrow.

[*Exit* POLONIUS *with all the* PLAYERS *except the* FIRST.]

Dost thou hear me, old friend; can you play the Murder of Gonzago?

FIRST PLAYER. Ay, my lord.

HAMLET. We'll ha't tomorrow night. You could, for a need, study a speech of some dozen or sixteen lines, which I would set down and insert in't, could you not?

FIRST PLAYER. Ay, my lord.

HAMLET. Very well. Follow that lord; and look you mock him not, [*Exit First Player*] My good friends, I'll leave you till night: You are welcome to Elsinore.

ROSENCRANTZ. Good my lord!

HAM. Ay, so, God be wi' ye!   [*Exeunt* ROSEN. *and* GUIL.]
   Now I am alone.

O, what a rogue and peasant slave am I!   495
Is it not monstrous, that this player here,
But in a fiction, in a dream of passion,
Could force his soul so to his own conceit,
That from her working all his visage wann'd,
Tears in his eyes, distraction in's aspect,   500
A broken voice, and his whole function suiting
With forms to his conceit? and all for nothing!
For Hecuba!
What's Hecuba to him, or he to Hecuba,
That he should weep for her? What would he do,   505
Had he the motive and the cue for passion
That I have? He would drown the stage with tears,
And cleave the general ear with horrid speech,
Make mad the guilty and appal the free,
Confound the ignorant, and amaze indeed   510
The very faculties of eyes and ears.
Yet I,
A dull and muddy-mettled rascal, peak,
Like John-a-dreams, unpregnant of my cause,
And can say nothing; no, not for a king,   515
Upon whose property and most dear life
A damn'd defeat was made. Am I a coward?
Who calls me villian? Breaks my pate across?
Plucks off my beard, and blows it in my face?
Tweaks me by the nose? Gives me the lie i' the throat,   520
As deep as to the lungs? Who does me this, ha?
'Swounds, I should take it: For it cannot be
But I am pigeon-liver'd, and lack gall
To make oppression bitter, or ere this

I should have fatted all the region kites   525
With this slave's offal: bloody, bloody villain!
Remorseless, treacherous, lecherous, kindless villain!
O, vengeance!
Why, what an ass am I! This is most brave,
That I, the son of a dear father murder'd,   530
Prompted to my revenge by heaven and hell,
Must, like a shrew, unpack my heart with words,
And fall a-cursing, like a very drab,
A scullion!
Fie upon't! foh! About, my brain! I have heard   535
That guilty creatures sitting at a play
Have by the very cunning of the scene
Been struck so to the soul, that presently
They have proclaim'd their malefactions;
For murder, though it have no tongue, will speak   540
With most miraculous organ. I'll have these players
Play something like the murder of my father
Before mine uncle: I'll observe his looks;
I'll tent him to the quick: If he but blench,
I know my course. The spirit that I have seen   545
May be the devil: And the devil hath power
To assume a pleasing shape; yea, and perhaps
Out of my weakness and my melancholy,
As he is very potent with such spirits,
Abuses me to damn me: I'll have grounds   550
More relative than this: The play's the thing
Wherein I'll catch the conscience of the king.   [*Exit.*]

Act III

SCENE I   A ROOM IN THE CASTLE

(*Enter* KING, QUEEN, POLONIUS, OPHELIA, ROSENCRANTZ,
and GUILDENSTERN.)

KING.   And can you, by no drift of circumstance,
Get from him why he puts on this confusion,
Grating so harshly all his days of quiet
With turbulent and dangerous lunacy?

ROS.   He does confess he feels himself distracted;   5
But from what cause he will by no means speak.

GUIL.   Nor do we find him forward to be sounded:

But, with a crafty madness, keeps aloof,
When we would bring him on to some confession
Of his true state.

    QUEEN.   Did he receive you well?   10

    ROSENCRANTZ.   Most like a gentleman.

    GUILDENSTERN.   But with much forcing of his disposition.

    ROSENCRANTZ.   Niggard of question; but, of our demands,
Most free in his reply.

    QUEEN.   Did you assay him
To any pastime?   15

    ROSENCRANTZ.   Madam, it so fell out, that certain players
We o'er-raught on the way: of these we told him;
And there did seem in him a kind of joy
To hear of it: They are about the court;
And, as I think, they have already order   20
This night to play before him.

    POLONIUS.   'Tis most true:
And he beseech'd me to entreat your majesties
To hear and see the matter.

    KING.   With all my heart; and it doth much content me
To hear him so inclined.   25
Good gentlemen, give him a further edge,
And drive his purpose on to these delights.

    ROS.   We shall, my lord.

                     [*Exeunt* ROSENCRANTZ *and* GUILDENSTERN.]

    KING.   Sweet Gertrude, leave us too;
For we have closely sent for Hamlet hither,
That he, as 'twere by accident, may here   30
Affront Ophelia:
Her father and myself, lawful espials,
Will so bestow ourselves that, seeing, unseen,
We may of their encounter frankly judge,
And gather by him, as he is behaved,   35
If't be the affliction of his love or no
That thus he suffers for.

    QUEEN.   I shall obey you:
And for your part, Ophelia, I do wish
That your good beauties be the happy cause
Of Hamlet's wildness: So shall I hope your virtues   40
Will bring him to his wonted way again,
To both your honours.

OPHELIA.   Madam, I wish it may.   [*Exit* QUEEN.]

POL.   Ophelia, walk you here. Gracious, so please you,
We will bestow ourselves.   [*To* OPHELIA]   Read on this book;
That show of such an exercise may colour   45
Your loneliness. We are oft to blame in this—
'Tis too much proved—that with devotion's visage
And pious action we do sugar o'er
The devil himself.

KING.   [*Aside*]   O, 'tis too true!
How smart a lash that speech doth give my conscience!   50
The harlot's cheek, beautied with plastering art,
Is not more ugly to the thing that helps it
Than is my deed to my most painted word:
O heavy burden!

POLONIUS.   I hear him coming: Let's withdraw, my lord.   55

[*Exeunt* KING *and* POLONIUS.]
(*Enter* HAMLET.)

HAMLET.   To be, or not to be: That is the question:
Whether 'tis nobler in the mind to suffer
The slings and arrows of outrageous fortune,
Or to take arms against a sea of troubles,
And by opposing end them? To die; to sleep;   60
No more; and by a sleep to say we end
The heart-ache and the thousand natural shocks
That flesh is heir to, 'tis a consummation
Devoutly to be wish'd. To die, to sleep;
To sleep! perchance to dream: Ay, there's the rub;   65
For in that sleep of death what dreams may come,
When we have shuffled off this mortal coil,
Must give us pause: There's the respect
That makes calamity of so long life,
For who would bear the whips and scorns of time,   70
The oppressor's wrong, the proud man's contumely,
The pangs of despised love, the law's delay,
The insolence of office and the spurns
The patient merit of the unworthy takes,
When he himself might his quietus make   75
With a bare bodkin? Who would fardels bear,
To grunt and sweat under a weary life,
But that the dread of something after death,
The undiscover'd country, from whose bourn
No traveller returns, puzzles the will,   80

And makes us rather bear those ills we have
Than fly to others that we know not of?
Thus conscience does make cowards of us all;
And thus the native hue of resolution
Is sicklied o'er with the pale cast of thought,   85
And enterprises of great pitch and moment
With this regard their currents turn awry,
And lose the name of action. Soft you now!
The fair Ophelia! Nymph, in thy orisons
Be all my sins remember'd.

OPHELIA.   Good my lord,   90
How does your honour for this many a day?

HAMLET.   I humbly thank you; well, well, well.

OPHELIA.   My lord, I have remembrances of yours,
That I have longed long to re-deliver;
I pray you, now receive them.

HAMLET.   No, not I;   95
I never gave you aught.

OPHELIA.   My honour'd lord, you know right well you did;
And, with them, words of so sweet breath composed
As made the things more rich; their perfume lost,
Take these again; for to the noble mind   100
Rich gifts wax poor when givers prove unkind.
There, my lord.

HAMLET.   Ha, ha! Are you honest?

OPHELIA.   My lord?

HAMLET.   Are you fair?   105

OPHELIA.   What means your lordship?

HAMLET.   That if you be honest and fair, your honesty should admit
no discourse to your beauty.

OPHELIA.   Could beauty, my lord, have better commerce than with
honesty?   110

HAMLET.   Ay, truly; for the power of beauty will sooner transform
honesty from what it is than the force of honesty can translate beauty
into his likeness: This was sometimes a paradox, but now the time gives
it proof. I did love you once.

OPHELIA.   Indeed, my lord, you made me believe so.   115

HAMLET.   You should not have believed me; for virtue cannot so
inoculate our old stock, but we shall relish of it: I loved you not.

OPHELIA.   I was the more deceived.

HAMLET.   Get thee to a nunnery. Why wouldst thou be a breeder of sinners? I am myself indifferent honest; but yet I could accuse me of such things, that it were better my mother had not borne me: I am very proud, revengeful, ambitious, with more offenses at my beck than I have thoughts to put them in, imagination to give them shape, or time to act them in. What should such fellows as I do crawling between earth and heaven? We are arrant knaves, all; believe none of us. Go thy ways to a nunnery. Where's your father?

OPHELIA.   At home, my lord.

HAMLET.   Let the doors be shut upon him, that he may play the fool no where but in's own house. Farewell.

OPHELIA.   O, help him, you sweet heavens!   130

HAMLET.   If thou dost marry, I'll give thee this plague for thy dowry: Be thou as chaste as ice, as pure as snow, thou shalt not escape calumny. Get thee to a nunnery, go: farewell. Or, if thou wilt needs marry, marry a fool: for wise men know well enough what monsters you make of them. To a nunnery, go; and quickly too. Farewell.   135

OPHELIA.   O heavenly powers, restore him!

HAMLET.   I have heard of your paintings too, well enough; God has given you one face, and you make yourselves another: You jig, you amble, and you lisp, and nickname God's creatures, and make your wantonness your ignorance. Go to, I'll no more on't; it hath made me mad. I say, we will have no more marriages. Those that are married already, all but one, shall live; the rest shall keep as they are. To a nunnery, go.   [*Exit.*]

OPHELIA.   O, what a noble mind is here o'erthrown!
The courtier's, soldier's, scholar's eye, tongue, sword;   145
The expectancy and rose of the fair state,
The glass of fashion and the mould of form,
The observed of all observers, quite, quite down!
And I, of ladies most deject and wretched,
That suck'd the honey of his music vows,   150
Now see that noble and most sovereign reason,
Like sweet bells jangled, out of tune and harsh;
That unmatch'd form and feature of blown youth
Blasted with ecstasy: O, woe is me
To have seen what I have seen, see what I see!   155

(*Reenter* KING *and* POLONIUS.)

KING.   Love! his affections do not that way tend;
Nor what he spake, though it lack'd form a little,

Was not like madness. There's something in his soul,
O'er which his melancholy sits on brood;
And I do doubt the hatch and the disclose   160
Will be some danger: Which for to prevent,
I have in quick determination
Thus set it down: He shall with speed to England,
For the demand of our neglected tribute:
Haply, the seas, and countries different,   165
With variable objects, shall expel
This something-settled matter in his heart;
Whereon his brains still beating puts him thus
From fashion of himself. What think you on't?

POLONIUS.   It shall do well: But yet do I believe   170
The origin and commencement of his grief
Sprung from neglected love. How now, Ophelia!
You need not tell us what Lord Hamlet said;
We heard it all. My lord, do as you please;
But, if you hold it fit, after the play,   175
Let his queen mother all alone entreat him
To show his grief: Let her be round with him;
And I'll be placed, so please you, in the ear
Of all their conference. If she find him not,
To England send him, or confine him where   180
Your wisdom best shall think.

KING.   It shall be so:
Madness in great ones must not unwatch'd go.   [*Exeunt.*]

SCENE II   A HALL IN THE SAME

(*Enter* HAMLET *and several* PLAYERS.)

HAMLET.   Speak the speech, I pray you, as I pronounced it to you,
trippingly on the tongue: But if you mouth it, as many of your players do,
I had as lief the town-crier spoke my lines. Nor do not saw the air too
much with your hand, thus, but use all gently: For in the very torrent,
tempest, and, as I may say, the whirlwind of passion, you must acquire
and beget a temperance that may give it smoothness. O, it offends me to
the soul to hear a robustious periwig-pated fellow tear a passion to tat-
ters, to very rags, to split the ears of the groundlings, who, for the most
part, are capable of nothing but inexplicable dumb-shows and noise: I
would have such a fellow whipped for o'erdoing Termagant; it out-herods
Herod. Pray you, avoid it.

FIRST PLAYER.   I warrant your honour.

HAMLET.   Be not too tame neither, but let your own discretion be your tutor. Suit the action to the word, the word to the action; with this special observance, that you o'erstep not the modesty of nature. For any thing so overdone is from the purpose of playing, whose end, both at the first and now, was and is, to hold, as 'twere, the mirror up to nature; to show virtue her own feature, scorn her own image, and the very age and body of the time his form and pressure. Now, this overdone, or come tardy off, though it make the unskilful laugh, cannot but make the judicious grieve; the censure of the which one must in your allowance o'erweigh a whole theatre of others. O, there be players that I have seen play, and heard others praise, and that highly, not to speak it profanely, that, neither having the accent of Christians nor the gait of Christian, pagan, nor man, have so strutted and bellowed, that I have thought some of nature's journeymen had made men, and not made them well, they imitated humanity so abominably.

FIRST PLAYER.   I hope we have reformed that indifferently with us, sir.

HAMLET.   O, reform it altogether. And let those that play your clowns speak no more than is set down for them: For there be of them that will themselves laugh, to set on some quantity of barren spectators to laugh too; though, in the mean time, some necessary question of the play be then to be considered. That's villanous, and shows a most pitiful ambition in the fool that uses it. Go, make you ready.

[*Exeunt* PLAYERS.]
(*Enter* POLONIUS, ROSENCRANTZ, *and* GUILDENSTERN.)

How now, my lord! Will the king hear this piece of work?   35

POLONIUS.   And the queen too, and that presently.

HAMLET.   Bid the players make haste.   [*Exit* POLONIUS.]
Will you two help to hasten them?

ROSENCRANTZ, GUILDENSTERN.   We will, my lord.

[*Exeunt* ROSENCRANTZ *and* GUILDENSTERN.]

HAMLET.   What, ho, Horatio!

(*Enter* HORATIO.)

HORATIO.   Here, sweet lord, at your service.   40

HAMLET.   Horatio, thou art e'en as just a man
As e'er my conversation coped withal.

HORATIO.   O, my dear lord—

HAMLET.   Nay, do not think I flatter;
For what advancement may I hope from thee,

That no revenue hast but thy good spirits,   45
To feed and clothe thee? Why should the poor be flatter'd?
No, let the candied tongue lick absurd pomp,
And crook the pregnant hinges of the knee
Where thrift may follow fawning. Dost thou hear?
Since my dear soul was mistress of her choice,   50
And could of men distinguish, her election
Hath seal'd thee for herself: For thou hast been
As one, in suffering all, that suffers nothing,
A man that fortune's buffets and rewards
Hast ta'en with equal thanks; and bless'd are those   55
Whose blood and judgment are so well commingled,
That they are not a pipe for fortune's finger
To sound what stop she please. Give me that man
That is not passion's slave, and I will wear him
In my heart's core, ay, in my heart of heart,   60
As I do thee. Something too much of this.
There is a play tonight before the king;
One scene of it comes near the circumstance
Which I have told thee of my father's death:
I prithee, when thou seest that act a-foot,   65
Even with the very comment of thy soul
Observe my uncle: If his occulted guilt
Do not itself unkennel in one speech,
It is a damned ghost that we have seen,
And my imaginations are as foul   70
As Vulcan's stithy. Give him heedful note:
For I mine eyes will rivet to his face;
And, after, we will both our judgments join
In censure of his seeming.

    HORATIO.   Well, my lord:
If he steal aught the whilst this play is playing,   75
And scape detecting, I will pay the theft.

    HAMLET.   They are coming to the play; I must be idle:
Get you a place.

        (*Danish march. A flourish. Enter* KING, QUEEN, POLONIUS,
                OPHELIA, ROSENCRANTZ, GUILDENSTERN, *and others.*)

    KING.   How fares our cousin Hamlet?

    HAMLET.   Excellent, i' faith: of the chameleon's dish: I eat the air,
promise-crammed: You cannot feed capons so.

KING.   I have nothing with this answer, Hamlet; these words are not mine.

HAMLET.   No, nor mine now.   [*To Polonius*]   My lord, you played once i' the university, you say?   85

POLONIUS.   That did I, my lord; and was accounted a good actor.

HAMLET.   And what did you enact?

POLONIUS.   I did enact Julius Cæsar; I was killed i' the Capitol; Brutus killed me.

HAMLET.   It was a brute part of him to kill so capital a calf there. Be the players ready?

ROSENCRANTZ.   Ay, my lord; they stay upon your patience.

QUEEN.   Come hither, my dear Hamlet, sit by me.

HAMLET.   No, good mother; here's metal more attractive.

[*Lying down at* OPHELIA'S *feet.*]

POLONIUS.   [*To the* KING]   O, ho! do you mark that?   95

HAMLET.   Lady, shall I lie in your lap?

OPHELIA.   No, my lord.

HAMLET.   I mean, my head upon your lap?

OPHELIA.   Ay, my lord. . . . You are merry, my lord.

HAMLET.   Who, I?   100

OPHELIA.   Ay, my lord.

HAMLET.   O God, your only jig-maker. What should a man do but be merry? For, look you, how cheerfully my mother looks, and my father died within these two hours.

OPHELIA.   Nay, 'tis twice two months, my lord.   105

HAMLET.   So long? Nay then, let the devil wear black, for I'll have a suit of sables. O heavens! Die two months ago, and not forgotten yet? Then there's hope a great man's memory may outlive his life half a year: But, by'r lady, he must build churches, then; or else shall he suffer not thinking on, with the hobby-horse, whose epitaph is, "For, O, for, O, the hobby-horse is forgot."

(*Hautboys play. The dumb-show enters.*)
Enter a KING *and a* QUEEN; *very lovingly; the* QUEEN *embracing him, and he her. She kneels, and makes show of protestation unto him. He takes her up, and declines his head upon her neck; lays him down upon a bank of flowers. She, seeing him asleep, leaves him. Anon comes in a fellow, takes off his crown, kisses*

> *it, and pours poison in the King's ears, and exit. The* QUEEN
> *returns; finds the* KING *dead, and makes passionate action. The*
> POISONER, *with some two or three* MUTES, *comes in again,*
> *seeming to lament with her. The dead body is carried away.*
> *The* POISONER *wooes the* QUEEN *with gifts: She seems loth and*
> *unwilling awhile, but in the end accepts his love.*
>
> > [*Exeunt.*]

OPHELIA.   What means this, my lord?

HAMLET.   Marry, this is miching mallecho; it means mischief.

OPHELIA.   Belike this show imports the argument of the play.

> (*Enter* PROLOGUE.)

HAMLET.   We shall know by this fellow: The players cannot keep
counsel; they'll tell all.

OPHELIA.   Will he tell us what this show meant?

HAMLET.   Ay, or any show that you'll show him.

OPHELIA.   You are naught, you are naught: I'll mark the play.

PRO.   For us, and for our tragedy,   120
    Here stooping to your clemency,
    We beg your hearing patiently.

HAMLET.   Is this a prologue, or the posy of a ring?

OPHELIA.   'Tis brief, my lord.

HAMLET.   As woman's love.   125

> (*Enter a* KING *and a* QUEEN.)

P. KING.   Full thirty times hath Phoebus' cart gone round
Neptune's salt wash and Tellus' orbed ground,
And thirty dozen moons with borrow'd sheen
About the world have times twelve thirties been,
Since love our hearts and Hymen did our hands,   130
Unite commutual in most sacred bands.

P. QUEEN.   So many journeys may the sun and moon
Make us again count o'er ere love be done!
But, woe is me, you are so sick of late,
So far from cheer and from your former state,   135
That I distrust you. Yet, though I distrust,
Discomfort you, my lord, it nothing must:
For women's fear and love holds quantity;
In neither aught, or in extremity.
Now, what my love is, proof hath made you know;   140
And as my love is sized, my fear is so:

Where love is great, the littlest doubts are fear;
Where little fears grow great, great love grows there.

    P. KING.   Faith, I must leave thee, love, and shortly too;
My operant powers their functions leave to do: 145
And thou shalt live in this fair world behind,
Honour'd, beloved; and haply one as kind
For husband shalt thou—

    P. QUEEN.   O, confound the rest!
Such love must needs be treason in my breast:
In second husband let me be accurst!   150
None wed the second but who kill'd the first.

HAMLET.   [*Aside*]   Wormwood, wormwood.

    P. QUEEN.   The instances that second marriage move
Are base respects of thrift, but none of love:
A second time I kill my husband dead   155
When second husband kisses me in bed.

    P. KING.   I do believe you think what now you speak;
But what we do determine oft we break.
Purpose is but the slave to memory,
Of violent birth, but poor validity: 160
Which now, like fruit unripe, sticks on the tree;
But fall, unshaken, when they mellow be.
Most necessary 'tis that we forget
To pay ourselves what to ourselves is debt:
What to ourselves in passion we propose,   165
The passion ending, doth the purpose lose.
The violence of either grief or joy
Their own enactures with themselves destroy:
Where joy most revels, grief doth most lament;
Grief joys, joy grieves, on slender accident.   170
This world is not for aye; nor 'tis not strange
That even our loves should with our fortunes change;
For 'tis a question left us yet to prove,
Whether love lead fortune, or else fortune love.
The great man down, you mark his favourite flies;   175
The poor advanced makes friends of enemies.
And hitherto doth love on fortune tend:
For who not needs shall never lack a friend;
And who in want a hollow friend doth try,
Directly seasons him his enemy.   180
But, orderly to end where I begun,
Our wills and fates do so contrary run,

That our devices still are overthrown;
Our thoughts are ours, their ends none of our own:
So think thou wilt no second husband wed;   185
But die thy thoughts when thy first lord is dead.

   P. QUEEN.   Nor earth to me give food, nor heaven light!
Sport and repose lock from me day and night!
To desperation turn my trust and hope!
An anchor's cheer in prison be my scope!   190
Each opposite that blanks the face of joy,
Meet what I would have well, and it destroy!
Both here and hence pursue me lasting strife,
If, once a widow, ever I be wife!

HAMLET.   If she should break it now!   195

   P. KING.   'Tis deeply sworn. Sweet, leave me here awhile;
My spirits grow dull, and fain I would beguile
The tedious day with sheep.   [*Sleeps.*]

   P. QUEEN.   Sleep rock thy brain;
And never come mischance between us twain!   [*Exit.*]

HAMLET.   Madam, how like you this play?   200

QUEEN.   The lady doth protest too much, methinks.

HAMLET.   O, but she'll keep her word.

KING.   Have you heard the argument? Is there no offence in't?

HAMLET.   No, no, they do but jest, poison in jest; no offense i' the
world.   205

KING.   What do you call the play?

HAMLET.   The Mouse-trap. Marry, how? Tropically. This play is the
image of a murder done in Vienna: Gonzago is the duke's name; his wife,
Baptista: You shall see anon; 'tis a knavish piece of work. But what o'
that? Your majesty and we that have free souls, it touches us not: Let the
galled jade wince, our withers are unwrung.

                                          [*Enter* LUCIANUS.]

This is one Lucianus, nephew to the king.

OPHELIA.   You are as good as a chorus, my lord.

HAMLET.   I could interpret between you and your love, if I could
see the puppets dallying.   215

OPHELIA.   You are keen, my lord, you are keen.

HAMLET.   Begin, murderer; leave thy damnable faces, and begin.
Come: "the croaking raven doth bellow for revenge."

   LUCIANUS. Thoughts black, hands apt, drugs fit, and time agreeing;

Confederate season, else no creature seeing;   220
Thou mixture rank, of midnight weeds collected,
With Hecate's ban thrice blasted, thrice infected,
Thy natural magic and dire property,
On wholesome life usurp immediately.

[*Pours the poison into the sleeper's ears.*]

HAMLET.   He poisons him i' the garden for's estate. His name's Gonzago: The story is extant, and writ in choice Italian: You shall see anon how the murderer gets the love of Gonzago's wife.

OPHELIA.   The king rises.

HAMLET.   What, frighted with false fire!

QUEEN.   How fares my lord?   230

POLONIUS.   Give o'er the play.

KING.   Give me some light: away!

ALL.   Lights, lights, lights!

[*Exeunt all except* HAMLET *and* HORATIO.]

HAM.   Why, let the stricken deer go weep,
             The hart ungalled play;   235
        For some must watch, while some must sleep:
             So runs the world away.
Would not this, sir, and a forest of feathers—if the rest of my fortunes turn Turk with me—with two Provincial roses on my razed shoes, get me a fellowship in a cry of players, sir?   240

HORATIO.   Half a share.

HAMLET.   A whole one, I.
             For thou dost know, O Damon dear,
                  This realm dismantled was
             Of Jove himself; and now reigns here   245
                  A very, very—pajock.

HORATIO.   You might have rhymed.

HAMLET.   O good Horatio, I'll take the ghost's word for a thousand pound. Didst perceive?

HORATIO.   Very well, my lord.   250

HAMLET.   Upon the talk of the poisoning?

HORATIO.   I did very well note him.

HAMLET.   Ah, ha! Come, some music! Come, the recorders!
             For if the king like not the comedy,
                  Why, then, belike—he likes it not, perdy.   255
Come, some music!

(*Reenter* ROSENCRANTZ *and* GUILDENSTERN.)

GUIL.   Good my lord, vouchsafe me a word with you.

HAMLET.   Sir, a whole history.

GUILDENSTERN.   The king, sir—

HAMLET.   Ay, sir, what of him?   260

GUIL.   Is, in his retirement, marvellous distempered.

HAMLET.   With drink, sir?

GUILDENSTERN.   No, my lord, with choler.

HAMLET.   Your wisdom should show itself more richer to signify this to his doctor; for, for me to put him to his purgation would perhaps plunge him into more choler.

GUILDENSTERN.   Good my lord, put your discourse into some frame, and start not so wildly from my affair.

HAMLET.   I am tame, sir: Pronounce.

GUILDENSTERN.   The queen, your mother, in most great affliction of spirit, hath sent me to you.

HAMLET.   You are welcome.

GUILDENSTERN.   Nay, good my lord, this courtesy is not of the right breed. If it shall please you to make me a wholesome answer, I will do your mother's commandment: If not, your pardon and my return shall be the end of my business.

HAMLET.   Sir, I cannot.

GUILDENSTERN.   What, my lord?

HAMLET.   Make you a wholesome answer; my wit's diseased. But, sir, such answer as I can make, you shall command; or rather, as you say, my mother: therefore no more, but the matter: my mother, you say—

ROSENCRANTZ.   Then thus she says; your behaviour hath struck her into amazement and admiration.

HAMLET.   O wonderful son, that can so astonish a mother! But is there no sequel at the heels of this mother's admiration? Impart.   285

ROSENCRANTZ.   She desires to speak with you in her closet, ere you go to bed.

HAMLET.   We shall obey, were she ten times our mother. Have you any further trade with us?

ROSENCRANTZ.   My lord, you once did love me.   290

HAMLET.   And do still, by these pickers and stealers.

ROSENCRANTZ.   Good my lord, what is your cause of distemper? You do, surely, bar the door upon your own liberty, if you deny your griefs to your friend.

HAMLET.   Sir, I lack advancement.   295

ROSENCRANTZ.   How can that be, when you have the voice of the king himself for your succession in Denmark?

HAMLET.   Ay, sir, but "While the grass grows"—the proverb is something musty.

(Reenter PLAYERS *with recorders.)*

O, the recorders: Let me see one. To withdraw with you:—Why do you go about to recover the wind of me, as if you would drive me into a toil?

GUILDENSTERN.   O, my lord, if my duty be too bold, my love is too unmannerly.

HAMLET.   I do not well understand that. Will you play upon this pipe?

GUILDENSTERN.   My lord, I cannot.

HAMLET.   I pray you.

GUILDENSTERN.   Believe me, I cannot.

HAMLET.   I do beseech you.

GUILDENSTERN.   I know no touch of it, my lord.   310

HAMLET.   'Tis as easy as lying: Govern these ventages with your finger and thumb, give it breath with your mouth, and it will discourse most eloquent music. Look you, these are the stops.

GUILDENSTERN.   But these cannot I command to any utterance of harmony; I have not the skill.   315

HAMLET.   Why, look you now, how unworthy a thing you make of me! You would play upon me; you would seem to know my stops; you would pluck out the heart of my mystery; you would sound me from my lowest note to the top of my compass: And there is much music, excellent voice, in this little organ; yet cannot you make it speak. 'Sblood, do you think I am easier to be played on than a pipe? Call me what instrument you will, though you can fret me, you cannot play upon me.

(Enter POLONIUS.*)*

God bless you, sir!

POLONIUS.   My lord, the queen would speak with you, and presently.

HAMLET.   Do you see yonder cloud that's almost in shape of a camel?

POLONIUS.   By the mass, and 'tis like a camel, indeed.

HAMLET.   Methinks it is like a weasel.

POLONIUS.   It is backed like a weasel.

HAMLET.   Or like a whale?

POLONIUS.   Very like a whale.   330

HAMLET.   Then will I come to my mother by and by.
They fool me to the top of my bent. I will come by
and by.

POLONIUS.   I will say so.

HAMLET.   By and by is easily said.   [*Exit* POLONIUS.]
Leave me, friends.   [*Exeunt all but* HAMLET.]
'Tis now the very witching time of night,
When churchyards yawn, and hell itself breathes out
Contagion to this world: Now could I drink hot blood,
And do such bitter business as the day   340
Would quake to look on. Soft! now to my mother.
O heart, lose not thy nature; let not ever
The soul of Nero enter this firm bosom:
Let me be cruel, not unnatural:
I will speak daggers to her, but use none;   345
My tongue and soul in this be hypocrites;
How in my words soever she be shent,
To give them seals never, my soul, consent!   [*Exit.*]

SCENE III   A ROOM IN THE SAME

(*Enter* KING, ROSENCRANTZ, *and* GUILDENSTERN.)

KING.   I like him not, nor stands it safe with us
To let his madness range. Therefore prepare you;
I your commission will forthwith dispatch,
And he to England shall along with you:
The terms of our estate may not endure   5
Hazard so dangerous as doth hourly grow
Out of his lunacies.

GUILDENSTERN.   We will ourselves provide:
Most holy and religious fear it is
To keep those many many bodies safe
That live and feed upon your majesty.   10

ROSENCRANTZ.   The single and peculiar life is bound,
With all the strength and armour of the mind,
To keep itself from noyance; but much more
That spirit upon whose weal depends and rests
The lives of many. The cease of majesty   15
Dies not alone; but, like a gulf, doth draw
What's near it with it; 'tis a massy wheel,

Fix'd on the summit of the highest mount,
To whose huge spokes ten thousand lesser things
Are mortised and adjoin'd; which, when it falls,   20
Each small annexment, petty consequence,
Attends the boisterous ruin. Ne'er alone
Did the king sigh, but with a general groan.

    KING.   Arm you, I pray you, to this speedy voyage;
For we will fetters put upon this fear,   25
Which now goes too free-footed.

    ROSENCRANTZ, GUILDENSTERN.   We will haste us.

                     [*Exeunt* ROSENCRANTZ *and* GUILDENSTERN.]
                             (*Enter* POLONIUS.)

    POLONIUS.   My lord, he's going to his mother's closet:
Behind the arras I'll convey myself,
To hear the process; I'll warrant she'll tax him home:
And, as you said, and wisely was it said,   30
'Tis meet that some more audience than a mother,
Since nature makes them partial, should o'erhear
The speech, of vantage. Fare you well, my liege:
I'll call upon you ere you go to bed,
And tell you what I know.

    KING.   Thanks, dear my lord.   35

                                 [*Exit* POLONIUS.]

O, my offence is rank, it smells to heaven;
It hath the primal eldest curse upon't,
A brother's murder! Pray can I not,
Though inclination be as sharp as will:
My stronger guilt defeats my strong intent;   40
And, like a man to double business bound,
I stand in pause where I shall first begin,
And both neglect. What if this cursed hand
Were thicker than itself with brother's blood,
Is there not rain enough in the sweet heavens   45
To wash it white as snow? Whereto serves mercy
But to confront the visage of offence?
And what's in prayer but this twofold force,
To be forestalled ere we come to fall,
Or pardon'd being down? Then I'll look up;   50
My fault is past. But, O, what form of prayer

Can serve my turn? "Forgive me my foul murder"?
That cannot be; since I am still possess'd
Of those effects for which I did the murder,
My crown, mine own ambition, and my queen.   55
May one be pardon'd, and retain the offence?
In the corrupted currents of this world
Offence's gilded hand may shove by justice,
And oft 'tis seen the wicked prize itself
Buys out the law: But 'tis not so above;   60
There is no shuffling, there the action lies
In his true nature; and we ourselves compell'd,
Even to the teeth and forehead of our faults,
To give in evidence. What then? What rests?
Try what repentance can: What can it not?   65
Yet what can it when one can not repent?
O wretched state! O bosom black as death!
O limed soul, that, struggling to be free,
Art more engaged! Help, angels! Make assay:
Bow, stubborn knees; and, heart with strings of steel,   70
Be soft as sinews of the new-born babe!
All may be well.

                                            [*Retires and kneels.*]
                                            (*Enter* HAMLET.)

    HAMLET.   Now might I do it pat, now he is praying;
And now I'll do't: And so he goes to heaven;
And so am I revenged; that would be scann'd.   75
A villain kills my father; and for that,
I, his sole son, do this same villain send
To heaven.
O, this is hire and salary, not revenge.
He took my father grossly, full of bread;   80
With all his crimes broad blown, as flush as May;
And how his audit stands who knows save heaven?
But, in our circumstance and course of thought,
'Tis heavy with him: And am I then revenged,
To take him in the purging of his soul,   85
When he is fit and season'd for his passage?
No.
Up, sword; and know thou a more horrid hent:
When he is drunk, asleep, or in his rage;
At gaming, swearing, or about some act   90
That has no relish of salvation in't;
Then trip him, that his heels may kick at heaven,

And that his soul may be as damn'd and black
As hell, whereto it goes. My mother stays:
This physic but prolongs thy sickly days.   [*Exit.*]
                                        [*The* KING *rises and advances.*]

    KING.   My words fly up, my thoughts remain below;
Words without thoughts never to heaven go.   [*Exit.*]

    SCENE IV   ANOTHER ROOM IN THE SAME

                                        (*Enter* QUEEN *and* POLONIUS.)

    POL.   He will come straight. Look you lay home to him:
Tell him his pranks have been too broad to bear with,
And that your grace hath screen'd and stood between
Much heat and him. I'll sconce me even here.
Pray you, be round with him.   5
    HAM. [*Within*]   Mother, mother, mother!
    QUEEN.   I'll warrant you;
Fear me not: Withdraw, I hear him coming.

                                        [POLONIUS *goes behind the arras.*]
                                                   (*Enter* HAMLET.)

    HAMLET.   Now, mother, what's the matter?
    QUEEN.   Hamlet, thou hast thy father much offended.
    HAMLET.   Mother, you have my father much offended.   10
    QUEEN.   Come, come, you answer with an idle tongue.
    HAMLET.   Go, go, you question with a wicked tongue.
    QUEEN.   Why, how now, Hamlet!
    HAMLET.   What's the matter now?
    QUEEN.   Have you forgot me?
    HAMLET.   No, by the rood, not so:
You are the queen, your husband's brother's wife;   15
And—would it were not so!—You are my mother.
    QUEEN.   Nay, then, I'll set those to you that can speak.
    HAMLET.   Come, come, and sit you down; you shall not budge;
You go not till I set you up a glass
Where you may see the inmost part of you.   20
    QUEEN.   What wilt thou do? Thou wilt not murder me?
Help, help, ho!
    POL. [*Behind*]   What, ho! help, help, help!

HAMLET.   [*Drawing*]   How now! a rat? Dead for a ducat, dead!
                                    [*Makes a pass through the arras.*]

POLONIUS.   [*Behind*]   O, I am slain!   [*Falls and dies.*]

QUEEN.   O, me, what hast thou done?

HAMLET.   Nay, I know not: 25
Is it the king?

QUEEN.   O, what a rash and bloody deed is this!

HAMLET.   A bloody deed! Almost as bad, good mother,
As kill a king, and marry with his brother.

QUEEN.   As kill a king!

HAMLET.   Ay, lady, 'twas my word.   30

                            [*Lifts up the arras, and sees* POLONIUS.]

Thou wretched, rash, intruding fool, farewell!
I took thee for thy better: Take thy fortune;
Thou find'st to be too busy is some danger.
Leave wringing of your hands; peace; sit you down,
And let me wring your heart: For so I shall,   35
If it be made of penetrable stuff;
If damned custom have not brass'd it so,
That it is proof and bulwark against sense.

QUEEN.   What have I done, that thou darest wag thy tongue
In noise so rude against me?

HAMLET.   Such an act   40
That blurs the grace and blush of modesty,
Calls virtue hypocrite, takes off the rose
From the fair forehead of an innocent love,
And sets a blister there, makes marriage-vows
As false as dicers' oaths: O, such a deed   45
As from the body of contraction plucks
The very soul, and sweet religion makes
A rhapsody of words: Heaven's face doth glow;
Yea, this solidity and compound mass,
With tristful visage, as against the doom,   50
Is thought-sick at the act.

QUEEN.   Ay me, what act,
That roars so loud and thunders in the index?

HAMLET.   Look here, upon this picture, and on this,
The counterfeit presentment of two brothers.
See, what a grace was seated on this brow;   55
Hyperion's curls; the front of Jove himself;

An eye like Mars, to threaten and command;
A station like the herald Mercury
New-lighted on a heaven-kissing hill;
A combination and a form indeed,   60
Where every god did seem to set his seal,
To give the world assurance of a man:
This was your husband. Look you now, what follows:
Here is your husband; like a mildew'd ear,
Blasting his wholesome brother. Have you eyes?   65
Could you on this fair mountain leave to feed,
And batten on this moor? Ha! Have you eyes?
You cannot call it love; for at your age
The hey-day in the blood is tame, it's humble,
And waits upon the judgment; and what judgment   70
Would step from this to this? Sense, sure, you have,
Else could you not have motion; but, sure, that sense
Is apoplex'd. For madness would not err,
Nor sense to ecstasy was ne'er so thrall'd
But it reserv'd some quantity of choice,   75
To serve in such a difference. What devil was't
That thus hath cozen'd you at hoodman-blind?
Eyes without feeling, feeling without sight,
Ears without hands or eyes, smelling sans all,
Or but a sickly part of one true sense   80
Could not so mope.
O shame! Where is thy blush? Rebellious hell,
If thou canst mutine in a matron's bones,
To flaming youth let virtue be as wax,
And melt in her own fire. Proclaim no shame   85
When the compulsive ardour gives the charge,
Since frost itself as actively doth burn,
And reason panders will.
    QUEEN.   O Hamlet, speak no more:
Thou turn'st mine eyes into my very soul;
And there I see such black and grained spots   90
As will not leave their tinct.
    HAMLET.   Nay, but to live
Stew'd in corruption, honeying and making love
Over the nasty sty—
    QUEEN.   O, speak to me no more;
These words, like daggers, enter in mine ears;
No more, sweet Hamlet!

HAMLET.   A murderer and a villain;   95
A slave that is not twentieth part the tithe
Of your precedent lord; a vice of kings;
A cutpurse of the empire and the rule,
That from a shelf the precious diadem stole,
And put it in his pocket!

QUEEN.   No more!   100

HAMLET.   A king of shreds and patches—

                                              (*Enter* GHOST.)

Save me, and hover o'er me with your wings,
You heavenly guards! What would your gracious figure?

QUEEN.   Alas, he's mad!

HAMLET.   Do you not come your tardy son to chide,   105
That, lapsed in time and passion, lets go by
The important acting of your dread command?
O, say!

GHOST.   Do not forget: This visitation
Is but to whet thy almost blunted purpose.   110
But, look, amazement on thy mother sits:
O, step between her and her fighting soul;
Conceit in weakest bodies strongest works:
Speak to her, Hamlet.

HAMLET.   How is it with you, lady?

QUEEN.   Alas, how is't with you,   115
That you do bend your eye on vacancy,
And with the incorporal air do hold discourse?
Forth at your eyes your spirits wildly peep;
And, as the sleeping soldiers in the alarm,
Your bedded hair, like life in excrements,   120
Start up, and stand an end. O gentle son,
Upon the heat and flame of thy distemper
Sprinkle cool patience. Whereon do you look?

HAM.   On him, on him! Look you, how pale he glares!
His form and cause conjoin'd, preaching to stones,   125
Would make them capable. Do not look upon me;
Lest with this piteous action you convert
My stern effects: Then what I have to do
Will want true colour; tears perchance for blood.

QUEEN.   To whom do you speak this?

HAMLET.   Do you see nothing there?   130

QUEEN.   Nothing at all; yet all that is I see.

HAM.   Nor did you nothing hear?

QUEEN.   No, nothing but ourselves.

HAMLET.   Why, look you there! look, how it steals away!
My father, in his habit as he lived!
Look, where he goes, even now, out at the portal!   135

[*Exit* GHOST.]

QUEEN.   This is the very coinage of your brain:
This bodiless creation ecstasy
Is very cunning in.

HAMLET.   Ecstasy!
My pulse, as yours, doth temperately keep time,
And makes as healthful music: 'Tis not madness   140
That I have utter'd: Bring me to the test,
And I the matter will re-word; which madness
Would gambol from. Mother, for love of grace
Lay not that flattering unction to your soul,
That not your trespass, but my madness speaks: 145
It will but skin and film the ulcerous place,
Whilst rank corruption, mining all within,
Infects unseen. Confess yourself to heaven;
Repent what's past; avoid what is to come;
And do not spread the compost on the weeds,   150
To make them ranker. Forgive me this my virtue;
For in the fatness of these pursy times
Virtue itself of vice must pardon beg,
Yea, curb and woo for leave to do him good.

QUEEN.   O Hamlet, thou hast cleft my heart in twain.   155

HAMLET.   O, throw away the worser part of it,
And live the purer with the other half.
Good night: But go not to my uncle's bed;
Assume a virtue, if you have it not.
That monster, custom, who all sense doth eat,   160
Of habits devil, is angel yet in this,
That to the use of actions fair and good
He likewise gives a frock or livery,
That aptly is put on. Refrain tonight;
And that shall lend a kind of easiness   165
To the next abstinence. The next more easy;
For use almost can change the stamp of nature,

And either master the devil, or throw him out
With wondrous potency. Once more, good night:
And when you are desirous to be bless'd,   170
I'll blessing beg of you—For this same lord,

[*Pointing to* POLONIUS.]

I do repent: But heaven hath pleased it so,
To punish me with this, and this with me,
That I must be their scourge and minister.
I will bestow him, and will answer well   175
The death I gave him. So, again, good night.
I must be cruel, only to be kind:
Thus bad begins, and worse remains behind.
One word more, good lady.
    QUEEN.   What shall I do?
    HAMLET.   Not this, by no means, that I bid you do: 180
Let the bloat king tempt you again to bed;
Pinch wanton on your cheek; call you his mouse;
And let him, for a pair of reechy kisses,
Or paddling in your neck with his damn'd fingers,
Make you to ravel all this matter out,   185
That I essentially am not in madness,
But mad in craft. 'Twere good you let him know;
For who, that's but a queen, fair, sober, wise,
Would from a paddock, from a bat, a gib,
Such dear concernings hide? Who would do so?   190
No, in despite of sense and secrecy,
Unpeg the basket on the house's top,
Let the birds fly, and, like the famous ape,
To try conclusions, in the basket creep,
And break your own neck down.   195
    QUEEN.   Be thou assured, if words be made of breath,
And breath of life, I have no life to breathe
What thou hast said to me.
    HAMLET.   I must to England; you know that?
    QUEEN.   Alack,
I had forgot: 'Tis so concluded on.   200
    HAM.   There's letters seal'd: And my two schoolfellows,
Whom I will trust as I will adders fang'd,
They bear the mandate; they must sweep my way,
And marshal me to knavery. Let it work;
For 'tis the sport to have the enginer   205

Hoist with his own petar: And't shall go hard
But I will delve one yard below their mines,
And blow them at the moon: O, 'tis most sweet
When in one line two crafts directly meet.
This man shall set me packing: 210
I'll lug the corpse into the neighbour room.
Mother, good night. Indeed, this counsellor
Is now most still, most secret, and most grave,
Who was in life a foolish prating knave.
Come, sir, to draw toward an end with you.   215
Good night, mother.

        [*Exeunt severally*; HAMLET *dragging in* POLONIUS.]

Act IV

SCENE I   A ROOM IN THE CASTLE

      (ENTER KING, QUEEN, ROSENCRANTZ *and* GUILDENSTERN.)

KING.   There's matter in these sighs, these profound heaves:
You must translate: 'Tis fit we understand them.
Where is your son?

    QUEEN.   Bestow this place on us a little while.

        [*Exeunt* ROSENCRANTZ *and* GUILDENSTERN.]

Ah, mine own lord, what have I seen tonight!   5

    KING.   What, Gertrude? How does Hamlet?

    QUEEN.   Mad as the sea and wind, when both contend
Which is the mightier: In his lawless fit,
Behind the arras hearing something stir,
Whips out his rapier, cries "A rat, a rat!"   10
And, in this brainish apprehension, kills
The unseen good old man.

    KING.   O heavy deed!
It had been so with us, had we been there:
His liberty is full of threats to all;
To you yourself, to us, to every one.   15
Alas, how shall this bloody deed be answer'd?
It will be laid to us, whose providence
Should have kept short, restrain'd, and out of haunt
This mad young man: But so much was our love,
We would not understand what was most fit,   20

But, like the owner of a foul disease,
To keep it from divulging, let it feed
Even on the pith of life. Where is he gone?

QUEEN.   To draw apart the body he hath kill'd:
O'er whom his very madness, like some ore   25
Among a mineral of metals base,
Shows itself pure; he weeps for what is done.

KING.   O Gertrude, come away!
The sun no sooner shall the mountains touch,
But we will ship him hence: And this vile deed   30
We must, with all our majesty and skill,
Both countenance and excuse. Ho, Guildenstern!

(*Reenter* ROSENCRANTZ *and* GUILDENSTERN.)

Friends both, go join you with some further aid:
Hamlet in madness hath Polonius slain,
And from his mother's closet hath he dragg'd him: 35
Go seek him out; speak fair, and bring the body
Into the chapel. I pray you, haste in this.

[*Exeunt* ROSENCRANTZ *and* GUILDENSTERN.]

Come, Gertrude, we'll call up our wisest friends;
And let them know, both what we mean to do,
And what's untimely done: [so, haply slander—]   40
Whose whisper o'er the world's diameter,
As level as the cannon to his blank,
Transports his poison'd shot—may miss our name,
And hit the woundless air. O, come away!
My soul is full of discord and dismay.   [*Exeunt.*]

SCENE II   ANOTHER ROOM IN THE CASTLE

(*Enter* HAMLET.)

HAMLET.   Safely stowed.

ROS., GUIL.   [*Within*]   Hamlet! Lord Hamlet!

HAMLET.   What noise? who calls on Hamlet? O, here they come.

(*Enter* ROSENCRANTZ *and* GUILDENSTERN.)

ROS.   What have you done, my lord, with the dead body?   5

HAM.   Compounded it with dust, whereto 'tis kin.

ROS.   Tell us where 'tis; that we may take it thence,
And bear it to the chapel.

HAMLET.   Do not believe it.

ROSENCRANTZ.   Believe what? 10

HAMLET.   That I can keep your counsel, and not mine own. Besides, to be demanded of a sponge! What replication should be made by the son of a king?

ROSENCRANTZ.   Take you me for a sponge, my lord?

HAMLET.   Ay, sir: that soaks up the king's countenance, his rewards, his authorities. But such officers do the king best service in the end: He keeps them, like an ape, in the corner of his jaw; first mouthed, to be last swallowed: When he needs what you have gleaned, it is but squeezing you, and, sponge, you shall be dry again.

ROSENCRANTZ.   I understand you not, my lord. 20

HAMLET.   I am glad of it: A knavish speech sleeps in a foolish ear.

ROSENCRANTZ.   My lord, you must tell us where the body is, and go with us to the king.

HAMLET.   The body is with the king, but the king is not with the body. The king is a thing— 25

GUILDENSTERN.   A thing, my lord!

HAMLET.   Of nothing: Bring me to him. Hide fox, and all after.

[*Exeunt.*]

SCENE III   ANOTHER ROOM IN THE CASTLE

(*Enter* KING, *attended.*)

KING.   I have sent to seek him, and to find the body.
How dangerous is it that this man goes loose:
Yet must not we put the strong law on him:
He's loved of the distracted multitude,
Who like not in their judgment, but their eyes; 5
And where 'tis so, the offender's scourge is weigh'd,
But never the offence. To bear all smooth and even,
This sudden sending him away must seem
Deliberate pause: Diseases desperate grown
By desperate appliance are relieved, 10
Or not at all.

(*Enter* ROSENCRANTZ.)

How now! what hath befall'n?

ROSENCRANTZ.   Where the dead body is bestow'd, my lord,
We cannot get from him.

KING.   But where is he?

ROS.   Without, my lord; guarded, to know your pleasure.

KING.   Bring him before us.   15

ROSENCRANTZ.   Ho, Guildenstern! Bring in my lord.

> (*Enter* HAMLET *and* GUILDENSTERN.)

KING.   Now, Hamlet, where's Polonius?

HAMLET.   At supper.

KING.   At supper! Where?

HAMLET.   Not where he eats, but where he is eaten: A certain con-
vocation of politic worms are e'en at him. Your worm is your only em-
peror for diet: We fat all creatures else to fat us, and we fat ourselves
for maggots: Your fat king and your lean beggar is but variable service,
two dishes, but to one table. That's the end.

KING.   Alas, alas!   25

HAMLET.   A man may fish with the worm that hath eat of a king, and
eat of the fish that hath fed of that worm.

KING.   What dost thou mean by this?

HAMLET.   Nothing but to show you how a king may go a progress
through a beggar.   30

KING.   Where is Polonius?

HAM.   In heaven; send thither to see. If your messenger find him not
there, seek him i' the other place yourself. But indeed, if you find him
not within this month, you shall nose him as you go up the stairs into the
lobby.   35

KING.   Go seek him there.   [*To some* ATTENDANTS.]

HAM.   He will stay till ye come.   [*Exeunt* ATTENDANTS.]

KING.   Hamlet, this deed, for thine especial safety—
Which we do tender, as we dearly grieve
For that which thou hast done—must send thee hence   40
With fiery quickness: Therefore prepare thyself;
The bark is ready, and the wind at help,
The associates tend, and every thing is bent
For England.

HAMLET.   For England!

KING.   Ay, Hamlet.

HAMLET.   Good.

KING.   So is it, if thou knew'st our purposes.   45

HAMLET.   I see a cherub that sees them. But, come; for England!
Farewell, dear mother.

KING.   Thy loving father, Hamlet.

HAMLET.   My mother: Father and mother is man and wife; man and
wife is one flesh; and so, my mother.   50
Come, for England!   [*Exit.*]

KING.   Follow him at foot; tempt him with speed aboard;
Delay it not; I'll have him hence tonight:
Away! For every thing is seal'd and done
That else leans on the affair: Pray you, make haste.   55

[*Exeunt* ROSENCRANTZ *and* GUILDENSTERN.]

And, England, if my love thou hold'st at aught—
As my great power thereof may give thee sense,
Since yet thy cicatrice looks raw and red
After the Danish sword, and thy free awe
Pays homage to us—thou mayst not coldly set   60
Our sovereign process; which imports at full,
By letters congruing to that effect,
The present death of Hamlet. Do it, England;
For like the hectic in my blood he rages,
And thou must cure me: Till I know 'tis done,   65
Howe'er my haps, my joys were ne'er begun.   [*Exit.*]

SCENE IV   A PLAIN IN DENMARK

(*Enter* FORTINBRAS, *a* CAPTAIN, *and* FORCES, *marching*.)

FORTINBRAS.   Go, captain, from me greet the Danish king;
Tell him that, by his license, Fortinbras
Claims the conveyance of a promised march
Over his kingdom. You know the rendezvous.
If that his majesty would aught with us,   5
We shall express our duty in his eye;
And let him know so.

CAPTAIN.   I will do't, my lord.

FOR.   Go softly on.   [*Exeunt* FORTINBRAS *and* FORCES.]

(*Enter* HAMLET, ROSENCRANTZ, GUILDENSTERN, *and others*.)

HAMLET.   Good sir, whose powers are these?

CAPTAIN.   They are of Norway, sir.   10

HAMLET.   How purposed, sir, I pray you?

CAPTAIN.   Against some part of Poland.

HAMLET.   Who commands them, sir?

CAPTAIN.   The nephew to old Norway, Fortinbras.

HAMLET.   Goes it against the main of Poland, sir,   15
Or for some frontier?

CAPTAIN.   Truly to speak, sir, and with no addition,
We go to gain a little patch of ground
That hath in it no profit but the name.
To pay five ducats, five, I would not farm it;   20
Nor will it yield to Norway or the Pole
A ranker rate, should it be sold in fee.

HAMLET.   Why, then, the Polack never will defend it.

CAPTAIN.   Yes, 'tis already garrison'd.

HAM.   Two thousand souls and twenty thousand ducats   25
Will not debate the question of this straw:
This is the imposthume of much wealth and peace,
That inward breaks, and shows no cause without
Why the man dies. I humbly thank you, sir.

CAP.   God be wi' you, sir.   [*Exit.*]

ROSENCRANTZ.   Will't please you go, my lord?   30

HAM.   I'll be with you straight. Go a little before.

                      [*Exeunt all except* HAMLET.]

How all occasions do inform against me,
And spur my dull revenge! What is a man,
If his chief good and market of his time
Be but to sleep and feed? A beast, no more.   35
Sure, he that made us with such large discourse,
Looking before and after, gave us not
That capability and godlike reason
To fust in us unused. Now, whether it be
Bestial oblivion, or some craven scruple   40
Of thinking too precisely on the event—
A thought which, quarter'd, hath but one part wisdom,
And ever three parts coward—I do not know
Why yet I live to say "This thing's to do";
Sith I have cause and will and strength and means   45
To do't. Examples, gross as earth, exhort me:
Witness this army, of such mass and charge,
Led by a delicate and tender prince,
Whose spirit, with divine ambition puff'd,
Makes mouths at the invisible event,   50
Exposing what is mortal and unsure

To all that fortune, death and danger dare,
Even for an egg-shell. Rightly to be great
Is not to stir without great argument,
But greatly to find quarrel in a straw   55
When honour's at the stake. How stand I then,
That have a father kill'd, a mother stain'd,
Excitements of my reason and my blood,
And let all sleep? While, to my shame, I see
The imminent death of twenty thousand men,   60
That for a fantasy and trick of fame
Go to their graves like beds, fight for a plot
Whereon the numbers cannot try the cause,
Which is not tomb enough and continent
To hide the slain? O, from this time forth,   65
My thoughts be bloody, or be nothing worth!   [*Exit.*]

SCENE V   ELSINORE, A ROOM IN THE CASTLE

(*Enter* QUEEN, HORATIO, *and a* GENTLEMAN.)

QUEEN.   I will not speak with her.

GENTLEMAN.   She is importunate, indeed distract;
Her mood will needs be pitied.

QUEEN.   What would she have?

GENT.   She speaks much of her father; says she hears
There's tricks i' the world; and hems, and beats her heart;   5
Spurns enviously at straws; speaks things in doubt,
That carry but half sense: Her speech is nothing,
Yet the unshaped use of it doth move
The hearers to collection; they aim at it,
And botch the words up fit to their own thoughts;   10
Which, as her winks and nods and gestures yield them,
Indeed would make one think there might be thought,
Though nothing sure, yet much unhappily.

HORATIO.   'Twere good she were spoken with; for she may strew
Dangerous conjectures in ill-breeding minds.   15

QUEEN.   Let her come in.   [*Exit* HORATIO.]
To my sick soul, as sin's true nature is,
Each toy seems prologue to some great amiss:
So full of artless jealousy is guilt,
It spills itself in fearing to be spilt.   20

(*Reenter* HORATIO, *with* OPHELIA.)

OPHELIA.   Where is the beauteous majesty of Denmark?

QUEEN.   How now, Ophelia!

OPHELIA.   [*Sings*]   How should I your true love know
From another one?
By his cockle hat and staff,   25
And his sandal shoon.

QUEEN.   Alas, sweet lady, what imports this song?

OPHELIA.   Say you? nay, pray you, mark.
[*Sings*]   He is dead and gone, lady,
He is dead and gone;   30
At his head a grass-green turf,
At his heels a stone.

QUEEN.   Nay, but, Ophelia—

OPHELIA.   Pray you, mark.
[*Sings*]   White his shroud as the mountain snow—   35

(*Enter* KING.)

QUEEN.   Alas, look here, my lord.

OPH.   [*Sings*]   Larded with sweet flowers;
Which bewept to the grave did go
With true-love showers.

KING.   How do you, pretty lady?   40

OPHELIA.   Well, God 'ild you! They say the owl was a baker's daughter. Lord, we know what we are, but know not what we may be. God be at your table!

KING.   Conceit upon her father.

OPHELIA.   Pray you, let's have no words of this; but when they ask you what it means, say you this:
[*Sings*]   Tomorrow is Saint Valentine's day,
All in the morning betime,
And I a maid at your window,
To be your Valentine.   50

KING.   Pretty Ophelia! How long hath she been thus?

OPHELIA.   I hope all will be well. We must be patient; but I cannot choose but weep, to think they should lay him i' the cold ground. My brother shall know of it: And so I thank you for your good counsel. Come, my coach! Good night, ladies; good night, sweet ladies; good night, good night.

[*Exit.*]

KING.   Follow her close; give her good watch, I pray you.

[Exit HORATIO.]

O, this is the poison of deep grief; it springs
All from her father's death. O Gertrude, Gertrude,
When sorrows come, they come not single spies,   60
But in battalions! First, her father slain:
Next, your son gone; and he most violent author
Of his own just remove: The people muddied,
Thick and unwholesome in their thoughts and whispers,
For good Polonius' death; and we have done but greenly,   65
In hugger-mugger to inter him. Poor Ophelia
Divided from herself and her fair judgment,
Without the which we are pictures, or mere beasts:
Last, and as much containing as all these,
Her brother is in secret come from France;   70
Feeds on his wonder, keeps himself in clouds,
And wants not buzzers to infect his ear
With pestilent speeches of his father's death;
Wherein necessity, of matter beggar'd,
Will nothing stick our person to arraign   75
In ear and ear. O my dear Gertrude, this,
Like to a murdering-piece, in many places
Gives me superfluous death.   *[A noise within.]*

QUEEN.   Alack, what noise is this?

KING.   Where are my Switzers? Let them guard the door.

(Enter a GENTLEMAN.)*

What is the matter?

GENTLEMAN.   Save yourself, my lord: 80
The ocean, overpeering of his list,
Eats not the flats with more impetuous haste
Than young Laertes, in a riotous head,
O'erbears your officers. The rabble call him lord;
And, as the world were now but to begin,   85
Antiquity forgot, custom not known,
The ratifiers and props of every word,
They cry, "Choose we; Laertes shall be king!"
Caps, hands, and tongues applaud it to the clouds,
"Laertes shall be king, Laertes king!"   90

QUEEN.   How cheerfully on the false trail they cry!
O, this is counter, you false Danish dogs!

KING.   The doors are broke.   *[Noise within.]*

(Enter LAERTES, armed; DANES following.)

LAERTES.   Where is this king? Sirs, stand you all without.

DANES.   No, let's come in.

LAERTES.   I pray you, give me leave.   95

DANES.   We will, we will.   [*They retire without the door.*]

LAERTES.   I thank you: Keep the door. O thou vile king,
Give me my father!

QUEEN.   Calmly, good Laertes.

LAERTES..   That drop of blood that's calm proclaims me bastard;   100
Cries cuckold to my father; brands the harlot
Even here, between the chaste unsmirched brow
Of my true mother.

KING.   What's the cause, Laertes,
That thy rebellion looks so giant-like?
Let him go, Gertrude; do not fear our person: 105
There's such divinity doth hedge a king,
That treason can but peep to what it would,
Acts little of his will. Tell me, Laertes,
Why thou art thus incensed: Let him go, Gertrude:
Speak, man.   110

LAERTES.   Where is my father?

KING.   Dead.

QUEEN.   But not by him.

KING.   Let him demand his fill.

LAERTES.   How came he dead? I'll not be juggled with:
To hell, allegiance! vows, to the blackest devil!
Conscience and grace, to the profoundest pit!   115
I dare damnation: To this point I stand,
That both the worlds I give to negligence,
Let come what comes; only I'll be revenged
Most throughly for my father.

KING.   Who shall stay you?

LAERTES.   My will, not all the world: 120
And for my means, I'll husband them so well,
They shall go far with little.

KING.   Good Laertes,
If you desire to know the certainty
Of your dear father's death, is't writ in your revenge   125
That, swoopstake, you will draw both friend and foe,
Winner and loser?

LAERTES.   None but his enemies.

KING.   Will you know them then?

LAERTES.   To his good friends thus wide I'll ope my arms,
And, like the kind life-rendering pelican,
Repast them with my blood.

KING.   Why, now you speak   130
Like a good child and a true gentleman.
That I am guiltless of your father's death,
And am most sensibly in grief for it,
It shall as level to your judgment pierce
As day does to your eye.

DANES.   [*Within*]   Let her come in.   135

LAERTES.   How now! what noise is that?

                              (*Reenter* OPHELIA.)

O heat, dry up my brains! tears seven-times salt,
Burn out the sense and virtue of mine eye!
By heaven, thy madness shall be paid by weight,
Till our scale turn the beam. O rose of May!   140
Dear maid, kind sister, sweet Ophelia!
O heavens! Is't possible a young maid's wits
Should be as mortal as an old man's life?
Nature is fine in love, and where 'tis fine,
It sends some precious instance of itself   145
After the thing it loves.

OPH.   [*Sings*]   They bore him barefaced on the bier;
                     Hey non nonny, nonny, hey nonny;
                     And in his grave rain'd many a tear—
Fare you well, my dove!   150

LAER.   Hadst thou thy wits, and didst persuade revenge,
It could not move thus.

OPH.   [*Sings*]   You must sing a-down a-down,
                     An you call him a-down-a.
O, how the wheel becomes it! It is the false steward, that stole his
master's daughter.   155

LAERTES.   This nothing's more than matter.

OPHELIA.   There's rosemary, that's for remembrance; pray you, love,
remember: And there is pansies, that's for thoughts.

LAERTES.   A document in madness, thoughts and remembrance fitted.

OPHELIA.   There's fennel for you, and columbines: There's rue for
you; and here's some for me: We may call it herb of grace o' Sundays:

O, you must wear your rue with a difference. There's a daisy: I would
give you some violets, but they withered all when my father died: they
say he made a good end—   165
[*Sings*]   For bonny sweet Robin is all my joy—

  LAERTES.   Thought and affliction, passion, hell itself,
She turns to favour and to prettiness.

  OPHELIA.   [*Sings*]

       And will he not come again?
       And will he not come again?   170
        No, no, he is dead:
        Go to thy death-bed:
        He never will come again.

       His beard was as white as snow,
       All flaxen was his poll: 175
        He is gone, he is gone,
        And we cast away moan:
        God ha' mercy on his soul!
And of all Christian souls, I pray God. God be wi' ye.

                [*Exit.*]

  LAERTES.   Do you see this, O God?   180
  KING.   Laertes, I must commune with your grief,
Or you deny me right. Go but apart,
Make choice of whom your wisest friends you will,
And they shall hear and judge 'twixt you and me:
If by direct or by collateral hand   185
They find us touch'd, we will our kingdom give,
Our crown, our life, and all that we call ours,
To you in satisfaction; but if not,
Be you content to lend your patience to us,
And we shall jointly labour with your soul   190
To give it due content.

  LAERTES.   Let this be so;
His means of death, his obscure burial—
No trophy, sword, nor hatchment o'er his bones,
No noble rite nor formal ostentation—
Cry to be heard, as 'twere from heaven to earth,   195
That I must call't in question.

  KING.   So you shall;
And where the offence is let the great axe fall.
I pray you, go with me.   [*Exeunt.*]

SCENE VI   ANOTHER ROOM IN THE CASTLE

(*Enter* HORATIO *and a* SERVANT.)

HORATIO.   What are they that would speak with me?

SERVANT.   Sailors, sir: they say they have letters for you.

HORATIO.   Let them come in.   [*Exit* SERVANT.]
I do not know from what part of the world
I should be greeted, if not from Lord Hamlet.   5

(*Enter* SAILORS.)

FIRST SAILOR.   God bless you, sir.

HORATIO.   Let him bless thee too.

FIRST SAILOR.   He shall, sir, an't please him. There's a letter for you
sir: It comes from the ambassador that was bound for England; if your
name be Horatio, as I am let to know it is.   10

HORATIO.   [*Reads*] "Horatio, when thou shalt have overlooked this,
give these fellows some means to the king: They have letters for him.
Ere we were two days old at sea, a pirate of very warlike appointment
gave us chase. Finding ourselves too slow of sail, we put on a compelled
valour, and in the grapple I boarded them: On the instant they got clear
of our ship; so I alone became their prisoner. They have dealt with me like
thieves of mercy: But they knew what they did; I am to do a good turn
for them. Let the king have the letters I have sent; and repair thou to
me with as much haste as thou wouldest fly death. I have words to speak
in thine ear will make thee dumb; yet are they much too light for the
bore of the matter. These good fellows will bring thee where I am. Rosencrantz and Guildenstern hold their course for England: Of them I have
much to tell thee. Farewell.

"He that thou knowest thine, HAMLET."
Come, I will make you way for these your letters;   25
And do't the speedier, that you may direct me
To him from whom you brought them.   [*Exeunt.*]

SCENE VII   ANOTHER ROOM IN THE CASTLE

(*Enter* KING *and* LAERTES.)

KING.   Now must your conscience my acquittance seal,
And you must put me in your heart for friend,
Sith you have heard, and with a knowing ear,

That he which hath your noble father slain
Pursued my life.

LAERTES.   It well appears: But tell me   5
Why you proceeded not against these feats,
So crimeful and so capital in nature,
As by your safety, wisdom, all things else,
You mainly were stirr'd up.

KING.   O, for two special reasons;
Which may to you, perhaps, seem much unsinew'd,   10
But yet to me they are strong. The queen his mother
Lives almost by his looks; and for myself—
My virtue or my plague, be't either which—
She's so conjunctive to my life and soul,
That, as the star moves not but in his sphere,   15
I could not but by her. The other motive,
Why to a public count I might not go,
Is the great love the general gender bear him;
Who, dipping all his faults in their affection,
Would, like the spring that turneth wood to stone,   20
Convert his gyves to graces; so that my arrows,
Too slightly timber'd for so loud a wind,
Would have reverted to my bow again,
And not where I had aim'd them.

LAERTES.   And so have I a noble father lost;   25
A sister driven into desperate terms,
Whose worth, if praises may go back again,
Stood challenger on mount of all the age
For her perfections: But my revenge will come.

KING.   Break not your sleeps for that: You must not think   30
That we are made of stuff so flat and dull,
That we can let our beard be shook with danger
And think it pastime. You shortly shall hear more:
I loved your father, and we love ourself;
And that, I hope, will teach you to imagine—   35

(*Enter a* MESSENGER.)

How now! what news?

MESSENGER.   Letters, my lord, from Hamlet:
This to your majesty; this to the queen.

KING.   From Hamlet! Who brought them?

MESSENGER.   Sailors, my lord, they say; I saw them not:

They were given me by Claudio; he received them   40
Of him that brought them.

    KING.   Laertes, you shall hear them.
Leave us.   [*Exit* MESSENGER.]

    [*Reads*]   "High and mighty, You shall know I am set naked on your
kingdom. Tomorrow shall I beg leave to see your kingly eyes: When I
shall, first asking your pardon thereunto, recount the occasion of my sudden and more strange return.

                                                 "HAMLET."

What should this mean? Are all the rest come back?
Or is it some abuse, and no such thing?

    LAER.   Know you the hand?

    KING.   'Tis Hamlet's character. "Naked"—
And in a postscript here, he says, "alone."   50
Can you advise me?

    LAERTES.   I am lost in it, my lord. But let him come;
It warms the very sickness in my heart,
That I shall live and tell him to his teeth,
"Thus diddest thou."

    KING.   If it be so, Laertes—   55
As how should it be so? how otherwise?—
Will you be ruled by me?

    LAERTES.   Ay, my lord;
So you will not o'errule me to a peace.

    KING.   To thine own peace. If he be now return'd,
As checking at his voyage, and that he means   60
No more to undertake it, I will work him
To an exploit, now ripe in my device,
Under the which he shall not choose but fall:
And for his death no wind of blame shall breathe,
But even his mother shall uncharge the practice,   65
And call it accident.

    LAERTES.   My lord, I will be ruled;
The rather, if you could devise it so,
That I might be the organ.

    KING.   It falls right.
You have been talk'd of since your travel much,
And that in Hamlet's hearing, for a quality   70
Wherein, they say, you shine: Your sum of parts
Did not together pluck such envy from him,

As did that one, and that, in my regard,
Of the unworthiest siege.

LAERTES.   What part is that, my lord?

KING.   A very riband in the cap of youth,   75
Yet needful too; for youth no less becomes
The light and careless livery that it wears
Than settled age his sables and his weeds,
Importing health and graveness. Two months since,
Here was a gentleman of Normandy,   80
I have seen myself, and serv'd against, the French,
And they can well on horseback: But this gallant
Had witchcraft in't; he grew unto his seat;
And to such wondrous doing brought his horse,
As he had been incorpsed and demi-natured   85
With the brave beast: So far he topp'd my thought,
That I, in forgery of shapes and tricks,
Come short of what he did.

LAERTES.   A Norman was't?

KING.   A Norman.

LAERTES.   Upon my life, Lamond.

KING.   The very same.   90

LAERTES.   I know him well: He is the brooch indeed
And gem of all the nation.

KING.   He made confession of you,
And gave you such a masterly report,
For art and exercise in your defence,   95
And for your rapier most especially,
That he cried out, 'twould be a sight indeed,
If one could match you: The scrimers of their nation,
He swore, had neither motion, guard, nor eye,
If you opposed them. Sir, this report of his   100
Did Hamlet to envenom with his envy,
That he could nothing do but wish and beg
Your sudden coming o'er, to play with him.
Now, out of this—

LAERTES.   What out of this, my lord?

KING.   Laertes, was your father dear to you?   105
Or are you like the painting of a sorrow,
A face without a heart?

LAERTES.   Why ask you this?

KING.   Not that I think you did not love your father;
But that I know love is begun by time;
And that I see, in passages of proof,   110
Time qualifies the spark and fire of it.
There lives within the very flame of love
A kind of wick or snuff that will abate it;
And nothing is at a like goodness still;
For goodness, growing to a plurisy,   115
Dies in his own too-much: That we would do.
We should do when we would; for this "would" changes,
And hath abatements and delays as many
As there are tongues, are hands, are accidents;
And then this "should" is like a spendthrift sigh,   120
That hurts by easing. But, to the quick o' the ulcer:—
Hamlet comes back. What would you undertake,
To show yourself your father's son in deed
More than in words?

    LAERTES.   To cut his throat i' the church.

    KING.   No place, indeed, should murder sanctuarize;   125
Revenge should have no bounds. But, good Laertes,
Will you do this, keep close within your chamber.
Hamlet return'd shall know you are come home:
We'll put on those shall praise your excellence,
And set a double varnish on the fame   130
The Frenchman gave you; bring you in fine together,
And wager on your heads. He, being remiss.
Most generous, and free from all contriving,
Will not peruse the foils; so that with ease,
Or with a little shuffling, you may choose   135
A sword unbated, and in a pass of practice
Requite him for your father.

    LAERTES.   I will do't:
And for that purpose I'll anoint my sword.
I bought an unction of a mountebank,
So mortal, that but dip a knife in it,   140
Where it draws blood no cataplasm so rare,
Collected from all simples that have virtue
Under the moon, can save the thing from death
That is but scratch'd withal: I'll touch my point
With this contagion, that, if I gall him slightly,   145
It may be death.

    KING.   Let's further think of this:

Weigh what convenience both of time and means
May fit us to our shape: If this should fail,
And that our drift look through our bad performance,
'Twere better not assay'd: Therefore this project   150
Should have a back or second, that might hold,
If this should blast in proof. Soft! let me see:
We'll make a solemn wager on your cunnings.
I ha't:
When in your motion you are hot and dry—   155
As make your bouts more violent to that end—
And that he calls for drink, I'll have prepared him
A chalice for the nonce; whereon but sipping,
If he by chance escape your venom'd stuck,
Our purpose may hold there.

                                        (*Enter* QUEEN.)

                    How now, sweet queen!   160

QUEEN.   One woe doth tread upon another's heel,
So fast they follow: Your sister's drown'd, Laertes.

LAERTES.   Drown'd! O, where?

QUEEN.   There is a willow grows aslant a brook,
That shows his hoar leaves in the glassy stream;   165
There with fantastic garlands did she come
Of crow-flowers, nettles, daisies, and long purples
That liberal shepherds give a grosser name,
But our cold maids do dead men's fingers call them:
There, on the pendent boughs her coronet weeds   170
Clambering to hang, an envious sliver broke:
When down her weedy trophies and herself
Fell in the weeping brook. Her clothes spread wide,
And, mermaid-like, awhile they bore her up;
Which time she chanted snatches of old tunes,   175
As one incapable of her own distress,
Or like a creature native and indued
Unto the element. But long it could not be
Till that her garments, heavy with their drink,
Pull'd the poor wretch from her melodious lay   180
To muddy death.

LAERTES.   Alas, then, she is drown'd?

QUEEN.   Drown'd, drown'd.

LAERTES.   Too much of water hast thou, poor Ophelia,
And therefore I forbid my tears: But yet

It is our trick; nature her custom holds,   185
Let shame say what it will. When these are gone,
The woman will be out. Adieu, my lord:
I have a speech of fire, that fain would blaze,
But that this folly douts it.   [*Exit.*]

KING.   Let's follow, Gertrude:
How much I had to do to calm his rage!   190
Now fear I this will give it start again;
Therefore let's follow.   [*Exeunt.*]

ACT V

SCENE I   ELSINORE, A CHURCHYARD

(*Enter two* CLOWNS, *with spades, and so on.*)

FIRST CLOWN.   Is she to be buried in Christian burial that wilfully
seeks her own salvation?

SECOND CLOWN.   I tell thee she is; and therefore make her grave
straight: The crowner hath sat on her, and finds it Christian burial.

FIRST CLOWN.   How can that be, unless she drowned herself in her
own defence?

SECOND CLOWN.   Why 'tis found so.

FIRST CLOWN.   It must be *se offendendo*; it cannot be else. For here
lies the point: If I drown myself wittingly, it argues an act; and an act
hath three branches; it is, to act, to do, to perform. Argal, she drowned
herself wittingly.

SECOND CLOWN.   Nay, but hear you, goodman delver—

FIRST CLOWN.   Give me leave. Here lies the water; good: Here stands
the man; good. If the man go to this water and drown himself, it is, will
he, nill he, he goes—mark you that; but if the water come to him and
drown him, he drowns not himself. Argal, he that is not guilty of his own
death shortens not his own life.

SECOND CLOWN.   But is this law?

FIRST CLOWN.   Ay, marry, is't; crowner's quest law.

SECOND CLOWN.   Will you ha' the truth on't? If this had not been a
gentlewoman, she should have been buried out of Christian burial.

FIRST CLOWN.   Why, there thou say'st: And the more pity that great
folk should have countenance in this world to drown or hang themselves,
more than their even Christian. Come, my spade. There is no ancient
gentlemen but gardeners, ditchers, and grave-makers: They hold up
Adam's profession.

SECOND CLOWN.   Was he a gentleman?

FIRST CLOWN.   He was the first that ever bore arms.

SECOND CLOWN.   Why, he had none.

FIRST CLOWN.   What, art a heathen? How dost thou understand the Scripture? The Scripture says, Adam digged: Could he dig without arms? I'll put another question to thee: If thou answerest me not to the purpose, confess thyself—

SECOND CLOWN.   Go to.

FIRST CLOWN.   What is he that builds stronger than either the mason, the shipwright, or the carpenter?

SECOND CLOWN.   The gallows-maker; for that frame outlives a thousand tenants.

FIRST CLOWN.   I like thy wit well, in good faith: The gallows does well; but how does it well? It does well to those that do ill: Now, thou dost ill to say the gallows is built stronger than the church. Argal, the gallows may do well to thee. To't again, come.

SECOND CLOWN.   "Who builds stronger than a mason, a shipwright, or a carpenter?"

FIRST CLOWN.   Ay, tell me that, and unyoke.   45

SECOND CLOWN.   Marry, now I can tell.

FIRST CLOWN.   To't.

SECOND CLOWN.   Mass, I cannot tell.

(Enter HAMLET *and* HORATIO, *at some distance.)*

FIRST CLOWN.   Cudgel thy brains no more about it, for your dull ass will not mend his pace with beating; and when you are asked this question next, say "a grave-maker." The houses that he makes last till doomsday. Go, get thee to Yaughan; fetch me a stoup of liquor.

[Exit SECOND CLOWN.]
[He digs, and sings.]

> In youth when I did love, did love,
>   Methought it was very sweet,
>   To contract, O, the time, for, ah, my behove,   55
>   O, methought there was nothing meet.

HAMLET.   Has this fellow no feeling of his business, that he sings at grave-making?

HORATIO.   Custom hath made it in him a property of easiness.

HAMLET.   'Tis e'en so: The hand of little employment hath the daintier sense.

FIRST CLOWN.   [*Sings*]
    But age, with his stealing steps,
     Hath claw'd me in his clutch,
    And hath shipped me intil the land,
     As if I had never been such.   65

        [*Throws up a skull.*]

HAMLET.   That skull had a tongue in it, and could sing once: How the knave jowls it to the ground, as if it were Cain's jaw-bone, that did the first murder! It might be the pate of a politician, which this ass now o'er-reaches; one that would circumvent God, might it not?

HORATIO.   It might, my lord.   70

HAMLET.   Or of a courtier; which could say "Good morrow, sweet lord! How dost thou, good lord?" This might be my lord such-a-one, that praised my lord such-a-one's horse, when he meant to beg it—might it not?

HORATIO.   Ay, my lord.   75

HAMLET.   Why, e'en so: And now my Lady Worm's; chapless, and knocked about the mazzard with a sexton's spade. Here's fine revolution, an we had the trick to see't. Did these bones cost no more the breeding, but to play at loggats with 'em? Mine ache to think on't.

FIRST CLOWN.   [*Sings*]
    A pickaxe, and a spade, a spade,   80
     For and a shrouding-sheet:
    O, a pit of clay for to be made
     For such a guest is meet.

       [*Throws up another skull.*]

HAMLET.   There's another: Why may not that be the skull of a lawyer? Where be his quiddities now, his quillets, his cases, his tenures, and his tricks? Why does he suffer this rude knave now to knock him about the sconce with a dirty shovel, and will not tell him of his action of battery? Hum! This fellow might be in's time a great buyer of land, with his statutes, his recognizances, his fines, his double vouchers, his recoveries: Is this the fine of his fines, and the recovery of his recoveries, to have his fine pate full of fine dirt? Will his vouchers vouch him no more of his purchases, and double ones too, than the length and breadth of a pair of indentures? The very conveyances of his lands will hardly lie in this box; and must the inheritor himself have no more, ha?

HORATIO.   Not a jot more, my lord.   95

HAMLET.   Is not parchment made of sheep-skins?

HORATIO.   Ay, my lord, and of calf-skins too.

HAMLET.   They are sheep and calves which seek out assurance in that. I will speak to this fellow. Whose grave's this, sirrah?

FIRST CLOWN.   Mine, sir.   100
[*Sings*]   O, a pit of clay for to be made
                     For such a guest is meet.

HAMLET.   I think it be thine, indeed; for thou liest in't.

FIRST CLOWN.   You lie out on't, sir, and therefore it is not yours: For my part, I do not lie in't, and yet it is mine.   105

HAMLET.   Thou dost lie in't, to be in't, and say it is thine. 'Tis for the dead, not for the quick; therefore thou liest.

FIRST CLOWN.   'Tis a quick lie, sir; 'twill away again, from me to you.

HAMLET.   What man dost thou dig it for?

FIRST CLOWN.   For no man, sir.   110

HAMLET.   What woman, then?

FIRST CLOWN.   For none, neither.

HAMLET.   Who is to be buried in't?

FIRST CLOWN.   One that was a woman, sir; but, rest her soul, she's dead.   115

HAMLET.   How absolute the knave is! We must speak by the card, or equivocation will undo us. By the Lord, Horatio, these three years I have taken note of it; the age is grown so picked that the toe of the peasant comes so near the heel of the courtier, he galls his kibe. How long hast thou been a grave-maker?   120

FIRST CLOWN.   Of all the days i' the year, I came to't that day that our last king Hamlet o'ercame Fortinbras.

HAMLET.   How long is that since?

FIRST CLOWN.   Cannot you tell that? every fool can tell that: It was the very day that young Hamlet was born; he that is mad, and sent into England.

HAMLET.   Ay, marry, why was he sent into England?

FIRST CLOWN.   Why, because he was mad: He shall recover his wits there; or, if he do not, it's no great matter there.

HAMLET.   Why?   130

FIRST CLOWN.   'Twill not be seen in him there; there the men are as mad as he.

HAMLET.   How came he mad?

FIRST CLOWN.   Very strangely, they say.

HAMLET.   How strangely?   135

FIRST CLOWN.   Faith, e'en with losing his wits.

HAMLET.   Upon what ground?

FIRST CLOWN.   Why, here in Denmark: I have been sexton here, man and boy, thirty years.

HAMLET.   How long will a man lie i' the earth ere he rot?   140

FIRST CLOWN.   I' faith, if he be not rotten before he die—as we have many corses now-a-days that will scarce hold the laying in—he will last you some eight year or nine year: A tanner will last you nine year.

HAMLET.   Why he more than another?   145

FIRST CLOWN.   Why, sir, his hide is so tanned with his trade that he will keep out water a great while; and your water is a sore decayer of your dead body. Here's a skull now; this skull has lain in the earth three-and-twenty years.

HAMLET.   Whose was it?   150

FIRST CLOWN.   A mad fellow's it was: Whose do you think it was?

HAMLET.   Nay, I know not.

FIRST CLOWN.   A pestilence on him for a mad rogue! 'A poured a flagon of Rhenish on my head once. This same skull, sir, was Yorick's skull, the king's jester.   155

HAMLET.   This?

FIRST CLOWN.   E'en that.

HAMLET.   Let me see.   [*Takes the skull*]   Alas, poor Yorick! I knew him, Horatio; a fellow of infinite jest, of most excellent fancy. He hath borne me on his back a thousand times; and now how abhorred in my imagination it is! My gorge rises at it. Here hung those lips that I have kissed I know not how oft. Where be your gibes now? your gambols? your songs? your flashes of merriment, that were wont to set the table on a roar? Not one now, to mock your own grinning? quite chap-fallen? Now get you to my lady's chamber, and tell her, let her paint an inch thick, to this favour she must come; make her laugh at that. Prithee, Horatio, tell me one thing.

HORATIO.   What's that, my lord?

HAMLET.   Dost thou think Alexander looked o' this fashion i' the earth?   170

HORATIO.   E'en so.

HAMLET.   And smelt so? pah!   [*Puts down the skull.*]

HORATIO.   E'en so, my lord.

HAMLET.   To what base uses we may return, Horatio! Why may not imagination trace the noble dust of Alexander till he find it stopping a bung-hole?

HORATIO.   'Twere to consider too curiously, to consider so.

HAMLET.   No, faith, not a jot; but to follow him thither with modesty enough, and likelihood to lead it: As thus; Alexander died, Alexander was buried, Alexander returneth into dust; the dust is earth; of earth we make loam; and why of that loam whereto he was converted might they not stop a beer-barrel?

> Imperious Cæsar, dead and turn'd to clay,
> Might stop a hole to keep the wind away:
> O, that that earth which kept the world in awe   185
> Should patch a wall to expel the winter's flaw!

But soft! but soft! aside: Here comes the king,

> (*Enter* PRIESTS, *and so on, in procession; the Corpse of* OPHELIA,
> LAERTES *and* MOURNERS *following*; KING, QUEEN, *their
> trains, and others.*)

The queen, the courtiers: Who is this they follow?
And with such maimed rites? This doth betoken
The corse they follow did with desperate hand   190
Fordo it own life:'Twas of some estate.
Couch we awhile, and mark.   [*Retiring with* HORATIO.]

LAERTES.   What ceremony else?

HAMLET.   That is Laertes,
A very noble youth: mark.

LAERTES.   What ceremony else?   195

FIRST PRIEST.   Her obsequies have been as far enlarged
As we have warrantise: Her death was doubtful;
And, but that great command o'ersways the order,
She should in ground unsanctified have lodged
Till the last trumpet; for charitable prayers,   200
Shards, flints and pebbles should be thrown on her:
Yet here she is allow'd her virgin crants,
Her maiden strewments, and the bringing home
Of bell and burial

LAERTES.   Must there no more be done?

FIRST PRIEST.   No more be done: 205
We should profane the service of the dead
To sing a requiem and such rest to her
As to peace-parted souls.

LAERTES.   Lay her i' the earth;
And from her fair and unpolluted flesh

May violets spring! I tell thee, churlish priest,   210
A ministering angel shall my sister be,
When thou liest howling.

    HAMLET.   What, the fair Ophelia!

    QUEEN.   Sweets to the sweet: farewell!

                                                [*Scattering flowers.*]

I hoped thou shouldst have been my Hamlet's wife;
I thought thy bride-bed to have deck'd, sweet maid,   215
And not have strew'd thy grave.

    LAERTES.   O, treble woe
Fall ten times treble on that cursed head
Whose wicked deed thy most ingenious sense
Deprived thee of! Hold off the earth awhile,
Till I have caught her once more in mine arms: 220

                                                [*Leaps into the grave.*]

Now pile your dust upon the quick and dead,
Till of this flat a mountain you have made
To o'ertop old Pelion or the skyish head
Of blue Olympus.

    HAM.   [*Advancing*]   What is he whose grief
Bears such an emphasis; whose phrase of sorrow   225
Conjures the wandering stars and makes them stand
Like wonder-wounded hearers? This is I,
Hamlet the Dane.   [*Leaps into the grave.*]

    LAERTES.   The devil take thy soul!

                                                [*Grappling with him.*]

    HAMLET.   Thou pray'st not well.
I prithee, take thy fingers from my throat;   230
For, though I am not splenitive and rash,
Yet have I something in me dangerous,
Which let thy wisdom fear: Hold off thy hand!

    KING.   Pluck them asunder.

    QUEEN.   Hamlet, Hamlet!   235

    ALL.   Gentlemen—

    HORATIO.   Good my lord, be quiet.

                            [*The* ATTENDANTS *part them, and they
                                        come out of the grave.*]

    HAMLET.   Why, I will fight with him upon this theme
Until my eyelids will no longer wag.

QUEEN.   O my son, what theme?

HAMLET.   I loved Ophelia. Forty thousand brothers   240
Could not, with all their quantity of love,
Make up my sum. What wilt thou do for her?

KING.   O, he is mad, Laertes.

QUEEN.   For love of God, forbear him.

HAMLET.   'Swounds, show me what thou'lt do: 245
Woo't weep? Woo't fight? Woo't fast? Woo't tear thyself?
Woo't drink up eisel? Eat a crocodile?
I'll do't. Dost thou come here to whine?
To outface me with leaping in her grave?
Be buried quick with her, and so will I: 250
And if thou prate of mountains, let them throw
Millions of acres on us, till our ground,
Singeing his pate against the burning zone,
Make Ossa like a wart! Nay, an thou'lt mouth,
I'll rant as well as thou.

QUEEN.   This is mere madness: 255
And thus awhile the fit will work on him;
Anon, as patient as the female dove
When that her golden couplets are disclosed,
His silence will sit drooping.

HAMLET.   Hear you, sir;
What is the reason that you use me thus?   260
I loved you ever: But it is no matter;
Let Hercules himself do what he may,
The cat will mew, and dog will have his day.   [*Exit.*]

KING.   I pray you, good Horatio, wait upon him.

[*Exit* HORATIO.]

[*To* LAERTES] Strengthen your patience in our last night's speech;265
We'll put the matter to the present push.
Good Gertrude, set some watch over your son.
This grave shall have a living monument:
An hour of quiet shortly shall we see;
Till then, in patience our proceeding be.   [*Exeunt.*]

SCENE II   A HALL IN THE CASTLE

(*Enter* HAMLET *and* HORATIO.)

HAM.   So much for this, sir: Now shall you see the other;
You do remember all the circumstance?

HORATIO.   Remember it, my lord!

HAMLET.   Sir, in my heart there was a kind of fighting,
That would not let me sleep: Methought I lay   5
Worse than the mutines in the bilboes. Rashly,
And praised be rashness for it, let us know,
Our indiscretion sometimes serves us well,
When our deep plots do pall; and that should learn us
There's a divinity that shapes our ends,   10
Rough-hew them how we will—

HORATIO.   That is most certain.

HAMLET.   Up from my cabin,
My sea-gown scarf'd about me, in the dark
Groped I to find out them: Had my desire,
Finger'd their packet, and in fine withdrew   15
To mine own room again; making so bold,
My fears forgetting manners, to unseal
Their grand commission; where I found, Horatio—
O royal knavery!—an exact command,
Larded with many several sorts of reasons,   20
Importing Denmark's health and England's too,
With ho! Such bugs and goblins in my life,
That on the supervise, no leisure bated,
No, not to stay the grinding of the axe,
My head should be struck off.

HORATIO.   Is't possible?   25

HAMLET.   Here's the commission: Read it at more leisure.
But wilt thou hear me how I did proceed?

HORATIO.   I beseech you.

HAMLET.   Being thus be-netted round with villanies—
Ere I could make a prologue to my brains,   30
They had begun the play—I sat me down,
Devised a new commission, wrote it fair:
I once did hold it, as our statists do,
A baseness to write fair, and labour'd much
How to forget that learning; but, sir, now   35
It did me yeoman's service. Wilt thou know
The effect of what I wrote?

HORATIO.   Ay, good my lord.

HAMLET.   An earnest conjuration from the king,
As England was his faithful tributary,
As love between them like the palm might flourish,   40

As peace should still her wheaten garland wear
And stand a comma 'tween their amities;
And many such-like "as'es" of great charge,
That, on the view and knowing of these contents,
Without debatement further, more or less,   45
He should the bearers put to sudden death,
Not shriving-time allow'd.

    HORATIO.   How was this seal'd?

    HAMLET.   Why, even in that was heaven ordinant.
I had my father's signet in my purse,
Which was the model of that Danish seal;   50
Folded the writ up in form of the other,
Subscribed it, gave't the impression, placed it safely,
The changeling never known. Now, the next day
Was our sea-fight; and what to this was sequent
Thou know'st already.   55

    HORATIO.   So Guildenstern and Rosencrantz go to't.

    HAMLET.   Why, man, they did make love to this employment;
They are not near my conscience; their defeat
Doth by their own insinuation grow:
'Tis dangerous when the baser nature comes   60
Between the pass and fell incensed points
Of mighty opposites.

    HORATIO.   Why, what a king is this!

    HAM.   Does it not, think'st thee, stand me now upon—
He that hath kill'd my king, and stain'd my mother,
Popp'd in between the election and my hopes,   65
Thrown out his angle for my proper life,
And with such cozenage—is't not perfect conscience
To quit him with this arm? And is't not to be damn'd
To let this canker of our nature come
In further evil?   70

    HOR.   It must be shortly known to him from England
What is the issue of the business there.

    HAMLET.   It will be short: The interim is mine;
And a man's life's no more than to say "one."
But I am very sorry, good Horatio,   75
That to Laertes I forgot myself;
For, by the image of my cause, I see
The portraiture of his: I'll court his favours:
But, sure, the bravery of his grief did put me
Into a towering passion.

HORATIO.   Peace! who comes here?   80

(*Enter* OSRIC.)

OSRIC.   Your lordship is right welcome back to Denmark.

HAMLET.   I humbly thank you, sir. [*Aside to* HORATIO]
Dost know this water-fly?

HORATIO.   [*Aside to* HAMLET]   No, my good lord.

HAMLET.   [*Aside to* HORATIO]   Thy state is the more gracious; for
'tis a vice to know him. He hath much land, and fertile: Let a beast be
lord of beasts, and his crib shall stand at the king's mess. 'Tis a chough;
but, as I say, spacious in the possession of dirt.

OSRIC.   Sweet lord, if your lordship were at leisure, I should impart
a thing to you from his majesty.   90

HAMLET.   I will receive it, sir, with all diligence of spirit.
Put your bonnet to his right use; 'tis for the head.

OSRIC.   I thank your lordship, it is very hot.

HAM.   No, believe me, 'tis very cold; the wind is northerly.

OSRIC.   It is indifferent cold, my lord, indeed.   95

HAMLET.   But yet methinks it is very sultry and hot, or
my complexion—

OSRIC.   Exceedingly, my lord; it is very sultry—as 'twere—I cannot
tell how. But, my lord, his majesty bade me signify to you, that he has
laid a great wager on your head. Sir, this is the matter—   100

HAMLET.   I beseech you, remember—

[HAMLET *moves him to put on his hat.*]

OSRIC.   Nay, in good faith; for mine ease, in good faith. Sir, here is
newly come to court Laertes; believe me, an absolute gentleman, full of
most excellent differences, of very soft society and great showing. Indeed, to speak feelingly of him, he is the card or calendar of gentry, for
you shall find in him the continent of what part a gentleman would see.

HAMLET.   Sir, his definement suffers no perdition in you; though, I
know, to divide him inventorially would dizzy the arithmetic of memory,
and yet but yaw neither, in respect of his quick sail. But, in the verity of
extolment, I take him to be a soul of great article; and his infusion of
such dearth and rareness, as, to make true diction of him, his semblable is
his mirror, and who else would trace him, his umbrage, nothing more.

OSRIC.   Your lordship speaks most infallibly of him.

HAMLET.   The concernancy, sir? Why do we wrap the gentleman in
our more rawer breath?   115

OSRIC.   Sir?

HORATIO. Is't not possible to understand in another tongue? You will do't, sir, really.

HAM. What imports the nomination of this gentleman?

OSRIC. Of Laertes? 120

HORATIO. His purse is empty already: All's golden words are spent.

HAMLET. Of him, sir.

OSRIC. I know you are not ignorant—

HAMLET. I would you did, sir; yet, in faith, if you did, it would not much approve me: well, sir. 125

OSR. You are not ignorant of what excellence Laertes is—

HAMLET. I dare not confess that, lest I should compare with him in excellence; but, to know a man well, were to know himself.

OSRIC. I mean, sir, for his weapon; but in the imputation laid on him by them, in his meed he's unfellowed. 130

HAMLET. What's his weapon?

OSRIC. Rapier and dagger.

HAMLET. That's two of his weapons: but, well.

OSRIC. The king, sir, hath wagered with him six Barbary horses; against the which he has imponed, as I take it, six French rapiers and poniards, with their assigns, as girdle, hangers, and so. Three of the carriages, in faith, are very dear to fancy, very responsive to the hilts, most delicate carriages, and of very liberal conceit.

HAMLET. What call you the carriages?

HORATIO. I knew you must be edified by the margent ere you had done.

OSRIC. The carriages, sir, are the hangers.

HAMLET. The phrase would be more germane to the matter, if we could carry cannon by our sides: I would it might be hangers till then. But, on: six Barbary horses against six French swords, their assigns, and three liberal-conceited carriages; that's the French bet against the Danish. Why is this "imponed," as you call it?

HAMLET. Yours, yours, [*Exit* OSRIC] He does well to commend it self and him, he shall not exceed you three hits. He hath laid on twelve for nine; and it would come to immediate trial, if your lordship would vouchsafe the answer.

HAMLET. How if I answer no?

OSRIC. I mean, my lord, the opposition of your person in trial.

HAMLET. Sir, I will walk here in the hall: If it please his majesty, 'tis the breathing time of day with me; let the foils be brought, the gentle-man willing, and the king hold his purpose, I will win for him an I can; if not, I will gain nothing but my shame and the odd hits.

OSRIC.   Shall I re-deliver you e'en so?

HAMLET.   To this effect, sir; after what flourish your nature will.

OSRIC.   I commend my duty to your lordship.   160

HAMLET.   Yours, yours. [*Exit* OSRIC]   He does well to commend it himself; there are no tongues else for's turn.

HORATIO.   This lapwing runs away with the shell on his head.

HAMLET.   He did comply with his dug, before he sucked it. Thus has he—and many more of the same bevy, that I know the drossy age dotes on —only got the tune of the time and outward habit of encounter; a kind of yeasty collection, which carries them through and through the most fond and winnowed opinions; and do but blow them to their trial, the bubbles are out.

(*Enter a* LORD.)

LORD.   My lord, his majesty commended him to you by young Osric, who brings back to him, that you attend him in the hall: He sends to know if your pleasure hold to play with Laertes, or that you will take longer time.

HAMLET.   I am constant to my purposes; they follow the king's pleasure: If his fitness speaks, mine is ready; now or whensoever, provided I be so able as now.

LORD.   The king and queen and all are coming down.

HAMLET.   In happy time.

LORD.   The queen desires you to use some gentle entertainment to Laertes before you fall to play.   180

HAMLET.   She well instructs me.   [*Exit* LORD.]

HORATIO.   You will lose this wager, my lord.

HAMLET.   I do not think so; since he went into France, I have been in continual practice; I shall win at the odds. But thou wouldst not think how ill all's here about my heart: But it is no matter.   185

HORATIO.   Nay, good my lord—

HAMLET.   It is but foolery; but it is such a kind of gain-giving as would perhaps trouble a woman.

HORATIO.   If your mind dislike anything, obey it: I will forestall their repair hither, and say you are not fit.   190

HAMLET.   Not a whit, we defy augury: There's a special providence in the fall of a sparrow. If it be now, 'tis not to come; if it be not to come,

it will be now; if it be not now, yet it will come. The readiness is all;
since no man has aught of what he leaves, what is't to leave betimes?

(*Enter* KING, QUEEN, LAERTES, LORDS, OSRIC, *and* ATTENDANTS
with foils, and so on.)

KING.   Come, Hamlet, come, and take this hand from me.   195

[*The* KING *puts* LAERTES'S *hand into* HAMLET'S.]

HAMLET.   Give me your pardon, sir: I have done you wrong;
But pardon't, as you are a gentleman
This presence knows,
And you must needs have heard, how I am punish'd
With sore distraction. What I have done,   200
That might your nature, honour and exception
Roughly awake, I here proclaim was madness.
Was't Hamlet wrong'd Laertes? Never Hamlet:
If Hamlet from himself be ta'en away,
And when he's not himself does wrong Laertes,   205
Then Hamlet does it not, Hamlet denies it.
Who does it, then? His madness: If't be so,
Hamlet is of the faction that is wrong'd;
His madness is poor Hamlet's enemy.
Sir, in this audience,   210
Let my disclaiming from a purposed evil
Free me so far in your most generous thoughts,
That I have shot mine arrow o'er the house,
And hurt my brother.

LAERTES.   I am satisfied in nature,
Whose motive, in this case, should stir me most   215
To my revenge: But in my terms of honour
I stand aloof, and will no reconcilement
Till by some elder masters, of known honour,
I have a voice and precedent of peace,
To keep my name ungored. But till that time   220
I do receive your offer'd love like love,
And will not wrong it.

HAMLET.   I embrace it freely,
And will this brother's wager frankly play.
Give us the foils. Come on.

LAERTES.   Come, one for me.

HAMLET.   I'll be your foil, Laertes: In mine ignorance   225
Your skill shall, like a star i' the darkest night,
Stick fiery off indeed.

LAERTES.   You mock me, sir.

HAMLET.   No, by this hand.

KING.   Give them the foils, young Osric. Cousin Hamlet,
You know the wager?

HAMLET.   Very well, my lord;   230
Your grace hath laid the odds o' the weaker side.

KING.   I do not fear it; I have seen you both:
But since he's better'd, we have therefore odds.

LAERTES.   This is too heavy, let me see another.

HAM.   This likes me well. These foils have all a length?   235

[*They prepare to play.*]

OSRIC.   Ay, my good lord.

KING.   Set me the stoups of wine upon that table.
If Hamlet give the first or second hit,
Or quit in answer of the third exchange,
Let all the battlements their ordnance fire;   240
The king shall drink to Hamlet's better breath;
And in the cup an union shall he throw,
Richer than that which four successive kings
In Denmark's crown have worn. Give me the cups,
And let the kettle to the trumpet speak,   245
The trumpet to the cannoneer without,
The cannons to the heavens, the heavens to earth,
"Now the king drinks to Hamlet." Come, begin;
And you, the judges, bear a wary eye.

HAMLET.   Come on, sir.

LAERTES.   Come, my lord.   [*They play.*]

HAMLET.   One.

LAERTES.   No.

HAMLET.   Judgment.   250

OSRIC.   A hit, a very palpable hit.

LAERTES.   Well; again.

KING.   Stay; give me drink. Hamlet, this pearl is thine;
Here's to thy health.

[*Trumpets sound, and cannon shot off within.*]

Give him the cup.

HAMLET.   I'll play this bout first; set it by awhile.
Come.   [*They play*]   Another hit; what say you?

LAERTES.   A touch, a touch, I do confess.   255

KING.   Our son shall win.

QUEEN.   He's fat, and scant of breath.
Here, Hamlet, take my napkin, rub thy brows:
The queen carouses to thy fortune, Hamlet.

HAMLET.   Good madam!

KING.   Gertrude, do not drink.

QUEEN.   I will, my lord; I pray you, pardon me.   260

[*Drinks.*]

KING.   [*Aside*]   It is the poison'd cup; it is too late.

HAMLET.   I dare not drink yet, madam; by and by.

QUEEN.   Come, let me wipe thy face.

LAERTES.   My lord, I'll hit him now.

KING.   I do not think't.

LAER.   [*Aside*] And yet 'tis almost 'against my conscience.   265

HAMLET.   Come, for the third, Laertes: You but dally;
I pray you, pass with your best violence;
I am afeard you make a wanton of me.

LAERTES.   Say you so? come on.   [*They play.*]

OSRIC.   Nothing, neither way.   270

LAERTES.   Have at you now!

[LAERTES *wounds* HAMLET; *then, in scuffling,
they change rapiers, and* HAMLET *wounds* LAERTES.]

KING.   Part them; they are incensed.

HAMLET.   Nay, come, again.   [*The* QUEEN *falls.*]

OSRIC.   Look to the queen there, ho!

HORATIO.   They bleed on both sides. How is it, my lord?

OSRIC.   How is't, Laertes?

LAERTES.   Why, as a woodcock to mine own springe, Osric;   275
I am justly kill'd with mine own treachery.

HAM.   How does the queen?

KING.   She swoons to see them bleed.

QUEEN.   No, no, the drink, the drink—O my dear Hamlet—
The drink, the drink!—I am poison'd.   [*Dies.*]

HAMLET.   O villany! Ho! let the door be lock'd: 280
Treachery! seek it out.

LAERTES.   It is here, Hamlet: Hamlet, thou art slain;
No medicine in the world can do thee good,

In thee there is not half an hour of life;
The treacherous instrument is in thy hand,   285
Unbated and envenom'd: The foul practice
Hath turn'd itself on me; lo, here I lie,
Never to rise again: Thy mother's poison'd:
I can no more: The king, the king's to blame.

    HAMLET.   The point envenom'd too!   290
Then, venom, do thy work.   [*Stabs the* KING.]

    ALL.   Treason! treason!

    KING.   O, yet defend me, friends; I am but hurt.

    HAM.   Here, thou incestuous, murderous, damned Dane,
Drink off this potion: Is thy union here?   295
Follow my mother.   [KING *dies.*]

    LAERTES.   He is justly served;
It is a poison temper'd by himself.
Exchange forgiveness with me, noble Hamlet:
Mine and my father's death come not upon thee,
Nor thine on me!   [*Dies.*]

    HAMLET.   Heaven make thee free of it! I follow thee.
I am dead, Horatio. Wretched queen, adieu!
You that look pale and tremble at this chance,
That are but mutes or audience to this act,
Had I but time—as this fell sergeant, death,   305
Is strict in his arrest—O, I could tell you—
But let it be. Horatio, I am dead;
Thou livest; report me and my cause aright
To the unsatisfied.

    HORATIO.   Never believe it:
I am more an antique Roman than a Dane: 310
Here's yet some liquor left.

    HAMLET.   As thou'rt a man,
Give me the cup. Let go; by heaven, I'll have't.
O good Horatio, what a wounded name,
Things standing thus unknown, shall live behind me!
If thou didst ever hold me in thy heart,   315
Absent thee from felicity awhile,
And in this harsh world draw thy breath in pain,
To tell my story.

          [*March at some distance, and shot within.*]
        What warlike noise is this?

OSRIC.   Young Fortinbras, with conquest come from Poland,
To the ambassadors of England gives   320
This warlike volley.

HAMLET.   O, I die, Horatio;
The potent poison quite o'er-crows my spirit:
I cannot live to hear the news from England;
But I do prophesy the election lights
On Fortinbras: He has my dying voice;   325
So tell him, with the occurrents, more and less,
Which have solicited—the rest is silence.   [*Dies.*]

HORATIO.   Now cracks a noble heart: Good night, sweet prince;
And flights of angels sing thee to thy rest!
Why does the drum come hither?   [*March within.*]

(*Enter* FORTINBRAS, *the* ENGLISH AMBASSADORS, *and others.*)

FORTINBRAS.   Where is this sight?

HORATIO.   What is it ye would see?
If aught of woe or wonder, cease your search.

FORTINBRAS.   This quarry cries on havoc. O proud Death,
What feast is toward in thine eternal cell,
That thou so many princes at a shot   335
So bloodily hast struck?

FIRST AMBASSADOR.   The sight is dismal;
And our affairs from England come too late:
The ears are senseless that should give us hearing,
To tell him his commandment is fulfill'd,
That Rosencrantz and Guildenstern are dead: 340
Where should we have our thanks?

HORATIO.   Not from his mouth,
Had it the ability of life to thank you:
He never gave commandment for their death.
But since, so jump upon this bloody question,
You from the Polack wars, and you from England,   345
Are here arrived, give order that these bodies
High on a stage be placed to the view;
And let me speak to the yet unknowing world
How these things came about: So shall you hear
Of carnal, bloody and unnatural acts,   350
Of accidental judgments, casual slaughters,

Of deaths put on by cunning and forced cause;
And, in this upshot, purposes mistook
Fall'n on the inventors' heads: All this can I
Truly deliver.

    FORTINBRAS.   Let us haste to hear it,   355
And call the noblest to the audience.
For me, with sorrow I embrace my fortune:
I have some rights of memory in this kingdom,
Which now to claim my vantage doth invite me.

    HORATIO.   Of that I shall have also cause to speak,   360
And from his mouth whose voice will draw on more:
But let this same be presently perform'd,
Even while men's minds are wild; lest more mischance,
On plots and errors, happen.

    FORTINBRAS.   Let four captains
Bear Hamlet, like a soldier, to the stage;   365
For he was likely had he been put on,
To have proved most royally: And, for his passage,
The soldiers' music and the rites of war
Speak loudly for him.
Take up the bodies: Such a sight as this   370
Becomes the field, but here shows much amiss.
Go, bid the soldiers shoot.

               (*A dead march. Exeunt, bearing off the dead bodies;*
               after which a peal of ordnance is shot off.)

Notes

    I, i   13 *rivals*: companions; 15 *Dane*: King of Denmark; 61 *Norway*: King of Norway; 62 *parle*: parley; 63 *sledded Polacks*: Polish soldiers on sleds; 65 *jump*: just; 72 *subject*: people; 74 *mart for*: buying of; 75 *impress*: forced labor; 89 *seized of*: possessed of; 90 *moiety*: half; 96 *unimproved*: undisciplined; 99 *for food and diet*: for keep but without pay; 100 *stomach*: courage; 107 *romage*: turmoil; 109 *sort*: suit; 118 *moist star*: the moon; 125 *climatures*: regions; 140 *partisan*: a spear with curved lobes at the base; 154 *extravagant*: wandering beyond limits; 156 *probation*: proof

    I, ii   18 *supposal*: opinion; 21 *colleagued with* . . . : with no ally but this imaginary advantage; 33 *subject*: people; 38 *delated*: detailed; 57 *native*: naturally related; 65 *kin*: kinsman; *kind*: kindly, *but also* of our race, our type; 70 *vailed*: downcast; 81 *behaviour*: behavior; 92 *obsequious*: funeral; 93 *condolement*: mourning; 107 *unprevailing*: unavailing; 113 *Wittenberg*: a German university; 114 *retrograde*: contrary; 127 *rouse*s cup of wine; *bruit*: spread abroad; 132 *canon*: commandment; 137 *merely*: absolutely; 140

Hyperion: Apollo; *satyr*: a lecherous, deformed god; 141 *beteem*: allow; 149 *Niobe*: Niobe's children were all slain by Apollo and Artemis; 150 *discourse of reason*: the reasoning faculty; 155 *flushing*: redness; 162 *change*: exchange; 191 *season*: temper; 197 *vast*: void; 199 *at point*: at all points; *cap-a-pe*: from head to foot; 229 *beaver*: movable front of the helmet; 247 *tenable*: kept; 249 *understanding*: thought; 255 *doubt*: suspect

I, iii 3 *convoy is assistant*: conveyance is ready; 6 *toy in blood*: a fancy; 7 *primy*: early; 8 *forward*: premature; 9 *suppliance*: pastime; 11 *crescent*: increasing; 15 *cautel*: craft, deceit; 19 *unvalued*: of low birth; 35 *chariest*: most scrupulous; 38 *canker*: canker-worm; 39 *buttons*: buds; 41 *blastments*: blights; 49 *recks not . . .* : heeds not his own advice; 50 *fear me not*: fear not for me; 58 *character*: write; 60 *vulgar*: with everyone; 61 *tried*: tested; 76 *husbandry*: thrift; 82 *tend*: are waiting; 93 *put on me*: impressed upon me; 101 *unsifted*: untried; 114 *springes*: snares; *woodcock*: a bird proverbially stupid; 125 *in few*: briefly; 128 *implorators*: implorers

I, iv 9 *wassail*: drinking bout; *upspring reels*: wild dances; 10 *Rhenish*: wine; 15 *manner*: custom; 18 *tax'd*: censured; 19 *clepe*: call; 20 *addition*: title; 24 *mole of nature*: natural blemish; 27 *complexion*: temperament; 30 *plausive*: pleasing; 36 *dram of eale . . .* : the one small spot of evil colors the entire character; 47 *hearsed*: coffined; 48 *cerements*: cloths wrapped about the body; 52 *corse*: corpse; 58 *impartment*: communication; 75 *toys*: freaks; 83 *Nemean lion*: a mythic beast, noted for ferocity; 85 *lets*: hinders

I, v 20 *porpentine*: porcupine; 21 *blazon*: public description; 33 *Lethe wharf*: banks of Lethe, the river of forgetfulness; 37 *forged process*: a false but official account; 61 *secure*: careless, unsuspicious; 62 *hebenon*: henbane, a poisonous plant; 68 *posset*: coagulate; 69 *eager*: sour; 71 *most instant tetter . . .* : an eruption covered my whole body, instantly; 75 *dispatch'd*: deprived; 77 *unhousel'd . . .* : unprepared, without receiving the eucharist or extreme unction; 81 *nature*: natural feeling; 83 *luxury*: lust; 85 *taint not . . .* : deprave not your own soul; 89 *matin*: morning; 99 *fond*: foolish; 107 *My tables*: a writing tablet carried by students; 116 *Hillo, ho, ho*: cry of the falconer to the hawk; 147 *Upon my sword*: that is, on the cross and as soldiers; 150 *truepenny*: good man; 156 *Hic et ubique?*: Here and everywhere?; 163 *pioner*: one who digs; 172 *antic*: fantastic; 174 *encumber'd*: entwined with

II, i 7 *Danskers*: Danes; 26 *quaintly*: oddly; 29 *unreclaimed*: undisciplined; 33 *fetch of warrant*: a warranted device; 55 *house of sale*: brothel; 59 *assays*: attempts; 65 *observe . . .* : see for yourself what he does; 71 *closet*: private chamber; 72 *doublet*: coat; *unbraced*: unfastened; 74 *down-gyved*: fallen down; 97 *fordoes*: destroys

II, ii 13 *vouchsafe your rest*: please to stay; 120 *numbers*: verses; 123 *machine*: body; 135 *play'd the desk . . .* : concealed; 158 *try*: test; 163 *arras*: a hanging, probably a tapestry; 182 *good kissing carrion*: dead bodies fit for kissing by the sun; 201 *out of the air*: out into the air; 248 *fay*: faith; 250 *sort you*: class you; 270 *consonancy of our youth*: we are the same age; 287 *express*: exact; 296 *coted*: passed beyond; 301 *tickle o' the sere*: light on the trigger; 308 *inhibition*: formal prohibition; 315 *eyrie*: nest; *eyases*: young hawks; *top of question*: drown out all others; 320 *escoted*: maintained; 325 *tarre*: set on; 326 *cuffs*: fisticuffs; 331 *Hercules and his load too*: Hercules carried the world on his shoulders (also the sign on the Globe Theatre); 333 *mows*: mouths, grimaces; 340 *extent*: showing kindness; 345 *mad north-north-west*: mad only at times and in a certain direction; 349 *clouts*: clothes; 358 *Buz, buz!*: indicates out of date news or gossip; 364 *Seneca*: Latin tragedian, imitated by Renaissance playwrights; *Plautus*: Latin writer of comedy, imitated by Renaissance playwrights; 366 *Jephthah*: sacrificed his own daughter because of an oath he had taken; 380 *pious chanson*: a song from the Bible; 381 *abridgment*: means for cutting this short; 383 *valanced*: fringed (that is, bearded); 386 *altitude of a chopine*: the height of an Italian shoe with a raised heel; 387 *uncurrent*: no longer legal tender; 394 *general*: the many; 397 *sallets*: salads, or the spices put on them; 401 *Aeneas and Dido*: this passage is imitated from Marlowe and Nashe's *Dido, Queen of Carthage*, to make it even more fulsome; 402 *Priam*: King of Troy; 405 *Pyrrhus*: a Greek hero in the Trojan War; *Hyrcanian beast*: tiger; 411 *gules*: red; *trick'd*: smeared; 446 *fellies*: jointed wooden rim of a wheel; 447 *nave*: hub; 451 *Hecuba*: wife of Priam; 452 *mobled*: muffled 456 *bisson rheum*: blinding tears; 467 *milch*: moist; 477 *God's bodykins*: by the body of God; 499 *wann'd*: grew pale; 513 *peak*: mope; 514 *John-a-dreams*: a dreamer; 522 *'S wounds*: by the wounds of Christ; 527 *kindless*: unnatural; 533 *drab*: whore; 534 *scullion*: kitchen worker; 544 *tent*: investigate; *blench*: flinch; 551 *relative*: definite

III, *i*   17 *o'er-raught*: overtook; 26 *edge*: incitement; 29 *closely*: secretly; 32 *espials*: spies; 76 *bodk*in: dagger; *fardels*: burdens; 79 *bourn*: limit; 89 *orisons*: prayers; 103 *honest*: chaste and truthful; 117 *inoculate*: graft; *relish of*: like; 147 *glass*: mirror; 150 *music*: melodious; 153 *blown*: blooming; 165 *Haply*: by chance; 179 *find him*: discover, understand

III, *ii*   8 *groundlings*: those who stood (and paid the least) to watch plays; 10 *Termagant*: who beat a thief and produced screams; 11 *Herod*: in mystery plays, the part of Herod was played loudly and fulsomely; 28 *indifferently*: fairly; 48 *pregnant hinges*: hinges made quick to open; 67 *occulted*: secret; 71 *stithy*: smithy; 74 *censure*: judgment; 80 *chameleon's dish*: chameleons were thought to feed on air; 107 *suit of sables*: trimmed with rich, black fur; 113 *miching mallecho*: sneaking mischief; 123 *posy of a ring*: sentimental mottoes engraved inside a ring; 126 *Phoebus' cart*: the sun; 127 *Neptune's salt wash*: the sea; *Tellus' orbed ground*: the earth; 130 *Hymen*: god of marriage; 152 *wormwood*: bitter wood; 168 *enactures*: fulfillments; 207 *Tropically*: figuratively; 211 *galled jade*: horse with saddle sores; 222 *Hecate*: goddess of witchcraft; 239 *turn Turk with*: betray; *provincial roses*: roses of Provence, very decorative; *razed shoes*: cut to decorate; 240 *cry of players*: as in a pack of crying hounds; 246 *pajock*: peacock; 255 *perdy*: by God; 263 *choler*: anger; 291 *pickers and stealers*: hands; 298 *"While the grass grows"*: "the silly horse starves"; 300 *withdraw with you*: speak to you privately; 301 *recover the wind*: go to the windward side, get the advantage; 302 *toil*: snare; 343 *Nero*: murdered his mother; 347 *shent*: rebuked; 348 *give them seals*: act accordingly

III, *iii*   68 *limed*: entrapped with lime, as with birds; 75 *scann'd*: examined closely; 88 *hent*: point of seizure

III, *iv*   4 *sconce*: hide; 14 *rood*: cross; 37 *custom*: habit; *brass'd*: hardened; 46 *contraction*: marriage contract; 50 *tristful*: sad; 52 *index*: prologue;

64 *mildew'd* ear: of corn, as in *Genesis* 41:5–7; 67 *batten*: grow fat; 77 *cozen'd*: tricked; *hoodman-blind*: blindman's buff; 81 *mope*: be depressed; 91 *leave their tinct*: be erased; 152 *pursy*: fat, short; 183 *reechy*: dirty; 184 *paddling*: fumbling; 189 *paddock* . . . gib: toad and tomcat; 193 *famous ape*: the ape that let birds out of a cage one by one and could only stare as the beauty fled him; 203 *sweep*: clear; 205 *enginer* . . . : artilleryman blown up by his own explosives

IV, i   18 *out of haunt*: hidden; 42 *blank*: the white center of a target

IV, ii   12 *replication*: reply

IV, iii   6 *scourge*: punishment; 21 *politic*: shrewd; 58 *cicatrice*: scar; 64 *hectic*: fever

IV, iv   27 *imposthume*: abscess; 39 *fust*: mould

IV, v   6 *spurns*: kicks; 9 *collection*: inference; 41 *God 'ild you*: God reward you; 72 *buzzers*: gossips; 75 *stick*: refrain from; 77 *murdering-piece*: small cannon; 79 *Switzers*: mercenary guards; 81 *list*: limit; 83 *riotous head*: at the head of rioters; 92 *counter*: opposite to the true trail (a hunting term); 129 *life-rendering pelican*: the pelican was thought to feed its young from the blood of its own breast; 185 *collaterial*: indirect; 193 *hatchment*: a grave tablet bearing the coat of arms of the dead

IV, vi   11 *overlooked*: looked over

IV, vii   1 *acquitance*: acquittal; 18 *general gender*: the people; 20 *the spring* . . . : a snare coated with lime; 21 *gyves*: fetters; 28 *challenger on mount*: a knightly champion; 60 *checking*: turning from his goal; 98 *scrimers*: fencers; 115 *plurisy*: excess; 136 *unbated*: with a protective button; 139 *unction*: salve; 141 *cataplasm*: poultice; 189 *douts*: extinguishes

V, i   1 *wilfully* . . . : commits suicide; 4 *straight*: immediately; *crowner*: coroner; 8 *se offendendo*: as opposed to *se defendendo*, defending oneself in causing death; 10 *argal*: ergo (therefore); 52 *Yaughan*: probably the owner of a tavern; 76 *chapless*: without cheeks; 77 *mazzard*: head; 79 *loggats*: a game in which sticks are thrown at a stake; 85 *quiddities* . . . *quillets*: quibbles; 116 *by the card*: with precision; 118 *picked*: refined; 119 *kibe*: chillblain; 175 *bung-hole*: pouring hole in a barrel; 189 *maimed*: shortened; 202 *crants*: circles of flowers laid on the coffins of unmarried women; 203 *strewments*: strewing of flowers; 223 *Pelion*: mountain in Greece; 231 *splenitive*: quick to anger; 247 *eisel*: vinegar; 254 *Ossa*: mountain in Greece; 258 *golden couplets*: pigeons hatch two chicks covered with yellow down

V, ii   6 *bilboes*: fetters; 22 *bugs*: fears, bugbears; 23 *supervise*: exact examination; 33 *statists*: statesmen; 34 *write fair*: write legibly; 42 *comma*: smallest break; 48 *ordinant*: directing; 59 *insinuation*: insertion, intervention; 61 *the pass* . . . : between fencing blades; 66 *angle*: fishhook; 83 *water-fly*: busy and ineffectual insect; 87 *crib*: trough; *mess*: dining table; *chough*: a noisy bird; 107 *definement* . . . : Hamlet uses the same inflated and inaccurate diction as Osric; 155 *breathing*: exercise; 163 *this lapwing*: a bird, the peewit;

164 *comply*: paid compliments to; 167 *yesty*: frothy; 217 *reconcilement*: Laertes wishes to consult authorities before saying that his honor is satisfied; 242 *union*: pearl; 245 *kettle*: kettledrum; 258 *napkin*: handkerchief; 268 *wanton*: spoiled child; 304 *mutes*: hired mourners, or those in a play who have no lines; 310 *antique Roman*: one who will kill himself at the death of his master; 333 *havoc*: slaughter

Hamlet

For Analysis

1. This is a revenge play. Hamlet finds several obstacles preventing his revenge:
   a. The nature of the ghost. It was real, but what was it?
      What are the alternatives Hamlet sees, in a speech such as:
         Angels and ministers of grace defend us!
         Be thou a spirit of health or goblin damn'd,
         Bring with thee airs from heaven or blasts from hell,
         Be they intents wicked or charitable . . . .
   b. The guilt of Gertrude. What may she be guilty of? What does the ghost command Hamlet to do about her?
   c. The nature of complete revenge. If Hamlet is to revenge the king (supposing the ghost told the truth), then Claudius must die in the same state that King Hamlet died. In what spiritual condition did Hamlet's father die? How does this explain Hamlet's refusal to kill Claudius after the play within a play?
2. In what way is Laertes used as a foil to illustrate the comparative nobility of Hamlet? Consider the similarities: Both are young nobles, both are university students, both wish to leave the kingdom; there is the death of a father in each case, the need for revenge. In the ways that the two travel to revenge, what illustrates their basic difference? Is Fortinbras also a foil to Hamlet?
3. Why is the play within a play necessary to Hamlet?
4. After the play within a play, the course of action shifts. Now Hamlet knows Claudius is guilty, but what also does Claudius now know? Past this point in the play do you see Hamlet acting (action) or fending off others' actions (counteraction)?
5. Does Hamlet develop in the play? Consider that after early frustrations and a consuming haste for revenge, he finally comes to say "The readiness is all."
6. Readers are sometimes bothered by Hamlet's tendency to generalize his situation: Instead of concentrating on killing the king, he spends a great deal of time talking and thinking about the world and the times. Is his view of the world borne out dramatically by supporting characters and subplots? Consider, for example, that his mother has made an incestuous marriage; his girl friend is being used as a tool against him; her father instructs his son, pompously, to be true to himself—and then sends a spy to watch him; his two friends, Rosencrantz and Guildenstern, become willing tools of his enemy.

Can you add other instances of this wholesale corruption? Does this justify Hamlet's tendency to generalize?

7. Is Gertrude guilty of complicity in the murder? How does she react to the play within a play?

8. How does Horatio function in the play? If Hamlet can speak the truth as he sees it in soliloquy, why is Horatio necessary?

9. Why does Hamlet decide to put on an "antic disposition"? What is protective about feigning madness?

10. Claudius is likely to seem an unworthy opponent unless one notes his influence on supporting characters. How did he get to be king, when Hamlet was the king's son? What in his handling of Rosencrantz and Guildenstern, Laertes, Gertrude, and Polonius suggests that this is a formidable man? What in his talk with Laertes before the duel shows that he is a man who (unlike Hamlet) leaves little to chance?

11. When Claudius is finally killed, does Hamlet achieve revenge in the eye-for-an-eye fashion he was bound to? After stabbing Claudius, why does he make him drink the poison too?

Tennessee Williams

The Glass
Menagerie

CHARACTERS

AMANDA WINGFIELD, *the mother.*

> *A little woman of great but confused vitality clinging frantically to another time and place. Her characterization must be carefully created, not copied from type. She is not paranoiac, but her life is paranois. There is much to admire in* AMANDA, *and as much to love and pity as there is to laugh at. Certainly she has endurance and a kind of heroism, and though her foolishness makes her unwittingly cruel at times, there is tenderness in her slight person.*

LAURA WINGFIELD, *her daughter.*

> AMANDA, *having failed to establish contact with reality, continues to live vitally in her illusions, but* LAURA'S *situation is even graver. A childhood illness has left her crippled, one leg slightly shorter than the other and held in a brace. This defect need not be more than suggested on the stage. Stemming from this,* LAURA'S *separation increases till she is like a piece of her own glass collection, too exquisitely fragile to move from the shelf.*

TOM WINGFIELD, *her son, and the narrator of the play. A poet with a job in a warehouse. His nature is not remorseless but to escape from a trap he has to act without pity.*

JIM O'CONNOR, *the gentleman caller. A nice, ordinary, young man.*

> SCENE   AN ALLEY IN ST. LOUIS
>
> PART I.   Preparation for a Gentleman Caller.
> PART II.   The Gentleman Calls.
>   *Time: Now and the Past.*

Production Notes

Being a "memory play," *The Glass Menagerie* can be presented with unusual freedom of convention. Because of its considerably delicate or tenuous material, atmospheric touches and subtleties of direction play a particularly important part. Expressionism and all other unconventional techniques in drama have only one valid aim and that is a closer approach to truth. When a play employs unconventional techniques, it is not, or certainly shouldn't be, trying to escape its responsibility of dealing with reality, or interpreting experience, but is actually or should be attempting to find a closer approach, a more penetrating and vivid expression of things as they are. The straight realistic play with its genuine frigidaire and authentic ice-cubes, its characters that speak exactly as its audience speaks, corresponds to the academic landscape and has the same virtue of a photographic likeness. Everyone should know nowadays the unimportance of the photographic in art: that truth, life, or reality is an organic thing which the poetic imagination can represent or suggest, in essence, only through transformation, through changing into other forms than those that were merely present in appearance.

These remarks are not meant as a preface only to this particular play. They have to do with a conception of a new, plastic theatre that must take the place of the exhausted theatre of realistic conventions if the theatre is to resume vitality as a part of our culture.

THE SCREEN DEVICE

There is *only one important difference between the original and acting versions of the play* and that is the *omission* in the latter of the device that I tentatively included in my *original* script. This device was the use of a screen on which were projected magic-lantern slides bearing images or titles. I do not regret the omission of this device from the Broadway production. The extraordinary power of Miss Taylor's performance made it suitable to have the utmost simplicity in the physical production. But I think it may be interesting to some readers to see how this device was conceived. So I am putting it into the published manuscript. These images and legends, projected from behind, were cast on a section of wall between the front-room and dining-room areas, which should be indistinguishable from the rest when not in use.

The purpose of this will probably be apparent. It is to give accent to certain values in each scene. Each scene contains a particular point (or several) that is structurally the most important. In an episodic play, such as this, the basic structure or narrative line may be obscured from the audience; the effect may seem fragmentary rather than architectural. This may not be the fault of the play so much as a lack of attention in the audience. The legend or image upon the screen will strengthen the effect of what is merely allusion in the writing and allow the primary point to be made more simply and lightly than if the entire responsibility were on the spoken lines. Aside from this structural value, I think the screen will have a definite emotional appeal, less definable but just as important. An imaginative producer or director may invent many other uses for this device than those indicated in the present script. In fact the possibilities of the device seem much larger to me than the instance of this play can possibly utilize.

THE MUSIC

Another extraliterary accent in this play is provided by the use of music. A single recurring tune, "The Glass Menagerie," is used to give emotional emphasis to suitable passages. This tune is like circus music, not when you are on the grounds or in the immediate vicinity of the parade, but when you are at some distance and very likely thinking of something else. It seems under those circumstances to continue almost interminably and it weaves in and out of your preoccupied consciousness; then it is the lightest, most delicate music in the world and perhaps the saddest. It expresses the surface vivacity of life with the underlying strain of immutable and inexpressible sorrow. When you look at a piece of delicately spun glass you think of two things: How beautiful it is and how easily it can be broken. Both of those ideas should be woven into the recurring tune, which dips in and out of the play as if it were carried on a wind that changes. It serves as a thread of connection and allusion between the narrator with his separate point in time and space and the subject of his story. Between each episode it returns as reference to the emotion, nostalgia, which is the first condition of the play. It is primarily Laura's music and therefore comes out most clearly when the play focuses upon her and the lovely fragility of glass which is her image.

THE LIGHTING

The lighting in the play is not realistic. In keeping with the atmosphere of memory, the stage is dim. Shafts of light are focused on selected areas or actors, sometimes in contradistinction to what is the apparent center. For instance, in the quarrel scene between Tom and Amanda, in which Laura has no active part, the clearest pool of light is on her figure. This is also true of the supper scene, when her silent figure on the sofa should remain the visual center. The light upon Laura should be distinct from the others, having a peculiar pristine clarity such as light used in early religious portraits of female saints or madonnas. A certain correspondence to light in religious paintings, such as El Greco's, where the figures are radiant in atmosphere that is relatively dusky, could be effectively used throughout the play. (It will also permit a more effective use of the screen.) A free, imaginative use of light can be of enormous value in giving a mobile, plastic quality to plays of a more or less static nature.

T.W.

SCENE I

The Wingfield apartment is in the rear of the building, one of those vast hive-like conglomerations of cellular living-units that flower as warty growths in overcrowded urban centers of lower middle-class population and are symptomatic of the impulse of this largest and fundamentally enslaved section of American society to avoid fluidity and differentiation and to exist and function as one interfused mass of automatism.

The apartment faces an alley and is entered by a fire escape, a structure whose name is a touch of accidental poetic truth, for all of these huge buildings are always burning with the slow and implacable fires of human desperation. The fire escape is included in the set—that is, the landing of it and steps descending from it.

The scene is memory and is therefore nonrealistic. Memory takes a lot of poetic license. It omits some details; others are exaggerated, according to the emotional value of the articles it touches, for memory is seated predominantly in the heart. The interior is therefore rather dim and poetic.

At the rise of the curtain, the audience is faced with the dark, grim rear wall of the Wingfield tenement. This building, which runs parallel to the footlights, is flanked on both sides by dark, narrow alleys that run into murky canyons of tangled clotheslines, garbage cans, and the sinister lattice-work of neighboring fire escapes. It is up and down these side alleys that exterior entrances and exits are made, during the play. At the end of TOM'S *opening commentary, the dark tenement wall slowly reveals (by means of a transparency) the interior of the ground floor Wingfield apartment.*

Downstage is the living room, which also serves as a sleeping room for LAURA, *the sofa unfolding to make her bed. Upstage, center, and divided by a wide arch or second proscenium with transparent faded portieres (or second curtain), is the dining room. In an old-fashioned what-not in the living room are seen scores of transparent glass animals. A blown-up photograph of the father hangs on the wall of the living room, facing the audience, to the left of the archway. It is the face of a very handsome young man in a doughboy's First World War cap. He is gallantly smiling, ineluctably smiling, as if to say, "I will be smiling forever."*

The audience hears and sees the opening scene in the dining room through both the transparent fourth wall of the building and the transparent gauze portieres of the dining-room arch. It is during this revealing scene that the fourth wall slowly ascends, out of sight.

This transparent exterior wall is not brought down again until the very end of the play, during TOM'S *final speech. The narrator is an undisguised convention of the play. He takes whatever license with dramatic convention is convenient to his purposes.* (TOM *enters dressed as a merchant sailor from alley, stage left, and strolls across the front of the stage to the fire escape. There he stops and lights a cigarette. He addresses the audience.*)

TOM. Yes, I have tricks in my pocket, I have things up my sleeve. But I am the opposite of a stage magician. He gives you illusion that has the appearance of truth. I give you truth in the pleasant disguise of illusion.

To begin with, I turn back time. I reverse it to that quaint period, the thirties, when the huge middle class of America was matriculating in a school for the blind. Their eyes had failed them, or they had failed their eyes, and so they were having their fingers pressed forcibly down on the fiery Braille alphabet of a dissolving economy.

In Spain there was revolution. Here there was only shouting and confusion.

In Spain there was Guernica. Here there were disturbances of labor, sometimes pretty violent, in otherwise peaceful cities such as Chicago, Cleveland, Saint Louis. . . .

This is the social background of the play.   (*Music*)

The play is memory.

Being a memory play, it is dimly lighted, it is sentimental, it is not realistic.

In memory everything seems to happen to music. That explains the fiddle in the wings.

I am the narrator of the play and also a character in it.

The other characters are my mother, Amanda, my sister, Laura, and a gentleman caller who appears in the final scenes.

He is the most realistic character in the play, being an emissary from a world of reality that we were somehow set apart from.

But since I have a poet's weakness for symbols, I am using this character also as a symbol; he is the long delayed but always expected something that we live for.

There is a fifth character in the play who doesn't appear except in this larger-than-life-size photograph over the mantel.

This is our father who left us a long time ago.

He was a telephone man who fell in love with long distances; he gave up his job with the telephone company and skipped the light fantastic out of town. . . .

The last we heard of him was a picture post card from Mazatlan, on

the Pacific coast of Mexico, containing a message of two words—
"Hello——Good-bye!" and no address.

I think the rest of the play will explain itself. . . .

(AMANDA'S *voice becomes audible through the portieres.* LEGEND
ON SCREEN: "OÙ SONT LES NEIGES?" *He divides the portieres and
enters the upstage area.* AMANDA *and* LAURA *are seated at a drop-
leaf table. Eating is indicated by gestures without food or utensils.*
AMANDA *faces the audience.* TOM *and* LAURA *are seated in profile.
The interior has lit up softly and through the scrim we see* AMANDA
and LAURA *seated at the table in the upstage area.*)

AMANDA   (*calling*).   Tom?

TOM.   Yes, Mother.

AMANDA.   We can't say grace until you come to the table!

TOM.   Coming, Mother.

(*He bows slightly and withdraws, reappearing a few moments later in
his place at the table.*)

AMANDA   (*to her son*).   Honey, don't *push* with your fingers.
If you have to push with something, the thing to push with is a crust of
bread. And chew—chew! Animals have sections in their stomachs which
enable them to digest food without mastication, but human beings are
supposed to chew their food before they swallow it down. Eat food leisurely
son, and really enjoy it. A well-cooked meal has lots of delicate flavors
that have to be held in the mouth for appreciation. So chew your food
and give your salivary glands a chance to function!

(TOM *deliberately lays his imaginary fork down and pushes his chair
back from the table.*)

TOM.   I haven't enjoyed one bite of this dinner because of your constant directions on how to eat it. It's you that make me rush through meals
with your hawk-like attention to every bite I take. Sickening— spoils my
appetite—all this discussion of—animals' secretion—salivary glands—
mastication!

AMANDA   (*lightly*).   Temperament like a Metropolitan star! (*He
rises and crosses downstage.*) You're not excused from the table.

TOM.   I'm getting a cigarette.

AMANDA.   You smoke too much.

(LAURA *rises.*)

LAURA.   I'll bring in the blanc mange.

(He remains standing with his cigarette by the portieres during the following.)

AMANDA *(rising)*.   No, sister, no, sister—you be the lady this time and I'll be the darky.

LAURA.   I'm already up.

AMANDA.   Resume your seat, little sister—I want you to stay fresh and pretty—for gentlemen callers!

LAURA.   I'm not expecting any gentlemen callers.

AMANDA *(crossing out to kitchenette; airily)*.   Sometimes they come when they are least expected! Why, I remember one Sunday afternoon in Blue Mountain—

(Enters kitchenette.)

TOM.   I know what's coming!

LAURA.   Yes. But let her tell it.

TOM.   Again?

LAURA.   She loves to tell it.

(AMANDA returns with bowl of dessert.)

AMANDA.   One Sunday afternoon in Blue Mountain—your mother received—*seventeen!*—gentlemen callers! Why, sometimes there weren't chairs enough to accommodate them all. We had to send the nigger over to bring in folding chairs from the parish house.

TOM *(remaining at portieres)*.   How did you entertain those gentlemen callers?

AMANDA.   I understood the art of conversation!

TOM.   I bet you could talk.

AMANDA.   Girls in those days *knew* how to talk, I can tell you.

TOM.   Yes?

(IMAGE: AMANDA AS A GIRL ON A PORCH, GREETING CALLERS)

AMANDA.   They knew how to entertain their gentlemen callers. It wasn't enough for a girl to be possessed of a pretty face and a graceful figure—although I wasn't slighted in either respect. She also needed to have a nimble wit and a tongue to meet all occasions.

TOM.   What did you talk about?

AMANDA.   Things of importance going on in the world! Never anything coarse or common or vulgar. *(She addresses* TOM *as though he were seated in the vacant chair at the table though he remains by portieres. He plays this scene as though he held the book.*) My callers were gentlemen—all! Among my callers were some of the most prominent young planters of the Mississippi Delta—planters and sons of planters!

(TOM *motions for music and a spot of light on* AMANDA. *Her eyes lift, her face glows, her voice becomes rich and elegiac.* SCREEN LEGEND: "OÙ SONT LES NEIGES?")

There was young Champ Laughlin, who later became vice-president of the Delta Planters Bank.

Hadley Stevenson, who was drowned in Moon Lake and left his widow one hundred and fifty thousand in Government bonds.

There were the Cutrere brothers, Wesley and Bates. Bates was one of my bright particular beaux! He got in a quarrel with that wild Wainwright boy. They shot it out on the floor of Moon Lake Casino. Bates was shot through the stomach. Died in the ambulance on his way to Memphis. His widow was also well-provided for, came into eight or ten thousand acres, that's all. She married him on the rebound—never loved her—carried my picture on him the night he died!

And there was that boy that every girl in the Delta had set her cap for! That beautiful, brilliant young Fitzhugh boy from Greene County!

TOM. What did he leave his widow?

AMANDA. He never married! Gracious, you talk as though all of my old admirers had turned up their toes to the daisies!

TOM. Isn't this the first you've mentioned that still survives?

AMANDA. That Fitzhugh boy went North and made a fortune—came to be known as the Wolf of Wall Street! He had the Midas touch, whatever he touched turned to gold! And I could have been Mrs. Duncan J. Fitzhugh, mind you! But—I picked your *father!*

LAURA (*rising*). Mother, let me clear the table.

AMANDA. No, dear, you go in front and study your typewriter chart. Or practice your shorthand a little. Stay fresh and pretty!—It's almost time for our gentlemen callers to start arriving. (*She flounces girlishly toward the kitchenette.*) How many do you suppose we're going to entertain this afternoon?

(TOM *throws down the paper and jumps up with a groan.*)

LAURA (*alone in the dining room*). I don't believe we're going to receive any, Mother.

AMANDA (*reappearing, airily*). What? no one—not one? You must be joking!

LAURA *nervously echoes her laugh. She slips in a fugitive manner through the half-open portieres and draws them gently behind her. A shaft of very clear light is thrown on her face against the faded tapestry of the curtains.* MUSIC: *"*THE GLASS MENAGERIE*" UNDER FAINTLY. Lightly.)*

Not one gentleman caller? It can't be true! There must be a flood, there must have been a tornado!

LAURA.   It isn't a flood, it's not a tornado, Mother. I'm just not popular like you were in Blue Mountain. . . . (TOM *utters another groan.* LAURA *glances at him with a faint, apologetic smile. Her voice catching a* little.) Mother's afraid I'm going to be an old maid.

(THE SCENE DIMS OUT WITH "GLASS
MENAGERIE" MUSIC.)

SCENE II

LEGEND: "LAURA, HAVEN'T YOU EVER LIKED SOME BOY?"

On the dark stage the screen is lighted with the image of blue roses. Gradually LAURA'S *figure becomes apparent and the screen goes out. The music subsides.*

LAURA *is seated in the delicate ivory chair at the small clawfoot table. She wears a dress of soft violet material for a kimono—her hair tied back from her forehead with a ribbon.*

She is washing and polishing her collection of glass.

(AMANDA *appears on the fire-escape steps. At the sound of her ascent,* LAURA *catches her breath, thrusts the bowl of ornaments away and seats herself stiffly before the diagram of the typewriter keyboard as though it held her spellbound.*

Something has happened to AMANDA. *It is written in her face as she climbs to the landing: a look that is grim and hopeless and a little absurd.*

She has on one of those cheap or imitation velvety-looking cloth coats with imitation fur collar. Her hat is five or six years old, one of those dreadful cloche hats that were worn in the late twenties, and she is clasping an enormous black patent-leather pocketbook with nickel clasps and initials. This is her full-dress outfit, the one she usually wears to the D.A.R.

Before entering she looks through the door. She purses her lips, opens her eyes very wide, rolls them upward and shakes her head. Then she slowly lets herself in the door. Seeing her mother's expression LAURA *touches her lips with a nervous gesture.)*

LAURA.   Hello, Mother, I was—

(*She makes a nervous gesture toward the chart on the wall.* AMANDA *leans against the shut door and stares at* LAURA *with a martyred look.*)

AMANDA.   Deception? Deception?

(*She slowly removes her hat and gloves, continuing the sweet suffering stare. She lets the hat and gloves fall on the floor—a bit of acting.*)

LAURA   (*shakily*).   How was the D.A.R. meeting? (AMANDA *slowly opens her purse and removes a dainty white handkerchief, which she shakes out delicately and delicately touches to her lips and nostrils.*) Didn't you go to the D.A.R. meeting, Mother?

AMANDA   (*faintly, almost inaudibly*).   —No.—No. (*Then more forcibly.*) I did not have the strength—to go to the D.A.R. In fact, I did not have the courage! I wanted to find a hole in the ground and hide myself in it forever!

(*She crosses slowly to the wall and removes the diagram of the typewriter keyboard. She holds it in front of her for a second, staring at it sweetly and sorrowfully—then bites her lips and tears it in two pieces.*)

LAURA   (*faintly*).   Why did you do that, Mother? (AMANDA *repeats the same procedure with the chart of the Gregg Alphabet.*) Why are you—

AMANDA.   Why? Why? How old are you, Laura?

LAURA.   Mother, you know my age.

AMANDA.   I thought that you were an adult; it seems that I was mistaken.

(*She crosses slowly to the sofa and sinks down and stares at* LAURA.)

LAURA.   Please don't stare at me, Mother.

(AMANDA *closes her eyes and lowers her head. Count ten.*)

AMANDA.   What are we going to do, what is going to become of us, what is the future?

(*Count ten.*)

LAURA.   Has something happened, Mother?

(AMANDA *draws a long breath and takes out the handkerchief again. Dabbing process.*)

Mother, has—something happened?

AMANDA.   I'll be all right in a minute, I'm just bewildered—(*Count five.*)—by life. . . .

LAURA.   Mother, I wish that you would tell me what's happened!

AMANDA.   As you know, I was supposed to be inducted into my office at the D.A.R. this afternoon. (IMAGE: A SWARM OF TYPEWRITERS) But I stopped off at Rubicam's Business College to speak to your teachers about your having a cold and ask them what progress they thought you were making down there.

LAURA.   Oh. . . .

AMANDA.   I went to the typing instructor and introduced myself as your mother. She didn't know who you were. Wingfield, she said. We don't have any such student enrolled at the school!

I assured her she did, that you had been going to classes since early in January.

"I wonder," she said, "if you could be talking about that terribly shy little girl who dropped out of school after only a few days' attendance?"

"No," I said, "Laura, my daughter, has been going to school every day for the past six weeks!"

"Excuse me," she said. She took the attendance book out and there was your name, unmistakably printed, and all the dates you were absent until they decided that you had dropped out of school.

I still said, "No, there must have been some mistake! There must have been some mix-up in the records!"

And she said, "No—I remember her perfectly now. Her hands shook so that she couldn't hit the right keys! The first time we gave a speed-test, she broke down completely—was sick at the stomach and almost had to be carried into the washroom! After that morning she never showed up any more. We phoned the house but never got any answer"—while I was working at Famous and Barr, I suppose, demonstrating those——Oh!

I felt so weak I could barely keep on my feet!

I had to sit down while they got me a glass of water!

Fifty dollars' tuition, all of our plans—my hopes and ambitions for you —just gone up the spout, just gone up the spout like that.

(LAURA *draws a long breath and gets awkwardly to her feet. She crosses to the victrola and winds it up.*)

What are you doing?

LAURA.   Oh!

(*She releases the handle and returns to her seat.*)

AMANDA.   Laura, where have you been going when you've gone out pretending that you were going to business college?

LAURA.   I've just been going out walking.

AMANDA.   That's not true.

LAURA.   It is. I just went walking.

AMANDA.   Walking? Walking? In winter? Deliberately courting pneumonia in that light coat? Where did you walk to, Laura?

LAURA.   All sorts of places—mostly in the park.

AMANDA.   Even after you'd started catching that cold?

LAURA.   It was the lesser of two evils, Mother. (IMAGE: WINTER SCENE IN PARK) I couldn't go back up. I—threw up—on the floor!

AMANDA.   From half past seven till after five every day you mean to tell me you walked around the park, because you wanted to make me think that you were still going to Rubicam's Business College?

LAURA.   It wasn't as bad as it sounds. I went inside places to get warmed up.

AMANDA.   Inside where?

LAURA.   I went in the art museum and the bird-houses at the Zoo. I visited the penguins every day! Sometimes I did without lunch and went to the movies. Lately I've been spending most of my afternoons in the Jewel-box, that big glass house where they raise the tropical flowers.

AMANDA.   You did all this to deceive me, just for deception? (LAURA *looks down.*)   Why?

LAURA.   Mother, when you're disappointed, you get that awful suffering look on your face, like the picture of Jesus' mother in the museum!

AMANDA.   Hush!

LAURA.   I couldn't face it.

(*Pause. A whisper of strings.* LEGEND: "THE CRUST OF HUMILITY")

AMANDA   (*hopelessly fingering the huge pocketbook*).   So what are we going to do the rest of our lives? Stay home and watch the parades go by? Amuse ourselves with the glass menagerie, darling? Eternally play those worn-out phonograph records your father left as a painful reminder of him?

We won't have a business career—we've given that up because it gave us nervous indigestion! (*Laughs wearily.*) What is there left but dependency all our lives? I know so well what becomes of unmarried women who aren't prepared to occupy a position. I've seen such pitiful cases in the South—barely tolerated spinsters living upon the grudging patronage of sister's husband or brother's wife!—stuck away in some little mouse-trap of a room—encouraged by one in-law to visit another—little bird-like women without any nest—eating the crust of humility all their life!

Is that the future that we've mapped out for ourselves?

I swear it's the only alternative I can think of!

It isn't a very pleasant alternative, is it?

Of course—some girls *do marry.* (LAURA *twists her hands nervously.*)

Haven't you ever liked some boy?

LAURA.   Yes. I liked one once. (*Rises.*)   I came across his picture a while ago.

AMANDA   (*with some interest*).   He gave you his picture?

LAURA.   No, it's in the year-book.

AMANDA   (*disappointed*).   Oh—a high-school boy.

(SCREEN IMAGE: JIM AS HIGH-SCHOOL HERO BEARING A SILVER CUP)

LAURA.   Yes. His name was Jim. (LAURA *lifts the heavy annual from the claw-foot table.*) Here he is in *The Pirates of Penzance.*

AMANDA   (*absently*).   The what?

LAURA.   The operetta the senior class put on. He had a wonderful voice and we sat cross the aisle from each other Mondays, Wednesdays, and Fridays in the Aud. Here he is with the silver cup for debating! See his grin?

AMANDA   (*absently*).   He must have had a jolly disposition.

LAURA.   He used to call me—Blue Roses.

(IMAGE: BLUE ROSES)

AMANDA.   Why did he call you such a name as that?

LAURA.   When I had that attack of pleurosis—he asked me what was the matter when I came back. I said pleurosis—he thought that I said Blue Roses! So that's what he always called me after that. Whenever he saw me, he'd holler, "Hello, Blue Roses!" I didn't care for the girl that he went out with. Emily Meisenbach. Emily was the best-dressed girl at Soldan. She never struck me, though, as being sincere. . . . It says in the Personal Section—they're engaged. That's—six years ago! They must be married by now.

AMANDA.   Girls that aren't cut out for business careers usually wind up married to some nice man. (*Gets up with a spark of revival.*) Sister, that's what you'll do!

(LAURA *utters a startled, doubtful laugh. She reaches quickly for a piece of glass.*)

LAURA.   But, Mother—

AMANDA.   Yes? (*Crossing to photograph.*)

LAURA   (*in a tone of frightened apology*).   I'm—crippled!

(IMAGE: SCREEN)

AMANDA.   Nonsense! Laura, I've told you never, never to use that word. Why, you're not crippled, you just have a little defect—hardly noticeable, even! When people have some slight disadvantage like that, they cultivate other things to make up for it—develop charm—and vivacity—and—*charm!* That's all you have to do! *(She turns again to the photograph.)* One thing your father had *plenty of*—was *charm!*

(TOM *motions to the fiddle in the wings.*)

(THE SCENE FADES OUT WITH MUSIC.)

SCENE III

(LEGEND ON SCREEN: "AFTER THE FIASCO———"
TOM *speaks from the fire-escape landing.*)

TOM.   After the fiasco at Rubicam's Business College, the idea of getting a gentleman caller for Laura began to play a more and more important part in Mother's calculations.

It became an obsession. Like some archetype of the universal unconscious, the image of the gentleman caller haunted our small apartment
. . . .

(IMAGE: YOUNG MAN AT DOOR WITH FLOWERS)

An evening at home rarely passed without some allusion to this image, this spectre, this hope. . . .

Even when he wasn't mentioned, his presence hung in Mother's preoccupied look and in my sister's frightened, apologetic manner—hung like a sentence passed upon the Wingfields!

Mother was a woman of action as well as words.

She began to take logical steps in the planned direction.

Late that winter and in the early spring—realizing that extra money would be needed to properly feather the nest and plume the bird—she conducted a vigorous campaign on the telephone, roping in subscribers to one of those magazines for matrons called *The Homemaker's Companion,* the type of journal that features the serialized sublimations of ladies of letters who think in terms of delicate cup-like breasts, slim, tapering waists, rich, creamy thighs, eyes like wood-smoke in autumn, fingers that soothe and caress like strains of music, bodies as powerful as Etruscan sculpture.

(SCREEN IMAGE: GLAMOR MAGAZINE COVER.
AMANDA *enters with phone on long extension cord. She is spotted in the dim stage.*)

AMANDA.   Ida Scott? This is Amanda Wingfield!

We *missed* you at the D.A.R. last Monday!

I said to myself: She's probably suffering with that sinus condition! How is that sinus condition?

Horrors! Heaven have mercy!—You're a Christian martyr, yes, that's what you are, a Christian martyr!

Well, I just now happened to notice that your subscription to the *Companion's* about to expire! Yes, it expires with the next issue, honey! —just when that wonderful new serial by Bessie Mae Hopper is getting off to such an exciting start. Oh, honey, it's something that you can't miss! You remember how *Gone With the Wind* took everybody by storm? You simply couldn't go out if you hadn't read it. All everybody *talked* was Scarlett O'Hara. Well, this is a book that critics already compare to *Gone With the Wind*. It's the *Gone With the Wind* of the post-World War generation!—What?—Burning?—Oh, honey, don't let them burn, go take a look in the oven and I'll hold the wire! Heavens—I think she's hung up!

(DIM OUT.)

(LEGEND ON SCREEN: "YOU THINK I'M IN LOVE WITH CONTINENTAL SHOEMAKERS?")

Before the stage is lighted the violent voices of TOM *and* AMANDA *are heard. They are quarreling behind the portieres. In front of them stands* LAURA *with clenched hands and panicky expression. A clear pool of light on her figure throughout this scene.*)

TOM.   What in Christ's name am I——

AMANDA   (*shrilly*).   Don't you use that——

TOM.   Supposed to do!

AMANDA.   Expression! Not in my——

TOM.   Ohhh!

AMANDA.   Presence! Have you gone out of your senses?

TOM.   I have, that's true, *driven* out!

AMANDA.   What is the matter with you, you—big—big—IDIOT!

TOM.   Look!—I've got *no thing,* no single thing——

AMANDA.   Lower your voice!

TOM.   In my life here that I can call my OWN! Everything is——

AMANDA.   Stop that shouting!

TOM.   Yesterday you confiscated my books! You had the nerve to——

AMANDA.   I took that horrible novel back to the library—yes! That hideous book by that insane Mr. Lawrence. (TOM *laughs wildly.*) I cannot

control the output of diseased minds or people who cater to them—
(TOM *laughs still more wildly.*) BUT I WON'T ALLOW SUCH FILTH BROUGHT
INTO MY HOUSE! No, no, no, no, no!

TOM.   House, house! Who pays rent on it, who makes a slave of
himself to——

AMANDA   (*fairly screeching*).   Don't you DARE to——

TOM.   No, no, *I* mustn't say things! *I've* got to just——

AMANDA.   Let me tell you——

TOM.   I don't want to hear any more!

(*He tears the portieres open. The upstage area is lit with a turgid
smoky red glow.* AMANDA'S *hair is in metal curlers and she wears
a very old bathrobe, much too large for her slight figure, a relic of
the faithless Mr. Wingfield. An upright typewriter and a wild dis-
array of manuscripts is on the drop-leaf table. The quarrel was
probably precipitated by* AMANDA'S *interruption of his creative labor. A chair lying overthrown on the floor. Their gesticulating shadows are cast on the ceiling by the fiery glow.*)

AMANDA.   You *will* hear more, you——

TOM.   No, I won't hear more, I'm going out!

AMANDA.   You come right back in——

TOM.   Out, out, out! Because I'm——

AMANDA.   Come back here, Tom Wingfield! I'm not through talking
to you!

TOM.   Oh go——

LAURA   (*desperately*).   —Tom!

AMANDA.   You're going to listen, and no more insolence from you!
I'm at the end of my patience! (*He comes back toward her.*)

TOM.   What do you think I'm at? Aren't I supposed to have any
patience to reach the end of, Mother? I know, I know. It seems unimportant to you, what I'm *doing*—what I *want* to do—having a little
difference between them! You don't think that——

AMANDA.   I think you've been doing things that you're ashamed of.
That's why you act like this. I don't believe that you go every night to
the movies. Nobody goes to the movies night after night. Nobody in
their right minds goes to the movies as often as you pretend to. People
don't go to the movies at nearly midnight, and movies don't let out at
two A.M. Come in stumbling. Muttering to yourself like a maniac! You
get three hours' sleep and then go to work. Oh, I can picture the way

you're doing down there. Moping, doping, because you're in no condition.

TOM   (*wildly*).   No, I'm in no condition!

AMANDA.   What right have you got to jeopardize your job? Jeopardize the security of us all? How do you think we'd manage if you were——

TOM.   Listen! You think I'm crazy *about* the *warehouse*? (*He bends fiercely toward her slight figure.*) You think I'm in love with the Continental Shoemakers? You think I want to spend fifty-five *years* down there in that—*celotex interior*! with—*fluorescent—tubes*! Look! I'd rather somebody picked up a crowbar and battered out my brains—than go back mornings! I *go*! Every time you come in yelling that Goddamn "*Rise and Shine!*" "*Rise and Shine!*" I say to myself, "How *lucky dead* people are!" But I get up. I *go*! For sixty-five dollars a month I give up all that I dream of doing and being *ever*! And you say self—*self's* all I ever think of. Why, listen, if self is what I thought of, Mother, I'd be where he is—GONE! (*Pointing to father's picture.*) As far as the system of transportation reaches! (*He starts past her. She grabs his arm.*) Don't grab at me, Mother!

AMANDA.   Where are you going?

TOM.   I'm going to the *movies*!

AMANDA.   I don't believe that lie!

TOM   (*crouching toward her, overtowering her tiny figure; she backs away, gasping*). I'm going to opium dens! Yes, opium dens, dens of vice and criminals' hang-outs, Mother. I've joined the Hogan gang, I'm a hired assassin, I carry a tommy-gun in a violin case! I run a string of cathouses in the Valley! They call me Killer, Killer Wingfield, I'm leading a double-life: a simple, honest warehouse worker by day, by night a dynamic *czar* of the *underworld, Mother*. I go to gambling casinos, I spin away fortunes on the roulette table! I wear a patch over one eye and a false mustache; sometimes I put on green whiskers. On those occasions they call me—*El Diablo*! Oh, I could tell you things to make you sleepless! My enemies plan to dynamite this place. They're going to blow us all sky-high some night! I'll be glad, very happy, and so will you! You'll go up, up on a broomstick, over Blue Mountain with seventeen gentlemen callers! You ugly—babbling old—*witch*. . . .

(*He goes through a series of violent, clumsy movements, seizing his overcoat, lunging to the door, pulling if fiercely open. The* WOMEN *watch him, aghast. His arm catches in the sleeve of the coat as he struggles to pull it on. For a moment he is pinioned by the bulky garment. With an outraged groan he tears the coat off again, splitting the shoulder of it, and hurls it across the room. It strikes against the shelf of* LAURA'S *glass collection, there is a tinkle of shattering glass.* LAURA *cries out as if wounded.* MUSIC. LEGEND: "THE GLASS MENAGERIE")

LAURA   (*shrilly*).   My glass!—menagerie. . . .
(*She covers her face and turns away. But* AMANDA *is still stunned and stupefied by the "ugly witch" so that she barely notices this occurrence. Now she recovers her speech.*)

AMANDA   (*in an awful voice*).   I won't speak to you—until you apologize!

(*She crosses through portieres and draws them together behind her.* TOM *is left with* LAURA. LAURA *clings weakly to the mantel with her face averted.* TOM *stares at her stupidly for a moment. Then he crosses to shelf. Drops awkwardly on his knees to collect the fallen glass, glancing at* LAURA *as if he would speak but couldn't.*)

("THE GLASS MENAGERIE" *steals in as* THE SCENE DIMS OUT.)

SCENE IV

*The interior is dark. Faint light in the alley. A deep-voiced bell in a church is tolling the hour of five as the scene commences. (*TOM *appears at the top of the alley. After each solemn boom of the bell in the tower, he shakes a little noisemaker or rattle as if to express the tiny spasm of man in contrast to the sustained power and dignity of the Almighty. This and the unsteadiness of his advance make it evident that he has been drinking.*
As he climbs the few steps to the fire-escape landing, light steals up inside. LAURA *appears in night-dress, observing* TOM'S *empty bed in the front room.*
TOM *fishes in his pockets for door key, removing a motley assortment of articles in the search, including a perfect shower of movie-ticket stubs and an empty bottle. At last he finds the key, but just as he is about to insert it, it slips from his fingers. He strikes a match and crouches below the door.*)

TOM   (*bitterly*).   One crack—and it falls through!

(LAURA *opens the door.*)

LAURA.   Tom! Tom, what are you doing?
TOM.   Looking for a door key.

LAURA.   Where have you been all this time?

TOM.   I have been to the movies.

LAURA.   All this time at the movies?

TOM.   There was a very long program. There was a Garbo picture and a Mickey Mouse and a travelogue and a newsreel and a preview of coming attractions. And there was an organ solo and a collection for the milk-fund—simultaneously—which ended up in a terrible fight between a fat lady and an usher!

LAURA   (*innocently*).   Did you have to stay through everything?

TOM.   Of course! And, oh, I forgot! There was a big stage show! The headliner on this stage show was Malvolio the Magician. He performed wonderful tricks, many of them, such as pouring water back and forth between pitchers. First it turned to wine and then it turned to beer and then it turned to whiskey. I know it was whiskey it finally turned into because he needed somebody to come up out of the audience to help him, and I came up—both shows! It was Kentucky Straight Bourbon. A very generous fellow, he gave souvenirs. (*He pulls from his back pocket a shimmering rainbow-colored scarf.*) He gave me this. This is his magic scarf. You can have it, Laura. You wave it over a canary cage and you get a bowl of goldfish. You wave it over the goldfish bowl and they fly away canaries. . . . But the wonderfullest trick of all was the coffin trick. We nailed him into a coffin and he got out of the coffin without removing one nail. (*He has come inside.*) There is a trick that would come in handy for me—get me out of this 2 by 4 situation!

(*Flops onto bed and starts removing shoes.*)

LAURA.   Tom—Shhh!

TOM.   What're you shushing me for?

LAURA.   You'll wake up Mother.

TOM.   Goody, goody! Pay 'er back for all those "Rise an' Shines." (*Lies down, groaning.*) You know it don't take much intelligence to get yourself into a nailed-up coffin, Laura. But who in hell ever got himself out of one without removing one nail?

(*As if in answer, the father's grinning photograph lights up.*) (SCENE DIMS OUT.)

(*Immediately following: The church bell is heard striking six. At the sixth stroke the alarm clock goes off in* AMANDA'S *room, and after a few moments we hear her calling: "Rise and Shine! Rise and Shine! Laura, go tell your brother to rise and shine!"*)

TOM   (*sitting up slowly*).   I'll rise—but I won't shine.

(The light increases.)

AMANDA. Laura, tell your brother his coffee is ready. (LAURA *slips into front room.)*

LAURA. Tom—It's nearly seven. Don't make Mother nervous. *(He stares at her stupidly. Beseechingly.)* Tom, speak to Mother this morning. Make up with her, apologize, speak to her!

TOM. She won't to me. It's her that started not speaking.

LAURA. If you just say you're sorry she'll start speaking.

TOM. Her not speaking—is that such a tragedy?

LAURA. Please—please!

AMANDA *(calling from kitchenette).* Laura, are you going to do what I asked you to do, or do I have to get dressed and go out myself?

LAURA. Going, going—soon as I get on my coat! *(She pulls on a shapeless felt hat with nervous, jerky movement, pleadingly glancing at TOM. Rushes awkwardly for coat. The coat is one of AMANDA'S, inaccurately madeover, the sleeves too short for LAURA.)* Butter and what else?

AMANDA *(entering upstage).* Just butter. Tell them to charge it.

LAURA. Mother, they make such faces when I do that.

AMANDA. Sticks and stones can break our bones, but the expression on Mr. Garfinkel's face won't harm us! Tell your brother his coffee is getting cold.

LAURA *(at door).* Do what I asked you, will you, will you, Tom?

(He looks sullenly away.)

AMANDA. Laura, go now or just don't go at all!

LAURA *(rushing out).* Going—going!

(A second later she cries out. TOM springs up and crosses to door. AMANDA rushes anxiously in. TOM opens the door.)

TOM. Laura?

LAURA. I'm all right. I slipped, but I'm all right.

AMANDA *(peering anxiously after her).* If anyone breaks a leg on those fire-escape steps, the landlord ought to be sued for every cent he possesses!

(She shuts door. Remembers she isn't speaking and returns to other room. As TOM enters listlessly for his coffee, she turns her back to him and stands rigidly facing the window on the gloomy gray vault of the areaway. Its light on her face with its aged but childish fea-

tures is cruelly sharp, satirical as a Daumier print. MUSIC UNDER: "AVE MARIA." TOM *glances sheepishly but sullenly at her averted figure and slumps at the table. The coffee is scalding hot; he sips it and gasps and spits it back in the cup. At his gasp,* AMANDA *catches her breath and half turns. Then catches herself and turns back to window.* TOM *blows on his coffee, glancing sidewise at his mother. She clears her throat.* TOM *clears his. He starts to rise. Sinks back down again, scratches his head, clears his throat again.* AMANDA *coughs.* TOM *raises his cup in both hands to blow on it, his eyes staring over the rim of it at his mother for several moments. Then he slowly sets the cup down and awkwardly and hesitantly rises from the chair.)*

TOM (*hoarsely*). Mother. I—I apologize, Mother. (AMANDA *draws a quick shuddering breath. Her face works grotesquely. She breaks into childlike tears.*) I'm sorry for what I said, for everything that I said, I didn't mean it.

AMANDA (*sobbingly*). My devotion has made me a witch and so I make myself hateful to my children!

TOM. *No, you don't.*

AMANDA. I worry so much, don't sleep, it makes me nervous!

TOM (*gently*). I understand that.

AMANDA. I've had to put up a solitary battle all these years. But you're my righthand bower! Don't fall down, don't fail!

TOM (*gently*). I'll try, Mother.

AMANDA (*with great enthusiasm*). Try and you will SUCCEED! (*The notion makes her breathless.*) Why, you—you're just *full* of natural endowments! Both of my children—they're *unusual* children! Don't you think I know it? I'm so—*proud!* Happy and—feel I've—so much to be thankful for but——Promise me one thing, Son!

TOM. What, Mother?

AMANDA. Promise, son, you'll—never be a drunkard!

TOM (*turns to her, grinning*). I will never be a drunkard, Mother.

AMANDA. That's what frightened me so, that you'd be drinking! Eat a bowl of Purina!

TOM. Just coffee, Mother.

AMANDA. Shredded wheat biscuit?

TOM. No. No, Mother, just coffee.

AMANDA. You can't put in a day's work on an empty stomach. You've got ten minutes — don't gulp! Drinking too-hot liquids makes cancer of the stomach. . . . Put cream in.

TOM.   No, thank you.

AMANDA.   To cool it.

TOM.   No! No, thank you, I want it black.

AMANDA.   I know, but it's not good for you. We have to do all that we can to build ourselves up. In these trying times we live in, all that we have to cling to is—each other. . . . That's why it's so important to— Tom, I——I sent out your sister so I could discuss something with you. If you hadn't spoken I would have spoken to you.

(*Sits down.*)

TOM   (*gently*).   What is it, Mother, that you want to discuss?

AMANDA.   *Laura!*

(TOM *puts his cup down slowly.* LEGEND ON SCREEN: "LAURA." MUSIC: "THE GLASS MENAGERIE")

TOM.   —Oh.—Laura. . . .

AMANDA   (*touching his sleeve*).   You know how Laura is. So quiet but—still water runs deep! She notices things and I think she—broods about them. (TOM *looks up.*) A few days ago I came in and she was crying.

TOM.   What about?

AMANDA.   You.

TOM.   Me?

AMANDA.   She has an idea that you're not happy here.

TOM.   What gave her that idea?

AMANDA.   What gives her any idea? However, you do act strangely. I—I'm not criticizing, understand that! I know your ambitions do not lie in the warehouse, that like everybody in the whole wide world—you've had to—make sacrifices, but—Tom—Tom—life's not easy, it calls for —Spartan endurance! There's so many things in my heart that I cannot describe to you! I've never told you but I—*loved* your father. . . .

TOM   (*gently*).   I know that, Mother.

AMANDA.   And you—when I see you taking after his ways! Staying out late—and—well, you *had* been drinking the night you were in that —terrifying condition! Laura says that you hate the apartment and that you go out nights to get away from it! Is that true, Tom?

TOM.   No. You say there's so much in your heart that you can't describe to me. That's true of me, too. There's so much in my heart that I can't describe to *you!* So let's respect each other's—

AMANDA.   But, why—*why*, Tom—are you always so *restless*? Where do you *go* to, nights?

TOM.   I—go to the movies.

AMANDA.   Why do you go to the movies so much, Tom?

TOM.   I go to the movies because—I like adventure. Adventure is something I don't have much of at work, so I go to the movies.

AMANDA.   But, Tom, you go to the movies *entirely* too *much!*

TOM.   I like a lot of adventure.

(AMANDA *looks baffled, then hurt. As the familiar inquisition resumes he becomes hard and impatient again.* AMANDA *slips back into her querulous attitude toward him.* IMAGE ON SCREEN: SAILING VESSEL WITH JOLLY ROGER)

AMANDA.   Most young men find adventure in their careers.

TOM.   Then most young men are not employed in a warehouse.

AMANDA.   The world is full of young men employed in warehouses and offices and factories.

TOM.   Do all of them find adventure in their careers?

AMANDA.   They do or they do without it! Not everybody has a craze for adventure.

TOM.   Man is by instinct a lover, a hunter, a fighter, and none of those instincts are given much play at the warehouse!

AMANDA.   Man is by instinct! Don't quote instinct to me! Instinct is something that people have got away from! It belongs to animals! Christian adults don't want it!

TOM.   What do Christian adults want, then, Mother?

AMANDA.   Superior things! Things of the mind and the spirit! Only animals have to satisfy instincts! Surely your aims are somewhat higher than theirs! Than monkeys—pigs——

TOM.   I reckon they're not.

AMANDA.   You're joking. However, that isn't what I wanted to discuss.

TOM   (*rising*).   I haven't much time.

AMANDA   (*pushing his shoulders*).   Sit down.

TOM.   You want me to punch in red at the warehouse, Mother?

AMANDA.   You have five minutes. I want to talk about Laura.

(LEGEND: "PLANS AND PROVISIONS")

TOM.   All right! What about Laura?

AMANDA.   We have to be making some plans and provisions for her. She's older than you, two years, and nothing has happened. She just drifts along doing nothing. It frightens me terribly how she just drifts along.

TOM.   I guess she's the type that people call home girls.

AMANDA.   There's no such type, and if there is, it's a pity! That is unless the home is hers, with a husband!

TOM.   What?

AMANDA.   Oh, I can see the handwriting on the wall as plain as I see the nose in front of my face! It's terrifying!

More and more you remind me of your father! He was out all hours without explanation!—Then *left! Good-bye!*

And me with the bag to hold. I saw that letter you got from the Merchant Marine. I know what you're dreaming of. I'm not standing here blindfolded.

Very well, then. Then *do* it!

But not till there's somebody to take your place.

TOM.   What do you mean?

AMANDA.   I mean that as soon as Laura has got somebody to take care of her, married, a home of her own, independent—why, then you'll be free to go wherever you please, on land, on sea, whichever way the wind blows you!

But until that time you've got to look out for your sister. I don't say me because I'm old and don't matter! I say for your sister because she's young and dependent.

I put her in business college—a dismal failure! Frightened her so it made her sick at the stomach.

I took her over to the Young People's League at the church. Another fiasco. She spoke to nobody, nobody spoke to her. Now all she does is fool with those pieces of glass and play those worn-out records. What kind of a life is that for a girl to lead?

TOM.   What can I do about it?

AMANDA.   Overcome selfishness!

Self, self, self is all that you ever think of!

(TOM *springs up and crosses to get his coat. It is ugly and bulky. He pulls on a cap with earmuffs.*) Where is your muffler? Put your wool muffler on! (*He snatches it angrily from the closet and tosses it around his neck and pulls both ends tight.*) Tom! I haven't said what I had in mind to ask you.

Tom.   I'm too late to——

Amanda.   (*catching his arm—very importunately; then shyly*).   Down at the warehouse, aren't there some—nice young men?

Tom.   No!

Amanda.   There *must* be—*some*. . . .

Tom.   Mother——   (*Gesture.*)

Amanda.   Find out one that's clean-living—doesn't drink and—ask him out for sister!

Tom.   What?

Amanda.   For *sister!* To *meet!* Get *acquainted!*

Tom   (*stamping to door*).   Oh, my *go-osh!*

Amanda.   Will you?   (*He opens door. Imploringly.*)   Will you? (*He starts down.*) Will you? *Will* you, dear?

Tom   (*calling back*).   Yes!

> (Amanda *closes the door hesitantly and with a troubled but faintly hopeful expression.* SCREEN IMAGE: GLAMOUR MAGAZINE COVER. *Spot* Amanda *at phone.*)

Amanda.   Ella Cartwright? This is Amanda Wingfield!
How are you, honey?
How is that kidney condition?

                                                    (*Count five.*)

Horrors!   (*Count five.*)

You're a Christian martyr, yes, honey, that's what you are, a Christian martyr!

Well, I just now happened to notice in my little red book that your subscription to the *Companion* has run out! I knew that you wouldn't want to miss out on the wonderful serial starting in this new issue. It's by Bessie Mae Hopper, the first thing she's written since *Honeymoon for Three*.

Wasn't that a strange and interesting story. Well, this one is even lovelier, I believe. It has a sophisticated, society background. It's all about the horsey set on Long Island!

                                                    (FADE OUT)

Scene V

> LEGEND ON SCREEN: "ANNUNCIATION." *Fade with music.*
> *It is early dusk of a spring evening. Supper has just been finished in the Wingfield apartment.* Amanda *and* Laura *in light-colored dresses*

are removing dishes from the table, in the upstage area, which is shadowy, their movements formalized almost as a dance or ritual, their moving forms as pale and silent as moths.

TOM, *in white shirt and trousers, rises from the table and crosses toward the fire escape.*)

AMANDA (*as he passes her*). Son, will you do me a favor?

TOM. What?

AMANDA. Comb your hair! You look so pretty when your hair is combed! (TOM *slouches on sofa with evening paper. Enormous caption "Franco Triumphs."*) There is only one respect in which I would like you to emulate your father.

TOM. What respect is that?

AMANDA. The care he always took of his appearance. He never allowed himself to look untidy. (*He throws down the paper and crosses to fire escape.*) Where are you going?

TOM. I'm going out to smoke.

AMANDA. You smoke too much. A pack a day at fifteen cents a pack. How much would that amount to in a month? Thirty times fifteen is how much, Tom? Figure it out and you will be astounded at what you could save. Enough to give you a night-school course in accounting at Washington U! Just think what a wonderful thing that would be for you, Son!

(TOM *is unmoved by the thought.*)

TOM. I'd rather smoke.

(*He steps out on landing, letting the screen door slam.*)

AMANDA (*sharply*). I know! That's the tragedy of it. . . .

(*Alone, she turns to look at her husband's picture.* DANCE MUSIC: "ALL THE WORLD IS WAITING FOR THE SUNRISE!")

TOM (*to the audience*). Across the alley from us was the Paradise Dance Hall. On evenings in spring the windows and doors were open and the music came outdoors. Sometimes the lights were turned out except for a large glass sphere that hung from the ceiling. It would turn slowly about and filter the dusk with delicate rainbow colors. Then the orchestra played a waltz or a tango, something that had a slow and sensuous rhythm. Couples would come outside, to the relative privacy of the alley. You could see them kissing behind ashpits and telephone poles.

This was the compensation for lives that passed like m
any change or adventure.

Adventure and change were imminent in this year. They were waiting around the corner for all these kids.

Suspended in the mist over Berchtesgaden, caught in the folds of
Chamberlain's umbrella——

In Spain there was Guernica!

But here there was only hot swing music and liquor, dance halls, bars,
and movies, and sex that hung in the gloom like a chandelier and flooded
the world with brief, deceptive rainbows. . . .

All the world was waiting for bombardments!

(AMANDA *turns from the picture and comes outside.*)

AMANDA (*sighing*). A fire-escape landing's a poor excuse for a
porch. (*She spreads a newspaper on a step and sits down, gracefully
and demurely as if she were settling into a swing on a Mississippi veranda.*) What are you looking at?

TOM. The moon.

AMANDA. Is there a moon this evening?

TOM. It's rising over Garfinkel's Delicatessen.

AMANDA. So it is! A little silver slipper of a moon. Have you made
a wish on it yet?

TOM. Um-hum.

AMANDA. What did you wish for?

TOM. That's a secret.

AMANDA. A secret, huh? Well, I won't tell mine either. I will be just
as mysterious as you.

TOM. I bet I can guess what yours is.

AMANDA. Is my head so transparent?

TOM. You're not a sphinx.

AMANDA. No, I don't have secrets. I'll tell you what I wished for on
the moon. Success and happiness for my precious children! I wish for
that whenever there's a moon, and when there isn't a moon, I wish for
it, too.

TOM. I thought perhaps you wished for a gentleman caller.

AMANDA. Why do you say that?

TOM. Don't you remember asking me to fetch one?

AMANDA.   I remember suggesting that it would be nice for your sister if you brought home some nice young man from the warehouse. I think that I've made that suggestion more than once.

TOM.   Yes, you have made it repeatedly.

AMANDA.   Well?

TOM.   We are going to have one.

AMANDA.   *What?*

TOM.   A gentleman caller!

> *(The annunciation is celebrated with music.* AMANDA *rises.* IMAGE ON SCREEN: CALLER WITH BOUQUET)

AMANDA.   You mean you have asked some nice young man to come over?

TOM.   Yep. I've asked him to dinner.

AMANDA.   You really did?

TOM.   I did!

AMANDA.   You did, and did he—*accept?*

TOM.   He did!

AMANDA.   Well, well—well, well! That's—lovely!

TOM.   I thought that you would be pleased.

AMANDA.   It's definite, then?

TOM.   Very definite.

AMANDA.   Soon?

TOM.   Very soon.

AMANDA.   For heaven's sake, stop putting on and tell me some things, will you?

TOM.   What things do you want me to tell you?

AMANDA.   *Naturally* I would like to know when he's *coming!*

TOM.   He's coming tomorrow.

AMANDA.   *Tomorrow?*

TOM.   Yep. Tomorrow.

AMANDA.   But, Tom!

TOM.   Yes, Mother?

AMANDA.   Tomorrow gives me no time!

TOM.   Time for what?

AMANDA.   Preparations! Why didn't you phone me at once, as soon as you asked him, the minute that he accepted? Then, don't you see, I could have been getting ready!

Tom. You don't have to make any fuss.

Amanda. Oh, Tom, Tom, Tom, of course I have to make a fuss! I want things nice, not sloppy! Not thrown together. I'll certainly have to do some fast thinking, won't I?

Tom. I don't see why you have to think at all.

Amanda. You just don't know. We can't have a gentleman caller in a pig-sty! All my wedding silver has to be polished, the monogrammed table linen ought to be laundered! The windows have to be washed and fresh curtains put up. And how about clothes? We have to *wear* something, don't we?

Tom. Mother, this boy is no one to make a fuss over!

Amanda. Do you realize he's the first young man we've introduced to your sister?

It's terrible, dreadful, disgraceful that poor little sister has never received a single gentleman caller! Tom, come inside!

(*She opens the screen door.*)

Tom. What for?

Amanda. I want to ask you some things.

Tom. If you're going to make such a fuss, I'll call it off, tell him not to come!

Amanda. You certainly won't do anything of the kind. Nothing offends people worse than broken engagements. It simply means I'll have to work like a Turk! We won't be brilliant, but we will pass inspection. Come on inside. (Tom *follows, groaning.*) Sit down.

Tom. Any particular place you would like me to sit?

Amanda. Thank heavens I've got that new sofa! I'm also making payments on a floor lamp I'll have sent out! And put the chintz covers on, they'll brighten things up! Of course I'd hoped to have these walls repapered. . . . What is the young man's name?

Tom. His name is O'Connor.

Amanda. That, of course, means fish—tomorrow is Friday! I'll have that salmon loaf—with Durkee's dressing! What does he do? He works at the warehouse?

Tom. Of course! How else would I—

Amanda. Tom, he—doesn't drink?

Tom. Why do you ask me that?

Amanda. Your father *did*!

Tom. Don't get started on that!

Amanda. He *does* drink, then?

TOM.   Not that I know of!

AMANDA.   Make sure, be certain! The last thing I want for my daughter's a boy who drinks!

TOM.   Aren't you being a little bit premature? Mr. O'Connor has not yet appeared on the scene!

AMANDA.   But will tomorrow. To meet your sister, and what do I know about his character? Nothing! Old maids are better off than wives of drunkards!

TOM.   Oh, my God!

AMANDA.   Be still!

TOM *(leaning forward to whisper)*.   Lots of fellows meet girls whom they don't marry!

AMANDA.   Oh, talk sensibly, Tom—and don't be sarcastic!

(She has gotten a hairbrush.)

TOM.   What are you doing?

AMANDA.   I'm brushing that cow-lick down! What is this young man's position at the warehouse?

TOM *(submitting grimly to the brush and the interrogation)*.   This young man's position is that of a shipping clerk, Mother.

AMANDA.   Sounds to me like a fairly responsible job, the sort of a job *you* would be in if you just had more *get-up*.
What is his salary? Have you any idea?

TOM.   I would judge it to be approximately eighty-five dollars a month.

AMANDA.   Well—not princely, but——

TOM.   Twenty more than I make.

AMANDA.   Yes, how well I know! But for a family man, eighty-five dollars a month is not much more than you can just get by on. . . .

TOM.   Yes, but Mr. O'Connor is not a family man.

AMANDA.   He might be, mightn't he? Some time in the future?

TOM.   I see. Plans and provisions.

AMANDA.   You are the only young man that I know of who ignores the fact that the future becomes the present, the present the past, and the past turns into everlasting regret if you don't plan for it!

TOM.   I will think that over and see what I can make of it.

AMANDA.   Don't be supercilious with your mother! Tell me some more about this—what do you call him?

TOM.   James D. O'Connor. The D. is for Delaney.

AMANDA.   Irish on *both* sides! *Gracious!* And doesn't drink?

TOM.   Shall I call him up and ask him right this minute?

AMANDA.   The only way to find out about those things is to make discreet inquiries at the proper moment. When I was a girl in Blue Mountain and it was suspected that a young man drank, the girl whose attentions he had been receiving, if any girl *was*, would sometimes speak to the minister of his church, or rather her father would if her father was living, and sort of feel him out on the young man's character. That is the way such things are discreetly handled to keep a young woman from making a tragic mistake!

TOM.   Then how did you happen to make a tragic mistake?

AMANDA.   That innocent look of your father's had everyone fooled! He *smiled*—the world was *enchanted!*

No girl can do worse than put herself at the mercy of a handsome appearance!

I hope that Mr. O'Connor is not too good-looking.

TOM.   No, he's not too good-looking. He's covered with freckles and hasn't too much of a nose.

AMANDA.   He's not right-down homely, though?

TOM.   Not right-down homely. Just medium homely, I'd say.

AMANDA.   Character's what to look for in a man.

TOM.   That's what I've always said, Mother.

AMANDA.   You've never said anything of the kind and I suspect you would never give it a thought.

TOM.   Don't be so suspicious of me.

AMANDA.   At least I hope he's the type that's up and coming.

TOM.   I think he really goes in for self-improvement.

AMANDA.   What reason have you to think so?

TOM.   He goes to night school.

AMANDA   (*beaming*).   Splendid! What does he do, I mean study?

TOM.   Radio engineering and public speaking!

AMANDA.   Then he has visions of being advanced in the world!

Any young man who studies public speaking is aiming to have an executive job someday!

And radio engineering? A thing for the future!

Both of these facts are very illuminating. Those are the sort of things that a mother should know concerning any young man who comes to call on her daughter. Seriously or—not.

TOM.   One little warning. He doesn't know about Laura. I didn't let on that we had dark ulterior motives. I just said, why don't you come and have dinner with us? He said okay and that was the whole conversation.

AMANDA.   I bet it was! You're eloquent as an oyster.

However, he'll know about Laura when he gets here. When he sees how lovely and sweet and pretty she is, he'll thank his lucky stars he was asked to dinner.

TOM.   Mother, you mustn't expect too much of Laura.

AMANDA.   What do you mean?

TOM.   Laura seems all those things to you and me because she's ours and we love her. We don't even notice she's crippled any more.

AMANDA.   Don't say crippled! You know that I never allow that word to be used!

TOM.   But face facts, Mother. She is and—that's not all—

AMANDA.   What do you mean "not all"?

TOM.   Laura is very different from other girls.

AMANDA.   I think the difference is all to her advantage.

TOM.   Not quite all—in the eyes of others—strangers—she's terribly shy and lives in a world of her own and those things make her seem a little peculiar to people outside the house.

AMANDA.   Don't say peculiar.

TOM.   Face the facts. She is.

(THE DANCE-HALL MUSIC CHANGES TO A TANGO THAT HAS A MINOR
                                        SOMEWHAT OMINOUS TONE.)

AMANDA.   In what way is she peculiar—may I ask?

TOM   (*gently*).   She lives in a world of her own—a world of—little glass ornaments, Mother. . . . (*Gets up.* AMANDA *remains holding brush, looking at him, troubled.*) She plays old phonograph records and—that's about all——

(*He glances at himself in the mirror and crosses to door.*)

AMANDA   (*sharply*).   Where are you going?

TOM.   I'm going to the movies.

(*Out screen door.*)

AMANDA.   Not to the movies, every night to the movies! (*Follows quickly to screen door.*) I don't believe you always go to the movies!

(*He is gone.* AMANDA *looks worriedly after him for a moment. Then vitality and optimism return and she turns from the door. Crossing
                                        to   portieres.*)

Laura! Laura!

(LAURA *answers from kitchenette.*)

LAURA.   Yes, Mother.

AMANDA.   Let those dishes go and come in front! (LAURA *appears with dish towel. Gaily.*) Laura, come here and make a wish on the moon!

(SCREEN IMAGE: MOON)

LAURA   (*entering*).   Moon—moon?

AMANDA.   A little silver slipper of a moon.
Look over your left shoulder, Laura, and make a wish!

(LAURA *looks faintly puzzled as if called out of sleep.* AMANDA *seizes her shoulders and turns her at an angle by the door.*)

Now!

Now, darling, *wish!*

LAURA.   What shall I wish for, Mother?

AMANDA   (*her voice trembling and her eyes suddenly filling with tears*). Happiness! Good fortune!

(*The violin rises and the stage dims out.*)
(CURTAIN)

SCENE VI

(IMAGE: HIGH-SCHOOL HERO)

TOM.   And so the following evening I brought Jim home to dinner. I had known Jim slightly in high school. In high school Jim was a hero. He had tremendous Irish good nature and vitality with the scrubbed and polished look of white chinaware. He seemed to move in a continual spotlight. He was a star in basketball, captain of the debating club, president of the senior class and the glee club and he sang the male lead in the annual light operas. He was always running or bounding, never just walking. He seemed always at the point of defeating the law of gravity. He was shooting with such velocity through his adolescence that you would logically expect him to arrive at nothing short of the White House by the time he was thirty. But Jim apparently ran into more interference after his graduation from Soldan. His speed had definitely slowed. Six years after he left high school he was holding a job that wasn't much better than mine.

(IMAGE: CLERK)

He was the only one at the warehouse with whom I was on friendly terms. I was valuable to him as someone who could remember his former glory, who had seen him win basketball games and the silver cup in debating. He knew of my secret practice of retiring to a cabinet of the washroom to work on poems when business was slack in the warehouse. He called me Shakespeare. And while the other boys in the warehouse regarded me with suspicious hostility, Jim took a humorous attitude toward me. Gradually his attitude affected the others; their hostility wore off and they also began to smile at me as people smile at an oddly fashioned dog who trots across their path at some distance.

I knew that Jim and Laura had known each other at Soldan, and I had heard Laura speak admiringly of his voice. I didn't know if Jim remembered her or not. In high school Laura had been as unobtrusive as Jim had been astonishing. If he did remember Laura, it was not as my sister, for when I asked him to dinner, he grinned and said, "You know, Shakespeare, I never thought of you as having folks!"

He was about to discover that I did. . . .

LIGHT UP STAGE. LEGEND ON SCREEN: "THE ACCENT OF A COMING FOOT." *Friday evening. It is about five o'clock of a late spring evening which comes "scattering poems in the sky." A delicate lemony light is in the Wingfield apartment.* AMANDA *has worked like a Turk in preparation for the gentleman caller. The results are astonishing. The new floor lamp with its rose-silk shade is in place, a colored paper lantern conceals the broken light fixture in the ceiling, new billowing white curtains are at the windows, chintz covers are on chairs and sofa, a pair of new sofa pillows make their initial appearance. Open boxes and tissue paper are scattered on the floor.* LAURA *stands in the middle with lifted arms while* AMANDA *crouches before her, adjusting the hem of the new dress, devout and ritualistic. The dress is colored and designed by memory. The arrangement of* LAURA's *hair is changed; it is softer and more becoming. A fragile, unearthly prettiness has come out in* LAURA: *She is like a piece of translucent glass touched by light, given a momentary radiance, not actual, not lasting.*)

AMANDA   (*impatiently*).   Why are you trembling?

LAURA.   Mother, you've made me so nervous!

AMANDA.   How have I made you nervous?

LAURA.   By all this fuss! You make it seem so important!

AMANDA.   I don't understand you, Laura. You couldn't be satisfied with just sitting home, and yet whenever I try to arrange something for you, you seem to resist it.

(*She gets up.*)

Now take a look at yourself.
No, wait! Wait just a moment—I have an idea!

LAURA.   What is it now?

(AMANDA *produces two powder puffs, which she wraps in handker-chiefs and stuffs in* LAURA'S *bosom.*)

LAURA.   Mother, what are you doing?

AMANDA.   They call them "Gay Deceivers"!

LAURA.   I won't wear them!

AMANDA.   You will!

LAURA.   Why should I?

AMANDA.   Because, to be painfully honest, your chest is flat.

LAURA.   You make it seem like we were setting a trap.

AMANDA.   All pretty girls are a trap, a pretty trap, and men expect them to be.

(LEGEND: "A PRETTY TRAP")

Now look at yourself, young lady. This is the prettiest you will ever be!

I've got to fix myself now! You're going to be surprised by your mother's appearance!

(*She crosses through portieres, humming gaily.* LAURA *moves slowly to the long mirror and stares solemnly at herself. A wind blows the white curtains inward in a slow, graceful motion and with a faint, sorrowful sighing.*)

AMANDA   (*off stage*).   It isn't dark enough yet.

(LAURA *turns slowly before the mirror with a troubled look.* LEGEND ON SCREEN: "THIS IS MY SISTER: "CELEBRATE HER WITH STRINGS!" MUSIC)

AMANDA   (*laughing, off*).   I'm going to show you something. I'm going to make a spectacular appearance!

LAURA.   What is it, Mother?

AMANDA.   Possess your soul in patience—you will see!

Something I've resurrected from that old trunk! Styles haven't changed so terribly much after all. . . .

(*She parts the portieres.*)

Now just look at your mother!

(*She wears a girlish frock of yellowed voile with a blue silk sash. She carries a bunch of jonquils—the legend of her youth is nearly revived. Feverishly.*)

This is the dress in which I led the cotillion. Won the cakewalk twice at Sunset Hill, wore one spring to the Governor's ball in Jackson! See how I sashayed around the ballroom, Laura?

(*She raises her skirt and does a mincing step around the room.*)

I wore it on Sundays for my gentlemen callers! I had it on the day I met your father——

I had malaria fever all that spring. The change of climate from East Tennessee to the Delta—weakened resistance—I had a little temperature all the time—not enough to be serious—just enough to make me restless and giddy!—Invitations poured in—parties all over the Delta!—"Stay in bed," said Mother, "you have a fever!" — but I just wouldn't.—I took quinine but kept on going, going!—Evenings, dances!—Afternoons, long, long rides! Picnics—lovely!—So lovely, that country in May.—All lacy with dogwood, literally flooded with jonquils!—That was the spring I had the craze for jonquils. Jonquils became an absolute obsession. Mother said, "Honey, there's no more room for jonquils." And still I kept on bringing in more jonquils. Whenever, wherever I saw them, I'd say, "Stop! Stop! I see jonquils!" I made the young men help me gather the jonquils! It was a joke. Amanda and her jonquils! Finally there were no more vases to hold them; every available space was filled with jonquils. No vases to hold them? All right, I'll hold them myself! And then I——(*She stops in front of the picture.* MUSIC) met your father!

Malaria fever and jonquils and then—this—boy. . . .

(*She switches on the rose-colored lamp.*)

I hope they get here before it starts to rain.

(*She crosses upstage and places the jonquils in bowl on table.*)

I gave your brother a little extra change so he and Mr. O'Connor could take the service car home.

LAURA   (*with altered look*).   What did you say his name was?

AMANDA.   O'Connor.

LAURA.   What is his first name?

AMANDA.   I don't remember. Oh, yes, I do. It was—Jim.

(LAURA *sways slightly and catches hold of a chair.* LEGEND ON SCREEN: "NOT JIM!")

LAURA   (*faintly*).   Not—Jim!

AMANDA.   Yes, that was it, it was Jim! I've never known a Jim that wasn't nice!

(MUSIC: OMINOUS)

LAURA.   Are you sure his name is Jim O'Connor?

AMANDA.   Yes. Why?

LAURA.   Is he the one that Tom used to know in high school?

AMANDA.   He didn't say so. I think he just got to know him at the warehouse.

LAURA.   There was a Jim O'Connor we both knew in high school——(*Then, with effort.*) If that is the one that Tom is bringing to dinner—you'll have to excuse me, I won't come to the table.

AMANDA.   What sort of nonsense is this?

LAURA.   You asked me once if I'd ever liked a boy. Don't you remember I showed you this boy's picture?

AMANDA.   You mean the boy you showed me in the year book?

LAURA.   Yes, that boy.

AMANDA.   Laura, Laura, were you in love with that boy?

LAURA.   I don't know, Mother. All I know is I couldn't sit at the table if it was him!

AMANDA.   It won't be him! It isn't the least bit likely. But whether it is or not, you will come to the table. You will not be excused.

LAURA.   I'll have to be, Mother.

AMANDA.   I don't intend to humor your silliness, Laura. I've had too much from you and your brother, both!

So just sit down and compose yourself till they come. Tom has forgotten his key so you'll have to let them in, when they arrive.

LAURA   (*panicky*).   Oh, Mother—*you* answer the door!

AMANDA   (*lightly*).   I'll be in the kitchen—busy!

LAURA.   Oh, Mother, please answer the door, don't make me do it!

AMANDA.   (*crossing into kitchenette*).   I've got to fix the dressing for the salmon. Fuss, fuss—silliness!—over a gentleman caller!

(*Door swings shut.* LAURA *is left alone.* LEGEND: "TERROR!" *She utters a low moan and turns off the lamp—sits stiffly on the edge of the sofa, knotting her fingers together.* LEGEND ON SCREEN: "THE OPENING OF A DOOR!" TOM *and* JIM *appear on the fire-escape steps and climb to landing. Hearing their approach,* LAURA *rises with a panicky gesture. She retreats to the portieres. The doorbell.* LAURA *catches her breath and touches her throat. Low drums.*)

AMANDA   (*calling*).   Laura, sweetheart! The door!

(LAURA *stares at it without moving.*)

JIM.   I think we just beat the rain.

TOM.   Uh-huh.

(*He rings again, nervously.* JIM *whistles and fishes for a cigarette.*)

AMANDA (*very, very gaily*).   Laura, that is your brother and Mr. O'Connor! Will you let them in, darling?

(LAURA *crosses toward kitchenette door.*)

LAURA (*breathlessly*).   Mother—you go to the door!

(AMANDA *steps out of kitchenette and stares furiously at* LAURA. *She points imperiously at the door.*)

LAURA.   Please, please!

AMANDA (*in a fierce whisper*).   What is the matter with you, you silly thing?

LAURA (*desperately*).   Please, you answer it, *please!*

AMANDA.   I told you I wasn't going to humor you, Laura. Why have you chosen this moment to lose your mind?

LAURA.   Please, please, please, you go!

AMANDA.   You'll have to go to the door because I can't!

LAURA (*desperately*).   I can't either!

AMANDA.   *Why?*

LAURA.   I'm *sick!*

AMANDA.   I'm sick, too—of your nonsense! Why can't you and your brother be normal people? Fantastic whims and behavior!

(TOM *gives a long ring.*)

Preposterous goings on! Can you give me one reason—(*Calls out lyrically.*) COMING! JUST ONE SECOND!—why you should be afraid to open a door? Now you answer it, Laura!

LAURA.   Oh, oh, oh. . .

(*She returns through the portieres. Darts to the victrola and winds it frantically and turns it on.*)

AMANDA.   Laura Wingfield, you march right to that door!

LAURA.   Yes—yes, Mother!

(*A faraway, scratchy rendition of "Dardanella" softens the air and gives her strength to move through it. She slips to the door and draws it cautiously open.* TOM *enters with the caller,* JIM O'CON-NOR.)

TOM.   Laura, this is Jim. Jim, this is my sister, Laura.

JIM (*stepping inside*).   I didn't know that Shakespeare had a sister!

LAURA (*retreating stiff and trembling from the door*).   How—how do you do?

JIM *(heartily extending his hand).* Okay!

(LAURA *touches it hesitantly with hers.*)

JIM. Your hand's *cold*, Laura!

LAURA. Yes, well—I've been playing the victrola. . . .

JIM. Must have been playing classical music on it! You ought to play a little hot swing music to warm you up!

LAURA. Excuse me—I haven't finished playing the victrola. . . .

(She turns awkwardly and hurries into the front room. She pauses a second by the victrola. Then catches her breath and darts through the portieres like a frightened deer.)

JIM *(grinning).* What was the matter?

TOM. Oh—with Laura? Laura is—terribly shy.

JIM. Shy, huh? It's unusual to meet a shy girl nowadays. I don't believe you ever mentioned you had a sister.

TOM. Well, now you know. I have one. Here is the *Post Dispatch.* You want a piece of it?

JIM. Uh-huh.

TOM. What piece? The comics?

JIM. Sports! *(Glances at it.)* Ole Dizzy Dean is on his bad behavior.

TOM *(disinterest).* Yeah?

(*Lights cigarette and crosses back to fire-escape door.*)

JIM. Where are *you* going?

TOM. I'm going out on the terrace.

JIM *(goes after him).* You know, Shakespeare—I'm going to sell you a bill of goods!

TOM. What goods!

JIM. A course I'm taking.

TOM. Huh?

JIM. In public speaking! You and me, we're not the warehouse type.

TOM. Thanks—that's good news. But what has public speaking got to do with it?

JIM. It fits you for—executive positions!

TOM. Awww.

JIM. I tell you it's done a helluva lot for me.

(IMAGE: EXECUTIVE AT DESK)

TOM.   In what respect?

JIM.   In every! Ask yourself what is the difference between you an' me and men in the office down front? Brains?—No!—Ability?—No! Then what? Just one little thing——

TOM.   What is that one little thing?

JIM.   Primarily it amounts to—social poise! Being able to square up to people and hold your own on any social level!

AMANDA   (*off stage*).   Tom?

TOM.   Yes, Mother?

AMANDA.   Is that you and Mr. O'Connor?

TOM.   Yes, Mother.

AMANDA.   Well, you just make yourselves comfortable in here.

TOM.   Yes, Mother.

AMANDA.   Ask Mr. O'Connor if he would like to wash his hands.

JIM.   Aw, no—no—thank you—I took care of that at the warehouse. Tom——

TOM.   Yes?

JIM.   Mr. Mendoza was speaking to me about you.

TOM.   Favorably?

JIM.   What do you think?

TOM.   Well——

JIM.   You're going to be out of a job if you don't wake up.

TOM.   I am waking up——

JIM.   You show no signs.

TOM.   The signs are interior.

(IMAGE ON SCREEN: THE SAILING VESSEL WITH JOLLY ROGER AGAIN)

TOM.   I'm planning to change. (*He leans over the rail speaking with quiet exhilaration. The incandescent marquees and signs of the first-run movie houses light his face from across the alley. He looks like a voyager.*) I'm right at the point of committing myself to a future that doesn't include the warehouse and Mr. Mendoza or even a night-school course in public speaking.

JIM.   What are you gassing about?

TOM.   I'm tired of the movies.

JIM.   Movies!

TOM.   Yes, movies! Look at them—— (*A wave toward the marvels of Grand Avenue.*) All of those glamorous people—having adventures—

hogging it all, gobbling the whole thing up! You know what happens? People go to the *movies* instead of *moving!* Hollywood characters are supposed to have all the adventures for everybody in America, while everybody in America sits in a dark room and watches them have them! Yes, until there's a war. That's when adventure becomes available to the masses! *Everyone's* dish, not only Gable's! Then the people in the dark room come out of the dark room to have some adventures themselves— Goody, goody!—It's our turn now, to go to the South Sea Islands—to make a safari—to be exotic, far-off!—But I'm not patient. I don't want to wait till then. I'm tired of the *movies* and I am *about* to *move!*

JIM   *(incredulously).*   Move?

TOM.   Yes.

JIM.   When?

TOM.   Soon!

JIM.   Where? Where?

(THEME THREE MUSIC SEEMS TO ANSWER THE QUESTION, WHILE TOM
        THINKS IT OVER. HE SEARCHES AMONG HIS POCKETS.)

TOM.   I'm starting to boil inside. I know I seem dreamy, but inside— well, I'm boiling!—Whenever I pick up a shoe, I shudder a little thinking how short life is and what I am doing!—Whatever that means, I know it doesn't mean shoes—except as something to wear on a traveler's feet! *(Finds paper.)* Look——

JIM.   What?

TOM.   I'm a member.

JIM   *(reading).*   The Union of Merchant Seamen.

TOM.   I paid my dues this month, instead of the light bill.

JIM.   You will regret it when they turn the lights off.

TOM.   I won't be here.

JIM.   How about your mother?

TOM.   I'm like my father. The bastard son of a bastard! See how he grins? And he's been absent going on sixteen years!

JIM.   You're just talking, you drip. How does your mother feel about it?

TOM.   Shhh!—Here comes Mother! Mother is not acquainted with my plans!

AMANDA   *(enters portieres).*   Where are you all?

TOM.   On the terrace, Mother.

   (They start inside. She advances to them. TOM *is distinctly shocked*

at her appearance. Even JIM *blinks a little. He is making his first
contact with girlish Southern vivacity and in spite of the night-school
course in public speaking is somewhat thrown off the beam by the
unexpected outlay of social charm. Certain responses are attempted
by* JIM *but are swept aside by* AMANDA'S *gay laughter and chatter.*
TOM *is embarrassed but after the first shock* JIM *reacts very warmly.
Grins and chuckles, is altogether won over.* IMAGE: AMANDA AS A
GIRL)

AMANDA   (*coyly smiling, shaking her girlish ringlets*). Well, well, well,
so this is Mr. O'Connor. Introductions entirely unnecessary. I've heard
so much about you from my boy. I finally said to him, Tom—good gracious!—why don't you bring this paragon to supper? I'd like to meet
this nice young man at the warehouse!—Instead of just hearing him sing
your praises so much!

I don't know why my son is so standoffish—that's not Southern behavior!

Let's sit down and—I think we could stand a little more air in here!
Tom, leave the door open. I felt a nice fresh breeze a moment ago. Where
has it gone to?

Mmm, so warm already! And not quite summer, even. We're going to
burn up when summer really gets started.

However, we're having—we're having a very light supper. I think
light things are better fo' this time of year. The same as light clothes are,
Light clothes an' light food are what warm weather calls fo'. You know
our blood gets so thick during th' winter—it takes a while fo' us to *adjust*
ou'selves!—when the season changes. . . .

It's come so quick this year. I wasn't prepared. All of a sudden—
heavens! Already summer!—I ran to the trunk an' pulled out this light
dress—Terribly old! Historical almost! But feels so good—so good an'
co-ol, y'know. . . .

TOM.   Mother——

AMANDA.   Yes, honey?

TOM.   How about—supper?

AMANDA.   Honey, you go ask Sister if supper is ready. You know that
Sister is in full charge of supper!

Tell her you hungry boys are waiting for it.   (*To* JIM)
Have you met Laura?

JIM.   She——

AMANDA.   Let you in? Oh, good, you've met already! It's rare for a
girl as sweet an' pretty as Laura to be domestic! But Laura is, thank
heavens, not only pretty but also very domestic. I'm not at all. I never

was a bit. I never could make a thing but angelfood cake. Well, in the South we had so many servants. Gone, gone, gone. All vestige of gracious living! Gone completely! I wasn't prepared for what the future brought me. All of my gentlemen callers were sons of planters and so of course I assumed that I would be married to one and raise my family on a large piece of land with plenty of servants. But man proposes—and women accepts the proposal!—To vary that old, old saying a little bit—I married no planter! I married a man who worked for the telephone company!—That gallantly smiling gentleman over there! (*Points to the picture.*) A telephone man who—fell in love with long-distance!—Now he travels and I don't even know where!—But what am I going on for about my—tribulations?

Tell me yours—I hope you don't have any!

Tom?

TOM   (*returning*).   Yes, Mother?

AMANDA.   Is supper nearly ready?

TOM.   It looks to me like supper is on the table.

AMANDA.   Let me look———(*She rises prettily and looks through portieres.*) Oh, lovely!—But where is Sister?

TOM.   Laura is not feeling well and she says that she thinks she'd better not come to the table.

AMANDA.   What?—Nonsense!—Laura? Oh, Laura!

LAURA   (*off stage, faintly*).   Yes, Mother.

AMANDA.   You really must come to the table. We won't be seated until you come to the table!

Come in, Mr. O'Connor. You sit over there, and I'll———

Laura? Laura Wingfield!

You're keeping us waiting, honey! We can't say grace until you come to the table!

(*The back door is pushed weakly open and* LAURA *comes in. She is obviously quite faint, her lips trembling, her eyes wide and staring. She moves unsteadily toward the table.* LEGEND "TERROR!" *Outside a summer storm is coming abruptly. The white curtains billow inward at the windows and there is a sorrowful murmur and deep blue dusk.* LAURA *suddenly stumbles—she catches at a chair with a faint moan.*)

TOM.   Laura!

AMANDA.   Laura!

(*There is a clap of thunder.* LEGEND: "AH!"
Despairingly.)

Why, Laura, you *are* sick, darling! Tom, help your sister into the living room, dear!

Sit in the living room, Laura—rest on the sofa.

Well!   (*To the gentleman caller*)

Standing over the hot stove made her ill!—I told her that it was just too warm this evening, but——

(TOM *comes back in.* LAURA *is on the sofa.*)

Is Laura all right now?

TOM.   Yes.

AMANDA.   What *is* that? Rain? A nice cool rain has come up!

(*She gives the gentleman caller a frightened look.*)

I think we may—have grace—now. . . .

(TOM *looks at her stupidly.*)

Tom, honey—you say grace!

TOM.   Oh. . . .

"For these and all thy mercies——

(*They bow their heads,* AMANDA *stealing a nervous glance at* JIM. *In the living room* LAURA, *stretched on the sofa, clenches her hand to her lips, to hold back a shuddering sob.*)

God's Holy Name be praised"——

(THE SCENE DIMS OUT.)

SCENE VII

LEGEND: A SOUVENIR

Half an hour later. Dinner is just being finished in the upstage area which is concealed by the drawn portieres.

As the curtain rises LAURA *is still huddled upon the sofa, her feet drawn under her, her head resting on a pale blue pillow, her eyes wide and mysteriously watchful. The new floor lamp with its shade of rose-colored silk gives a soft, becoming light to her face, bringing out the fragile, unearthly prettiness which usually escapes attention. There is a steady murmur of rain, but it is slackening and stops soon after the scene begins; the air outside becomes pale and luminous as the moon breaks out.*

A moment after the curtain rises, the lights in both rooms flicker and go out.

JIM.   Hey, there, Mr. Light Bulb!

(AMANDA *laughs nervously.* LEGEND: "SUSPENSION OF A PUBLIC
SERVICE")

AMANDA.   Where was Moses when the lights went out? Ha-ha. Do
you know the answer to that one, Mr. O'Connor?

JIM.   No, Ma'am, what's the answer?

AMANDA.   In the dark!

(JIM *laughs appreciatively.*)

Everybody sit still. I'll light the candles. Isn't it lucky we have them on
the table? Where's a match? Which of you gentlemen. can provide a
match?

JIM.   Here.

AMANDA.   Thank you, sir.

JIM.   Not at all, Ma'am!

AMANDA.   I guess the fuse has burnt out. Mr. O'Connor, can you tell
a burnt-out fuse? I know I can't and Tom is a total loss when it comes
to mechanics.

(SOUND:GETTING UP: VOICES RECEDE A LITTLE TO KITCHENETTE)

Oh, be careful you don't bump into something. We don't want our
gentleman caller to break his neck. Now wouldn't that be a fine howdy-
do?

JIM.   Ha-ha!

Where is the fuse-box?

AMANDA.   Right here next to the stove. Can you see anything?

JIM.   Just a minute.

AMANDA.   Isn't electricity a mysterious thing?
Wasn't it Benjamin Franklin who tied a key to a kite?
We live in such a mysterious universe, don't we? Some people say that
science clears up all the mysteries for us. In my opinion it only creates
more!
Have you found it yet?

JIM.   No, Ma'am. All these fuses look okay to me.

AMANDA.   Tom!

TOM.   Yes, Mother?

AMANDA.   That light bill I gave you several days ago. The one I told
you we got the notices about?

(LEGEND "HA!")

TOM.   Oh.—Yeah.

AMANDA.   You didn't neglect to pay it by any chance?

Tom.   Why, I——

Amanda.   Didn't! I might have known it!

Jim.   Shakespeare probably wrote a poem on that light bill, Mrs. Wingfield.

Amanda.   I might have known better than to trust him with it! There's such a high price for negligence in this world!

Jim.   Maybe the poem will win a ten-dollar prize.

Amanda.   We'll just have to spend the remainder of the evening in the nineteenth century, before Mr. Edison made the Mazda lamp!

Jim.   Candlelight is my favorite kind of light.

Amanda.   That shows you're romantic! But that's no excuse for Tom.

Well, we got through dinner. Very considerate of them to let us get through dinner before they plunged us into everlasting darkness, wasn't it, Mr. O'Connor?

Jim.   Ha-ha!

Amanda.   Tom, as a penalty for your carelessness you can help me with the dishes.

jim.   Let me give you a hand.

Amanda.   Indeed you will not!

Jim.   I ought to be good for something.

Amanda.   Good for something?

(*Her tone is rhapsodic.*)

You? Why, Mr. O'Connor, nobody, *nobody's* given me this much entertainment in years—as you have!

Jim.   Aw, now, Mrs. Wingfield!

Amanda.   I'm not exaggerating, not one bit! But Sister is all by her lonesome. You go keep her company in the parlor!

I'll give you this lovely old candelabrum that used to be on the altar at the Church of the Heavenly Rest. It was melted a little out of shape when the church burnt down. Lighting struck it one spring. Gypsy Jones was holding a revival at the time and he intimated that the church was destroyed because the Episcopalians gave card parties.

Jim.   Ha-ha.

Amanda.   And how about you coaxing Sister to drink a little wine? I think it would be good for her! Can you carry both at once?

Jim.   Sure. I'm Superman!

Amanda.   Now, Thomas, get into this apron!

(*The door of kitchenette swings closed on* Amanda's *gay laughter;*

the flickering light approaches the portieres. LAURA *sits up nervously as he enters. Her speech at first is low and breathless from the almost intolerable strain of being alone with a stranger.* [THE LEGEND: "I DON'T SUPPOSE YOU REMEMBER ME AT ALL!"] *In her first speeches in this scene, before* JIM'S *warmth overcomes her paralyzing shyness,* LAURA'S *voice is thin and breathless as though she has just run up a steep flight of stairs.* JIM'S *attitude is gently humorous. In playing this scene it should be stressed that while the incident is apparently unimportant, it is to* LAURA *the climax of her secret life.*)

JIM.   Hello, there, Laura.

LAURA   *(faintly).*   Hello.

(*She clears her throat.*)

JIM.   How are you feeling now? Better?

LAURA.   Yes. Yes, thank you.

JIM.   This is for you. A little dandelion wine.

(*He extends it toward her with extravagant gallantry.*)

LAURA.   Thank you.

JIM.   Drink it—but don't get drunk!

(*He laughs heartily.* LAURA *takes the glass uncertainly, laughs shyly.*)

Where shall I set the candles?

LAURA.   Oh—oh, anywhere. . . .

JIM.   How about here on the floor? Any objections?

LAURA.   No.

JIM.   I'll spread a newspaper under to catch the drippings. I like to sit on the floor. Mind if I do?

LAURA.   Oh, no.

JIM.   Give me a pillow?

LAURA.   What?

JIM.   A pillow!

LAURA.   Oh. . . .   (*Hands him one quickly.*)

JIM.   How about you? Don't you like to sit on the floor?

LAURA.   Oh—yes.

JIM.   Why don't you, then?

LAURA.   I—will.

JIM.   Take a pillow! (LAURA *does. Sits on the other side of the can-*

delabrum. JIM *crosses his legs and smiles engagingly at her.*) I can't
hardly see you sitting way over there.

LAURA.   I can—see you.

JIM.   I know, but that's not fair; I'm in the limelight. (LAURA *moves
her pillow closer.*)
Good! Now I can see you! Comfortable?

LAURA.   Yes.

JIM.   So am I. Comfortable as a cow! Will you have some gum?

LAURA.   No, thank you.

JIM.   I think that I will indulge, with your permission. (*Musingly
unwraps it and holds it up.*) Think of the fortune made by the guy that
invented the first piece of chewing gum. Amazing, huh? The Wrigley
Building is one of the sights of Chicago.—I saw it summer before last
when I went up to the Century of Progress. Did you take in the Century
of Progress?

LAURA.   No, I didn't.

JIM.   Well, it was quite a wonderful exposition. What impressed me
most was the Hall of Science. Gives you an idea of what the future will
be in America, even more wonderful than the present time is! (*Pause.
Smiling at her.*) Your brother tells me you're shy. Is that right, Laura?

LAURA.   I—don't know.

JIM.   I judge you to be an old-fashioned type of girl. Well, I think
that's a pretty good type to be. Hope you don't think I'm being too
personal—do you?

LAURA   *(hastily, out of embarrassment).*   I believe I *will* take a piece
of gum, if you—don't mind. (*Clearing her throat.*)   Mr. O'Connor, have
you— kept up with your singing?

JIM.   Singing? Me?

LAURA.   Yes. I remember what a beautiful voice you had.

JIM.   When did you hear me sing?

(VOICE OFF STAGE IN THE PAUSE)

VOICE   (*off stage*).

> O blow, ye winds, heigh-ho,
> A-roving I will go!
> I'm off to my love
> With a boxing glove—
> Ten thousand miles away!

JIM.   You say you've heard me sing?

LAURA.   Oh, yes! very often . . . . I—don't suppose—you remember me—at all?

JIM   (*smiling doubtfully*).   You know I have an idea I've seen you before. I had that idea soon as you opened the door. It seemed almost like I was about to remember your name. But the name that I started to call you—wasn't a name! And so I stopped myself before I said it.

LAURA.   Wasn't it—Blue Roses?

JIM   (*springs up; grinning*).   Blue Roses!—My gosh, yes—Blue Roses!

That what I had on my tongue when you opened the door!

Isn't it funny what tricks your memory plays? I didn't connect you with high school somehow or other.

But that's where it was; it was high school. I didn't even know you were Shakespeare's sister!

Gosh, I'm sorry.

LAURA.   I didn't expect you to. You—barely knew me!

JIM.   But we did have a speaking acquaintance, huh?

LAURA.   Yes, we—spoke to each other.

JIM.   When did you recognize me?

LAURA.   Oh, right away!

JIM.   Soon as I came in the door?

LAURA.   When I heard your name I thought it was probably you. I knew that Tom used to know you a little in high school. So when you came in the door—

Well, then I was—sure.

JIM.   Why didn't you *say* something, then?

LAURA   (*breathlessly*).   I didn't know what to say, I was—too surprised!

JIM.   For goodness' sake! You know, this sure is funny!

LAURA.   Yes! Yes, isn't it, though . . . .

JIM.   Didn't we have a class in something together?

LAURA.   Yes, we did.

JIM.   What class was that?

LAURA.   It was—singing—Chorus!

JIM.   Aw!

LAURA.   I sat across the aisle from you in the Aud.

JIM.   Aw.

LAURA.   Mondays, Wednesdays, and Fridays.

JIM.   Now I remember—you always came in late.

LAURA.   Yes, it was so hard for me, getting upstairs. I had that brace on my leg—it clumped so loud!

JIM.   I never heard any clumping.

LAURA   (*wincing at the recollection*).   To me it sounded like—thunder!

JIM.   Well, well, well, I never even noticed.

LAURA.   And everybody was seated before I came in. I had to walk in front of all those people. My seat was in the back row. I had to go clumping all the way up the aisle with everyone watching!

JIM.   You shouldn't have been self-conscious.

LAURA.   I know, but I was. It was always such a relief when the singing started.

JIM.   Aw, yes, I've placed you now! I used to call you Blue Roses. How was it that I got started calling you that?

LAURA.   I was out of school a little while with pleurosis. When I came back you asked me what was the matter. I said I had pleurosis—you thought I said Blue Roses. That's what you always called me after that!

JIM.   I hope you didn't mind.

LAURA.   Oh, no—I liked it. You see, I wasn't acquainted with many —people. . . .

JIM.   As I remember you sort of stuck by yourself.

LAURA.   I—I—never have had much luck at—making friends.

JIM.   I don't see why you wouldn't.

LAURA.   Well, I—started out badly.

JIM.   You mean being——

LAURA.   Yes, it sort of—stood between me——

JIM.   You shouldn't have let it!

LAURA.   I know, but it did, and——

JIM.   You were shy with people!

LAURA.   I tried not to be but never could——

JIM.   Overcome it?

LAURA.   No, I—I never could!

JIM.   I guess being shy is something you have to work out of kind of gradually.

LAURA   (*sorrowfully*).   Yes—I guess it——

JIM.   Takes time!

LAURA.   Yes——

JIM.   People are not so dreadful when you know them. That's what you have to remember! And everybody has problems, not just you, but practically everybody has got some problems.
You think of yourself as having the only problems, as being the only

one who is disappointed. But just look around you and you will see lots of people as disappointed as you are. For instance, I hoped when I was going to high school that I would be further along at this time, six years later, than I am now——You remember that wonderful write-up I had in *The Torch?*

LAURA.   Yes!

(She rises and crosses to table.)

JIM.   It said I was bound to succeed in anything I went into! (LAURA *returns with the annual.*) Holy Jeez! *The Torch!*

(He accepts it reverently. They smile across it with mutual wonder. LAURA crouches beside him and they begin to turn through it. LAURA'S shyness is dissolving in his warmth.)

LAURA.   Here you are in *The Pirates of Penzance!*

JIM   *(wistfully).*   I sang the baritone lead in that operetta.

LAURA   *(raptly).*   So—*beautifully!*

JIM   *(protesting).*   Aw——

LAURA.   Yes, yes—beautifully—beautifully!

JIM.   You heard me?

LAURA.   All three times!

JIM.   No!

LAURA.   Yes!

JIM.   All three performances?

LAURA   *(looking down).*   Yes.

JIM.   Why?

LAURA.   I—wanted to ask you to—autograph my program.

JIM.   Why didn't you ask me to?

LAURA.   You were always surrounded by your own friends so much that I never had a chance to.

JIM.   You should have just——

LAURA.   Well, I—thought you might think I was—

JIM.   Thought I might think you was—what?

LAURA.   Oh——

JIM   *(with reflective relish).*   I was beleaguered by females in those days.

LAURA.   You were terribly popular!

JIM.   Yeah——

LAURA.   You had such a—friendly way——

JIM.   I was spoiled in high school.

LAURA.   Everybody—liked you!

JIM.   Including you?

LAURA.   I—yes, I—I did, too——

(*She gently closes the book in her lap.*)

JIM.   Well, well, well!—Give me that program, Laura. (*She hands it to him. He signs it with a flourish.*) There you are—better late than never!

LAURA.   Oh, I——what a—surprise!

JIM.   My signature isn't worth very much right now.
But some day—maybe—it will increase in value!
Being disappointed is one thing and being discouraged is something else. I am disappointed but I am not discouraged.
I'm twenty-three years old.
How old are you?

LAURA.   I'll be twenty-four in June.

JIM.   That's not old age!

LAURA.   No, but——

JIM.   You finished high school?

LAURA   (*with difficulty*).   I didn't go back.

JIM.   You mean you dropped out?

LAURA.   I made bad grades in my final examinations. (*She rises and replaces the book and the program. Her voice strained.*) How is— Emily Meisenbach getting along?

JIM.   Oh, that kraut-head!

LAURA.   Why do you call her that?

JIM.   That's what she was.

LAURA.   You're not still—going with her?

JIM.   I never see her.

LAURA.   It said in the Personal Section that you were—engaged!

JIM.   I know, but I wasn't impressed by that—propaganda!

LAURA.   It wasn't—the truth?

JIM.   Only in Emily's optimistic opinion!

LAURA.   Oh——

(LEGEND: "WHAT HAVE YOU DONE SINCE HIGH SCHOOL?" JIM *lights a cigarette and leans indolently back on his elbows smiling at* LAURA *with a warmth and charm which lights her inwardly with altar candles. She remains by the table and turns in her hands a piece of glass to cover her tumult.*)

JIM (*after several reflective puffs on a cigarette*).   What have you done since high school? (*She seems not to hear him.*) Huh? (LAURA *looks up.*) I said what have you done since high school, Laura?

LAURA.   Nothing much.

JIM.   You must have been doing something these six long years.

LAURA.   Yes.

JIM.   Well, then, such as what ?

LAURA.   I took a business course at business college——

JIM.   How did that work out?

LAURA.   Well, not very—well—I had to drop out, it gave me—indigestion——

(JIM *laughs gently.*)

JIM.   What are you doing now?

LAURA.   I don't do anything—much. Oh, please don't think I sit around doing nothing! My glass collection takes up a good deal of time. Glass is something you have to take good care of.

JIM.   What did you say—about glass?

LAURA.   Collection I said—I have one——

(*She clears her throat and turns away again, acutely shy.*)

JIM (*abruptly*).   You know what I judge to be the trouble with you? Inferiority complex! Know what that is? That's what they call it when someone low-rates himself!

I understand it because I had it, too. Although my case was not so aggravated as yours seems to be. I had it until I took up public speaking, developed my voice, and learned that I had an aptitude for science. Before that time I never thought of myself as being outstanding in any way whatsoever!

Now I've never made a regular study of it, but I have a friend who says I can analyze people better than doctors that make a profession of it. I don't claim that to be necessarily true, but I can sure guess a person's psychology, Laura! (*Takes out his gum.*)   Excuse me, Laura. I always take it out when the flavor is gone. I'll use this scrap of paper to wrap it in. I know how it is to get it stuck on a shoe.

Yep—that's what I judge to be your principal trouble. A lack of confidence in yourself as a person. You don't have the proper amount of faith in yourself. I'm basing that fact on a number of your remarks and also on certain observations I've made. For instance that clumping you thought was so awful in high school. You say that you even dreaded to walk into class. You see what you did? You dropped out of school, you gave up an education because of a clump, which as far as I know was practically nonexistent! A little physical defect is what you have. Hardly noticeable even! Magnified thousands of times by imagination!

You know what my strong advice to you is? Think of yourself as *superior* in some way!

LAURA.   In what way would I think?

JIM.   Why, man alive, Laura! Just look about you a little. What do you see? A world full of common people! All of 'em born and all of 'em going to die!

Which of them has one-tenth of your good points? Or mine? Or anyone else's, as far as that goes—Gosh!

Everybody excels in some one thing. Some in many!

> (*Unconsciously glances at himself in the mirror.*)

All you've got to do is discover in *what!*

Take me, for instance.

> (*He adjusts his tie at the mirror.*)

My interest happens to lie in electrodynamics. I'm taking a course in radio engineering at night school, Laura, on top of a fairly responsible job at the warehouse. I'm taking that course and studying public speaking.

LAURA.   Ohhhh.

JIM.   Because I believe in the future of television!

> (*Turning back to her.*)

I wish to be ready to go up right along with it. Therefore I'm planning to get in on the ground floor. In fact I've already made the right connections and all that remains is for the industry itself to get under way! Full steam——

> (*His eyes are starry.*)

Knowledge—Zzzzzp! Money—Zzzzzzp!—Power!
That's the cycle democracy is built on!

> (*His attitude is convincingly dynamic.* LAURA *stares at him, even her shyness eclipsed in her absolute wonder. He suddenly grins.*)

I guess you think I think a lot of myself!

LAURA.   No—o-o-o, I——

JIM.   Now how about you? Isn't there something you take more interest in than anything else?

LAURA.   Well, I do—as I said—have my—glass collection——

> (*A peal of girlish laughter from the kitchen.*)

JIM.   I'm not right sure I know what you're talking about.
What kind of glass is it?

LAURA.   Little articles of it, they're ornaments mostly!
Most of them are little animals made out of glass, the tiniest little animals in the world. Mother calls them a glass menagerie!
Here's an example of one, if you'd like to see it!
This one is one of the oldest. It's nearly thirteen.

(MUSIC: "THE GLASS MENAGERIE." *He stretches out his hand.*)

Oh, be careful—if you breathe, it breaks!

JIM.   I'd better not take it. I'm pretty clumsy with things.

LAURA.   Go on, I trust you with him!

(*Places it in his palm.*)

There now—you're holding him gently!
Hold him over the light, he loves the light! You see how the light shines through him?

JIM.   It sure does shine!

LAURA.   I shouldn't be partial, but he is my favorite one.

JIM.   What kind of a thing is this one supposed to be?

LAURA.   Haven't you noticed the single horn on his forehead?

JIM.   A unicorn, huh?

LAURA.   Mmm-hmmm!

JIM.   Unicorns, aren't they extinct in the modern world?

LAURA.   I know!

JIM.   Poor little fellow, he must feel sort of lonesome.

LAURA   (*smiling*).   Well, if he does he doesn't complain about it. He stays on a shelf with some horses that don't have horns and all of them seem to get along nicely together.

JIM.   How do you know?

LAURA   (*lightly*).   I haven't heard any arguments among them!

JIM   (*grinning*).   No arguments, huh? Well, that's a pretty good sign! Where shall I set him?

LAURA.   Put him on the table. They all like a change of scenery once in a while!

JIM   (*stretching*).   Well, well, well, well——
Look how big my shadow is when I stretch!

LAURA.   Oh, oh, yes—it stretches across the ceiling!

JIM   (*crossing to door*).   I think it's stopped raining. (*Opens fire-escape door.*) Where does the music come from?

LAURA.   From the Paradise Dance Hall across the alley.

JIM.   How about cutting the rug a little, Miss Wingfield?

LAURA.   Oh, I——

JIM.   Or is your program filled up? Let me have a look at it. (*Grasps imaginary card.*) Why, every dance is taken! I'll just have to scratch some out. (WALTZ MUSIC: "LA GOLONDRINA.") Ahh, a waltz!

> (*He executes some sweeping turns by himself then holds his arms toward* LAURA.)

LAURA   (*breathlessly*).   I—can't dance!

JIM.   There you go, that inferiority stuff!

LAURA.   I've never danced in my life!

JIM.   Come on, try!

LAURA.   Oh, but I'd step on you!

JIM.   I'm not made out of glass.

LAURA.   How—how—how do we start?

JIM.   Just leave it to me. You hold your arms out a little.

LAURA.   Like this?

JIM.   A little bit higher. Right. Now don't tighten up, that's the main thing about it—relax.

LAURA   (*laughing breathlessly*).   It's hard not to.

JIM.   Okay.

LAURA.   I'm afraid you can't budge me.

JIM.   What do you bet I can't?

> (*He swings her into motion.*)

LAURA.   Goodness, yes, you can!

JIM.   Let yourself go, now, Laura, just let yourself go.

LAURA.   I'm——

JIM.   Come on!

LAURA.   Trying!

JIM.   Not so stiff——Easy does it!

LAURA.   I know but I'm——

JIM.   Loosen th' backbone! There now, that's a lot better.

LAURA.   Am I?

JIM.   Lots, lots better!

> (*He moves her about the room in a clumsy waltz.*)

LAURA.   Oh, my!

JIM.   Ha-ha!

LAURA.   Oh, my goodness!

JIM. Ha-ha-ha! (*They suddenly bump into the table.* JIM *stops.*)
What did we hit on?

LAURA. Table.

JIM. Did something fall off it? I think——

LAURA. Yes.

JIM. I hope that it wasn't the little glass horse with the horn!

LAURA. Yes.

JIM. Aw, aw, aw. Is it broken?

LAURA. Now it is just like all the other horses.

JIM. It's lost its——

LAURA. Horn!
It doesn't matter. Maybe it's a blessing in disguise.

JIM. You'll never forgive me. I bet that that was your favorite piece
of glass.

LAURA. I don't have favorites much. It's no tragedy, Freckles.
Glass breaks so easily. No matter how careful you are. The traffic jars
the shelves and things fall off them.

JIM. Still I'm awfully sorry that I was the cause.

LAURA (*smiling*). I'll just imagine he had an operation.
The horn was removed to make him feel less—freakish!

(*They both laugh.*)

Now he will feel more at home with the other horses, the ones that
don't have horns. . .

JIM. Ha-ha, that's very funny!

(*Suddenly serious.*)

I'm glad to see that you have a sense of humor.
You know—you're—well—very different!
Surprisingly different from anyone else I know!

(*His voice becomes soft and hesitant with a genuine feeling.*)

Do you mind me telling you that?

(LAURA *is abashed beyond speech.*)

I mean it in a nice way. . . .

(LAURA *nods shyly, looking away.*)

You make me feel sort of—I don't know how to put it!
I'm usually pretty good at expressing things, but——
This is something that I don't know how to say!

(LAURA *touches her throat and clears it—turns the broken uni-*
corn in her hands. Even softer.)

Has anyone ever told you that you were pretty?

(PAUSE: MUSIC. LAURA *looks up slowly, with wonder, and shakes*
her head.)

Well, you are! In a very different way from anyone else.
And all the nicer because of the difference, too.

(*His voice becomes low and husky.* LAURA *turns away, nearly*
faint with the novelty of her emotions.)

I wish that you were my sister. I'd teach you to have some confidence
in yourself. The different people are not like other people, but being
different is nothing to be ashamed of. Because other people are not such
wonderful people. They're one hundred times one thousand. You're one
times one! They walk all over the earth. You just stay here. They're common as—weeds, but—you—well, you're—*Blue Roses!*

(IMAGE ON SCREEN: BLUE ROSES. MUSIC CHANGES.)

LAURA.   But blue is wrong for—roses . . . .

JIM.   It's right for you! You're—pretty!

LAURA.   In what respect am I pretty?

JIM.   In all respects—believe me! Your eyes—your hair—are pretty!
Your hands are pretty! (*He catches hold of her hand.*)
You think I'm making this up because I'm invited to dinner and have
to be nice. Oh, I could do that! I could put on an act for you, Laura, and
say lots of things without being very sincere. But this time I am. I'm talking to you sincerely. I happened to notice you had this inferiority complex that keeps you from feeling comfortable with people. Somebody
needs to build your confidence up and make you proud instead of shy
and turning away and—blushing——
Somebody—ought to——
Ought to—*kiss* you, Laura!

(*His hand slips slowly up her arm to her shoulder.* MUSIC SWELLS
TUMULTUOUSLY. *He suddenly turns her about and kisses her on*
the lips. When he releases her, LAURA *sinks on the sofa with a*
bright, dazed look. JIM *backs away and fishes in his pocket for a*
cigarette. LEGEND ON SCREEN: "SOUVENIR.")

Stumble-john!

(*He lights the cigarette, avoiding her look: There is a peal of girlish*
laughter from AMANDA *in the kitchen.* LAURA *slowly raises and*

opens her hand. It still contains the little broken glass animal. She looks at it with a tender, bewildered expression.)

Stumble-john!
I shouldn't have done that—That was way off the beam.
You don't smoke, do you?

(*She looks up, smiling, not hearing the question. He sits beside her a little gingerly. She looks at him speechlessly—waiting. He coughs decorously and moves a little farther aside as he considers the situation and senses her feelings, dimly, with perturbation. Gently.*)

Would you—care for a—mint?

(*She doesn't seem to hear him but her look grows brighter even.*)

Peppermint—Life-Saver?
My pocket's a regular drug store—wherever I go. . . .

(*He pops a mint in his mouth. Then gulps and decides to make a clean breast of it. He speaks slowly and gingerly.*)

Laura, you know, if I had a sister like you, I'd do the same thing as Tom. I'd bring out fellows and—introduce her to them. The right type of boys of a type to—appreciate her.
Only—well—he made a mistake about me.
Maybe I've got no call to be saying this. That may not have been the idea in having me over. But what if it was?
There's nothing wrong about that. The only trouble is that in my case —I'm not in a situation to—do the right thing.
I can't take down your number and say I'll phone.
I can't call up next week and—ask for a date.
I thought I had better explain the situation in case you—misunderstood it and—hurt your feelings. . . .

(*Pause. Slowly, very slowly,* LAURA'S *look changes, her eyes returning slowly from his to the ornament in her palm.* AMANDA *utters another gay laugh in the kitchen.*)

LAURA   (*faintly*).   You—won't—call again?

JIM.   No, Laura, I can't.

(*He rises from the sofa.*)

As I was just explaining, I've—got strings on me.
Laura, I've—been going steady!
I go out all of the time with a girl named Betty. She's a home-girl like you, and Catholic, and Irish, and in a great many ways we—get along fine.

I met her last summer on a moonlight boat trip up the river to Alton, on the *Majestic.*

Well—right away from the start it was—love!

(LEGEND: LOVE! LAURA *sways slightly forward and grips the arm of the sofa. He fails to notice, now enrapt in his own comfortable being.*)

Being in love has made a new man of me!

(*Leaning stiffly forward, clutching the arm of the sofa,* LAURA *struggles visibly with her storm. But* JIM *is oblivious; she is a long way off.*)

The power of love is really pretty tremendous!

Love is something that—changes the whole world, Laura!

(*The storm abates a little and* LAURA *leans back. He notices her again.*)

It happened that Betty's aunt took sick; she got a wire and had to go to Centralia. So Tom—when he asked me to dinner—I naturally just accepted the invitation, not knowing that you—that he—that I——

(*He stops awkwardly.*)

Huh—I'm a stumble-john!

(*He flops back on the sofa. The holy candles in the altar of* LAURA'S *face have been snuffed out. There is a look of almost infinite desolation.* JIM *glances at her uneasily.*)

I wish that you would—say something.

(*She bites her lip, which was trembling, and then bravely smiles. She opens her hand again on the broken glass ornament. Then she gently takes his hand and raises it level with her own. She carefully places the unicorn in the palm of his hand, then pushes his fingers closed upon it.*)

What are you—doing that for? You want me to have him?— Laura? (*She nods.*) What for?

LAURA.   A—souvenir. . . .

(*She rises unsteadily and crouches beside the victrola to wind it up.* LEGEND ON SCREEN: "THINGS HAVE A WAY OF TURNING OUT SO BADLY!" OR IMAGE: "GENTLEMAN CALLER WAVING GOOD-BYE!— GAILY." *At this moment* AMANDA *rushes brightly back in the front room. She bears a pitcher of fruit punch in an old-fashioned cut-glass pitcher and a plate of macaroons. The plate has a gold border and poppies painted on it.*)

AMANDA. Well, well, well! Isn't the air delightful after the shower? I've made you children a little liquid refreshment.

(*Turns gaily to the gentleman caller.*)

Jim, do you know that song about lemonade? "Lemonade, lemonade Made in the shade and stirred with a spade—Good enough for any old maid!"

JIM (*uneasily*). Ha-ha! No—I never heard it.

AMANDA. Why, Laura! You look so serious!

JIM. We were having a serious conversation.

AMANDA. Good! Now you're better acquainted!

JIM (*uncertainly*). Ha-ha! Yes.

AMANDA. You modern young people are much more serious-minded than my generation. I was so gay as a girl!

JIM. You haven't changed, Mrs. Wingfield.

AMANDA. Tonight I'm rejuvenated! The gaiety of the occasion, Mr. O'Connor!

(*She tosses her head with a peal of laughter. Spills lemonade.*)

Oooo! I'm baptizing myself!

JIM. Here—let me——

AMANDA (*setting the pitcher down*). There now. I discovered we had some maraschino cherries. I dumped them in, juice and all!

JIM. You shouldn't have gone to that trouble, Mrs. Wingfield.

AMANDA. Trouble, trouble? Why, it was loads of fun! Didn't you hear me cutting up in the kitchen? I bet your ears were burning! I told Tom how outdone with him I was for keeping you to himself so long a time! He should have brought you over much, much sooner! Well, now that you've found your way, I want you to be a very frequent caller! Not just occasional but all the time.

Oh, we're going to have a lot of gay times together! I see them coming!

Mmm, just breathe that air! So fresh, and the moon's so pretty!

I'll skip back out—I know where my place is when young folks are having a—serious conversation!

JIM. Oh, don't go out, Mrs. Wingfield. The fact of the matter is I've got to be going.

AMANDA. Going, now? You're joking! Why, it's only the shank of the evening, Mr. O'Connor!

JIM. Well, you know how it is.

AMANDA. You mean you're a young workingman and have to keep workingmen's hours. We'll let you off early tonight. But only on the condition that next time you stay later.

What's the best night for you? Isn't Saturday night the best night for you workingmen?

JIM. I have a couple of time-clocks to punch, Mrs. Wingfield. One at morning, another one at night!

AMANDA. My, but you *are* ambitious! You work at night, too?

JIM. No, Ma'am, not work but—Betty!

(*He crosses deliberately to pick up his hat. The band at the Paradise Dance Hall goes into a tender waltz.*)

AMANDA. Betty? Betty? Who's—Betty?

(*There is an ominous cracking sound in the sky.*)

JIM. Oh, just a girl. The girl I go steady with!

(*He smiles charmingly. The sky falls.*
LEGEND: "THE SKY FALLS")

AMANDA (*a long-drawn exhalation*). Ohhh . . . Is it a serious romance, Mr. O'Connor?

JIM. We're going to be married the second Sunday in June.

AMANDA. Ohhhh—how nice!

Tom didn't mention that you were engaged to be married.

JIM. The cat's not out of the bag at the warehouse yet.

You know how they are. They call you Romeo and stuff like that.

(*He stops at the oval mirror to put on his hat. He carefully shapes the brim and the crown to give a discreetly dashing effect.*)

It's been a wonderful evening, Mrs. Wingfield. I guess this is what they mean by Southern hospitality.

AMANDA. It really wasn't anything at all.

JIM. I hope it don't seem like I'm rushing off. But I promised Betty I'd pick her up at the Wabash depot, an' by the time I get my jalopy down there her train'll be in. Some women are pretty upset if you keep 'em waiting.

AMANDA. Yes, I know——The tyranny of women!

(*Extends her hand.*)

Good-bye, Mr. O'Connor.

I wish you luck—and happiness—and success! All three of them, and so does Laura!—Don't you, Laura?

LAURA. Yes!

JIM   (*taking her hand*).   Good-bye, Laura. I'm certainly going to treasure that souvenir. And don't you forget the good advice I gave you.

(*Raises his voice to a cheery shout.*)

So long, Shakespeare!
Thanks again, ladies——Good night!

(*He grins and ducks jauntily out. Still bravely grimacing,* AMANDA *closes the door on the gentleman caller. Then she turns back to the room with a puzzled expression. She and* LAURA *don't dare to face each other.* LAURA *crouches beside the victrola to wind it.*)

AMANDA   (*faintly*).   Things have a way of turning out so badly.
I don't believe that I would play the victrola.
Well, well—well——
Our gentleman caller was engaged to be married!
Tom!

TOM   (*from back*).   Yes, Mother?

AMANDA.   Come in here a minute. I want to tell you something awfully funny.

TOM   (*enters with macaroon and a glass of the lemonade*).   Has the gentleman caller gotten away already?

AMANDA.   The gentleman caller has made an early departure.
What a wonderful joke you played on us!

TOM.   How do you mean?

AMANDA.   You didn't mention that he was engaged to be married.

TOM.   Jim? Engaged?

AMANDA.   That's what he just informed us.

TOM.   I'll be jiggered! I didn't know about that.

AMANDA.   That seems very peculiar.

TOM.   What's peculiar about it?

AMANDA.   Didn't you call him your best friend down at the warehouse?

TOM.   He is, but how did I know?

AMANDA.   It seems extremely peculiar that you wouldn't know your best friend was going to be married!

TOM.   The warehouse is where I work, not where I know things about people!

AMANDA.   You don't know things anywhere! You live in a dream; you manufacture illusions!   (*He crosses to the door.*)
Where are you going?

TOM.   I'm going to the movies.

AMANDA.   That's right, now that you've had us make such fools of ourselves. The effort, the preparations, all the expense! The new floor lamp, the rug, the clothes for Laura! All for what? To entertain some other girl's fiancé!

Go to the movies, go! Don't think about us, a mother deserted, an unmarried sister who's crippled and has no job! Don't let anything interfere with your selfish pleasure!

Just go, go, go—to the movies!

TOM.   All right, I will! The more you shout about my selfishness to me the quicker I'll go, and I won't go to the movies!

AMANDA.   Go, then! Then go to the moon—you selfish dreamer!

(TOM *smashes his glass on the floor. He plunges out on the fire escape, slamming the door.* LAURA *screams—cut off by door. Dance-hall music up.* TOM *goes to the rail and grips it desperately, lifting his face in the chill white moonlight penetrating the narrow abyss of the alley.* LEGEND ON SCREEN: "AND SO GOOD-BYE. . . ." TOM'S *closing speech is timed with the interior pantomime. The interior scene is played as though viewed through soundproof glass.* AMANDA *appears to be making a comforting speech to* LAURA *who is huddled upon the sofa. Now that we cannot hear the mother's speech, her silliness is gone and she has dignity and tragic beauty.* LAURA'S *dark hair hides her face until at the end of the speech she lifts it to smile at her mother.* AMANDA'S *gestures are slow and graceful, almost dancelike, as she comforts the daughter. At the end of her speech she glances a moment at the father's picture—then withdraws through the portieres. At close of* TOM'S *speech,* LAURA blows out the candles, ending the play.)

TOM.   I didn't go to the moon, I went much further—for time is the longest distance between two places——

Not long after that I was fired for writing a poem on the lid of a shoebox.

I left Saint Louis. I descended the steps of this fire escape for the last time and followed, from then on, in my father's footsteps, attempting to find in motion what was lost in space——

I travelled around a great deal. The cities swept about me like dead leaves, leaves that were brightly colored but torn away from the branches.

I would have stopped, but I was pursued by something.

It always came upon me unawares, taking me altogether by surprise. Perhaps it was a familiar bit of music. Perhaps it was only a piece of transparent glass——

Perhaps I am walking along a street at night, in some strange city, before I have found companions. I pass the lighted window of a shop where perfume is sold. The window is filled with pieces of colored glass, tiny transparent bottles in delicate colors, like bits of a shattered rainbow.

Then all at once my sister touches my shoulder. I turn around and look into her eyes. . . .

Oh, Laura, Laura, I tried to leave you behind me, but I am more faithful than I intended to be!

I reach for a cigarette, I cross the street, I run into the movies or a bar, I buy a drink, I speak to the nearest stranger—anything that can blow your candles out!

(LAURA *bends over the candles.*)

—for nowadays the world is lit by lightning! Blow out your candles, Laura—and so good-bye. . . .

(*She blows the candles out.*)
(THE SCENE DISSOLVES.)

The Glass Menagerie

For Analysis

For a discussion of this play, see the introduction to the drama section, 499–507.

1. How is Tom's final escape foreshadowed and justified in the early scenes?

2. In what way is the father an actor in the play?

3. What developing figure characterizing first Amanda and then Laura begins in Scene II with Laura's remark about her mother's appearance? How is that figure continued in the scenes that follow by means of dialogue and the screen legends? How is it peculiarly fitting, if a little startling?

4. What do Jim and Amanda have in common?

5. How much truth is there in Jim's analysis of Laura's problem? of his own earlier problem?

6. Every character in this play has an escape hatch of some kind; for Laura it is the glass menagerie. What is it for Tom, before he leaves? for Amanda? for Jim?

7. The play is tied closely to the world situation of the 1930's. Is that

setting necessary to the play? Or does the play have more universal
validity than that?

8. What in Amanda's reaction to the dinner fiasco helps justify Tom's
   leaving?

9. Refer to the discussion of the play in the introduction to the drama
   section. Can you now answer the final questions in that introduction?
   What, for example, is the effect of the last lengthy stage direction
   in the play, in which Williams writes, "Now that we cannot hear the
   mother's speech, her silliness is gone and she has dignity and tragic
   beauty"? Is there a character in the play whose "dignity and tragic
   beauty" existed only in his words, not in his actions?

Lorraine Hansberry

A Raisin
in the Sun

What happens to a dream deferred?
Does it dry up
Like a raisin in the sun?
Or fester like a sore—
And then run?
Does it stink like rotten meat?
Or crust and sugar over—
Like a syrupy sweet?

Maybe it just sags
Like a heavy load.

Or does it explode?
                            —Langston Hughes

A RAISIN IN THE SUN: © Copyright as an unpublished work, 1958 by Lorraine
Hansberry. © Copyright 1959 by Lorraine Hansberry. Reprinted from FOUR
CONTEMPORARY AMERICAN PLAYS by permission of Random House,
Inc.

A RAISIN IN THE SUN was first presented by Philip Rose and David J. Cogan
at the Ethel Barrymore Theatre, New York City, March 11, 1959, with the
listed cast.

Characters

RUTH YOUNGER, Ruby Dee. TRAVIS YOUNGER, Glynn Turman. WALTER LEE YOUNGER (BROTHER), Sidney Poitier. BENEATHA YOUNGER, Diana Sands. LENA YOUNGER (MAMA), Claudia McNeil. JOSEPH ASAGAI, Ivan Dixon. GEORGE MURCHISON, Louis Gossett. KARL LINDNER, John Fiedler. BOBO, Lonne Elder III. MOVING MEN, Ed Hall, Douglas Turner.

Directed by Lloyd Richards.

Designed and lighted by Ralph Alswang.

Costumes by Virginia Volland.

> *The action of the play is set in Chicago's Southside, sometime between World War II and the present.*

ACT I

SCENE 1. *Friday morning.*
SCENE 2. *The following morning.*

ACT II

SCENE 1. *Later, the same day.*
SCENE 2. *Friday night, a few weeks later.*
SCENE 3. *Moving day, one week later.*

ACT III

An hour later.

ACT I

SCENE 1

The YOUNGER *living room would be a comfortable and well-ordered room if it were not for a number of indestructible contradictions to this state of being. Its furnishings are typical and undistinguished and their primary feature now is that they have clearly had to accommodate the living of too many people for too many years—and they are tired. Still, we can see that at some time, a time probably no longer remembered by the family (except per-*

haps for MAMA) *the furnishings of this room were actually selected with care and love and even hope—and brought to this apartment and arranged with taste and pride.*

That was a long time ago. Now the once loved pattern of the couch upholstery has to fight to show itself from under acres of crocheted doilies and couch covers that have themselves finally come to be more important than the upholstery. And here a table or a chair has been moved to disguise the worn places in the carpet; but the carpet has fought back by showing its weariness, with depressing uniformity, elsewhere on its surface.

Weariness has, in fact, won in this room. Everything has been polished, washed, sat on, used, scrubbed too often. All pretenses but living itself have long since vanished from the very atmosphere of this room.

Moreover, a section of this room, for it is not really a room unto itself, though the landlord's lease would make it seem so, slopes backward to provide a small kitchen area, where the family prepares the meals that are eaten in the living room proper, which must also serve as dining room. The single window that has been provided for these "two" rooms is located in this kitchen area. The sole natural light the family may enjoy in the course of a day is only that which fights its way through this little window.

At left, a door leads to a bedroom which is shared by MAMA *and her daughter,* BENEATHA. *At right, opposite, is a second room (which in the beginning of the life of this apartment was probably a breakfast room), which serves as a bedroom for* WALTER *and his wife,* RUTH.

Time: Sometime between World War II and the present.

Place: Chicago's Southside.

At Rise: It is morning dark in the living room. TRAVIS *is asleep on the make-down bed at center. An alarm clock sounds from within the bedroom at right, and presently* RUTH *enters from that room and closes the door behind her. She crosses sleepily toward the window. As she passes her sleeping son she reaches down and shakes him a little. At the window she raises the shade and a dusky Southside morning light comes in feebly. She fills a pot with water and puts it on to boil. She calls to the boy, between yawns, in a slightly muffled voice.*

RUTH *is about thirty. We can see that she was a pretty girl, even exceptionally so, but now it is apparent that life has been little that she expected, and disappointment has already begun to hang in her face. In a few years, before thirty-five even, she will be known among her people as a "settled woman."*

She crosses to her son and gives him a good, final, rousing shake.

RUTH.   Come on now, boy, it's seven thirty! (*Her son sits up at last, in a stupor of sleepiness.*) I say hurry up, Travis! You ain't the only person in the world got to use a bathroom! (*The child, a sturdy, handsome little boy of ten or eleven, drags himself out of the bed and almost blindly takes his towels and "today's clothes" from drawers and a closet and goes out to the bathroom, which is in an outside hall and which is shared by another family or families on the same floor.* RUTH *crosses to the bedroom door at right and opens it and calls in to her husband*) Walter Lee! . . . It's after seven thirty! Lemme see you do some waking up in there now! (*She waits.*) You better get up from there, man! It's after seven thirty I tell you. (*She waits again.*) All right, you just go ahead and lay there and next thing you know Travis be finished and Mr. Johnson'll be in there and you'll be fussing and cussing round here like a mad man! And be late too! (*She waits, at the end of patience.*) Walter Lee—it's time for you to get up!

(*She waits another second and then starts to go into the bedroom, but is apparently satisfied that her husband has begun to get up. She stops, pulls the door to, and returns to the kitchen area. She wipes her face with a moist cloth and runs her fingers through her sleep-disheveled hair in a vain effort and ties an apron around her housecoat. The bedroom door at right opens and her husband stands in the doorway in his pajamas, which are rumpled and mismated. He is a lean, intense young man in his middle thirties, inclined to quick nervous movements and erratic speech habits—and always in his voice there is a quality of indictment.*)

WALTER.   Is he out yet?

RUTH.   What you mean *out!* He ain't hardly got in there good yet.

WALTER   (*wandering in, still more oriented to sleep than to a new day*). Well, what was you doing all that yelling for if I can't even get in there yet? (*Stopping and thinking*) Check coming today?

RUTH.   They *said* Saturday and this is just Friday and I hopes to God you ain't going to get up here first thing this morning and start talking to me 'bout no money— 'cause I 'bout don't want to hear it.

WALTER.   Something the matter with you this morning?

RUTH.   No—I'm just sleepy as the devil. What kind of eggs you want?

WALTER.   Not scrambled. (*RUTH starts to scramble eggs.*) Paper come? (*RUTH points impatiently to the rolled up Tribune on the table, and he*

gets it and spreads it out and vaguely reads the front page.) Set off another
bomb yesterday.

RUTH   *(maximum indifference).*   Did they?

WALTER   *(looking up).*   What's the matter with you?

RUTH.   Ain't nothing the matter with me. And don't keep asking
me that this morning.

WALTER.   Ain't nobody bothering you. *(Reading the news of the day
absently again)* Say Colonel McCormick is sick.

RUTH   *(affecting tea-party interest).*   Is he now? Poor thing.

WALTER   *(sighing and looking at his watch).*   Oh me. *(He waits.)*
Now what is that boy doing in that bathroom all this time? He just going
to have to start getting up earlier. I can't be being late to work on account of him fooling around in there.

RUTH   *(turning on him).*   Oh, no he ain't going to be getting up no
earlier no such thing! It ain't his fault that he can't get to bed no earlier
nights 'cause he got a bunch of crazy good-for-nothing clowns sitting
up running their mouths in what is supposed to be his bedroom after ten
o'clock at night. . . .

WALTER.   That's what you mad about, ain't it? The things I want
to talk about with my friends just couldn't be important in your mind,
could they?

> *(He rises and finds a cigarette in her handbag on the table
> and crosses to the little window and looks out, smoking and deeply
> enjoying this first one.)*

RUTH   *(almost matter of factly, a complaint too automatic to deserve emphasis).* Why you always got to smoke before you eat in the
morning?

WALTER   *(at the window).*   Just look at 'em down there. . . . Running
and racing to work. . . . *(He turns and faces his wife and watches her a
moment at the stove, and then, suddenly.)* You look young this morning,
baby.

RUTH   *(indifferently).*   Yeah?

WALTER.   Just for a second—stirring them eggs. It's gone now—just
for a second it was—you looked real young again. *(Then, drily)* It's gone
now—you look like yourself again.

RUTH.   Man, if you don't shut up and leave me alone.

WALTER   *(looking out to the street again).*   First thing a man ought
to learn in life is not to make love to no colored woman first thing in
the morning. You all some evil people at eight o'clock in the morning.

(TRAVIS *appears in the hall doorway, almost fully dressed and quite wide awake now, his towels and pajamas across his shoulders. He opens the door and signals for his father to make the bathroom in a hurry.*)

TRAVIS (*watching the bathroom*). Daddy, come on!

(WALTER *gets his bathroom utensils and flies out to the bathroom.*)

RUTH. Sit down and have your breakfast, Travis.

TRAVIS. Mama, this is Friday. (*Gleefully*) Check coming tomorrow, huh?

RUTH. You get your mind off money and eat your breakfast.

TRAVIS (*eating*). This is the morning we supposed to bring the fifty cents to school.

RUTH. Well, I ain't got no fifty cents this morning.

TRAVIS. Teacher say we have to.

RUTH. I don't care what teacher say. I ain't got it. Eat your breakfast, Travis.

TRAVIS. I *am* eating.

RUTH. Hush up now and just eat!

(*The boy gives her an exasperated look for her lack of understanding and eats grudgingly.*)

TRAVIS. You think Grandmama would have it?

RUTH. No! And I want you to stop asking your grandmother for money, you hear me?

TRAVIS (*outraged*). Gaaalcce! I don't ask her, she just gimme it sometimes!

RUTH. Travis Willard Younger—I got too much on me this morning to be—

TRAVIS. Maybe Daddy—

RUTH. *Travis!*

(*The boy hushes abruptly. They are both quiet and tense for several seconds.*)

TRAVIS (*presently*). Could I maybe go carry some groceries in front of the supermarket for a little while after school then?

RUTH. Just hush, I said. (TRAVIS *jabs his spoon into his cereal bowl viciously and rests his head in anger upon his fists.*) If you through eating, you can get over there and make up your bed.

(*The boy obeys stiffly and crosses the room, almost mechanically, to the bed and more or less carefully folds the covering. He carries the bedding into his mother's room and returns with his books and cap.)*

TRAVIS *(sulking and standing apart from her unnaturally).* I'm gone.

RUTH *(looking up from the stove to inspect him automatically).* Come here. *(He crosses to her and she studies his head.)* If you don't take this comb and fix this here head, you better! *(TRAVIS puts down his books with a great sigh of oppression, and crosses to the mirror. His mother mutters under her breath about his "slubbornness.")* 'Bout to march out of here with that head looking just like chickens slept in it! I just don't know where you get your slubborn ways. . . . And get your jacket, too. Looks chilly out this morning.

TRAVIS *(with conspicuously brushed hair and jacket).* I'm gone.

RUTH. Get carfare and milk money—*(Waving one finger)*—and not a single penny for no caps, you hear me?

TRAVIS *(with sullen politeness).* Yes'm.

(He turns in outrage to leave. His mother watches after him as in his frustration he approaches the door almost comically. When she speaks to him, her voice has become a very gentle tease.)

RUTH *(mocking; as she thinks he would say it).* Oh, Mama makes me so mad sometimes, I don't know what to do! *(She waits and continues to his back as he stands stock-still in front of the door.)* I wouldn't kiss that woman good-bye for nothing in this world this morning! *(The boy finally turns around and rolls his eyes at her, knowing the mood has changed and he is vindicated; he does not, however, move toward her yet.)* Not for nothing in this world! *(She finally laughs aloud at him and holds out her arms to him and we see that it is a way between them, very old and practiced. He crosses to her and allows her to embrace him warmly but keeps his face fixed with masculine rigidity. She holds him back from her presently and looks at him and runs her fingers over the features of his face. With utter gentleness—)* Now—whose little old angry man are you?

TRAVIS *(the masculinity and gruffness start to fade at last).* Aw gaalee—Mama. . . .

RUTH *(mimicking).* Aw—gaaaaalleeeee, Mama! *(She pushes him, with rough playfulness and finality, toward the door.)* Get on out of here or you going to be late.

TRAVIS *(in the face of love, new aggressiveness).* Mama, could I *please* go carry groceries?

RUTH. Honey it's starting to get so cold evenings.

WALTER   (*coming in from the bathroom and drawing a make-believe gun from a make-believe holster and shooting at his son*). What is it he wants to do?

RUTH.   Go carry groceries after school at the supermarket.

WALTER.   Well, let him go. . . .

TRAVIS   (*quickly, to the ally*).   I *have* to—she won't gimme the fifty cents. . . .

WALTER   (*to his wife only*).   Why not?

RUTH   (*simply and with flavor*).   'Cause we don't have it.

WALTER   (*to* RUTH *only*).   What you tell the boy things like that for? (*Reaching down into his pants with a rather important gesture.*) Here, son—

> (*He hands the boy the coin, but his eyes are directed to his wife's.*
> TRAVIS *takes the money happily.*)

TRAVIS.   Thanks, Daddy.

> (*He starts out.* RUTH *watches both of them with murder in her eyes.*
> WALTER *stands and stares back at her with defiance, and suddenly reaches into his pocket again on an afterthought.*)

WALTER   (*without even looking at his son, still staring hard at his wife*).   In fact, here's another fifty cents. . . . Buy yourself some fruit to-day—or take a taxicab to school or something!

TRAVIS.   Whoopee—

> (*He leaps up and clasps his father around the middle with his legs, and they face each other in mutual appreciation; slowly* WALTER
> LEE *peeks around the boy to catch the violent rays from his wife's eyes and draws his head back as if shot.*)

WALTER.   You better get down now—and get to school, man.

TRAVIS   (*at the door*).   O.K. Good-bye.

> (*He exits.*)

WALTER   (*after him, pointing with pride*).   That's *my* boy. (*She looks at him in disgust and turns back to her work.*) You know what I was thinking 'bout in the bathroom this morning?

RUTH.   No.

WALTER.   How come you always try to be so pleasant!

RUTH.   What is there to be pleasant 'bout!

WALTER.   You want to know what I was thinking 'bout in the bathroom or not!

RUTH.   I know what you thinking 'bout.

WALTER   (*ignoring her*).   'Bout what me and Willy Harris was talking about last night.

RUTH   (*immediately—a refrain*).   Willy Harris is a good-for-nothing loud mouth.

WALTER.   Anybody who talks to me has got to be a good-for-nothing loud mouth, ain't he? And what you know about who is just a good-for-nothing loud mouth? Charlie Atkins was just a "good-for-nothing loud mouth" too, wasn't he! When he wanted me to go in the dry-cleaning business with him. And now—he's grossing a hundred thousand a year. A hundred thousand dollars a year! You still call *him* a loud mouth!

RUTH   (*bitterly*).   Oh, Walter Lee. . . .

(*She folds her head on her arms over the table.*)

WALTER   (*rising and coming to her and standing over her*).   You tired, ain't you? Tired of everything. Me, the boy, the way we live—this beat-up hole—everything. Ain't you? (*She doesn't look up, doesn't answer.*) So tired—moaning and groaning all the time, but you wouldn't do nothing to help, would you? You couldn't be on my side that long for nothing, could you?

RUTH.   Walter, please leave me alone.

WALTER.   A man needs for a woman to back him up. . . .

RUTH.   Walter—

WALTER.   Mama would listen to you. You know she listen to you more than she do me and Bennie. She think more of you. All you have to do is just sit down with her when you drinking your coffee one morning and talking 'bout things like you do and—(*He sits down beside her and demonstrates graphically what he thinks her methods and tone should be.*)—you just sip your coffee, see, and say easy like that you been thinking 'bout that deal Walter Lee is so interested in, 'bout the store and all, and sip some more coffee, like what you saying ain't really that important to you—And the next thing you know, she be listening good and asking you questions and when I come home—I can tell her the details. This ain't no fly-by-night proposition, baby. I mean we figured it out, me and Willy and Bobo.

RUTH   (*with a frown*).   Bobo?

WALTER.   Yeah. You see, this little liquor store we got in mind cost seventy-five thousand and we figured the initial investment on the place be 'bout thirty thousand, see. That be ten thousand each. Course, there's a couple of hundred you got to pay so's you don't spend your life just waiting for them clowns to let your license get approved—

RUTH.   You mean graft?

WALTER (*frowning impatiently*). Don't call it that. See there, that just goes to show you what women understand about the world. Baby, don't *nothing* happen for you in this world 'less you pay *somebody* off!

RUTH. Walter, leave me alone! (*She raises her head and stares at him vigorously—then says, more quietly.*) Eat your eggs, they gonna be cold.

WALTER (*straightening up from her and looking off*). That's it. There you are. Man say to his woman: I got me a dream. His woman say: Eat your eggs. (*Sadly, but gaining in power*) Man say: I got to take hold of this here world, baby! And a woman will say: Eat your eggs and go to work. (*Passionately now*) Man say: I got to change my life, I'm choking to death, baby! And his woman say—(*In utter anguish as he brings his fists down on his thighs*)—Your eggs is getting cold!

RUTH (*softly*). Walter, that ain't none of our money.

WALTER (*not listening at all or even looking at her*). This morning, I was lookin' in the mirror and thinking about it. . . . I'm thirty-five years old; I been married eleven years and I got a boy who sleeps in the living room—(*Very, very quietly*)—and all I got to give him is stories about how rich white people live . . . .

RUTH. Eat your eggs, Walter.

WALTER. *Damn my eggs . . . damn all the eggs that ever was!*

RUTH. Then go to work.

WALTER (*looking up at her*). See—I'm trying to talk to you 'bout myself—(*Shaking his head with the repetition*)—and all you can say is eat them eggs and go to work.

RUTH (*wearily*). Honey, you never say nothing new. I listen to you every day, every night and every morning, and you never say nothing new. (*Shrugging*) So you would rather *be* Mr. Arnold than be his chauffeur. So—I would *rather* be living in Buckingham Palace.

WALTER. That is just what is wrong with the colored woman in this world. . . . Don't understand about building their men up and making 'em feel like they somebody. Like they can do something.

RUTH (*drily, but to hurt*). There *are* colored men who do things.

WALTER. No thanks to the colored woman.

RUTH. Well, being a colored woman, I guess I can't help myself none.

(*She rises and gets the ironing board and sets it up and attacks a huge pile of rough-dried clothes, sprinkling them in preparation for the ironing and then rolling them into tight fat balls.*)

WALTER (*mumbling*). We one group of men tied to a race of women with small minds.

(*His sister BENEATHA enters. She is about twenty, as slim and in-*

tense as her brother. She is not as pretty as her sister-in-law, but her lean, almost intellectual face has a handsomeness of its own. She wears a bright-red flannel nightie, and her thick hair stands wildly about her head. Her speech is a mixture of many things; it is different from the rest of the family's insofar as education has permeated her sense of English—and perhaps the Midwest rather than the South has finally—at last—won out in her inflection; but not altogether, because over all of it is a soft slurring and transformed use of vowels which is the decided influence of the Southside. She passes through the room without looking at either RUTH *or* WALTER *and goes to the outside door and looks, a little blindly, out to the bathroom. She sees that it has been lost to the Johnsons. She closes the door with a sleepy vengeance and crosses to the table and sits down a little defeated.*)

BENEATHA.   I am going to start timing those people.

WALTER.   You should get up earlier.

BENEATHA   (*her face in her hands; she is still fighting the urge to go back to bed*). Really—would you suggest dawn? Where's the paper?

WALTER   (*pushing the paper across the table to her as he studies her almost clinically, as though he has never seen her before*). You a horrible-looking chick at this hour.

BENEATHA   (*drily*).   Good morning, everybody.

WALTER   (*senselessly*).   How is school coming?

BENEATHA   (*in the same spirit*).   Lovely. Lovely. And you know, biology is the greatest. (*Looking up at him*) I dissected something that looked just like you yesterday.

WALTER.   I just wondered if you've made up your mind and everything.

BENEATHA   (*gaining in sharpness and impatience*).   And what did I answer yesterday morning—and the day before that?

RUTH   (*from the ironing board, like someone disinterested and old*). Don't be so nasty, Bennie.

BENEATHA   (*still to her brother*).   And the day before that and the day before that!

WALTER   (*defensively*).   I'm interested in you. Something wrong with that? Ain't many girls who decide—

WALTER *and* BENEATHA   (*in unison*).   —"to be a doctor."

(*Silence*)

WALTER.   Have we figured out yet just exactly how much medical school is going to cost?

RUTH.   Walter Lee, why don't you leave that girl alone and get out of here to work?

BENEATHA   (*exits to the bathroom and bangs on the door*).   Come on out of there, please!

(*She comes back into the room.*)

WALTER   (*looking at his sister intently*).   You know the check is coming tomorrow.

BENEATHA   (*turning on him with a sharpness all her own*).   That money belongs to Mama, Walter, and it's for her to decide how she wants to use it. I don't care if she wants to buy a house or a rocket ship or just nail it up somewhere and look at it. It's hers. Not ours—*hers*.

WALTER   (*bitterly*).   Now ain't that fine! You just got your mother's interest at heart, ain't you, girl? You such a nice girl—but if Mama got that money she can always take a few thousand and help you through school too—can't she?

BENEATHA.   I have never asked anyone around here to do anything for me!

WALTER.   No! And the line between asking and just accepting when the time comes is big and wide—ain't it!

BENEATHA   (*with fury*).   What do you want from me, Brother—that I quit school or just drop dead, which!

WALTER.   I don't want nothing but for you to stop acting holy 'round here. Me and Ruth done made some sacrifices for you—why can't you do something for the family?

RUTH.   Walter, don't be dragging me in it.

WALTER.   You are in it—Don't you get up and go work in somebody's kitchen for the last three years to help put clothes on her back?

RUTH.   Oh, Walter—that's not fair. . . .

WALTER.   It ain't that nobody expects you to get on your knees and say thank you, Brother; thank you, Ruth; thank you, Mama—and thank you, Travis, for wearing the same pair of shoes for two semesters—

BENEATHA   (*dropping to her knees*).   Well—I *do*—all right?—thank everybody . . . and forgive me for ever wanting to be anything at all . . . forgive me, forgive me!

RUTH.   Please stop it! Your mama'll hear you.

WALTER.   Who the hell told you you had to be a doctor? If you so crazy 'bout messing 'round with sick people—then go be a nurse like other women—or just get married and be quiet. . . .

BENEATHA.   Well—you finally got it said. . . . It took you three years but you finally got it said. Walter, give up; leave me alone—it's Mama's money.

WALTER.   *He was my father, too!*

BENEATHA.   So what? He was mine, too—and Travis's grandfather —but the insurance money belongs to Mama. Picking on me is not going to make her give it to you to invest in any liquor stores—(*Underbreath, dropping into a chair*)—and I for one say, God bless Mama for that!

WALTER   (*to* RUTH).   See—did you hear? Did you hear!

RUTH.   Honey, please go to work.

WALTER.   Nobody in this house is ever going to understand me.

BENEATHA.   Because you're a nut.

WALTER.   Who's a nut?

BENEATHA.   You—you are a nut. Thee is mad, boy.

WALTER   (*looking at his wife and his sister from the door, very sadly*). The world's most backward race of people, and that's a fact.

BENEATHA   (*turning slowly in her chair*).   And then there are all those prophets who would lead us out of the wilderness—(WALTER *slams out of the house.*)—into the swamps!

RUTH.   Bennie, why you always gotta be pickin' on your brother? Can't you be a little sweeter sometimes? (*Door opens.* WALTER *walks in.*)

WALTER   (*to Ruth*). I need some money for carfare.

RUTH   (*looks at him, then warms; teasing, but tenderly*). Fifty cents? (*She goes to her bag and gets money.*) Here, take a taxi.

(WALTER *exits.* MAMA *enters. She is a woman in her early sixties, full-bodied and strong. She is one of those women of a certain grace and beauty who wear it so unobtrusively that it takes a while to notice. Her dark-brown face is surrounded by the total whiteness of her hair, and, being a woman who has adjusted to many things in life and overcome many more, her face is full of strength. She has, we can see, wit and faith of a kind that keep her eyes lit and full of interest and expectancy. She is, in a word, a beautiful woman. Her bearing is perhaps most like the noble bearing of the women of the Hereros of Southwest Africa—rather as if she imagines that as she walks she still bears a basket or a vessel upon her head. Her speech, on the other hand, is as careless as her carriage is precise— she is inclined to slur everything—but her voice is perhaps not so much quiet as simply soft.*)

MAMA.   Who that 'round here slamming doors at this hour?

(*She crosses through the room, goes to the window, opens it, and brings in a feeble little plant growing doggedly in a small pot on the window sill. She feels the dirt and puts it back out.)*

RUTH.   That was Walter Lee. He and Bennie was at it again.

MAMA.   My children and they tempers. Lord if this little old plant don't get more sun than it's been getting it ain't never going to see spring again. (*She turns from the window.*) What's the matter with you this morning, Ruth? You looks right peaked. You aiming to iron all them things? Leave some for me. I'll get to 'em this afternoon. Bennie honey, it's too drafty for you to be sitting 'round half dressed. Where's your robe?

BENEATHA.   In the cleaners.

MAMA.   Well, go get mine and put it on.

BENEATHA.   I'm not cold, Mama, honest.

MAMA.   I know—but you so thin. . . .

BENEATHA (*irritably*).   Mama, I'm not cold.

MAMA (*seeing the make-down bed as* TRAVIS *has left it*).   Lord have mercy, look at that poor bed. Bless his heart—he tries, don't he?

(*She moves to the bed* TRAVIS *has sloppily made up.*)

RUTH.   No—he don't half try at all 'cause he knows you going to come along behind him and fix everything. That's just how come he don't know how to do nothing right now—you done spoiled that boy so.

MAMA.   Well—he's a little boy. Ain't supposed to know 'bout housekeeping. My baby, that's what he is. What you fix for his breakfast this morning?

RUTH (*angrily*).   I feed my son, Lena!

MAMA.   I ain't meddling—(*Underbreath; busy-bodyish*) I just noticed all last week he had cold cereal, and when it starts getting this chilly in the fall a child ought to have some hot grits or something when he goes out in the cold—

RUTH (*furious*).   I gave him hot oats—is that all right!

MAMA.   I ain't meddling. (*Pause*) Put a lot of nice butter on it? (RUTH *shoots her an angry look and does not reply.*) He likes lots of butter.

RUTH (*exasperated*).   Lena—

MAMA (*to* BENEATHA; MAMA *is inclined to wander conversationally sometimes*). What was you and your brother fussing 'bout this morning?

BENEATHA.   It's not important, Mama.

(*She gets up and goes to look out at the bathroom, which is apparently free, and she picks up her towels and rushes out.*)

MAMA.   What was they fighting about?

RUTH.   Now you know as well as I do.

MAMA   (*shaking her head*).   Brother still worrying hisself sick about that money?

RUTH.   You know he is.

MAMA.   You had breakfast?

RUTH.   Some coffee.

MAMA.   Girl, you better start eating and looking after yourself better. You almost thin as Travis.

RUTH.   Lena—

MAMA.   Uh-hunh?

RUTH.   What are you going to do with it?

MAMA.   Now don't you start, child. It's too early in the morning to be talking about money. It ain't Christian.

RUTH.   It's just that he got his heart set on that store—

MAMA.   You mean that liquor store that Willy Harris want him to invest in?

RUTH.   Yes—

MAMA.   We ain't no business people, Ruth. We just plain working folks.

RUTH.   Ain't nobody business people till they go into business. Walter Lee say colored people ain't never going to start getting ahead till they start gambling on some different kinds of things in the world—investments and things.

MAMA.   What done got into you, girl? Walter Lee done finally sold you on investing.

RUTH.   No. Mama, something is happening between Walter and me. I don't know what it is—but he needs something—something I can't give him any more. He needs this chance, Lena.

MAMA   (*frowning deeply*).   But liquor, honey—

RUTH.   Well—like Walter say—I spec people going to always be drinking themselves some liquor.

MAMA.   Well—whether they drinks it or not ain't none of my business. But whether I go into business selling it to 'em *is*, and I don't want that on my ledger this late in life. (*Stopping suddenly and studying her daughter-in-law*) Ruth Younger, what's the matter with you today? You look like you could fall over right there.

RUTH.   I'm tired.

MAMA.   Then you better stay home from work today.

RUTH. I can't stay home. She'd be calling up the agency and scream-ing at them, "My girl didn't come in today—send me somebody! My girl didn't come in!" Oh, she just have a fit. . . .

MAMA. Well, let her have it. I'll just call her up and say you got the flu—

RUTH (*laughing*). Why the flu?

MAMA. 'Cause it sounds respectable to 'em. Something white people get, too. They know 'bout the flu. Otherwise they think you been cut up or something when you tell 'em you sick.

RUTH. I got to go in. We need the money.

MAMA. Somebody would of thought my children done all but starved to death the way they talk about money here late. Child, we got a great big old check coming tomorrow.

RUTH (*sincerely but also self-righteously*). Now that's your money. It ain't got nothing to do with me. We all feel like that—Walter and Ben-nie and me—even Travis.

MAMA (*thoughtfully and suddenly very far away*). Ten thousand dollars—

RUTH. Sure is wonderful.

MAMA. Ten thousand dollars.

RUTH. You know what you should do, Miss Lena? You should take yourself a trip somewhere. To Europe or South America or someplace—

MAMA (*throwing up her hands at the thought*). Oh, child!

RUTH. I'm serious. Just pack up and leave! Go on away and enjoy yourself some. Forget about the family and have yourself a ball for once in your life—

MAMA (*drily*). You sound like I'm just about ready to die. Who'd go with me? What I look like wandering 'round Europe by myself?

RUTH. Shoot—these rich white women do it all the time. They don't think nothing of packing up they suitcases and piling on one of them big steamships and—swoosh!—they gone, child.

MAMA. Something always told me I wasn't no rich white woman.

RUTH. Well—what are you going to do with it then?

MAMA. I ain't rightly decided. (*Thinking. She speaks now with em-phasis.*) Some of it got to be put away for Beneatha and her schoolin'— and ain't nothing going to touch that part of it. Nothing. (*She waits sev-eral seconds, trying to make up her mind about something, and looks at RUTH a little tentatively before going on.*) Been thinking that we may-be could meet the notes on a little old two-story somewhere, with a yard where Travis could play in the summertime, if we use part of the insurance for a down payment and everybody kind of pitch in. I could maybe take on a little day work again, few days a week—

RUTH (*studying her mother-in-law furtively and concentrating on her ironing, anxious to encourage without seeming to*). Well, Lord knows, we've put enough rent into this here rat trap to pay for four houses by now . . . .

MAMA (*looking up at the words "rat trap" and then looking around and leaning back and sighing—in a suddenly reflective mood—*). "Rat trap"—yes, that's all it is. (*Smiling*) I remember just as well the day me and Big Walter moved in here. Hadn't been married but two weeks and wasn't planning on living here no more than a year. (*She shakes her head at the dissolved dream*). We was going to set away, little by little, don't you know, and buy a little place out in Morgan Park. We had even picked out the house. (*Chuckling a little*) Looks right dumpy today. But Lord, child, you should know all the dreams I had 'bout buying that house and fixing it up and making me a little garden in the back—(*She waits and stops smiling.*) And didn't none of it happen.

(*Dropping her hands in a futile gesture.*)

RUTH (*keeps her head down, ironing*). Yes, life can be a barrel of disappointments, sometimes.

MAMA. Honey, Big Walter would come in here some nights back then and slump down on that couch there and just look at the rug, and look at me and look at the rug and then back at me—and I'd know he was down then . . . really down. (*After a second very long and thoughtful pause; she is seeing back to times that only she can see.*) And then, Lord, when I lost that baby—little Claude—I almost though I was going to lose Big Walter too. Oh, that man grieved hisself! He was one man to love his children.

RUTH. Ain't nothin' can tear at you like losin' your baby.

MAMA. I guess that's how come that man finally worked hisself to death like he done. Like he was fighting his own war with this here world that took his baby from him.

RUTH. He sure was a fine man, all right. I always liked Mr. Younger.

MAMA. Crazy 'bout his children! God knows there was plenty wrong with Walter Younger—hard-headed, mean, kind of wild with women —plenty wrong with him. But he sure loved his children. Always wanted them to have something—be something. That's where Brother gets all these notions, I reckon. Big Walter used to say, he'd get right wet in the eyes sometimes, lean his head back with the water standing in his eyes and say, "Seem like God didn't see fit to give the black man nothing but dreams—but He did give us children to make them dreams seem worth while."

(She smiles.) He could talk like that, don't you know.

RUTH. Yes, he sure could. He was a good man, Mr. Younger.

MAMA. Yes, a fine man—just couldn't never catch up with his dreams, that's all.

(BENEATHA *comes in, brushing her hair and looking up to the ceiling, where the sound of a vacuum cleaner has started up.*)

BENEATHA. What could be so dirty on that woman's rugs that she has to vacuum them every single day?

RUTH. I wish certain young women 'round here who I could name would take inspiration about certain rugs in a certain apartment I could also mention.

BENEATHA *(shrugging)*. How much cleaning can a house need, for Christ's sakes.

MAMA *(not liking the Lord's name used thus)*. Bennie!

RUTH. Just listen to her—just listen!

BENEATHA. Oh, God!

MAMA. If you use the Lord's name just one more time—

BENEATHA *(a bit of a whine)*. Oh, Mama—

RUTH. Fresh—just fresh as salt, this girl!

BENEATHA *(drily)*. Well—if the salt loses its savor—

MAMA. Now that will do. I just ain't going to have you 'round here reciting the scriptures in vain—you hear me?

BENEATHA. How did I manage to get on everybody's wrong side by just walking into a room?

RUTH. If you weren't so fresh—

BENEATHA. Ruth, I'm twenty years old.

MAMA. What time you be home from school today?

BENEATHA. Kind of late. *(With enthusiasm)* Madeline is going to start my guitar lessons today.

(MAMA *and* RUTH *look up with the same expression.*)

MAMA. Your *what* kind of lessons?

BENEATHA. Guitar.

RUTH. Oh, Father!

MAMA. How come you done take it in your mind to learn to play the guitar?

BENEATHA.   I just want to, that's all.

MAMA   (*smiling*).   Lord, child, don't you know what to do with yourself? How long it going to be before you get tired of this now—like you got tired of that little play-acting group you joined last year? (*Looking at Ruth*) And what was it the year before that?

RUTH.   The horseback-riding club for which she bought that fifty-five-dollar riding habit that's been hanging in the closet ever since!

MAMA   (*to* BENEATHA).   Why you got to flit so from one thing to another, baby?

BENEATHA   (*sharply*).   I just want to learn to play the guitar. Is there anything wrong with that?

MAMA.   Ain't nobody trying to stop you. I just wonders sometimes why you has to flit so from one thing to another all the time. You ain't never done nothing with all that camera equipment you brought home—

BENEATHA.   I don't flit. I—I experiment with different forms of expression—

RUTH.   Like riding a horse?

BENEATHA.   —People have to express themselves one way or another.

MAMA.   What is it you want to express?

BENEATHA   (*angrily*).   Me! (MAMA *and* RUTH *look at each other and burst into raucous laughter.*) Don't worry—I don't expect you to understand.

MAMA   (*to change the subject*). Who you going out with tomorrow night?

BENEATHA   (*with displeasure*).   George Murchison again.

MAMA   (*pleased*).   Oh—you getting a little sweet on him?

RUTH.   You ask me, this child ain't sweet on nobody but herself— (*Underbreath*) Express herself!

(*They laugh.*)

BENEATHA.   Oh—I like George all right, Mama. I mean I like him enough to go out with him and stuff, but—

RUTH   (*for devilment*).   What does *and stuff* mean?

BENEATHA.   Mind your own business.

MAMA.   Stop picking at her now, Ruth. (*A thoughtful pause, and then a suspicious sudden look at her daughter as she turns in her chair for emphasis.*) What *does* it mean?

BENEATHA   (*wearily*).   Oh, I just mean I couldn't ever really be serious about George. He's—he's so shallow.

RUTH.   Shallow—what do you mean he's shallow? He's *Rich!*

MAMA.   Hush, Ruth.

BENEATHA.   I know he's rich. He knows he's rich, too.

RUTH.   Well—what other qualities a man got to have to satisfy you, little girl?

BENEATHA.   You wouldn't even begin to understand. Anybody who married Walter could not possibly understand.

MAMA   (*outraged*).   What kind of way is that to talk about your brother?

BENEATHA.   Brother is a flip—let's face it.

MAMA   (*to* RUTH, *helplessly*).   What's a flip?

RUTH   (*glad to add kindling*).   She's saying he's crazy.

BENEATHA.   Not crazy. Brother isn't really crazy yet—he—he's an elaborate neurotic.

MAMA.   Hush your mouth!

BENEATHA.   As for George. Well, George looks good—he's got a beautiful car and he takes me to nice places and, as my sister-in-law says, he is probably the richest boy I will ever get to know and I even like him sometimes—but if the Youngers are sitting around waiting to see if their little Bennie is going to tie up the family with the Murchisons, they are wasting their time.

RUTH.   You mean you wouldn't marry George Murchison if he asked you someday? That pretty, rich thing? Honey, I knew you was odd—

BENEATHA.   No I would not marry him if all I felt for him was what I feel now. Besides, George's family wouldn't really like it.

MAMA.   Why not?

BENEATHA.   Oh, Mama—The Murchisons are honest-to-God-real-*live*-rich colored people, and the only people in the world who are more snobbish than rich white people are rich colored people. I thought everybody knew that. I've met Mrs. Murchison. She's a scene!

MAMA.   You must not dislike people 'cause they well off, honey.

BENEATHA.   Why not? It makes just as much sense as disliking people 'cause they are poor, and lots of people do that.

RUTH   (*a wisdom-of-the-ages manner; to* MAMA).   Well, she'll get over some of this—

BENEATHA.   Get over it? What are you talking about, Ruth? Listen, I'm going to be a doctor. I'm not worried about who I'm going to marry yet—if I ever get married.

MAMA *and* RUTH.   *If!*

MAMA.   Now, Bennie—

BENEATHA.   Oh, I probably will . . . but first I'm going to be a doctor, and George, for one, still thinks that's pretty funny. I couldn't be bothered with that. I am going to be a doctor and everybody around here better understand that!

MAMA   (*kindly*).   'Course you going to be a doctor, honey, God willing.

BENEATHA   (*drily*).   God hasn't got a thing to do with it.

MAMA.   Beneatha—that just wasn't necessary.

BENEATHA.   Well—neither is God. I get sick of hearing about God.

MAMA.   Beneatha!

BENEATHA.   I mean it! I'm just tired of hearing about God all the time. What has He got to do with anything? Does he pay tuition?

MAMA.   You 'bout to get your fresh little jaw slapped!

RUTH.   That's just what she needs, all right!

BENEATHA.   Why? Why can't I say what I want to around here, like everybody else?

MAMA.   It don't sound nice for a young girl to say things like that— you wasn't brought up that way. Me and your father went to trouble to get you and Brother to church every Sunday.

BENEATHA.   Mama, you don't understand. It's all a matter of ideas, and God is just one idea I don't accept. It's not important. I am not going out and be immoral or commit crimes because I don't believe in God. I don't even think about it. It's just that I get tired of Him getting credit for all the things the human race achieves through its own stubborn effort. There simply is no blasted God—there is only man and it is he who makes miracles!

(MAMA *absorbs this speech, studies her daughter and rises slowly and crosses to* BENEATHA *and slaps her powerfully across the face. After, there is only silence and the daughter drops her eyes from her mother's face, and* MAMA *is very tall before her.*)

MAMA.   Now—you say after me, in my mother's house there is still God. (*There is a long pause and* BENEATHA *stares at the floor wordlessly.* MAMA *repeats the phrase with precision and cool emotion.*) In my mother's house there is still God.

BENEATHA.   In my mother's house there is still God.

(*A long pause*)

MAMA.   (*walking away from* BENEATHA, *too disturbed for triumphant posture; stopping and turning back to her daughter).* There are some ideas we ain't going to have in this house. Not long as I am at the head of this family.

BENEATHA.   Yes, ma'am.

(MAMA *walks out of the room.*)

RUTH   (*almost gently, with profound understanding*).   You think you a woman, Bennie—but you still a little girl. What you did was childish—so you got treated like a child.

BENEATHA.   I see. *(Quietly)* I also see that everybody thinks it's all right for Mama to be a tyrant. But all the tryanny in the world will never put a God in the heavens!

(She picks up her books and goes out.)

RUTH   (*goes to* MAMA'S *door*).   She said she was sorry.

MAMA   (*coming out, going to her plant*).   They frightens me, Ruth. My children.

RUTH.   You got good children, Lena. They just a little off sometimes—but they're good.

MAMA.   No—there's something come down between me and them that don't let us understand each other and I don't know what it is. One done almost lost his mind thinking 'bout money all the time and the other done commence to talk about things I can't seem to understand in no form or fashion. What is it that's changing, Ruth?

RUTH   (*soothingly, older than her years*).   Now . . . you taking it all too seriously. You just got strong-willed children and it takes a strong woman like you to keep 'em in hand.

MAMA   (*looking at her plant and sprinkling a little water on it*).   They spirited all right, my children. Got to admit they got spirit—Bennie and Walter. Like this little old plant that ain't never had enough sunshine or nothing—and look at it. . . .

(She has her back to RUTH, *who has had to stop ironing and lean against something and put the back of her hand to her forehead.)*

RUTH   (*trying to keep* MAMA *from noticing*).   You . . . sure . . . loves that little old thing, don't you? . . .

MAMA.   Well, I always wanted me a garden like I used to see sometimes at the back of the houses down home. This plant is close as I ever got to having one. (*She looks out of the window as she replaces the plant.*) Lord, ain't nothing as dreary as the view from this window on a dreary day, is there? Why ain't you singing this morning, Ruth? Sing that

"No Ways Tired." That song always lifts me up so—(*She turns at last to see that* RUTH *has slipped quietly into a chair, in a state of semiconsciousness.*) Ruth! Ruth honey—what's the matter with you . . . Ruth!

(CURTAIN)

SCENE 2

It is the following morning; a Saturday morning, and house cleaning is in progress at the YOUNGERS. *Furniture has been shoved hither and yon and* MAMA *is giving the kitchen-area walls a washing down.* BENEATHA, *in dungarees, with a handkerchief tied around her face, is spraying insecticide into the cracks in the walls. As they work, the radio is on and a Southside disk-jockey program is inappropriately filling the house with a rather exotic saxophone blues.* TRAVIS, *the sole idle one, is leaning on his arms, looking out of the window.*

TRAVIS.   Grandmama, that stuff Bennie is using smells awful. Can I go downstairs, please?

MAMA.   Did you get all them chores done already? I ain't seen you doing much.

TRAVIS.   Yes'm—finished early. Where did Mama go this morning?

MAMA   (*looking at* BENEATHA).   She had to go on a little errand.

TRAVIS.   Where?

MAMA.   To tend to her business.

TRAVIS.   Can I go outside then?

MAMA.   Oh, I guess so. You better stay right in front of the house, though . . . and keep a good lookout for the postman.

TRAVIS.   Yes'm. (*He starts out and decides to give his* AUNT BENEATHA *a good swat on the legs as he passes her.*) Leave them poor little old cockroaches alone, they ain't bothering you none.

(*He runs as she swings the spray gun at him both viciously and playfully.* WALTER *enters from the bedroom and goes to the phone.*)

MAMA.   Look out there, girl, before you be spilling some of that stuff on that child!

TRAVIS   (*teasing*).   That's right—look out now!

(*He exits.*)

BENEATHA   (*drily*).   I can't imagine that it would hurt him—it has never hurt the roaches.

MAMA.   Well, little boys' hides ain't as tough as Southside roaches.

WALTER   (*into phone*).   Hello—Let me talk to Willy Harris.

MAMA.   You better get over there behind the bureau. I seen one marching out of there like Napoleon yesterday.

WALTER.   Hello, Willy? It ain't come yet. It'll be here in a few minutes. Did the lawyer give you the papers?

BENEATHA.   There's really only one way to get rid of them, Mama—

MAMA.   How?

BENEATHA.   Set fire to this building.

WALTER.   Good. Good. I'll be right over.

BENEATHA.   Where did Ruth go, Walter?

WALTER.   I don't know.

(He exits abruptly.)

BENEATHA.   Mama, where did Ruth go?

MAMA   (*looking at her with meaning*).   To the doctor, I think.

BENEATHA.   The doctor? What's the matter? (*They exchange glances.*) You don't think—

MAMA   (*with her sense of drama*).   Now I ain't saying what I think. But I ain't never been wrong 'bout a woman neither.

(The phone rings.)

BENEATHA   (*at the phone*).   Hay-lo . . . . (*Pause, and a moment of recognition*) Well—when did you get back! . . . And how was it? . . . Of course I've missed you—in my way. . . . This morning? No . . . house cleaning and all that and Mama hates it if I let people come over when the house is like this . . . . You *have*? Well, that's different. . . . What is it—Oh, what the hell, come on over . . . . Right, see you then.

(She hangs up.)

MAMA   (*who has listened vigorously, as is her habit*).   Who is that you inviting over here with this house looking like this? You ain't got the pride you was born with!

BENEATHA.   Asagai doesn't care how houses look, Mama—he's an intellectual.

MAMA.   *Who?*

BENEATHA.   Asagai—Joseph Asagai. He's an African boy I met on campus. He's been studying in Canada all summer.

MAMA.   What's his name?

BENEATHA.   Asagai, Joseph. Ah-sah-guy. . . . He's from Nigeria.

MAMA.   Oh, that's the little country that was founded by slaves way back. . . .

BENEATHA.   No, Mama—that's Liberia.

MAMA.   I don't think I never met no African before.

BENEATHA.   Well, do me a favor and don't ask him a whole lot of ignorant questions about Africans. I mean, do they wear clothes and all that—

MAMA.   Well, now, I guess if you think we so ignorant 'round here maybe you shouldn't bring your friends here—

BENEATHA.   It's just that people ask such crazy things. All anyone seems to know about when it comes to Africa is Tarzan—

MAMA   (*indignantly*).   Why should I know anything about Africa?

BENEATHA.   Why do you give money at church for the missionary work?

MAMA.   Well, that's to help save people.

BENEATHA.   You mean save them from *heathenism*—

MAMA   (*innocently*).   Yes.

BENEATHA.   I'm afraid they need more salvation from the British and the French.

(RUTH *comes in forlornly and pulls off her coat with dejection. They both turn to look at her.*)

RUTH   (*dispiritedly*).   Well, I guess from all the happy faces—everybody knows.

BENEATHA.   You pregnant?

MAMA.   Lord have mercy, I sure hope it's a little old girl. Travis ought to have a sister.

(BENEATHA *and* RUTH *give her a hopeless look for this grandmotherly enthusiasm.*)

BENEATHA.   How far along are you?

RUTH.   Two months.

BENEATHA.   Did you mean to? I mean did you plan it or was it an accident?

MAMA.   What do you know about planning or not planning?

BENEATHA.   Oh, Mama.

RUTH   (*wearily*).   She's twenty years old, Lena.

BENEATHA.   Did you plan it, Ruth?

RUTH.   Mind your own business.

BENEATHA.   It is my business—where is he going to live, on the *roof*? (*There is silence following the remark as the three women react to the sense of it).* Gee—I didn't mean that, Ruth, honest, Gee, I don't feel like that at all. I—I think it is wonderful.

RUTH   *(dully).*   Wonderful.

BENEATHA.   Yes—really.

MAMA   *(looking at* RUTH, *worried).*   Doctor say everything going to be all right?

RUTH   *(far away).*   Yes—she says everything is going to be fine. . . .

MAMA   *(immediately suspicious).*   "She"—What doctor you went to?

(RUTH folds over, near hysteria.)

MAMA   *(worriedly hovering over* RUTH).   Ruth honey—what's the matter with you—you sick?

(RUTH has her fists clenched on her thighs and is fighting hard to suppress a scream that seems to be rising in her.)

BENEATHA.   What's the matter with her, Mama?

MAMA   *(working her fingers in* RUTH's *shoulder to relax her).*   She be all right. Women gets right depressed sometimes when they get her way. *(Speaking softly, expertly, rapidly)*   Now you just relax. That's right . . . just lean back, don't think 'bout nothing at all . . . nothing at all—

RUTH.   I'm all right . . . .

(The glassy-eyed look melts and then she collapses into a fit of heavy sobbing. The bell rings.)

BENEATHA.   Oh, my God—that must be Asagai.

MAMA   *(to* RUTH).   Come on now, honey. You need to lie down and rest awhile . . . then have some nice hot food.

(They exit, RUTH's weight on her mother-in law. BENEATHA, herself profoundly disturbed, opens the door to admit a rather dramatic-looking young man with a large package.)

ASAGAI.   Hello, Alaiyo—

BENEATHA.   *(holding the door open and regarding him with pleasure).*   Hello . . . . *(Long pause)* Well—come in. And please excuse everything. My mother was very upset about my letting anyone come here with the place like this.

ASAGAI   *(coming into the room).*   You look disturbed too. . . . Is something wrong?

BENEATHA   *(still at the door, absently).*   Yes . . . we've all got acute ghetto-itus. *(She smiles and comes toward him, finding a cigarette and sitting.)* So—sit down! How was Canada?

ASAGAI   *(a sophisticate).*   Canadian.

BENEATHA.   *(looking at him).*   I'm very glad you are back.

ASAGAI   *(looking back at her in turn).*   Are you really?

BENEATHA.   Yes—very.

ASAGAI.   Why—you were quite glad when I went away. What happened?

BENEATHA.   You went away.

ASAGAI.   Ahhhhhhhh.

BENEATHA.   Before—you wanted to be so serious before there was time.

ASAGAI.   How much time must there be before one knows what one feels?

BENEATHA   *(stalling this particular conversation; her hands pressed together, in a deliberately childish gesture).* What did you bring me?

ASAGAI   *(handing her the package).*   Open it and see.

BENEATHA   *(eagerly opening the package and drawing out some records and the colorful robes of a Nigerian woman).* Oh, Asagai! . . . You got them for me! . . . How beautiful . . . and the records too! *(She lifts out the robes and runs to the mirror with them and holds the drapery up in front of herself.)*

ASAGAI   *(coming to her at the mirror).*   I shall have to teach you how to drape it properly. *(He flings the material about her for the moment and stands back to look at her.)*   Ah—Oh-pay-gay-day, oh-gbah-mu-shay. *(A Yoruba exclamation for admiration)* You wear it well . . . very well . . . mutilated hair and all.

BENEATHA   *(turning suddenly).*   My hair—what's wrong with my hair?

ASAGAI   *(shrugging).*   Were you born with it like that?

BENEATHA   *(reaching up to touch it).*   No . . . of course not.

                    (She looks back to the mirror, disturbed.)

ASAGAI   *(smiling).*   How then?

BENEATHA.   You know perfectly well how . . . as crinkly as yours . . . that's how.

ASAGAI.   And it is ugly to you that way?

BENEATHA   *(quickly).*   Oh, no—not ugly. . . . *(More slowly, apologetically)* But it's so hard to manage when it's, well—raw.

ASAGAI.   And so to accommodate that—you mutilate it every week?

BENEATHA.   It's not mutilation.

ASAGAI   (*laughing aloud at her seriousness*). Oh . . . please! I am only teasing you because you are so very serious about these things. (*He stands back from her and folds his arms across his chest as he watches her pulling at her hair and frowning in the mirror.*)   Do you remember the first time you met me at school? . . . (*He laughs.*) You came up to me and you said—and I thought you were the most serious little thing I had ever seen —you said: (*He imitates her*) "Mr. Asagai—I want very much to talk with you. About Africa. You see, Mr. Asagai, I am looking for my *identity!*"

(*He laughs.*)

BENEATHA   (*turning to him, not laughing*). Yes—

(*Her face is quizzical, profoundly disturbed.*)

ASAGAI   (*still teasing and reaching out and taking her face in his hands and turning her profile to him*).   Well . . . it is true that this is not so much a profile of a Hollywood queen as perhaps a queen of the Nile —(*A mock dismissal of the importance of the question*) But what does it matter? Assimilationism is so popular in your country.

BENEATHA   (*wheeling, passionately, sharply*).   I am not an assimilationist!

ASAGAI   (*the protest hangs in the room for a moment and* ASAGAI *studies her, his laughter fading*). Such a serious one. (*There is a pause.*) So you like the robes? You must take excellent care of them—they are from my sister's personal wardrobe.

BENEATHA   (*with incredulity*).   You—you sent all the way home— for me?

ASAGAI   (*with charm*). For you—I would do much more. . . . Well, that is what I came for. I must go.

BENEATHA.   Will you call me Monday?

ASAGAI.   Yes. . . . We have a great deal to talk about. I mean about identity and time and all that.

BENEATHA.   Time?

ASAGAI.   Yes. About how much time one needs to know what one feels.

BENEATHA.   You never understood that there is more than one kind of feeling which can exist between a man and a woman—or, at least, there should be.

ASAGAI   (*shaking his head negatively but gently*).   No. Between a

man and a woman there need be only one kind of feeling. I have that
for you. . . . Now even . . . right this moment . . .

BENEATHA.   I know—and by itself—it won't do. I can find that
anywhere.

ASAGAI.   For a woman it should be enough.

BENEATHA.   I know—because that's what it says in all the novels that
men write. But it isn't. Go ahead and laugh—but I'm not interested in
being someone's little episode in America or—(*With feminine vengeance*)—one of them! (ASAGAI *has burst into laughter again.*)   That's
funny as hell, huh!

ASAGAI.   It's just that every American girl I have known has said
that to me. White—black—in this you are all the same. And the same
speech, too!

BENEATHA   (*angrily*).   Yuk, yuk, yuk!

ASAGAI.   It's how you can be sure that the world's most liberated
women are not liberated at all. You all talk about it too much!

(MAMA *enters and is immediately all social charm because of the
presence of a guest.*)

BENEATHA.   Oh—Mama—this is Mr. Asagai.

MAMA.   How do you do?

ASAGAI   (*total politeness to an elder*).   How do you do, Mrs. Younger. Please forgive me for coming at such an outrageous hour on a Saturday.

MAMA.   Well, you are quite welcome. I just hope you understand
that our house don't always look like this. (*Chatterish*) You must come
again. I would love to hear all about—(*Not sure of the name*)—your
country. I think it's so sad the way our American Negroes don't know
nothing about Africa 'cept Tarzan and all that. And all that money they
pour into these churches when they ought to be helping you people
over there drive out them French and Englishmen done taken away your
land.

(*The mother flashes a slightly superior look at her daughter upon
completion of the recitation.*)

ASAGAI   (*taken aback by this sudden and acutely unrelated expression of sympathy*).   Yes . . . yes . . . .

MAMA   (*smiling at him suddenly and relaxing and looking him over*).
How many miles is it from here to where you come from?

ASAGAI.   Many thousands.

MAMA   (*looking at him as she would* WALTER).   I bet you don't half look after yourself, being away from your mama either. I spec you better come 'round here from time to time and get yourself some decent home-cooked meals. . . .

ASAGAI (*moved*).   Thank you. Thank you very much. (*They are all quiet, then*—) Well . . . I must go. I will call you Monday, Alaiyo.

MAMA. What's that he call you?

ASAGAI.   Oh—"Alaiyo." I hope you don't mind. It is what you would call a nickname, I think. It is a Yoruba word. I am a Yoruba.

MAMA (*looking at* BENEATHA).   I—I thought he was from—

ASAGAI (*understanding*).   Nigeria is my country. Yoruba is my tribal origin—

BENEATHA.   You didn't tell us what Alaiyo means . . . for all I know, you might be calling me Little Idiot or something . . . .

ASAGAI.   Well . . . let me see . . . I do not know how just to explain it . . . The sense of a thing can be so different when it changes languages.

BENEATHA.   You're evading.

ASAGAI.   No—really it is difficult. . . . (*Thinking*) It means . . . it means One for Whom Bread—Food—Is Not Enough. (*He looks at her.*) Is that all right?

BENEATHA (*understanding, softly*).   Thank you.

MAMA (*looking from one to the other and not understanding any of it.* . . . The sense of a thing can be so different when it changes languages.

ASAGAI.   Ah-sah-guy . . . .

MAMA.   Yes . . . . Do come again.

ASAGAI.   Good-bye.

(*He exits.*)

MAMA (*after him*).   Lord, that's a pretty thing just went out here! (*Insinuatingly, to her daughter*) Yes, I guess I see why we done commence to get so interested in Africa 'round here. Missionaries my aunt Jenny!

(*She exits.*)

BENEATHA.   Oh, Mama! . . .

(*She picks up the Nigerian dress and holds it up to her in front of the mirror again. She sets the headdress on haphazardly and then notices her hair again and clutches at it and then replaces the headdress and frowns at herself. Then she starts to wriggle in front of the mirror as she thinks a Nigerian woman might.* TRAVIS *enters and regards her.*)

TRAVIS.   You cracking up?

BENEATHA.   Shut up.

(She pulls the headdress off and looks at herself in the mirror and clutches at her hair again and squinches her eyes as if trying to imagine something. Then, suddenly, she gets her raincoat and kerchief and hurriedly prepares for going out.)

MAMA   *(coming back into the room)*.   She's resting now. Travis, baby, run next door and ask Miss Johnson to please let me have a little kitchen cleanser. This here can is empty as Jacob's kettle.

TRAVIS.   I just came in.

MAMA.   Do as you told. *(He exits and she looks at her daughter.)* Where you going?

BENEATHA   *(halting at the door)*.   To become a queen of the Nile!

(She exits in a breathless blaze of glory. RUTH appears in the bedroom doorway.)

MAMA.   Who told you to get up?

RUTH.   Ain't nothing wrong with me to be lying in no bed for. Where did Bennie go?

MAMA   *(drumming her fingers)*. Far as I could make out—to Egypt. *(RUTH just looks at her.)* What time is it getting to?

RUTH.   Ten twenty. And the mailman going to ring that bell this morning just like he done every morning for the last umpteen years.

(TRAVIS comes in with the cleanser can.)

TRAVIS.   She say to tell you that she don't have much.

MAMA   *(angrily)*.   Lord, some people I could name sure is tight-fisted! *(Directing her grandson)* Mark two cans of cleanser down on the list there. If she that hard up for kitchen cleanser, I sure don't want to forget to get her none!

RUTH.   Lena—maybe the woman is just short on cleanser—

MAMA   *(not listening)*.   —Much baking powder as she done borrowed from me all these years, she could of done gone into the baking business!

(The bell sounds suddenly and sharply and all three are stunned— serious and silent—mid-speech. In spite of all the other conversations and distractions of the morning, this is what they have been wating for, even TRAVIS, who looks helplessly from his mother to his grandmother. RUTH is the first to come to life again.)

RUTH   *(to TRAVIS)*.   Get down them steps, boy!

(TRAVIS snaps to life and flies out to get the mail.)

MAMA   (*her eyes wide, her hand to her breast*).   You mean it done really come?

RUTH   (*excited*).   Oh, Miss Lena!

MAMA   (*collecting herself*).   Well . . . I don't know what we all so excited about 'round here for. We known it was coming for months.

RUTH.   That's a whole lot different from having it come and being able to hold it in your hands . . . a piece of paper worth ten thousand dollars . . . . (TRAVIS *bursts back into the room. He holds the envelope high above his head, like a little dancer, his face is radiant and he is breathless. He moves to his grandmother with sudden slow ceremony and puts the envelope into her hands. She accepts it, and then merely holds it and looks at it.*) Come on! Open it . . . . Lord have mercy, I wish Walter Lee was here!

TRAVIS.   Open it, Grandmama!

MAMA   (*staring at it*).   Now you all be quiet. It's just a check.

RUTH.   Open it . . . .

MAMA   (*still staring at it*).   Now don't act silly. . . . We ain't never been no people to act silly 'bout no money—

RUTH   (*swiftly*).   We ain't never had none before—*open it!*

(MAMA *finally makes a good strong tear and pulls out the thin blue slice of paper and inspects it closely. The boy and his mother study it raptly over* MAMA'S *shoulders.*)

MAMA.   *Travis!* (*She is counting off with doubt.*) Is that the right number of zeros.

TRAVIS.   Yes'm . . . ten thousand dollars. Gaalee, Grandmama, you rich.

MAMA   (*she holds the check away from her, still looking at it; slowly her face sobers into a mask of unhappiness*).   Ten thousand dollars. (*She hands it to* RUTH.)   Put it away somewhere, Ruth. (*She does not look at* RUTH; *her eyes seem to be seeing something somewhere very far off.*) Ten thousand dollars they give you. Ten thousand dollars.

TRAVIS   (*to his mother, sincerely*).   What's the matter with Grandmama—don't she want to be rich?

RUTH   (*distractedly*).   You go on out and play now, baby. (TRAVIS *exits.* MAMA *starts wiping dishes absently, humming intently to herself.* RUTH *turns to her, with kind exasperation.*)   You've gone and got yourself upset.

MAMA   (*not looking at her*).   I spec if it wasn't for you all. . . . I would just put that money away or give it to the church or something.

RUTH.   Now what kind of talk is that. Mr. Younger would just be plain mad if he could hear you talking foolish like that.

MAMA   (*stopping and staring off*).   Yes . . . he sure would. (*Sighing*) We got enough to do with that money, all right. (*She halts then, and turns and looks at her daughter-in-law hard;* RUTH *avoids her eyes and* MAMA *wipes her hands with finality and starts to speak firmly to* RUTH.) Where did you go today, girl?

RUTH.   To the doctor.

MAMA   (*impatiently*).   Now, Ruth . . . you know better than that. Old Doctor Jones is strange enough in his way but there ain't nothing 'bout him make somebody slip and call him "she"—like you done this morning.

RUTH.   Well, that's what happened—my tongue slipped.

MAMA.   You went to see that woman, didn't you?

RUTH   (*defensively, giving herself away*).   What woman you talking about?

MAMA   (*angrily*).   That woman who—

(WALTER *enters in great excitement.*)

WALTER.   Did it come?

MAMA   (*quietly*).   Can't you give people a Christian greeting before you start asking about money?

WALTER   (*to* RUTH).   Did it come? (RUTH *unfolds the check and lays it quietly before him, watching him intently with thoughts of her own.* WALTER *sits down and grasps it close and counts off the zeros.*) Ten thousand dollars—(*He turns suddenly, frantically to his mother and draws some papers out of his breast pocket.*) Mama—look. Old Willy Harris put everything on paper—

MAMA.   Son—I think you ought to talk to your wife . . . . I'll go on out and leave you alone if you want—

WALTER.   I can talk to her later—Mama, look—

MAMA.   Son—

WALTER.   WILL SOMEBODY PLEASE LISTEN TO ME TODAY!

MAMA   (*quietly*).   I don't 'low no yellin' in this house, Walter Lee, and you know it—(WALTER *stares at them in frustration and starts to speak several times.*) And there ain't going to be no investing in no liquor stores. I don't aim to have to speak on that again.

(*A long pause*)

WALTER.   Oh—so you don't aim to have to speak on that again? So *you* have decided . . . (*Crumpling his papers*) Well, *you* tell that to my boy tonight when you put him to sleep on the living-room couch. . . . (*Turning to* MAMA *and speaking directly to her*) Yeah—and tell it to my wife, Mama, tomorrow when she has to go out of here to look after somebody else's kids. And tell it to *me*, Mama, every time we need a new pair of curtains and I have to watch *you* go out and work in somebody's kitchen. Yeah, you tell me then!

(WALTER *starts out.*)

RUTH.   Where you going?

WALTER.   I'm going out!

RUTH.   Where?

WALTER.   Just out of this house somewhere—

RUTH   (*getting her coat*).   I'll come too.

WALTER.   I don't want you to come!

RUTH.   I got something to talk to you about, Walter.

WALTER.   That's too bad.

MAMA   (*still quietly*).   Walter Lee—(*She waits and he finally turns and looks at her.*) Sit down.

WALTER.   I'm a grown man, Mama.

MAMA.   Ain't nobody said you wasn't grown. But you still in my house and my presence. And as long as you are—you'll talk to your wife civil. Now sit down.

RUTH   (*suddenly*).   Oh let him go on out and drink himself to death! He makes me sick to my stomach! (*She flings her coat against him.*)

WALTER   (*violently*).   And you turn mine too, baby! (RUTH *goes into their bedroom and slams the door behind her.*) That was my greatest mistake—

MAMA   (*still quietly*).   Walter, what is the matter with you?

WALTER.   Matter with me? Ain't nothing the matter with *me!*

MAMA.   Yes there is. Something eating you up like a crazy man. Something more than me not giving you this money. The past few years I been watching it happen to you. You get all nervous acting and kind of wild in the eyes—(WALTER *jumps up impatiently at her words.*) I said sit there now, I'm talking to you!

WALTER.   Mama—I don't need no nagging at me today.

MAMA.   Seem like you getting to a place where you always tied up in some kind of knot about something. But if anybody ask you 'bout it you just yell at 'em and bust out the house and go out and drink somewheres. Walter Lee, people can't live with that. Ruth's a good, patient girl in her way—but you getting to be too much. Boy, don't make the mistake of driving that girl away from you.

WALTER.   Why—what she do for me?

MAMA.   She loves you.

WALTER.   Mama—I'm going out. I want to go off somewhere and be by myself for a while.

MAMA.   I'm sorry 'bout your liquor store, son. It just wasn't the thing for us to do. That's what I want to tell you about—

WALTER.   I got to go out, Mama—

(*He rises.*)

MAMA.   It's dangerous, son.

WALTER.   What's dangerous?

MAMA.   When a man goes outside his home to look for peace.

WALTER   (*beseechingly*).   Then why can't there never be no peace in this house then?

MAMA.   You done found it in some other house?

WALTER.   No—there ain't no woman! Why do women always think there's a woman somewhere when a man gets restless. (*Coming to her*) Mama—Mama—I want so many things . . . .

MAMA.   Yes, son—

WALTER.   I want so many things that they are driving me kind of crazy. . . . Mama—look at me.

MAMA.   I'm looking at you. You a good-looking boy. You got a job, a nice wife, a fine boy and—

WALTER.   A job. (*Looks at her.*) Mama, a job? I open and close car doors all day long. I drive a man around in his limousine and I say, "Yes, sir; no, sir; very good, sir; shall I take the Drive, sir?" Mama, that ain't no kind of job . . . that ain't nothing at all. (*Very quietly*) Mama, I don't know if I can make you understand.

MAMA.   Understand what, baby?

WALTER   (*quietly*).   Sometimes it's like I can see the future stretched out in front of me—just plain as day. The future, Mama. Hanging over there at the edge of my days. Just waiting for me—a big, looming blank space—full of *nothing*. Just waiting for *me*. (*Pause*) Mama—sometimes when I'm downtown and I pass them cool, quiet-looking restaurants where them white boys are sitting back and talking 'bout things . . . sitting there turning deals worth millions of dollars . . . sometimes I see guys don't look much older than me—

MAMA.   Son—how come you talk so much 'bout money?

WALTER   (*with immense passion*).   Because it is life, Mama!

MAMA   (*quietly*).   Oh—(*Very quietly*)So now it's life. Money is life. Once upon a time freedom used to be life—now it's money. I guess the world really do change. . . .

WALTER.   No—it was always money, Mama. We just didn't know about it.

MAMA.   No . . . something has changed. (*She looks at him.*) You something new, boy. In my time we was worried about not being lynched and getting to the North if we could and how to stay alive and still have a pinch of dignity too . . . Now here come you and Beneatha—talking 'bout things we ain't never even thought about hardly, me and your daddy. You ain't satisfied or proud of nothing we done. I mean that you had a home; that we kept you out of trouble till you was grown; that you don't have to ride to work on the back of nobody's streetcar—You my children—but how different we done become.

WALTER.   You just don't understand, Mama, you just don't understand.

MAMA.   Son—do you know your wife is expecting another baby? (*WALTER stands, stunned, and absorbs what his mother has said.*) That's what she wanted to talk to you about. (*WALTER sinks down into a chair.*) This ain't for me to be telling—but you ought to know. (*She waits.*) I think Ruth is thinking 'bout getting rid of that child.

WALTER   (*slowly understanding*).   No—no—Ruth wouldn't do that.

MAMA.   When the world gets ugly enough—a woman will do anything for her family. *The part that's already living.*

WALTER.   You don't know Ruth, Mama, if you think she would do that.

(*RUTH opens the bedroom door and stands there a little limp.*)

RUTH   (*beaten*).   Yes I would too, Walter. (*Pause*) I gave her a five-dollar down payment.

(*There is total silence as the man stares at his wife and the mother stares at her son.*)

MAMA   (*presently*). Well—(*Tightly*) Well—son, I'm waiting to hear you say something. . . . I'm waiting to hear how you be your father's son. Be the man he was. . . . (*Pause*)   Your wife say she going to destroy your child. And I'm waiting to hear you talk like him and say we a people who give children life, not who destroys them—(*She rises.*) I'm waiting to see you stand up and look like your daddy and say we done give up one baby to poverty and that we ain't going to give up nary another one. . . . I'm waiting.

WALTER.   Ruth—

MAMA.   If you a son of mine, tell her! (WALTER *turns, looks at her and can say nothing. She continues, bitterly.*) You . . . you are a disgrace to your father's memory. Somebody get me my hat.

(CURTAIN)

ACT II

SCENE 1

Time: Later the same day.

At rise: RUTH *is ironing again. She has the radio going. Presently* BENEATHA'S *bedroom door opens and* RUTH'S *mouth falls and she puts down the iron in fascination.*

RUTH.   What have we got on tonight!

BENEATHA   (*emerging grandly from the doorway so that we can see her thoroughly robed in the costume Asagai brought*). You are looking at what a well-dressed Nigerian woman wears—(*She parades for* RUTH, *her hair completely hidden by the headdress; she is coquettishly fanning herself with an ornate oriental fan, mistakenly more like Butterfly than any Nigerian that ever was.*) Isn't it beautiful? (*She promenades to the radio and, with an arrogant flourish, turns off the good loud blues that is playing.*) Enough of this assimilationist junk! (*RUTH follows her with her eyes as she goes to the phonograph and puts on a record and turns and waits ceremoniously for the music to come up. Then, with a shout—*) OCOMOGOSIAY!

(*RUTH jumps. The music comes up, a lovely Nigerian melody.*

BENEATHA *listens, enraptured, her eyes far away—"back to the past."*
She begins to dance. RUTH *is dumfounded.*)

RUTH.   What kind of dance is that?

BENEATHA.   A folk dance.

RUTH   (*Pearl Bailey*).   What kind of folks do that, honey?

BENEATHA.   It's from Nigeria. It's a dance of welcome.

RUTH.   Who you welcoming?

BENEATHA.   The men back to the village.

RUTH.   Where they been?

BENEATHA.   How should I know—out hunting or something. Anyway, they are coming back now . . . .

RUTH.   Well, that's good.

BENEATHA   (*with the record*).
  Alundi, alundi
  Alundi alunya
  Jop pu a jeepua
  Ang gu soooooooooo

  Ai yai yae . . .
  Ayehaye—alundi . . .

(WALTER *comes in during this performance; he has obviously been drinking. He leans against the door heavily and watches his sister, at first with distaste. Then his eyes look off — "back to the past" —as he lifts both his fists to the roof, screaming.*)

WALTER.   YEAH . . . AND ETHIOPIA STRETCH FORTH HER HANDS AGAIN! . . .

RUTH   (*drily, looking at him*).   Yes—and Africa sure is claiming her own tonight. (*She gives them both up and starts ironing again.*)

WALTER   (*all in a drunken, dramatic shout*).   Shut up! . . . I'm digging them drums . . . them drums move me! . . . (*He makes his weaving way to his wife's face and leans in close to her*) In my heart of hearts—(*He thumps his chest*)—I am much warrior!

RUTH   (*without even looking up*).   In your heart of hearts you are much drunkard.

WALTER   (*coming away from her and starting to wander around the room, shouting*). Me and Jomo. . . . (*Intently, in his sister's face. She has stopped dancing to watch him in this unknown mood.*) That's my man, Kenyatta. (*Shouting and thumping his chest*) FLAMING SPEAR! HOT DAMN! (*He is suddenly in possession of an imaginary spear and actively spearing enemies all over the room.*) OCOMOGOSIAY. . . . THE LION IS WAKING . . . OWIMOWEH! (*He pulls his shirt open and leaps up on a table and gestures with his spear. The bell rings.* RUTH *goes to answer.*)

BENEATHA   (*to encourage* WALTER, *thoroughly caught up with this side of him*).   OCOMOGOSIAY, FLAMING SPEAR!

WALTER   (*on the table, very far gone, his eyes pure glass sheets; he sees what we cannot, that he is a leader of his people, a great chief, a descendant of Chaka, and that the hour to march has come*).   Listen, my black brothers—

BENEATHA.   OCOMOGOSIAY!

WALTER.   —Do you hear the waters rushing against the shores of the coastlands—

BENEATHA.   OCOMOGOSIAY!

WALTER.   —Do you hear the screeching of the cocks in yonder hills beyond where the chiefs meet in council for the coming of the mighty war—

BENEATHA.   OCOMOGOSIAY!

WALTER.   —Do you hear the beating of the wings of the birds flying low over the mountains and the low places of our land—

(RUTH *opens the door.* GEORGE MURCHISON *enters.*)

BENEATHA.   OCOMOGOSIAY!

WALTER.   —Do you hear the singing of the women, singing the war songs of our fathers to the babies in the great houses . . . singing the sweet war songs? OH, DO YOU HEAR, MY BLACK BROTHERS!

BENEATHA (*completely gone*).   We hear you, Flaming Spear—

WALTER.   Telling us to prepare for the greatness of the time—(*To* GEORGE) Black Brother!

(*He extends his hand for the fraternal clasp.*)

GEORGE.   Black Brother, hell!

RUTH (*having had enough, and embarrassed for the family*). Beneatha, you got company—what's the matter with you? Walter Lee Younger, get down off that table and stop acting like a fool. . . .

(WALTER *comes down off the table suddenly and makes a quick exit to the bathroom.*)

RUTH.   He's had a little to drink. . . . I don't know what her excuse is.

GEORGE (*to* BENEATHA).   Look honey, we're going *to* the theatre —we're not going to be *in* it . . . so go change, huh?

RUTH.   You expect this boy to go out with you looking like that?

BENEATHA (*looking at* GEORGE).   That's up to George. If he's ashamed of his heritage—

GEORGE.   Oh, don't be so proud of yourself, Bennie—just because you look eccentric.

BENEATHA.   How can something that's natural be eccentric?

GEORGE.   That's what being eccentric means—being natural. Get dressed.

BENEATHA.   I don't like that, George.

RUTH.   Why must you and your brother make an argument out of everything people say?

BENEATHA.   Because I hate assimilationist Negroes!

RUTH. Will somebody please tell me what assimila-who-ever means!

GEORGE. Oh, it's just a college girl's way of calling people Uncle Toms—but that isn't what it means at all.

RUTH. Well, what does it mean?

BENEATHA (*cutting* GEORGE *off and staring at him as she replies to* RUTH). It means someone who is willing to give up his own culture and submerge himself completely in the dominant, and in this case, *oppressive* culture!

GEORGE. Oh, dear, dear, dear! Here we go! A lecture on the African past! On our Great West African Heritage! In one second we will hear all about the great Ashanti empires; the great Songhay civilizations; and the great sculpture of Bénin—and then some poetry in the Bantu—and the whole monologue will end with the word *heritage!* (*Nastily*) Let's face it, baby, your heritage is nothing but a bunch of raggedy-assed spirituals and some grass huts!

BENEATHA. *Grass huts!* (RUTH *crosses to her and forcibly pushes her toward the bedroom.*) See there . . . you are standing there in your splendid ignorance talking about people who were the first to smelt iron on the face of the earth! (RUTH *is pushing her through the door.*) The Ashanti were performing surgical operations when the English—(RUTH *pulls the door to, with* BENEATHA *on the other side, and smiles graciously at* GEORGE. BENEATHA *opens the door and shouts the end of the sentence defiantly at* GEORGE.)—were still tattooing themselves with blue dragons. . . . (*She goes back inside.*)

RUTH. Have a seat, George. (*They both sit.* RUTH *folds her hands rather primly on her lap, determined to demonstrate the civilization of the family.*) Warm, ain't it? I mean for September. (*Pause*) Just like they always say about Chicago weather: If it's too hot or cold for you, just wait a minute and it'll change. (*She smiles happily at this cliché of clichés.*) Everybody say it's got to do with them bombs and things they keep setting off. (*Pause*) Would you like a nice cold beer?

GEORGE. No, thank you. I don't care for beer. (*He looks at his watch.*) I hope she hurries up.

RUTH. What time is the show?

GEORGE. It's an eight-thirty curtain. That's just Chicago, though. In New York standard curtain time is eight forty.

(*He is rather proud of this knowledge.*)

RUTH (*properly appreciating it*). You get to New York a lot?

GEORGE (*offhand*). Few times a year.

RUTH. Oh—that's nice. I've never been to New York.

(WALTER *enters. We feel he has relieved himself, but the edge of unreality is still with him.*)

WALTER.   New York ain't got nothing Chicago ain't. Just a bunch of hustling people all squeezed up together—being "Eastern."

(*He turns his face into a screw of displeasure.*)

GEORGE.   Oh—you've been?

WALTER.   *Plenty* of times.

RUTH   (*shocked at the lie*).   Walter Lee Younger!

WALTER   (*staring her down*).   Plenty! (*Pause*) What we got to drink in this house? Why don't you offer this man some refreshment. (*To* GEORGE) They don't know how to entertain people in this house, man.

GEORGE.   Thank you—I don't really care for anything.

WALTER   (*feeling his head; sobriety coming*).   Where's Mama?

RUTH.   She ain't come back yet.

WALTER   (*looking* MURCHISON *over from head to toe, scrutinizing his carefully casual tweed sports jacket over cashmere V-neck sweater over soft eyelet shirt and tie, and soft slacks, finished off with white buckskin shoes*).   Why all you college boys wear them fairyish-looking white shoes?

RUTH.   Walter Lee!

(GEORGE MURCHISON *ignores the remark.*)

WALTER (*to* RUTH).   Well, they look crazy as hell—white shoes, cold as it is.

RUTH   (*crushed*).   You have to excuse him—

WALTER.   No he don't! Excuse me for what? What you always excusing me for! I'll excuse myself when I needs to be excused! (*A pause*) They look as funny as them black knee socks Beneatha wears out of here all the time.

RUTH.   It's the college *style,* Walter.

WALTER.   Style, hell. She looks like she got burnt legs or something!

RUTH.   Oh, Walter—

WALTER   (*an irritable mimic*).   Oh, Walter! Oh, Walter! (To MURCHISON) How's your old man making out? I understand you all going to buy that big hotel on the Drive? (*He finds a beer in the refrigerator, wanders over to* MURCHISON, *sipping and wiping his lips with the back of his hand, and straddling a chair backwards to talk to the other man.*) Shrewd move. Your old man is all right, man. (*Tapping his head and half winking for emphasis*) I mean he knows how to operate. I mean he thinks *big*, you know what I mean, I mean for a *home*, you know? But I think he's kind of running out of ideas now. I'd like to talk to him. Listen, man, I got some plans that could turn this city upside down. I mean I think like he does. *Big*. Invest big, gamble big, hell, lose *big* if you have to, you know what I mean. It's hard to find a man on this whole Southside who understands my kind of thinking—you dig? *(He scrutinizes* MURCHISON *again, drinks his beer, squints his eyes and leans in close, confidential, man to man.)* Me and you ought to sit down and talk sometimes, man. Man, I got me some ideas. . . .

MURCHISON   *(with boredom).*   Yeah—sometimes we'll have to do that, Walter.

WALTER   *(understanding the indifference and offended).*   Yeah—well, when you get the time, man. I know you a busy little boy.

RUTH.   Walter, please—

WALTER   *(bitterly, hurt).*   I know ain't nothing in this world as busy as you colored college boys with your fraternity pins and white shoes. . . .

RUTH   *(covering her face with humiliation).*   Oh, Walter Lee—

WALTER.   I see you all all the time—with the books tucked under your arms—going to your *(British A—a mimic)* "clahsses." And for what! What the hell you learning over there? Filling up your heads— *(Counting off on his fingers)*—with the sociology and the psychology— but they teaching you how to be a man? How to take over and run the world? They teaching you how to run a rubber plantation or a steel mill? Naw—just to talk proper and read books and wear white shoes. . . .

GEORGE   *(looking at him with distaste, a little above it all).*   You're all wacked up with bitterness, man.

WALTER   *(intently, almost quietly, between the teeth, glaring at the boy).*   And you—ain't you bitter, man? Ain't you just about had it yet? Don't you see no stars gleaming that you can't reach out and grab? You happy—You contented son-of-a-bitch—you happy? You got it made? Bitter? Man, I'm a volcano. Bitter? Here I am a giant—surrounded by ants! Ants who can't even understand what it is the giant is talking about.

RUTH   *(passionately and suddenly).*   Oh, Walter—ain't you with no-body!

WALTER   *(violently).*   No! 'Cause ain't nobody with me! Not even my own mother!

RUTH.   Walter, that's a terrible thing to say!

(BENEATHA *enters, dressed for the evening in a cocktail dress and earrings.)*

GEORGE.   Well—hey, you look great.

A Raisin in the Sun

BENEATHA. Let's go, George. See you all later.

RUTH. Have a nice time.

GEORGE. Thanks. Good night. *(To WALTER, sarcastically.)* Good night, *Prometheus.*

(BENEATHA and GEORGE exit.)

WALTER *(to RUTH).* Who is Prometheus?

RUTH. I don't know. Don't worry about it.

WALTER *(in fury, pointing after GEORGE).* See there—they get to a point where they can't insult you man to man—they got to go talk about something ain't nobody never heard of!

RUTH. How do you know it was an insult? *(To humor him)* Maybe Prometheus is a nice fellow.

WALTER. Prometheus! I bet there ain't even no such thing! I bet that simple-minded clown—

RUTH. Walter—

(She stops what she is doing and looks at him.)

WALTER *(yelling).* Don't start!

RUTH. Start what?

WALTER. Your nagging! Where was I? Who was I with? How much money did I spend?

RUTH *(plaintively).* Walter Lee—why don't we just try to talk about it. . . .

WALTER *(not listening).* I been out talking with people who understand me. People who care about the things I got on my mind.

RUTH *(wearily).* I guess that means people like Willy Harris.

WALTER. Yes, people like Willy Harris.

RUTH *(with a sudden flash of impatience).* Why don't you all just hurry up and go into the banking business and stop talking about it!

WALTER. Why? You want to know why? 'Cause we all tied up in a race of people that don't know how to do nothing but moan, pray and have babies!

(The line is too bitter even for him and he looks at her and sits down.)

RUTH. Oh, Walter. . . . *(Softly)* Honey, why can't you stop fighting me?

WALTER *(without thinking).* Who's fighting you? Who even cares about you?

(This line begins the retardation of his mood.)

RUTH.   Well—(*She waits a long time, and then with resignation starts to put away her things.*) I guess I might as well go on to bed. . . . *(More or less to herself)* I don't know where we lost it . . . but we have . . . . (*Then, to him*) I—I'm sorry about this new baby, Walter. I guess maybe I better go on and do what I started. . . . I guess I just didn't realize how bad things was with us. . . . I guess I just didn't really realize—(*She starts out to the bedroom and stops.*) You want some hot milk?

WALTER.   Hot milk?

RUTH.   Yes—hot milk.

WALTER.   Why hot milk?

RUTH.   'Cause after all that liquor you come home with you ought to have something hot in your stomach.

WALTER.   I don't want no milk.

RUTH.   You want some coffee then?

WALTER.   No, I don't want no coffee. I don't want nothing hot to drink. *(Almost plaintively)* Why you always trying to give me something to eat?

RUTH   (*standing and looking at him helplessly*).   What else can I give you, Walter Lee Younger?

> (*She stands and looks at him and presently turns to go out again. He lifts his head and watches her going away from him in a new mood that began to emerge when he asked her "Who cares about you?"*)

WALTER.   It's been rough, ain't it, baby? (*She hears and stops but does not turn around, and he continues to her back.*) I guess between two people there ain't never as much understood as folks generally thinks there is. I mean like between me and you—(*She turns to face him.*) How we gets to the place where we scared to talk softness to each other. (*He waits, thinking hard himself.*) Why you think it got to be like that? (*He is thoughtful, almost as a child would be.*) Ruth, what is it gets into people ought to be close?

RUTH.   I don't know, honey. I think about it a lot.

WALTER.   On account of you and me, you mean? The way things are with us. The way something done come down between us.

RUTH.   There ain't so much between us, Walter. . . . Not when you come to me and try to talk to me. Try to be with me . . . a little even.

WALTER   (*total honesty*).   Sometimes . . . sometimes . . . . I don't even know how to try.

RUTH.   Walter—

WALTER.   Yes?

RUTH   (*coming to him, gently and with misgiving, but coming to him*).
Honey . . . life don't have to be like this. I mean sometimes people can
do things so that things are better. . . . You remember how we used to
talk when Travis was born . . . about the way we were going to live . . .
the kind of house. . . . (*She is stroking his head.*) Well, it's all starting to slip
away from us . . . .

(MAMA *enters, and* WALTER *jumps up and shouts at her.*)

WALTER.   Mama, where have you been?

MAMA.   My—them steps is longer than they used to be. Whew! (*She
sits down and ignores him.*) How you feeling this evening, Ruth?

(RUTH *shrugs, disturbed some at having been prematurely interrupted and watching her husband knowingly.*)

WALTER.   Mama, where have you been all day?

MAMA   (*still ignoring him and leaning on the table and changing to
more comfortable shoes*).   Where's Travis?

RUTH.   I let him go out earlier and he ain't come back yet. Boy, is
he going to get it!

WALTER.   Mama!

MAMA   (*as if she has heard him for the first time*).   Yes, son?

WALTER.   Where did you go this afternoon?

MAMA.   I went downtown to tend to some business that I had to tend
to.

WALTER.   What kind of business?

MAMA.   You know better than to question me like a child, Brother.

WALTER   (*rising and bending over the table*).   Where were you,
Mama? (*Bringing his fists down and shouting*) Mama, you didn't go do
something with that insurance money, something crazy?

(*The front door opens slowly, interrupting him, and* TRAVIS *peeks his
head in, less than hopefully.*)

TRAVIS   (*to his mother*).   Mama, I—

RUTH.   "Mama I" nothing! You're going to get it, boy! Get on in
that bedroom and get yourself ready!

TRAVIS.   But I—

MAMA.   Why don't you all never let the child explain hisself.

RUTH.   Keep out of it now, Lena.

(MAMA *clamps her lips together, and* RUTH *advances toward her
son menacingly.*)

RUTH.   A thousand times I have told you not to go off like that—

MAMA   (*holding out her arms to her grandson*).   Well—at least let me tell him something. I want him to be the first one to hear . . . . Come here, Travis. (*The boy obeys, gladly.*) Travis—(*She takes him by the shoulder and looks into his face.*)—you know that money we got in the mail this morning?

TRAVIS.   Yes'm—

MAMA.   Well—what you think your grandmama gone and done with that money?

TRAVIS.   I don't know, Grandmama.

MAMA   (*putting her finger on his nose for emphasis*).   She went out and she bought you a house! (*The explosion comes from* WALTER *at the end of the revelation and he jumps up and turns away from all of them in a fury.* MAMA *continues, to* TRAVIS.) You glad about the house? It's going to be yours when you get to be a man.

TRAVIS.   Yeah—I always wanted to live in a house.

MAMA.   All right, gimme some sugar then—(TRAVIS *puts his arms around her neck as she watches her son over the boy's shoulder. Then, to* TRAVIS, *after the embrace*) Now when you say your prayers tonight, you thank God and your grandfather—'cause it was him who give you the house—in his way.

RUTH   (*taking the boy from* MAMA *and pushing him toward the bedroom*).   Now you get out of here and get ready for your beating.

TRAVIS.   Aw, Mama—

RUTH.   Get on in there—(*Closing the door behind him and turning radiantly to her mother-in-law*) So you went and did it!

MAMA   (*quietly, looking at her son with pain*).   Yes, I did.

RUTH   (*raising both arms classically*).   Praise God! (*Looks at* WALTER *a moment, who says nothing. She crosses rapidly to her husband.*) Please, honey—let me be glad . . . you be glad too. (*She has laid her hands on his shoulders, but he shakes himself free of her roughly, without turning to face her.*) Oh, Walter . . . a home . . . *a home.* (*She comes back to* MAMA.) Well—where is it? How big is it? How much it going to cost?

MAMA.   Well—

RUTH.   When we moving?

MAMA   (*smiling at her*). First of the month.

RUTH   (*throwing back her head with jubliance*).   Praise God!

MAMA   (*tentatively, still looking at her son's back turned against her and* RUTH). It's—it's a nice house too . . . . (*She cannot help speaking directly to him. An imploring quality in her voice, her manner, makes her almost like a girl now.*) Three bedrooms—nice big one for you and Ruth. . . . Me and Beneatha still have to share our room, but Travis have one of his own—and (*With difficulty*) I figure if the—new baby—is a boy, we could get one of them double-decker outfits. . . . And there's a yard with a little patch of dirt where I could maybe get to grow me a few flowers. . . . And a nice big basement. . . .

RUTH.   Walter honey, be glad—

MAMA   (*still to his back, fingering things on the table*). 'Course I don't want to make it sound fancier than it is . . . It's just a plain little old house—but it's made good and solid—and it will be *ours*. Walter Lee—it makes a difference in a man when he can walk on floors that belong to *him*. . . .

RUTH.   Where is it?

MAMA   (*frightened at this telling*).   Well—well—it's out there in Clybourne Park—

> (RUTH'S *radiance fades abruptly, and* WALTER *finally turns slowly to face his mother with incredulity and hostility.*)

RUTH.   Where?

MAMA   (*matter-of-factly*).   Four o six Clybourne Street, Clybourne Park.

RUTH.   Clybourne Park? Mama, there ain't no colored people living in Clybourne Park.

MAMA   (*almost idiotically*).   Well, I guess there's going to be some now.

WALTER   (*bitterly*).   So that's the peace and comfort you went out and bought for us today!

MAMA   (*raising her eyes to meet his finally*).   Son—I just tried to find the nicest place for the least amount of money for my family.

RUTH   (*trying to recover from the shock*).   Well—well—'course I ain't one never been 'fraid of no crackers, mind you—but—well, wasn't there no other houses nowhere?

MAMA.   Them houses they put up for colored in them areas way out all seem to cost twice as much as other houses. I did the best I could.

RUTH   (*struck senseless with the news, in its various degrees of goodness and trouble, she sits a moment, her fists propping her chin in thought, and then she starts to rise, bringing her fists down with vigor, the radiance spreading from cheek to cheek again*). Well—well!—All I can say is—if this is my time in life—*my time*—to say good-bye—(*And she builds with momentum as she starts to circle the room with an ex-uberant, almost tearfully happy release.)*—to these Goddamned crack-ing walls!—(*She pounds the walls.*)—and these marching roaches!—(*She wipes at an imaginary army of marching roaches.*)—and this cramped little closet which ain't now or never was no kitchen! . . . then I say it loud and good, *Hallelujah! and good-bye misery. . . . I don't never want to see your ugly face again! (She laughs joyously, having practically de-stroyed the apartment, and flings her arms up and lets them come down happily, slowly, reflectively, over her abdomen, aware for the first time perhaps that the life therein pulses with happiness and not despair.)* Lena?

MAMA   (*moved, watching her happiness*).   Yes, honey?

RUTH   (*looking off*).   Is there—is there a whole lot of sunlight?

MAMA   (*understanding*).   Yes, child, there's a whole lot of sunlight.

(Long pause)

RUTH   (*collecting herself and going to the door of the room* TRAVIS *is in*). Well—I guess I better see 'bout Travis. *(To* MAMA*)* Lord, I sure don't feel like whipping nobody today!

(She exits.)

MAMA   (*the mother and son are left alone now and the mother waits a long time, considering deeply, before she speaks*). Son—you—you un-derstand what I done, don't you? (WALTER *is silent and sullen.*) I—I just seen my family falling apart today . . . just falling to pieces in front of my eyes. . . . We couldn't of gone on like we was today. We was going backwards 'stead of forwards—talking 'bout killing babies and wish-ing each other was dead. . . . When it gets like that in life—you just got to do something different, push on out and do something bigger. . . . *(She waits.)* I wish you say something, son . . . I wish you'd say how deep inside you you think I done the right thing—

WALTER   (*crossing slowly to his bedroom door and finally turning there and speaking measuredly*).   What you need me to say you done right for? *You* the head of this family. You run our lives like you want to. It was your money and you did what you wanted with it. So what you need for me to say it was all right for? *(Bitterly, to hurt her as deeply as he knows is possible)* So you butchered up a dream of mine—you—who al-ways talking 'bout your children's dreams. . . .

MAMA.   Walter Lee—

(He just closes the door behind him. MAMA *sits alone, thinking heavily.)*

(CURTAIN)

SCENE 2

Time: Friday night. A few weeks later.

At rise: Packing crates mark the intention of the family to move. BENEATHA *and* GEORGE *come in, presumably from an evening out*
again.

GEORGE.   O.K. . . . O.K., whatever you say. . . . *(They both sit on the couch. He tries to kiss her. She moves away.)* Look, we've had a nice evening; let's not spoil it, huh? . . .

(He again turns her head and tries to nuzzle in and she turns away from him, not with distaste but with momentary lack of interest; in a mood to pursue what they were talking about.)

BENEATHA.   I'm *trying* to talk to you.

GEORGE.   We always talk.

BENEATHA.   Yes—and I love to talk.

GEORGE   *(exasperated; rising)*.   I know it and I don't mind it sometimes. . . . I want you to cut it out, see—The moody stuff, I mean. I don't like it. You're a nice-looking girl . . . all over. That's all you need, honey, forget the atmosphere. Guys aren't going to go for the atmosphere —they're going to go for what they see. Be glad for that. Drop the Garbo routine. It doesn't go with you. As for myself, I want a nice—*(Groping)* —simple *(Thoughtfully)*—sophisticated girl . . . not a poet—O.K.?

(She rebuffs him again and he starts to leave.)

BENEATHA.   Why are you angry?

GEORGE.   Because this is stupid! I don't go out with you to discuss the nature of "quiet desperation" or to hear all about your thoughts—because the world will go on thinking what it thinks regardless—

BENEATHA.   Then why read books? Why go to school?

GEORGE   *(with artificial patience, counting on his fingers)*.   It's simple. You read books—to learn facts—to get grades—to pass the course—to get a degree. That's all—it has nothing to do with thoughts.

(A long pause)

BENEATHA.   I see. *(A longer pause as she looks at him)* Good night, George.

GEORGE *looks at her a little oddly, and starts to exit. He meets* MAMA
coming in.)

GEORGE.   Oh—hello, Mrs. Younger.

MAMA.   Hello, George, how you feeling?

GEORGE.   Fine—fine, how are you?

MAMA.   Oh a little tired. You know them steps can get you after a day's work. You all have a nice time tonight?

GEORGE.   Yes—a fine time. Well, good night.

MAMA.   Good night. (*He exits.* MAMA *closes the door behind her.*) Hello, honey. What you sitting like that for?

BENEATHA.   I'm just sitting.

MAMA.   Didn't you have a nice time?

BENEATHA.   No.

MAMA.   No? What's the matter?

BENEATHA.   Mama, George is a fool—honest. (*She rises.*)

MAMA (*hustling around unloading the packages she has entered with; she stops*). Is he, baby?

BENEATHA.   Yes.

> (BENEATHA *makes up* TRAVIS'S *bed as she talks.*)

MAMA.   You sure?

BENEATHA.   Yes.

MAMA.   Well—I guess you better not waste your time with no fools.

> BENEATHA *looks up at her mother, watching her put groceries in the refrigerator. Finally she gathers up her things and starts into the bedroom. At the door she stops and looks back at her mother.*)

BENEATHA.   Mama—

MAMA.   Yes, baby—

BENEATHA.   Thank you.

MAMA.   For what?

BENEATHA.   For understanding me this time.

> (*She exits quickly and the mother stands, smiling a little, looking at the place where* BENEATHA *just stood.* RUTH *enters.*)

RUTH.   Now don't you fool with any of this stuff, Lena—

MAMA.   Oh, I just thought I'd sort a few things out.

> (*The phone rings.* RUTH *answers.*)

RUTH (*at the phone*). Hello—Just a minute. (*Goes to door*) Walter, it's Mrs. Arnold. (*Waits. Goes back to the phone. Tense*) Hello. Yes, this is his wife speaking. . . . He's lying down now. Yes . . . well, he'll be in tomorrow. He's been very sick. Yes—I know we should have called, but we were so sure he'd be able to come in today. Yes—yes, I'm very sorry. Yes. . . . Thank you very much. (*She hangs up.* WALTER *is standing in the doorway of the bedroom behind her.*) That was Mrs. Arnold.

WALTER   (*indifferently*).   Was it?

RUTH.   She said if you don't come in tomorrow that they are getting a new man . . . .

WALTER.   Ain't that sad—ain't that crying sad.

RUTH.   She said Mr. Arnold has had to take a cab for three days. . . . Walter, you ain't been to work for three days! (*This is a revelation to her.*) Where you been, Walter Lee Younger? (WALTER *looks at her and starts to laugh.*) You're going to lose your job.

WALTER.   That's right . . . .

RUTH.   Oh Walter, and with your mother working like a dog every day—

WALTER.   That's sad too—Everything is sad.

MAMA.   What you been doing for these three days, son?

WALTER.   Mama—you don't know all the things a man what got leisure can find to do in this city. . . . What's this—Friday night? Well—Wednesday I borrowed Willy Harris's car and I went for a drive. . . . Just me and myself and I drove and drove . . . . Way out . . . way past South Chicago, and I parked the car and I sat and looked at the steel mills all day long. I just sat in the car and looked at them big black chimneys for hours. Then I drove back and I went to the Green Hat. (*Pause*) And Thursday—Thursday I borrowed the car again and I got in it and I pointed it the other way and I drove the other way—for hours—way, way up to Wisconsin, and I looked at the farms. I just drove and looked at the farms. Then I drove back and I went to the Green Hat. (*Pause*) And today today I didn't get the car. Today I just walked. All over the Southside. And I looked at the Negroes and they looked at me and finally I just sat down on the curb at Thirty-ninth and South Parkway and I just sat there and watched the Negroes go by. And then I went to the Green Hat. You all sad? You all depressed? And you know where I am going right now—

(RUTH *goes out quietly.*)

MAMA.   Oh, Big Walter, is this the harvest of our days?

WALTER.   You know what I like about the Green Hat? (*He turns the radio on and a steamy, deep blues pours into the room.*) I like this little cat they got there who blows a sax. . . . He blows. He talks to me. He ain't but 'bout five feet tall and he's got a conked head and his eyes is always closed and he's all music—

MAMA   (*rising and getting some papers out of her handbag*). Walter—

WALTER.   And there's this other guy who plays the piano . . . and they got a sound. I mean they can work on some music. . . . They got the best little combo in the world in the Green Hat. . . .You can just sit there and drink and listen to them three men play and you realize that don't nothing matter worth a damn, but just being there—

MAMA.   I've helped do it to you, haven't I, son? Walter, I been wrong.

WALTER.   Naw—you ain't never been wrong about nothing, Mama.

MAMA.   Listen to me, now. I say I been wrong, son. That I been doing to you what the rest of the world been doing to you. (*She stops and he looks up slowly at her and she meets his eyes pleadingly.*) Walter —what you ain't never understood is that I ain't got nothing, don't own nothing, ain't never really wanted nothing that wasn't for you. There ain't nothing as precious to me . . . There ain't nothing worth holding on to, money, dreams, nothing else—if it means—if it means it's going to destroy my boy. (*She puts her papers in front of him and he watches her without speaking or moving.*) I paid the man thirty-five hundred dollars down on the house. That leaves sixty-five hundred dollars. Monday morning I want you to take this money and take three thousand dollars and put it in a savings account for Beneatha's medical schooling. The rest you put in a checking account—with your name on it. And from now on any penny that come out of it or that go in it is for you to look after. For you to decide. (*She drops her hands a little helplessly.*) It ain't much, but it's all I got in the world and I'm putting it in your hands. I'm telling you to be the head of this family from now on like you supposed to be.

WALTER   (*stares at the money*).   You trust me like that, Mama?

MAMA.   I ain't never stop trusting you. Like I ain't never stop loving you.

> (*She goes out, and* WALTER *sits looking at the money on the table as the music continues in its idiom, pulsing in the room. Finally, in a decisive gesture, he gets up, and, in mingled joy and desperation, picks up the money. At the same moment,* TRAVIS *enters for bed.*)

TRAVIS.   What's the matter, Daddy? You drunk?

WALTER   (*sweetly, more sweetly than we have ever known him*). No, Daddy ain't drunk. Daddy ain't going to never be drunk again. . . .

TRAVIS.   Well, good night, Daddy.

> (*The* FATHER *has come from behind the couch and leans over, embracing his son.*)

WALTER.   Son, I feel like talking to you tonight.

TRAVIS.   About what?

WALTER.   Oh, about a lot of things. About you and what kind of man you going to be when you grow up . . . . Son—son, what do you want to be when you grow up?

TRAVIS.   A bus driver.

WALTER   (*laughing a little*).   A what? Man, that ain't nothing to want to be!

TRAVIS.   Why not?

WALTER.   'Cause, man—it ain't big enough—you know what I mean.

TRAVIS.   I don't know then. I can't make up my mind. Sometimes Mama asks me that too. And sometimes when I tell you I just want to be like you—she says she don't want me to be like that and sometimes she says she does. . . .

WALTER   (*gathering him up in his arms*).   You know what, Travis? In seven years you going to be seventeen years old. And things is going to be very different with us in seven years, Travis. . . .One day when you are seventeen I'll come home—home from my office downtown some-where—

TRAVIS.   You don't work in no office, Daddy.

WALTER.   No—but after tonight. After what your daddy gonna do tonight, there's going to be offices—a whole lot of offices. . . .

TRAVIS.   What you gonna do tonight, Daddy?

WALTER.   You wouldn't understand yet, son, but your daddy's gon-na make a transaction . . . a business transaction that's going to change our lives. . . . That's how come one day when you 'bout seventeen years old I'll come home and I'll be pretty tired, you know what I mean, after a day of conferences and secretaries getting things wrong the way they do . . . 'cause an executive's life is hell, man—(*The more he talks the farther away he gets.*) And I'll put the car up on the driveway . . . just a plain black Chrysler, I think, with white walls—no—black tires. More elegant. Rich people don't have to be flashy . . . though I'll have to get something a little sportier for Ruth—maybe a Cadillac convertible to do her shopping in. . . . And I'll come up the steps to the house and the gardener will be clipping away at the hedges and he'll say, "Good eve-ning, Mr. Younger." And I'll say, "Hello, Jefferson, how are you this eve-ning?" And I'll go inside and Ruth will come downstairs and meet me at the door and we'll kiss each other and she'll take my arm and we'll go up to your room to see you sitting on the floor with the catalogues of all the great schools in America around you. . . . All the great schools in the world! And—and I'll say, all right son—it's your seventeenth birth-day, what is it you've decided? . . . Just tell me where you want to go to school and you'll *go*. Just tell me, what it is you want to be—and you'll *be* it. . . . Whatever you want to be—Yessir! *(He holds his arms open for* TRAVIS.*)* You just name it, son . . . (TRAVIS *leaps into them.)* and I hand you the world!

> *(*WALTER'S *voice has risen in pitch and hysterical promise, and on the last line he lifts* TRAVIS *high.)*
> (BLACKOUT)

SCENE 3

Time: *Saturday, moving day, one week later.*

Before the curtain rises, RUTH'S *voice, a strident, dramatic church alto, cuts through the silence.*

It is, in the darkness, a triumphant surge, a penetrating statement of expectation: "Oh, Lord, I don't feel no ways tired! Children, oh, glory hallelujah!"

As the curtain rises we see that RUTH *is alone in the living room, finishing up the family's packing. It is moving day. She is nailing crates and tying cartons.* BENEATHA *enters, carrying a guitar case, and watches her exuberant sister-in-law.*

RUTH.   Hey!

BENEATHA   *(putting away the case)*.   Hi.

RUTH   *(pointing at a package)*.   Honey—look in that package there and see what I found on sale this morning at the South Center. (RUTH *gets up and moves to the package and draws out some curtains.)* Look-ahere—hand-turned hems!

BENEATHA.   How do you know the window size out there?

RUTH   *(who hadn't thought of that)*.   Oh—Well, they bound to fit something in the whole house. Anyhow, they was too good a bargain to pass up. (RUTH *slaps her head, suddenly remembering something.)* Oh, Bennie—I meant to put a special note on that carton over there. That's your mama's good china and she wants 'em to be very careful with it.

BENEATHA.   I'll do it.

> *(*BENEATHA *finds a piece of paper and starts to draw large letters on it.)*

RUTH.   You know what I'm going to do soon as I get in that new house?

BENEATHA.   What?

RUTH.   Honey—I'm going to run me a tub of water up to here. . . . *(With her fingers practically up to her nostrils)* And I'm going to get in it—and I am going to sit . . . and sit . . . and sit in that hot water and the first person who knocks to tell *me* to hurry up and come out—

BENEATHA.   Gets shot at sunrise.

RUTH   *(laughing happily).*   You said it, sister! *(Noticing how large* BENEATHA *is absent-mindedly making the note)* Honey, they ain't going to read that from no airplane.

BENEATHA   *(laughing herself).*   I guess I always think things have more emphasis if they are big, somehow.

RUTH   *(looking up at her and smiling).*   You and your brother seem to have that as a philosophy of life. Lord, that man—done changed so 'round here. You know—you know what we did last night? Me and Walter Lee?

BENEATHA.   What?

RUTH   *(smiling to herself).*   We went to the movies. *(Looking at* BENEATHA *to see if she understands.)* We went to the movies. You know the last time me and Walter went to the movies together?

BENEATHA.   No.

RUTH.   Me neither. That's how long it been. *(Smiling again)* But we went last night. The picture wasn't much good, but that didn't seem to matter. We went—and we held hands.

BENEATHA.   Oh, Lord!

RUTH.   We held hands—and you know what?

BENEATHA.   What?

RUTH.   When we come out of the show it was late and dark and all the stores and things was closed up . . . and it was kind of chilly and there wasn't many people on the streets . . . and we was still holding hands, me and Walter.

BENEATHA.   You're killing me.

(WALTER *enters with a large package. His happiness is deep in him; he cannot keep still with his new-found exuberance. He is singing and wiggling and snapping his fingers. He puts his package in a corner and puts a phonograph record, which he has brought in with him, on the record player. As the music comes up he dances over to* RUTH *and tries to get her to dance with him. She gives in at last to his raunchiness and in a fit of giggling allows herself to be drawn into his mood and together they deliberately burlesque an old social dance of their youth.)*

BENEATHA (*regarding them a long time as they dance, then drawing in her breath for a deeply exaggerated comment that she does not particularly mean*). Talk about—olddddddddddd-fashioneddddddddd—Negroes!

WALTER (*stopping momentarily*). What kind of Negroes? (*He says this in fun. He is not angry with her today, nor with anyone. He starts to dance with his wife again.*)

BENEATHA. Old-fashioned.

WALTER (*as he dances with* RUTH). You know, when these *New Negroes* have their convention–(*Pointing at his sister*)–that is going to be the chairman of the Committee on Unending Agitation. (*He goes on dancing, then stops.*) Race, race, race! . . . Girl, I do believe you are the first person in the history of the entire human race to successfully brainwash yourself. (BENEATHA *breaks up and he goes on dancing. He stops again, enjoying his tease.*) Damn, even the N double A C P takes a holiday sometimes! (BENEATHA *and* RUTH *laugh. He dances with* RUTH *some more and starts to laugh and stops and pantomimes someone over an operating table.*) I can just see that chick someday looking down at some poor cat on an operating table before she starts to slice him, saying. . . . (*Pulling his sleeves back maliciously.*) "By the way, what are your views on civil rights down there? . . ."

(*He laughs at her again and starts to dance happily. The bell sounds.*)

BENEATHA. Sticks and stones may break my bones but . . . words will never hurt me!

(BENEATHA *goes to the door and opens it as* WALTER *and* RUTH *go on with the clowning.* BENEATHA *is somewhat surprised to see a quiet-looking middle-aged white man in a business suit holding his hat and a briefcase in his hand and consulting a small piece of paper.*)

MAN. Uh—how do you do, miss. I am looking for a Mrs.—(*He looks at the slip of paper.*) Mrs. Lena Younger?

BENEATHA (*smoothing her hair with slight embarrassment*). Oh—yes, that's my mother. Excuse me (*She closes the door and turns to quiet the other two.*) Ruth! Brother! Somebody's here. (*Then she opens the door. The man casts a curious quick glance at all of them*). Uh—come in please.

MAN (*coming in*). Thank you.

BENEATHA. My mother isn't here just now. Is it business?

MAN. Yes . . . well, of a sort.

WALTER (*freely, the Man of the House*). Have a seat. I'm Mrs. Younger's son. I look after most of her business matters.

(RUTH *and* BENEATHA *exchange amused glances.*)

MAN   (*regarding* WALTER *and sitting*).   Well—My name is Karl
Lindner . . . .

WALTER   (*stretching out his hand*).   Walter Younger. This is my
wife—(RUTH *nods politely.*)—and my sister.

LINDNER.   How do you do.

WALTER   (*amiably, as he sits himself easily on a chair, leaning
with interest forward on his knees and looking expectantly into the newcomer's face*).   What can we do for you, Mr. Lindner!

LINDNER   (*some minor shuffling of the hat and briefcase on his knees*).
Well—I am a representative of the Clybourne Park Improvement
Association—

WALTER   (*pointing*).   Why don't you sit your things on the floor?

LINDNER.   Oh—yes. Thank you. (*He slides the briefcase and hat
under the chair.*) And as I was saying—I am from the Clybourne Park
Improvement Association and we have had it brought to our attention at
the last meeting that you people—or at least your mother—has bought
a piece of residential property at—(*He digs for the slip of paper again.*)—
four o six Clybourne Street . . . .

WALTER.   That's right. Care for something to drink? Ruth, get Mr.
Lindner a beer.

LINDNER   (*upset for some reason*).   Oh—no, really. I mean thank
you very much, but no thank you.

RUTH   (*innocently*).   Some coffee?

LINDNER.   Thank you, nothing at all.

(BEANEATHA *is watching the man carefully.*)

LINDNER.   Well, I don't know how much you folks know about our
organization. (*He is a gentle man; thoughtful and somewhat labored in
his manner.*) It is one of these community organizations set up to look
after—oh, you know, things like block upkeep and special projects and
we also have what we call our New Neighbors Orientation Committee. . . .

BEANEATHA   (*drily*).   Yes—and what do they do?

LINDNER   (*turning a little to her and then returning the main force
to* WALTER).   Well—it's what you might call a sort of welcoming committee, I guess. I mean they, we, I'm the chairman of the committee—
go around and see the new people who move into the neighborhood and
sort of give them the lowdown on the way we do things out in Clybourne
Park.

BEANEATHA   (*with appreciation of the two meanings, which escape*
RUTH *and* WALTER).   Uh-huh.

LINDNER.   And we also have the category of what the association calls —(*He looks elsewhere.*)—uh—special community problems . . . .

BENEATHA.   Yes—and what are some of those?

WALTER.   Girl, let the man talk.

LINDNER   (*with understated relief*).   Thank you. I would sort of like to explain this thing in my own way. I mean I want to explain to you in a certain way.

WALTER.   Go ahead.

LINDNER.   Yes. Well. I'm going to try to get right to the point. I'm sure we'll all appreciate that in the long run.

BENEATHA.   Yes.

WALTER.   Be still now!

LINDNER.   Well—

RUTH   (*still innocently*).   Would you like another chair—you don't look comfortable.

LINDNER   (*more frustrated than annoyed*).   No, thank you very much. Please. Well—to get right to the point I—(*A great breath and he is off at last.*) I am sure you people must be aware of some of the incidents which have happened in various parts of the city when colored people have moved into certain areas—(BENEATHA *exhales heavily and starts tossing a piece of fruit up and down in the air.*) Well—because we have what I think is going to be a unique type of organization in American community life—not only do we deplore that kind of thing—but we are trying to do something about it. (BENEATHA *stops tossing and turns with a new and quizzical interest to the man.*) We feel — (*gaining confidence in his mission because of the interest in the faces of the people he is talking to*)—we feel that most of the trouble in this world, when you come right down to it—(*He hits his knee for emphasis.*) — most of the trouble exists because people just don't sit down and talk to each other.

RUTH   (*nodding as she might in church, pleased with the remark*). You can say that again, mister.

LINDNER   (*more encouraged by such affirmation*).   That we don't try hard enough in this world to understand the other fellow's problem. The other guy's point of view.

RUTH.   Now that's right.

(BENEATHA *and* WALTER *merely watch and listen with genuine interest.*)

LINDNER.   Yes—that's the way we feel out in Clybourne Park. And that's why I was elected to come here this afternoon and talk to you people. Friendly like, you know, the way people should talk to each other and see if we couldn't find some way to work this thing out. As I say, the whole business is a matter of *caring* about the other fellow. Anybody can see that you are a nice family of folks, hard working and honest I'm sure. (BENEATHA *frowns slightly, quizzically, her head tilted regarding him.*) Today everybody knows what it means to be on the outside of *something.* And of course, there is always somebody who is out to take the advantage of people who don't always understand.

WALTER.   What do you mean?

LINDNER.   Well—you see our community is made up of people who've worked hard as the dickens for years to build up that little community. They're not rich and fancy people; just hard-working, honest people who don't really have much but those little homes and a dream of the kind of community they want to raise their children in. Now, I don't say we are perfect and there is a lot wrong in some of the things they want. But you've got to admit that a man, right or wrong, has the right to want to have the neighborhood he lives in a certain kind of way. And at the moment the overwhelming majority of our people out there feel that people get along better, take more of a common interest in the life of the community, when they share a common background. I want you to believe me whan I tell you that race prejudice simply doesn't enter into it. It is a matter of the people of Clybourne Park believing, rightly or wrongly, as I say, that for the happiness of all concerned that our Negro families are happier when they live in their *own* communities.

BENEATHA   (*with a grand and bitter gesture*).   This, friends, is the Welcoming Committee!

WALTER   (*dumfounded, looking at* LINDNER).   Is this what you came marching all the way over here to tell us?

LINDNER.   Well, now we've been having a fine conversation. I hope you'll hear me all the way through.

WALTER   (*tightly*).   Go ahead, man.

LINDNER.   You see—in the face of all things I have said, we are prepared to make your family a very generous offer. . . .

BENEATHA.   Thirty pieces and not a coin less!

WALTER.   Yeah?

LINDNER   (*putting on his glasses and drawing a form out of the briefcase*).   Our association is prepared, through the collective effort of our people, to buy the house from you at a financial gain to your family.

RUTH.   Lord have mercy, ain't this the living gall!

WALTER.   All right, you through?

LINDNER.   Well, I want to give you the exact terms of the financial arrangement—

WALTER.   We don't want to hear no exact terms of no arrangements. I want to know if you got any more to tell us 'bout getting together?

LINDNER   (*taking off his glasses*).   Well—I don't suppose that you feel. . . .

WALTER.   Never mind how I feel—you got any more to say 'bout how people ought to sit down and talk to each other? . . . Get out of my house, man.

(He turns his back and walks to the door.)

LINDNER   (*looking around at the hostile faces and reaching and assembling his hat and briefcase*).   Well—I don't understand why you people are reacting this way. What do you think you are going to gain by moving into a neighborhood where you just aren't wanted and where some elements—well—people can get awful worked up when they feel that their whole way of life and everything they've ever worked for is threatened.

WALTER.   Get out.

LINDNER   (*at the door, holding a small card*).   Well—I'm sorry it went like this.

WALTER.   Get out.

LINDNER   (*almost sadly regarding* WALTER).   You just can't force people to change their hearts, son.

(He turns and puts his card on a table and exits. WALTER *pushes the door to with stinging hatred, and stands looking at it.* RUTH *just sits and* BENEATHA *just stands. They say nothing.* MAMA *and* TRAVIS *enter.)*

MAMA.   Well—this all the packing got done since I left out of here this morning. I testify before God that my children got all the energy of the dead. What time the moving men due?

BENEATHA.   Four o'clock. You had a caller, Mama.

(She is smiling, teasingly.)

MAMA.   Sure enough—who?

BENEATHA   (*her arms folded saucily*).   The Welcoming Committee.

*(*WALTER *and* RUTH *giggle.)*

MAMA   (*innocently*).   Who?

BENEATHA.   The Welcoming Committee. They said they're sure going to be glad to see you when you get there.

WALTER   (*devilishly*).   Yeah, they said they can't hardly wait to see your face.

(*Laughter*)

MAMA   (*sensing their facetiousness*).   What's the matter with you all?

WALTER.   Ain't nothing the matter with us. We just telling you 'bout the gentleman who came to see you this afternoon. From the Clybourne Park Improvement Association.

MAMA.   What he want?

RUTH   (*in the same mood as* BENEATHA *and* WALTER).   To welcome you, honey.

WALTER.   He said they can't hardly wait. He said the one thing they don't have, that they just *dying* to have out there is a fine family of colored people! (*To* RUTH *and* BENEATHA) Ain't that right!

RUTH *and* BENEATHA (*mockingly*). Yeah! He left his card in case—

(*They indicate the card, and* MAMA *picks it up and throws it on the floor—understanding and looking off as she draws her chair up to the table on which she has put her plant and some sticks and some cord.*)

MAMA.   Father, give us strength. (*Knowingly—and without fun*) Did he threaten us?

BENEATHA.   Oh—Mama—they don't do it like that anymore. He talked Brotherhood. He said everybody ought to learn how to sit down and hate each other with good Christian fellowship.

(*She and* WALTER *shake hands to ridicule the remark.*)

MAMA   (*sadly*).   Lord, protect us. . . .

RUTH.   You should hear the money those folks raised to buy the house from us. All we paid and then some.

BENEATHA.   What they think we going to do—eat 'em?

RUTH.   No, honey, marry 'em.

MAMA   (*shaking her head*).   Lord, Lord, Lord . . . .

RUTH.   Well—that's the way the crackers crumble. Joke.

BENEATHA   (*laughingly noticing what her mother is doing*). Mama, what are you doing?

MAMA.   Fixing my plant so it won't get hurt none on the way . . . .

BENEATHA.   Mama, you going to take *that* to the new house?

MAMA.   Uh-huh—

BENEATHA.   That raggedy-looking old thing?

MAMA   (*stopping and looking at her*).   It expresses *me*.

RUTH   (*with delight, to* BENEATHA).   So there, Miss Thing!

(WALTER *comes to* MAMA *suddenly and bends down behind her and squeezes her in his arms with all his strength. She is overwhelmed by the suddenness of it and, though delighted, her manner is like that of* RUTH *with* TRAVIS).

MAMA.   Look out now, boy! You make me mess up my thing here!

WALTER   (*his face lit, he slips down on his knees beside her, his arms still about her*). Mama . . . you know what it means to climb up in the chariot?

MAMA   (*gruffly, very happy*).   Get on away from me now. . . .

RUTH   (*near the gift-wrapped package, trying to catch* WALTER'S *eye*).   Psst—

WALTER.   What the old song say, Mama . . . .

RUTH.   Walter—Now?

(*She is pointing at the package.*)

WALTER   (*speaking the lines, sweetly, playfully, in his mother's face*).
        I got wings . . . you got wings . . .
        All God's Children got wings . . . .

MAMA.   Boy—get out of my face and do some work . . . .

WALTER.
        When I get to heaven gonna put on my wings,
        Gonna fly all over God's heaven . . . .

BENEATHA   (*teasingly, from across the room*).   Everybody talking 'bout heaven ain't going there!

WALTER   (*to* RUTH, *who is carrying the box across to them*).   I don't know, you think we ought to give her that. . . . Seems to me she ain't been very appreciative around here.

MAMA   (*eyeing the box, which is obviously a gift*).   What is that?

WALTER   (*taking it from* RUTH *and putting it on the table in front of* MAMA). Well—what you all think? Should we give it to her?

RUTH.   Oh—she was pretty good today.

MAMA.   I'll good you—

(*She turns her eyes to the box again.*)

BENEATHA.   Open it, Mama.

(*She stands up, looks at it, turns and looks at all of them, and then presses her hands together and does not open the package.*)

WALTER   (*sweetly*).   Open it, Mama. It's for you. (MAMA *looks in his eyes. It is the first present in her life without its being Christmas. Slowly she opens her package and lifts out, one by one, a brand-new sparkling set of gardening tools.* WALTER *continues, prodding.*) Ruth made up the note—read it . . . .

MAMA   (*picking up the card and adjusting her glasses*).   "To our own Mrs. Miniver—Love from Brother, Ruth and Beneatha." Ain't that lovely. . . .

TRAVIS   (*tugging at his father's sleeve*).   Daddy, can I give her mine now?

WALTER.   All right, son. (TRAVIS *flies to get his gift*).   Travis didn't want to go in with the rest of us, Mama. He got his own. (*Somewhat amused*) We don't know what it is . . . .

TRAVIS   (*racing back in the room with a large hatbox and putting it in front of his grandmother*).   Here!

MAMA.   Lord have mercy, baby. You done gone and bought your grandmother a hat?

TRAVIS   (*very proud*).   Open it!

> (*She does and lifts out an elaborate, but very elaborate, wide gardening hat, and all the adults break up at the sight of it.*)

RUTH.   Travis, honey, what is that?

TRAVIS   (*who thinks it is beautiful and appropriate*).   It's a gardening hat! Like the ladies always have on in the magazines when they work in their gardens.

BENEATHA   (*giggling fiercely*).   Travis—we were trying to make Mama Mrs. Miniver—not Scarlett O'Hara!

MAMA   (*indignantly*).   What's the matter with you all! This here is a beautiful hat! (*Absurdly*) I always wanted me one just like it!

> (*She pops it on her head to prove it to her grandson, and the hat is ludicrous and considerably oversized.*)

RUTH.   Hot dog! Go, Mama!

WALTER   (*doubled over with laughter*).   I'm sorry, Mama—but you look like you ready to go out and chop you some cotton sure enough!

> (*They all laugh except* MAMA, *out of deference to* TRAVIS's *feelings.*)

MAMA   (*gathering the boy up to her*).   Bless your heart—this is the prettiest hat I ever owned—(WALTER, RUTH *and* BENEATHA *chime in—noisily, festively and insincerely congratulating* TRAVIS *on his gift.*) What are we all standing around here for? We ain't finished packin' yet. Bennie, you ain't packed one book.

> (*The bell rings.*)

BENEATHA.   That couldn't be the movers . . . it's not hardly two good yet—

> (BENEATHA *goes into her room.* MAMA *starts for door.*)

WALTER   (*turning, stiffening*).   Wait—wait—I'll get it.

> (*He stands and looks at the door.*)

MAMA.   You expecting company, son?

WALTER   (*just looking at the door*).   Yeah—yeah. . . .

> (MAMA *looks at* RUTH, *and they exchange innocent and unfrightened glances.*)

MAMA   (*not understanding*).   Well, let them in, son.

BENEATHA   (*from her room*).   We need some more string.

MAMA.   Travis—you run to the hardware and get me some string cord.

> (MAMA *goes out and* WALTER *turns and looks at* RUTH. TRAVIS *goes to a dish for money.*)

RUTH.   Why don't you answer the door, man?

WALTER   (*suddenly bounding across the floor to her*).   'Cause sometimes it hard to let the future begin!

> (*Stooping down in her face.*)

> *I got wings! You got wings!*
> *All God's children got wings!*

(*He crosses to the door and throws it open. Standing there is a very slight little man in a not too prosperous business suit and with haunted frightened eyes and a hat pulled down tightly, brim up, around his forehead.* TRAVIS *passes between the men and exits.* WALTER *leans deep in the man's face, still in his jubilance.*)

> *When I get to heaven gonna put on my wings,*
> *Gonna fly all over God's heaven . . . .*

> (*The little man just stares at him.*)

> *Heaven—*

(*Suddenly he stops and looks past the little man into the empty hallway.*) Where's Willy, man?

BOBO.   He ain't with me.

WALTER   (*not disturbed*).   Oh—come on in. You know my wife.

BOBO   (*dumbly, taking off his hat*).   Yes—h'you, Miss Ruth.

RUTH   (*quietly, a mood apart from her husband already, seeing* BOBO). Hello, Bobo.

WALTER.   You right on time today. . . . Right on time. That's the way! *(He slaps* BOBO *on his back.)* Sit down . . . lemme hear.

>   (RUTH *stands stiffly and quietly in back of them, as though some-how she senses death, her eyes fixed on her husband.)*

BOBO   *(his frightened eyes on the floor, his hat in his hands)*.   Could I please get a drink of water, before I tell you about it, Walter Lee?

>   (WALTER *does not take his eyes off the man.* RUTH *goes blindly to the tap and gets a glass of water and brings it to* BOBO.*)*

WALTER.   There ain't nothing wrong, is there?

BOBO.   Lemme tell you—

WALTER.   Man—didn't nothing go wrong?

BOBO.   Lemme tell you—Walter Lee. *(Looking at* RUTH *and talking to her more than to* WALTER.*)* You know how it was. I got to tell you how it was. I mean first I got to tell you how it was all the way. . . . I mean about the money I put in, Walter Lee . . . .

WALTER   *(with taut agitation now)*.   What about the money you put in?

BOBO.   Well—it wasn't much as we told you—me and Willy—*(He stops.)* I'm sorry, Walter. I got a bad feeling about it. I got a real bad feeling about it. . . .

WALTER.   Man, what you telling me about all this for? . . . Tell me what happened in Springfield. . . .

BOBO.   Springfield.

RUTH   *(like a dead woman)*.   What was supposed to happen in Springfield?

BOBO   *(to her)*.   This deal that me and Walter went into with Willy—Me and Willy was going to go down to Springfield and spread some money 'round so's we wouldn't have to wait so long for the liquor license. . . . That's what we were going to do. Everybody said that was the way you had to do, you understand, Miss Ruth?

WALTER.   Man—what happened down there?

BOBO   *(a pitiful man, near tears)*.   I'm trying to tell you, Walter.

WALTER   *(screaming at him suddenly)*.   THEN TELL ME, GOD-DAMMIT. . . . WHAT'S THE MATTER WITH YOU?

BOBO.   Man . . . I didn't go to no Springfield, yesterday.

WALTER   *(halted, life hanging in the moment)*.   Why not?

BOBO   *(the long way, the hard way to tell)*.   'Cause I didn't have no reasons to . . . .

WALTER.   Man, what are you talking about!

BOBO.   I'm talking about the fact that when I got to the train station yesterday morning—eight o'clock like we planned . . . . Man—*Willy didn't never show up.*

WALTER.   Why . . . where was he . . . where is he?

BOBO.   That's what I'm trying to tell you. . . . I don't know. . . . I waited six hours. . . . I called his house . . . and I waited . . . six hours . . . I waited in that train station six hours. . . . (*Breaking into tears*) That was all the extra money I had in the world . . . . (*Looking up at* WALTER *with the tears running down his face) Man, Willy is gone.*

WALTER.   Gone, what you mean Willy is gone? Gone where? You mean he went by himself. You mean he went off to Springfield by himself—to take care of getting the license—(*Turns and looks anxiously at* RUTH.) You mean maybe he didn't want too many people in on the business down there? (*Looks to* RUTH *again, as before.*) You know Willy got his own ways. (*Looks back to* BOBO.) Maybe you was late yesterday and he just went on down there without you. Maybe—maybe—he's been callin' you at home tryin' to tell you what happened or something. Maybe —maybe—he just got sick. He's somewhere—he's got to be somewhere. We just got to find him—me and you got to find him. (*Grabs* BOBO *senselessly by the collar and starts to shake him.*) We got to!

BOBO   (*in sudden angry, frightened agony*).   What's the matter with you, Walter! *When a cat take off with your money he don't leave you no maps!*

WALTER   (*turning madly, as though he is looking for* WILLY *in the very room*).   Willy! . . . Willy . . . don't do it. . . . Please don't do it. . . . Man, not with that money . . . Man, please, not with that money . . . . Oh, God. . . . Don't let it be true. . . . (*He is wandering around, crying out for* WILLY *and looking for him or perhaps for help from God.*) Man . . . I trusted you. . . . Man, I put my life in your hands. . . . (*He starts to crumple down on the floor as* RUTH *just covers her face in horror.* MAMA *opens the door and comes into the room, with* BENEATHA *behind her.*) Man. . . .(*He starts to pound the floor with his fists, sobbing wildly.*) That money is made out of my father's flesh . . . .

BOBO   (*standing over him helplessly*).   I'm sorry, Walter. . . . (*Only* WALTER'S *sobs reply.* BOBO *puts on his hat.*) I had my life staked on this deal, too. . . .

(He exits.)

MAMA   (*to* WALTER).   Son—(*She goes to him, bends down to him, talks to his bent head.*) Son . . . . Is it gone? Son, I gave you sixty-five hundred dollars. Is it gone? All of it? Beneatha's money too?

WALTER   *(lifting his head slowly).*   Mama . . . I never . . . went to the bank at all . . . .

MAMA   *(not wanting to believe him).*   You mean . . . your sister's school money . . . you used that too. . . . Walter?. . .

WALTER.   Yessss! . . . All of it. . . . It's all gone. . . .

> *(There is total silence.* RUTH *stands with her face covered with her hands;* BENEATHA *leans forlornly against a wall, fingering a piece of red ribbon from the mother's gift.* MAMA *stops and looks at her son without recognition and then, quite without thinking about it, starts to beat him senselessly in the face.* BENEATHA *goes to them and stops it.)*

BENEATHA.   Mama!

> *(MAMA stops and looks at both of her children and rises slowly and wanders vaguely, aimlessly away from them.)*

MAMA.   I seen . . . him . . . night after night . . . come in . . . and look at that rug . . . and then look at me . . . the red showing in his eyes . . . the veins moving in his head . . . I seen him grow thin and old before he was forty . . . working and working and working like somebody's old horse . . . killing himself . . . and you—you give it all away in a day . . . .

BENEATHA.   Mama—

MAMA.   Oh, God . . . *(She looks up to Him.)* Look down here—and show me the strength.

BENEATHA.   Mama—

MAMA   *(folding over).*   Strength. . . .

BENEATHA   *(plaintively).*   Mama. . . .

MAMA.   Strength!

(CURTAIN)

ACT III

An hour later.

At curtain, there is a sullen light of gloom in the living room, gray light not unlike that which began the first scene of Act I. At left we can see WALTER *within his room, alone with himself. He is stretched out on the bed, his shirt out and open, his arms under his head. He does not smoke, he does not cry out, he merely lies there, looking up at the ceiling, much as if he were alone in the world.*

In the living room BENEATHA *sits at the table, still surrounded by the now almost ominous packing crates. She sits looking off. We feel that this is a mood struck perhaps an hour before, and it lingers now, full of the empty sound of profound disappointment. We see on a line from her brother's bedroom the sameness of their attitudes. Presently the bell rings, and* BENEATHA *rises without ambition or interest in answering. It is* ASAGAI, *smiling broadly, striding into the room with energy and happy expectation and conversation.*

ASAGAI.   I came over. . . . I had some free time. I thought I might help with the packing. Ah, I like the look of packing crates! A household in preparation for a journey! It depresses some people. . . but for me . . . it is another feeling. Something full of the flow of life, do you understand? Movement, progress. . . . It makes me think of Africa.

BENEATHA.   Africa!

ASAGAI.   What kind of a mood is this? Have I told you how deeply you move me?

BENEATHA.   He gave away the money, Asagai . . . .

ASAGAI.   Who gave away what money?

BENEATHA.   The insurance money. My brother gave it away.

ASAGAI.   Gave it away?

BENEATHA.   He made an investment! With a man even Travis wouldn't have trusted.

ASAGAI.   And it's gone?

BENEATHA.   Gone!

ASAGAI.   I'm very sorry . . . . And you, now?

BENEATHA.   Me? . . . Me? . . . Me I'm nothing . . . . Me. When I was very small . . . we used to take our sleds out in the wintertime and the only hills we had were the ice-covered stone steps of some houses down the street. And we used to fill them in with snow and make them smooth and slide down them all day . . . and it was very dangerous you know . . . far too steep . . . and sure enough one day a kid named Rufus came down too fast and hit the sidewalk . . . and we saw his face just split open right there in front of us. . . . And I remember standing there looking at his bloody open face thinking that was the end of Rufus. But the ambulance came and they took him to the hospital and they fixed the broken bones and they sewed it all up . . . and the next time I saw Rufus he just had a little line down the middle of his face. . . . I never got over that . . .

(WALTER *sits up, listening on the bed. Throughout this scene it is important that we feel his reaction at all times, that he visibly respond to the words of his sister and* ASAGAI.)

ASAGAI.   What?

BENEATHA.   That that was what one person could do for another, fix him up—sew up the problem, make him all right again. That was the most marvelous thing in the world. . . . I wanted to do that. I always thought it was the one concrete thing in the world that a human being could do. Fix up the sick, you know—and make them whole again. This was truly being God. . . .

ASAGAI.   You wanted to be God?

BENEATHA.   No—I wanted to cure. It used to be so important to me. I wanted to cure. It used to matter. I used to care. I mean about people and how their bodies hurt . . . .

ASAGAI.   And you've stopped caring?

BENEATHA.   Yes—I think so.

ASAGAI.   Why?

(WALTER *rises, goes to the door of his room and is about to open it, then stops and stands listening, leaning on the door jamb.*)

BENEATHA.   Because it doesn't seem deep enough, close enough to what ails mankind—I mean this thing of sewing up bodies or administering drugs. Don't you understand? It was a child's reaction to the world. I thought that doctors had the secret to all the hurts. . . .That's the way a child sees things—or an idealist.

ASAGAI.   Children see things very well sometimes—and idealists even better.

BENEATHA.   I know that's what you think. Because you are still where I left off—you still care. This is what you see for the world, for Africa. You with the dreams of the future will patch up all Africa—you are going to cure the Great Sore of colonialism with Independence——

ASAGAI.   Yes!

BENEATHA.   Yes—and you think that one word is the penicillin of the human spirit: "Independence!" But then what?

ASAGAI.   That will be the problem for another time. First we must get there.

BENEATHA.   And where does it end?

ASAGAI.   End? Who even spoke of an end? To life? To living?

BENEATHA.   An end to misery!

ASAGAI   (*smiling*).   You sound like a French intellectual.

BENEATHA.   No! I sound like a human being who just had her future taken right out of her hands! While I was sleeping in my bed in there, things were happening in this world that directly concerned me—and nobody asked me, consulted me—they just went out and did things—and changed my life. Don't you see there isn't any real progress, Asagai, there is only one large circle that we march in, around and around, each of us with our own little picture—in front of us—our own little mirage that we think is the future.

ASAGAI.   That is the mistake.

BENEATHA.   What?

ASAGAI.   What you just said—about the circle. It isn't a circle—it is simply a long line—as in geometry, you know, one that reaches into infinity. And because we cannot see the end—we also cannot see how it changes. And it is very odd but those who see the changes are called "idealists"—and those who cannot, or refuse to think, they are the "realists." It is very strange, and amusing too, I think.

BENEATHA.   You—you are almost religious.

ASAGAI.   Yes . . . I think I have the religion of doing what is necessary in the world—and of worshipping man—because he is so marvelous, you see.

BENEATHA.   Man is foul! And the human race deserves its misery!

ASAGAI.   You see: *You* have become the religious one in the old sense. Already, and after such a small defeat, you are worshipping despair.

BENEATHA.   From now on, I worship the truth—and the truth is that people are puny, small and selfish. . . .

ASAGAI.   Truth? Why is it that you despairing ones always think that only you have the truth? I never thought to see *you* like that. You! Your brother made a stupid, childish mistake—and you are grateful to him. So that now you can give up the ailing human race on account of it. You talk about what good is struggle; what good is anything? Where are we all going? And why are we bothering?

BENEATHA.   *And you cannot answer it!* All your talk and dreams about Africa and Independence. Independence and then what? What about all the crooks and petty thieves and just plain idiots who will come into power to steal and plunder the same as before—only now they will be black and do it in the name of the new Independence—You cannot answer that.

ASAGAI   (*shouting over her*).   *I live the answer!* (*Pause*). In my village at home it is the exceptional man who can even read a newspaper . . . or who ever *sees* a book at all. I will go home and much of what I will have to say will seem strange to the people of my village. . . . But I will teach and work and things will happen, slowly and swiftly. At times it will seem that nothing changes at all . . . and then again . . . the sudden dramatic events which make history leap into the future. And then quiet again. Retrogression even. Guns, murder, revolution. And I even will have moments when I wonder if the quiet was not better than all that death and hatred. But I will look about my village at the illiteracy and disease and ignorance and I will not wonder long. And perhaps . . . perhaps I will be a great man. . . . I mean perhaps I will hold on to the substance of truth and find my way always with the right course . . . and perhaps for it I will be butchered in my bed some night by the servants of empire. . . .

BENEATHA. *The martyr!*

ASAGAI. . . . or perhaps I shall live to be a very old man, respected and esteemed in my new nation. . . . And perhaps I shall hold office and this is what I'm trying to tell you, Alaiyo; perhaps the things I believe now for my country will be wrong and outmoded, and I will not understand and do terrible things to have things my way or merely to keep my power. Don't you see that there will be young men and women, not British soldiers then, but my own black countrymen . . . to step out of the shadows some evening and slit my then useless throat? Don't you see they have always been there . . . that they always will be. And that such a thing as my own death will be an advance? They who might kill me even . . . actually replenish me!

BENEATHA.   Oh, Asagai, I know all that.

ASAGAI.   Good! Then stop moaning and groaning and tell me what you plan to do.

BENEATHA.   Do?

ASAGAI.   I have a bit of a suggestion.

BENEATHA.   What?

ASAGAI (*rather quietly for him*).   That when it is all over—that you come home with me—

BENEATHA (*slapping herself on the forehead with exasperation born of misunderstanding*).   Oh—Asagai—at this moment you decide to be romantic!

ASAGAI (*quickly understanding the misunderstanding*).   My dear, young creature of the New World—I do not mean across the city—I mean across the ocean; home—to Africa.

BENEATHA (*slowly understanding and turning to him with murmured amazement*).   To—to Nigeria?

ASAGAI. Yes! . . . (*Smiling and lifting his arms playfully*) Three hundred years later the African Prince rose up out of the seas and swept the maiden back across the middle passage over which her ancestors had come—

BENEATHA (*unable to play*). Nigeria?

ASAGAI. Nigeria. Home. *(Coming to her with genuine romantic flippancy)* I will show you our mountains and our stars; and give you cool drinks from gourds and teach you the old songs and the ways of our people—and, in time, we will pretend that—*(Very softly)*—you have only been away for a day—

(*She turns her back to him, thinking. He swings her around and takes her full in his arms in a long embrace which proceeds to passion.*)

BENEATHA (*pulling away*). You're getting me all mixed up—

ASAGAI. Why?

BENEATHA. Too many things—too many things have happened today. I must sit down and think. I don't know what I feel about anything right this minute.

(*She promptly sits down and props her chin on her fist.*)

ASAGAI (*charmed*). All right, I shall leave you. No—don't get up. *(Touching her, gently, sweetly)* Just sit awhile and think. . . . Never be afraid to sit awhile and think. *(He goes to door and looks at her.)* How often I have looked at you and said, "Ah—so this is what the New World hath finally wrought. . . ."

(*He exits. BENEATHA sits on alone. Presently WALTER enters from his room and starts to rummage through things, feverishly looking for something. She looks up and turns in her seat.*)

BENEATHA (*hissingly*). Yes—just look at what the New World hath wrought! . . . Just look! *(She gestures with bitter disgust.)* There he is! *Monsieur le petit bourgeois noir*—himself! There he is—Symbol of a Rising Class! Entrepreneur! Titan of the system! (WALTER *ignores her completely and continues frantically and destructively looking for something and hurling things to floor and tearing things out of their place in his search.* BENEATHA *ignores the eccentricity of his actions and goes on with the monologue of insult.*) Did you dream of yachts on Lake Michigan, Brother? Did you see yourself on that Great Day sitting down at the Conference Table, surrounded by all the mighty bald-headed men in America? All halted, waiting, breathless, waiting for your pronouncements on industry? Waiting for you—Chairman of the Board? (WALTER *finds what he is looking for—a small piece of white paper—and pushes*

*it in his pocket and puts on his coat and rushes out without ever having
looked at her. She shouts after him.)* I look at you and I see the final triumph of stupidity in the world!

>   *(The door slams and she returns to just sitting again.* RUTH *comes
>   quickly out of* MAMA'S *room.)*

RUTH.   Who was that?

BENEATHA.   Your husband.

RUTH.   Where did he go?

BENEATHA.   Who knows—maybe he has an appointment at U.S. Steel.

RUTH *(anxiously, with frightened eyes).* You didn't say nothing bad to
him, did you?

BENEATHA.   Bad? Say anything bad to him? No—I told him he was
a sweet boy and full of dreams and everything is strictly peachy keen, as
the ofay kids say!

>   *(*MAMA *enters from her bedroom. She is lost, vague, trying to catch
>   hold, to make some sense of her former command of the world, but
>   it still eludes her. A sense of waste overwhelms her gait; a measure
>   of apology rides on her shoulders. She goes to her plant, which has
>   remained on the table, looks at it, picks it up and takes it to the
>   window sill and sits it outside, and she stands and looks at it a long
>   moment. Then she closes the window, straightens her body with ef-
>   fort and turns around to her children.)*

MAMA.   Well—ain't it a mess in here, though? *(A false cheerfulness,
a beginning of something)* I guess we all better stop moping around and
get some work done. All this unpacking and everything we got to do.
*(*RUTH *raises her head slowly in response to the sense of the line; and*
BENEATHA *in similar manner turns very slowly to look at her mother.)*
One of you all better call the moving people and tell 'em not to come.

RUTH.   Tell 'em not to come?

MAMA.   Of course, baby. Ain't no need in 'em coming all the way
here and having to go back. They charges for that too. *(She sits down,
fingers to her brow, thinking.)* Lord, ever since I was a little girl, I always remembers people saying, "Lena—Lena Eggleston, you aims too
high all the time. You needs to slow down and see life a little more like
it is. Just slow down some." That's what they always used to say down
home—"Lord, that Lena Eggleston is a high-minded thing. She'll get her
due one day!"

RUTH.   No, Lena. . . .

MAMA.   Me and Big Walter just didn't never learn right.

RUTH. Lena, no! We gotta go. Bennie—tell her. . . . *(She rises and crosses to* BENEATHA *with her arms outstretched.* BENEATHA *doesn't respond.)* Tell her we can still move . . . the notes ain't but a hundred and twenty-five a month. We got four grown people in this house—we can work. . . .

MAMA *(to herself).* Just aimed too high all the time—

RUTH *(turning and going to* MAMA *fast—the words pouring out with urgency and desperation).* Lena—I'll work . . . I'll work twenty hours a day in all the kitchens in Chicago. . . . I'll strap my baby on my back if I have to and scrub all the floors in America and wash all the sheets in America if I have to—but we got to move. . . . We got to get out of here . . . .

(MAMA *reaches out absently and pats* RUTH's *hand.)*

MAMA. No—I sees things differently now. Been thinking 'bout some of the things we could do to fix this place up some. I seen a second-hand bureau over on Maxwell Street just the other day that could fit right there. *(She points to where the new furniture might go.* RUTH *wanders away from her.)* Would need some new handles on it and then a little varnish and then it look like something brand-new. And—we can put up them new curtains in the kitchen. . . . Why this place be looking fine. Cheer us all up so that we forget trouble ever came . . . *(To* RUTH*)* And you could get some nice screens to put up in your room round the baby's bassinet. . . . *(She looks at both of them, pleadingly.)* Sometimes you just got to know when to give up some things . . . and hold on to what you got.

(WALTER *enters from the outside, looking spent and leaning against the door, his coat hanging from him.)*

MAMA. Where you been, son?

WALTER *(breathing hard).* Made a call.

MAMA. To who, son?

WALTER. To The Man.

MAMA. What man, baby?

WALTER. The Man, Mama. Don't you know who The Man is?

RUTH. Walter Lee?

WALTER. *The Man.* Like the guys in the streets say—The Man. Captain Boss—Mistuh Charley . . . Old Captain Please Mr. Bossman. . . .

BENEATHA *(suddenly).* Lindner!

WALTER. That's right! That's good. I told him to come right over.

BENEATHA *(fiercely, understanding).* For what? What do you want to see him for!

WALTER *(looking at his sister).* We going to do business with him.

MAMA. What you talking 'bout son?

WALTER. Talking 'bout life, Mama. You all always telling me to see life like it is. Well—I laid in there on my back today . . . and I figured it out. Life just like it is. Who gets and who don't get. *(He sits down with his coat on and laughs.)* Mama, you know it's all divided up. Life is. Sure enough. Between the takers and the "tooken." *(He laughs.)* I've figured it out finally. *(He looks around at them.)* Yeah. Some of us always getting "tooken." *(He laughs.)* People like Willy Harris, they don't never get "tooken." And you know why the rest of us do? 'Cause we all mixed up. Mixed up bad. We get to looking 'round for the right and the wrong; and we worry about it and cry about it and stay up nights trying to figure out 'bout the wrong and the right of things all the time. . . . And all the time, man, them takers is out there operating, just taking and taking. Willy Harris? Shoot—Willy Harris don't even count. He don't even count in the big scheme of things. But I'll say one thing for old Willy Harris . . . he's taught me something. He's taught me to keep my eye on what counts in this world. Yeah—(*Shouting out a little*) Thanks, Willy!

RUTH. What did you call that man for, Walter Lee?

WALTER. Called him to tell him to come on over to the show. Gonna put on a show for the man. Just what he wants to see. You see, Mama, the man came here today and he told us that them people out there where you want us to move—well they so upset they willing to pay us not to move out there. *(He laughs again.)* And—and oh, Mama—you would of been proud of the way me and Ruth and Bennie acted. We told him to get out. . . . Lord have mercy! We told the man to get out. Oh, we was some proud folks this afternoon, yeah. *(He lights a cigarette.)* We were still full of that old-time stuff. . . .

RUTH *(coming toward him slowly).* You talking 'bout taking them people's money to keep us from moving in that house?

WALTER. I ain't just talking 'bout it, baby—I'm telling you that's what's going to happen.

BENEATHA. Oh, God! Where is the bottom! Where is the real honest to-God bottom so he can't go any farther!

WALTER. See—that's the old stuff. You and that boy that was here today. You all want everybody to carry a flag and a spear and sing some marching songs, huh? You wanna spend your life looking into things and trying to find the right and the wrong part, huh? Yeah. You know what's going to happen to that boy someday—he'll find himself sitting in a dungeon, locked in forever—and the takers will have the key! Forget it, baby! There ain't no causes—there ain't nothing but taking in this world, and he who takes most is smartest—and it don't make a damn bit of difference *how*.

MAMA.   You making something inside me cry, son. Some awful pain inside me.

WALTER.   Don't cry, Mama. Understand. That white man is going to walk in that door able to write checks for more money than we ever had. It's important to him and I'm going to help him. . . . I'm going to put on the show, Mama.

MAMA.   Son—I come from five generations of people who was slaves and sharecroppers—but ain't nobody in my family never let nobody pay 'em no money that was a way of telling us we wasn't fit to walk the earth. We ain't never been that poor. (*Raising her eyes and looking at him*) We ain't never been that dead inside.

BENEATHA.   Well—we are dead now. All the talk about dreams and sunlight that goes on in this house. All dead.

WALTER.   What's the matter with you all! I didn't make this world! It was give to me this way! Hell, yes, I want me some yachts someday! Yes, I want to hang some real pearls 'round my wife's neck. Ain't she supposed to wear no pearls? Somebody tell me—tell me, who decides which women is suppose to wear pearls in this world. I tell you I am a *man*—and I think my wife should wear some pearls in this world!

(*This last line hangs a good while and* WALTER *begins to move about the room. The word "Man" has penetrated his consciousness; he mumbles it to himself repeatedly between strange agitated pauses as he moves about.*)

MAMA.   Baby, how you going to feel on the inside?

WALTER.   Fine! . . . Going to feel fine . . . a man. . . .

MAMA.   You won't have nothing left then, Walter Lee.

WALTER (*coming to her*).   I'm going to feel fine, Mama. I'm going to look that son-of-a-bitch in the eyes and say—(*He falters.*)—and say, "All right, Mr. Lindner—(*He falters even more.*)—that's your neighborhood out there. You got the right to keep it like you want. You got the right to have it like you want. Just write the check and—the house is yours." And, and I am going to say—(*His voice almost breaks.*) And you—you people just put the money in my hand and you won't have to live next to this bunch of stinking niggers! . . . (*He straightens up and moves away from his mother, walking around the room.*) Maybe—maybe I'll just get down on my black knees. . . . (*He does so;* RUTH *and* BENNIE *and* MAMA *watch him in frozen horror.*) Captain, Mistuh. Bossman. (*He starts crying.*) A-hee-hee-hee! (*Wringing his hands in profoundly anguished imitation*) Yasssssuh!

Great White Father, just gi' ussen de money, fo' God's sake, and we's ain't gwine come out deh and dirty up yo' white folks neighborhood. . . .

(He breaks down completely, then gets up and goes into the bedroom.)

BENEATHA.   That is not a man. That is nothing but a toothless rat.

MAMA.   Yes—death done come in this here house. *(She is nodding, slowly, reflectively.)* Done come walking in my house. On the lips of my children. You what supposed to be my beginning again. You—what supposed to be my harvest. *(To* BENEATHA*)* You—you mourning your brother?

BENEATHA.   He's no brother of mine.

MAMA.   What you say?

BENEATHA.   I said that that individual in that room is no brother of mine.

MAMA.   That's what I thought you said. You feeling like you better than he is today? (BENEATHA *does not answer.*) Yes? What you tell him a minute ago? That he wasn't a man? Yes? You give him up for me? You done wrote his epitaph too—like the rest of the world? Well, who give you the privilege?

BENEATHA.   Be on my side for once! You saw what he just did, Mama! You saw him—down on his knees. Wasn't it you who taught me—to despise any man who would do that. Do what he's going to do.

MAMA.   Yes—I taught you that. Me and your daddy. But I thought I taught you something else too. . . . I thought I taught you to love him.

BENEATHA.   Love him? There is nothing left to love.

MAMA.   There is always something left to love. And if you ain't learned that, you ain't learned nothing. *(Looking at her)* Have you cried for that boy today? I don't mean for yourself and for the family 'cause we lost the money. I mean for him; what he been through and what it done to him. Child, when do you think is the time to love somebody the most; when they done good and made things easy for everybody? Well then, you ain't through learning—because that ain't the time at all. It's when he's at his lowest and can't believe in hisself 'cause the world done whipped him so. When you starts measuring somebody, measure him right, child, measure him right. Make sure you done taken into account what hills and valleys he come through before he got to wherever he is.

*(*TRAVIS *bursts into the room at the end of the speech, leaving the door open.)*

TRAVIS.   Grandmama—the moving men are downstairs! The truck just pulled up.

MAMA *(turning and looking at him).* Are they, baby? They downstairs?

(She sighs and sits. LINDNER appears in the doorway. He peers in and knocks lightly, to gain attention, and comes in. All turn to look at him.)

LINDNER *(hat and briefcase in hand).* Uh—hello. . . . (RUTH *crosses mechanically to the bedroom door and opens it and lets it swing open freely and slowly as the lights come up on* WALTER *within, still in his coat, sitting at the far corner of the room. He looks up and out through the room to* LINDNER.)

RUTH. He's here.

(A long minute passes and WALTER *slowly gets up.)*

LINDNER *(coming to the table with efficiency, putting his briefcase on the table and starting to unfold papers and unscrew fountain pens).* Well, I certainly was glad to hear from you people. (WALTER *has begun the trek out of the room, slowly and awkwardly, rather like a small boy, passing the back of his sleeve across his mouth from time to time.)* Life can really be so much simpler than people let it be most of the time. Well—with whom do I negotiate? You, Mrs. Younger, or your son here? (MAMA *sits with her hands folded on her lap and her eyes closed as* WALTER *advances.* TRAVIS *goes close to* LINDNER *and looks at the papers curiously.)* Just some official papers, sonny.

RUTH. Travis, you go downstairs.

MAMA *(opening her eyes and looking into* WALTER'S). No. Travis, you stay right here. And you make him understand what you doing, Walter Lee. You teach him good. Like Willy Harris taught you. You show where our five generations done come to. Go ahead, son—

WALTER *(looks down into his boy's eyes;* TRAVIS *grins at him merrily, and* WALTER *draws him beside him with his arm lightly around his shoulders).* Well, Mr. Lindner. (BENEATHA *turns away.)* We called you— *(There is a profound, simple groping quality in his speech.)*—because, well, me and my family *(He looks around and shifts from one foot to the other).* Well—we are very plain people. . . .

LINDNER. Yes—

WALTER. I mean—I have worked as a chauffeur most of my life— and my wife here, she does domestic work in people's kitchens. So does my mother. I mean—we are plain people . . . .

LINDNER. Yes, Mr. Younger—

WALTER *(really like a small boy, looking down at his shoes and then up at the man).* And—uh—well, my father, well, he was a laborer most of his life.

LINDNER   *(absolutely confused).* Uh, yes—

WALTER   *(looking down at his toes once again).*   My father almost beat a man to death once because this man called him a bad name or something, you know what I mean?

LINDNER.   No, I'm afraid I don't.

WALTER   *(finally straightening up).*   Well, what I mean is that we come from people who had a lot of pride. I mean—we are very proud people. And that's my sister over there and she's going to be a doctor—and we are very proud—

LINDNER.   Well—I am sure that is very nice, but—

WALTER   *(starting to cry and facing the man eye to eye).*   What I am telling you is that we called you over here to tell you that we are very proud and that this is—this is my son, who makes the sixth generation of our family in this country, and that we have all thought about your offer and we have decided to move into our house because my father— —my father—he earned it. *(MAMA has her eyes closed and is rocking back and forth as though she were in church, with her head nodding the amen yes.)* We don't want to make no trouble for nobody or fight no causes—but we will try to be good neighbors. That's all we got to say. *(He looks the man absolutely in the eyes.)* We don't want your money.

(He turns and walks away from the man.)

LINDNER   *(looking around at all of them).*   I take it then that you have decided to occupy.

BENEATHA.   That's what the man said.

LINDNER   *(to MAMA in her reverie).*   Then I would like to appeal to you, Mrs. Younger. You are older and wiser and understand things better I am sure . . . .

MAMA   *(rising).*   I am afraid you don't understand. My son said we was going to move and there ain't nothing left for me to say. *(Shaking her head with double meaning)* You know how these young folks is nowadays, mister. Can't do a thing with 'em. Good-bye.

LINDNER   *(folding up his materials).*   Well—if you are that final about it . . . . There is nothing left for me to say. *(He finishes. He is almost ignored by the family, who are concentrating on WALTER LEE. At the door LINDNER halts and looks around.)* I sure hope you people know what you're doing.

(He shakes his head and exits.)

RUTH   *(looking around and coming to life).*   Well, for God's sake—

if the moving men are here—LET'S GET THE HELL OUT OF HERE!

MAMA (*into action*). Ain't it the truth! Look at all this here mess. Ruth put Travis's good jacket on him . . . Walter Lee, fix your tie and tuck your shirt in, you look just like somebody's hoodlum. Lord have mercy, where is my plant? (*She flies to get it amid the general bustling of the family, who are deliberately trying to ignore the nobility of the past moment.*) You all start on down . . . . Travis child, don't go empty-handed. . . . Ruth, where did I put that box with my skillets in it? I want to be in charge of it myself. . . . I'm going to make us the biggest dinner we ever ate tonight . . . . Beneatha, what's the matter with them stockings? Pull them things up, girl . . .

(*The family starts to file out as two moving men appear and begin to carry out the heavier pieces of furniture, bumping into the family as they move about.*)

BENEATHA. Mama, Asagai—asked me to marry him today and go to Africa—

MAMA (*in the middle of her getting-ready activity*). He did? You ain't old enough to marry nobody—(*Seeing the moving men lifting one of her chairs precariously*) Darling, that ain't no bale of cotton, please handle it so we can sit in it again. I had that chair twenty-five years. . . .

(*The movers sigh with exasperation and go on with their work.*)

BENEATHA (*girlishly and unreasonably trying to pursue the conversation*). To go to Africa, Mama—be a doctor in Africa . . . .

MAMA (*distracted.*) Yes, baby—

WALTER. Africa! What he want you to go to Africa for?

BENEATHA. To practice there . . . .

WALTER. Girl, if you don't get all them silly ideas out your head! You better marry yourself a man with some loot . . . .

BENEATHA (*angrily, precisely as in the first scene of the play*). What have you got to do with who I marry!

WALTER. Plenty. Now I think George Murchison—

(*He and* BENEATHA *go out yelling at each other vigorously;* BENEATHA *is heard saying that she would not marry* GEORGE MURCHISON *if he were Adam and she were Eve, and so on. The anger is loud and real till their voices diminish.* RUTH *stands at the door and turns to* MAMA *and smiles knowingly.*)

MAMA (*fixing her hat at last*). Yeah—they something all right, my children . . . .

RUTH.   Yeah—they're something. Let's go, Lena.

MAMA   (*stalling, starting to look around at the house*).   Yes—I'm coming. Ruth—

RUTH.   Yes?

MAMA   (*quietly, woman to woman*). He finally come into his manhood today, didn't he? Kind of like a rainbow after the rain . . . .

RUTH   (*biting her lip lest her own pride explode in front of* MAMA). Yes, Lena.

(WALTER'S *voice calls for them raucously.*)

MAMA   (*waving* RUTH *out vaguely*).   All right, honey—go on down. I be down directly.

> (RUTH *hesitates, then exits.* MAMA *stands, at last alone in the living room, her plant on the table before her as the lights start to come down. She looks around at all the walls and ceilings and suddenly, despite herself, while the children call below, a great heaving thing rises in her and she puts her fist to her mouth, takes a final desperate look, pulls her coat about her, pats her hat and goes out. The lights dim down. The door opens and she comes back in, grabs her plant, and goes out for the last time.*)
>
> (CURTAIN)

A Raisin in the Sun

For Analysis

A Raisin in the Sun, a problem play, was the first play by a black woman playwright to be produced on Broadway (1958–59).

What is the problem in this problem play? The interesting thing about the play is that the characters have to discover the problem just as the audience does. Before Act III, no character understands what the problem is, with the possible exception of the mother.

The question the play poses, as indicated in the title and the Langston Hughes poem from which it is taken is, "What happens to a dream deferred"?

1. Does the Younger family have *a* dream or separate dreams?
2. Do any of the dreams lead to positive accomplishments? For example:
   a. What happens when Walter Lee puts $6500 into his dream?
   b. When Mama takes decisive action and puts $3500 into her dream does a solution or the need for a greater decision result?

3. Do members of the family form alliances with each other against other members? Do these alliances shift?

4. What signs do you have that the problem seems at first to be money? Consider the youngest member of the family, Travis. Does he too think that money is the problem? Consider the man, Walter Lee. Mama says: "Son—how come you talk so much 'bout money?" and Walter replies, "Because it is life, Mama!" Later, when Willy betrays him, he says, "Man, I put my life in your hands." In Act I, Walter Lee says, "Baby, don't *nothing* happen for you in this world 'less you pay *somebody* off!" Does he maintain this value system?

5. We see, then, in the play a family that is rapidly disintegrating but that finally pulls itself together, despite the fact that their investments are seemingly disastrous. Can the basic problem, then, be money?

6. The problem might be racial. Asagai, the most sophisticated character in the play, is not only black but an African black and happy and secure at that. George Murchison is an American black, but he is represented as a kind of Super-white, a parody of whiteness in dress and speech. If Asagai is largely separate from white American values and George has largely assimilated white American culture, where do the Youngers fit in this pattern?

Consider what the following lines—one by a black African, one by a black American, one by a white American—tell you about the Youngers' problem:

Asagai: "It's just that every American girl I have known has said that to me. White—black—in this you are all the same. And the same speech, too!"

George: "That's what being eccentric means—being natural."

Karl Lindner: " . . . people get along better . . . when they share a common background."

Remember Mama's remark, "I don't think I never met no African before."

7. Does Beneatha's line, "You see, Mr. Asagai, I am looking for my *identity!*" summarize the real problem in the play? What concrete signs do you see that Beneatha is not sure of her identity?

8. One aspect of the problem of identity is the question of a heritage. When Lindner talks of "a common background" what background is he assuming the Youngers have? Is he right? What is the heritage of a black if he is a sixth generation American?

9. How is the identity problem symbolized in Mama's plant? (See the end of Act I, Scene 1, and the end of the play.) Is it significant that the plant is movable?

10. Consider how the identity problem is symbolized by clothes:

    a. What is suggested by Beneatha's riding habit, hanging in the closet? by her wearing Asagai's tribal dress?

    b. What does Walter's reaction to his chauffeur's uniform tell you of his dream? (Notice that he appears first in "rumpled and mismated" pajamas.)

    c. What do Ruth's actions with the "huge pile of rough-dried clothes" suggest about her dream?

(Note that Walter says Ruth works to keep clothes on Beneatha's back, and Mama offers Beneatha her robe, which Beneatha refuses.)

11. Is the identity problem ever solved by the Youngers? In Act III Mama says, "Son—I come from five generations of people who was slaves and sharecroppers—but ain't nobody in my family never let nobody pay 'em no money that was a way of telling us we wasn't fit to walk the earth. We ain't never been that poor." Does Walter finally get the problem in perspective when he says, "I tell you I am a *man*"? What does Mama mean when, after the last confrontation with Lindner, she says of Walter, "He finally come into his manhood today, didn't he? Kind of like a rainbow after the rain. . . . "? (Is there a connection here with the Negro spiritual that says, "God gave Noah the rainbow sign: No more water. The fire next time."?) What, then, in the end does the play say about the basic identity of the Younger family?

12. How many characters in this play are function characters? Who are the major characters?

13. Is there a clearly defined crisis and climax in the play? What major character is central in them? Who, then, is the major character in the play? Is his change greater than that of any other character in the play? Does Mama undergo change?

14. What character holds the key to the identity problem throughout the play but is unable to communicate it?

Index to
Authors, Titles,
and First Lines

Index to
Literary Terms